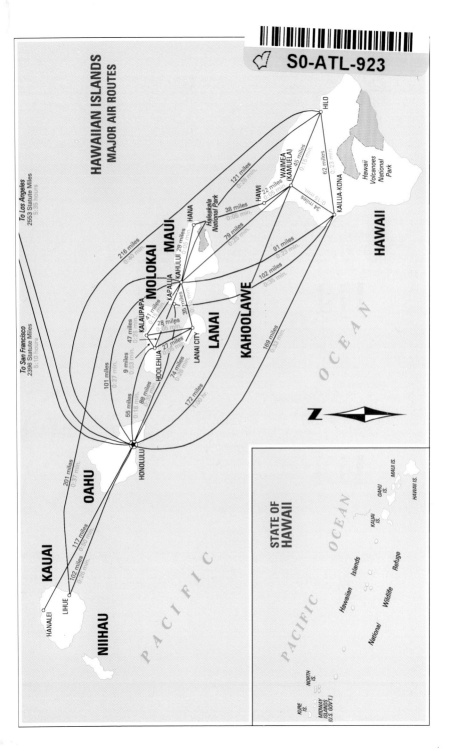

HAWAIIAN ISLANDS
MAJOR AIR ROUTES

S0-ATL-923

To Los Angeles
2553 Statute Miles
5:35 hours

To San Francisco
2396 Statute Miles
5:10 hours

KAUAI

HANALEI
LIHUE

NIIHAU

OAHU

HONOLULU

MOLOKAI

KALAUPAPA
KAPALUA
HOOLEHUA
LANAI CITY

LANAI

MAUI
KAHULUI
HANA
Haleakala National Park

KAHOOLAWE

HAWI
WAIMEA (KAMUELA)
KAILUA-KONA

HILO

Hawaii Volcanoes National Park

HAWAII

PACIFIC OCEAN

117 miles
0:30 min.

102 miles
0:26 min.

201 miles
0:37 min.

101 miles
0:27 min.

55 miles
0:18 min.

88 miles
0:30 min.

74 miles
0:25 min.

172 miles
1:00 hr.

9 miles
0:03 min.

47 miles
0:33 min.

28 miles
0:06 min.

27 miles
0:09 min.

41 miles

36 miles

216 miles
0:40 min.

28 miles
0:05 min.

121 miles
0:35 min.

38 miles
0:05 min.

79 miles
0:25 min.

91 miles
0:25 min.

102 miles
0:35 min.

169 miles
0:55 min.

22 miles
0:06 min.

45 miles
0:15 min.

34 miles
0:15 min.

62 miles
0:23 min.

N

STATE OF HAWAII

PACIFIC OCEAN

KURE IS.
MIDWAY ISLANDS (U.S. GOVT.)
NORTH IS.

Hawaiian Islands National Wildlife Refuge

KAUAI IS.
OAHU IS.
MAUI IS.
HAWAII IS.

PACIFIC OCEAN

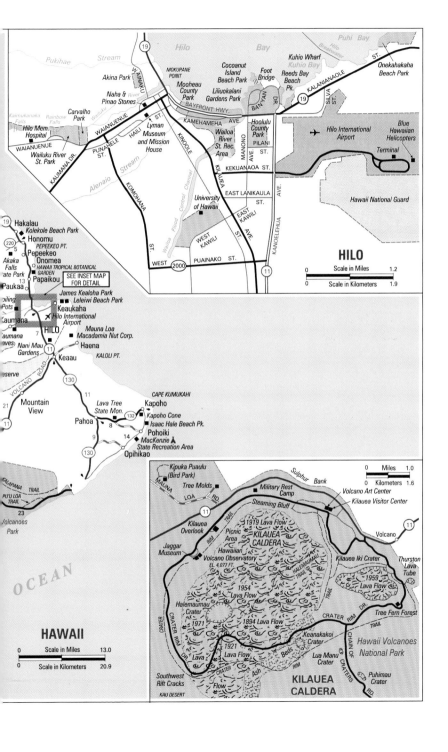

HILO

Puhi Bay

Hilo Breakwater

Onekahakaha Beach Park

Kuhio Wharf

Kuhio Bay

Reeds Bay Beach Pk.

Foot Bridge

Cocoanut Island Beach Park

Liliuokalani Gardens Park

Mooheau County Park

Mokupane Point

Akina Park

Naha & Pinao Stones

Carvalho Park

Hilo Mem. Hospital

Wailuku River St. Park

Lyman Museum and Mission House

Wailoa River St. Rec. Area

Hoolulu County Park

Blue Hawaiian Helicopters

Hilo International Airport

Terminal

Hawaii National Guard

University of Hawaii

Scale in Miles 1.2
Scale in Kilometers 1.9

Hakalau
Kolekole Beach Park
Honomu
PEPEEKEO PT.
Pepeekeo
Onomea
Akaka Falls ate Park
HAWAII TROPICAL BOTANICAL GARDEN
Papaikou
Paukaa
SEE INSET MAP FOR DETAIL
oiling Pots
James Kealoha Park
Leleiwi Beach Park
Keaukaha
Hilo International Airport
aumana
Kaumana
aves
Nani Mau Gardens
Mauna Loa Macadamia Nut Corp.
Haena
KALOLI PT.
Keaau
eserve
VOLCANO ROAD
Mountain View
Lava Tree State Mon.
Kapoho
CAPE KUMUKAHI
Kapoho Cone
Isaac Hale Beach Pk.
Pahoa
Pohoiki
MacKenzie State Recreation Area
Opihikao
olcanoes Park

HAWAII

Scale in Miles 13.0
Scale in Kilometers 20.9

O C E A N

KALAPANA TRAIL
PU'U LOA TRAIL

KILAUEA CALDERA

Kipuka Puaulu (Bird Park)
Tree Molds
MAUNA LOA RD
Military Rest Camp
Sulphur Bank
Volcano Art Center
Kilauea Visitor Center
Steaming Bluff
Kilauea Overlook
Picnic Area
1919 Lava Flow
KILAUEA CALDERA
Volcano
Jaggar Museum
Hawaiian Volcano Observatory
EL. 4,077 FT.
HALEMAUMAU TRAIL
Kilauea Iki Crater
Thurston Lava Tube
1959 Lava Flow
1954 Lava Flow
1894 Lava Flow
Halemaumau Crater
1971 Lava
1921 Lava Flow
Keanakakoi Crater
Ash Beds
Lua Manu Crater
Tree Fern Forest
CRATER RIM TRAIL
CHAIN OF CRATERS RD.
Hawaii Volcanoes National Park
Puhimau Crater
Southwest Rift Cracks
Flow
KAU DESERT
CRATER RIM DR.

Miles 1.0
Kilometers 1.6

HIDDEN® Hawaii

"A bible."
—*Honolulu Advertiser*

"The perfect choice for the visitor who wants an active vacation in the islands."
—*Travel & Leisure*

"Paints a vivid picture of each island's history, natural wonders and unique qualities."
—*Travel Holiday*

"Explores even deeper for the hidden places at the heart of island life."
—*American Bookseller*

"A view no travel agent can offer. Riegert's adventures are crammed with fascinating insider's advice."
—*Los Angeles Times*

"A polished, authoritative and thoroughly enjoyable handbook for travelers."
—*Our World*

"Unlike many guides that claim to offer inside information, this one actually delivers."
—*Vancouver Sun*

"Offers the best of all worlds to the Hawaii visitor."
—*Dallas Morning News*

HIDDEN ®

Hawaii

Ray Riegert

ELEVENTH EDITION

Ulysses Press ®

BERKELEY, CALIFORNIA

Published by: ULYSSES PRESS
P.O. Box 3440
Berkeley, CA 94703
www.ulyssespress.com

ISSN 1097-3222
ISBN 1-56975-218-4

Printed in Canada by Transcontinental Printing

30 29 28 27 26

EDITORIAL DIRECTOR: Leslie Henriques
MANAGING EDITOR: Claire Chun
PROJECT DIRECTOR: Marin Van Young
COPY EDITORS: Lily Chou, Steven Zah Schwartz
EDITORIAL ASSOCIATES: Shola Ogunlana, Ryan Gowland,
    Melissa Millar, Lisa Kester
TYPESETTERS: Steven Zah Schwartz, Lindsay Mugglestone
CARTOGRAPHY: Pease Press
HIDDEN BOOKS DESIGN: Sarah Levin
INDEXER: Sayre Van Young
COVER PHOTOGRAPHY: Front: Robert Holmes
    (Tunnels Beach, Kauai's North Shore)
    Back and circle: Robert Holmes (hibiscus)
COLOR INSERT: Robert Holmes
ILLUSTRATOR: Jen-Ann Kirchmeier

Distributed in the United States by Publishers Group West, in Canada by Raincoast Books, and in Great Britain and Europe by World Leisure Marketing

All color maps copyright © 2000 AAA. All rights reserved. Used with permission. www.aaa.com AAA

Hidden Hawaii was produced by Ulysses Press in association with VIA Books. VIA Books is a division of the California State Automobile Association (CSAA), 150 Van Ness Avenue, San Francisco, CA 94102. VIA

HIDDEN is a federally registered trademark of BookPack, Inc.

Ulysses Press 🏯 is a federally registered trademark of BookPack, Inc.

Acknowledgments

Since this book is now entering its eleventh edition, there are several generations of people to thank. The person to whom I owe the deepest gratitude has been working on the project since the very beginning. I met my wife Leslie when I first arrived in the islands to write *Hidden Hawaii*. Since then she has contributed to the book as an editor, writer, researcher and innovator. Her energy and spirit have been an inspiration throughout.

The current edition results from the efforts of several people. Claire Chun skillfully shepherded the book through many stages. Marin Van Young worked her magic as the project director. Sayre Van Young once again lent her skill as indexer; my wife Leslie and Sarah Levin devoted their talents to the cover design (while I'm at it, Leslie deserves an extra thanks for all her help with the researching and writing of this edition); Robert Holmes provided outstanding cover and interior photos. Lily Chou, Steven Schwartz, Shola Ogunlana, Ryan Gowland, Melissa Millar and Lindsay Muggle-stone aided and abetted with research and other matters large and small. Glenn and Liz Johnson, Ken Henriques and Nancy Mathey suggested several great spots. My son Keith and daughter Alice also merit a warm note of thanks for their encouraging smiles and infectious energy.

People to whom I am indebted for prior work on *Hidden Hawaii* include Carlene Scnabel, the project coordinator for the earlier editions; Jen-Ann Kirchmeier, who contributed her boundless enthusiasm as well as a collection of marvelous drawings; Marlyn Amann and Alison McDonald, who worked on the first edition; and Ed Silberstang, who offered expert assistance above and beyond the call of friendship.

To everyone, I want to extend a *mahalo nui loa*—thank you a thousand times for your *kokua*.

*

What's Hidden?

At different points throughout this book, you'll find special listings marked with a hidden symbol:

◀ HIDDEN

This means that you have come upon a place off the beaten tourist track, a spot that will carry you a step closer to the local people and natural environment of Hawaii.

The goal of this guide is to lead you beyond the realm of everyday tourist facilities. While we include traditional sightseeing listings and popular attractions, we also offer alternative sights and adventure activities. Instead of filling this guide with reviews of standard hotels and chain restaurants, we concentrate on one-of-a-kind places and locally owned establishments.

Our authors seek out locales that are popular with residents but usually overlooked by visitors. Some are more hidden than others (and are marked accordingly), but all the listings in this book are intended to help you discover the true nature of Hawaii and put you on the path of adventure.

Write to us!

If in your travels you discover a spot that captures the spirit of Hawaii, or if you live in the region and have a favorite place to share, or if you just feel like expressing your views, write to us and we'll pass your note along to the author.

We can't guarantee that the author will add your personal find to the next edition, but if the writer does use the suggestion, we'll acknowledge you in the credits and send you a free copy of the new edition.

ULYSSES PRESS
3286 Adeline Street, Suite 1
Berkeley, CA 94703
E-mail: readermail@ulyssespress.com

Contents

Preface   xiv
Introduction   xvi

1 THE ALOHA STATE   I
Where to Go   2
When to Go   4
Seasons   4
Calendar of Events   5
Before You Go   10
Visitors Centers   10
Packing   10
Lodging   11
Condos   12
Dining   13
Traveling with Children   13
Women Traveling Alone   15
Gay & Lesbian Travelers   16
Senior Travelers   17
Disabled Travelers   17
Foreign Travelers   18
Mail   19
Transportation   19
Getting to the Islands   19
Getting between Islands   20
Car Rentals   21

2 THE LAND AND OUTDOOR ADVENTURES   22
Flora   23
Fauna   27
Outdoor Adventures   29
Fishing   29
Crabbing   30
Squidding   30
Shellfish Gathering   30
Seaweed Gathering   32
Ocean Safety   32
Camping & Hiking   33

3 HISTORY AND CULTURE   35
History   35
Culture   49
People   51
Cuisine   52

Language   53
Music   56
Hula   57

4 OAHU   59

Waikiki   64
Downtown Honolulu   87
Greater Honolulu   103
Southeast Oahu   114
Windward Coast   120
North Shore   131
Leeward Coast   142
Outdoor Adventures   149
Transportation   160

5 HAWAII   164

Hilo   166
Hamakua Coast   178
Waimea   183
Kohala Coast   186
Kailua-Kona Area   198
Kona/Kau District   211
Hawaii Volcanoes National Park   224
Puna District   230
Outdoor Adventures   233
Transportation   244

6 MAUI   247

Lahaina   250
Kaanapali–Kapalua Area   266
Northwest Maui   278
Kihei–Wailea–Makena Area   281
Kahului–Wailuku Area   294
Hana Highway   302
Upcountry   319
Haleakala National Park   325
Outdoor Adventures   328
Transportation   343

7 LANAI   347

Lanai City   350

Northeast—Shipwreck Beach and Naha   356
Southeast—Manele Bay   358
Southwest—Kaumalapau Harbor & Kaunolu   362
Northwest—Polihua Beach   364
Outdoor Adventures   364
Transportation   367

8 **MOLOKAI**   **369**
Kaunakakai to East End   372
Kaunakakai to West End   380
Outdoor Adventures   392
Transportation   395

9 **KAUAI**   **397**
Lihue Area   400
Poipu Area   409
Waimea Area   420
Wailua–Kapaa Area   432
North Shore   441
Outdoor Adventures   456
Transportation   466

Recommended Reading   468
Index   470
Lodging Index   482
Dining Index   485
About the Author   492

Maps

Hawaiian Islands	3
Oahu	61
Waikiki	67
Downtown Honolulu	89
Greater Honolulu	105
Southeast Oahu	115
Windward Coast	123
North Shore	133
Leeward Coast & Central Oahu	143
Hawaii	167
Hilo	171
Hamakua Coast	179
Waimea	183
Kohala Coast	189
Kailua-Kona Area	201
Kailua	205
Kona/Kau District	213
Hawaii Volcanoes National Park	225
Puna District	231
Maui	249
Lahaina–Kaanapali Area	253
Lahaina	257
Kaanapali–Kapalua Area	269
Northwest Maui	279
Kihei–Wailea–Makena Area	283
Kahului–Wailuku Area	297
Hana Highway	303
Upcountry	321
Haleakala National Park	327
Lanai	349
Lanai City	351
Northeast—Shipwreck Beach & Naha	357
Southeast—Manele Bay	359
Southwest—Kaumalapau Harbor & Kaunolu	363
Northwest—Polihua Beach	365
Molokai	371
Kaunakakai to East End	373
Kaunakakai	375
Kaunakakai to West End	381
Kauai	399
Lihue Area	403
Poipu Area	411
Waimea Area	423
Waimea Canyon—Kokee Trails	431
Wailua–Kapaa Area	433
North Shore	443

OUTDOOR ADVENTURE SYMBOLS

The following symbols accompany national, state and regional park listings, as well as beach descriptions throughout the text.

Camping

Hiking

Swimming

Snorkeling or Scuba Diving

Surfing

Waterskiing

Windsurfing

Fishing

Preface

Hawaii. What images does the word bring to mind? Crystal blue waters against a white sand beach. Palm trees swaying in a soft ocean breeze. Volcanic mountains rising in the hazy distance. Bronzed beach boys and luscious Polynesian women. Serenity. Luxury. Paradise.

To many it conjures still another dream—the perfect vacation. There is no more beautiful hideaway than this spectacular chain of tropical islands. For over a century Hawaii has been the meeting place of East and West, a select spot among savvy travelers. These adventurers are attracted not by Hawaii's famed tourist resorts—which are usually crowded and expensive—but by the opportunity to travel naturally and at low cost to an exotic locale.

As you'll find in the following pages, it is possible to tour economically through Hawaii's major sightseeing centers. It's even easier to explore the archipelago's more secluded realms. Few people realize that most of Hawaii's land is either rural or wilderness, and there's no price tag on the countryside. You can flee the multitudes and skip the expense by heading into the islands' endless backcountry. And if you venture far enough, you'll learn the secret that lies at the heart of this book: The less money you spend, the more likely you are to discover paradise.

Quite simply, that's the double-barreled purpose of *Hidden Hawaii*—to save you dollars while leading you to paradise. Whatever you're after, you should be able to find it right here. When you want to relax amid the comforts of civilization, this book will show you good restaurants, comfortable hotels, quaint shops and intriguing nightspots.

When you're ready to depart the beaten track, *Hidden Hawaii* will guide you to untouched beaches, remote campsites, underwater grottoes and legendary fishing holes. It will take you to the Pacific's greatest surfing beaches, on hiking trails across live volcanoes, into flower-choked jungles, through desert canyons and up to the top of the world's most massive mountain.

Hidden Hawaii is a handbook for living both in town and in the wild. The first chapter covers the nuts and bolts—how to get to the islands, what to bring and what to expect when you arrive. Chapter Two prepares you for outdoor life—swimming, hiking, camping, skindiving and living off the land. The third chapter, covering Hawaii's history and language, will familiarize you with the rich tropical culture.

The last six chapters describe individual islands. Each island is divided geographically. Here you'll find specific information on sightseeing, hotels, restaurants, shops, nightspots and beaches.

This book is not intended for those tourists in plastic leis who plop down on a Waikiki beach, toast for two weeks, then claim they've seen Hawaii when all they've really seen is some bizarre kind of Pacific Disneyland. No, *Hidden Hawaii* is for adventurers: people who view a vacation not as an escape from everyday routine, but rather as an extension of the most exciting aspects of their daily lives. People who travel to faraway places to learn more about their own homes. Folks like you and me who want to sit back and relax, but also seek to experience and explore.

Ray Riegert
Honolulu, 1979

Introduction

Reading *Hidden Hawaii* brought back memories of my long and frustratingly unconsummated love affair with the islands. Throughout my childhood I listened spellbound as my father and uncles swapped tales of sun-washed beaches far across the Pacific. Like millions of other sailors and GIs, they had toured distant lands courtesy of that great travel agent, Uncle Sam. Between battles they recuperated under swaying coco palms, swilling warm beer and bartering with the natives. Stale Lucky Strikes were traded for hand-forged bolo knives and intricately carved hardwood spears. And though their travels took them far beyond "Pearl," to me the atolls, jungles and magical reefs of which they spoke all spelled Hawaii.

"Hawaii Granted Statehood," the headline ran. I folded the damp newspaper, hurled it toward my customer's front porch and pedaled angrily along my paper route. *They* had done it, by a simple stroke of an administrative pen. My dream of retiring to the islands at age fifteen gave a violent lurch. Hawaii suddenly shifted from the distant edge of the unknown Orient to just another state. The Iowa of the Pacific. Offshore California. No more need for a passport or an interpreter. No gorging on exotic mahimahi and poi—the fabled Sandwich Islands would now feed me on McBurgers and cola.

I survived the disillusionment of statehood and though, two years later, I squandered my meager savings (earmarked for passage to the islands) on a battered motorbike, the dream did not fade entirely. Friends-of-friends returned from two-week Hawaiian idylls, faces and arms tanned to an improbable richness. Wilted leis would be casually draped over lampshades and mantlepieces, a not-so-subtle reminder of their brief fling in the sun. I could only wait.

Later, the islands subverted my college career. In the storm clouds gathering above the campus, I saw the foam of a turquoise wave curling around a slender surfer. Rain-washed ivy dissolved into frangipani and bougainvillea. The neo-Gothic monstrosity of the campus library became a battered volcanic grotto, rumbling with echoes of ocean rollers. My instructors, unable to see beyond the tips of their umbrellas, rewarded my visions of paradise with neat lines of zeroes.

Flunking out of college, however, almost brought me my dream. I found myself low man on the totem pole on a disabled fishing boat, drifting helplessly across the gulf of Alaska. There seemed little promise of sunburns and coco palms in those cold, relentless waves. And then the captain took a close look at the charts.

"Well, boys, if this keeps up, we'll just have to head for Hawaii," he muttered. It had already been two endless weeks. Given the force of wind and current, we would hail the islands' sparkling shores within a month.

But it was just another lost chance, thwarted by an annoyingly efficient Norwegian chief engineer who dreamed of cod and boiled salmon heads rather than pineapple and passion fruit. The ancient engine coughed to life and took us north, back into the Big Grey.

Like many early explorers before me, I now took the only reasonable alternative left in my unsuccessful quest for the islands: I gave up. I went south instead, to a land where coconuts and tequila create a dream of their own. I traded my vision of a Polynesian outrigger for a ticket on the Greyhound, drawn to the irresistible warmth of a Mexican sun. Hawaii receded over the horizon.

A few years later, returning north through California, land of surprises, the dream suddenly reappeared. My partner Lorena and I were invited to a birthday luau honoring King Kamehameha, father of the islands. In the shade of a redwood forest we feasted on rich, greasy barbecued pork, delicate raw fish, tropical fruits, palm hearts and that exotic beverage, Budweiser-on-tap. Frustrated Hawaiians weaving another year's dream from Maui smoke, we lay back on soft aromatic pine needles, lulled into fantasies of graceful sea canoes, the melancholy summons of conch shell trumpets, the rhythmic sweep of the paddles . . . carrying us off to the islands.

We could resist no longer; we determined to make the big break with the mainland. Having already written a travel book on Mexico, I now had the ultimate justification. We would go to Hawaii and return with knowledge and advice to pass on to others—while also earning a royalty that would guarantee a long rest on a hidden beach. Lorena was enthusiastic; between the native herbs and tropical sunsets, she could pass many many days. The final lure was thrown to us by our publisher: the promise of an advance to finance the journey. "But only when you've finished your camping book on Mexico," he warned.

• • •

"Hey, Carl, remember the book you were going to do on Hawaii?" I held the phone in a white-knuckled grip. Publishers are notorious for their twisted humor. Surely "remember" and "were going to do" were just sad attempts to cheer me toward my deadline.

"Yeah," I answered, "I have my Hawaiian shirt on right now. The one you bought me at Goodwill. *Remember?*"

There was a short, cynical laugh.

"Well, Ray Riegert just wrote it for you. Looks like it's time to play spin-the-globe again."

I slammed the phone down. Moments later I was trudging through the dusty Mexican streets, snarling at burros and stray dogs. At least my new recipe for mai tais wouldn't be wasted!

• • •

Good travel writers must constantly walk a tightrope between telling too much and not telling enough. The lazy tourist demands to be led by the nose to a comfortable yet inexpensive hotel and from there to a tasteful, quaint café. Nothing can be left to the demons of surprise and chance. Restless natives laboring over tom-toms in the middle of the night must be courtesy of the local tourist bureau, a civic contribution to amuse the traveler, rather than an inconvenient rebellion.

And with the distance between the islands and the continental U.S. reduced to nothing more than a quick lunch and a few drinks on a passenger jet, the pressures of tourism have become enormous. Hawaii's very lure is in danger of becoming its downfall.

This has created a situation in which a responsible and imaginative writer can perform a service both to adventurers and to the places they travel to see. A sensitive and aware guidebook like *Hidden Hawaii* helps educate and, in so doing, creates sensitive and aware travelers. The vast majority of guidebooks are not actually guides but consumer directories: where to spend your money with a minimum of distraction. That type of book actually steers us away from the heart of a place and an understanding of its peoples, on to nothing more than a superficial tour of the "sights." Ray Riegert shows us a Hawaii blessed with an incredible richness of cultures, history, topography and climates.

Hidden Hawaii not only points out attractive and inexpensive alternatives in meals, lodging, entertainment and shopping, but also takes us beyond Hawaii's often overdeveloped facade: where to watch whales; how to find the best parks, trails and campsites; how to live on the beach, foraging, fishing and diving; where to go shell collecting, volcano gazing . . . a variety of information as broad as the interests of travelers who want a lot out of a trip without going bankrupt. *Hidden Hawaii* demonstrates a very encouraging trend: I like guidebooks that are starting points for my own explorations, not addictive crutches. A little help can, and should, go a long way. Travel is a creative activity, one that should enhance the traveler as well as the places and people visited.

This is a book with an underlying attitude of respect and an awareness that it is more often one's attitude, rather than physical presence, that can be destructive. The hiker's motto, "Walk softly on the earth," is just as valid to the traveler strolling the streets of Lahaina as it is to the explorer on the trails of Kauai or the hidden beaches of Molokai.

It's up to *us* to keep hidden Hawaii unspoiled and enjoyable for everyone.

Carl Franz
San Miguel de Allende, 1979

No alien land in all the world has any deep, strong charm for me but that one, no other land could so longingly and so beseechingly haunt me, sleeping and waking, through half a lifetime, as that one has done. Other things leave me, but it abides; other things change, but it remains the same. . . . In my nostrils still lives the breath of flowers that perished twenty years ago.

—*Mark Twain, 1889*

ONE

The Aloha State

Hawaii is an archipelago that stretches more than 1500 miles across the North Pacific Ocean. Composed of 132 islands, it has eight major islands, clustered at the southeastern end of the chain. Together these larger islands are about the size of Connecticut and Rhode Island combined.

Each island, in a sense, is a small continent. Volcanic mountains rise in the interior, while the coastline is fringed with coral reefs and white-sand beaches. In the parlance of the Pacific, they are "high islands," very different from the low-lying atolls found elsewhere in Polynesia.

The northeastern face of each island, buffeted by trade winds, is the wet side. The contrast between this side and an island's southwestern sector is sometimes startling. Dense rainforests in the northeast are teeming with exotic tropical plants, while across the island you're liable to see cactus growing in a barren landscape!

Deciding to take a vacation in Hawaii is easy; the hard part comes when you have to choose which islands to visit. All six are remarkably beautiful places, each with unique features to offer the traveler. Eventually, you should try to tour them all, but on a single trip you'll probably choose only one, two or three. Traveling to more in the course of a typical vacation is counterproductive.

To help you decide which to see, I'll briefly describe the key features of each. For more detailed information, you can turn to the introductory notes in each of the island chapters.

My personal favorites are the Big Island and Kauai, the easternmost and westernmost islands in the chain, and I often recommend to friends unfamiliar with Hawaii that they visit these two islands. That way they manage to travel to both ends of the chain, experiencing the youngest and most rugged, and the oldest and most lush, of all the islands. The two offer a startling contrast, one that quickly shatters any illusion that all the islands are alike.

▼▼▼▼▼▼▼▼▼▼
Where to Go

Oahu, Hawaii's most populous island, is dominated by the capital city of Honolulu. Featuring the Waikiki tourist center, this is the most heavily touristed island. It's too crowded for many visitors. But Oahu *is* a prime place to mix city living with country exploring. It's also rich in history, culture and beautiful beaches.

The island of Hawaii, or the **Big Island**, is true to its nickname. Located at the southeastern end of the Hawaiian chain, and dominated by two 13,000-foot volcanoes, this giant measures more than twice the size of all the other islands combined. It's a great place to mountain climb and explore live volcanoes, to snorkel along the sun-splashed Kona Coast, or to tour orchid farms in the verdant city of Hilo.

Since Hawaii does not practice daylight-saving, their time difference becomes one hour greater during the summer months.

Maui, the second largest island, is one of Hawaii's favorite destinations for young visitors. Haleakala alone, the extraordinary crater that dominates the island, makes the "Valley Isle" worth touring. The island also sports many of Hawaii's nicest beaches and provides an offshore breeding ground for rare humpback whales.

Directly to the west, lying in Maui's wind shadow, sits the third smallest and most secluded island. **Lanai** is an explorer's paradise, with a network of jeep trails leading to hidden beaches and scenic mountain ridges. There are only 2800 people and about 20 miles of paved road here. If you are seeking an idyllic retreat, this is the place.

Molokai, slightly larger but nearly as remote, provides another extraordinary hideaway. With white-sand beaches, a mountainous interior and a large population of Hawaiians, the "Friendly Isle" retains a unique sense of old Hawaii. Here you can visit a former leper colony on the windswept Kalaupapa Peninsula, a pilgrimage that could prove to be the most inspiring of all your experiences in Hawaii.

The oldest island in the chain, **Kauai** is also the archipelago's prettiest, most luxuriant island. Located at the northwestern end of the chain, it is filled with jewel-like beaches and uninhabited valleys. Along the north shore are misty cliffs that fall precipitously to the sea; from the island's center rises a mountain that receives more rainfall than any place on earth; and along Kauai's southern flank there's a startling desert region reminiscent of the Southwest.

They're located 2500 miles southwest of Los Angeles, on the same 20th latitude as Hong Kong and Mexico City. It's two hours earlier in Hawaii than in Los Angeles, four hours before Chicago and five hours earlier than New York.

For years, sugar was king in Hawaii, the most lucrative part of the island economy. Today, tourism is number one. About four million Americans, and almost seven million travelers worldwide visit

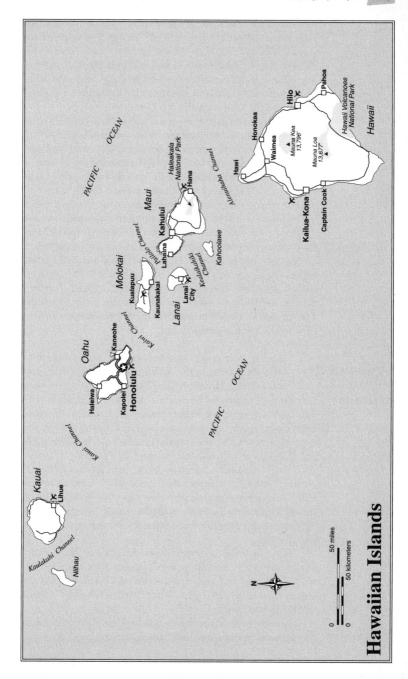

Hawaiian Islands

the Aloha State every year. It's now a $10.9 billion business that expanded exponentially during the 1970s and 1980s, leveled off in the 1990s and is now on the rise again.

With 44,542 personnel stationed in Hawaii, the U.S. military is another large industry. Concentrated on Oahu, where they control one-quarter of the land, the armed forces pour more than $3 billion into the local economy every year.

While the $200 million sugar industry is small potatoes compared to tourism and the military, Hawaii remains one of America's largest sugar-producing states. But sugar, like everything else in the islands, is threatened by urban development. A ton of water is required to produce a pound of sugar. Since the construction industry is now a $4.8 billion business, new housing developments are competing more and more with sugar cane for the precious liquid.

Pineapple is another crop that's ailing. Stiff competition from the Philippines, where labor is relatively cheap, has reduced Hawaii's pineapple plantations to a few relatively small operations.

Hawaii is one of the only places in the United States that grows coffee. The islands do a booming business in macadamia nuts, orchids, anthuriums, guava nectar and passion fruit juice. Together, these industries have created a stable economy in the 50th state. The per capita income is greater than the national average, and the standard of living is generally higher.

▼▼▼▼▼▼▼▼▼▼
When to Go

SEASONS

There are two types of seasons in Hawaii, one keyed to tourists and the other to the climate. The peak tourist seasons run from mid-December until Easter, then again from mid-June through Labor Day. Particularly around the Christmas holidays and in August, the visitors centers are crowded. Prices increase, hotel rooms and rental cars become harder to reserve, and everything moves a bit more rapidly. Shop around, however; package deals that include discounts on published rates are available.

If you plan to explore Hawaii during these seasons, make reservations several months in advance; actually, it's a good idea to make advance reservations whenever you visit. Without doubt, the off-season is the best time to hit the islands. Not only are hotels more readily available, but campsites and hiking trails are also less crowded.

Climatologically, the ancient Hawaiians distinguished between two seasons—*kau*, or summer, and *hooilo*, or winter. Summer extends from May to October, when the sun is overhead and the temperatures are slightly higher. Winter brings more variable winds and cooler weather.

The important rule to remember about Hawaii's beautiful weather is that it changes very little from season to season but varies dramatically from place to place. The average yearly temperature is about 78°, and during the coldest weather in January and the warmest in August, the thermometer rarely moves more than 5° or 6° in either direction. Similarly, sea water temperatures range comfortably between 74° and 80° year-round.

Crucial to this luxurious semitropical environment is the trade wind that blows with welcome regularity from the northeast, providing a natural form of air-conditioning. When the trades stop blowing, they are sometimes replaced by *kona* winds carrying rain and humid weather from the southwest. These are most frequent in the winter, when the Hawaiian islands receive their heaviest rainfall.

While summer showers are less frequent and shorter in duration, winter storms are sometimes quite nasty. I've seen it pour for five consecutive days, until hiking trails disappeared and city streets were awash. If you visit in winter, particularly from December to March, you're risking the chance of rain.

A wonderful factor to remember through this wet weather is that if it's raining where you are, you can often simply go someplace else. And I don't mean another part of the world, or even a different island. Since the rains generally batter the northeastern sections of each island, you can usually head over to the south or west coast for warm, sunny weather.

Sometimes nasty weather engulfs the entire chain, but there's usually a sunny refuge somewhere. I once spent a strenuous period along the Kona Coast working on a suntan. Across the island near Hilo, flood warnings were up. Twenty-five inches of rain dropped in 24 hours; five feet of water fell in seven days. Toward the end of the week, when my major problem was whether the tan would peel, officials in Hilo declared a state of emergency.

CALENDAR OF EVENTS

Something else to consider in planning a visit to Hawaii is the amazing lineup of annual cultural events. For a thumbnail idea of what's happening when, check the calendar below. You might

SOME ISLANDS ARE OFF-LIMITS

Only seven of the major islands are inhabited: the eighth, Kahoolawe, although sacred to Hawaiians, was used for decades as a bombing range for the U.S. Navy, then was finally turned over to the state of Hawaii in 1994. The seventh island, Niihau, is inhabited but is privately owned and off-limits to the public.

just find that special occasion to climax an already dynamic vacation. For a comprehensive listing with current updates, check the Hawaii Visitors & Convention Bureau website at www.go hawaii.com.

JANUARY

Early January   At Maui's **Annual Festival of Hula** local Hula *Halaus* compete for Halau of the Year.

During January   On Maui, the Four Seasons Resort Wailea sponsors the **Whales Alive Celebration**, an international gathering with discussions, whale watching, entertainment and an art exhibit.

Mid-January or February   The month-long **Narcissus Festival** begins with the Chinese New Year. During the weeks of festivities, there are open houses, street parties and parades in Honolulu's Chinatown.

Late January   **Makahiki** was traditionally a time when wars paused, taxes were paid, and partying was plentiful. Molokai celebrates this legacy with its annual **Hawaiian Games**; in addition to the sports competitions, there are crafts, food booths and entertainment. The **Pipeline Bodysurfing Classic** takes place on Oahu's North Shore.

FEBRUARY

Early February   Usher in **Chinese New Year** with Lahaina locals: a colorful lion dance, food booths, Chinese calligraphy and the traditional fireworks are among the festivities.

February through March   The Japanese community celebrates its **Cherry Blossom Festival** in Honolulu with tea ceremonies, kabuki theater presentations, martial arts demonstrations and crafts exhibits.

Late February   The world's greatest female bodyboarders compete in the **Extreme Bodyboard Series** at the birthplace of the sport, The Pipeline in Oahu. The annual **Whale Day Celebration** on Maui includes food by Maui's top chefs, a Hawaiian craft fair and a carnival for the kids.

MARCH

During March   On Maui, you can volunteer to help the Pacific Whale Foundation count humpbacks during **The Great Whale Count** in late February/early March. Athletes compete in Kauai's **Prince Kuhio Ironman/Ironwoman Canoe Race**. **Art Maui** is a month-long juried art show featuring new work by local artists.

Mid-March   Celebrate the "Mother of Hawaii" with exhibits, entertainment and storytelling at Maui's **Queen Kaahumanu Festival**. The **Maui Marathon** is run from the Kaahumanu Shopping Center in Kahului to Kaanapali.

March 26   Major festivities on Kauai mark the **Prince Kuhio Festival**, commemorating the birthdate of Prince Jonah Kuhio Kalanianaole, Hawaii's first delegate to the U.S. Congress.

Late March/Early April   The **East Maui Taro Festival** in Hana celebrates taro, the staple of the Hawaiian diet, with exhibits, lectures, music, hula, and, of course, food.

April 1–22   For the eco- and creative-minded, the Kaahumanu Center in Kahului, Maui sponsors the **Trash Art Show**, a glimpse into the wonders of—what else—trash art.

APRIL

Early April   The **International Pro Board Windsurfing Competition** is a popular ten-day tournament that's held at Hookipa Beach Park on Maui. The week-long **Merrie Monarch Festival** on the Big Island pays tribute to David Kalakaua, Hawaii's last king. Festivities include musical performances, pageants and a parade. Buddhist temples on all the islands mark **Buddha Day**, the luminary's birthday, with special services. Included among the events are pageants, dances and flower festivals. Maui's annual birthday party for **Lahaina's Banyan** honors the famous tree with cake and exhibits.

During May   **Molokai Ka Hula Piko** marks the birth of hula on Molokai. Hula dancers, local musicians and Hawaiian craftspeople display their many talents. Held for four weekends in May (and sometimes in June), the **50th State Fair** in Oahu features agricultural exhibits, food stalls, dances, music and displays of island arts and crafts.

MAY

May 1   **Lei Day** is celebrated in the islands by people wearing flower leis and colorful Hawaiian garb. In Oahu's Kapiolani Park, there are pageants and concerts.

Mid-May   Maui's **Mother's Day Orchid Show** presents award-winning orchids. The **Maui Music Festival** fills two days and nights with jazz at the Kaanapali resort.

Late May   The Molokai **Ka Hula Piko Festival** honors Maunaloa's art form with hula performances.

During June   In Honolulu, the music, dance and customs of more than 40 Pacific Rim areas are showcased at the annual **International Festival of the Pacific**. This two-week event features performers from American Samoa, New Zealand, Guam and Hawaii. Also on Oahu, the **Aloha State Games**, featuring Olympic-style events, take place statewide. *Halaus* from around the world participate in Oahu's **Annual King Kamehameha Hula Competition**. On Maui, the **Kapalua Chamber Music Festival** features chamber music by internationally acclaimed artists. Staged at the Eddie Tam Complex in Makawao, the **Upcountry Fair** is where the 4-H crowd swings into action. Enjoy the live entertainment and local delicacies and, if you're an aspiring performer, don't miss the Star Search.

JUNE

June 10–11 **King Kamehameha Day**, honoring Hawaii's first king, is celebrated on all six islands with parades, chants, hula dances and exhibits.

Mid-June In Lahaina, the annual **Shapers Phoai Na Keiki Nalu** showcases surfers under 12.

June through August On Oahu and the other islands, Buddhists perform colorful **Bon Dances** every weekend to honor the dead.

Early July "Cowboy Town" Makawao, in Maui's ranchland, promotes its **Parade & Rodeo** as a Maui-style Fourth of July.

JULY

During July On the Big Island, the **Hilo Orchid Society Flower Show** is a showy demonstration of tropical colors. On Maui, more than 100 different wines from California, Oregon and Washington, as well as Australia, are sampled at the **Kapalua Wine & Food Symposium**. The **Pineapple Festival**, held in Lanai City, features contemporary Hawaiian music, pineapple cooking contests and arts and crafts.

Late July **Ocean Concepts Bayfest**, one of Oahu's biggest water carnivals, presents three days of rides, games and watersports.

AUGUST

During August On Oahu, you can see the dramatic **Haleiwa Cup**, a one-mile ocean swim from Haleiwa Beach Park to Puena Point and back, which draws more than 350 swimmers. In Honolulu, dancers six to twelve years old gather to compete in the **Queen Liliuokalani Keiki Hula Festival**. In addition to a raw onion–eating contest, **The Maui Onion Festival** features food booths, live music, a farmers market and an onion recipe contest.

August 21 Local residents celebrate **Admission Day**, the date in 1959 when Hawaii became the 50th state.

Late August Visitors to Molokai won't want to miss the **Molokai Ranch Professional Rodeo**, a full two-day rodeo with barbecues and live bands.

SEPTEMBER

During September The six-person **Hana Relay**, a 54-mile Maui swim from Kahului to Hana, is one of autumn's more challenging events. The **Haleakala Run to the Sun** is a 38-mile run from the ocean to the 10,023-foot peak of Haleakala. Molokai's **Bankoh Na Wahine** draws canoers from around the world for a grueling race from Molokai to Oahu.

Early September The **Queen Liliuokalani Canoe Regatta** is staged on Oahu. Everyone keeps their eyes on Maui's **Wilson Kapalua Open Tennis Tournament**; it has Hawaii's largest tennis purse. A six-person relay across the nine-mile channel from Lanai to Kaanapali draws 50 international teams to the **Maui Channel Relay Swim**.

Late September The **Hawaii County Fair** in Hilo on the Big Isle features an orchid show, steer show, lei contest, agricultural displays, plus exhibits of Hawaiian arts and crafts.

Late September and during October   The highlight of Hawaii's cultural season is the **Aloha Week** festival, a series of week-long celebrations featuring parades, street parties and pageants. Each week, a different island stages the festival and the entire sequence ends with a **Molokai-to-Oahu Canoe Race**. The **Maui County Fair** features agricultural exhibits and arts-and-crafts displays at the Wailuku War Memorial Complex.

During October   The **Honolulu Orchid Show** in Honolulu presents thousands of orchids and other tropical plants. The EMC **Kaanapali Classic** tournament on Maui draws top stars from the PGA Tour.   **OCTOBER**
Mid-October   The **Ironman Triathlon World Championship** on the Big Island tests the stamina of the world's best-conditioned athletes.
Late October   **Halloween in Lahaina** is a memorable street party with a parade, food fair, music and dancing on Front Street.

Early November   The Big Island's **Kona Coffee Festival** celebrates the coffee harvest with a parade, international food bazaar and musical entertainment.   **NOVEMBER**
Mid-November   Sail out to snorkel with over 200 Hawaiian spinner dolphins during Oahu's **Dolphin Rendezvous**.
During November   **Hula O Na Keiki**, a children's hula performance on Maui, gives prizes for top performers in traditional and modern forms of the dance. Surfers and landlubbers alike gather for the **Hawaiian Pro Surfing Championships** on Oahu. The **Aloha Classic Windsurfing** at Hookipa Beach on Maui is a key event during the Pro Boardsailing Association World Tour.
November through December   The world's greatest surfers compete on Oahu's north shore in a series of contests including the **Pipeline Masters**, **World Cup of Surfing** and the **Hawaiian Pro Surfing Classic**. With 20-foot waves and prize money topping $50,000, these are spectacular events. Hawaiian and other crafts are showcased at the **Lokahi Pacific Christmas Craft Fair**, held at the War Memorial Sports Complex in Wailuku, Maui.

During December   **Honolulu City Lights** at Honolulu's City Hall marks the Christmas season. Maui celebrates with arts and crafts, music and dance at the **Na Mele O Maui Festival**. On Molokai, local communities take turns hosting **Christmas crafts fairs**. Oahu puts on the two-day **Festival of Art & Fine Crafts** at Thomas Square Park featuring over 110 arts and crafts vendors.   **DECEMBER**
Early December   Buddha's enlightenment is commemorated on all the islands with **Bodhi Day** ceremonies and religious services.
Mid-December   Runners by the thousands turn out for the **Honolulu Marathon**.

▼▼▼▼▼▼▼▼▼▼▼▼
Before You Go

**VISITORS
CENTERS**

The **Hawaii Visitors & Convention Bureau**, a state-run agency, is a valuable resource from which to obtain free information on Hawaii. With offices nationwide and branches on each of the four largest islands, the Bureau can help plan your trip and then offer advice once you reach Hawaii.

Details concerning the island offices appear in the "Addresses and Phone Numbers" section at the end of the Oahu, Hawaii, Maui and Kauai chapters. You can always contact the **Hawaii Visitors & Convention Bureau**. ~ 2270 Kalakaua Avenue, Suite 801, Honolulu, HI 96815; 808-923-1811; www.gohawaii.com.

Another excellent resource is the **Hawaii State Public Library System**. With a network of libraries on all the islands, this government agency provides facilities for residents and non-residents alike. The libraries are good places to find light beach-reading material as well as books on Hawaii. Visitors can check out books by simply applying for a library card with a valid identification card.

PACKING

When I get ready to pack for a trip, I sit down and make a list of everything I'll need. It's a very slow, exact procedure: I look in closets, drawers and shelves, and run through in my mind the activities in which I'll participate, determining which items are required for each. After all the planning is complete and when I have the entire inventory collected in one long list, I sit for a minute or two, basking in my wisdom and forethought.

Then I tear the hell out of the list, cut out the ridiculous items I'll never use, halve the number of spares among the necessary items, and reduce the entire contents of my suitcase to the bare essentials.

Before I developed this packing technique, I once traveled overland from London to New Delhi carrying two suitcases and a knapsack. I lugged those damned bundles onto trains, buses, jitneys, taxis and rickshaws. When I reached Turkey, I started shipping things home, but by then I was buying so many market goods that it was all I could do to keep even.

I ended up carrying so much crap that one day, when I was sardined in a crowd pushing its way onto an Indian train, someone managed to pick my pocket. When I felt the wallet slipping out, not only was I unable to chase the culprit—I was so weighted down with baggage that I couldn't even turn around to see who was robbing me!

I'll never travel that way again, and neither should you. Particularly when visiting Hawaii, where the weather is mild, you should pack very light. The airlines permit two suitcases and a carry-on bag; try to take one suitcase and maybe an accessory bag that can double as a beach bag. Dress styles are very informal in the islands, and laundromats are frequent, so you don't need a broad range of clothing items.

Remember, you're packing for a semitropical climate. Take along a sweater or light jacket for the mountains, and a poncho to protect against rain. But otherwise, all that travelers in Hawaii require are shorts, bathing suits, lightweight slacks, short-sleeved shirts and blouses, and summer dresses or muumuus. Rarely do visitors require sport jackets or formal dresses. Wash-and-wear fabrics are the most convenient.

Seeking a cooler climate? Head up to the mountains; for every thousand feet in elevation, the temperature drops about 3°F. If you climb high enough on Maui or the Big Island, you might even encounter snow!

For footwear, I suggest soft, comfortable shoes. Low-cut hiking boots or tennis shoes are preferable for hiking; for beachgoing, there's nothing as good as sandals.

There are several other items to squeeze in the corners of your suitcase—sunscreen, sunglasses, a towel and, of course, your copy of *Hidden Hawaii*. You might also consider packing a mask, fins and snorkel, and possibly a camera.

If you plan on camping, you'll need most of the equipment required for mainland overnighting. In Hawaii, you can get along quite comfortably with a lightweight tent and sleeping bag. You'll also need a knapsack, canteen, camp stove and fuel, mess kit, first-aid kit (with insect repellent, water purification tablets and Chapstick), toilet kit, a pocket knife, hat, waterproof matches, flashlight and ground cloth.

LODGING

Accommodations in Hawaii range from funky cottages to bed-and-breakfast inns to highrise condos. You will find inexpensive family-run hotels, middle-class tourist facilities and world-class resorts. Generally, the farther a hotel is from the beach, the less it costs.

Whichever you choose, there are a few guidelines to help save money. Try to visit during the off-season, avoiding the high-rate periods during the summer and from Christmas to Easter. Rooms with mountain views are less expensive than ocean view accommodations. Another way to economize is by reserving a room with a kitchen. In any case, try to reserve far in advance.

To help you decide on a place to stay, I've described the accommodations not only by area but also according to price (prices listed are for double occupancy during the high season; prices may decrease in low season). *Budget* hotels are generally less than $60 per night for two people; the rooms are clean and comfortable, but lack luxury. The *moderately* priced hotels run $60 to $120, and provide larger rooms, plusher furniture and more attractive surroundings. At *deluxe*-priced accommodations you can expect to spend between $120 and $180 for a double in a hotel or resort. You'll check into a spacious, well-appointed room with all modern facilities; downstairs the lobby will be a fashionable affair, and you'll usually see a restaurant, lounge and a cluster of shops. If you want to spend your time (and money) in the island's very finest hotels, try an *ultra-deluxe* facility, which will include all the amenities and price above $180.

Bed-and-Breakfast Inns   The bed-and-breakfast business in Hawaii becomes more diverse and sophisticated every year. Today there are several referral services that can find you lodging on any of the islands. Claiming to be the biggest clearinghouse in the state, **Bed and Breakfast Honolulu (Statewide)** represents over 400 properties. ~ 3242 Kaohinani Drive, Honolulu, HI 96817; 808-595-7533, 800-288-4666, fax 808-595-2030; www.hawaiibnb.com.

> When traveling around Christmas, Easter and during the summer high season, it's wise to book reservations as far in advance as possible.

The original association, **Bed and Breakfast Hawaii**, claims more than 200 locations. This Kauai-based service was founded in 1979 and is well known throughout Hawaii. ~ P.O. Box 449, Kapaa, HI 96746; 808-822-7771, 800-733-1632, fax 808-822-2723; www.bandb-hawaii.com. For other possibilities, contact **Hawaiian Islands Bed & Breakfast**. ~ 808-261-7895, 800-258-7895, fax 808-262-2181; www.flyhi.com.

You can also try the Maui-based **Affordable Accommodations**, which offers help finding all types of lodging. ~ 2825 Kauhale Street, Kihei, HI 96753; 808-879-7865, 888-333-9747, fax 808-874-0831; www.affordablemaui.com. Or call **All Islands Bed & Breakfast**, an Oahu-based reservation service that represents over 700 bed and breakfasts. ~ 463 Iliwahi Loop, Kailua, HI 96734; 808-263-2342, 800-542-0344, fax 808-263-0308; home.hawaii.rr.com/allislands.

While the properties represented by these agencies range widely in price, **Hawaii's Best Bed & Breakfasts** specializes in small, upscale accommodations on all the islands. With about 100 establishments to choose from, it places guests in a variety of privately owned facilities; most are deluxe priced. ~ P.O. Box 563, Kamuela, HI 96743; 808-885-4550, 800-262-9912, fax 808-885-0559; www.bestbnb.com.

CONDOS   Many people visiting Hawaii, especially those traveling with families, find that condominiums are often cheaper than hotels. While some hotel rooms come with kitchenettes, few provide all the amenities of condominiums. A condo, in essence, is an apartment away from home. Designed as studio, one-, two- or three-bedroom apartments, they come equipped with full kitchen facilities and complete kitchenware collections. Many also feature washer/dryers, dishwashers, air-conditioning, color televisions, telephones, lanais and community swimming pools.

Utilizing the kitchen will save considerably on your food bill; by sharing the accommodations among several people, you'll also cut your lodging bill. While the best way to see Hawaii is obviously by hiking and camping, when you're ready to come in from the wilds, consider reserving a place that provides more than a bed and a night table.

DINING

A few guidelines will help you chart a course through Hawaii's countless dining places. Within a particular chapter, the restaurants are categorized geographically, with each restaurant entry describing the establishment as budget, moderate, deluxe or ultra-deluxe in price.

To establish a pattern for Hawaii's parade of dining places, I've described not only the cuisine but also the ambience of each establishment. Restaurants listed offer lunch and dinner unless otherwise noted.

Dinner entrées at *budget* restaurants usually cost $8 or less. The ambience is informal café style and the crowd is often a local one. *Moderately* priced restaurants range between $8 and $16 at dinner and offer pleasant surroundings, a more varied menu and a slower pace. *Deluxe* establishments tab their entrées above $16, featuring sophisticated cuisines, plush decor and more personalized service. *Ultra-deluxe* restaurants generally price above $24.

Breakfast and lunch menus vary less in price from restaurant to restaurant. Even deluxe-priced kitchens usually offer light breakfasts and lunch sandwiches, which place them within a few dollars of their budget-minded competitors. These early meals can be a good time to test expensive restaurants.

TRAVELING WITH CHILDREN

Hawaii is an ideal vacation spot for family holidays. The pace is slow, the atmosphere casual. A few guidelines will help ensure that your trip to the islands brings out the joys rather than the strains of parenting, allowing everyone to get into the *aloha* spirit.

Use a travel agent to help with arrangements; they can reserve spacious bulkhead seats on airlines and determine which flights are least crowded. They can also seek out the best deals on inexpensive condominiums, saving you money on both room and board.

Planning the trip with your kids stimulates their imagination. Books about travel, airplane rides, beaches, whales, volcanoes and Hawaiiana help prepare even a two-year-old for an adventure. This preparation makes the "getting there" part of the trip more exciting for children of all ages.

And "getting there" means a long-distance flight. Plan to bring everything you need on board the plane—diapers, food, books, toys, and extra clothing for kids and parents alike. I found it helpful to carry a few new toys and books as treats to distract my son and daughter when they got bored. When they were young children, I also packed extra snacks.

Allow extra time to get places. Book reservations in advance and make sure that the hotel or condominium has the extra crib, cot or bed you require. It's smart to ask for a room at the end of the hall to cut down on noise. And when reserving a rental car, inquire to see if they provide car seats and if there is an added charge. Hawaii has a strictly enforced car seat law.

Besides the car seat you may have to bring along, also pack shorts and T-shirts, a sweater, sun hat, sundresses and waterproof sandals. A stroller with sunshade for little ones helps on sightseeing sojourns; a shovel and pail are essential for sandcastle building. Most importantly, remember to bring a good sunblock. The quickest way to ruin a family vacation is with a bad sunburn. Also plan to bring indoor activities such as books and games for evenings and rainy days.

Most towns have stores that carry diapers, food and other essentials. However, prices are much higher in Hawaii. To economize, some people take along an extra suitcase filled with diapers and wipes, baby food, peanut butter and jelly, etc. If you're staying in Honolulu, ABC stores carry a limited selection of disposables and baby food. ~ 2432 Koa Avenue, Honolulu; 808-921-2799. Shopping outside Waikiki in local supermarkets will save you a considerable sum: Star Market is open from 5 a.m. to 2 a.m. ~ 2470 South King Street, Honolulu; 808-973-1666.

A first-aid kit is always a good idea. Also check with your pediatrician for special medicines and dosages for colds and diarrhea. If your child does become sick or injured in the Honolulu area, contact Kapiolani Medical Center (808-983-6000). On the Windward Coast of Oahu, call Castle Medical Center (808-263-5500); on the North Shore, Kahuku Hospital (808-293-9221); and on

KEIKI CAMP

Some resorts and hotels have daily programs for kids during the summer and holiday seasons. Hula lessons, lei making, storytelling, sandcastle building and various sports activities keep *keikis* (kids) over six happy while also giving Mom and Dad a break. As an added bonus, these resorts offer family plans, providing discounts for extra rooms or permitting children to share a room with their parents at no extra charge. Check with your travel agent.

the leeward side, **Wahiawa General Hospital** (808-621-8411). On the Big Island's east side, there's **Hilo Medical Center** (808-974-4700); in Kona, **Kona Community Hospital** (808-322-9311); Maui, **Maui Memorial Hospital** (808-242-2343); Lanai, **Lanai Community Hospital** (808-565-6411); Molokai, **Molokai General Hospital** (808-553-5331); and Kauai, **Wilcox Memorial Hospital and Health Center** (808-245-1100). There's also a **Hawaii Poison Center** in Honolulu. ~ 808-941-4411.

Hotels often provide access to babysitters. On Oahu, **Aloha Babysitting Service** is a bonded babysitting agency. ~ 808-732-2029, fax 808-735-1958.

When choosing which island to visit, consider how many diversions it will take to keep your children happy. Oahu offers numerous options, from the Honolulu Zoo to theme parks to museums, while the outer islands have fewer attractions. It might be helpful to read the introductory passages to each of the island chapters before planning your vacation.

Traveling solo grants an independence and freedom different from that of traveling with a partner, but single travelers are more vulnerable to crime and should take additional precautions. An option for those who are alone but prefer not to be is to join a tour group. A multitude abound that are tailored to your specific interests; see "The New Travel" section in Chapter Two for ideas.

WOMEN TRAVELING ALONE

It's unwise to hitchhike and probably best to avoid inexpensive accommodations on the outskirts of town; the money saved does not outweigh the risk. Bed and breakfasts, youth hostels and YWCAs are generally your safest bet for lodging, and they also foster an environment ideal for bonding with fellow travelers.

Keep all valuables well-hidden and hold on to cameras and purses. Avoid late-night treks or strolls through undesirable parts of town, but if you find yourself in this situation, continue walking with a confident air until you reach a safe haven. A fierce scowl never hurts.

These hints should by no means deter you from seeking out adventure. Wherever you go, stay alert, use your common sense and trust your instincts.

Throughout the islands there are many organizations that can help you in case of emergency. On Oahu, contact the **Sex Abuse Treatment Center**. ~ 808-524-7273. **Women Helping Women**, a domestic violence shelter on Maui, can provide referrals. ~ 808-579-9581; www.whwmaui.net.

For more helpful hints, get a copy of *Safety and Security for Women Who Travel* (Traveler's Tales, 1998).

GAY & LESBIAN TRAVELERS

The Gay & Lesbian Community Center, specializing in support groups and community outreach, supplies Oahu visitors with gay-relevant information. Stop by during office hours to pick up lesbian and gay newspapers and brochures. It's located in the YWCA; call for office hours. ~ 2424 Beretania Street, Honolulu; 808-951-7000, fax 808-951-7001; www.glcc-hawaii.org.

For monthly updates on the gay and lesbian scene in Hawaii, pick up a copy of *Da Kine* at bars and clubs in Waikiki, the main library and the Academy of Arts Theater. Along with coverage of news and entertainment, it provides a calendar of events and a listing of services. ~ 2410 Cleghorn Street #2302, Honolulu, HI 96815; 808-923-7378, fax 808-922-6124; e-mail ha@gte.net.

The *Pocket Guide to Hawaii*, published by **Pacific Ocean Holidays**, is also helpful for gay travelers. It comes out three times a year and lists the best and hottest establishments and beaches that Hawaii has to offer. Send $5 per copy (via mail only) if ordering from the mainland; otherwise, it's distributed free by local gay businesses. This outfit can also help book vacation packages. ~ P.O. Box 88245, Honolulu, HI 96830; 808-923-2400, 800-735-6600 reservations only; www.gayhawaii.com.

Hawaiinet Tour & Travel Services Network, Inc. offers special tour packages to both gays and straights. They can help decide on hotels, condos and restaurants. This gay-owned company also delivers Hawaiian paper order baskets to the mainland. ~ P.O. Box 15671, Honolulu, HI 96830; 808-545-1119, fax 808-524-9572; www.hawaiinet.com.

Spanning the entire Hawaiian chain, the Big Island–based **Black Bamboo Guest Services** unearths the best cottages and houses for gay and straight travelers. This service also arranges car rentals, hiking tours, birdwatching trips and other sporting activities for its guests. ~ P.O. Box 211, Kealakekua, HI; 808-328-9607, 800-527-7789; e-mail bbamboo@aloha.net. For information on the gay and lesbian scene on Maui, contact **Both Sides Now, Inc.** They can

CRUISING THE ISLANDS

Hawaii's grand oceanliner tradition is carried on today by **American Hawaii Cruises**. The S.S. *Independence* cruises the inter-island waters, docking at Maui, the Big Island, Kauai and Pier 2 in Honolulu. The cruises are three-day, four-day and week-long affairs that evoke memories of the old steamship era. ~ P.O. Box 56729, New Orleans, LA 70156; 800-765-7000, reservations 800-513-5022; www.cruisehawaii.com.

provide details on lodging, upcoming events and social gatherings. ~ P.O. Box 5042, Kahului, HI 96733; 808-244-4566, fax 808-573-0045; www.maui-tech.com/glom. Lesbians can also call **Contact Dykes.** ~ 808-879-2971.

Women can call the **Women's Events Information Line** for goings-on around Maui. ~ 808-573-3077.

For further information, be sure to look under "gay and lesbian travelers" in the index at the end of the book.

SENIOR TRAVELERS

Hawaii is a hospitable place for senior citizens to visit. Countless museums, historic sights and even restaurants and hotels offer senior discounts that can cut a substantial chunk off vacation costs. The national park system's Golden Age Passport, which must be applied for in person, allows free admission for anyone 62 and older to the two national parks in the islands.

The **American Association of Retired Persons** (AARP) offers membership to anyone over 50. AARP's benefits include travel discounts with a number of firms. ~ 601 E Street NW, Washington, DC 20049; 800-424-3410; www.aarp.org.

Elderhostel offers reasonably priced, all-inclusive educational programs in a variety of locations throughout the year. ~ 75 Federal Street, Boston, MA 02110; 877-426-8056; www.elderhostel.org.

Be extra careful about health matters. Consider carrying a medical record with you—including your medical history and current medical status as well as your doctor's name, phone number and address. Make sure your insurance covers you while you are away from home.

DISABLED TRAVELERS

The **Commission on Persons with Disabilities** publishes a survey of the city, county, state and federal parks in Hawaii that are accessible to travelers with disabilities. They also provide "Aloha Guides to Accessibility," which cover Oahu, Maui, Kauai and the Big Island, and give information on various hotels, shopping centers, and restaurants that are accessible. ~ 919 Ala Moana Boulevard, Room 101, Honolulu, HI 96814; 808-586-8121, fax 808-586-8129; e-mail accesshi@aloha.net.

The **Society for the Advancement of Travel for the Handicapped** offers information for travelers with disabilities. ~ 347 5th Avenue, Suite 610, New York, NY 10016; 212-447-7284, fax 212-725-8253; www.sath.org. **Travelin' Talk,** a network of people and organizations, also provides assistance. ~ P.O. Box 1796, Wheatridge, CO 80034; 303-232-2979; www.travelintalk.net. **Access-Able Travel Source** has worldwide information online. ~ 303-232-2979; www.access-able.com.

Be sure to check in advance when making room reservations. Some hotels feature facilities for those in wheelchairs.

FOREIGN TRAVELERS

Passports and Visas   Most foreign visitors are required to obtain a passport and tourist visa to enter the United States. Contact your nearest United States Embassy or Consulate well in advance to obtain a visa and to check on any other entry requirements.

Customs Requirements   Foreign travelers are allowed to carry in the following: 200 cigarettes (1 carton), 50 cigars or 2 kilograms (4.4 pounds) of smoking tobacco; one liter of alcohol for personal use only (you must be 21 years of age to bring in alcohol); and US$100 worth of duty-free gifts that include an additional quantity of 100 cigars. You may bring in any amount of currency, but must fill out a form if you bring in over US $10,000. Carry any prescription drugs in clearly marked containers. (You may have to produce a written prescription or doctor's statement for the customs officer.) Meat or meat products, seeds, plants, fruits and narcotics are not allowed to be brought into the United States. Contact the **United States Customs Service** for further information. ~ 1301 Constitution Avenue NW, Washington, DC 20229; 202-927-6724; www.customs.treas.gov.

The island of Kauai boasts one of the wettest spots on earth, but its southwestern flank resembles the Arizona desert!

Driving   If you plan to rent a car, an international driver's license should be obtained prior to arrival. Some rental car companies require both a foreign license and an international driver's license. Many car rental agencies require that the lessee be at least 25 years of age; all require a major credit card. Seat belts are mandatory for the driver and all passengers. Children under the age of 5 or weighing less than 40 pounds should be in the back seat in approved child safety restraints.

Currency   United States money is based on the dollar. Bills come in six denominations: $1, $5, $10, $20, $50 and $100. Every dollar is divided into 100 cents. Coins are the penny (1 cent), nickel (5 cents), dime (10 cents), quarter (25 cents) and dollar (100 cents).

You may not use foreign currency to purchase goods and services in the United States. Consider buying traveler's checks in dollar amounts. You may also use credit cards affiliated with an American company such as Interbank, Barclay Card, VISA, MasterCard and American Express.

Electricity and Electronics   Electric outlets use currents of 110 volts, 60 cycles. For appliances made for other electrical systems, you need a transformer or adapter. Travelers who use laptop computers for telecommunication should be aware that modem configurations for U.S. telephone systems may be different from their European counterparts. Similarly, the U.S. format for videotapes is different from that in Europe; U.S. Park Service visitors centers and other stores that sell souvenir videos often have them available in European format.

Weights and Measurements   The United States uses the English system of weights and measures. American units and their metric equivalents are as follows: 1 inch = 2.5 centimeters; 1 foot (12 inches) = 0.3 meter; 1 yard (3 feet) = 0.9 meter; 1 mile (5280 feet) = 1.6 kilometers; 1 ounce = 28 grams; 1 pound (16 ounces) = 0.45 kilogram; 1 quart (liquid) = 0.9 liter.

MAIL

If you're staying in a particular establishment during your visit, you can usually have personal mail sent there. Otherwise, for cardholders, **American Express** will hold letters for no charge at its Honolulu office for 30 days, and will provide forwarding services. If you decide to use their facilities, have mail addressed to American Express, Client Mail, 2424 Kalakaua Avenue, Honolulu, HI 96815. ~ 808-922-4718. If you don't use this service, your only other recourse is to have mail sent to a particular post office in care of general delivery.

▼ ▼ ▼ ▼ ▼ ▼ ▼ ▼ ▼ ▼

Transportation

GETTING TO THE ISLANDS

During the 19th century, sleek clipper ships sailed from the West Coast to Hawaii in about 11 days. Today, you'll be traveling by a less romantic but far swifter conveyance—the jet plane. Rather than days at sea, it will be about five hours in the air from California, nine hours from Chicago, or around 11 hours if you're coming from New York.

There's really nothing more rewarding than catching a plane to Hawaii. Air Canada, American, Continental, Delta, Hawaiian, Northwest, TWA and United fly regular schedules to Honolulu. American and Delta also offer flights to Maui, and United flies to Maui as well as the Big Island and Kauai. This nonstop service is particularly convenient for travelers who are interested in visiting the outer islands while bypassing Honolulu.

Whichever carrier you choose, ask for the economy or excursion fare, and try to fly during the week; weekend flights are generally higher in price. To qualify for the lower price fares, it is sometimes necessary to book your flight two weeks in advance and to stay in the islands at least one week. Generally, however, the restrictions are minimal. Children under two years of age can fly for free, but they will not have a seat of their own. Each passenger is permitted two large pieces of luggage plus a carry-on bag. Shipping a bike or surfboard will cost extra.

In planning a Hawaiian sojourn, one potential moneysaver is the package tour, which combines air transportation with a hotel room and other amenities. Generally, it is a style of travel that I avoid. However, if you can find a package that provides air transportation, a hotel or condominium accommodation and a rental car, all at one low price—it might be worth considering. Just try to avoid the packages that preplan your entire visit, dragging you around on air-conditioned tour buses. Look for the package that provides only the bare necessities, namely transportation and lodging, while allowing you the greatest freedom.

However you decide to go, be sure to consult a travel agent. They are professionals in the field, possessing the latest information on rates and facilities, and their service to you is usually free.

GETTING BETWEEN ISLANDS

Since cruise ships are the only commercial boats serving all six Hawaiian islands, most of the transportation is by plane. **Aloha Airlines** and **Hawaiian Airlines**, the state's major carriers, provide frequent inter-island jet service. If you're looking for smooth, rapid, comfortable service, this is certainly it. You'll be buckled into your seat, offered a low-cost cocktail and whisked to your destination within about 20 minutes.

Without doubt, the best service aboard any inter-island carrier is on Aloha Airlines. They have an excellent reputation for flying on time and offer a seven-day, unlimited travel pass for island-hopping travelers. I give them my top recommendation.

Now that you know how to fly quickly and comfortably, let me tell you about the most exciting way to get between islands. **Aloha IslandAir** flies twin-engine propeller planes. These small airplanes travel at low altitudes and moderate speeds over the islands. Next to chartering a helicopter, they are one of the finest ways to see Hawaii from the air.

The service is very personalized; often the pilot will point out landmarks along the route, and sometimes he'll fly out of his way to show you points of particular interest. I often fly this way when I'm in the islands and highly recommend these small planes to anyone with a sense of adventure.

Let me describe a typical flight I took between Honolulu and Kona. So that I'd get a better view, the captain suggested that I sit up front in the copilot's seat. After taking off in a wide arc around Honolulu, we passed close enough to Diamond Head to gaze down into the crater, then headed across the Kaiwi Channel to Molokai. Since we had to pick up passengers at Molokai's lonely airstrip, the pilot gave us a tour of the island. We paralleled the island's rugged north face, where sharp cliffs laced with waterfalls drop thousands of feet to the sea. Then we swept in toward Maui for a view of Haleakala Crater, and continued past the Big Island's snowtipped volcanoes before touching down in Kona. All for the price of an airline ticket!

Rates for these twin-engine propeller planes are very competitive when compared with the inter-island jets. Coupled with the fact that your ticket on the smaller carriers is worth a guided tour as well as a trip between islands, you really can't do better than booking your flights on these sturdy little planes.

Renting a car is as easy in Hawaii as anywhere. Every island supports at least several rental agencies, which compete fiercely with one another in price and quality of service. So before renting, shop around: check the listings in this book, and also look for special temporary offers that many rental companies sometimes feature.

CAR RENTALS

There are several facts to remember when renting a car. First of all, a major credit card is essential. Also, many agencies don't rent at all to people under 25. Regardless of your age, many companies charge several dollars a day extra for insurance. The insurance is optional and expensive, and in many cases, unnecessary (many credit cards provide the same coverage when a rental is charged to the card). Find out if you credit card company offers this coverage. Your personal insurance policy may also provide for rental cars and, if necessary, have a clause added that will include rental car protection. Check on this before you leave home. But remember, whether you have insurance or not, you are liable for the first several thousand dollars in accident damage.

Rates fluctuate with the season; slack tourist seasons are great times for good deals. Also, three-day, weekly and monthly rates are almost always cheaper than daily rentals; cars with standard shifts are generally less than automatics; and compacts are more economical than the larger four-door models.

Other than on the island of Lanai, I don't recommend renting a jeep. They're more expensive and less comfortable than automobiles, and won't get you to very many more interesting spots. In addition, the rental car collision insurance provided by most credit cards does not cover jeeps. Except in extremely wet weather when roads are muddy, all the places mentioned in this book, including the hidden locales, can be reached by car.

The Land
and Outdoor Adventures

GEOLOGY More than 25 million years ago a fissure opened along the Pacific floor. Beneath tons of sea water molten lava poured from the rift. This liquid basalt, oozing from a hot spot in the earth's center, created a crater along the ocean bottom. As the tectonic plate that comprises the ocean floor drifted over the earth's hot spot, numerous other craters appeared. Slowly, in the seemingly endless procession of geologic time, a chain of volcanic islands, now stretching almost 2000 miles, has emerged from the sea.

On the continents it was also a period of terrible upheaval. The Himalayas, Alps and Andes were rising, but these great chains would reach their peaks long before the Pacific mountains even touched sea level. Not until about 25 million years ago did the first of these underwater volcanoes, today's Kure and Midway atolls, break the surface and become islands. It was not until about five million years ago that the first of the main islands of the archipelago, Niihau and Kauai, broke the surface to become high islands.

For a couple of million more years, the mountains continued to grow. The forces of erosion cut into them, creating knife-edged cliffs and deep valleys. Then plants began germinating: mosses and ferns, springing from windblown spores, were probably first, followed by seed plants carried by migrating birds and on ocean currents. The steep-walled valleys provided natural greenhouses in which unique species evolved, while transoceanic winds swept insects and other life from the continents.

Some islands never survived this birth process: the ocean simply washed them away. The first islands that did endure, at the northwestern end of the Hawaiian chain, proved to be the smallest. Today these islands, with the exception of Midway, are barren uninhabited atolls. The volcanoes that rose last, far to the southeast, became the mountainous archipelago generally known as the Hawaiian Islands.

With its luxurious parks, mountain retreats and deserted beaches, Hawaii is a paradise for campers and backpackers. Because of the varied terrain and the islands' microenvironments, it's possible to experience all kinds of outdoor adventures. One day you'll hike through a steaming rainforest filled with tropical flowers; the next night you'll camp atop a volcanic crater in a stark, windblown area that resembles the moon's surface; then you'll descend to a curving white-sand beach populated only by shorebirds and tropical fish.

Paradise means more than physical beauty, however. It also involves an easy life and a bountiful food supply. The easy living is up to you; just slow down from the frantic pace of mainland life and you'll discover that island existence can be relaxing. As for wild food—you'll find it hanging from trees, swimming in the ocean and clinging to coral reefs. Just be sure to use the proper techniques in taking from the environment and always keep Hawaii's delicate ecosystem in mind.

In this chapter, I'll detail some of the outdoor skills necessary to camp, hike and live naturally in Hawaii. This is certainly not a comprehensive study of how to survive on a Pacific island; I'm just passing along a few facts I've learned while exploring Hawaii. I don't advise that you plan to live entirely off the land. Hawaii's environment is too fragile to support you full-time. Anyway, living that way is a hell of a lot of work! I'll just give a few hints on how to supplement your provisions with a newly caught fish or a fresh fruit salad. That way, not only will you save on food bills, you'll also get a much fuller taste of the islands.

Obviously, none of these techniques were developed by me personally. In fact, most of them date back centuries to the early days, when Polynesian explorers applied the survival skills they had learned in Tahiti and the Marquesas to the newly discovered islands of Hawaii. So as you set out to fish along a coral reef, hunt for shellfish in tidepools or gather seaweed at low tide, give a prayerful thanks to the generations of savvy islanders who have come before you.

Flora and Fauna

FLORA

Many of the plants you'll see in Hawaii are not indigenous. In fact, much of the lush vegetation of this tropical island found its way here from locations all over the world. Sea winds, birds and seafaring settlers brought many of the seeds, plants, flowers and trees from the islands of the South Pacific, as well as from other, more distant regions. Over time, some plants adapted to Hawaii's unique ecosystem and climate, creating strange new lineages and evolving into a completely new ecosystem. This process has long interested scientists, who call the Hawaiian Islands one of the best natural labs for studies of plant evolution.

Sugar cane arrived in Hawaii with the first Polynesian settlers, who appreciated its sweet juices. By the late 1800s, it was well established as a lucrative crop. The pineapple was first planted during the same century. A member of the bromeliad family, this spiky plant is actually a collection of beautiful pink, blue and purple flowers, each of which develops into a fruitlet. The pineapple is a collection of these fruitlets, grown together into a single fruit that takes 14 to 17 months to mature. Sugar cane and pineapple are still the main crops in Hawaii, although competition from other countries and environmental problems caused by pesticides have taken their toll.

Visitors to Hawaii will find the islands a perpetual flower show. Sweetly scented plumeria, deep red, shiny anthurium, exotic ginger, showy birds of paradise, small lavender crown flowers, highly fragrant gardenias and the brightly hued hibiscus run riot on the islands and add color and fragrance to the surrounding area. Scarlet and purple bougainvillea vines, and the aromatic lantana, with its dense clusters of flowers, are also found in abundance.

Each of the main islands has designated a specific bloom as its island flower. Oahu has the *ilima*, a small golden blossom, and the Big Island has the red *lehua*, a furry flower with needle petals resembling a bottlebrush plant. Maui spotlights the *lokelani*, or pink cottage rose while Kauai's pick is the *mokihana*, which is actually a light green berry. Molokai's flower of choice is the small, white *kukui* blossom and Lanai's is the vibrant orange *kaunaoa*.

The beautiful, delicate orchid thrives in Hawaii's tropical heat and humidity. Cultivated primarily on the Big Island, the most popular orchids are the *dendrobium*, which can come in white, purple, lavender, or yellow; the *vanda* (bamboo orchid), which is lavender with white lavender and often used for making leis; and the popcorn, which has small, yellow flowers. The wild *vanda*, with its white and lavender petals, can be spotted along the side of the road year-round.

Hawaii's most unique plant is the silversword. Delicate looking, this silvery green plant is actually very hardy. It thrives on the moonscape of Haleakala, 6000 to 10,000 feet above sea level on Maui. Very adaptable, it can survive in extreme hot and cold temperatures with little moisture. Its silvery hairs reflect the sun and its leaves curl inward, protecting the stalk and creating a sort of bowl where rain is collected and stored. The plant lives from five to thirty years, waiting until the right moment before sprouting a three- to nine-foot stalk composed of hundreds of small, reddish flowers—and then it dies. In the same family as the sunflower, this particular type of silversword lives only on Haleakala and has been close to extinction for many years. Now protected, it is currently making a comeback.

Another curious specimen found on the leeward slopes of Haleakala and on the Big Island is the protea. With 1500 varieties, this remarkable plant comes in a myriad of shapes, sizes and colors. Some look like pin cushions, others resemble corn cobs. Originally from South Africa and Australia, the Hawaiian plant is a hybrid.

> The state tree is the *kukui* or candlenut tree, which provided early Hawaiians with oil, light and a natural remedy.

Although many people equate the tropics with the swaying palm tree, Hawaii is home to a variety of exotic trees. The famed banyan tree, known for pillar-like aerial roots that grow vertically downward from the branches, spreads to form a natural canopy. When the roots touch the ground, they thicken, providing support for the tree's branches to continue expanding. The candlenut, or *kukui*, tree, originally brought to Hawaii from the South Pacific islands, is big, bushy and prized for its nuts, which can be used for oil or polished and strung together to make leis. With its cascades of bright yellow or pink flowers, the cassia tree earns its moniker—the shower tree. Covered with tiny pink blossoms, the canopied monkeypod tree has fernlike leaves that close up at night.

Found in a variety of shapes and sizes, the ubiquitous palm does indeed sway to the breezes on white-sand beaches, but it also comes in a short, stubby form featuring more frond than trunk. The fruit, or nuts, of these trees are prized for their oil, which can be utilized for making everything from margarine to soap. The wood (rattan for example) is often used for making furniture.

FRUITS AND VEGETABLES There's a lot more to Hawaii's tropical wonderland than gorgeous flowers and overgrown rainforests. The islands are also teeming with edible plants. Roots, fruits, vegetables, herbs and spices grow like weeds from the shoreline to the mountains. Following is a list of some of the more commonly found edibles.

Avocado: Covered with either a tough green or purple skin, this pear-shaped fruit sometimes weighs as much as three pounds. It grows on ten- to forty-foot-high trees, and ripens from June through November.

Bamboo: The bamboo plant is actually a grass with a sweet root that is edible and a long stem frequently used for making furniture. Often exceeding eight feet in height, bamboo is green until picked, when it turns a golden brown.

Banana: Polynesians use banana trees not only for food but also for clothing, medicines, dyes and even alcohol. The fruit, which grows upside down on broad-leaved trees, can be harvested as soon as the first banana in the bunch turns yellow.

Breadfruit: This large round fruit grows on trees that reach up to 60 feet in height. Breadfruit must be boiled, baked or fried.

Coconut: The coconut tree is probably the most important plant in the entire Pacific. Every part of the towering palm is used. Most people are concerned only with the hard brown nut, which yields delicious milk as well as a tasty meat. If the coconut is still green, the meat is a succulent jellylike substance. Otherwise, it's a hard but delicious white rind.

Guava: A roundish yellow fruit that grows on a small shrub or tree, guavas are extremely abundant in the wild. They ripen between June and October.

Lychee: Found hanging in bunches from the lychee tree, this popular fruit is encased in red, prickly skin that peels off to reveal the sweet-tasting, translucent flesh.

Mango: Known as the king of fruits, the mango grows on tall shade trees. The oblong fruit ripens in the spring and summer.

Maui onion: Resembling an ordinary yellow onion in size and color, these bulbs are uncommonly mild. They are grown on the south side of Haleakala in rich volcanic soil, and enjoy enough sun and altitude to make them very sweet. A member of the lily family, the Maui onion is best eaten raw.

Mountain apple: This sweet fruit grows in damp, shaded valleys at an elevation of about 1800 feet. The flowers resemble fluffy crimson balls; the fruit, which ripens from July to December, is also a rich red color.

Papaya: This delicious fruit, which is picked as it begins to turn yellow, grows on unbranched trees. The sweet flesh can be bright orange or coral pink in color. Summer is the peak harvesting season.

Passion fruit: Oval in shape, this tasty yellow fruit grows to a length of about two or three inches. It's produced on a vine and ripens in summer or fall.

Taro: The tuberous root of this Hawaiian staple is pounded, then made into a grayish purple paste known as *poi*. One of the

FROM SURF TO SNOW

With several distinct biological regions, there's much more to the islands than lush tropics. Rainforests give way to dry forests, and to coastal habitats where the vegetation is specially suited to withstand wind and salt. Higher in altitude are the bogs, pools of standing water containing rare life forms that have been forced to adapt to a difficult environment. Highest in altitude is the alpine zone, consisting of bare volcanic surfaces scattered with clumps of low-growing herbs and shrubs. Subzero temperatures, frost and even snow help keep this region desolate.

most nutritious foods, it has a rather bland taste. The plant has wide, shiny, thick leaves with reddish stems; the root is white with purple veins.

In Hawaii, it seems there is more wildlife in the water and air than on land. A scuba diver's paradise, the ocean is also a promised land for many other creatures. Coral, colorful fish and migrating whales are only part of this underwater community. Sadly, many of Hawaii's coral reefs have been dying mysteriously in the last several years. No one is sure why, but many believe this is partially due to runoff from pesticides used in agriculture.

FAUNA

For adventure lovers, Maui, and to a lesser extent the Big Island, offer excellent opportunities for whale watching. Every year, humpback whales converge in the warm waters off the islands to give birth to their calves. Beginning their migration in Alaska, they can be spotted in Hawaiian waters from November through May. The humpback, named for its practice of showing its dorsal fin when diving, is quite easy to spy. They feed in shallow waters, usually diving for periods of no longer than 15 minutes. They often sleep on the surface and breathe fairly frequently. Unlike other whales, humpbacks have the ability to sing. Loud and powerful, their songs carry above and below the water for miles. The songs change every year, yet, incredibly, all the whales always seem to know the current one. Quite playful, they can be seen leaping, splashing and flapping their 15-foot tails over their backs. The best time for whale watching is from January to April.

Spinner dolphins are also favorites among visitors. Named for their "spinning" habit, they can revolve as many as six times during one leap. They resemble the spotted dolphin, another frequenter of Hawaiian waters, but are more likely to venture closer to the shore. Dolphins have clocked in with speeds ranging from 9 to 25 mph, a feat they often achieve by propelling themselves out of the water (or even riding the bow wave of a ship). Their thick, glandless skin also contributes to this agility. The skin is kept smooth by constant renewal and sloughing (bottlenoses replace their epidermis every two hours). Playful and intelligent, dolphins are a joy to watch. Many research centers are investigating the mammals' ability to imitate, learn and communicate; some believe that dolphin intelligence may be comparable to that of humans.

One of the few animals to live in the Hawaiian islands before the Polynesians' arrival, the Hawaiian monk seal has been hunted to the point of extinction. Now protected as an endangered species, this tropical seal is found mostly on the outer islands, although it is occasionally spotted on Kauai, and more rarely, on Oahu. Closely related to the elephant seal, the monk seal is not as agile or as fond of land as other seals.

Green sea turtles are common on all of the Hawaiian islands, although this was not always the case. Due to the popularity of their shells, they spent many years on the endangered species list, but are now making a comeback. Measuring three to four feet in diameter, these large reptiles frolic in saltwater only, and are often visible from the shore.

Hawaii is also home to many rare and endangered birds. Like the flora, the birds on the islands are highly specialized. The state bird, the nene, or Hawaiian goose, is a cousin to the Canadian goose and mates for life. Extinct on Maui for many years, several nenes were reintroduced here in the late 1960s. There's still some doubt as to whether they will produce a self-sustaining wild population. They currently live in the wild in the West Maui Mountains, on the Big Island and on Kauai. Once thought to be native to high-elevation habitats, biologists now believe that these rare birds may be more suited to a sea-level environment. The slopes of Haleakala are also home to two other endangered birds: the crested honeycreeper and the parrotbill.

On the endangered species list for many years, the Hawaiian hawk, or *io*, has had its status changed to "threatened." Existing exclusively on the Big Island, the regal *io* is found in a variety of habitats from forest to grassland, but is most often sighted on the slopes of Mauna Kea and Mauna Loa.

There *are* a few birds native to Hawaii that have thus far avoided the endangered species list. Two of the most common birds are the yellow-green *amakihi* and the red *iiwi*.

Known in Hawaiian mythology for its protective powers, the *pueo*, or Hawaiian owl, a brown-and-white-feathered bird, resides on Kauai, the Big Island and in Haleakala crater. On Oahu the Hawaiian owl is considered an endangered species.

The *koae kea*, or "tropic bird," lives on Haleakala, as well as in Kilauea Crater and Kauai's Waimea Canyon. Resembling a sea-

AQUACULTURE THE ANCIENT WAY

Ancient Hawaiians would have fared well on the television series *Survivor;* they had fishtrapping down pat. Using enclosed brackish water off the coast, fish were bred and maintained in fishponds through ingenious use of *makaha*, sluice gates that controlled the in- and outflow of water. Designed to allow young fish in and keep the ready-to-eat fish from escaping, the gates also helped control the growth of algae, the lowest but most vital rung on the pond food ladder. This ancient technique is still practiced in Oahu's Kaneohe Bay, where the **Kualoa Ranch** maintains an operational pond and sells its produce. ~ Kualoa Ranch, Kaneohe; 800-231-7321; www.kualoa.com.

gull in size, it has a long, thin white tail and a striking striping pattern on the back of the wings.

Another common bird is the *iwa*, or frigate, a very large creature measuring three to four feet in length, with a wing span averaging seven feet. The males are solid black, while the females have a large white patch on their chest and tail. A predatory bird, they're easy to spot raiding the nesting colonies of other birds along the offshore rocks. If you see one, be careful not to point at it; legend has it that it's bad luck. Other birds that make the islands their home are the Hawaiian stilt and the Hawaiian coot—both water birds—along with the black noddy, American plover and wedge-tailed shearwater.

Not many wild four-footed creatures roam the islands. Deer, feral goats and pigs were brought here early on and have found a home in the forests. Some good news for people fearful of snakes: There is nary a serpent (or a sea serpent) in Hawaii, although lizards such as skinks and geckos abound.

One can only hope that with the renewed interest in Hawaiian culture, and growing environmental awareness, Hawaii's plants and animals will continue to exist as they have for centuries.

Outdoor Adventures

FISHING

While you're exploring the islands, the sea will be your prime food source. Fishing in Hawaii is good year-round, and the offshore waters are crowded with many varieties of edible fish. For deep-sea fishing you'll have to charter a boat, and freshwater angling requires a license; so I'll concentrate on surf-casting. It costs nothing to fish this way.

In the individual island chapters, you'll find information on the best spots to fish for different species; in the "Addresses" section of those chapters, you'll usually see a fishing supply store listed. For information on seasons, licenses and official regulations, check with the Aquatic Resources Division of the State Department of Land and Natural Resources. This agency has offices on most of the major islands.

The easiest, most economical way to fish is with a hand-held line. Just get a 50- to 100-foot line, and attach a hook and a ten-ounce sinker. Wind the line loosely around a smooth block of wood, then remove the wood from the center. If your coil is free from snags, you'll be able to throw-cast it easily. You can either hold the line in your hand, feeling for a strike, or tie it to the frail end of a bamboo pole.

Beaches and rocky points are generally good places to surf-cast; the best times are during the incoming and outgoing tides. Popular baits include octopus, eel, lobster, crab, frozen shrimp and sea worms.

TORCHFISHING & SPEARFISHING The old Hawaiians also fished at night by torchlight. They fashioned torches by inserting nuts from the *kukui* tree into the hollow end of a bamboo pole, then lighting the flammable nuts. When fish swam like moths to the flame, the Hawaiians speared, clubbed or netted them.

Today, it's easier to use a lantern and spear. (In fact, it's all *too* easy and tempting to take advantage of this willing prey: Take only edible fish and only what you will eat.) It's also handy to bring a facemask or a glass-bottomed box to aid in seeing underwater. The best time for torchfishing is a dark night when the sea is calm and the tide low.

During daylight hours, the best place to spearfish is along coral reefs and in areas where the bottom is a mixture of sand and rock. Equipped with speargun, mask, fins and snorkel, you can explore underwater grottoes and spectacular coral formations while seeking your evening meal. Spearguns can be purchased inexpensively throughout the islands.

CRABBING For the hungry adventurer, there are several crab species in Hawaii. The most sought after are the Kona and Samoan varieties. Kona crabs are found in relatively deep water, and can usually be caught only from a boat. Samoan crabs inhabit sandy and muddy areas in bays and near river mouths. All you need to catch them are a boat and a net fastened to a round wire hoop secured by a string. The net is lowered to the bottom; then, after a crab has gone for the bait, the entire contraption is raised to the surface.

SQUIDDING Between June and December, squidding is another popular sport. Actually, the term is a misnomer: squid inhabit deep water and are not usually hunted. What you'll really be after are octopuses. There are two varieties in Hawaii, both of which are commonly found in water three or four feet deep: the *hee*, a greyish-brown animal that changes color like a chameleon, and the *puloa*, a red-colored mollusk with white stripes on its head.

Both are nocturnal and live in holes along coral reefs. At night by torchlight you can spot them sitting exposed on the bottom. During the day, they crawl inside the holes, covering the entrances with shells and loose coral.

The Hawaiians used to pick the octopus up, letting it cling to their chest and shoulders. When they were ready to bag their prize, they'd dispatch the creature by biting it between the eyes. You'll probably feel more comfortable spearing the beast.

SHELLFISH GATHERING Other excellent food sources are the shellfish that inhabit coastal waters. The ancient Hawaiians used pearl shells to attract the fish, and hooks, some made from human bones, to snare them.

The New Travel

Travel has become a personal art form. A destination no longer serves as just a place to relax: It's also a point of encounter. To many, this new wave in travel customs is labeled "adventure travel" and involves trekking glaciers or dusting the cliffs in a hang glider; to others, it connotes nothing more daring than a restful spell in a secluded resort. Actually, it's a state of mind, a willingness not only to accept but seek out the uncommon and unique.

Few places in the world are more conducive to this imaginative travel than Hawaii. Several organizations in the islands cater specifically to people who want to add local customs and unusual adventures to their vacation itineraries.

The **Nature Conservancy of Hawaii** conducts natural history day hikes of Oahu, Maui and Molokai. Led by expert guides, small groups explore untrammeled beaches, rainforest and an ancient bog. The tours provide a singular insight into the plant and animal life of the Islands. Reservations should be made at least one month in advance. ~ P.O. Box 1716, Makawao, HI 96768, 537-4508 on Oahu; 808-572-7849 on Maui; and P.O. Box 220, Kualapuu, HI 96757, 808-553-5236 on Molokai; www.tnc.org/hawaii.

Hawaiian Adventure Tours features a ten-day tour of Kauai, Maui and the Big Island, including hiking and snorkeling. ~ P.O. Box 1269, Kapaau, HI 96755; 808-889-0227, 800-659-3544; www.hawaiianadventuretours.com.

Paradise Safaris offers a sunset stargazing trip. Small groups enjoy a sunset view at the summit of Mauna Kea, and learn about the mountaintop observatory's telescope. ~ P.O. Box 9027, Kailua-Kona, HI 96745; 808-322-2366, 888-322-2366; www.maunakea.com.

EarthVoice Hawaii is an environmentally and culturally active nonprofit that aims to generate respect and responsibility for the natural world and interest in Hawaiian culture and customs. Activities run the gamut from nature walks to volcano watches to stepping through waterfalls. ~ P.O. Box 1433, Honokaa, HI 96727; 888-464-1080; www.earthmediahawaii.com.

When you're ready to take up the challenge of this style of freewheeling travel, check with these outfits. Or plan your own trip. To traditional tourists, Hawaii means souvenir shops and fast-food restaurants. But for those with spirit and imagination, it's a land of untracked beaches and ancient volcanoes waiting to be explored.

Your friends will probably be quite content to see you angling with store-bought artificial lures. Oysters and clams, which use their muscular feet to burrow into sand and soft mud, can be collected along the bottom of Hawaii's bays. Spiny lobsters, rarely found in Hawaii waters, are illegal to spear, but can be taken with short poles to which cable leaders and baited hooks are attached. You can also just grab them with a gloved hand but be careful—spiny lobsters live up to their name! You can also gather limpets, though I don't recommend it. These tiny black shellfish, locally known as *opihi*, cling tenaciously to rocks in the tidal zone. In areas of very rough surf, the Hawaiians gather them by leaping into the water after one set of waves breaks, then jumping out before the next set arrives. Being a coward myself, I simply order them in Hawaiian restaurants.

SEAWEED GATHERING

There are still some people who don't think of seaweed as food, but it's very popular among Japanese, and it once served as an integral part of the Hawaiian diet. It's extremely nutritious, easy to gather and very plentiful.

Rocky shores are the best places to find the edible species of seaweed. Some of them float in to shore and can be picked up; other species cling stubbornly to rocks and must be freed with a knife; still others grow in sand or mud. Low tide is the best time to collect seaweed: more plants are exposed, and some can be taken without even getting wet.

OCEAN SAFETY

For swimming, surfing, snorkeling and diving, there's no place quite like Hawaii. With endless miles of white-sand beach, the islands attract aquatic enthusiasts from all over the world. They come to enjoy Hawaii's colorful coral reefs and matchless surf conditions.

Many water lovers, however, never realize how awesome the sea can be. Particularly in Hawaii, where waves can reach 30-foot heights and currents flow unobstructed for thousands of miles,

SERVICE IN THE SUN

If you're looking for a fun and fulfilling way to spend ten days, contact **Sierra Club Outings**. Their guided service trips lead you into the islands' most desolate wilderness areas, through lush tropical forests and to coastal waters, restoring natural settings by removing manmade structures and fencing and conducting research on marine wildlife. Adventurers are able to snorkel, hike and enjoy beautiful views while helping to preserve Hawaii's paradise. ~ 85 2nd Street, 2nd Floor, San Francisco, CA 94105; 415-977-5522, fax 415-977-5795; www.sierraclub.org/outings/national.

the ocean is sometimes as treacherous as it is spectacular. Dozens of people drown every year in Hawaii, many others are dragged from the crushing surf with broken backs, and countless numbers sustain minor cuts and bruises.

These accidents can be entirely avoided if you approach the ocean with a respect for its power as well as an appreciation of its beauty. All you have to do is heed a few simple guidelines. First, never turn your back on the sea. Waves come in sets: one group may be small and quite harmless, but the next set could be large enough to sweep you out to sea. Never swim alone.

Don't try to surf, or even bodysurf, until you're familiar with the sports' techniques and precautionary measures. Be extremely careful when the surf is high.

If you get caught in a rip current, don't swim *against* it: swim *across* it, parallel to the shore. These currents, running from the shore out to sea, can often be spotted by their ragged-looking surface water and foamy edges.

Around coral reefs, wear something to protect your feet against coral cuts. Particularly good are the inexpensive Japanese *tabis*, or reef slippers. If you do sustain a coral cut, clean it with hydrogen peroxide, then apply an antiseptic or antibiotic substance. This is also a good procedure for octopus bites.

When stung by a Portuguese man-of-war or a jellyfish, rub on Adolph's unseasoned meat tenderizer, leave it on the sting for ten or twenty minutes, then rinse it off with alcohol. The old Hawaiian remedies, which are reputedly quite effective, involve applying urine or green papaya.

If you step on the sharp, painful spines of a sea urchin, soak the affected area in very hot water for 15 to 90 minutes. Another remedy calls for applying urine or undiluted vinegar. If the pain persists for more than a day, or you notice swelling or other signs of infection, consult a doctor.

Oh, one last thing. The chances of encountering a shark are about as likely as sighting a UFO. But should you meet one of these ominous creatures, stay calm. He'll be no happier to see you than you are to confront him. Simply swim quietly to shore. By the time you make it back to terra firma, you'll have a hell of a story to tell.

CAMPING & HIKING

Camping in Hawaii usually means pitching a tent or reserving a cabin. Throughout the islands there are secluded spots and hidden beaches, plus numerous county, state and federal parks. All of these campsites, together with hiking trails, are described in the individual island chapters; it's a good idea to consult those detailed listings when planning your trip. The camping equipment you'll require is listed in the "Packing" section of the preceding chapter. You might also want to obtain some hiking maps; they are available from **Hawaii Geographic Maps & Books**. ~ 49 South Hotel Street #215, Honolulu; 808-538-3952, 800-538-3950.

Before you set out on your camping trip, there are a few very important matters that I want to explain more fully. First, bring a campstove: firewood is scarce in most areas and soaking wet in others. It's advisable to wear long pants when hiking in order to protect your legs from rock outcroppings, spiny plants and insects. Also, if you are going to explore the Mauna Kea, Mauna Loa or Haleakala volcanoes, be sure to bring cold-weather gear; temperatures are often significantly lower than at sea level and these peaks occasionally receive snow.

Most trails you'll be hiking are composed of volcanic rock. Since this is a very crumbly substance, be extremely cautious when climbing any rock faces. In fact, you should avoid steep climbs if possible. Stay on the trails: Hawaii's dense undergrowth makes it very easy to get lost. If you get lost at night, stay where you are. Because of the low latitude, night descends rapidly here; there's practically no twilight. Once darkness falls, it can be very dangerous to move around. You should also be careful to purify all of your drinking water. And be extremely cautious near streambeds as flash-flooding sometimes occurs, particularly on the windward coasts. This is particularly true during the winter months, when heavy storms from the northeast lash the islands.

Another problem that you're actually more likely to encounter are those nasty varmints that buzz your ear just as you're falling asleep—mosquitoes. Hawaii contains neither snakes nor poison ivy, but it has plenty of these dive-bombing pests. Like me, you probably consider that it's always open season on the little bastards.

With most of the archipelago's other species, however, you'll have to be a careful conservationist. You'll be sharing the wilderness with pigs, goats, tropical birds, deer and mongooses, as well as a spectacular array of exotic and indigenous plants. All exist in one of the world's most delicate ecological balances. There are more endangered species in Hawaii than in all the rest of the United States. So keep in mind the maxim that the Hawaiians try to follow. *Ua mau ke ea o ka aina i ka pono:* The life of the land is preserved in righteousness.

THREE

History and Culture

POLYNESIAN ARRIVAL   The island of Hawaii, the Big Island, was the last land mass created in the ongoing dramatic geologic upheaval that formed the Hawaiian islands. But it was most likely the first island to be inhabited by humans. Perhaps as early as the third century, Polynesians sailing from the Marquesas Islands, and then later from Tahiti, landed on Hawaii's southern tip. The boats were formidable structures, catamaran-like vessels with a cabin built on the platform between the wooden hulls. The sails were woven from *hala* (pandanus) leaves. Some of the vessels were a hundred feet long and could do 20 knots, making the trip to Hawaii in a month.

The Polynesians had originally come from the coast of Asia about 3000 years before. They had migrated through Indonesia, then pressed inexorably eastward, leapfrogging across archipelagoes until they finally reached the last chain, the most remote—Hawaii.

These Pacific migrants were undoubtedly the greatest sailors of their day, and stand among the finest in history. When close to land they could smell it, taste it in the seawater, see it in a lagoon's turquoise reflection on the clouds above an island. They knew 150 stars. From the color of the water they determined ocean depths and current directions. They had no charts, no compasses, no sextants; sailing directions were simply recorded in legends and chants. Yet Polynesians discovered the Pacific, from Indonesia to Easter Island, from New Zealand to Hawaii. They made the Vikings and Phoenicians look like landlubbers.

CAPTAIN COOK   They were high islands, rising in the northeast as the sun broke across the Pacific. First one, then a second and, finally, as the tall-masted ships drifted west, a third island loomed before them. Landfall! The British crew was ecstatic. It meant fresh water, tropical fruits, solid ground on which to set their boots and a chance to carouse with the native women. For their captain, James Cook, it was another in an amazing career of discoveries. The man whom many call history's greatest explorer was about to land in one of the last spots on earth to be discovered by the West.

He would name the place for his patron, the British earl who became famous by pressing a meal between two crusts of bread. The Sandwich Islands. Later they would be called Owhyhee, and eventually, as the Western tongue glided around the uncharted edges of a foreign language, Hawaii.

It was January 1778, a time when the British Empire was still basking in a sun that never set. The Pacific had been opened to Western powers over two centuries before, when a Portuguese sailor named Magellan crossed it. Since that time, the British, French, Dutch and Spanish had tracked through in search of future colonies.

They happened upon Samoa, Fiji, Tahiti and the other islands that spread across this third of the globe, but somehow they had never sighted Hawaii. Even when Cook finally spied it, he little realized how important a find he had made. Hawaii, quite literally, was a jewel in the ocean, rich in fragrant sandalwood, ripe for agricultural exploitation and crowded with sea life. But it was the archipelago's isolation that would prove to be its greatest resource. Strategically situated between Asia and North America, it was the only place for thousands of miles to which whalers, merchants and bluejackets could repair for provisions and rest.

Cook was 49 years old when he shattered Hawaii's quiescence. The Englishman hadn't expected to find islands north of Tahiti. Quite frankly, he wasn't even trying. It was his third Pacific voyage and Cook was hunting bigger game, the fabled Northwest Passage that would link this ocean with the Atlantic.

But these mountainous islands were still an interesting find. He could see by the canoes venturing out to meet his ships that the lands were inhabited; when he finally put ashore on Kauai, Cook discovered a Polynesian society. He saw irrigated fields, domestic animals and high-towered temples. The women were bare-breasted, the men wore loincloths. As his crew bartered for pigs, fowls and bananas, he learned that the natives knew about metal and coveted iron like gold.

If iron was gold to these "Indians," then Cook was a god. He soon realized that his arrival had somehow been miraculously timed, coinciding with the Makahiki festival, a months-long celebration highlighted by sporting competitions, feasting, hula and exaltation of the ruling chiefs. Even war ceased during this gala affair. Makahiki honored the roving deity Lono, whose return to Hawaii on "trees that would move over seas" was foretold in ancient legend. Cook was a strange white man sailing tall-masted ships—obviously he was Lono. The Hawaiians gave him gifts, fell in his path and rose only at his insistence.

But even among religious crowds, fame is often fickle. After leaving Hawaii, Cook sailed north to the Arctic Sea, where he failed to discover the Northwest Passage. He returned the next year to Kealakekua Bay on the Big Island, arriving at the tail end of another exhausting Makahiki festival. By then the Hawaiians had tired of his constant demands for provisions and were suffering from a new disease that was obviously carried by Lono's archangelic crew—syphilis. This Lono was proving something of a freeloader.

Tensions ran high. The Hawaiians stole a boat. Cook retaliated with gunfire. A scuffle broke out on the beach and in a sudden violent outburst, which surprised the islanders as much as the interlopers, the Hawaiians discovered that their god could bleed. The world's finest mariner lay face down in foot-deep water, stabbed and bludgeoned to death.

Cook's end marked the beginning of an era. He had put the Pacific on the map, his map, probing its expanses and defining its fringes. In Hawaii he ended a thousand years of solitude. The archipelago's geographic isolation, which has always played a crucial role in Hawaii's development, had finally failed to protect it, and a second theme had come into play—the islands' vulnerability. Together with the region's "backwardness," these conditions would now mold Hawaii's history. All in turn would be shaped by another factor, one which James Cook had added to Hawaii's historic equation: the West.

KAMEHAMEHA AND KAAHUMANU The next man whose star would rise above Hawaii was present at Cook's death. Some say he struck the Englishman, others that he took a lock of the great leader's hair and used its residual power, its *mana*, to become king of all Hawaii.

Kamehameha was a tall, muscular, unattractive man with a furrowed face, a lesser chief on the powerful island of Hawaii. When he began his career of conquest a few years after Cook's death, he was a mere upstart, an ambitious, arrogant young chief. But he fought with a general's skill and a warrior's cunning, often plunging into the midst of a melee. He had an astute sense of technology, an intuition that these new Western metals and firearms could make him a king.

In Kamehameha's early years, the Hawaiian islands were composed of many fiefdoms. Several kings or great chiefs, continu-

SAILORS EXTRAORDINAIRE

Centuries before Columbus happened upon the New World, and during a time when European mariners were rarely venturing outside the Mediterranean Sea, entire families of Polynesians were crossing 2500 miles of untracked ocean in hand-carved canoes.

ally warring among themselves, ruled individual islands. At times, a few kings would carve up one island or a lone king might seize several. Never had one monarch controlled all the islands.

But fresh players had entered the field: Westerners with ample firepower and awesome ships. During the decade following Cook, only a handful had arrived, mostly Englishmen and Americans, and they had not yet won the influence they soon would wield. However, even a few foreigners were enough to upset the balance of power. They sold weapons and hardware to the great chiefs, making several of them more powerful than any of the others had ever been. War was imminent.

While British sailors were discovering Hawaii, the English army was battling a ragtag band of revolutionaries for control of the American colonies.

Kamehameha stood in the center of the hurricane. Like any leader suddenly caught up in the terrible momentum of history, he never quite realized where he was going or how fast he was moving. And he cared little that he was being carried in part by Westerners who would eventually want something for the ride. Kamehameha was no fool. If political expedience meant Western intrusion, then so be it. He had enemies among chiefs on the other islands; he needed the guns.

When two white men came into his camp in 1790, he had the military advisers to complement a fast expanding arsenal. Within months he cannonaded Maui. In 1792, Kamehameha seized the Big Island by inviting his main rival to a peaceful parley, then slaying the hapless chief. By 1795, he had consolidated his control of Maui, grasped Molokai and Lanai, and begun reaching greedily toward Oahu. He struck rapidly, landing near Waikiki and sweeping inland, forcing his enemies to their deaths over the precipitous cliffs of the Nuuanu Pali.

The warrior had become a conqueror, controlling all the islands except Kauai, which he finally gained in 1810 by peaceful negotiation. Kamehameha proved to be as able a bureaucrat as he had been a general. He became a benevolent despot who, with the aid of an ever-increasing number of Western advisers, expanded Hawaii's commerce, brought peace to the islands and moved his people inexorably toward the modern age.

He came to be called Kamehameha the Great, and history first cast him as the George Washington of Hawaii, a wise and resolute leader who gathered a wartorn archipelago into a kingdom. Kamehameha I. But with the revisionist history of the 1960s and 1970s, as Third World people questioned both the Western version of events and the virtues of progress, Kamehameha began to resemble Benedict Arnold. He was seen as an opportunist, a megalomaniac who permitted the Western powers their initial foothold in Hawaii. He used their technology and then, in the manner of great men who depend on stronger allies, was eventually used by them.

As long a shadow as Kamehameha cast across the islands, the event that most dramatically transformed Hawaiian society occurred after his death in 1819. The kingdom had passed to Kamehameha's son Liholiho, but Kamehameha's favorite wife, Kaahumanu, usurped the power. Liholiho was a prodigal son, dissolute, lacking self-certainty, a drunk. Kaahumanu was a woman for all seasons, a canny politician who combined brilliance with boldness, the feminist of her day. She had infuriated Kamehameha by eating forbidden foods and sleeping with other chiefs, even when he placed a taboo on her body and executed her lovers. She drank liquor, ran away, proved completely uncontrollable and won Kamehameha's love.

It was only natural that when he died, she would take his *mana*, or so she reckoned. Kaahumanu gravitated toward power with the drive of someone whom fate has unwisely denied. She carved her own destiny, announcing that Kamehameha's wish had been to give her a governmental voice. There would be a new post and she would fill it, becoming in a sense Hawaii's first prime minister.

And if the power, then the motion. Kaahumanu immediately marched against Hawaii's belief system, trying to topple the old idols. For years she had bristled under a polytheistic religion regulated by taboos, or *kapus*, which severely restricted women's rights. Now Kaahumanu urged the new king, Liholiho, to break a very strict *kapu* by sharing a meal with women.

Since the act might help consolidate Liholiho's position, it had a certain appeal to the king. Anyway, the *kapus* were weakening: these white men, coming now in ever greater numbers, defied them with impunity. Liholiho vacillated, went on a two-day drunk before gaining courage, then finally sat down to eat. It was a last supper, shattering an ancient creed and opening the way for a radically new divinity. As Kaahumanu had willed, the old order collapsed, taking away a vital part of island life and leaving the Hawaiians more exposed than ever to foreign influence.

Already Western practices were gaining hold. Commerce from Honolulu, Lahaina and other ports was booming. There was a fortune to be made dealing sandalwood to China-bound merchants, and the chiefs were forcing the common people to strip Hawaii's forests. The grueling labor might make the chiefs rich, but it gained the commoners little more than a barren landscape. Western diseases struck virulently. The Polynesians in Hawaii, who numbered 300,000 in Cook's time, were extremely susceptible. By 1866, their population had dwindled to less than 60,000. It was a difficult time for the Hawaiian people.

MISSIONARIES AND MERCHANTS   Hawaii was not long without religion. The same year that Kaahumanu shattered tradition, a group of New England missionaries boarded the brig *Thaddeus* for a voyage around Cape Horn. It was a young company—many were in their twenties or thirties—and included a doctor, a printer and several teachers. They were all strict Calvinists, fearful that the second coming was at hand and possessed of a mission. They were bound for a strange land called Hawaii, 18,000 miles away.

Hawaii, of course, was a lost paradise, a hellhole of sin and savagery where men slept with several wives and women neglected to wear dresses. To the missionaries, it mattered little that the Hawaiians had lived this way for centuries. The churchmen would save these heathens from hell's everlasting fire whether they liked it or not.

The delegation arrived in Kailua on the Big Island in 1820 and then spread out, establishing important missions in Honolulu and Lahaina. Soon they were building schools and churches, conducting services in Hawaiian and converting the natives to Christianity.

The missionaries rapidly became an integral part of Hawaii, despite the fact that they were a walking contradiction to everything Hawaiian. They were a contentious, self-righteous, fanatical people whose arrogance toward the Hawaiians blinded them to the beauty and wisdom of island lifestyles. Where the natives lived in thatch homes open to the soothing trade winds, the missionaries built airless clapboard houses with New England–style fireplaces. While the Polynesians swam and surfed frequently, the new arrivals, living near the world's finest beaches, stank from not bathing. In a region where the thermometer rarely drops much below seventy degrees, they wore long-sleeved woolens, ankle-length dresses and claw-hammer coats. At dinner they preferred salt pork to fresh beef, dried meat to fresh fish. They considered coconuts an abomination and were loath to eat bananas.

And yet the missionaries were a brave people, selfless and God-fearing. Their dangerous voyage from the Atlantic had brought them into a very alien land. Many would die from disease and overwork; most would never see their homeland again. Bigoted though they were, the Calvinists committed their lives to the Hawaiian people. They developed the Hawaiian alphabet, rendered Hawaiian into a written language and, of course, translated the Bible. Theirs was the first printing press west of the Rockies. They introduced Western medicine throughout the islands and created such an effective school system that, by the mid-19th century, 80 percent of the Hawaiian population was literate. Unlike almost all the other white people who came to Hawaii, they not only took from the islanders, they also gave.

But to these missionaries, *giving* meant ripping away everything repugnant to God and substituting it with Christianity. They would have to destroy Hawaiian culture in order to save it. Though instructed by their church elders not to meddle in island politics, the missionaries soon realized that heavenly wars had to be fought on earthly battlefields. Politics it would be. After all, wasn't government just another expression of God's bounty?

They allied with Kaahumanu and found it increasingly difficult to separate church from state. Kaahumanu converted to Christianity, while the missionaries became government advisers and helped pass laws protecting the sanctity of the Sabbath. Disgusting practices such as hula dancing were prohibited.

Politics can be a dangerous world for a man of the cloth. The missionaries were soon pitted against other foreigners who were quite willing to let the clerics sing hymns, but were damned opposed to permitting them a voice in government. Hawaii in the 1820s had become a favorite way station for the whaling fleet. As the sandalwood forests were decimated, the island merchants began looking for other industries. By the 1840s, when over 500 ships a year anchored in Hawaiian ports, whaling had become the islands' economic lifeblood.

During the heyday of the whaling industry, more American ships visited Hawaii than any other port in the world.

Like the missionaries, the whalers were Yankees, shipping out from bustling New England ports. But they were a hell of a different cut of Yankee. These were rough, crude, boisterous men who loved rum and music, and thought a lot more of fornicating with island women than saving them. After the churchmen forced the passage of laws prohibiting prostitution, the sailors rioted along the waterfront and fired cannons at the mission homes. When the smoke cleared, the whalers still had their women.

Religion simply could not compete with commerce, and other Westerners were continuously stimulating more business in the islands. By the 1840s, as Hawaii adopted a parliamentary form of government, American and British fortune hunters were replacing missionaries as government advisers. It was a time when anyone, regardless of ability or morality, could travel to the islands and become a political powerhouse literally overnight. A consumptive American, fleeing the mainland for reasons of health, became chief justice of the Hawaiian Supreme Court while still in his twenties. Another lawyer, shadowed from the East Coast by a checkered past, became attorney general two weeks after arriving.

The situation was no different internationally. Hawaii was subject to the whims and terrors of gunboat diplomacy. The archipelago was solitary and exposed, and Western powers were beginning to eye it covetously. In 1843, a maverick British naval officer actually annexed Hawaii to the Crown, but the London government later countermanded his actions. Then, in the early 1850s, the threat of American annexation arose. Restless Californians, fresh from the gold fields and hungry for revolution, plotted unsuccessfully in Honolulu. Even the French periodically sent gunboats in to protect their small Catholic minority.

Finally, the three powers officially stated that they wanted to maintain Hawaii's national integrity. But independence seemed increasingly unlikely. European countries had already begun claiming other Pacific islands, and with the influx of Yankee missionaries and whalers, Hawaii was being steadily drawn into the American orbit.

THE SUGAR PLANTERS   There is an old Hawaiian saying that describes the 19th century: The missionaries came to do good, and they did very well. Actually the early evangelists, few of whom profited from their work, lived out only half the maxim. Their sons would give the saying its full meaning.

This second generation, quite willing to sacrifice glory for gain, fit neatly into the commercial society that had rendered their fathers irrelevant. They were shrewd, farsighted young Christians who had grown up in Hawaii and knew both the islands' pitfalls and potentials. They realized that the missionaries had never quite found Hawaii's pulse, and they watched uneasily as whaling became the lifeblood of the islands. Certainly it brought wealth, but whaling was too tenuous—there was always a threat that it might dry up entirely. A one-industry economy would never do; the mission boys wanted more. Agriculture was the obvious answer, and eventually they determined to bind their providence to a plant that grew wild in the islands—sugar cane.

The first sugar plantation was started on Kauai in 1835, but not until the 1870s did the new industry blossom. By then, the Civil War had wreaked havoc with the whaling fleet, and a devastating winter in the Arctic whaling grounds practically destroyed it. The mission boys, who had prophesied the storm, weathered it quite comfortably. They had already begun fomenting an agricultural revolution.

Agriculture, of course, means land, and until the 19th century all Hawaii's acreage was held by chiefs. So in 1848, the mission sons, together with other white entrepreneurs, pushed through the Great Mahele, one of the slickest real estate laws in history. Rationalizing that it would grant chiefs the liberty to sell land to Hawaiian commoners and white men, the mission sons established a western system of private property.

The Hawaiians, who had shared their chiefs' lands communally for centuries, had absolutely no concept of deeds and leases. What resulted was the old $24-worth-of-beads story. The benevolent Westerners wound up with the land, while the lucky Hawaiians got practically nothing. Large tracts were purchased for cases of whiskey; others went for the cost of a hollow promise. The entire island of Niihau, which is still owned by the same family, sold for $10,000. It was a bloodless coup, staged more than 40 years before the revolution that would topple Hawaii's monarchy. In a sense it made the 1893 uprising anticlimactic. By then Hawaii's future would already be determined: white interlopers would own four times as much land as Hawaiian commoners.

Following the Great Mahele, the mission boys, along with other businessmen, were ready to become sugar planters. The *mana* once again was passing into new hands. Obviously, there was money to be made in cane, a lot of it, and now that they had land, all they needed was labor. The Hawaiians would never do. Cook might have recognized them as industrious, hardworking people, but the sugar planters considered them shiftless. Disease was killing them off anyway, and the Hawaiians who survived seemed to lose the will to live. Many made appointments with death, stating that in a week they would die; seven days later they were dead.

> Between 1850 and 1930, 180,000 Japanese, 125,000 Filipinos, 50,000 Chinese and 20,000 Portuguese immigrated to Hawaii.

Foreign labor was the only answer. In 1850, the Masters and Servants Act was passed, establishing an immigration board to import plantation workers. Cheap Asian labor would be brought over. It was a crucial decision, one that would ramify forever through Hawaiian history and change the very substance of island society. Eventually these Asian workers transformed Hawaii from a chain of Polynesian islands into one of the world's most varied and dynamic locales, a meeting place of East and West.

The Chinese were the first to come, arriving in 1852 and soon outnumbering the white population. Initially, with their long pigtails and uncommon habits, the Chinese were a joke around the islands. They were poor people from southern China whose lives were directed by clan loyalty. They built schools and worked hard so that one day they could return to their native villages in glory. They were ambitious, industrious and—ultimately—successful.

Too successful, according to the sugar planters, who found it almost impossible to keep the coolies down on the farm. The Chinese came to Hawaii under labor contracts, which forced them to work for five years. After their indentureship, rather than reenlisting as the sugar bosses had planned, the Chinese moved to the city and became merchants. Worse yet, they married Hawaiian women and were assimilated into the society.

These coolies, the planters decided, were too uppity, too ready to fill social roles that were really the business of white men. So in the 1880s, they began importing Portuguese. But the Portuguese thought they already *were* white men, while any self-respecting American or Englishman of the time knew they weren't.

The Portuguese spelled trouble, and in 1886 the sugar planters turned to Japan, with its restricted land mass and burgeoning population. The new immigrants were peasants from Japan's southern islands, raised in an authoritarian, hierarchical culture in which the father was a family dictator and the family was strictly defined by its social status. Like the Chinese, they built schools to protect their heritage and dreamed of returning home someday; but unlike their Asian neighbors, they only married other Japanese. They sent home for "picture brides," worshipped their ancestors and Emperor and paid ultimate loyalty to Japan, not Hawaii.

The Japanese, it soon became evident, were too proud to work long hours for low pay. Plantation conditions were atrocious; workers were housed in hovels and frequently beaten. The Japanese simply did not adapt. Worst of all, they not only bitched, they organized, striking in 1909.

So in 1910, the sugar planters turned to the Philippines for labor. For two decades the Filipinos arrived, seeking their fortunes and leaving their wives behind. They worked not only with sugar cane but also with pineapples, which were becoming a big business in the 20th century. They were a boisterous, fun-loving people, hated by the immigrants who preceded them and used by the whites who hired them. The Filipinos were given the most menial jobs, the worst working conditions and the shoddiest housing. In time, another side of their character began to show—a despondency, a hopeless sense of their own plight, their inability to raise passage money back home. They became the untouchables of Hawaii.

REVOLUTIONARIES AND ROYALISTS   Sugar, by the late 19th century, was king. It had become the center of island economy, the principal fact of life for most islanders. Like the earlier whaling industry, it was drawing Hawaii ever closer to the American sphere. The sugar planters were selling the bulk of their crops in California; having already signed several tariff treaties to protect their American market, they were eager to further strengthen mainland ties. Besides, many sugar planters were second-, third- and fourth-generation descendants of the New England missionaries; they had a natural affinity for the United States.

There was, however, one group that shared neither their love for sugar nor their ties to America. To the Hawaiian people, David Kalakaua was king, and America was the nemesis that had long threatened their independence. The whites might own the land, but the Hawaiians, through their monarch, still held substantial political power. During Kalakaua's rule in the 1870s and 1880s, anti-colonialism was rampant.

The sugar planters were growing impatient. Kalakaua was proving very antagonistic; his nationalist drumbeating was becoming louder in their ears. How could the sugar merchants convince the United States to annex Hawaii when all these silly Hawaiian royalists were running around pretending to be the Pacific's answer to the British Isles? They had tolerated this long enough. The Hawaiians were obviously unfit to rule, and the planters soon joined with other businessmen to form a secret revolutionary organization. Backed by a force of well-armed followers, they pushed through the "Bayonet Constitution" of 1887, a self-serving document that weakened the king and strengthened the white landowners. If Hawaii was to remain a monarchy, it would have a Magna Carta.

But Hawaii would not be a monarchy long. Once revolution is in the air, it's often difficult to clear the smoke. By 1893, Kalakaua was dead and his sister, Liliuokalani, had succeeded to the throne. She was an audacious leader, proud of her heritage, quick to defend it and prone to let immediate passions carry her onto dangerous ground. At a time when she should have hung fire, she charged, proclaiming publicly that she would abrogate the new constitution and reestablish a strong monarchy. The revolutionaries had the excuse they needed. They struck in January, seized government buildings and, with four boatloads of American marines and the support of the American minister, secured Honolulu. Liliuokalani surrendered.

Hawaii's first president was Sanford Dole, a missionary's son whose name eventually became synonymous with pineapples.

It was a highly illegal coup; legitimate government had been stolen from the Hawaiian people. But given an island chain as isolated and vulnerable as Hawaii, the revolutionaries reasoned, how much did it really matter? It would be weeks before word reached Washington of what a few Americans had done without official sanction, then several more months before a new American president, Grover Cleveland, denounced the renegade action. By then the revolutionaries would already be forming a republic.

Not even revolution could rock Hawaii into the modern age. For years, an unstable monarchy had reigned; now an oligarchy composed of the revolution's leaders would rule. Officially, Hawaii was a democracy; in truth, the Chinese and Japanese were hindered from voting, and the Hawaiians were encouraged not to bother. Hawaii, reckoned its new leaders, was simply not ready for democracy. Even when the islands were finally annexed by the United States in 1898 and granted territorial status, they remained a colony.

More than ever before, the sugar planters, alias revolutionaries, held sway. By the early 20th century, they had linked their plantations into a cartel, the Big Five. It was a tidy monopoly composed of five companies that owned not only the sugar and pineapple industries, but the docks, shipping companies and many of the stores, as well. Most of these holdings, happily, were the property of a few interlocking, intermarrying mission families—the Doles, Thurstons, Alexanders, Baldwins, Castles, Cookes and others—who had found heaven right here on earth. They golfed together and dined together, sent their daughters to Wellesley and their sons to Yale. All were proud of their roots, and as blindly paternalistic as their forefathers. It was their destiny to control Hawaii, and they made very certain, by refusing to sell land or provide services, that mainland firms did not gain a foothold in their domain.

Don't get confused—that's not the British Union Jack you see flying but the state flag of Hawaii.

What was good for the Big Five was good for Hawaii. Competition was obviously not good for Hawaii. Although the Chinese and Japanese were establishing successful businesses in Honolulu and some Chinese were even growing rich, they posed no immediate threat to the Big Five. And the Hawaiians had never been good at capitalism. By the early 20th century, they had become one of the world's most urbanized groups. But rather than competing with white businessmen in Honolulu, unemployed Hawaiians were forced to live in hovels and packing crates, cooking their poi on stoves fashioned from empty oil cans.

Political competition was also unhealthy. Hawaii was ruled by the Big Five, so naturally it should be run by the Republican Party. After all, the mission families were Republicans. Back on the mainland, the Democrats had always been cool to the sugar planters, and it was a Republican president, William McKinley, who eventually annexed Hawaii. The Republicans, quite simply, were good for business.

The Big Five set out very deliberately to overwhelm any political opposition. When the Hawaiians created a home-rule party around the turn of the century, the Big Five shrewdly co-opted it by running a beloved descendant of Hawaii's royal family as the Republican candidate. On the plantations they pitted one ethnic group against another to prevent the Asian workers from organizing. Then, when labor unions finally formed, the Big Five attacked them savagely. In 1924, police killed 16 strikers on Kauai. Fourteen years later, in an incident known as the "Hilo massacre," the police wounded 50 picketers.

The Big Five crushed the Democratic Party by intimidation. Polling booths were rigged. It was dangerous to vote Democratic—workers could lose their jobs, and if they were plantation workers, that meant losing their houses as well. Conducting Democratic meetings on the plantations was about as easy as holding a hula dance in an old missionary church. The Democrats went underground.

Those were halcyon days for both the Big Five and the Republican Party. In 1900, only five percent of Hawaii's population was white. The rest was composed of races that rarely benefitted from Republican policies. But for the next several decades, even during the Depression, the Big Five kept the Republicans in power.

While the New Deal swept the mainland, Hawaii clung to its colonial heritage. The islands were still a generation behind the rest of the United States—the Big Five enjoyed it that way. There was nothing like the status quo when you were already in power. Other factors that had long shaped Hawaii's history also played into the hands of the Big Five. The islands' vulnerability, which had always favored the rule of a small elite, permitted the Big Five to establish an awesome cartel. Hawaii's isolation, its distance from the mainland, helped protect their monopoly.

THE JAPANESE AND THE MODERN WORLD   All that ended on December 7, 1941. On what would afterwards be known as the "Day of Infamy," a flotilla of six aircraft carriers carrying over 400 planes unleashed a devastating assault on Pearl Harbor. Attacking the Pacific Fleet on a Sunday morning, when most of the American ships were unwisely anchored side by side, the Japanese sank or badly damaged six battleships, three destroyers and several other vessels. Over 2400 Americans were killed.

The Japanese bombers that attacked Pearl Harbor sent shock waves through Hawaii that are still rumbling today. World War II changed all the rules of the game, upsetting the conditions that had determined island history for centuries.

Ironically, no group in Hawaii would feel the shift more thoroughly than the Japanese. On the mainland, Japanese-Americans were rounded up and herded into relocation camps. But in Hawaii that was impossible; there were simply too many (160,000— fully one-third of the island's population), and they comprised too large a part of the labor force.

Many were second-generation Japanese, *nisei*, who had been educated in American schools and assimilated into Western society. Unlike their immigrant parents, the *issei*, they felt few ties to Japan. Their loyalties lay with America, and when war broke out they determined to prove it. They joined the U.S. armed forces and formed a regiment, the 442nd, which became the most frequently decorated outfit of the war. The Japanese were heroes, and when the war ended many heroes came home to the United States and ran for political office. Men like Daniel Inouye and Spark Matsunaga began winning elections and would eventually become United States senators.

By the time the 442nd returned to the home front, Hawaii was changing dramatically. The Democrats were coming to power. Leftist labor unions won crucial strikes in 1941 and 1946. Jack Burns, an ex-cop who dressed in tattered clothes and drove around Honolulu in a beat-up car, was creating a new Democratic coalition.

Burns, who would eventually become governor, recognized the potential power of Hawaii's ethnic groups. Money was flowing into the islands—first military expenditures and then tourist dollars, and non-whites were rapidly becoming a new middle class. The Filipinos still constituted a large part of the plantation force, and the Hawaiians remained disenchanted, but the Japanese and Chinese were moving up fast. Together they formed a majority of Hawaii's voters.

Burns organized them, creating a multiracial movement and thrusting the Japanese forward as candidates. By 1954, the Democrats controlled the legislature, with the Japanese filling one out of every two seats in the capital. Then, when Hawaii attained statehood five years later, the voters elected the first Japanese ever to serve in Congress. Today one of the state's U.S. senators and a congressman are Japanese. On every level of government, from municipal to federal, the Japanese predominate. They have arrived. The *mana*, that legendary power coveted by the Hawaiian chiefs and then lost to the sugar barons, has passed once again—to a people who came as immigrant farm-workers and stayed to become the leaders of the 50th state.

The Japanese and the Democrats were on the move, but in the period from World War II until the present day, everything was in motion. Hawaii was in upheaval. Jet travel and a population boom shattered the islands' solitude. While in 1939 about 500 people flew to Hawaii, now about seven million visitors land every year. The military population escalated as Oahu became a key base not only during World War II but throughout the Cold War and the Vietnam War, as well. Hawaii's overall population exploded from about a half-million just after World War II to over one million at the present time.

No longer did the islands lag behind the mainland; they rapidly acquired the dubious quality of modernity. Hawaii became America's 50th state in 1959, Honolulu grew into a bustling high-rise city, and hotels and condominiums mushroomed along the beaches of Maui, a neighboring island. Outside investors swallowed up two of the Big Five corporations, and several partners in the old monopoly began conducting most of their business outside Hawaii. Everything became too big and moved too fast for Hawaii to be entirely vulnerable to a small interest group.

A SLICE OF THE PIE

In ancient Hawaii, each island was divided like a pie into wedge-shaped plots, *ahupuaas*, which extended from the ocean to the mountain peaks. In that way, every chief's domain contained fishing spots, village sites, arable land and everything else necessary for the survival of his subjects.

Now, like the rest of the world, it would be prey to multinational corporations.

By the 1980s, it would also be of significant interest to investors from Japan. In a few short years they succeeded in buying up a majority of the state's luxury resorts, including every major beachfront hotel in Waikiki, sending real estate prices into an upward spiral that did not level off until the early 1990s. During the rest of the decade, the economy was stagnant, with real estate prices dropping, agriculture declining and tourism leveling off at seven million visitors annually; but by the year 2000 Hawaii was beginning to experience yet another boom.

One element that has not plateaued during the last ten years is the Native Hawaiian movement. Nativist sentiments were spurred in January 1993 by the 100th anniversary of the American overthrow of the Hawaiian monarchy. Over 15,000 people turned out to mark the illegal coup. Later that year, President Clinton signed a statement issued by Congress formally apologizing to the Hawaiian people. In 1994, the United States Navy returned the island of Kahoolawe to the state of Hawaii. Long a rallying symbol for the Native Hawaiian movement, the unoccupied island had been used for decades as a naval bombing target. By 1996, efforts to clean away bomb debris and make the island habitable were well under way, although completion of the clean-up is still years off. Then in 1998, the issue of Hawaii's monarchy arose again when demonstrators marched around the entire island of Oahu and staged rallies to protest the 100th anniversary of the United States' annexation of Hawaii.

Today, numerous perspectives remain to be reconciled, with grassroots movements working to secure a degree of autonomy for Hawaii's native people. The most common goal seems to be a status similar to that accorded the American Indians by the federal government, although there are still those who seek a return to an independent Hawaii, either as a restored monarchy or along democratic lines. Also pending resolution is the distribution of land to Native Hawaiians with documented claims, as well as a financial settlement with the state government. It's a complex situation involving the setting right of injustices of a century past.

Hawaii, according to Polynesian legend, was discovered by Hawaii-loa, an adventurous sailor who often disappeared on long fishing trips. On one voyage, urged along by his navigator, Hawaii-loa sailed toward the planet Jupiter. He crossed the "many-colored ocean," passed over the "deep-colored sea," and eventually came upon "flaming Hawaii," a mountainous island chain that spewed smoke and lava.

Culture

History is less romantic. The Polynesians who found Hawaii were probably driven from their home islands by war or some similar calamity. They traveled in groups, not as lone rangers, and shared their canoes with dogs, pigs and chickens, with which they planned to stock new lands. Agricultural plants such as coconuts, yams, taro, sugar cane, bananas and breadfruit were also stowed on board.

Most important, they transported their culture, an intricate system of beliefs and practices developed in the South Seas. After undergoing the stresses and demands of pioneer life, this traditional lifestyle was transformed into a new and uniquely Hawaiian culture.

It was based on a caste system that placed the *alii* or chiefs at the top and the slaves, *kauwas*, on the bottom. Between these two groups were the priests, *kahunas* and the common people or *makaainanas*. The chiefs, much like feudal lords, controlled all the land and collected taxes from the commoners who farmed it.

Life centered around the *kapu*, a complex group of regulations that dictated what was sacred or profane. For example, women were not permitted to eat pork or bananas; commoners had to prostrate themselves in the presence of a chief. These strictures were vital to Hawaiian religion; *kapu* breakers were directly violating the will of the gods and could be executed for their actions. And there were a lot of gods to watch out for, many quite vindictive. The four central gods were *Kane*, the creator; *Lono*, the god of agriculture; *Ku*, the war god; and *Kanaloa*, lord of the underworld. They had been born from the sky father and earth mother, and had in turn created many lesser gods and demigods who controlled various aspects of nature.

It was, in the uncompromising terminology of the West, a stone-age civilization. Though the Hawaiians lacked metal tools, the wheel and a writing system, they managed to include within their inventory of cultural goods everything necessary to sustain a large population on a chain of small islands. They fashioned fish nets from native *olona* fiber, made hooks out of bone, shell and ivory, and raised fish in rock-bound ponds. The men used irrigation in their farming. The women made clothing by pounding mulberry bark into a soft cloth called *tapa*, dyeing elaborate patterns into the fabric. They built peak-roofed thatch huts from native *pili* grass and *hala* leaves. The men fought wars with spears, slings, clubs and daggers. The women used mortars and pestles to pound the roots of the taro plant into poi, the islanders' staple food. Bread, fruit, yams and coconut were other menu standards.

The West labeled these early Hawaiians "noble savages." Actually, they often lacked nobility. The Hawaiians were cannibals who practiced human sacrifice during religious ceremonies and often used human bone to fashion fish hooks. They constantly warred among themselves and would mercilessly pursue a retreating army, murdering as many of the vanquished soldiers as possible.

But they weren't savages either. The Hawaiians developed a rich oral tradition of genealogical chants and created beautiful lilting songs to accompany their hula dancing. Their musicians mastered several instruments including the *ukeke* (a single-stringed device resembling a bow), an *ohe hano ihu* or nose flute, rattles and drums made from gourds, coconut shells or logs. Their craftsmen produced the world's finest featherwork, tying thousands of tiny feathers onto netting to produce golden cloaks and ceremonial helmets. The Hawaiians helped develop the sport of surfing. They also swam, boxed, bowled and devised an intriguing game called *konane*, a cross between checkers and the Japanese game of go. They built networks of trails across lava flows, and created an elemental art form in the images—petroglyphs—that they carved into lava rock along the trails.

Three out of every four Hawaii residents live on the island of Oahu, and almost half reside in Honolulu.

They also achieved something far more outstanding than their varied arts and crafts, something that the West, with its awesome knowledge and advanced technology, has never duplicated. The Hawaiians created a balance with nature. They practiced conservation, establishing closed seasons on certain fish species and carefully guarding their plant and animal resources. They led a simple life, without the complexities the outside world would eventually thrust upon them. It was a good life: food was plentiful, people were healthy and the population increased. For a thousand years, the Hawaiians lived in delicate harmony with the elements. It wasn't until the West entered the realm, transforming everything, that the fragile balance was destroyed. But that is another story entirely.

PEOPLE

Because of its unique history and isolated geography, Hawaii is truly a cultural melting pot. It's one of the few states in the union in which caucasians are a minority group. Whites, or *haoles* as they're called in the islands, comprise only about 22 percent of Hawaii's 1.2 million population. Japanese constitute 18 percent, Filipinos 13 percent, Hawaiians and part-Hawaiians account for 21 percent, Chinese about 3 percent and other racial groups 23 percent.

It's a very vital society, with one fifth of the people born of racially mixed parents.

One trait characterizing many of these people is Hawaii's famous spirit of aloha, a genuine friendliness, an openness to strangers, a willingness to give freely. Undoubtedly, it is one of the finest qualities any people has ever demonstrated. Aloha originated with the Polynesians and played an important role in ancient Hawaiian civilization.

The aloha spirit is alive and well in the islands, although bad attitudes toward *haoles*, the pejorative term used for whites, are not unknown. All parties, however, seem to understand the crucial role tourism has come to play in Hawaii's economy, which means you're not likely to experience unpleasantness from the locals you'll meet.

CUISINE Nowhere is the influence of Hawaii's melting pot population stronger than in the kitchen. While in the islands, you'll probably eat not only with a fork, but with chopsticks and fingers as well. You'll sample a wonderfully varied cuisine. In addition to standard American fare, hundreds of restaurants serve Hawaiian, Japanese, Chinese, Korean, Portuguese and Filipino dishes. There are also fresh fruits aplenty—pineapples, papayas, mangoes, bananas and tangerines—plus native fish such as mahimahi, marlin and snapper.

The mainstay of the traditional Hawaiian diet is poi, a purplish paste pounded from baked or steamed taro tubers. It's pretty bland fare, but it does make a good side dish with imu-cooked pork or tripe stew. You should also try *laulau*, a combination of fish, pork and taro leaves wrapped in a *ti* leaf and steamed. And don't neglect to taste baked *ulu* (breadfruit) and *opihi* (limpets). Among the other Hawaiian culinary traditions are *kalua* pig, a shredded pork dish baked in an *imu* (underground oven); *lomi-lomi* salmon, which is salted and mixed with onions and tomatoes; and chicken *luau*, prepared in taro leaves and coconut milk.

A good way to try all these dishes at one sitting is to attend a luau. I've always found the tourist luaus too commercial, but you might watch the newspapers for one of the special luaus sponsored by civic organizations.

Japanese dishes include sushi, sukiyaki, teriyaki and tempura, plus an island favorite—sashimi, or raw fish. On most any menu,

SOUNDS FISHY

What are all those strange-sounding fish dishes on the menu? A quick translation will help you when choosing a seafood platter from Hawaiian waters. Firm-textured with a light taste, the most popular fish is mahimahi, or dolphin fish (no, it's not one of those amazing creatures that do fancy tricks on the waves); its English equivalent is dorado. Ahi is yellowfin tuna and is especially delicious as sashimi (raw) or blackened. Opakapaka is pink snapper and is a staple of Pacific Rim cuisine. Other snappers include Uku (gray snapper), Onaga (ruby snapper) and Ehu (red snapper). Ono (which means delicious in Hawaiian) is king mackerel, a white fish that lives up to its name.

including McDonald's, you'll find *saimin*, a noodle soup filled with meat, vegetables and *kamaboko* (fishcake).

You can count on the Koreans for *kim chi*, a spicy salad of pickled cabbage and *kalbi*, barbecued beef short ribs prepared with soy and sesame oil. The Portuguese serve up some delicious sweets including *malasadas* (donuts minus the holes) and *pao doce*, or sweet bread. For Filipino fare, I recommend *adobo*, a pork or chicken dish spiced with garlic and vinegar, and *pochero*, a meat entrée cooked with bananas and several vegetables. In addition to a host of dinner dishes, the Chinese have contributed treats such as *manapua* (a steamed bun filled with barbecued pork) and oxtail soup. They also introduced crack seed to the islands. Made from dried and preserved fruit, it provides a treat as sweet as candy.

As the Hawaiians say, *"Hele mai ai."* Come and eat!

The language common to all Hawaii is English, but because of **LANGUAGE** its diverse cultural heritage, the archipelago also supports several other tongues. Foremost among these are Hawaiian and pidgin. Hawaiian, closely related to other Polynesian languages, is one of the most fluid and melodious languages in the world. It's composed of only twelve letters: five vowels—*a, e, i, o, u* and seven consonants—*h, k, l, m, n, p, w*. The glottal stop ('), when used, counts as a thirteenth letter.

At first glance, the language appears formidable: how the hell do you pronounce *humuhumunukunukuapuaa*? But actually it's quite simple. After you've mastered a few rules of pronunciation, you can take on any word in the language.

The first thing to remember is that every syllable ends with a vowel, and the next to last syllable usually receives the accent.

The next rule to keep in mind is that all the letters in Hawaiian are pronounced. Consonants are pronounced the same as in English (except for the *w*, which is pronounced as a *v* when it introduces the last syllable of a word—as in *ewa* or *awa*. Vowels are pronounced the same as in Spanish: *a* as in *among*, *e* as in *they*, *i* as in *machine*, *o* as in *no* and *u* as in *too*. Hawaiian has four vowel combinations or diphthongs: *au*, pronounced *ow*; *ae* and *ai*, which sound like *eye*; and *ei*, pronounced *ay*. As noted above, the glottal stop (') occasionally provides a thirteenth letter.

By now, you're probably wondering what I could possibly have meant when I said Hawaiian was simple. I think the glossary that follows will simplify everything while helping you pronounce common words and place names. Just go through the list, starting with words like aloha and luau that you already know. After you've practiced pronouncing familiar words, the rules will become second nature; you'll no longer be a *malihini*.

Just when you start to speak with a swagger, cocky about having learned a new language, some young Hawaiian will start talking at you in a tongue that breaks all the rules you've so carefully mastered. That's pidgin. It started in the 19th century as a lingua franca among Hawaii's many races. Pidgin speakers mix English and Hawaiian with several other tongues to produce a spicy creole. It's a fascinating language with its own vocabulary, a unique syntax and a rising inflection that's hard to mimic.

Pidgin is definitely the hip way to talk in Hawaii. A lot of young Hawaiians use it among themselves as a private language. At times they may start talking pidgin to you, acting as though they don't speak English; then if they decide you're okay, they'll break into English. When that happens, you be one *da kine brah*.

So *brah*, I take *da kine* pidgin words, put 'em together with Hawaiian, make one big list. Savvy?

aa (ah-**ah**)—a type of rough lava
ae (eye)—yes
aikane (eye-**kah**-nay)—friend, close companion
akamai (ah-kah-**my**)—wise
alii (ah-**lee**-ee)—chief
aloha (ah-**lo**-ha)—hello; greetings; love
aole (ah-**oh**-lay)—no
auwe (ow-**way**)—ouch!
brah (bra)—friend; brother; bro'
bumby (**bum**-bye)—after a while; by and by
da kine (da kyne)—whatdyacallit; thingamajig; that way
dah makule guys (da mah-**kuh**-lay guys)—senior citizens
diamondhead—in an easterly direction (Oahu only)
duh uddah time (duh **uh**-duh time)—once before
ewa (**eh**-vah)—in a westerly direction (Oahu only)
hale (**hah**-lay)—house
haole (**how**-lee)—Caucasian; white person
hapa (**hah**-pa)—half
hapa-haole (**hah**-pa **how**-lee)—half-Caucasian
heiau (hey-**yow**)—temple
hele on (**hey**-lay own)—hip; with it
hoaloha (ho-ah-**lo**-ha)—friend
holo holo (**ho**-low **ho**-low)—to visit
howzit? (hows-it)—how you doing? what's happening?
huhu (hoo-hoo)—angry
hukilau (**who**-key-lau)—community fishing party
hula (**who**-la)—Hawaiian dance
imu (ee-moo)—underground oven
ipo (ee-po)—sweetheart
kahuna (kah-**who**-nah)—priest; specialist or expert in any field

kai (kye)—ocean

kaka-roach (**kah**-kah roach)—ripoff; theft

kamaaina (kah-mah-**eye**-nah)—one born and raised in Hawaii; a longtime island resident

kane (**kah**-nay)—man

kapu (**kah**-poo)—taboo; forbidden

kaukau (cow-cow)—food

keiki (**kay**-key)—child

kiawe (key-**ah**-vay)—mesquite tree

kokua (ko-**coo**-ah)—help

kona winds (**ko**-nah winds)—winds that blow against the trades

lanai (lah-**nye**)—porch; also island name

lauhala (lau-**hah**-lah) or *hala* (**hah**-lah)—a pandanus tree whose leaves are used in weaving

lei (lay)—flower garland

lolo (low-low)—stupid

lomilomi (**low**-me-**low**-me)—massage; also raw salmon

luau (**loo**-ow)—feast

mahalo (mah-**hah**-low)—thank you

mahalo nui loa (mah-**ha**-low **new**-ee **low**-ah)—thank you very much

mahu (**mah**-who)—gay; homosexual

makai (mah-**kye**)—toward the sea

malihini (mah-lee-**hee**-nee)—newcomer; stranger

mauka (**mau**-kah)—toward the mountains

nani (**nah**-nee)—beautiful

ohana (oh-**hah**-nah)—family

okole (oh-**ko**-lay)—rear; ass

okolemaluna (oh-ko-lay-mah-**loo**-nah)—a toast: bottoms up!

ono (**oh**-no)—tastes good

pahoehoe (pah-**hoy**-hoy)—smooth or ropy lava

pakalolo (pah-kah-**low**-low)—marijuana

pakiki head (pah-**key**-key head)—stubborn

pali (**pah**-lee)—cliff

paniolo (pah-nee-**oh**-low)—cowboy

pau (pow)—finished; done

pilikia (pee-lee-**key**-ah)—trouble

puka (**poo**-kah)—hole

pupus (**poo**-poos)—hors d'oeuvres

shaka (**shah**-kah)—great; perfect

swell head—"big head"; egotistical

tapa (**tah**-pah)—also *kapa*; fabric made from the beaten bark of mulberry trees

wahine (wah-**hee**-nay)—woman

wikiwiki (**wee**-key-**wee**-key)—quickly; in a hurry

you get stink ear—you don't listen well

MUSIC

Music has long been an integral part of Hawaiian life. Most families keep musical instruments in their homes, gathering to play at impromptu living room or backyard jam sessions. Hawaiian folk tunes are passed down from generation to generation. In the earliest days, it was the sound of rhythm instruments and chants that filled the air. Drums were fashioned from hollowed-out gourds, coconut shells or hollowed sections of coconut palm trunks, then covered with sharkskin. Gourds and coconuts, adorned with tapa cloth and feathers, were also filled with shells or pebbles to produce a rattling sound. Other instruments included the nose flute, a piece of bamboo similar to a mouth flute, but played by exhaling through the nostril; the bamboo organ; and *puili*, sections of bamboo split into strips, which were struck rhythmically against the body.

Western musical scales and instruments were introduced by explorers and missionaries. As ancient Hawaiian music involved a radically different musical system, Hawaiians had to completely re-adapt. Actually, western music caught on quickly, and the hymns brought by missionaries fostered a popular musical style—the *himeni,* or Hawaiian church music.

Hawaii has been the birthplace of several different musical instruments and styles. The ukulele, modeled on a Portuguese guitar, quickly became the most popular Hawaiian instrument. Its small size made it easy to carry, and with just four strings, it was simple to play. During the early 1900s, the steel guitar was exported to the mainland. Common in country-and-western music today, it was invented by a young man who experimented by sliding a steel bar across guitar strings.

The slack-key style of guitar playing also comes from Hawaii, where it's called *ki ho'alu*. When the guitar was first brought to Hawaii in the 1830s by Mexican and Spanish cowboys, the Hawaiians adapted the instrument to their own special breed of music. In tuning, the six (or twelve) strings are loosened so that they sound a chord when strummed and match the vocal range of the singer. Slack-key is played in a variety of ways, from plucking or slapping the strings to sliding along them. A number of different tunings exist, and many have been passed down orally through families for generations.

NO OOMPAH-PAH! MO' BETTAH BRAH!
Strangely enough, a Prussian bandmaster named Henry Berger had a major influence on contemporary Hawaiian music. Brought over in the 19th century by King Kalakaua to lead the Royal Hawaiian Band, Berger helped Hawaiians make the transition to Western instruments.

During the late 19th century, "*hapa*-haole" songs became the rage. The ukulele was instrumental in contributing to this Hawaiian fad. Written primarily in English with pseudo-Hawaiian themes, songs like "Tiny Bubbles" and "Lovely Hula Hands" were later introduced to the world via Hollywood.

The Hawaiian craze continued on the mainland with radio and television shows such as "Hawaii Calls" and "The Harry Owens Show." In the 1950s, little mainland girls donned plastic hula skirts and danced along with Hilo Hattie and Ray Kinney.

It was not until the 1970s that both the hula and music of old Hawaii made a comeback. Groups such as the Sons of Hawaii and the Makaha Sons of Niihau, along with Auntie Genoa Keawe and the late Gabby Pahinui, became popular. Before long, a new form of Hawaiian music was being heard, a combination of ancient chants and contemporary sounds, performed by such islanders as Henry Kapono, Kalapana, Olomana, the Beamer Brothers, the Peter Moon Band and the Brothers Cazimero.

Today many of these groups, along with other notables such as Hapa, the Kaau Crater Boys, Brother Noland, Willie K., Butch Helemano and Obrien Eselu, bring both innovation to the Hawaiian music scene and contribute to the preservation of an ancient tradition. The trend continues with hybrid infusions of reggae and rock, while performers like Kealii Reichel and groups like Kapena maintain the soft-edged sounds so well-suited to the islands. An entire new category of music has become established in Hawaii: dubbed "Jawaiian," the sound incorporates Jamaican reggae and contemporary Hawaiian music, and is especially popular amongst the state's younger population. In addition, now-deceased masters of Hawaiian song like Gabby Pahinui and Israel Kamakawiwoole have gained renewed popularity and respect for the links they created between old and contemporary Hawaiian music.

For both classic and contemporary Hawaiian music, tune your radio dial to KCCN (1420 AM, 100.3 FM) or to KINE (105.1 FM).

HULA

Along with palm trees, the hula—swaying hips, grass skirts, colorful leis—is linked forever in people's minds with the Hawaiian Islands. This western idea of hula is very different from what the dance has traditionally meant to native Hawaiians.

Hula is an old dance form, its origin shrouded in mystery. The ancient hula, *hula kahiko*, was more concerned with religion and spirituality than entertainment. Originally performed only by men, it was used in rituals to communicate with a deity—a connection to nature and the gods. Accompanied by drums and chants, *hula kahiko* expressed the islands' culture, mythology and history in hand and body movements. It later evolved from a strictly religious rite to a method of communicating stories and legends. Over the years, women were allowed to study the rituals and eventually became the primary dancers.

When westerners arrived, the *hula kahiko* began another transformation. Explorers and sailors were more interested in its erotic element, ignoring the cultural significance. Missionaries simply found it scandalous and set out to destroy the tradition. They dressed Hawaiians in western garb and outlawed the *hula kahiko*.

The hula tradition was resurrected by King David Kalakaua. Known by the moniker "Merrie Monarch," Kalakaua loved music and dance. For his coronation in 1883, he called together the kingdom's best dancers to perform the chants and hulas once again. He was also instrumental in the development of the contemporary hula, the *hula auwana*, which added new steps and movements and was accompanied by ukeleles and guitars rather than drums.

By the 1920s, modern hula had been popularized by Hollywood, westernized and introduced as kitschy tropicana. Real grass skirts gave way to cellophane versions, plastic leis replaced fragrant island garlands, and exaggerated gyrations supplanted the hypnotic movements of the traditional dance.

Fortunately, with the resurgence of Hawaiian pride in recent decades, Polynesian culture has been reclaimed and *hula kahiko* and traditional chants have made a welcome comeback.

The most isolated population center on earth, Hawaii is 2390 miles from the mainland United States and 4900 miles from China.

Oahu

Honolulu, Somerset Maugham once remarked, is the meeting place of East and West. Today, with its highrise cityscape and crowded commercial center, Hawaii's capital is more the place where Hong Kong meets Los Angeles. It's the hub of Hawaii—a city that dominates the political, cultural and economic life of the islands.

And it's the focus of Oahu as well. Honolulu has given Oahu more than its nickname, The Capital Island. The city has drawn three-fourths of Hawaii's population to this third-largest island, making Oahu both a military stronghold and a popular tourist spot.

With military installations at Pearl Harbor and outposts seemingly everywhere, the armed forces control about one-quarter of the island. Most bases are off-limits to civilians; and tourists congregate in Honolulu's famed resort area—Waikiki. Both defense and tourism are big business on Oahu, and it's an ironic fact of island life that the staid, uniformly dressed military peacefully coexist here with crowds of sun-loving, scantily clad visitors.

The tourists are attracted by one of the world's most famous beaches, an endless white-sand ribbon that has drawn sun worshippers and water lovers since the days of Hawaiian royalty. In ancient times Waikiki was a swamp; now it's a spectacular region of world-class resorts.

Indeed, Waikiki is at the center of Pacific tourism, just as Honolulu is the capital of the Pacific. Nowhere else in the world will you find a population more varied or an ambience more vital. There are times when Waikiki's Parisian-size boulevards seem ready to explode from the sheer force of the crowds. People in bikinis and wild-colored aloha shirts stroll the streets, while others flash past on mopeds.

Since the 1980s this sun-splashed destination has also become a focal point for millions of wealthy tourists from Japan. As a result, Waikiki now has money-changing shops, restaurants displaying menus in Japanese only, stores where the clerks speak no English and an entire mall filled with duty-free shops.

Today the development that created modern-day Waikiki continues, albeit at a slower pace and on a less intense scale, at the Koolina Resort, along the south central Oahu coast near residential Ewa Beach, with the JW Marriott Ihilani Resort & Spa providing a flagship hotel for the resort. Nearby, work continues on the development of Kapolei as a "second city" for Oahu, planned for as many as 200,000 people and designed to reduce the population concentration on urban Honolulu.

So hurry. Visitors can still discover that just beyond Honolulu's bustling thoroughfares stretches a beautiful island, featuring countless beaches and two incredible mountain ranges. Since most of the tourists (and a vast majority of the island's 864,000 population) congregate in the southern regions around Honolulu, the north is rural. You can experience the color and velocity of the city, then head for the slow and enchanting country.

As you begin to explore for yourself, you'll find Oahu also has something else to offer: history. *Oahu* means "gathering place" in Hawaiian, and for centuries it has been an important commercial area and cultural center. First populated by Marquesans around 500 A.D., the island was later settled by seafaring immigrants from Tahiti. Waikiki, with its white-sand beaches and luxurious coconut groves, became a favored spot among early monarchs.

Warring chiefs long battled for control of the island. Kamehameha I seized power in 1795 after landing troops along the coast just east of Waikiki, proceeding inland and sweeping an opposing army over the cliffs of Nuuanu Pali north of Honolulu. Several years earlier the British had "discovered" Honolulu Harbor, a natural anchorage destined to be one of the Pacific's key seaports. Over the years the harbor proved ideal first for whalers and sandalwood traders and eventually for freighters and ocean liners.

By the 1840s, the city, originally a village called Kou, had grown into a shipping port and the commercial and political capital of the Hawaiian kingdom. Here in 1893 a band of white businessmen illegally overthrew the native monarchy. Almost a half-century later, in an ill-advised but brilliantly executed military maneuver, the Japanese drew the United States into World War II with a devastating air strike against the huge naval base at Pearl Harbor.

There are some fascinating historical monuments to tour throughout Honolulu, but I recommend you also venture outside the city to Oahu's less congested regions. Major highways lead from the capital along the east and west coasts of this 608-square-mile island, and several roads bisect the central plateau en route to the North Shore. Except for a five-mile strip in Oahu's northwest corner, you can drive completely around the island.

Closest to Honolulu is the east coast, where a spectacular seascape is paralleled by the Koolaus, a jagged and awesomely steep mountain range. This is Oahu's rainswept Windward Coast. Here, traveling up the coast past the bedroom communities of Kailua and Kaneohe, you'll discover beautiful and relatively untouched white-sand beaches. On the North Shore are some of the world's most famous surfing spots—Waimea Bay, Sunset, the Banzai Pipeline—where winter waves as high as 20 to 30 feet roll in with crushing force.

The Waianae Range, rising to 4040 feet, shadows Oahu's western coast. The sands are as white here, the beaches as uncrowded, but I've always felt slightly

Text continued on page 64.

Oahu

Hawaiian Getaway

Oahu Three-Day Itinerary

Day 1
• Check into a hotel or condo in Waikiki then make tour reservations for the next day for Iolani Palace and/or Pearl Harbor.

• Explore **Waikiki Beach**, take a stroll over to **Kapiolani Park** (page 66), or just kick back. In the evening, seek out a spot to listen to Hawaiian music. Dine in Waikiki.

Day 2
• Spend the morning sightseeing in Honolulu. If you are going to **Pearl Harbor** (page 107) try for an early-morning tour. (Allow 1.5 hours.)

• Head back downtown to visit the **Mission Houses Museum** (page 87) (allow .5 hour) and then continue along South King Street to **Iolani Palace** (page 88). (Allow 45 minutes for the tour of the palace, reservations needed.)

• If you opted not to go to Pearl Harbor earlier, drive up the Pali Highway to the **Nuuanu Pali Outlook** (page 107), stopping at **Queen Emma Summer Palace** (page 107) on the way.

• Return to Downtown Honolulu and have lunch, then stroll through the nooks and crannies of **Chinatown** (page 92).

• In the afternoon either visit the **Hawaii Maritime Museum** (page 90) and **Foster Botanical Garden** (page 92) or return to Waikiki for a canoe ride, a swim or a hike up **Diamond Head** (page 68).

• Hop on a bus and have dinner at an eatery in Ward Centre or Restaurant Row.

Day 3
• Drive around the island. Get up *early* in the morning (when the water is clear) and snorkel at **Hanauma Bay** (page 114). (Allow at least 1 hour.)

• Continue along the Kalanianaole Highway, Route 72, stopping at the **Halona Blowhole** (page 115) to see the ocean in its fury and **Makapuu** or **Sandy Beach** (page 119) to watch the body surfers.

- Continue on Route 72 to the bedroom community of **Kailua** (page 120), then take Route 83 (Kahekili Highway) to the **Byodo-In Temple** (page 121) for a short stroll through a peaceful oasis. (Allow .5 hour.)

- Continue along Route 83, stopping for a picnic lunch at **Kahana Bay** (page 122).

- Take a short hike through **Kahana Valley State Park** (page 129), past small Hawaiian farms. (Allow 1.5 hours.)

- Continue along Route 83 to **Sunset Beach** (page 140) or **Waimea Bay** (page 141) for a dip in the ocean. (If it's winter and the surf's up, don't go swimming—just watch the surfers ride those magnificent waves.)

- Next, drive through **Haleiwa** (page 134), stopping at **Matsumoto's** (page 135) for a shave ice (with azuki beans) and a stroll around town.

- Take Route 99 to H2 to Honolulu, stopping at the **Aloha Tower Marketplace** (page 101) for dinner.

uncomfortable on the Leeward Coast. Theft can be a problem here. Wherever you go on Oahu you have to be careful not to leave valuables unattended, but be particularly watchful around this coast.

Between the Koolau and Waianae ranges, remnants of the two volcanoes that created Oahu, spreads the Leilehua Plateau. This fertile region is occupied by sugar and pineapple plantations as well as several large military bases.

Geologically, Oahu is the second-oldest island in the chain; two million years ago it was two individual islands, which eventually were joined by the Leilehua Plateau. Among its geographic features is the *pali*, an awesome wall of sheer cliffs along the windward coastline, and three famous tuff-cone volcanoes—Diamond Head, Punchbowl and Koko Head.

Hosting millions of tourists each year, Oahu has become a favorite location among travel agents. Many people can't even conceive of visiting Hawaii without going to "the gathering place," and some never venture out to any of the other islands. Oahu does have its virtues. But if, like me, you think of a vacation in terms of experiencing the crowds, and then leaving them behind—plan on fully exploring Oahu and then continuing on to the neighbor islands.

▼ ▼ ▼ ▼ ▼ ▼ ▼ ▼
Waikiki

To understand the geography of Waikiki you need only know about Waikiki Beach. And to understand Waikiki Beach, you must know two things. The first is that major hotels line the beach, practically from one end to the other, and are used as landmarks by visitors and local residents alike. The other fact to remember is that to visitors Waikiki Beach is a single sandy ribbon two miles long, but to local folks it represents many beaches in one. When you park your beach towel here, consider that every few strides will carry you into another realm of Waikiki's culture and history.

Waikiki once served as a retreat for Hawaiian kings and queens. By the turn of the 20th century it was favored by writer-adventurers like Jack London and Robert Louis Stevenson. During World War II, GIs on leave soaked up its sun. Then in the jet age that followed, it became a highrise resort area. As a result, different sections of Waikiki Beach answer to different names.

This fabled peninsula extends two miles from the Ala Wai Yacht Harbor to Diamond Head and measures a half-mile in width from the Ala Wai Canal to the Pacific. Kalakaua Avenue, the main drag, is packed elbow to elbow with throngs of visitors. Paralleling the ocean, this broad boulevard is noisy, annoying, cosmopolitan and fascinating. Today visitors from Japan add to the international atmosphere.

But the main appeal is still the district's white-sand corridor. Dotting the beach are picnic areas, restrooms, showers, concession stands and beach equipment rentals. Most of the beach is protected by coral reefs and sea walls, so the swimming is excellent, the snorkeling fair. This is also a prime area for surfing. Two- to four-foot waves, good for beginners and still challenging to experienced surfers, are common here.

The western flank of Waikiki Beach sits near the Hilton Hawaiian Village. Here you will find a pretty lagoon fringed by palm trees.

The curving strand nearby, fronting Hilton Hawaiian Village at 2005 Kalia Road, is called **Kahanamoku Beach**. Named for Hawaii's great surfer, Duke Kahanamoku, it features numerous facilities. Beach stands rent everything from towels, chairs and air mattresses to snorkel sets, surfboards and Hobie-cat sailboats.

Fort DeRussy Beach, owned by the military but open to the public, features the area's widest swath of white sand. It is also beautifully backdropped by a grove of palm trees. There are restrooms, picnic tables and barbecues, plus tennis, squash and volleyball courts.

The nearby **U.S. Army Museum of Hawaii** has every weapon from Hawaiian shark teeth blades to modern-day instruments of destruction. You can also trace the United States' unending series of military campaigns from the uniforms (ours and theirs) on exhibit here. Closed Monday. ~ Kalia Road; 808-438-2821, fax 808-438-2819.

Tourists are relative newcomers to Hawaii: Not a single hotel in Waikiki was built before the 20th century.

Past Fort DeRussy Beach stretches a palisade of highrise hotels. Lining the beachfront, they provide numerous facilities for thirsty sunbathers or adventuresome athletes. Continue on and you will pass the Sheraton strip, a lengthy stretch of Waikiki Beach fronted entirely by hotels. This section marks Waikiki's center of action. The first hotel is the **Outrigger Reef on the Beach**, followed by the **Halekulani**, a pricey property that many consider Waikiki's best hotel. Next is the **Sheraton Waikiki**. A highrise structure built with two curving wings, it resembles a giant bird roosting on the beach.

The hotels here are so famous that the nearby strand is named **Royal-Moana Beach**. Stretching between the Royal Hawaiian and Moana hotels, it has been a sun-soaked gathering place for decades. That's because these two grand dames are Waikiki's oldest hotels. The **Royal Hawaiian Hotel** is Hawaii's "Pink Palace," a Spanish Moorish–style caravansary painted shocking pink. Built in 1927, it is a labyrinth of gardens, colonnades and balconies; the old place is certainly Waikiki's most interesting edifice. ~ 2259 Kalakaua Avenue; 808-923-7311, fax 808-924-7098; www.royalhawaiian.com.

The woodframe **Sheraton Moana Surfrider Resort**, built in 1901, was Waikiki's first resort. Its vaulted ceilings, tree-shaded courtyard and spacious accommodations reflect the days when Hawaii was a retreat for the rich. This beach is also the site of one of Waikiki's most renowned surfing spots, **Canoe's Surf.** ~ 2365 Kalakaua Avenue; 808-922-3111, fax 808-923-0308.

Just beyond the Moana is **Kuhio Beach Park**, which runs along Kalakaua Avenue from Kaiulani to Kapahulu avenues. In addition to a broad sandy beach and a creative layout that includes a banyan tree, traditional healing stones and a cascading fountain, there are numerous facilities here—picnic areas, beach equipment rentals, showers, restrooms and lifeguards on duty. The shady pavilions in this public park also attract local folks who come to play cards and chess. Needless to say, this convenient beach is often quite crowded. Diners like it because of its proximity to many Waikiki budget restaurants; parents favor the beach for its protective sea wall, which provides a secure area where children can swim; and people-watchers find it an ideal place to check out the crowds of tourists and local residents. The park has been gussied up recently; renovations so far include broader walkways, grassy areas and artificial waterfalls and tidepools. ~ Kalakaua Avenue.

HIDDEN ►
Tucked behind St. Augustine Catholic Church on a side street near the beach sits the tiny **Damien Museum**, a tribute to Father Damien, the Belgian priest best known for his work in Kalaupaupa, the leper colony on Molokai. Father Damien established churches throughout the islands, but his dedication to those suffering from Hansen's Disease (leprosy) is what made him a Hawaiian hero. The exhibits include his glasses, chalice and other unassuming belongings, as well as his prayer book and vestments. Photos depicting his final years on Molokai, where he, too, died of the disease, paint an evocative portrait of this selfless man. Closed weekends. ~ 130 Ohua Avenue; phone/fax 808-923-2690.

The strand just beyond Kuhio Beach Park is called **Queen's Surf**. Here also are picnic areas, shady pavilions, restroom facilities and showers. Something of a Bohemian quarter, this pretty plot draws gays, local artists and a wide array of intriguing characters. On the weekends, conga drummers may be pounding out rhythms along the beach while other people gather to soak in the scene.

Kapiolani Park next door extends across 140 acres on both sides of Kalakaua Avenue. Hawaii's oldest park, this tree-studded playland dates back more than 100 years. Perhaps more than anything else, it has come to serve as a jogger's paradise. From dawn 'til dark, runners of all ages, colors, sizes and shapes beat a path around its perimeter. But Kapiolani offers something to just about anyone. There are tennis courts, softball and soccer fields, an archery area, and much more. To fully explore the park, you must visit each of its features in turn.

First is the **Waikiki Aquarium**, the place where you can finally discover what a *humuhumunukunukuapuaa*, that impossibly named fish, really looks like. (Don't be surprised if the name proves

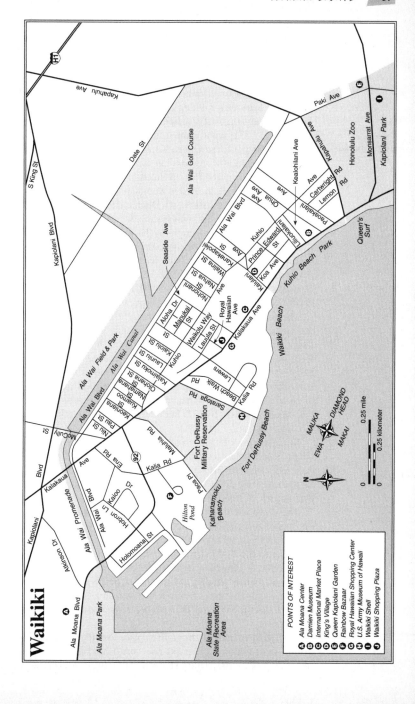

Waikiki

Ala Moana Park

Ala Moana State Recreation Area

Ala Moana Blvd

Atkinson Dr

Kapiolani

Kapiolani Blvd

Kalakaua Ave

Ala Wai Promenade

Ala Wai Blvd

McCully St

S King St

Kapahulu Ave

Date St

Kapiolani Blvd

Seaside Ave

Ala Wai Golf Course

Ala Wai Field & Park

Ala Wai Canal

Ala Wai Blvd

Niu St

Pau St

Kaiolu St

Kaiulani St

Keoniana St

Kuamoo St

Namahana St

Olohana St

Kalaimoku St

Launiu St

Kaiolu St

Aloha Dr

Makaloa St

Nohonani

Nahua St

Malina St

Kanekapolei St

Kealohilani Ave

Ohua Ave

Cartwright Rd

Paoakalani Ave

Lemon Rd

Kalakaua Ave

Kuhio Ave

Ala Wai Blvd

Prince Edward St

Liliuokalani

Kuhio

Koa Ave

Kaiulani

Kuhio Beach Park

Kuhio Beach Park

Waikiki Beach

Queen's Surf

Honolulu Zoo

Monsarrat Ave

Paki Ave

Kapiolani Park

Waikolu Way

Royal Hawaiian Ave

Lauula St

Kuhio Rd

Beach Walk

Lewers

Kalia Rd

Saratoga Rd

Maluhia Rd

Ena Rd

Kalia Rd

Paoa Pl

Fort DeRussy Military Reservation

Fort DeRussy Beach

Kahanamoku Beach

Hobron Ln

Kaioo Dr

Ala Wai Blvd

Holomoana St

Hilton Pond

MAUKA

DIAMOND HEAD

EWA

MAKAI

N

0   0.25 mile

0   0.25 kilometer

POINTS OF INTEREST

- Ala Moana Center
- Damien Museum
- International Market Place
- King's Village
- Queen Kapiolani Garden
- Rainbow Bazaar
- Royal Hawaiian Shopping Center
- U.S. Army Museum of Hawaii
- Waikiki Shell
- Waikiki Shopping Plaza

to be longer than the fish.) Within the aquarium's glass walls, you'll see more than 350 different species of fish originating from Hawaiian and South Pacific waters. Ranging from rainbow-hued tropical fish to blacktip reef sharks, they constitute a broad range of underwater species. Then there are Hawaiian monk seals (an endangered species) and other intriguing creatures. A biodiversity exhibit features a rotating display of creatures not native to Hawaii. Admission. ~ 2777 Kalakaua Avenue; 808-923-9741, fax 808-923-1771; www.waquarium.org.

HIDDEN ►   Across the park, the **Queen Kapiolani Garden**, with its colorful flowerbeds and shady pavilion, is a pretty place to stroll and picnic. ~ Monsarrat and Paki avenues.

The **Waikiki Shell**, located in Kapiolani Park, is a great place for an evening under the stars with Diamond Head as a backdrop. General admission means lawn seating, which is the perfect way to enjoy the Honolulu Symphony backing up headliners like Michael Feinstein, local favorites like the Brothers Cazimero, or megastars like Bob Dylan. Check with the Blaisdell Center box office to see if anything is scheduled for the Shell while you're in town and plan to go. ~ 808-527-5400, 808-591-2211, fax 808-591-8072; www.co.honolulu.hi.us/depts/aud.

The park's most outstanding feature is the **Honolulu Zoo**. Like city zoos everywhere, this tropical facility has a resident population of elephants, giraffes, ostriches, zebras, hippos, Sumatran tigers, lions, alligators and so on. But it also includes animals more common to the islands, creatures like the nene (a rare goose), Komodo dragons and Galápagos tortoises. Perhaps most interesting of all, there is an outstanding collection of tropical birds. Admission. ~ 808-971-7171, fax 808-971-7173; www.honolulu zoo.org.

Kapiolani Park includes a stretch of beach called **Sans Souci**, a popular spot where residents and visitors share the sand and reef-sheltered waters. It's also an easy place to set out for a kayak paddle to the marine preserve off Diamond Head or to head toward Waikiki, which stands in highrise silhouette.

The beach is bordered to the west by the **Natatorium**, a saltwater pool and grandstand built in the 1920s as a monument to those Hawaiians who lost their lives in World War I. Closed in 1979 due to slipshod maintenance and deterioration, it is slated to be restored. However, legal challenges have put the start of restoration on hold pending environmental, health and best-use issues. The City continues to say it will pursue a full restoration that includes the saltwater pool as well as the landmark arch at the entrance.

Sans Souci is certainly not a hard place to find, as one of the world's most famous landmarks rises just behind it. More than any other place in the islands, **Diamond Head** is the trademark of

Hawaii. A 760-foot crater, it is the work of a volcano that has been dead for about 100,000 years. To the Hawaiians it was known as *Leahi*. They saw in its sloping hillsides the face of an ahi, or yellowfin tuna. Then, in the 19th century, sailors mistook its volcanic glass rocks for rare gems and gave the promontory its present name. Formed 350,000 years ago, this natural landmark was a sacred place to the ancient Hawaiians. A *heiau* once graced its slopes and King Kamehameha is said to have worshiped here, offering a human sacrifice to the Polynesian war god.

It is possible to drive into the gaping maw of this old dragon. Just take Kalakaua Avenue until it meets Diamond Head Road, then follow the latter around to the inland site of the crater. From there a tunnel leads inside. Once within, there is a three-quarter-mile trail climbing to the rim of the crater. From here you can gaze along Oahu's southeast corner and back across the splendid little quarter called Waikiki.

LODGING

While it may no longer be the simple country retreat it was at the century's turn, Waikiki does have one advantage: believe it or not, it's a great place to find low-rent hotels. A lot of the cozy old hostelries have been torn down and replaced with highrises, but a few have escaped the urban assault. Some of those skyscrapers, too, are cheaper than you might think. The one thing to be aware of—the noise level is high. Ask for rooms off the street or high in the sky! Let's take a look at some of the better bargains Waikiki has to offer.

What better combination can you ask for than a place that is both a hotel *and* a hostel? At the **Island Hostel/Hotel**, located inside the Hawaiian Colony building, you can book a room with private bath or join fellow travelers in a coed dorm room. The dorm includes kitchen privileges. ~ 1946 Ala Moana Boulevard; phone/fax 808-942-8748. BUDGET.

BABES IN TOW

Waikiki is the perfect place to vacation with your toddler. Was there ever a better sandbox for making sandcastles? For a gentle, no-wave swimming area head to **Kuhio Beach Park** (page 66) with its protected seawall. When you (or your little one) tire of the ocean, walk or take the number 4, 8, 19, 20 or 43 bus to the **Honolulu Zoo** (page 68) or the **Waikiki Aquarium** (pages 66, 68). **Kapiolani Park** (page 66) also has oodles of space to run and play tag. In the evening, you can always hire a babysitter from a bonded service (see "Traveling with Children" in Chapter One) for a night on the town.

The Polynesian Hostel Beach Club offers both private and dormitory accommodations (baths are shared in either case) in this apartment building. Each room has its own refrigerator and bathroom and sleeps up to six people. Laundry facilities and a full kitchen are available for guests, as well as a barbecue and outdoor deck area. It is the closest hostel to the beach, which is one block away. ~ 2584 Lemon Road; 808-922-1340, fax 808-923-4146; www.hostelhawaii.com, e-mail polynesian@hostelhawaii.com. BUDGET.

An inexpensive place for both men and women in Waikiki is the YMCA Central Branch. It's handily situated across the street from Ala Moana Center and a block from the beach. And you're welcome to use the gym, pool, saunas, television room and coffee shop. You can also expect the usual Y ambience—long sterile hallways leading to an endless series of identical, cramped, uncarpeted rooms. You will pay several dollars more for a private bathroom, but low prices help make up for the lack of amenities. ~ 401 Atkinson Drive; 808-941-3344, fax 808-941-8821; www.centra lymcahonolulu.org, e-mail hidomen@aol.com. BUDGET.

Budget travelers should also consider a stay at **Hostelling International—Waikiki**. This helpful facility features single-sex dormitory-style accommodations and private studio units available for couples. The latter are plain cinder block rooms with private baths and mini-refrigerators. Open to both men and women, the hostel provides bedding and a common kitchen and creates a family-style atmosphere conducive to meeting other travelers. Internet access is available for a fee. Seven-day maximum stay. ~ 2417 Prince Edward Street; 808-926-8313, fax 808-922-3798; www.hiayh.com. BUDGET.

Interclub Waikiki is a sparkling clean, air-conditioned hostel close to the beach, featuring ten four-person dorms and ten private rooms. All quarters have refrigerators, TVs and baths; private rooms are equipped with hot plates and microwaves. There is a laundry. ~ 2426 Kuhio Avenue; 808-924-2636, fax 808-922-3993;

STAY AT SOMEBODY ELSE'S PLACE!

If you're planning on staying in Honolulu for a week or more and would like to do so in the comfort of someone else's fully furnished apartment, **Waikiki Vacation Rentals** offers studios as well as one- and two-bedroom condos. Places book up fast all year round, so be sure to call two or three months in advance. Closed Saturday and Sunday. ~ 1580 Makaloa Street, Suite 770; 808-946-9371, 800-543-5663, fax 808-943-6934; e-mail corasinc@aol.com. BUDGET TO MODERATE.

www.interclubwaikiki.com, e-mail interclubhawaii@yahoo.com.
BUDGET.

The **Malihini Hotel** will give you a feel for Honolulu's earlier, lowrise era. An attractive complex that spreads out instead of up, this 30-unit hotel is just a short stroll from the beach. Though pretty on the outside, its sparse furnishings, scant decoration and cinderblock walls give a vacant feel to the place. But the studios are spacious and come equipped with kitchenettes. The one-bedroom apartments have air conditioning and will sleep up to five people. ~ 217 Saratoga Road; 808-923-9644. BUDGET.

The walls are still cinderblock, but the price is right at the **Waikiki Prince Hotel**. All rooms have air conditioning and cable TV and many of the rooms are equipped with kitchenettes. ~ 2431 Prince Edward Street; 808-922-1544, fax 808-924-3712. BUDGET.

One budget-priced place that I particularly recommend is the small, intimate and close to the beach. **Hale Pua Nui**, a congenial home away from home. There are 22 studio apartments here, each spacious, well-furnished and cross-ventilated. The rooms are quaintly decorated, carpeted and equipped with kitchenettes, cable television and air conditioning. The personalized service you receive from the management makes the Hale Pua Nui an ideal vacation spot for budget-conscious travelers. ~ 228 Beach Walk; 808-923-9693, fax 808-923-9678. BUDGET.

Rising higher from the ground, while still keeping costs low, is the **Royal Grove Hotel**, a six-story, 87-unit establishment. If you can get past the garish pink exterior here, you'll find the rooms more tastefully designed. All are carpeted and comfortably furnished, and some are decorated in simple but appealing styles. There are televisions and telephones in all of the rooms, plus an almond-shaped pool and spacious lobby. Rents vary according to which wing of this sprawling building your bags are parked in. Most rooms even have kitchenettes with microwaves, as well as air conditioning, so it's hard to go wrong here. ~ 151 Uluniu Avenue; 808-923-7691, 800-922-7508, fax 808-922-7508; www.royalgrovehotel.com, e-mail rghawaii@gte.net. BUDGET.

Kai Aloha Apartment Hotel offers intimacy combined with modern convenience; each guest room has air conditioning, an all-electric kitchen, radio, telephone with voice mail, cable television and carpeting. Studio apartments have lovely rattan furniture and are attractively decorated with old drawings and paintings. The one-bedroom apartments will comfortably sleep four people. Daily maid service. ~ 235 Saratoga Road; 808-923-6723, fax 808-922-7592; e-mail kai.aloha@gte.net. MODERATE.

A lowrise hotel tucked away in the shadow of vaulting condominiums, **The Breakers** is truly a find. Dating to the 1950s, this   ◄ HIDDEN
Waikiki original consists of 64 rooms and 15 suites surrounding

a pool and landscaped patio. Shoji doors add to the ambience while kitchenettes in every room and a location one block from the beach round out the features. ~ 250 Beach Walk; 808-923-3181, 800-426-0494, fax 808-923-7174; www.breakers-hawaii.com. MODERATE.

Dominating the mid-range hotel scene in Waikiki are the Outrigger's Ohana hotels. It seems like everywhere you turn in this tourist enclave another one looms above: There are over a dozen. While prices range across the entire spectrum, one facility that offers a special value is the **Ohana Edgewater Hotel**. Located a stone's skip from the beach, this 184-unit colossus offers excellent accommodations at low prices. Each room comes with carpeting, telephone, TV, cable movies, refrigerator and shared lanai; many rooms also have a kitchenette. The decor is bland but the furniture comfy. Downstairs is an open-air lobby with adjoining restaurant and pool. ~ 2168 Kalia Road; 808-922-6424, 800-462-6262, fax 808-622-4852; www.ohanahotels.com. MODERATE.

If you're willing to sacrifice intimacy, you may find that the **Ohana Coral Seas Hotel** is one of the best deals in Waikiki. This seven-story hostelry is located just a hundred yards from the beach. They have appealing accommodations with air conditioning, telephones, wall-to-wall carpeting and small lanais. In some units you can add a kitchenette to the list of extras. There's a pool at another Ohana hotel next door that guests may use. If you want, just for the hell of it, to directly experience the Waikiki tourist scene, this is the place. The Ohana Coral Seas Hotel is at the heart of the action. ~ 250 Lewers Street; 808-923-3881, 800-462-6262, fax 808-922-2330; www.ohanahotels.com. MODERATE.

If the **Ohana Waikiki Surf** has no space in its central facility, they can probably fit you in their other building on Royal Hawaiian Road. Both are located in central Waikiki. The guest rooms are adequately, if unimaginatively, decorated and come with television, air conditioning, telephone and lanai; there are a pool and jacuzzi on-site. ~ 2200 Kuhio Avenue; 808-923-7671, 800-688-7444, fax 808-921-4959; www.ohanahotels.com. MODERATE.

The **Ewa Hotel** has 90 rooms. Tucked away on a back street one block from the beach, this pastel-and-rattan establishment has a spiffy 1980s aura about it. Close to Kapiolani Park and offering kitchenettes in many rooms, it is particularly convenient for families. ~ 2555 Cartwright Road; 808-922-1677, 800-359-8639, fax 808-923-8538; www.ethotel.com. MODERATE.

About the same size is the **Waikiki Hana Hotel**, a 73-room place that offers a restaurant and small lobby. Quiet (for Waikiki), friendly and comfortable, its rooms are brightly decorated and trimly appointed with air conditioning and color televisions. Some have kitchenettes and lanais. ~ 2424 Koa Avenue; 808-926-8841, 800-367-5004, fax 808-924-3770. MODERATE.

Author Picks

CHAPTER FAVORITES

When I want to glimpse the glamour of Hawaii's monarchy days, I take the behind-the-scenes tour at the **Bishop Museum** and gaze in awe at feathered capes and royal jewels. *page 106*

To me, Hawaii is much more than luxury hotels and sunshine. I go on the **Chinatown Walking Tour** for a taste of the islands' rich culture, taking in the acupuncture shops, herbalists, lei makers and smells and sounds that make up old Hawaii. *page 92*

I like to rinse the grit off after a long day of snorkeling and sand, and soak my senses in luxury at the **Royal Hawaiian Hotel**, better known as the "Pink Palace." *page 75*

When I feast on Pacific Rim delights at **Alan Wong's Restaurant**, the hardest part is trying to save room for dessert. Ultimately, however, nothing stands in the way of me and my "Banoffee Pie." *page 111*

My vacation wouldn't be complete without a visit to **Chai's Island Bistro**. Here I can enjoy Hawaiian contemporary musicians like Hapa and the Brothers Cazimero, whose sound is as distinct to Hawaii as rainbows and waterfalls. *page 96*

Waimea Beach provides me with endless activity. In winter, I breathlessly watch the pros ride the 20-foot-high surf, and in summer I lazily swim in the calm, still ocean. *page 141*

The **Aston Honolulu Prince Hotel** was once a college dormitory. Today it's a ten-story hotel with a comfortable lobby. The standard rooms are small and blandly decorated. Located two blocks from the beach, this hotel also has one- and two-bedroom apartments available with full kitchens. ~ 415 Nahua Street; 808-922-1616, 800-922-7866, fax 808-922-6223; www.aston-hotels.com. MODERATE TO DELUXE.

The **Ohana Village** is located on a busy street a block from the beach, but it offers rooms with or without kitchenettes at reasonable cost. You can expect street noise. The lobby contains about five different shops selling a variety of clothing and sundries. There is a pool. ~ 240 Lewers Street; 808-923-3881, 800-462-6262, fax 808-922-2330; www.ohanahotels.com. DELUXE.

Holiday Inn Waikiki, another good bargain, is easy walking distance from both Ala Moana Center and the beach. For the price, accommodations at this 17-story caravansary are relatively plush. Each room has air conditioning, television, telephone, decorations, carpeting, a shower-tub combination, a small refrigerator, a hair dryer, in-room coffee and an in-room safe. The room I saw was quite spacious and contained a king-size bed. There's also a fitness center. ~ 1830 Ala Moana Boulevard; 808-955-1111,

888-992-4545, fax 808-947-1799; www.holidayinnwaikiki.com.
MODERATE TO DELUXE.

The **Marc Waikiki Grand Hotel** is right across the street from lush Kapiolani Park. The standard rooms in this ten-story building are comfortable, pleasant places to park your bags. Downstairs there's a windswept lobby. ~ 134 Kapahulu Avenue; 808-923-1511, 800-535-0085, fax 808-922-2421; www.marcresorts.com. MODERATE TO DELUXE.

Ramada Vacation Suites is a modern, attractive complex of three low-slung buildings surrounding a garden and swimming pool. The rooms are decorated in a tropical theme with rattan furniture and come with all-electric kitchenette, telephone, color TV and air conditioning. ~ 431 Nohonani Street; 808-923-7336, 800-634-6981, fax 808-923-1622; www.ramadavacationsuites.com. MODERATE.

The **Coconut Plaza**, a ten-story highrise, has accommodations with kitchenettes; all guest rooms have refrigerators and microwaves; standard rooms have a wet bar. Decorated in Mexican tile and furnished with wicker, the rooms are attractively appointed. The lobby adds elements of elegance in the form of an open-air lounge and pool. Breakfast included. ~ 450 Lewers Street; 808-923-8828, 800-922-7866, fax 808-923-3473; www.aston-hotels.com, e-mail cocoplaza@lava.net. MODERATE.

The **Queen Kapiolani Hotel** is a 314-room facility that rises 19 stories above nearby Kapiolani Park. There's a spacious lobby, three floors of public rooms, several shops and a swimming pool here. The guest rooms are plainly decorated and modest in size. Located one block from the beach. ~ 150 Kapahulu Avenue; 808-922-1941, 800-367-5004, fax 808-596-0158. MODERATE TO ULTRA-DELUXE.

The **Hawaiiana Hotel** is an intimate, low-rise facility that offers a garden courtyard arrangement with rooms surrounding either of the hotel's two pools. Some of the rooms have a private lanai; all have wicker armoires, kitchenettes and pastel decor. ~ 260 Beach Walk; 808-923-3811, 800-367-5122, fax 808-926-5728. MODERATE.

If you'd like to stay directly across the street from the beach, check into the **Aston Waikiki Circle Hotel**. This 14-story hotel-in-the-round has air-conditioned rooms at reasonable rates. Many have an ocean view, which is the main advantage here. ~ 2464 Kalakaua Avenue; 808-923-1571, 800-922-7866, fax 808-926-8024; www.aston-hotels.com. DELUXE TO ULTRA-DELUXE.

The **Cabana at Waikiki** is a lodging option for gay and lesbian visitors. The hotel has 15 nicely decorated one-bedroom suites, with queen beds in the bedroom and a queen sofa-bed in the living room. Rattan furnishings and Hawaiian prints convey a tropical feel. All suites have TV/VCR/stereos and microwave-equipped kitchenettes, complete with toasters and blenders. There is an eight-person jacuzzi for guest use. Continental breakfast is included. ~ 2551 Cartwright Road; 808-926-5555, 877-902-2121, fax 808-926-5566; www.cabana-waikiki.com. MODERATE TO DELUXE.

There are three attractive facilities on the edge of Waikiki that are removed from the crowds. The **New Otani Kaimana Beach Hotel** rests beside beautiful Sans Souci Beach in the shadow of Diamond Head. Its two restaurants and oceanside bar lend the feel of a big hotel, but the friendly staff and standard rooms create a family atmosphere. ~ 2863 Kalakaua Avenue; 808-923-1555, 800-356-8264, fax 808-922-9404; www.kaimana.com, e-mail kaimana@pixi.com. DELUXE.

A throwback to colonial times, tea is served every afternoon at the Sheraton Moana Surfrider's Banyan Veranda.

Decorated with a tastefully tropical flair that hints of old Hawaii, the 20-room **Colony Surf Condominiums** feature spacious oceanfront studios. The complex is situated on the beach side of Kalakaua Avenue as it makes its way through Kapiolani Park; two vest-pocket beaches are within a minute's walk. Two restaurants, Michele's and the Diamond Head Grill are adjacent. Service is first rate. ~ 2885 Kalakaua Avenue; 808-924-3111, 888-924-7873, fax 808-923-2249; www.colonysurf.com. ULTRA-DELUXE.

Another hotel is equally secluded from the bustle of Waikiki. Located even closer to the fabled crater, the **Diamond Head Beach Hotel** is an ultra-contemporary establishment. The rooms are done in soft pastel tones and adorned with quilted beds and potted plants. Located on the ocean, this 13-story facility is one of the most chic resting places around. Continental breakfast is available to the guests and most rooms come with a kitchen. ~ 2947 Kalakaua Avenue; 808-922-1928, 800-367-2317, fax 808-924-8980; www.diamondheadbeach.com. ULTRA-DELUXE.

◄ HIDDEN

Two hotels right on the beach at Waikiki capture the sense of old Hawaii. Waikiki was little more than a thatch-hut village when its first deluxe hotel went up in 1901. Today the **Sheraton Moana Surfrider Resort** retains the aura of those early days in its Colonial architecture and Victorian decor. Insist on a room in the main building with its traditional appointments and turn-of-the-20th-century ambience. Downstairs are restaurants, bars, a lobby filled with wicker furniture, and an ancient banyan tree beneath which Robert Louis Stevenson once wrote. ~ 2365 Kalakaua Avenue; 808-922-3111, 800-325-3535, fax 808-923-0308; www.sheraton-hawaii.com. ULTRA-DELUXE.

Just down the beach resides the grand dame of Hawaiian hotels. Built in 1927 and affectionately known as "The Pink Palace," the **Royal Hawaiian Hotel** is an elegant, Spanish Moorish–style building complete with colonnaded walkways and manicured grounds. This castle away from home is decorated in French provincial fashion and features a fabulous lobby bedecked with chandeliers. Adjacent to the original building is a 17-story tower that brings the room count to 675. Worth visiting even if you never check in. ~ 2259 Kalakaua Avenue; 808-923-7311, 800-325-3535, fax 808-924-7098; www.royal-hawaiian.com. ULTRA-DELUXE.

If you'd prefer to go native and stay in a private home, contact one of the bed and breakfast referral numbers. These include **Bed & Breakfast Honolulu** (808-595-7533, 800-288-4666, fax 808-595-2030; www.hawaiibnb.com), or **Bed & Breakfast Hawaii** (808-822-7771, 800-733-1632, fax 808-822-2723; www.bandb-hawaii.com). They offer accommodations on all islands, priced from budget to deluxe.

For top-notch accommodations in out-of-the-way places, consider **Hawaii's Best Bed & Breakfasts** (808-885-0550, 800-262-9912, fax 808-885-0559; www.bestbnb.com).

CONDOS   The **Royal Kuhio**, a good bet for families, is a 389-unit highrise two blocks from Waikiki Beach. One-bedroom units feature fully equipped kitchens and balconies with ocean or mountain views. Prices start at $95. ~ 2240 Kuhio Avenue; 808-923-0555, 800-927-0555, fax 808-923-0720; www.waikikicondos.com.

Kaulana Kai Resort at Waikiki has 90 comfortable units with kitchenettes and private lanais. The suites, which include a full living room, are a good value for families. Studios run $99 to $120 and suites run $160 to $250. ~ 2425 Kuhio Avenue; 808-922-7777, 800-367-5666, fax 808-922-9473; www.marcresorts.com.

At the **Aston Waikiki Beach Tower** all 97 suites and penthouses feature contemporary furniture, wetbars, kitchens and beautiful lanais. The kids will enjoy the pool and paddle tennis court. One-bedroom units begin at $430. Suites for up to six guests start at

◆◆

THINK BIG

Offering over 2500 rooms, the **Hilton Hawaiian Village** is the largest resort in the islands and Waikiki's premier family hotel. The grounds provide a Disneyesque atmosphere that keeps children of all ages engaged—fireworks on Friday evening, shopping malls, restaurants and nightly entertainment, not to mention a penguin pool, flamingos, cockatoos and koi ponds. Seaside diversions include paddle boats, surfboards and sailing trips as well as numerous swimming pools to dip in, an acre of sand for sandcastle-making and an ocean of fun. Not to be overlooked, the rooms are attractively furnished and well-cared for and the service is friendly and welcoming. ~ 2005 Kalia Road; 808-949-4321, fax 808-947-7898; www.hilton.com. ULTRA-DELUXE.

$520. This is Waikiki's finest condominium. ~ 2470 Kalakaua Avenue; 808-926-6400, 800-922-7866, fax 808-926-7380; www.aston-hotels.com.

Offering kitchenettes and balconies, the **Aston Pacific Monarch** has studio apartments from $130 to $170 and one-bedroom units from $160 to $215 for up to four. There is a rooftop pool, jacuzzi and sauna, and the beach is just two blocks away. ~ 2427 Kuhio Avenue; 808-923-9805, 800-922-7866, fax 808-924-3220; e-mail lia.tauelangi@aston-hotels.com.

At **Winston's Waikiki Condos**, one-bedroom condos rent for $75 to $125 for one to four people. All suites are comfortably furnished with rattan furniture and feature lanais and full and complete kitchens. The units are recently renovated, well-maintained and clean. Eight of the thirteen units have washers and dryers. One block from the beach. Patrick Winston offers special deals for *Hidden Hawaii* readers, so make sure you call ahead and mention this book. He also offers an old-fashioned concierge and travel agency service to help you make the most of your stay. ~ 417 Nohonani Street, Suite 409; phone/fax 808-924-3332, 800-545-1948; www.winstonwaikikicondos.com, e-mail winston@iav.com.

Aston Waikiki Shore offers 90 studios as well as one- and two-bedroom units. These condos feature complete kitchens, washer/dryers and great views. Studios run $170 to $185. One bedroom units are $200 to $265. Two-bedroom units accommodating up to six cost $335 to $500. ~ 2161 Kalia Road; 808-926-4733, 800-922-7866, fax 808-922-2902.

At **Aston Waikiki Banyan** one-bedroom units are $210 to $280 for one to four people. These highrise ocean and mountain view units have full kitchens, rattan furniture and lanais. One block from the beach. ~ 201 Ohua Avenue; 808-922-0555, 800-922-7866, fax 808-922-0906; www.aston-hotels.com.

Several services rent condominiums on Oahu. They include **Condo Rentals of Waikiki** at 413 Seaside Avenue (808-923-0555, 800-927-0555, fax 808-923-0720) and **Marc Resorts** at 2155 Kalakaua Avenue (808-922-9700, 800-535-0085, fax 808-922-2421; www.marcresorts.com).

DINING

This tourist mecca is crowded with restaurants. Since the competition is so stiff, the cafés here are cheaper than anywhere else on the islands. There are numerous American restaurants serving moderately good food at modest prices, so diners looking for standard fare will have no problem. But as you're probably seeking something more exotic, I'll also list some interesting Asian, Hawaiian, health food and other offbeat restaurants.

If you decide to go to **Nick's Fishmarket**, plan on eating seafood. You have never seen such a list of fresh fish dishes. Not that much of it will seem familiar, but there is mahimahi, *opakapaka* and ahi. Or if you prefer to dine on something you recognize, how about shrimp scampi, abalone, lobster or scallops? The service is attentive. ~ 2070 Kalakaua Avenue; 808-955-6333; e-mail nicks waikiki@aol.com. ULTRA-DELUXE.

For a just-before-midnight snack—they close at 12:00—or to satisfy cravings for a hot bowl of noodle soup, you're never too far from an **Ezogiku**. Rub shoulders with Japanese tourists at the counter in one of these hole-in-the-wall eateries serving ramen in a variety of styles, including curry, pork and wonton. There are three locations to choose from in Waikiki. ~ 2420 Koa Avenue, 808-922-2473, fax 808-926-2207; www.ezogiku.com, e-mail info@ezogiku.com; 2546 Lemon Road, 808-923-2013; 2146 Kalakaua Avenue, 808-926-8616. BUDGET.

To find an affordable meal on Kalakaua Avenue, the ocean-front strip, try the bottom floor of the **Waikiki Shopping Plaza**. Here about a dozen ethnic and American restaurants offer take-out food as well as full course sitdown dinners. ~ 2250 Kalakaua Avenue; 808-923-1191, fax 808-922-4579. BUDGET.

The food is pretty standard fare at the Sheraton Waikiki's **Ocean Terrace** but the view deserves five stars. Set poolside next to the beach in one of the state's largest hotels, this open-air dining room provides a welcome means to dine on the water. Popular for breakfast, lunch and dinner, the Ocean Terrace's evening menu centers around rotating theme buffets, such as prime rib and clam night, steak and seafood night and crab night. ~ 2255 Kalakaua Avenue; 808-922-4422 ext. 71777. ULTRA-DELUXE.

The **International Food Court**, tucked into the northwest corner of the International Market Place, features a cluster of food stands and a patio for dining beneath a banyan tree. Here you will find **Bautista's Filipino Kitchen** (923-7220), where the specialties include noodles, beef stew, mixed vegetables and menudo with green fish. **Peking Garden** (926-6060) has traditional Chinese dishes including beef and broccoli, chicken chop suey and eggplant with chicken. For Japanese and Korean food, go to **Choi's Kitchen** (923-5614), where *saimin* and chicken teriyaki are popular dishes. ~ 2330 Kalakaua Avenue. BUDGET.

On a balcony in the International Market Place, **Coconut Willy's Bar & Grill** has a dinner menu that includes a teriyaki steak and shrimp platter, fish and chips, and mahimahi. There are also hamburgers, sandwiches and salads. Set beside the banyan tree that dominates the market, the place has a funky appeal. ~ 2330 Kalakaua Avenue; 808-923-9454. MODERATE.

For oceanfront dining, **The Beachside Café** is true to its name. With indoor and patio dining and a big buffet bar, it's a standard-fare American restaurant lacking in imagination but filled with beautiful views. Open for breakfast, lunch and dinner, the café serves steak, hamburgers and egg dishes, as well as offering a prime rib and crab leg dinner buffet. Ask for a table outside. ~ Sheraton Moana Surfrider Resort, 2365 Kalakaua Avenue; 808-922-3111, fax 808-924-4759; e-mail guy.villarosa@sheraton.com. MODERATE TO DELUXE.

Fans whirr overhead and a bar sits in the back; sheet music covers and old Matson oceanliner menus stand framed along the walls. Hard to believe someone would create this ambience for their restaurant, then name the place **Cheeseburger in Paradise**. But burgers it is, plus a selection of breakfast dishes for the morning. ~ 2500 Kalakaua Avenue; 808-923-3731, fax 808-923-1070; www.chzy-burger-waikiki.com, e-mail cipoahu@maui gateway.com. BUDGET TO MODERATE.

The cuisine at **Acqua** is Mediterranean/Pacific and the ambience dovetails with it neatly. Everything is pastels and primary colors with bright contemporary artwork and an ocean view to match. The menu features several pasta dishes and a host of "main attractions." That means you can order paella, tomato-basil capellini with garlic prawns, or rock shrimp risotto; or try pepper-crusted steak, honey-glazed chicken or bouillabaisse. Dinner only. ~ Hawaiian Regent Hotel, 2552 Kalakaua Avenue; 808-924-0123, fax 808-923-5848; www.acqua.com. MODERATE TO ULTRA-DELUXE.

Apart from the bustle of Waikiki but still right on the beach is the **Hau Tree Lanai**. Here beneath the interwoven branches of twin *hau* trees you can enjoy patio dining with a view that extends across Waikiki to the distant mountains. I favor the place for its breakfast (the French toast is delicious), but they also have a lunch and dinner menu that ranges from steamed vegetables to curried chicken to fresh island fish. In the evening the place is illuminated by torches, and soft breezes wisp off the water, adding to the enchantment. ~ New Otani Kaimana Beach Hotel, 2863 Kalakaua Avenue; 808-923-1555, fax 808-922-9404; www.kaimana.com. ULTRA-DELUXE.

Innovative, high-quality cuisine and excellent service make the **Diamond Head Grill** one of Hawaii's best restaurants. The Maui onion–crusted seared ahi is one of those oh-so-good dishes that makes you want to order it each time you visit. The refined and

CATCH A WAVE

All along Waikiki Beach, concessions offer rides on **outrigger canoes**. They are long, sleek fiberglass crafts resembling ancient Polynesian canoes. Each seats four to six passengers, plus a captain. For very cheap you can join the crew on a low-key wave-riding excursion that will have you paddling as hard and fast as you can to catch waves and ride them far into the shore.

artful presentation is complemented by the eatery's New Age decor with deco highlights. Nightly jazz adds to the dining pleasure. No lunch Saturday and Sunday. ~ Colony Surf Hotel, 2885 Kalakaua Avenue; 808-922-3734, fax 808-791-5165; e-mail www.diamond headgrill.com. ULTRA-DELUXE.

One of the ethnic restaurants most popular with local folks is **Keo's in Waikiki**. Fulfilling to all the senses, this intimate place is decorated with fresh flowers and tropical plants. The cuisine includes such Southeast Asian dishes as the "evil jungle prince," a sliced beef, shrimp or chicken entrée with coconut milk, fresh basil and red chili. You can choose from dozens of fish, shellfish, fowl and meat dishes. The menu offers a lot of variety, and is highly recommended. ~ 2028 Kuhio Avenue; 808-951-9355, fax 808-734-4652; www.keosthaicuisine.com, e-mail keos@hawaii.rr.com. MODERATE.

Among the movies filmed on Oahu are *Don Juan DeMarco*, *Like Water for Chocolate* and *Desperado*.

Davey Jones Ribs also serves pizza and pasta dishes as well as seafood and chicken. Informal and lively. ~ 250 Lewers Street; 808-923-7427, fax 808-922-7001. MODERATE.

Favored by both tourists and locals for its low prices, **Seaside Bar & Grill** has a budget-priced early-bird special nightly until 8 p.m. Choose any two items—lobster tail, crab legs, mahimahi, fried shrimp or New York steak—and they'll throw in a house salad as well. The fish is frozen and the place is actually two blocks from the "seaside," but for low-rent dining it's worth considering. Breakfast and dinner only. ~ 2256 Kuhio Avenue; 808-922-8227, fax 808-922-8166. BUDGET.

An L-shaped counter with swivel chairs is the most decor you can expect at **Fatty's Chinese Kitchen**. The prices on plate lunches and dinners are a throwback, too. With several dozen choices, including many "noodle in soup" dishes, Fatty aims to suit every palate. ~ Kuhio Mall at 2345 Kuhio Avenue; 808-922-9600. BUDGET.

The blue skies and green palms of the Caribbean never seem far away in Hawaii, and they feel even closer at **Cha Cha Cha Restaurant**. With its tropical color scheme and festive decor, this "Caribe/Mex" eatery serves up Mexican dishes such as burritos, tacos and quesadillas prepared Caribbean style with unusual spices and sauces. Dinner only. ~ 342 Seaside Avenue; 808-923-7797, fax 808-926-7007. BUDGET TO MODERATE.

A great place for breakfast, the **Waikiki Broiler** has inexpensive specials every morning. Dining is outdoors under thatched umbrellas or in a dining room with an outdoor feel. It's on a busy corner so the atmosphere is not exactly idyllic, but it's hard to match the prices —at dinner you can enjoy teriyaki steak, scallop and chicken entrées. ~ 200 Lewers Street; 808-923-8836, fax 808-924-3316. BUDGET TO DELUXE.

Perry's Smorgy, with its two locations—at the Ohana Coral Seas Hotel and on Kuhio Avenue—has an inexpensive buffet at dinner, lunch and breakfast. With an extensive salad bar, plus a host of meat and fish platters, this all-you-can-eat emporium is hard to beat. I'd suggest the Ohana branch; it's right on the waterfront. ~ Ohana Coral Seas Hotel, 250 Lewers Street, 808-922-8814; and also at 2380 Kuhio Avenue, 808-926-0184, phone/fax 808-922-1907; e-mail perrysrestaurants@hotmail.com. BUDGET TO MODERATE.

Northern Italian specialties at affordable prices draw nightly crowds to **Arancino's.** The place has the feel of a New York–style bistro, with excellent, home-style standards like eggplant parmigiana that are worth the likely 20-minute wait. The generous appetizer portions can easily become dinner. Owner/chef Riyoishi Kimura may be Japanese-born but his training in sophisticated Milano shows—great recipes are enhanced by quality cheeses and fresh ingredients. ~ 255 Beach Walk; 808-923-5557, fax 808-922-0105. BUDGET TO MODERATE.

Dishes like macadamia nut–crusted *opakapaka* and marinated chicken breast make **Bali-by-the-Sea** a special favorite. Plush seating, nautical lamps, fresh flowers and soft ocean breezes add to the charm of this elegant restaurant. Dress code. Closed Sunday. ~ Hilton Hawaiian Village, 2005 Kalia Road; 808-949-4321, fax 808-947-7926. ULTRA-DELUXE.

The **Shore Bird Beach Broiler** is a beachfront dining room that's a great place to enjoy a reasonably priced dinner and an ocean view. This is a cook-your-own-food facility that offers hand-carved steaks, fresh fish, teriyaki chicken and barbecued ribs. One of the best bargains on Waikiki Beach, the Shore Bird is inevitably crowded, so try to dine early. ~ Reef Hotel, 2169 Kalia Road; 808-922-2887, fax 808-923-8811. MODERATE.

It's not surprising that Waikiki's most fashionable hotel, the Halekulani, contains one of the district's finest restaurants. Situated on an open-air balcony overlooking the ocean, **La Mer** has a reputation for elegant dining in intimate surroundings. French-inspired dishes include confit tomato with truffle juice and fried basil and fillet of *kumu* in a rosemary salt crust with mushrooms, vegetables and an herb butter sauce. Add the filigree woodwork and sumptuous surroundings and La Mer is one of the island's most attractive waterfront dining rooms. Dinner only. ~ 2199 Kalia Road; 808-923-2311, fax 808-926-8004; www.halekulani.com. ULTRA-DELUXE.

Downstairs from La Mer is **Orchids,** serving a mix of Hawaiian and Continental cuisine like steamed oriental-style *onaga*, Indo-Chinese sauteed *opakapaka* and mustard herb–roasted lamb. Orchids is open for breakfast, lunch, dinner and Sunday brunch. ~ 2199 Kalia Road; 808-923-2311, fax 808-926-8004; www. halekulani.com. ULTRA-DELUXE.

GROCERIES   The best grocery store in Waikiki is also the biggest. Prices at **The Food Pantry** are inflated, but not as much as elsewhere in this tourist enclave. ~ 2370 Kuhio Avenue; 808-923-9831.

ABC **Discount Stores**, a chain of sundry shops with branches all around Waikiki, are convenient, but have a very limited stock and even higher prices.

If you are willing and able to shop outside Waikiki, you'll generally fare much better price-wise. Try the **Foodland** supermarket in the Ala Moana Center just outside Waikiki. Cheaper than Waikiki groceries, it's still more expensive than Greater Honolulu stores. ~ 1450 Ala Moana Boulevard; 808-949-5044, fax 808-949-5869.

Also in the Ala Moana Center, **Vim and Vigor** has a variety of vitamins, supplements and health foods, as well as a juice bar and lunch counter. ~ 1450 Ala Moana Boulevard; 808-955-3600, fax 808-941-1995; www.vimnvigor.com.

SHOPPING   This tourist mecca is a great place to look but not to buy. Browsing the busy shops is like studying a catalog of Hawaiian handicrafts. It's all here. You'll find everything but bargains. With a few noteworthy exceptions, the prices include the unofficial tourist surcharges that merchants worldwide levy against visitors. Windowshop Waikiki, but plan on spending your shopping dollars elsewhere.

One Waikiki shopping area I do recommend is **Duke's Lane**. This alleyway, running from Kalakaua Avenue to Kuhio Avenue near the International Market Place, may be the best place in all Hawaii to buy jade jewelry. Either side of the lane is flanked by mobile stands selling rings, necklaces, earrings, stick pins, bracelets and more. It's a prime place to barter for tiger's eyes, opals and mother-of-pearl pieces.

The main shopping scene is in the malls. **Waikiki Shopping Plaza** has five floors of stores and restaurants. Here are jewelers, sundries and boutiques, plus specialty shops like **Waldenbooks**, with an excellent line of magazines as well as paperbacks and bestsellers. ~ 2250 Kalakaua Avenue; 808-922-4154.

The **Royal Hawaiian Shopping Center** is a four-story complex that runs for two blocks along Kalakaua Avenue, from Lewers Street to the Outrigger Waikiki. On the *makai* side (facing the ocean), it fronts the grounds of the Royal Hawaiian and the Sheraton Waikiki. It is Waikiki's largest mall and features Euro-American designer boutiques, upscale shops, numerous restaurants and fast-food kiosks, as well as an indoor shooting gallery and showroom. A weekly schedule of Hawaiiana and other cultural performances provides an entertaining respite from the pressures of shopping. Two of Waikiki's more unique shops are in the center. Check out the **Little Hawaiian Crafts Shop** (808-926-2662,

fax 808-924-7874) on the third floor, where you'll find an interesting selection of traditional and contemporary Hawaiian crafts
including carved koa wood bowls, Niihau shell leis, Hawaiian
quilts, ceramics and glassware. If you're in the market for a ukulele,
try **The Ukulele House** (808-923-8587, fax 808-924-8587), on
the ground floor, which carries everything from children's souvenir ukes for $10–$20 to musically playable instruments ranging from $80 all the way to $2000-plus for vintage models. ~
2233 Kalakaua Avenue.

Then there's **King's Village**, a mock Victorian town that suggests how Britain might have looked had the 19th-century English
invented polyethylene. The motif may be trying to appear anti-
quated, but the prices are unfortunately quite contemporary. ~
131 Kaiulani Avenue at Kalakaua Avenue.

International Market Place is my favorite browsing spot.
With tiny shops and vending stands spotted around the sprawling grounds, it's a relief from the claustrophobic shopping complexes. There's an old banyan spreading across
the market, plus thatched treehouses, a carp
pond, brick sidewalks and woodfront stores. You
won't find many bargains, but the sightseeing is
priceless. ~ 2330 Kalakaua Avenue.

The tallest ceramic mural
in the world—30 stories
high—climbs the side of
the Hilton Hawaiian
Village Rainbow
Tower.

The **Waikiki Trade Center** is another strikingly attractive mall. With an air of Milanese splendor about
it, this glass-and-steel complex is a maze of mirrors. In
addition to the stained-glass windows and twinkling
lights, there are several worthwhile shops. ~ Kuhio and
Seaside avenues.

A nice selection of shops are located in the **Hyatt Regency
Waikiki**. This triple-tiered arcade is *the* place to look when you
are seeking the very best. Glamour and style are passwords around
here. There are fine-art shops, designer apparel stores, gem shops
and shops that feature made-in-Hawaii products. ~ 2424 Kalakaua Avenue.

Hilton Hawaiian Village contains the **Rainbow Bazaar**, an array
of shops spread around the grounds of Hawaii's largest resort
complex. This plaza contains a number of stores specializing in
island fashions, plus gift shops and import emporia. The shopping
center has been designed in Oriental style, with curving tile roofs
and brilliantly painted roof beams. You can stroll along an Asian
arcade, past lofty banyan trees and flowering gardens, to stores
filled with rare art and Far Eastern antiquities. ~ 2005 Kalia Road.

Island-based **Local Motion** has opened an architecturally distinguished flagship shop for its line of logowear and sporting gear,
including surfboards, body boards and backpacks. There's also
a pleasant alfresco café on the second floor. ~ 1958 Kalakaua
Avenue; 808-979-7873.

Island Treasures Antique Mall has Waikiki's best selection of Hawaiiana in a multilevel complex that's home to a number of individual vendors. Fun for browsing and a purchase if you find something priced right. The shops open in the early afternoon and stay open until 10 p.m., which makes it a good tie-in with an evening stroll. Closed Monday. ~ 2145 Kuhio Avenue; 808-922-8223.

HIDDEN ►

Looking for a vintage silk shirt? Those famous Hawaiian styles, like the one Montgomery Clift sported in *From Here to Eternity*, are among the alluring items at Bailey's Antiques and Aloha Shirts. If an original silky is beyond your means, they also have reproductions as well as collectibles like Zippo lighters. ~ 517 Kapahulu Avenue; 808-734-7628.

NIGHTLIFE   Hawaii has a strong musical tradition, kept alive by excellent groups performing their own compositions as well as old Polynesian songs. I'm not talking about the "Blue Hawaii"–"Tiny Bubbles"–"Beyond the Reef" medleys that draw tourists in droves, but *real* Hawaiian music as performed by Hapa, the Brothers Cazimero, Keola and Kapono Beamer, Marlene Sai, Melveen Leed and others.

If you spend any time in Honolulu, don't neglect to check out such authentic sounds. One or more of these musicians will probably be playing at a local club. Consult the daily newspapers.

Over at Nick's Fishmarket there's live entertainment nightly. Expect to hear light rock, jazz, soul or blues while munching on half-price *pupus*. ~ 2070 Kalakaua Avenue; 808-955-6333, fax 808-946-0478; e-mail nickswaikiki@aol.com.

On Wednesday, Friday and Saturday nights, a contemporary Hawaiian group stars at the Paradise Lounge. Other forms of live entertainment are offered nightly. Choose between table or lounge seating in this carpeted club, which is decorated with Hawaiian landscapes painted by local artists. ~ Hilton Hawaiian Village, 2005 Kalia Road; 808-949-4321, fax 808-947-7926.

The Esprit Nightclub is a congenial spot situated right on Waikiki Beach. This cozy club features bands that play music from different eras Tuesday through Saturday, features special

THE ROMANCE OF YESTERDAY TODAY

During the first part of the 20th century, the arrival of cruise ships was marked by a celebration. This elaborate welcome is making a comeback in the guise of Boat Days. When cruise ships arrive in port, the Royal Hawaiian Band plays music and there's singing and multicolored streamers. A modern-day touch is the helicopter dropping flower petals from above. ~ 808-566-2337.

guests on Sunday and Monday and offers spectacular ocean views every night of the week. ~ Sheraton Waikiki Hotel, 2255 Kalakaua Avenue; 808-922-4422, fax 808-923-8785.

Two groups perform mellow Hawaiian music nightly at the **Shorebird** at the Outrigger Reef: one in the restaurant, the other in the lounge. ~ Outrigger Reef, 2169 Kalia Road; 808-923-3111.

Tired of the old nine-to-five grind? For a change of pace try **Scruples**, where the schedule is eight to four. 8 p.m. to 4 a.m. that is. Promising "dance and romance," this popular night spot features dancing to Top-40 tunes. Cover and two-drink minimum. ~ 2310 Kuhio Avenue; 808-923-9530.

The Cellar specializes in dancing, with Top-40 hits spun by a deejay Tuesday through Sunday. It's a top spot for a hot night. Closed Monday, except during summer. Cover. ~ 205 Lewers Street; 808-923-9952.

Nearby, **Waikiki Broiler** has karaoke nightly. ~ 200 Lewers Street at Kalia Road; 808-923-8836, fax 808-924-3316.

If you like sophisticated jazz to accompany dinner or drinks, the **Diamond Head Grill** is the place to go. The vocalists and musicians are first rate, and the decibel level is suitable for either concentrating on the music, conversation or food, which is some of the best in the Islands. ~ Colony Surf Hotel, 2885 Kalakaua Avenue; 808-922-3734, fax 808-791-5165; www.diamondheadgrill.com.

Eurasia Night Club and Sports Bar has nightly deejays spinning hip-hop, Top-40 and R&B. The shows are broadcast live on KQMQ 93.1 FM and I94 93.9 FM on Friday and Saturday. Every night but Saturday is 18-and-over college night; Thursday is Latin night (salsa lessons are available). Cover. ~ Hawaiian Regent Hotel, 2552 Kalakaua Avenue; 808-921-5335, fax 808-926-2742.

Acqua offers live Latin music Friday and Saturday night in a plush setting. With an ocean view and relaxing ambience, this lounge in the Hawaiian Regent Hotel is part of a light, airy, Mediterranean restaurant. Cover. ~ 2552 Kalakaua Avenue; 808-924-0123, fax 808-923-5848.

Coconut Willy's Bar & Grill, situated on a balcony in the International Market Place, has a live band that starts in the afternoon and continues on into the night. The 35-and-over crowd turns out to dance to the '50s and '60s classics as well as Hawaiian and country tunes. Attractive setting. ~ 2330 Kalakaua Avenue; 808-923-9454.

Duke's Canoe Club in the Outrigger Waikiki offers a beachfront setting, a distant view of Diamond Head, and plenty of atmosphere. Duke refers to Duke Kahanamoku, the Olympic swimming champion and surfer who helped restore surfing to a position of cultural prominence. The decor documents his career with archival photography and memorabilia. It draws overflowing crowds, particularly on weekends and Sunday afternoons when Henry Kapono performs. ~ Outrigger Waikiki, 2335 Kalakaua Avenue; 808-922-2268, fax 808-923-4204.

With room for 300 of your closest friends, **Moose McGilly-cuddy's** is a prime place to dance to live bands Monday through Saturday. Deejays also spin Top-40 music. Known for its weird pictures, this establishment is easily spotted. Just look for the only building on Lewers Street sporting a stuffed moose head. Occasional cover. ~ 310 Lewers Street; 808-923-0751, fax 808-922-8931; www.moosemcgillycuddys.com.

GAY SCENE   The gay scene is centered around several clubs on Waikiki's Kuhio Avenue and in Eaton Square, near the corner of Eaton and Hobron streets, not far away.

Club goers hang in and out at **Angles Waikiki**, where a bar in the center of the room provides a place to socialize as does the lanai outside. There are pool tables and videos, as well as a dancefloor. Every Wednesday, crowds compete for cash prizes in the Best Chest/ Best Buns contest, and In-trigued, an all-male revue, entertains on Thursday and Sunday nights. ~ 2256 Kuhio Avenue; 808-926-9766.

Fusion Waikiki is another gay club open until 4 a.m. This hot spot taking up the second and third floors of the Paradise Building features dancing to house and underground deejay music. There are male strip shows and female impersonation performances on Friday and Saturday. Cover. ~ 2260 Kuhio Avenue; 808-924-2422.

Near Diamond Head, **Hula's Bar and Lei Stand,** with an ocean view and a disco complete with strobe-lit dancefloor and videos, rocks nightly until 2 a.m. Cover after 10 p.m. ~ Waikiki Grand Hotel, 134 Kapahulu Avenue; 808-923-0669.

Tucked away in the back of Eaton Square, a little hideaway off Ala Moana Boulevard, **P-10A,** a private coffee bar that gives gay guys an alternative place to meet. It's an alcohol- and smoke-free relaxing retreat, serving coffee and tea. For entertainment there

PIG ON FIRE

For an authentic *tourist* experience accompanied by a genuine aloha spirit join the busloads of Waikiki visitors who are caravanned to Barber's Point for **Germaine's Luau** in Campbell Industrial Park, the ultimate in Hawaiian kitsch. At Germaine's you'll get to participate in the unearthing ceremony of a pig from its underground *imu* (oven), dine on Hawaiian-style food, watch Polynesian dancers (or join them on stage), all at a beachfront site as the sun sets on the Pacific. Closed Monday from January through May and September through December. ~ Reservations: **808-949-6626, 800-367-5685,** fax **808-949-4218;** www.germainesluau.com.

are video games, a pool table, X-rated movies and, most importantly, conversation in this low-key, quiet hangout. Although it's a private club, it costs no more than a night at a bar. Open from 4 p.m. weekdays and from noon on weekends; there's live entertainment Friday and Saturday nights. Cover. ~ Eaton Square, Hobron and Eaton streets; 808-942-8536.

Michelangelo is a cozy old-fashioned gay cruise bar with video games, pool table and jukeboxes. ~ Eaton Square, Hobron and Eaton streets; 808-951-0008.

Dance any night of the week 'til 4 a.m. to DJ-spun house, disco and hip-hop mixes at **Venus Nightclub**. They feature a male revue and female impersonators. Cover. ~ 1349 Kapiolani Boulevard; 808-951-8671.

Downtown Honolulu

For a historical and cultural tour of Hawaii's state capital, simply head toward Downtown Honolulu. A financial center for the entire Pacific Rim, Honolulu's importance to both North America and Asia is manifest in the highrise cityscape. The historical significance of this port city is evident from the 19th-century buildings that lead to the financial district in the heart of the city.

SIGHTS

A fitting place to begin your tour is among the oldest homes in the islands. The buildings at the **Mission Houses Museum** seem to be borrowed from a New England landscape, and in a sense they were. The Frame House, a trim white wooden structure, was cut on the East Coast and shipped around the Horn to Hawaii. That was back in 1821, when this Yankee-style building was used to house missionary families.

Like the nearby Chamberlain House and Depository and other structures here, the Frame House represents one of the missionaries' earliest centers in Hawaii. It was in 1820 that Congregationalists arrived in the islands; they immediately set out to build and proselytize. In 1831, they constructed the Chamberlain House and Depository from coral and used it as the mission store. The neighborhood's Printing Office, built of the same durable material ten years later, was used by the first press ever to print in the Hawaiian language. The Mission Houses complex tells much about the missionaries, who converted Hawaiian into a written language, then proceeded to rewrite the entire history of the islands. The museum is run by the Hawaiian Mission Children's Society. Guided tours daily. Closed Sunday and Monday. Admission. ~ 553 South King Street; 808-531-0481, fax 808-545-2280; e-mail mhm@lava.net.

Opposite, at South King and Punchbowl streets, is the **Kawaiahao Church**. This imposing edifice required 14,000 coral blocks for its construction. Completed in 1842, it has been called the Westminster Abbey of Hawaii, because coronations and funerals for Hawaiian kings and queens were once conducted here. Services are still performed in Hawaiian and English every Sunday at 10:30 a.m.; attending them is not only a way to view the church interior, but also provides a unique cultural perspective on contemporary Hawaiian life. Also note that the tomb of King Lunalilo rises in front of the church, and behind the church lies the cemetery where early missionaries and converted Hawaiians were buried.

Across South King Street, the brick structure with stately white pillars is the **Mission Memorial Building**, constructed in 1916 to honor those same early church leaders. The nearby Renaissance-style building with the tile roof is **Honolulu Hale**, the City Hall. You might want to venture into the central courtyard, an open-air plaza surrounded by stone columns.

As you continue along South King Street in a westerly direction toward the center of Honolulu, **Iolani Palace** will appear on your right. Built for King Kalakaua in 1882, this stunning Renaissance-style mansion served as a royal residence until Queen Liliuokalani was overthrown in 1893. Later the ill-starred monarch was imprisoned here; eventually, after Hawaii became a territory of the United States, the palace was used as the capitol building. Guided tours lead you along the *koa* staircases and past the magnificent chandeliers and Corinthian columns that lend a touch of European grandeur to this splendid building. Reservations are recommended. Admission. ~ 808-522-0832.

Also located on the palace grounds are the **Iolani Barracks**, where the Royal Household Guards were stationed, and the **Coronation Pavilion** upon which the King was crowned. You can tour the palace grounds for free, but there's an admission charge for the building. Reservations are strongly advised; children under five are not allowed. Tours are given Tuesday through Saturday. Closed Sunday and Monday. ~ South King and Richards streets; 808-522-0832, fax 808-532-1051.

Directly across the street rises the **Kamehameha Statue**, honoring Hawaii's first king. A huge gilt-and-bronze figure cast in Italy, it is covered with flower leis on special occasions. The spear-carrying warrior wears a feather cape and helmet. Behind him stands **Aliiolani Hale**, better known as the Judiciary Building. Back in the days of the monarchy, it served as the House of Parliament. Docent-led tours of the Judiciary History Center are available Monday through Friday by reservation only. ~ 808-539-4999, fax 808-539-4996; www.jhchawaii.org, e-mail jhc@aloha.net.

Behind Iolani Palace is the **State Capitol Building**. Unlike the surrounding structures, this is an ultramodern building, completed in 1969. Encircled by flared pillars that resemble palm trees, the capitol represents a variety of themes. Near the entrance there's a statue of Father Damien, the leper martyr of Molokai Island and Queen Liliuokalani, Hawaii's last reigning monarch. The

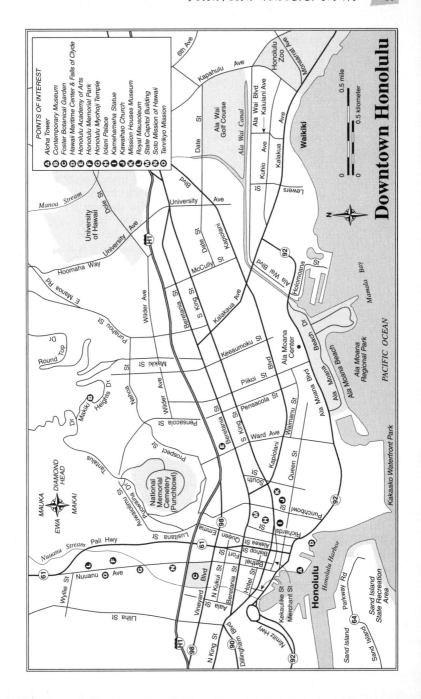

Downtown Honolulu

POINTS OF INTEREST

1. Aloha Tower
2. Contemporary Museum
3. Foster Botanical Garden
4. Hawaii Maritime Center & Falls of Clyde
5. Honolulu Academy of Arts
6. Honolulu Memorial Park
7. Honolulu Myohoji Temple
8. Iolani Palace
9. Kamehameha Statue
10. Kawaiahao Church
11. Mission Houses Museum
12. Royal Mausoleum
13. State Capitol Building
14. Soto Mission of Hawaii
15. Tenrikyo Mission

0   0.5 mile
0   0.5 kilometer

PACIFIC OCEAN

MAUKA / DIAMOND HEAD / EWA / MAKAI

National Memorial Cemetery (Punchbowl)

University of Hawaii

Waikiki

Honolulu

Honolulu Harbor

Mamala Bay

Sand Island State Recreation Area

House and Senate chambers are designed in a cone shape to resemble volcanoes, and the open-air courtyard is a commentary on the state's balmy weather. Tours of the capitol building and the legislature are given Monday through Friday. ~ Bounded by South Beretania, Richards and Punchbowl streets; 808-586-0178, fax 808-586-0046.

For a tour of Honolulu's waterfront, head down Richards Street from the State Capitol Building toward Pier 7. Next to the Aloha Tower Marketplace, the imposing and historic **Falls of Clyde** lies berthed. A completely restored century-old sailing ship, the *Falls of Clyde* is reputedly the only fully rigged four-masted ship in the world. In the old days it was used to carry sugar and oil across the Pacific. Honolulu was then a harbor filled with tall-masted ships, so crowded at the dock that they bumped one another's gunwales. Part of this proud fleet, the *Falls of Clyde* was built in Scotland and sailed halfway round the world.

For a single admission charge you can tour this marvelous piece of floating history and view the **Hokulea**, a double-hulled canoe that has sailed several times to Tahiti. A 60-foot replica of an ancient Polynesian craft, it follows the traditional designs of the boats used by the early Tahitians. Since 1975, this fragile craft has been sailed between Hawaii and French Polynesia by Hawaiian navigators, recreating more than 100,000 miles of historic sea voyages. Using no modern instruments, navigating by stars and wave patterns, they traced the course of their ancestors.

The **Hawaii Maritime Center** (adjacent to the *Falls of Clyde*) is an outstanding museum that traces the archipelago's maritime history from the era of Polynesian exploration to the days of the great ocean liners and beyond. Other displays focus on the old whaling trade, the invention of surfing and seaplanes. Admission. ~ Pier 7; 808-536-6373, fax 808-536-1519; e-mail bmoore@ bishopmuseum.org.

It's also fun to wander the nearby wharves, catching glimpses of the shops and pleasure boats that still tie up around Honolulu's historic port. You can take in the city's fishing fleet, as well as

THE MERRY MONARCH

The king who commissioned the Iolani Palace, David Kalakaua, was a world traveler with a taste for the good life. Known as the Merry Monarch, he planned for his coronation the greatest party Hawaii had ever seen. He liked to spend money with abandon and managed to amass in his lifetime a remarkable collection of material goods, not the least of which was his palace.

wander through a "prehistoric glen," a riot of ancient ferns and unusual palms. Or you can stroll through and marvel at the universe of color crowded into this small urban garden. Visitors are advised to bring insect repellent. Admission. ~ 50 North Vineyard Boulevard; 808-522-7065, fax 808-522-7050; www.co.honolulu. hi.us/parks/hbg.

When you're done enjoying Foster Botanical Garden, stop by the adjacent **Kwan Yin Temple**, where the smell of incense fills the air. For a brief moment you'll feel like you're in China rather than Honolulu. ~ 50 North Vineyard Boulevard. ◄ HIDDEN

On the way back to Chinatown, walk along the other side of Nuuanu Stream and stop at the **Cultural Plaza**. This Asian-style shopping mall is bounded by Kukui, Maunakea and Beretania streets, and by the stream. You'll find porcelain, Chinese jewelry, herbs and perhaps even acupuncture supplies.

Another important cultural point in the downtown district is the **Honolulu Academy of Arts**. This outstanding museum often displays author James Michener's collection of woodblocks from Japan. There are also works by European, Asian and American masters, as well as important art by local painters and sculptors. Renovated cases and lighting improve the views of these works; a pavilion houses diverse exhibits while other galleries focus on the East meeting the West. Several elegantly landscaped courtyards add to the beauty here. Closed Monday. Admission. ~ 900 South Beretania Street; 808-532-8700, fax 808-532-8787; www.honoluluacademy.org

If you're in the mood for a great film, head to the **Signature Theater** complex at Dole Cannery Square. Hawaii's largest cineplex with 18 screens, it also features Hawaii's best cinematic selection, including foreign films you'll find nowhere else on the Islands. ~ 735B Iwilei Road; 808-526-3456.

The **Pagoda Hotel** is sufficiently removed from the crowds but still only a ten-minute drive from the beach. Spacious studio and one-bedroom units put the accent on rattan furniture. The car- **LODGING**

◆◆

HEART OF A NEIGHBORHOOD

Some of Chinatown's woodframe buildings still suggest the old days and traditions. Wander down side streets like Maunakea Street and you will encounter import stores, Chinese groceries and noodle factories. You might also pop into one of the medicinal herb shops, which feature strange potions and healing powders. There are chop suey joints, acupuncturists and outdoor markets galore, all lending a priceless flavor of the Orient.

peted rooms feature views of the hotel garden or distant mountains. Two-bedroom units in the adjoining Pagoda Terrace offer kitchens. ~ 1525 Rycroft Street; 808-941-6611, 800-367-6060, fax 808-955-5067; www.pagoda hotel.com. MODERATE.

On the outskirts of Chinatown is the **Town Inn**. This is an excellent spot to capture the local color of Honolulu's Chinese section, though the hotel itself is rather nondescript. The 26 rooms are clean, carpeted and sparsely furnished—some even have air conditioning—and all are practically devoid of decoration. First-come, first-served. ~ 250 North Beretania Street; 808-536-2377. BUDGET.

In the mid-1840s, writer Herman Melville worked in Honolulu as a pin boy in a bowling alley.

DINING

Rather than list the city's restaurants according to price, I'll group them by area. As you get away from Waikiki you'll be dining with a more local crowd and tasting foods more representative of island cuisine, so I would certainly advise checking out some of Honolulu's eating places.

Right next to Waikiki, in Ala Moana Center, there are numerous ethnic takeout restaurants that share a large dining pavilion called **Makai Market**. Best of all is **Patti's Chinese Kitchen** (808-946-5002, fax 808-943-4355), a crowded and noisy gathering place. At Patti's you can choose from over 20 entrées plus a side order of fried rice, or *chow fun*. The courses include dim sum, orange chicken, beef and broccoli, tofu, beef tomato, sweet-and-sour ribs, barbecued pork and shrimp with vegetables. It's quite simply the best place near Waikiki for a low-cost meal. There's also the **Poi Bowl** (808-949-8444), a takeout stand serving Hawaiian dishes. **Schlotzsky's Deli** (808-944-8883) features a full line of deli sandwiches as well as pizzas and salads. ~ BUDGET.

HIDDEN ▶

Or you can ride the escalator to the upper level of Ala Moana Center. Here **Shirokiya**, a massive Asian department store, features an informal Japanese à la carte-style buffet. ~ 808-973-9111. MODERATE.

Hawaiian regional cuisine accented by island fruits is featured at the **Prince Court**. The Hawaii Prince Hotel's harborside restaurant, this dining room is known for dishes like sea scallops and lobster. A big wine list is another plus at this Polynesian-style dining room appointed with floral bouquets. ~ 100 Holomoana Street; 808-956-1111. DELUXE TO ULTRA-DELUXE.

Ward Centre, midway between Waikiki and Downtown Honolulu, is a focus for gourmet dining. A warren of wood-paneled restaurants, it features several outstanding eateries. Particularly recommended for the price is **Scoozee's**, a "pasta, pizza, pizzazz" restaurant with entrées averaging around $10. ~ 1200 Ala Moana Boulevard; 808-597-1777. BUDGET TO MODERATE.

Also consider **Compadres**, upstairs in the same complex. This attractive Mexican restaurant, with oak bar and patio dining, prepares dishes from south of the border as well as salads, steaks and seafood. It specializes in tropical ambience, good food and fishbowl-size margaritas. ~ 1200 Ala Moana Boulevard; 808-591-8307. MODERATE.

Ryan's Grill is one of Honolulu's hottest after-work hangouts for singles who want to become un-single, and the place is packed from 5 p.m. until after 1 a.m. Comfortable leather chairs and marble-topped tables create a cozy, modern atmosphere. Grilled and steamed fish and fowl, pizzas, salads and fettuccine are among the many culinary options for those who go to eat instead of drink. ~ 1200 Ala Moana Boulevard; 808-591-9132, fax 808-591-0034; e-mail ryansgrill@aol.com. MODERATE TO ULTRA-DELUXE.

Chef Jean Marie Josselin's version of Pacific Rim cuisine makes use of island-grown produce and herbs at **A Pacific Café** in the Ward Centre. The stylish decor, with a hint of retro, is well lit, highlighting floral displays and a rich play of colors. Artful presentation adds to the appeal of dishes like garlic- and sesame-crusted prime rib. Service is welcoming and the ambience one of casual elegance. Dinner only. ~ 1200 Ala Moana Boulevard; 808-593-0035, fax 808-593-1840. DELUXE TO ULTRA-DELUXE.

Tai Pan on the Boulevard is tucked away in a building on   ◄ HIDDEN
Kapiolani Boulevard, about a block from the Hawaii Convention Center. This quiet, modern-chic restaurant, with dramatic lighting that adds a sense of intimacy, is a perfect place for fine conversation. Fine dining too, with a French, Chinese and hybrid menu. You can't go wrong with the rich lobster and crab bisque or the slow-roasted duck confit with raspberry-ginger sauce. There are rarely crowds, which is a surprise considering the quality of the setting and the cuisine. This is one of Honolulu's hidden finds. ~ 1680 Kapiolani Boulevard; 808-943-1888, fax 808-943-1881. MODERATE TO ULTRA-DELUXE.

Located in the ultracontemporary Restaurant Row shopping mall, **Sunset Grill** is a minimalist's delight. Track lights, exposed pipes, raw wood and poured concrete establish a kind of early-21st-century motif. The only area devoted to excess is the kitchen, which serves up a lavish array of *kiawe*-grilled dishes, such as smoke-infused marinated salmon. No lunch Saturday or Sunday; Sunday brunch. ~ 500 Ala Moana Boulevard, #1-A; 8-521-4409, fax 808-523-5190. MODERATE TO DELUXE.

Honolulu has numerous seafood restaurants. Some of them, fittingly enough, are located right on the water. But for an authentic seafront feel, it's nice to be where the fishing boats actually come in. **Fisherman's Wharf** provides just such an atmosphere. This sprawling facility is festooned with nautical gear. The "Seafood Grotto" topside has a shoalful of seafood selections ranging from live Maine lobster to Dungeness crab. ~ 1009 Ala Moana Boulevard; 808-538-3808. MODERATE TO ULTRA-DELUXE.

Fresh *ono*, mahimahi, *opakapaka* and ahi highlight the vast seafood menu at **John Dominis**. A sprawling establishment midway between Waikiki and Downtown Honolulu, it features huge pools filled with live fish. The wood-paneled dining room overlooks the water and the chefs know as much about preparing seafood as the original Polynesians. For landlubbers, steak and veal are also on the menu. No lunch. ~ 43 Ahui Street; 808-523-0955, fax 808-526-3758; e-mail jdominis@lava.net. ULTRA-DELUXE.

For prime rib, Alaskan snow crab legs, shrimp and vegetable tempura, try the **Pagoda Floating Restaurant**. This restaurant-in-the-round sits above a pond populated with gaily colored koi fish. Several cascades and a fountain feed the pond. The surrounding grounds have been carefully landscaped. This dining room offers lunch and dinner buffets with themes such as prime rib night. ~ 1525 Rycroft Street; 808-941-6611, fax 808-946-6596. DELUXE.

Up on the second level of the Aloha Tower Marketplace, toward the back overlooking the water, there's the **Kau Kau Corner Food Lanai**. This cluster of food stands ranges from Villa Pizza to Belinda's Aloha Kitchen to Yokozuna and beyond. There is comfortable seating in an attractive setting, all at economical prices. ~ Aloha Tower Marketplace, Pier 8; 808-528-5700, fax 808-524-8334. BUDGET.

Satisfying your senses is easy at **Chai's Island Bistro**. Ample portions of distinctive dishes such as seafood risotto with Big Island heart of palm or Asian-style osso buco with kabocha squash sate the taste buds, while the presentation pleases the eyes. The service is friendly and evening brings the sounds of Hawaii's contemporary musicians to touch your heart. ~ Aloha Tower Marketplace, 1 Aloha Tower Drive; 808-585-0011. MODERATE TO DELUXE.

Auntie Pasto's is a popular Italian restaurant with oilcloth on the tables and a map of the mother country tacked to the wall. Pasta is served with any of a dozen different sauces—meat sauce, clams and broccoli, creamy pesto, carbonara and seafood. There are salads aplenty plus an assortment of entrées that includes veal marsala, chicken cacciatore and calamari piccata. Closed for lunch on weekends. ~ 1099 South Beretania Street; 808-523-8855, fax 808-524-6267; www.auntiepastos.com. BUDGET TO MODERATE.

For a taste of Southeast Asian cuisine, try the **Pae Thai**. At this café you can savor *tom yum* (spicy lemongrass soup), chicken satay or a tasty garlic shrimp dish. ~ 1246 South King Street; phone/fax 808-596-8106. BUDGET TO DELUXE.

McCully Chop Suey, one of Honolulu's best budget-priced Chinese restaurants, is rather bland but offers a menu that contains everything imaginable. There are over 160 items to choose from—two dozen poultry dishes, eight different sizzling platters, and a host of beef, noodle and seafood dishes. ~ 2005 South King Street; 808-946-4069. BUDGET.

Near the city's financial center there's a modest restaurant that I particularly like. **People's Café** is owned by an Okinawan family, but the food is primarily Polynesian: this is a splendid spot to order poi, *lomi* salmon, *kalua* pig and other island favorites. *Ono, ono!* Closed Sunday. ~ 1310 Pali Highway; phone/fax 808-536-5789. BUDGET TO MODERATE.

For Chinese food hereabouts, try **Yong Sing Restaurant**. This high-ceilinged establishment, catering to local businesspeople, has some delicious dishes. I thought the oyster sauce chicken particularly tasty. With its daily lunch specials, Yong Sing is a perfect stopoff when you're shopping or sightseeing downtown. ~ 1055 Alakea Street; 808-531-1367. BUDGET TO MODERATE.

But for the true flavor of China, head over to Chinatown, just a few blocks from the financial district. Amid the tumbledown buildings and jumble of shops, you'll happen upon **Double Eight Restaurant**. Although the service is forgettable and the decor nonexistent, they do know how to cook up Hong Kong–style delicacies. One fortuitous sign of quality is that few of the employees speak any English. Good luck and bon appetit! ~ 1113 Maunakea Street; 808-526-3887. BUDGET.

There's **A Little Bit of Saigon** right in the heart of Chinatown.   ◀ HIDDEN
Small it may be, but this café represents a triple threat to the competition—attractive decor, good prices and excellent food. Little wonder it has gained such a strong reputation among the local gentry. The menu covers the spectrum of Vietnamese dishes, with a smattering of Italian and vegetarian fare, and the interior, lined with tropical paintings, is easy on the eyes. ~ 1160 Maunakea Street; phone/fax 808-528-3663. BUDGET TO MODERATE.

MAESTRO MAVRO

A rising star on the Honolulu culinary scene is **Chef Mavro's**. Chef George Mavrothalassitis, formerly of the Four Seasons Resort in Wailea, now presides over his own corner in Honolulu. The unassuming building on South King Street does not hint at what awaits inside—an elegant yet understated dining room adorned with local artwork. The French-inspired cuisine arrives at the table in an equally sublime presentation. The dishes are five-star and the service impeccable. One claim to fame of Chef Mavro is the perfect pairing of the wine with every item on the menu. A place for that special night. Dinner only. ~ 1969 South King Street; 808-944-4714; www.chefmavro.com, e-mail mavro@gte.net. ULTRA-DELUXE.

A Hawaiian Cultural Tour

You're on the right island to get a true sense of what life was (and is) like for the Hawaiian people.

BISHOP MUSEUM   Our tour begins at the Bishop Museum (page 106), with its exceptional exhibits of Hawaiiana. Three floors of the grand hall give you a feel for Polynesian history over the centuries. Allow 1.5 hours.

IOLANI PALACE   Next, head downtown to Iolani Palace (page 88). Be sure to make reservations ahead of time if you want to see the phenomenal woodwork inside the palace. Stroll the grounds and imagine what it was like to be dressed in the long-sleeved outfits of the royal family in this heat! Most Friday afternoons the Royal Hawaiian Band plays at the Royal Bandstand. Allow 45 minutes for the tour. Stroll across the street to see the **statue** of King Kamehameha, Hawaii's first king. If you're lucky, it will be a holiday and he'll be draped in flower leis.

ROYAL MAUSOLEUM   It's about six blocks west (*ewa*) to Nuuanu Avenue. Head toward the mountains (*mauka*) and you'll arrive at the Royal Mausoleum (page 104), where Hawaii's royals are interred.

QUEEN EMMA SUMMER PALACE   After paying your respects, backtrack to Route H-1, head Diamond Head direction (east) and get off on the Pali Highway (Route 61) traveling *mauka* toward Kaneohe/Kailua. You'll soon come to Queen Emma Summer Palace (page 107). A comfortable

And there's a little bit of every other ethnic cuisine at the food stalls in **Maunakea Marketplace**. Here you'll find vendors dispensing steaming plates of Thai, Chinese, Japanese, Hawaiian, Filipino, Korean, Vietnamese and Italian food. Italian? Small tables are provided. ~ Hotel and Maunakea streets. BUDGET.

By way of Filipino food, **Mabuhay Cafe** comes recommended by several readers. It's a plainly adorned place on the edge of Chinatown that serves a largely local clientele. The menu is extensive, covering all types of Filipino dishes. ~ 1049 River Street; 808-545-1956. BUDGET.

For upscale dining in Chinatown, the address is **Indigo**. This Eurasian dining room casts an aura of the Orient with its dark wicker chairs, ornamental gong and intaglio-carved furnishings. Expect more than a dozen dim sum dishes plus "Peking pizzettas." The soups and salads include tea-smoked chicken jook and goat

New England–style home rather than a grand building, it was built in 1843 for the wife of King Kamehameha IV. Allow half an hour to tour her residence and lovely grounds.

NUUANU PALI LOOKOUT   Continue up the highway to the Nuuanu Pali Lookout (page 107). This is where King Kamehameha I overwhelmed his enemies. The view is not to be missed.

ULUPO HEIAU   You'll want to see at least one *heiau* (ancient temple) on this tour. Your best bet is to continue your drive on Route 61. As you descend into Kailua, you'll encounter Ulupo Heiau (page 120), located behind the YMCA. According to legend, this temple was built by the leprechaun-like *menehunes*.

HEEIA STATE PARK   Farther along Kaneohe Bay is Heeia State Park (page 122), where the ancient Hawaiians built one of the largest fishponds in the islands.

UNWINDING   Now that you've had a day of sightseeing, round things out with an invigorating canoe ride at **Waikiki Beach** (page 65) and then dine at **Ono Hawaiian Foods** (page 111) on poi and lomi salmon or kalua pig. Be sure to check out the Hawaiian music scene: Hapa or the Brothers Cazimero often perform at **Chai's Island Bistro** (page 96) in Aloha Tower Marketplace.

cheese wontons. Among the entrées, they offer miso-marinated seared salmon and Mongolian lamb chops with mint-tangerine sauce. What an adventure! No lunch Saturday; closed Sunday and Monday. ~ 1121 Nuuanu Avenue; 808-521-2900, fax 808-537-4164; www.indigo-hawaii.com. MODERATE TO DELUXE.

A giant red neon sign announces that you've arrived at **Sam Choy's Breakfast, Lunch & Crab,** a noisy, bustling restaurant with marine decor accentuated by a dry-docked fishing boat. Chef Sam Choy, a local boy who has helped Hawaii Regional cuisine establish an international reputation, serves crab (Dungeness, Maryland Blue, Florida Gold, Alaskan King) fresh from the open kitchen. There's also lobster, shrimp, fish and, for those unclear of the concept, chicken and beef dishes. ~ 580 North Nimitz Highway; 808-545-7979, fax 808-545-5997; www.samchoy. com, e-mail samchoy@lava.net. MODERATE TO ULTRA-DELUXE.

GROCERIES Midway between Waikiki and Downtown Honolulu there's a **Times Supermarket**. ~ 1290 South Beretania Street; 808-524-5711. Nearby is a **Safeway** store. ~ 1121 South Beretania Street; 808-591-8315. There's another **Safeway** in Downtown Honolulu. ~ 1360 Pali Highway; 808-538-3953.

Also look for **The Carrot Patch** with its health and diet products and sandwiches. ~ 700 Bishop Street; 808-531-4037.

R. Field Wine Co. specializes in fine wines and gourmet groceries. ~ 1460 South Beretania Street; 808-596-9463.

You might want to browse around the mom-and-pop grocery stores spotted throughout Chinatown. They're marvelous places to pick up Chinese foodstuffs and to capture the local color.

HIDDEN ►   Don't miss the **Open Market** in Chinatown. It's a great place to shop for fresh foods. There are numerous stands selling fish, produce, poultry, meat, baked goods and island fruits, all at low-overhead prices. ~ Along North King Street between River and Kekaulike streets.

SHOPPING **Ala Moana Center**, on the outskirts of Waikiki, is the state's largest shopping center. This multitiered complex has practically everything. Where most self-respecting malls have two department stores, Ala Moana has four: **Sears** (808-947-0211), **JC Penney** (808-946-8068), Hawaii's own **Liberty House** (808-941-2345) and a Japanese emporium called **Shirokiya** (808-973-9111). There's also a **Longs Drug Store** (808-941-4433), a good place to buy inexpensive Hawaiian curios. You'll also find an assortment of stores selling liquor, tennis and golf supplies, stationery, leather goods, cameras, shoes, art, tobacco, etc. You name it, they have it. The designer shops, appropriately, are located on the upper levels. ~ 1450 Ala Moana Boulevard.

One of Honolulu's sleeker shopping malls is **Ward Centre** on Ala Moana Boulevard. Streamlined and stylized, it's an elite enclave filled with designer shops, spiffy restaurants, boutiques and children's shops. Adorned with blond-wood facades, brick walkways and brass-rail restaurants, the shopping complex provides a touch of Beverly Hills. ~ 1200 Ala Moana Boulevard.

Anchoring Ward Centre at the far end is **Borders Books & Music** (808-591-8995), a superstore that is chockablock with everything for your reading and listening pleasure. They have two floors of paperbacks, hardbacks, audiotapes and CDs.

Just down the walkway in Ward Centre, you can home in on **Sedona**, the self-proclaimed "unique place to find yourself." It stocks aromatherapy oils, visionary music, inspirational gifts—and personal psychic readings. ~ 808-591-8010.

In the same complex, there's an excellent selection of women's clothing and accessories at **The Ultimate You**. This designer consignment store offers great bargains. ~ 808-591-8388.

Ala Moana may be the biggest, but the smaller **Ward Warehouse**, located on Ala Moana Boulevard between Waikiki and Downtown Honolulu, is another very interesting shopping center. It features stores such as **Mamo Howell** (808-592-0616), which stocks original Hawaiian wear—aloha shirts and dressy muumuus. **Out of Africa** (808-591-6260) is a gallery with art, masks and jewelry.

A California-style affair complete with white stucco walls and curved tile roof, **Aloha Tower Marketplace** is located on the waterfront overlooking Honolulu Harbor. With its flagstone walkways and open-air courtyards, it's worth visiting even if buying something is the last thing on your mind. Among the over 90 shops are about 25 devoted to apparel, a handful of galleries and perhaps three dozen specialty shops. There are also several full-service restaurants. Tucked between the Hawaii Maritime Museum and Aloha Tower, it's set near one of the busiest parts of the harbor. ~ Pier 8; 808-528-5700.

For crafts, sushi, fresh produce and even feng shui advice, visit the Honolulu Street Market. Open Saturday from 8 a.m. to 2 p.m. ~ 90 Pohukaina Street; 808-221-6042.

If you're seeking Asian items, then Chinatown is the place. Spotted throughout this refurbished neighborhood are small shops selling statuettes, pottery and other curios. It's also worthwhile wandering through the **Cultural Plaza,** on the corner of Beretania and Maunakea streets. This mall offers Asian jewelers, bookstores and knickknack shops. ~ 808-521-4934.

If you love those claustrophobic antique stores that have keepsakes stacked to the rafters and spilling into the aisles, then the 900 block of Maunakea Street is calling. Here **Aloha Antique & Collectibles** extends for seven storefronts with everything imaginable in the priceless-to-worthless range. ~ 920 Maunakea Street; 808-536-6187.

At the edge of Chinatown along Nuuanu Avenue are several galleries and shops worthy of a visit. The **Pegge Hopper Gallery** is here, displaying acrylic paintings and the female portraits for which she is renowned. Closed Saturday through Monday. ~ 1164 Nuuanu Avenue; 808-524-1160.

Actually it's the other 20 percent that predominates at **80% Straight Inc.** This gay and straight shop has cards, clothes, videos and gift items. ~ 1917 Kalakaua Avenue; 808-941-9996.

The first thing you'll see upon entering the Radisson Waikiki Prince Kuhio is **Cupid's Lobby Bar**. The lounge area features tropical palms, tapestries, rock walls and a small mirrored bar. Order drinks and *pupus* while enjoying nightly light piano music and vocalists. An outdoor garden is adjacent. ~ 2500 Kuhio Avenue; 808-922-0811.

NIGHTLIFE

At **Rumours**, theme nights are the spice of life. Ballroom dancing, college night and karaoke are all featured, along with

"Big Chill" night on Friday featuring '60s music. Located in the Ala Moana Hotel, this club is decorated with artwork and neon fixtures. Cover. ~ 410 Atkinson Drive; 808-955-4811.

A harbor view and Hawaiian contemporary music played on Thursday, Friday and Saturday by acoustic guitarists and bands make **Kincaid's** a good choice for a relaxing evening. This lounge is part of a popular Honolulu restaurant in Ward Centre. ~ 1050 Ala Moana Boulevard; 808-591-2005.

In the opening credits of *Gilligan's Island*, the ship set sail out of the harbor by Ala Moana Regional Park.

Located east of Waikiki, the **Hard Rock Cafe** is always a kick. Decorated with tons of rock-and-roll memorabilia, this restaurant/bar is a popular nightspot for those who like loud music and a big crowd. Live bands play on Friday night. ~ 1837 Kapiolani Boulevard; 808-955-7383.

Near downtown, the ultracontemporary Restaurant Row, offers several nightspots including a restaurant called **The Ocean Club**. This upscale club features nightly deejay dance music. Dress code. Cover. ~ 500 Ala Moana Boulevard; 808-526-9888.

Indigo, an attractive Asian restaurant with a patio, has hip-hop dancing and contemporary music Tuesday through Saturday. On several nights the sound is live; other nights it's deejay driven. Cover. ~ 1121 Nuuanu Avenue; 808-521-2900.

There's deejay dancing, theme nights and billiards at the **World Cafe**, which also regularly books national acts. ~ 1130 North Nimitz Highway, B-100; 808-599-4450.

For something more refined and classical, consider **Chamber Music Hawaii**, which presents a series of concerts annually at several different locations around the city. They also perform on the windward side of the island. ~ 808-543-0935.

The **Hawaii Theatre** offers the best in Broadway performances, dance troupes, classical music and much more. The Hawaii International Film Festival is held here every November. ~ 1130 Bethel Street; 808-528-0506.

The **Honolulu Symphony**, with a season that runs from September to May, provides a delightful schedule of programs. ~ 650 Ewalei Road; 808-524-0815, box office 808-538-8863.

At the **Hawaii Opera Theater**, you can see works like Saint-Saens' *Samson and Delilah*, Puccini's *Madame Butterfly* and *Die Fledermaus* by Strauss. This regional company features stars from the international opera scene. ~ 987 Waimanu Street; 808-596-7372, box office 808-596-7858.

A variety of youth- and family-oriented productions are performed by the **Honolulu Theater for Youth**, at a number of venues throughout Oahu. The company also tours the neighbor islands twice a year. Make reservations two weeks in advance. ~ 2846 Ualena Street; 808-839-9885.

At the other end of the cultural spectrum (and at the other end of town), the Honolulu red-light scene centers around Hotel Street in Chinatown. This partially refurbished, partially run-down strip is lined with hostess bars and adult bookstores. Prostitutes, straight and gay, are on the street regularly.

ALA MOANA REGIONAL PARK   This 119-acre park is a favorite with Hawaii residents. On weekends every type of outdoor enthusiast imaginable turns out to swim, snorkel, fish (common catches are *papio*, bonefish, goatfish and *moano*), jog, sail model boats and so on. It's also a good place to surf; there are three separate breaks here: "Concessions," "Tennis Courts" and "Baby Haleiwa" all have summer waves. There's a curving length of beach, a grassy park area, a helluva lot of local color and facilities that include a picnic area, restrooms, showers, concession stands, tennis courts, a recreation building, a bowling green and lifeguards. ~ On Ala Moana Boulevard at the west end of Waikiki, across from Ala Moana Center.

BEACHES & PARKS

◄ *HIDDEN*

KAKAAKO WATERFRONT PARK   Located near downtown Honolulu and popular with local picnickers, this rock-fringed park has a promenade with a view spanning from Diamond Head to the harbor. There are picnic tables, pavilions, showers, restrooms and large grassy plots. There's a surfing break offshore but no swimming. ~ End of Cooke Street off Ala Moana Boulevard.

◄ *HIDDEN*

SAND ISLAND STATE RECREATION AREA   This 140-acre park wraps around the south and east shores of Sand Island, with sections fronting both Honolulu Harbor and the open sea. Despite the name, there's only a small sandy beach here, and jet traffic from nearby Honolulu International might disturb your snoozing. But there is a great view of Honolulu. While the swimming and snorkeling are poor here, there are good surf breaks in summer and fishing is usually rewarding. *Papio* and *moano* are the prime catches. Facilities include restrooms and a picnic area. ~ From Waikiki, take Ala Moana Boulevard and Nimitz Highway several miles west to Sand Island Access Road.

◄ *HIDDEN*

▲ State permit required for tent camping in the grassy area facing the ocean.

Framed by the Waianae Range in the west and the Koolau Range to the east, Honolulu is a nonstop drama presented within a natural amphitheater. Honolulu Harbor sets the stage to the south; at the center lie Waikiki and Downtown Honolulu. Wrapped around these tourist and business centers is a rainbow-shaped congeries of sights and places that for lack of a better name constitutes "Greater Honolulu."

Greater Honolulu

It extends from navy-gray Pearl Harbor to the turquoise waters of the prestigious Kahala district and holds in its ambit some of the city's prettiest territory. These points of interest are dotted all across the city, and to see them you must ride buses or taxis or rent a car. But all are well worth the extra effort. Many are visited more by local residents than tourists and offer a singular perspective on island life and culture. Others contain an interesting mix of local folk and out-of-towners. In any case, be sure to visit a few of these outlying spots.

SIGHTS

NUUANU AVENUE   The first district is actually within walking distance of Downtown Honolulu, but it's a relatively long walk, so transportation is generally advised. Nuuanu Avenue begins downtown and travels uphill in a northeasterly direction past several noteworthy points. First stop is **Soto Mission of Hawaii**, home of a meditative Zen sect. Modeled after a temple in India where the Buddha gave his first sermon, this building is marked by dramatic towers, and beautiful Japanese bonsai plants decorate the landscape. ~ 1708 Nuuanu Avenue. Here and at nearby **Honolulu Myohoji Temple** the city seems like a distant memory. The latter building, placidly situated along a small stream, is capped by a peace tower. ~ 2003 Nuuanu Avenue.

Uphill from these shrines lies **Honolulu Memorial Park**. There is an ancestral monument here, bordered on three sides by a pond of flashing carp and a striking three-tiered pagoda. ~ 22 Craigside Place. This entire area is a center of simple yet beautiful Asian places of worship. For instance, **Tenrikyo Mission** is a woodframe temple that was moved here all the way from Japan. One intriguing fact about this fragile structure is that large sections were built without nails. ~ 2236 Nuuanu Avenue.

HIDDEN ►

The Hawaiian people also have an important center here. The **Royal Mausoleum** is situated across the street from the Tenrikyo Mission. This was the final resting place for two of Hawaii's royal families, the Kamehameha and Kalakaua clans. Together they ruled 19th-century Hawaii. Today the area is landscaped with palms, ginger, plumeria and other beautiful plants and flowers. ~ 2261 Nuuanu Avenue.

PUNCHBOWL AND TANTALUS   It is a few miles from Downtown Honolulu to **Punchbowl**, the circular center of an extinct volcano. You'll find it northeast of town, at the end of Ward Avenue and just off Prospect Drive, which circles the crater. A youngster in geologic terms, the volcano is a mere 150,000 years old. From the lip of the crater, there is a marvelous vista sweeping down to Diamond Head, across Honolulu and all the way out to the Waianae Range.

The most important feature here, however, is the **National Memorial Cemetery**, where over 32,000 war dead have been in-

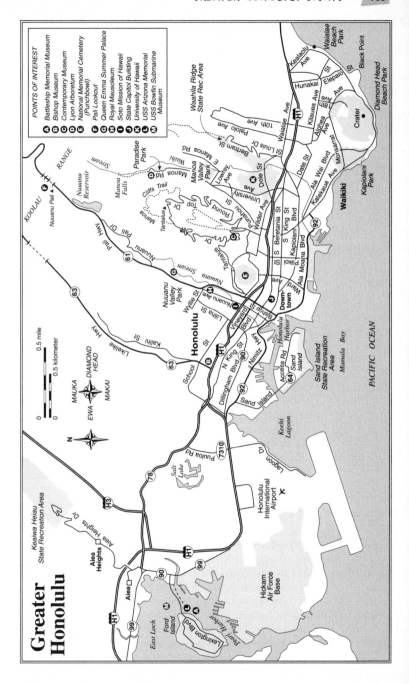

Greater Honolulu

POINTS OF INTEREST

- A Battleship Memorial Museum
- B Bishop Museum
- C Contemporary Museum
- D Lyon Arboretum
- E National Memorial Cemetery (Punchbowl)
- F Pali Lookout
- G Queen Emma Summer Palace
- H Royal Mausoleum
- I Soto Mission of Hawaii
- J State Capitol Building
- K University of Hawaii
- L USS Arizona Memorial
- M USS Bowfin Submarine Museum

terred. Victims of both World Wars, as well as the Korean, Spanish-American and Vietnam wars, are buried here. There is also an impressive monument to the "Courts of the Missing," which lists the names of soldiers missing in action. Ironically, of all the people buried here, the most famous was not a soldier but a journalist—Ernie Pyle, whose World War II stories about the average GI were eagerly followed by an entire nation. Near his grave you will also find the burial site of Hawaii's first astronaut, Ellison Onizuka, who died in the *Challenger* space shuttle disaster. Guided walking tours are offered by the American Legion. Fee. ~ 808-946-6383, fax 808-947-3957; e-mail aldepthi@gte.net.

HIDDEN ▶ You can explore the heights by following Tantalus Drive as it winds up the side of **Tantalus**, a 2013-foot mountain. Together with Round Top Drive, Tantalus Drive forms a loop that circles through the residential areas hidden within this rainforest. There are spectacular views all along the route, as well as hiking trails that lead from the road into verdant hilltop regions. Here you'll encounter guava, banana, eucalyptus and ginger trees as well as wildflowers and an occasional wild pig. One of the best views of all is found at **Puu Ualakaa Park**, a lovely retreat located along the drive. The vista here extends from Diamond Head west to Pearl Harbor, encompassing in its course a giant swath of Honolulu and the Pacific.

En route stop by the **Contemporary Museum**. In addition to changing exhibitions of contemporary art, the museum features the works of several well-known artists in its sculpture garden including David Hockney, Robert Arneson, Charles Arnoldi and Tom Wesselman. Boasting five galleries, an inspired gift shop and a gourmet café, the museum is nevertheless upstaged by its magnificently landscaped grounds. Closed Monday. Admission. ~ 2411 Makiki Heights Drive; 808-526-1322, fax 808-536-5973; www.tcmhi.org, e-mail lovliek@aol.com.

CROSS-ISLAND EXPRESS Along the outskirts of Honolulu, there are several more points of interest. The best way to tour them is while traveling along the two highways that cut across the Koolaus, connecting Honolulu directly with the island's Windward Coast.

The Likelike Highway, Route 63, can be reached from Route H-1, the superhighway that serves Honolulu. Before heading up into the mountains, you will encounter the **Bishop Museum** near the intersection of Routes 63 and H-1. Built around the turn of the 20th century, it houses an excellent collection of Hawaiian and Pacific artifacts.

Here you'll find outrigger canoes, thrones, primitive artworks, royal feather capes and fascinating natural-history exhibits. There are plaited mats woven from pandanus, drums made with shark skin, 19th-century surfboards, and helmets decorated with dog teeth and pearl shells. The 19th-century whaling trade is represented with menacing harpoons and yellowing photographs of the oil-laden ships. There are displays capturing the Japanese, Chinese and Filipino heritage in Hawaii and a hall devoted to other cultures of the Pacific.

The Bishop also offers a **"behind the scenes" tour**, which covers territory the general public doesn't get to see. Following a 25-minute dramatic presentation on the reign of King Kalakaua and Queen Kapiolani, a small group is ushered into the storage areas of the museum. Here they are treated to artifacts focusing on Hawaii's monarchy period: personal effects of Hawaii's kings and queens including royal jewels and garments and a series of other royal relics and treasures. Additional fee for the tour.

◄ *HIDDEN*

The museum also houses a planetarium, a Hall of Discovery with children's activities, and classes in quilting, hula dancing, lei-making and weaving. The Bishop is truly one of the finest museums of its kind in the world. Admission. ~ 1525 Bernice Street; 808-847-3511, fax 808-842-4703; www.bishopmuseum.org.

The other, more scenic road across the mountains is the Pali Highway, Route 61. As it ascends, it passes **Queen Emma Summer Palace**. Constructed in 1848, the palace was originally used by King Kamehameha IV and his wife, Queen Emma. Today the gracious white-pillared house is a museum. Here you can view the Queen's personal artifacts, as well as various other period pieces. Admission. ~ 808-595-3167, fax 808-595-4395; www.daughtersofhawaii. org, e-mail doh@pixi.com.

Of all the exhibits at the Bishop Museum, the most spectacular are cloaks worn by Hawaiian kings and fashioned from tens of thousands of tiny feathers.

You can also walk the tree-shaded grounds of **Nuuanu Pali Drive** and follow until it rejoins the highway. This residential boulevard, with its natural canopy and park-like atmosphere, is one of Honolulu's many idyllic hideaways.

◄ *HIDDEN*

Farther along Pali Highway, there is a turnoff to **Nuuanu Pali Lookout**. It is a point that must not be missed, and is without doubt Oahu's finest view. Gaze down the sheer, rugged face of the Koolau cliffs as they drop 3000 feet to a softly rolling coastal shelf. Your view will extend from Makapuu Point to the distant reaches of Kaneohe Bay, and from the lip of the cliff far out to sea. It was from these heights, according to legend, that a vanquished army was forced to plunge when Kamehameha I captured Oahu in 1795.

PEARL HARBOR Many people consider a trip to Pearl Harbor a pilgrimage. It was here on a sleepy Sunday morning, December 7, 1941, that the Japanese launched a sneak attack on the United States naval fleet anchored in the port, immediately plunging the nation into World War II. As Japanese planes bombed the harbor, over 2400 Americans lost their lives. Eighteen ships sank that day in the country's greatest military disaster.

The battleship USS *Arizona* was hit so savagely by aerial bombs and torpedoes that it plunged to the bottom, entombing over 1100 sailors within its hulk; today they remain in that watery grave. A special **USS Arizona Memorial** was built to honor them; it's constructed directly above the ship, right in the middle of Pearl Harbor. The memorial includes a shrine with the name of each sailor who died aboard the ship carved in marble. Gazing at this too, too long list of names, and peering over the side at the shadowy hull of the ship, it's hard not to be overcome by the tragic history of the place. Daily from 7:30 a.m. to 3 p.m., the United States Navy sponsors free boat tours out to this fascinating memorial. Before boarding, be sure to remember, no bathing suits or bare feet are permitted. Pearl Harbor, several miles northwest of Downtown Honolulu, can be reached by car or bus. ~ 808-422-2771, fax 808-483-8608; www.nps.gov/usar.

For another perspective on World War II, visit the **Battleship Missouri Memorial**. It was aboard this 887-foot vessel on September 2, 1945, that Admiral Chester Nimitz accepted the surrender of the Japanese forces, thus ending World War II. The decommissioned battleship is now docked in Pearl Harbor, off Ford Island, within sight of the USS *Arizona* Memorial. Tours depart from the ticket office of the *Bowfin* submarine. You can tour the Mighty Mo on your own, getting a first-hand glimpse of its massive armaments, the surrender deck and the commanding bridge. Plan to spend an hour on the self-guided tour. Admission. ~ 808-423-2263, 888-877-6477, fax 808-423-0700; www.ussmissouri.com, e-mail bigmo@pixi.com.

Launched in 1944, the *Missouri*, or Mighty Mo as it is usually called, was the last U.S. battleship ever built.

Anchored nearby the *Arizona* visitors center is the **USS Bowfin Submarine Museum**. This World War II–era submarine is a window into life beneath the waves. It provides an excellent opportunity to tour the claustrophobic quarters in which 80 men spent months at a time. The accompanying museum, filled with submarine-related artifacts, will help provide an even fuller perspective. Admission. ~ 808-423-1341, fax 808-422-5201; www.aloha.net/~bowfin.

Atlantis Adventures offers a 90-minute deluxe package that includes transfers from Waikiki, tours of the *Missouri* (including areas not normally open to the public) and lunch, with an optional dive stop. Transfers to the ship itself are by open-air trolley via the Ford Island Bridge. Fee. ~ 808-973-2494, 888-732-5782, fax 808-973-9840.

MANOA VALLEY   Residents of a different sort are found in the city's beautiful Manoa Valley, a couple of miles northeast of Waikiki. Among the elegant homes decorating the region are some owned by the New England families that settled in Hawaii in the 19th century.

The **University of Hawaii** has its main campus here; almost 20,000 students and 2000 faculty members attend classes and teach on these grounds, which are set amid rolling lawns and backdropped by the Koolau Mountains. ~ 2444 Dole Street; 808-956-8111; www.hawaii.edu.

On campus is the **East-West Center**, a private research facility. Designed by noted architect I. M. Pei, the center is devoted to the study of Asian and American cultures. The center also contains a number of priceless Asian artworks, well worth viewing. ~ John Burns Hall, 1601 East-West Road; 808-944-7111; www.ewc.hawaii.edu, e-mail ewcinfo@eastwestcenter.org.   ◄ HIDDEN

From here you can head deeper into Manoa Valley along Oahu Avenue and Manoa Road. You'll pass the **Waioli Tea Room** (808-988-5800), a cozy dining room tucked into a garden setting where you can enjoy breakfast or high tea, a bakery and a gift shop. Here also is the **Little Grass Shack** that was once occupied by novelist Robert Louis Stevenson (or so the story goes), and a small chapel replete with stained-glass windows. ~ 2950 Manoa Road.

Adjacent to Paradise Park is **Lyon Arboretum**, a magnificent 194-acre garden with over 8000 plant species, research greenhouses, hiking trails and perhaps the world's largest collection of palm trees. The arboretum also offers one-day classes on topics such as horticulture and lei-making. Closed Sunday. ~ 3860 Manoa Road; 808-988-0456; www.hawaii.edu/lyonarboretum.

KAHALA   On the far side of Diamond Head, along a string of narrow beaches, lie many of Honolulu's most admired addresses. To reach this residential promised land follow Diamond Head Road.

Diamond Head Beach Park, a twisting ribbon of white sand, nestles directly below the famous crater. Whenever the wind and waves are good, you'll see windsurfers and surfers galore sweeping in toward the shoreline. The coral reef here makes for good skindiving, too. It's a pretty beach, backdropped by the Kuilei cliffs and watched over by the **Diamond Head Lighthouse**.

From Diamond Head, continue east along Diamond Head Road and Kahala Avenue. These will lead through the Kahala District, home to the island's elite. Bordered by the ocean and the exclusive Waialae Country Club is a golden string of spectacular oceanfront homes with carefully manicured lawns.

The **Nuuanu** YMCA has inexpensive accommodations for men. Complete athletic facilities are available. ~ 1441 Pali Highway;   **LODGING**

808-536-3556, fax 808-521-1181; e-mail nuuanu-ymca@hot
mail.com. BUDGET.

HIDDEN ▶

Hawaii's foremost bed-and-breakfast inn rests in a magnificent old mansion near the University of Hawaii campus. Set in
the lush Manoa Valley, the **Manoa Valley Inn** is a 1915 cream-
colored Victorian featuring seven guest rooms and an adjacent
cottage. Decorated with patterned wallpaper and old-style artworks, the rooms are furnished in plump antique armchairs.
Guests enjoy a sunroom and parlor, as well as a spacious veranda
and lawn. For luxury and privacy, this historic jewel is one of the
island's finest spots. Continental breakfast and evening wine are
included. ~ 2001 Vancouver Drive; 808-947-6019, 800-634-5115,
fax 808-946-6168; www.aloha.net/~wery, e-mail manoavalley
inn@aloha.net. MODERATE TO ULTRA-DELUXE.

Also in Manoa Valley, the **Fernhurst YWCA** is an appealing
three-story lowrise that provides a residence for women. Rooms
are single or double occupancy with shared baths. Among the facilities are microwaves, refrigerators, laundry, dining room, swimming pool and lounge. Rates include breakfast and dinner Monday through Friday. ~ 1566 Wilder Avenue; 808-941-2231, fax
808-949-0266. BUDGET.

The **Atherton YWCA** is a coed facility with accommodations
for men and women. Across the street from the University of Hawaii campus, it's open year-round to full-time students (of any
institution, but you have to show registration and student ID) and
during the summer to the general public. There's a nonrefund-
able application fee and a refundable deposit. Facilities include
laundry, lounge and a full kitchen. Reservations must be booked
at least two weeks in advance and the facility is closed weekends
and holidays, so plan accordingly. ~ 1810 University Avenue;
808-946-0253, fax 808-941-7802; e-mail ymca@hawaii.edu.
BUDGET.

Hostelling International Honolulu is a dormitory-style crash
pad with separate living quarters for men and women, although
there are a few studios available. Shared kitchen facilities, television lounge, garden patio and laundry are available. Visitors can
book island tours through the hostel. ~ 2323-A Sea View Avenue; 808-946-0591, fax 808-946-5904; www.hiayh.org. BUDGET.

DINING

HIDDEN ▶

One of my favorite Japanese eateries is **Irifune**, a warm and
friendly place frequented by a local crowd. There are tasty curry,
sushi, teriyaki and tempura dishes, plus several other Asian de-
lectables. Closed Sunday and Monday. ~ 563 Kapahulu Avenue;
808-737-1141. BUDGET TO MODERATE.

Quantity and quality don't usually come together, particularly where gourmet restaurants are concerned. But at **Sam Choy**
you can count on platter-size portions of macadamia-crushed *ono*,

Oriental lamb chops or oven-roasted duck. Considered one of the top Hawaiian cuisine restaurants on the island, it sits with unassuming grace on the second floor of a strip mall. Eat heartily (and well)! Dinner and Sunday brunch. ~ 449 Kapahulu Avenue, Suite 201; 808-732-8645, fax 808-732-8682; www.samchoy. com. DELUXE TO ULTRA-DELUXE.

For local-style plate lunches, cruise in to **Rainbow Drive-In**. Popular with *kamaainas* and tourists alike, the menu includes hamburger steak, beef curry, breaded and grilled mahimahi, chili and fried chicken served with two scoops of rice and macaroni salad. ~ 3308 Kanaina Avenue; 808-737-0177. BUDGET.

Ono Hawaiian Foods is a must for all true Hawaii lovers. It's ◀ HIDDEN a hole-in-da-wall eatery on a busy street. But if you're lucky enough to get one of the few tables, you can feast on *laulau, kalua* pig, *pipikaula,* poi and *haupia*. The walls are papered with signed photographs of local notables and the place is packed with locals, notable and otherwise. Closed Sunday. ~ 726 Kapahulu Avenue; 808-737-2275. BUDGET TO MODERATE.

Near the University of Hawaii campus, there are pizzas, sub sandwiches and chicken dinners at **Magoo's**. Open for lunch on weekends and dinner daily, it's a great place to snack or stop for a cold beer. ~ Puck's Alley, 1015 University Avenue; 808-949-5381. BUDGET TO MODERATE.

Or you can check out **Anna Bannana's**, a combination bar and Mexican eatery that draws a swinging crowd. Located a half-mile from campus, this dim eatery serves burritos, enchiladas and other south-of-the-border favorites. Decorated in slapdash fashion with propellers, antlers, surfboards, boxing gloves and trophies, Anna's is the local center for slumming. ~ 2440 South Beretania Street; 808-946-5190. BUDGET.

HAUTE CUISINE WITH HUMOR

If you want to know where the local gentry dine, head to **Alan Wong's Restaurant**. "Appeteasers" in the form of quarter-sized burgers made from an ahi tuna combination hint at bigger and better things to come. Alan Wong himself will concoct a meal for you, surprising you with the Chef's Tasting Menu; or you can select from a menu filled with locally caught fish, home-grown produce and a wealth of meat and poultry dishes. You may find ginger-crusted onaga with miso-sesame vinaigrette or braised veal shank and smashed taro in poi sauce with lomi tomato relish. One of the *in* places to dine on Hawaiian Regional cuisine, so reservations are suggested. ~ 1857 South King Street; 808-949-2526, fax 808-951-9520; www.alanwongs.com. DELUXE.

Waialae Avenue, a neighborhood strip several miles outside Waikiki, has developed into a gourmet ghetto. **Azteca Mexican Restaurant** is a vinyl-booth-and-plastic-panel eatery that serves a delicious array of Mexican food. ~ 3617 Waialae Avenue; 808-735-2492. BUDGET TO MODERATE.

HIDDEN ▶ For spicy and delicious Asian dishes, it is hard to find a more appealing place than **Hale Vietnam**. A family restaurant that draws a local crowd, it features traditional Vietnamese soup and a host of excellent entrées. ~ 1140 12th Avenue; 808-735-7581. MODERATE.

GROCERIES A good place to shop near the University of Hawaii's Manoa campus is **Star Market**. ~ 2470 South King Street; 808-973-1666.

The best place in Honolulu to buy health foods is at **Down To Earth Natural Foods**. ~ 2525 South King Street; 808-947-7678. **Kokua Market** is another excellent choice. ~ 2643 South King Street; 808-941-1922.

SHOPPING Scattered around town are several shops that I recommend you check out. At **Lanakila Crafts** most of the goods are made by the disabled, and the craftsmanship is superb. There are shell necklaces, woven handbags, monkeypod bowls and homemade dolls. You'll probably see these items in other stores around the islands, with much higher price tags than here at the "factory." ~ 1809 Bachelot Street; 808-531-0555.

Out at the Bishop Museum be sure to stop by **Shop Pacifica**, which offers a fine selection of Hawaiiana. There are books on island history and geography, an assortment of instruments that include nose flutes and gourds, plus cards, souvenirs and wooden bowls. ~ 1525 Bernice Street, near the intersection of Routes 63 and H-1; 808-848-4158.

One of Honolulu's most upscale shopping centers is **Kahala Mall**, where you'll find designer shops galore. This attractive complex also hosts almost 100 moderately priced stores. ~ 4211 Waialae Avenue; 808-732-7736.

Barnes & Noble has a superstore here. In addition to a comprehensive line of books, they sell tapes and CDs and feature a

---

SWAP 'EM, BRAH

For secondhand items, try the **Kam Super Swap Meet**. It's a great place to barter for bargains, meet local folks and find items you'll never see in stores. It's open on Wednesday, Saturday, Sunday and some holidays. ~ 98-850 Moanalua Road; 808-483-5933, 808-483-5535.

café on the premises. ~ Kahala Mall, 4211 Waialae Avenue; 808-737-3323.

Outside Honolulu there are usually a couple of spots to hear Hawaiian music. Pick up a copy of *Spotlight's Oahu Gold* or *This Week Oahu* magazine to see what's going on.

NIGHTLIFE

Over by the University of Hawaii's Manoa campus, there's **Anna Bannana's**. A popular hangout for years, this wildly decorated spot has all types of live music on Thursday, Friday and Saturday nights. Cover for live shows. ~ 2440 South Beretania Street; 808-946-5190.

While away Friday and Saturday evening at **LaMariana Sailing Club**, where a festive bunch of locals takes over the floor to entertain you with their song and dance. There's live piano music Wednesday through Saturday evenings.

KEAIWA HEIAU STATE RECREATION AREA 🏃 Amazing as it sounds, this is a wooded retreat within easy driving distance of Honolulu. Situated in the Koolau foothills overlooking Pearl Harbor, it contains the remains of a *heiau*, a temple once used by Hawaiian healers. There's a forest extending to the far reaches of the mountains and a loop hiking trail. Facilities include picnic area, showers and restrooms. Markets and restaurants several miles away. ~ Located in Aiea Heights. To get there from Honolulu, take Route 90 west to Aiea, then follow Aiea Heights Drive to the park.

BEACHES & PARKS

◀ *HIDDEN*

▲ Tents only. State permit required.

DIAMOND HEAD BEACH PARK 🏄 ⛵ 🎣 🚿 💧 A heaven to windsurfers, this twisting ribbon of white sand sits directly below the crater. It's close enough to Waikiki for convenient access but far enough to shake most of the crowds. The Kuilei cliffs, covered with scrub growth, loom behind the beach. Snorkeling is good here as a coral reef extends offshore through this area. There's also a good year-round surf break called "Lighthouse." And for the anglers, your chances are good to reel in *ulua*, *papio* or *mamao*. A shower is the sole facility. Markets and restaurants in Waikiki are about two miles away. ~ Located just beyond Waikiki along Diamond Head Road at the foot of Diamond Head; watch for parked cars.

◀ *HIDDEN*

KUILEI CLIFFS BEACH PARK AND KAALAWAI BEACH 🏄 ⛵ 🎣 🚿 💧 Extending east from Diamond Head Beach Park, these sandy corridors are also flanked by sharp sea cliffs. Together they extend from Diamond Head Lighthouse to Black Point. The aquatic attractions are the same as at Diamond Head Beach Park and both beaches can be reached from it (or from cliff trails leading down from Diamond Head Road). A protecting reef makes for good swimming at Kaalawai Beach (which can also be reached via a public accessway off Kulumanu Place).

WAIALAE BEACH PARK Smack in the middle of Honolulu's prestigious Kahala district, where a million dollars buys a modest house, sits this tidy beach. Its white sand neatly groomed, its spacious lawn shaded by palms, Waialae is a true find. It has good swimming and fishing. There are bathhouse facilities, beachside picnic tables and a footbridge arching across the stream that divides the property. (Groceries are several miles away in Waikiki or along Waialae Avenue.) To the west of the park lies **Kahala Beach**, a long, thin swath of sand that extends all the way to Black Point. There's good snorkeling near the Kahala Mandarin Oriental Hotel. ~ Located on the 4900 block of Kahala Avenue in Kahala.

▼▼▼▼▼▼▼▼▼▼▼▼
Southeast Oahu

Out past Honolulu, beyond the lights of Waikiki and the gilded neighborhoods of Kahala, the pace slackens, the vistas open and Oahu begins to look more like a tropical island. As the sunny south shore gives way to the windward side of the island, you'll encounter volcanic craters, famous bodysurfing beaches and a dramatic blowhole. A major road, Route 72—the Kalanianaole Highway—leads from Honolulu along this southeastern coast.

SIGHTS   This thoroughfare streams through Hawaii Kai and other residential areas, then ascends the slopes of an extinct volcano, 642-foot **Koko Head**. Here Madame Pele is reputed to have dug a hole for the last time in search of fiery volcanic matter. **Koko Crater**, the second hump on the horizon, rises to over 1200 feet. This firepit, according to Hawaiian legend, is the vagina of Pele's sister. It seems that Pele, goddess of volcanoes, was being pursued by a handsome demigod. Her sister, trying to distract the hot suitor from Pele, spread her legs across the landscape.

From the top of Koko Head, a well-marked road and sidewalk lead down to **Hanauma Bay**, one of the prettiest beaches in all Hawaii. This breathtaking place is a marine preserve filled with multicolored coral and teeming with underwater life. Little wonder that Hollywood chose this spot as the prime location for Elvis Presley's movie, *Blue Hawaii*. Elvis' grass shack was right here, and the strand was also a setting in the classic film *From Here to Eternity*.

The swimming and snorkeling are unmatched anywhere and the mazework of coral formations along the bottom adds to the snorkeling adventure. Or you can stroll along the rock ledges that fringe the bay and explore **Toilet Bowl**, a tidepool that "flushes" as the waves wash through it. The best time to come is early morning before other swimmers stir up the waters. Hanauma Bay is an extremely popular picnic spot among local folks, so it is also advisable to visit on a weekday rather than face bucking the crowds on Saturday and Sunday. Because of its popularity, the preserve cuts off entrance to the park when the parking lot is full (another good reason to arrive early). Closed Tuesday. ~ Located on Kalanianaole Highway about 12 miles east of Waikiki; 808-396-4229.

From here the highway corkscrews along the coast. Among the remarkable scenes you'll enjoy en route are views of Lanai and Molokai, two of Oahu's sister islands. On a clear, clear day you can also see Maui, an island that requires no introduction.

At an overlook you will encounter **Halona Blowhole**, a lava tube through which geysers of seawater blast. During high tide

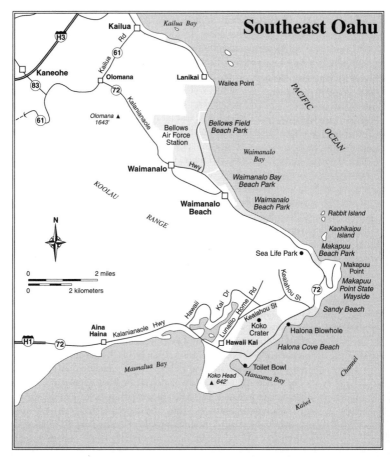

and when the sea is turbulent, these gushers reach dramatic heights. *Halona* means "peering place," and that is exactly what everyone seems to do here. You can't miss the spot, since the roadside parking lot is inevitably crowded with tourists. Between December and April this vista is also a prime whale-watching spot.

Just beyond spreads **Sandy Beach**, one of Hawaii's most renowned bodysurfing spots. It's a long, wide beach piled with fluffy sand and complete with picnic areas and showers. Inexperienced bodysurfers are better off enjoying the excellent sunbathing here, since the dramatic shorebreak that makes the beach so popular among bodysurfers can overwhelm beginners.

HIDDEN ▶

Across from the beach a side road leads up to **Koko Crater Botanical Gardens,** a 60-acre collection of cacti, plumeria and other water-thrifty plants. ~ Kealahou Street, off of Kalanianaole Highway; 808-522-7060.

Past this pretty spot, Route 72 rounds Oahu's southeastern corner and sets a course along the eastern shoreline. It also climbs to a scenic point from which you can take your first view of the Windward Coast. You will be standing on **Makapuu Point**. Above you rise sharp lava cliffs, while below are rolling sand dunes and open ocean. The slope-faced islet just offshore is Rabbit Island. The distant headland is Makapuu Peninsula, toward which you are bound.

The word *hanauma* means "the curved bay," and you will clearly see that Hanauma Bay was once a circular volcano, one wall of which was breached by the sea

From this perfect perch you can also spy a complex of buildings. That's **Sea Life Park**, a marine-world attraction comparable to those in California and Florida. Among the many features at this park is the "Hawaiian Reef," a 300,000-gallon oceanarium inhabited by about 4000 sea creatures. To see it you wind through a spiral viewing area that descends three fathoms along the tank's glass perimeter. At times a scuba diver will be hand-feeding the fish. Swimming about this underwater world are sharks, stingrays and a variety of lesser-known species. The park also features a turtle lagoon, penguin habitat and the only known *wholphin* (half whale, half dolphin) living in captivity. Admission. ~ Makapuu Point; 808-259-7933, fax 808-973-9840.

Across the road from Sea Life Park spreads **Makapuu Beach Park,** another fabled but daunting bodysurfing spot that is set in a particularly pretty location. Nearby black lava cliffs are topped by a white lighthouse and Rabbit Island is anchored just offshore. The beach itself is a short, wide rectangle of white sand. It's an ideal place to picnic, but when the surf is up, beware of the waves.

The road continues along the shoreline between soft sand beaches and rugged mountain peaks. For the next 30 miles your attention will be drawn back continually to those rocky crags.

They are part of the **Koolau Range,** a wall of precipitous mountains that vault up from Oahu's placid interior. Their spires, minarets and fluted towers are softened here and there by lush, green valleys, but never enough to detract from the sheer beauty and magnitude of the heights. Light and shade play games along their moss-covered surfaces, while rainbows hang suspended between the peaks. If wind and weather permit, you will see hang gliders dusting the cliffs as they sail from the mountains down to the distant beach.

The road continues through **Waimanalo,** an old ranching area that today has been turned to fruit and flower cultivation. Outside town you will see **Olomana Peak.** Favored by rock climbers, it is a double-barreled peak that seems to belong in the Swiss Alps.

Spotted along Oahu's southeastern shore are a number of moderately priced restaurants (and a couple of expensive but worthy ones) that may prove handy if you're beachcombing or camping. Most are located on or near Route 72 (Kalanianaole Highway). For the sake of convenience, I'll list the restaurants as they will appear when you travel east and north.

DINING

You're bound to feel Eurocentric at the **Swiss Inn,** where the menu includes wienerschnitzel, veal with a cream mushroom sauce and cheese fondue. On the dessert menu you'll find Swiss chocolate mousse, peach melba and fresh fruit tarts. The wood-paneled Old World look features pictures of villages that make you yearn for the Matterhorn. Closed Monday and Tuesday. ~ Niu Valley Shopping Center, 5730 Kalanianaole Highway; 808-377-5447, fax 808-377-1151. MODERATE TO DELUXE.

Tucked away in unassuming fashion in a business park is one of the area's top dining spots. You'll have to travel all the way to Hawaii Kai, several miles east of Waikiki, to find **Roy's Restaurant.** It is, to say the least, ultracontemporary, from the magazine clips framed on the walls to the cylindrical fish tank near the door. One of the most innovative of Hawaii's Pacific Rim cuisine dining rooms, it specializes in fresh local ingredients. Wildly popular, so reserve in advance. Dinner only. ~ 6600 Kalanianaole Highway, Hawaii Kai; 808-396-7697, fax 808-396-8706; www.roysrestaurant.com, e-mail info@roysrestaurant.com. DELUXE TO ULTRA-DELUXE.

Keneke's has breakfasts, plate lunches and sandwiches at greasy-spoon prices. No gourmet's delight, this tiny eatery is well placed for people enjoying Waimanalo's beaches. ~ 41-857 Kalanianaole Highway, Waimanalo; 808-259-5266. BUDGET.

Better yet, join the local crowd at **Koo's Kitchen** where Chinese dishes satisfy the hungriest diners. Tasty food and ample

◄ HIDDEN

servings. Closed Tuesday. ~ Behind the Waimanalo Post Office on Kalanianaole Highway, Waimanalo; 808-259-5493. BUDGET.

GROCERIES A convenient place to shop in Oahu's southeast corner is at the Koko Marina Shopping Center's **Foodland**. ~ 7192 Kalanianaole Highway, Hawaii Kai; 808-395-3131. Proceeding north along the coast, there's **Mel's Market,** a small store in Waimanalo. ~ 41-1029 Kalanianaole Highway, Waimanalo; 808-259-7550.

SHOPPING There aren't many places on Oahu more Hawaiian than Waimanalo, so **Naturally Hawaiian** fits the landscape nicely. Featuring fine art and homemade gifts, the shop sells puka necklaces, koa wood pieces, prints and paintings, and Hawaiian commemorative stamps. ~ 41-1025 Kalanianaole Highway, Waimanalo; 808-259-5354.

BEACHES & PARKS **HANAUMA BAY NATURE PRESERVE** One of Oahu's prettiest and most popular beaches, this curving swath of white sand extends for almost a half-mile. The bottom of the bay is a maze of coral reef, and the entire area has been designated a marine preserve; fishing is strictly prohibited. As a result, the skin-diving is unmatched and the fish are tame enough to eat from your hand. (Just beware of "Witch's Brew," a turbulent area on the bay's right side, and the "Molokai Express," a wicked current sweeping across the mouth of the bay.) You can also hike along rock ledges fringing the bay and explore some mind-boggling tidepools. Crowded though it is, this is one strand that should not be bypassed. Get here early—the beach closes at 6 p.m. (it opens at 6 a.m.). Facilities include a picnic area, restrooms, showers, a snack bar, snorkeling equipment rentals and lifeguards. Arrive early; once the parking lot fills up, entrance to the park is cut off. Parking fee, $1; nonresident day-use fee, $3 per person. Closed Tuesday. ~ Located about nine miles east of Waikiki. Take Kalanianaole Highway (Route 72) to Koko Head, then turn onto the side road near the top of the promontory. This leads to a parking lot; leave your vehicle and walk the several hundred yards down the path to the beach. ~ 808-396-4229.

HIDDEN ▶ **HALONA COVE BEACH** This is the closest you'll find to a hidden beach near Honolulu. It's a patch of white sand wedged between Halona Point and the Halona Blowhole lookout. Located directly below Kalanianaole Highway (Route 72), this is not exactly a wilderness area. But you can still escape the crowds massed on the nearby beaches. Swimming and snorkeling are good when the sea is gentle but extremely dangerous if it's rough. Prime catches are *ulua*, *papio* and *mamao*. There are no facilities. ~ Stop at the Halona Blowhole parking lot on Kalanianaole Highway (Route 72), about ten miles east of Waikiki. Follow the path from the right side of the lot down to the beach.

SANDY BEACH 🏖 🏄 ⛵ This long, wide beach is a favorite among Oahu's youth. The shorebreak makes it one of the finest, and most dangerous, bodysurfing beaches in the islands. Surfing is good and very popular but beware of rip currents. Lifeguards are on duty. It's a pleasant place to sunbathe, but if you go swimming, plan to negotiate a pounding shoreline. Anglers try for *ulua*, *papio* and *mamao*. There are picnic areas, restrooms and showers. Should you want to avoid the crowds, head over to **Wawamalu Beach Park** next door to the east. ~ Head out on Kalanianaole Highway (Route 72) about 12 miles east of Waikiki.

MAKAPUU POINT STATE WAYSIDE 🏃 This state park encompasses Makapuu Beach, lookout and the lighthouse that overlooks the east Oahu coast. The mile-long asphalted trail leading to the lighthouse has become a popular family excursion; you can take the trail's uphill segments at a leisurely pace. The heat can be draining by midday, so a morning or afternoon hike is recommended, particularly on weekends when crowds abound. Panoramic views are the reward, with brisk tradewinds likely. ~ Off Kalanianaole Highway between Sandy Beach and Makapuu Lookout.

MAKAPUU BEACH PARK 🏖 ⛵ Makapuu is set in a very pretty spot with lava cliffs in the background and Rabbit Island just offshore. This short, wide rectangle of white sand is Hawaii's most famous bodysurfing beach. With no protecting reef and a precipitous shoreline, Makapuu is inundated by awesome swells that send wave riders crashing onto shore. Necks and backs are broken with frightening regularity here, so if the waves are large and you're inexperienced—play the spectator. If you take the plunge, prepare for a battering! Snorkeling is usually poor and surfing is not permitted here. Common catches are *ulua*, *papio* and *mamao*. The only facilities are restrooms and a lifeguard. ~ Located on Kalanianaole Highway (Route 72) about 13 miles east of Waikiki.

> Rabbit Island, located off Makapuu Point, resembles a bunny's head, but was actually named for a former rabbit-raising farm there.

🔺 Currently not permitted, but it will probably reopen to the public so it's worth checking out.

WAIMANALO BEACH PARK AND WAIMANALO BAY BEACH PARK 🏖 🎣 ⛵ Located at the southeast end of Waimanalo's three-and-a-half-mile-long beach, this is a spacious 38-acre park. It's studded with ironwood trees and equipped with numerous recreation facilities including a playground, a basketball court and a baseball field. Waimanalo Beach Park and Waimanalo Bay Beach Park, a mile farther north, are both excellent spots for picnicking, swimming, snorkeling, bodysurfing and sunbathing.

The latter is farther removed from the highway in a grove of ironwood trees known to local residents as "Sherwood Forest." Waimanalo is a good place to fish for *papio*, bonefish, milkfish and goatfish. There are picnic areas, restrooms and showers at both. ~ Waimanalo Beach Park is located at 41-741 Kalanianaole Highway (Route 72) about 15 miles east of Waikiki. Waimanalo Bay Beach Park is on Aloiloi Street a mile farther north.

▲ A county permit required at both of the parks for tent and trailer camping.

HIDDEN ► **BELLOWS FIELD BEACH PARK** This is one of Oahu's prettiest parks. There's a broad white-sand beach bordered by ironwood trees, with a marvelous view of the Koolau mountains. It's a great place for swimming and snorkeling. It's also a good surf spot for beginners and fishing usually rewards with *papio*, bonefish, milkfish and goatfish. Sounds great, huh? The catch is that Bellows Park is situated on a military base and is open to visitors only from Friday noon until 8 a.m. Monday. Facilities include a picnic area, showers, a restroom and a lifeguard. ~ Turn off Kalanianaole Highway (Route 72) toward Bellows Air Force Station. The park is located near Waimanalo, about 17 miles east of Waikiki.

▲ County permit required.

▼▼▼▼▼▼▼▼▼▼▼▼
Windward Coast
Named for the trade winds that blow with soothing predictability from the northeast, this sand-rimmed shoreline lies on the far side of the *pali* from Honolulu. Between these fluted emerald cliffs and the turquoise ocean are the bedroom communities of Kailua and Kaneohe and the agricultural regions of the Waiahole and Waikane valleys. As suburbs give way to small farms, this florid region provides a relaxing transition between the busy boulevards of Honolulu and the wild surf of the North Shore.

SIGHTS

From the southeastern corner of the island, the Kalanianaole Highway flows into Kailua, where it intersects with Route 61, or Kailua Road. If you go right for a quarter of a mile along this *HIDDEN* ► road you will encounter **Ulupo Heiau** (it's behind the YMCA). According to Hawaiian legend, this temple (which stands 30 feet high and measures 150 feet in length) was built by *Menehunes*, who passed the building stones across a six-mile-long bucket brigade in a one-night construction project.

Heading back to the main highway, you will find that Route 72 immediately merges into Route 61, which then continues for two miles to Route 83, the Kamehameha Highway. Above this thoroughfare, spreading across 400 acres at the foot of the *pali* *HIDDEN* ► is **Hoomaluhia Botanical Garden,** a relaxing nature conservancy.

With sheer cliffs rising on one side and a panoramic ocean view opening in the distance, it is a special place indeed. There is a 32-acre lake (no swimming) as well as a visitors center and hiking trails. Camping is available on weekends (permit required—get one at the garden office, which is closed Sunday). The fruits, flowers and trees include hundreds of species native to Hawaii as well as tropical regions around the world. ~ Off Route 83 at the end of Luluku Road, Kaneohe; 808-233-7323, fax 808-233-7326; www.co.honolulu.hi.us/parks/hbg.

The Kahekili Highway will also carry you to the graceful **Haiku Gardens,** located just outside Kailua. Formerly a private estate, the gardens rest in a lovely spot with a lofty rockface backdrop. Within this preserve are acres of exotic plant life, including an enchanting lily pond as well as numerous species of flowers. Hawaii specializes in beautiful gardens; the frequent rains and lush terrain make for luxuriant growing conditions. This happens to be one of the prettiest gardens of all. ~ 46-336 Haiku Road, Kaneohe; 808-247-6671, fax 808-247-9796.

Farther along you'll encounter the "Valley of the Temples," a verdant chasm folded between the mountains and the sea. Part of the valley has been consecrated as a cemetery honoring the Japanese. Highlighting the region is the **Byodo-In Temple.** Rimmed by 2000-foot cliffs, this Buddhist shrine is a replica of a 900-year-old temple in Kyoto, Japan. It was constructed in 1968 in memory of the first Japanese immigrants to settle in Hawaii. The simple architecture is enhanced by a bronze bell weighing seven tons that visitors are permitted to ring. A statue of Buddha dominates the site. Walk along the placid reflecting pool with its swans, ducks and multihued carp and you will be drawn a million miles away from the bustle of Honolulu. Admission. ~ 47-200 Kahekili Highway, Kaneohe; 808-239-8811, fax 808-239-8997.

An alternate route through Kailua and Kaneohe will carry you near the water, though the only really pretty views of Kaneohe Bay come near the end. Simply follow North Kalaheo

MYTHICAL MAKERS

The *Menehunes,* in case you haven't been introduced, were tiny Hobbit-like creatures who inhabited Hawaii even before the Polynesians arrived. They were reputed to be superhumanly strong and would work all night to build dams, temples and other structures. Several mysterious manmade objects in the islands that archaeologists have trouble placing chronologically are claimed by mythmakers to be *Menehune* creations.

Avenue through Kailua, then pick up Kaneohe Bay Drive, and turn right on Route 836, which curves for miles before linking with Route 83. At Heeia Kea Boat Harbor on Route 836, you can take an hour-long glass bottom boat ride aboard the **Coral Queen**. ~ 808-235-2888, fax 808-247-8015.

Kaneohe Bay is renowned for its coral formations and schools of tropical fish that are as brilliantly colored as the coral. This expansive body of water possesses the only barrier reef in Hawaii. Along its shores are ancient Hawaiian fish ponds, rock-bound enclosures constructed by the early Polynesians to raise fresh seafood. Though they once lined the shores of Oahu, today only a quarter (about 100) remain in usable condition. Several rest along this Windward Coast. One of the largest is located near **Heeia State Park**. It's an impressive engineering feat that measures 500 feet in length and once contained an 88-acre fish farm. The stone walls in places are 12 feet thick. ~ Located along Kamehameha Highway (Route 836), a few hundred yards before it merges with Route 83. A view is available from the State Park.

High above Kaneohe, gazing down upon the bay, is **Senator Fong's Plantation and Gardens**. Here you can take a narrated tram tour of 725 acres of gardens and orchards. This luxurious preserve was donated by one of Hawaii's most famous U.S. senators, so be prepared to venture from Eisenhower Valley to Kennedy Valley (sugar cane) to the Johnson Plateau (fruit orchards) to Nixon Valley (gardens) to the Ford Plateau (pine trees). Admission. ~ 47-285 Pulama Road, Kaneohe; 808-239-6775.

Route 83 soon becomes known as the Kamehameha Highway as it courses past taro patches and lazy fishing boats, then enters **Waiahole Valley** and **Waikane Valley**, some of the last places on the island where Hawaiian farmers grow crops in the traditional way.

Just down the road, the **Old Sugar Mill**, Oahu's first, lies in ruin along the side of the road. Built during the 1860s, it fell into disuse soon after completion and has since served only as a local curiosity.

Three miles later you will arrive at a rock profile that resembles a **Crouching Lion**. To the ancient Hawaiians, who had never experienced the king of the jungle, the stone face was, in fact, that of Kauhi, a demigod from the island of Tahiti.

Next is coral-studded **Kahana Bay**. Then the road, still crowding the coastline, traverses the tiny towns of Punaluu and Hauula. The old **Hauula Door of Faith Church**, a small chapel of clapboard design, is surrounded by palms. Not far from here is another aging woodframe sanctuary, **Hauula Congregational Christian Church**, built of wood and coral back in 1862.

The nearby town of Laie is populated by Mormons. The Hawaii campus of **Brigham Young University** is located here, as

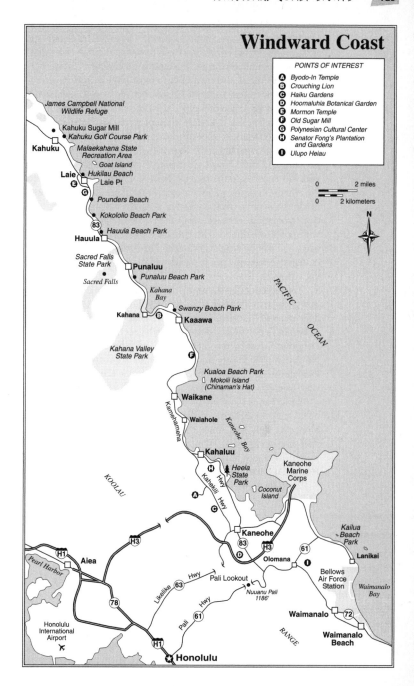

Windward Coast

POINTS OF INTEREST

- Ⓐ Byodo-In Temple
- Ⓑ Crouching Lion
- Ⓒ Haiku Gardens
- Ⓓ Hoomaluhia Botanical Garden
- Ⓔ Mormon Temple
- Ⓕ Old Sugar Mill
- Ⓖ Polynesian Cultural Center
- Ⓗ Senator Fong's Plantation and Gardens
- Ⓘ Ulupo Heiau

James Campbell National Wildlife Refuge

Kahuku Sugar Mill
Kahuku Golf Course Park
Kahuku
Malaekahana State Recreation Area
Goat Island
Laie   Hukilau Beach
Laie Pt
Pounders Beach
Kokololio Beach Park
(83)
Hauula Beach Park
Hauula

Sacred Falls State Park
Punaluu
Punaluu Beach Park
Sacred Falls
Kahana Bay
Swanzy Beach Park
Kahana   **Kaaawa**

Kahana Valley State Park

Kualoa Beach Park
Mokolii Island (Chinaman's Hat)
Waikane

Waiahole

Kaneohe Bay

Kahaluu
Heeia State Park
Coconut Island

Kaneohe Marine Corps

KOOLAU

Kamehameha

Kahekili Hwy

(H3)
(H3)

Pearl Harbor   **Aiea**

(H1)

(83)
Kaneohe
(H3)
(61)   Kailua Beach Park
Olomana   **Lanikai**

(78)

Likelike (63) Hwy
Pali Lookout
Nuuanu Pali 1186'

Bellows Air Force Station
Waimanalo Bay

Honolulu International Airport

Pali (61) Hwy

Waimanalo   (72)

RANGE
Waimanalo Beach

Ⓐ Honolulu

PACIFIC OCEAN

0   2 miles
0   2 kilometers

N

well as the **Mormon Temple**. The Mormons settled here back in 1864; today there are about 55,000 in Hawaii. The courtyards and grounds of the temple are open to the public, but only Mormons are permitted to enter the temple sanctuary.

The Mormons also own Oahu's most popular tourist attraction, the **Polynesian Cultural Center**. Set right on Kamehameha Highway in Laie, it represents one of the foremost theme parks in the entire Pacific, a 42-acre attempt to re-create ancient Polynesia. As you wander about the grounds you'll encounter ersatz villages portraying life in the Marquesas, Tahiti, Fiji, Tonga, New Zealand and old Hawaii. Step over to the Tahitian hamlet and you will experience the rocking *tamure* dance. Or wander onto the islands of Samoa where the local inhabitants demonstrate how to climb coconut trees. In Tonga a native will be beating tapa cloth from mulberry bark, while the Fijians are pounding rhythms with poles of bamboo. These mock villages are linked by waterways and can be visited in canoes. The boats will carry you past craftsmen preparing poi by mashing taro roots, and others husking coconuts.

The most popular shows are the "Pageant of the Long Canoes," in which the boats head up a lagoon amid a flurry of singing and dancing, and "Horizons." The latter is an evening show similar to Waikiki's Polynesian revues, though generally considered more elaborate. Most of the entertainers and other employees at this Hawaiian-style Disneyland are Mormon students attending the local university. Closed Sunday. Admission. ~ Kamehameha Highway, Laie; 808-293-3000, fax 808-239-3339; www.polynesia.com.

Be sure to take in the town's natural wonder, **Laie Point**. This headland provides extraordinary ocean views sweeping for miles along the shoreline. Since the breezes and surf are wilder here than elsewhere on the Windward Coast, you'll often encounter waves lashing at the two offshore islets with amazing force. ~ Anemoku Street, off Kamehameha Highway.

Then the main road goes to Kahuku, past the **Kahuku Sugar Mill**, a turn-of-the-20th-century plant. In an effort to refurbish

● ●

RORSCHACH TEST, HAWAIIAN STYLE

That cone-shaped island offshore is **Chinaman's Hat**. It was named for its resemblance to a coolie cap, though the Hawaiians had another name for it long before the Chinese arrived in the islands. They called it Mokolii Island, or "little dragon," and claimed it represented the tail of a beast that resided under the water. Watch for frigate birds and delicate Hawaiian stilts flying overhead.

the old mill several years ago, gears and crushers were painted tropical hues and the entire complex was turned into an entertaining museum-cum-shopping mall. The place has been struggling for years, and the shops never quite made it, but you will find a restaurant there.

Facilitating the recovery of four endangered bird species—the black-necked Hawaiian stilt, Hawaiian moorhen, Hawaiian coot and Hawaiian duck—is the **James Campbell National Wildlife Refuge** in Kahuku. Free guided tours of the wetlands are offered August to mid-February. Reservations required. ~ P.O. Box 340, Haleiwa, HI 96712; 808-637-6330.

Roadside vendors at locations along the way sell sweet corn, watermelon, papaya, mango and tropical flowers from local farms and gardens; fresh-caught fish; and shrimp from the area's aquaculture ponds. You'll get a warm welcome and a chance to "talk story" with the locals as well as the opportunity to enjoy some of Hawaii's natural treasures. For well-prepared fresh Kahuku shrimp, look for the **Shrimp Shack**. ~ Just off Kalanianaole Highway, near the entrance to the Kualoa Activity Club.

◀ *HIDDEN*

Out in the suburban town of Kailua, where trim houses front a beautiful white-sand beach, you'll discover **Kailua Beachside Cottages**. Overlooking Kailua Beach Park and about 100 yards from the beach sits a cluster of woodframe cottages. Each is equipped with a full kitchen, cable television and a telephone. Some of the furniture is nicked, but these duplex units are clean and cozy. They sit in a yard shaded with *hala*, coconut and breadfruit trees and provide an excellent value. ~ 204 South Kalaheo Avenue, Kailua; 808-262-4128, 808-261-1653, fax 808-261-0893. MODERATE.

LODGING

You can't get much closer to the water than **Schrader's Windward Marine Resort**. With about 50 units for rent, this unusual resting place consists of several woodframe buildings right on the edge of Kaneohe Bay. There are picnic tables, barbecue grills and a pool on the two-acre property, as well as a tour boat that can take you snorkeling, kayaking or sightseeing on the bay. The guest rooms are cottage style with kitchenettes; many have lanais and bay views. Prices include continental breakfast. ~ 47-039 Lihikai Drive, Kaneohe; 808-239-5711, 800-735-5711, fax 808-239-6658; www.hawaiiscene.com/schrader. MODERATE.

◀ *HIDDEN*

The **Ali'i Bluffs Bed & Breakfast** offers two rooms with private baths. The Victorian room features antiques and vintage paintings, while the Circus room has large circus posters, many of them originals, from around the world. This contemporary Hawaiian home has a shake roof and is furnished in antiques and Persian rugs. A full breakfast is served poolside every morning.

~ 46-251 Ikiiki Street, Kaneohe; 808-235-1124, 800-235-1151, fax 808-236-4877; www.hawaiiscene.com/aliibluffs, e-mail donm@lava.net. BUDGET TO MODERATE.

If you don't mind funky living, check out the **Countryside Cabins** in Punaluu, run by the Naii family since the '50s. The rustic cabins are set in beautiful garden surroundings across the street from the ocean. Depending on your taste, you'll find the one-room cottages either claustrophobic and untidy or quaint. But no one will find fault with the low prices on these units and the two-bedroom cottages. ~ 53-224 Kamehameha Highway, Punaluu; 808-293-8200, fax 808-293-2169. BUDGET

The old clapboard structures of the Countryside Cabins used to be World War II army barracks.

The **Best Inn Hukilau** is a low-slung motel with two floors of rooms surrounding a swimming pool. This is a standard Coke-machine-in-the-courtyard facility located next to the Polynesian Cultural Center. ~ 55-109 Laniloa Street, Laie; 808-293-9282, 800-526-4562, fax 808-293-8115; www.hawaii bestinn.com. MODERATE.

DINING   Kailua is a bedroom community with little to offer the adventurer. But since you might find yourself nearby at lunchtime or when returning from the beach, I'll briefly describe a few restaurants. You can try **Times Coffee Shop** for fried rice, hamburger steaks or sandwiches. ~ 43 Oneawa Street, Kailua, 808-262-7122; 153 Hamakua Street, Kailua, 808-262-0300. BUDGET.

Saeng's Thai Cuisine is a freshly decorated ethnic restaurant with a hardwood bar and potted plants all around. Located in a strip mall, it nevertheless conveys a sense of elegance. The menu focuses on vegetarian, seafood and curry dishes. No lunch on weekends. ~ 315 Hahani Street, Kailua; 808-263-9727. BUDGET TO MODERATE.

HIDDEN ►   One of Hawaii's great Mexican restaurants is **Bueno Nalo,** which may be short on looks, but it's definitely long on taste. ~ 20 Kainehe Street, Kailua; 808-263-1999. BUDGET TO MODERATE.

HIDDEN ►   Known for years as a prime breakfast and lunch place, **Cinnamon's Restaurant** draws a local crowd, which sits beneath the dining room gazebo or out on the patio. The menu is best described as Continental cuisine with local flavors. Try the chicken cashew sandwich or the carrot pancakes—all made from scratch! No dinner Sunday, closed Monday. ~ Kailua Square Shopping Center, 315 Uluniu Street, Kailua; 808-261-8724, fax 808-262-9910. MODERATE TO DELUXE.

Kailua residents will tell you the pastas at **Baci Bistro** are all homemade and beautifully prepared at this small dining room with greenhouse windows and romantic ambience. There are veal and fish entrées, risotto dishes and an array of antipasti. No lunch on Saturday and Sunday. ~ 30 Aulike Street, Kailua; 808-262-7555. MODERATE TO DELUXE.

In Kaneohe you might like **Koa Omelette House**. It's a tastefully appointed restaurant with a breakfast bill of fare that includes pancakes and crêpes suzette and a lunch menu with salads, sandwiches, teriyaki chicken and seafood. ~ 46-126 Kahuhipa Street, Kaneohe; 808-235-5772. BUDGET.

You don't need a map to find **Smokin' Bob Barr-B-Q**. The fragrant fumes pouring from the smoker stacked with succulent ribs and chicken act like a magnet, drawing anyone within several blocks. The barbecue and cole slaw are world class in flavor and tenderness. Besides that, the inventive metal sculptures crafted from car mufflers (one stands nearly 20 feet high) and the huge Wild West murals create a sense of fun that makes your meal all the more enjoyable. ~ 46-132A Kahuhipa, Kaneohe; 808-247-8811. MODERATE.

What sets **Haleiwa Joe's Seafood Grill** apart is its idyllic setting. A terraced dining area overlooks sharp cliffs and peaceful flower beds, making this a choice stop for dinner. Though the atmosphere varies from the average Chart House, the menu is quite similar: steak, seafood and prime rib, but with a Pan-Asian influence. ~ 46-336 Haiku Road, Kaneohe; 808-247-6671, fax 808-247-9796; e-mail joesiihoo1@hawaii.rr.com. MODERATE TO DELUXE.

The **Crouching Lion Inn**, set in a vintage 1927 wood-shingle house, serves sandwiches and hamburgers, rotisserie chicken, mahimahi and teriyaki steak for lunch. At dinner there's a surf-and-turf menu. Enjoying a beautiful ocean view, this attractive complex is popular with tour buses, so try to arrive at an off-hour. ~ 51-666 Kamehameha Highway, Kaaawa; 808-237-8511, fax 808-237-7061; www.honolulurestaurantguide.com/crouching lion. MODERATE TO ULTRA-DELUXE.

In Kailua and Kaneohe, you'll encounter large supermarkets. In **GROCERIES** the Kailua Shopping Center there's **Times Supermarket**. ~ Kailua Road, Kailua; 808-262-2366. **Foodland** is in the Windward City Shopping Center. ~ At Kamehameha Highway and Kaneohe Bay Drive, Kaneohe; 808-247-3357.

For health food, you might try the **Vim and Vigor** store. ~ 345 Hahani Street, Kailua; 261-3911.

These are good places to stock up, since the next large supermarket is **Lindy's Food**. ~ Hauula Kai Center on Kamehameha Highway, Hauula; 808-293-9722.

Between these major shopping complexes there are smaller facilities such as the **7-11**. ~ 51-484 Kamehameha Highway, Kaaawa; 808-237-8810.

You can get fresh fish at **Masa and Joyce Fish Market** in the Temple Valley Shopping Center. ~ Kahekili Highway (Route 83), just north of Kaneohe; 808-239-6966.

There's a large **Foodland** grocery store in the Laie Village Shopping Center. ~ Kamehameha Highway, Laie; 808-293-4443.

SHOPPING   **Kailua Shopping Center** offers a wide range of services at 20 stores. ~ Kailua Road and Hahani Street, Kailua.

Kaneohe Shopping Center serves the region with eight stores. ~ 45-934 Kamehameha Highway, Kaneohe; 808-847-2345.

HIDDEN ▶   Up in Punaluu, the **Punaluu Art Gallery** features pottery, oil paintings, photography, hand-carved candles and unusual pieces like landscapes made from banana leaves, all by local artists. ~ 53-352 Kamehameha Highway, Punaluu; 808-237-8221.

The nearby **Lance Fairly Gallery** has colorful island fabrics, handmade jewelry, paintings by local artists, and assorted gift items. ~ 53-839 Kamehameha Highway, Punaluu; 808-293-9009.

NIGHTLIFE   Nights on the Windward Coast are quiet and peaceful, and most people like it that way. For those who prefer a bit of action, however, head to Kailua, where you can catch live entertainment every Thursday, Friday and Saturday at **Jaron's Restaurant**. On Thursday, it's contemporary Hawaiian music and on the weekends dance tunes from reggae to rock. Occasional cover on Friday and Saturday. ~ 201 Hamakua Drive #A, Kailua; 808-261-4600.

BEACHES & PARKS   **KAILUA BEACH** Stretching for two miles with white sand all the way and tiny islands offshore, this is one of the prettiest beaches around. It's in the suburban town of Kailua, so you'll trade seclusion for excellent beach facilities. The center of activity is **Kailua Beach Park** at the end of Kailua Road near the south end of the beach. This 30-acre facility has a grassy expanse shaded by ironwood and coconut trees and perfect for picnicking. There are restrooms and a pavilion with a snack bar. **Kalama Beach County Park**, a small park with restrooms in the middle of Kailua Beach, is less crowded. Swimming, surfing and bodysurfing are good all along the strand and windsurfing is excellent, but exercise caution. ~ You can access Kailua Beach farther north via side streets off Kalaheo Avenue; Kalama Beach County Park is located at 250 North Kalaheo Avenue.

LANIKAI BEACH Everyone's dream house is on the beach at Lanikai. This sandy stretch, varying from 20 to 100 feet in width, extends for over a mile. The entire beach in this residential community is lined with those houses everybody wants. The water is the color of cobalt and the protecting reef offshore makes the entire beach safe for swimming. The nearest facilities are at

Kailua Beach. ~ The strand parallels Mokulua Drive in Lanikai, which in turn is reached by driving south along the beachfront roads in Kailua.

KUALOA BEACH PARK 🏊 🏄 ⛵ You could search the entire Pacific for a setting as lovely as this one. Just 500 yards offshore lies the islet of Mokolii, better known as Chinaman's Hat. Behind the beach the *pali* creates a startling background of fluted cliffs and tropical forest. The beach is a long and narrow strip of sand paralleled by a wide swath of grass parkland. Little wonder this is one of the Windward Coast's most popular picnic areas. It's also a favorite for swimming, snorkeling and fishing (common catches are *papio*, bonefish, milkfish and goatfish). Facilities include picnic areas, restrooms and showers. ~ 49-479 Kamehameha Highway (Route 83) about ten miles north of Kaneohe.

▲ Tent camping permitted. County permit required.

SWANZY BEACH PARK, PUNALUU BEACH PARK AND HAUULA BEACH PARK 🏊 🏄 🎣 ⛵ These three county facilities lie along Kamehameha Highway (Route 83) within seven miles of each other. Swimming is generally good at each. Along this coast the most abundant fish is *papio*, followed by bonefish, milkfish and goatfish. Camping is allowed at all except Punaluu, but none compare aesthetically with other beaches to the north and south. Swanzy (open weekends only) is located on the highway but lacks a sandy beach. However, it has the best diving. Its surf break, "Crouching Lion," is for experts only; Punaluu, though possessing a pretty palm-fringed beach, is cramped; and Hauula, a spacious park with a beach and a winter surf break for beginners, is visited periodically by tour buses. So put these beach parks near the bottom of your list, and bring them up only if the other beaches are too crowded. All three beaches have picnic areas and restrooms. ~ These parks are all located along Kamehameha Highway (Route 83). Swanzy lies about 12 miles north of Kaneohe, Punaluu is about four miles north of Swanzy, and Hauula is about three miles beyond that.

All along the Kamehameha Highway in Waiahole and Waikane valleys, there are small stands selling fresh fruit grown right in this lush area.

▲ Tent and trailer camping allowed at Hauula Beach Park, as well as at Swanzy Beach Park on weekends. A county permit is required.

KAHANA VALLEY STATE PARK 🚶 🏊 ⛵ This 5228-acre paradise, set on a white-sand beach, offers something for every adventurer. You can pick fruit in a lush forest, picnic in a coconut grove and sightsee the ancient **Huilua Fishpond**. Follow the five-mile trail up into the lush valley and you'll pass a succession of old Hawaiian farms. You can also fish for *papio*, bonefish, milkfish and goatfish. Swimming is generally good. Surfing is a possibility but is mediocre at best. There are picnic areas and restrooms. ~ 52-222 Kamehameha Highway (Route 83) about 14 miles north of Kaneohe.

▲ There's camping across the street at Kahana Beach Park. State permit required; 808-587-0300, fax 808-587-0311.

The "Twin Islands," tiny bird sanctuaries, rest off the shore of Lanikai Beach.

KOKOLOLIO BEACH PARK 🏊 🏕 Here's one of the prettiest beaches on the Windward Coast. With trees and a lawn that extends toward the white-sand beach, it's a highly recommended spot for day-tripping. It's also a good beach for swimming and bodysurfing and in winter there are breaks up to six feet, with right and left slide. Common catches include *papio*, bonefish, goatfish and milkfish. There are picnic areas and restrooms. ~ 55-017 Kamehameha Highway (Route 83) in Laie about 20 miles north of Kaneohe.

▲ Camping allowed with county permit.

POUNDERS BEACH 🏊 Named for the crushing shorebreak that makes it a popular bodysurfing beach, this quarter-mile-long strand features a corridor of white sand and a sandy bottom. Swimming is good near the old landing at the western end of the beach. Be careful of currents when swimming anywhere along the beach. Anglers try for *ono*, *moi* and *papio*. There are no facilities here. ~ Located along Kamehameha Highway north of Kakela Beach.

HUKILAU BEACH 🏊 🏕 This privately owned facility fronts a beautiful white-sand beach that winds for more than a mile. Part of the beach is lined with homes, but much of it is undeveloped. Several small islands lie offshore, and the park contains a lovely stand of ironwood trees. All in all this enchanting beach is one of the finest on this side of the island. Swimming is good; bodysurfing is also recommended. Snorkeling is usually fair and there are small surfable waves with left and right slides. The principal catch is *papio*; milkfish, bonefish and goatfish are also caught. There are no facilities here. ~ Located on Kamehameha Highway (Route 83) in Laie about 22 miles north of Kaneohe.

HIDDEN ► **MALAEKAHANA STATE RECREATION AREA AND GOAT ISLAND** 🏊 🏕 This is a rare combination. The Malaekahana facility is one of the island's prettiest parks. It's a tropical wonderland filled with palm, *hala* and ironwood trees, and graced with a curving, white-sand beach. Goat Island lies just offshore. It's a small, low-lying island covered with scrub growth and scattered ironwood trees. On the windward side is a coral beach; to leeward lies a crescent-shaped white-sand beach. It's a good place to swim because it is shallow and well-protected. There are also good places for snorkeling and in winter you can paddle out to a break with a left slide. Feel like fishing? You may well reel in *papio*, the most abundant fish along here; goatfish, milkfish and bonefish are also caught. Goat Island is now a state bird refuge, so you might see wedge-tailed shearwaters nesting. Whatever activity you choose, make sure you don't disturb the birds. Goat Island will return the favor—there'll be nothing here to disturb you either. Facilities include showers, bathrooms and barbecue pits. ~ Located on Kamehameha Highway (Route 83) in Laie about 23 miles north of Kaneohe.

▲ There are two sections to the park. The Laie section includes Goat Island and is administered by the state. The Kahuku section (Puuhonua o Malaekahana or Place of Refuge) is operated by the Friends of Malaekahana, the first native Hawaiian group to operate a park in the islands.

Laie Section: Tent camping allowed. State permit required.

Kahuku Section: There are very rustic cabins available here. These beachfront units include 40 campsites and 7 beach cabins —6 beach houses with two or three bedrooms, private baths and kitchens ($80 per night on weekends), and a six-room cabin with a game room and a commercial kitchen ($250 per night). Tent sites are $5 per person, per night. Cabins are equipped with beds, kitchen facilities and bathrooms. Bring your own bedding and cooking gear and be prepared for rustic accommodations. For information or reservations, call 808-293-1736, fax 808-293-2066.

KAHUKU GOLF COURSE PARK 🏊 🎣 ⛵ Other than Goat Island, this is about the closest you'll come to a hidden beach on the Windward Coast. Granted, there's a golf course paralleling the strand, but sand dunes hide you from the duffers. The beach is long, wide and sandy white. Swimming is fair, but exercise caution. In winter, surfers work the "Seventh Hole" breaks, which reach up to eight feet and have a right and left slide. *Papio*, bonefish, goatfish and milkfish are common catches. There are restrooms at the golf course. ~ In Kahuku, about 25 miles north of Kaneohe, turn off Kamehameha Highway (Route 83) toward the ocean. Park at the golf course, then walk the gated road to the beach.

Wide, wide beaches heaped with white, white sand roll for miles along the North Shore. Some of them have become famous throughout the world. Not, however, for their **North Shore** size or their sand, but rather because of their waves. If you have ever owned a surfboard, or even a Beach Boys album, you know Waimea Bay and Sunset Beach. The names are synonymous with surfing. They number among the most challenging and dangerous surf spots anywhere. During the winter 15- to 20-foot waves are as common as blond hair and beach buggies. The infamous

"Banzai Pipeline," where surfers risk limb and longevity as thunderous waves pass over a shallow reef, is here as well.

Curving in a bowl shape from Kahuku Point in the east to Kaena Point in the west, the coast is backdropped by both Oahu mountain ranges. Most dramatic are the Waianaes, dominated by 4025-foot Mt. Kaala, the island's highest peak.

While the aquatic oriented zero in on the international surfing competitions that occur annually, many other residents work the small farms and ranches that checkerboard the tableland between the mountains and sea. All of them look to Haleiwa, a refurbished plantation town, as their primary gathering place.

SIGHTS

Stretching for two miles and averaging 200 feet in width, **Sunset Beach** (Kamehameha Highway) is one of Hawaii's largest strands. When the surf is up you can watch world-class athletes shoot the curl. When it's not, Sunset becomes a great place to swim. The best place to go is **Ehukai Beach Park**, just off Kamehameha Highway about seven miles northeast of Haleiwa. Just 100 yards to the west sits the **Banzai Pipeline** (Ke Nui Road), where a shallow coral shelf creates tubular waves so powerful and perfect they resemble pipes. First surfed in 1957, it lays claim to cracked skulls, lacerated legs and some of the sport's greatest feats.

HIDDEN ►

On a plateau between Sunset Beach and Waimea Bay is **Puu o Mahuka Heiau**, Oahu's oldest temple. A split-level structure built of stone, it once was used for human sacrifices. Today you will encounter nothing more menacing than a spectacular view and perhaps a gentle breeze from the ocean. To get there from Kamehameha Highway, turn left near the Sunset Beach Fire Station onto Pupukea Road, then follow the Hawaii Visitors & Convention Bureau signs.

At **Waimea Valley Adventure Park** you can wander through a tropical preserve stretching across 1800 acres. Once a Hawaiian village, it is crisscrossed with hiking trails and archaeological ruins. A tram carries visitors to **Waimea Falls**, where you can picnic. There's an arboretum featuring tropical and subtropical trees from around the world, beautiful botanical gardens including one local Hawaiian species, and a butterfly encounter exhibit. Then there are the birds, caged and wild, that populate the complex; since this nature park serves as a bird sanctuary, it attracts a varied assortment. Activities for visitors include horseback riding, kayaking, mountain biking, ATV riding, craft classes and a hula show. Steep admission. ~ Kamehameha Highway, five miles northeast of Haleiwa; 808-638-8511, fax 808-638-7900.

Across the road looms **Waimea Bay**, another fabled place that sports the largest surfable waves in the world. When surf's up in winter, the monster waves that roll in are so big they make the ground tremble when they break. Salt spray reaches as far as the

North Shore

highway. Thirty-foot waves are not uncommon. Fifty-foot giants have been recorded; though unsurfable, these are not tidal waves, just swells rising along the incredible North Shore. In December, the Hawaiian Triple Crown—basically the Super Bowl of surfing—takes place. In summer, Waimea is a pretty blue bay with a white-sand beach. The water is placid and the area perfect for picnicking and sunbathing. So when you visit Waimea, remember: swim in summer, sunbathe in winter.

Next, the Kamehameha Highway crosses a double rainbow-shaped bridge en route to **Haleiwa**, an old plantation town with a new facelift. Fortunately, the designers who performed the surgery on this village had an eye for antiquity. They planned it so the modern shopping centers and other facilities blend comfortably into the rural landscape. The community that has grown up around the new town reflects a rare combination of past and future. The old Japanese, Filipinos and Hawaiians have been joined by blond-mopped surfers and laidback counterculturalists. As a result, this clapboard town with wooden sidewalks has established itself as the "in" spot on the North Shore. Its stylish nonchalance has also proved popular among canny travelers.

It's also a good town for surf history enthusiasts. Within the modern walls of a local shopping mall resides the **North Shore Surf and Cultural Museum**. This surfing nook displays related artifacts, boards and old photographs of the local community, and has a mini-theater showing videos of the sport. It also temporarily houses items from an 1824 shipwreck, providing a safe haven for the items while the wreck is being excavated. The museum's other claim to fame is its possession of the last two boards used by famed surfer Mark Foo before he was killed in a surfing accident in 1994. ~ North Shore Marketplace, 66-250 Kamehameha Highway; 808-637-8888.

Despite the hint of gentrification, Haleiwa holds on to its relaxed ambience with a dose of authenticity. The surf scene still adds a definite style to Haleiwa, an image that's been strengthened with *Baywatch Hawaii*'s North Shore setting. Needing a new venue to give the TV series *Baywatch* a fresh angle, the network producers ultimately chose Oahu's North Shore as the new location. The waves and surf scene have become familiar to households around the world as the ongoing drama about the lives of lifeguards has made its mark.

From here, head west and pick up Farrington Highway (Route 930). This country road parallels miles of unpopulated beachfront, and arrives at Dillingham Airfield, where you can take **The Original Glider Ride** along the Waianae Mountains. With nearly 30 years of experience, Mr. Bill knows the ins and outs of the countryside. He'll also provide you with a video of your ride. Reservations recommended. ~ 808-677-3404.

How to Beat the Heat
with a Sweet Treat

Since the early days of Hawaiian royalty, people have complained about Honolulu's shirt-sticking weather. Come summer, temperatures rise and the trade winds stop blowing. Visitors seeking a golden tan discover they're baking without browning. And residents begin to think that their city, renowned as a cultural melting pot, is actually a pressure cooker.

With the ocean all around, relief is never far away. But a lot of folks, when not heading for the beaches, have found another way to cool off: shave ice. Known as ice frappes among the Japanese originators and snow cones back on the mainland, these frozen treats are Hawaii's answer to the Good Humor man.

They're made with ice that's been shaved from a block into thin slivers, packed into a cone-shaped cup and covered with sweet syrup. Health-minded people eat the ice plain or with a low-calorie or sugar-free syrup, and some folks ask for a scoop of ice cream or sweet black beans (*azuki* beans) underneath the shavings. Most people just order it with their favorite syrup flavors—grape, root beer, cola, cherry, orange, lemon-lime, vanilla, fruit punch, banana, strawberry or whatever.

Whichever you choose, you'll find it only costs about a buck at the many stands sprinkled around town. Watch for stands up on the North Shore, too. No doubt you'll see a long line outside Oahu's most famous shave ice store, **Matsumoto's**. ~ 66-087 Kamehameha Highway, Haleiwa; 808-637-4827.

As a matter of fact, anyplace where the sun blazes overhead you're liable to find someone trying to beat the heat by slurping up a "snow cone" before it melts into mush.

Beyond this landing strip, the road continues for several miles between ocean and mountains before turning into a very rugged dirt track. Along this unpaved portion of roadway you can hike out about ten miles to **Kaena Point** on Oahu's northwest corner (see the "Hiking" section at the end of this chapter).

LODGING   For a resort experience in a rustic setting, consider the **Hilton Turtle Bay Golf and Tennis Resort**. This rural retreat sprawls across 808 acres on a dramatic peninsula. With a broad beach at the doorstep and mountains out back, it's an overwhelming spot. Add to that riding paths, two golf courses, tennis courts and a pair of swimming pools. Every guest room features an ocean view. ~ 57-091 Kamehameha Highway, Kahuku; 808-293-8811, 800-445-8667, fax 808-293-9147; www.turtlebayresort.hilton.com. ULTRA-DELUXE.

Located on the grounds of the Turtle Bay Hilton but independently operated, **The Estates at Turtle Bay** offers studio, as well as one-, two- and three-bedroom resort condominiums, each with stove, refrigerator, dishwasher, microwave, washer/dryer and cable television. There are five swimming pools and four tennis courts on the property, and guests can arrange golf and horseback riding through the Hilton. Closed Sunday. ~ 56-565 Kamehameha Highway, Kahuku; 808-293-0600, 888-200-4202, fax 808-293-0471; www.turtlebay-rentals.com, e-mail trtlbayest@aol.com. MODERATE TO DELUXE.

Turtle Bay Condos has one-, two- and three-bedroom units with kitchen facilities and private lanais that overlook a nine-hole golf course. Studios run $80 to $105; one-bedrooms units with a loft sleeping up to four guests are $110 to $140; two-bedroom units are $160; and three-bedroom units are $175. ~ 56-565 Kamehameha Highway, Kahuku; 808-293-2800, fax 808-293-2169; www.turtlebaycondos.com.

Surfers, scuba divers and budget-minded travelers will find **Backpacker's Vacation Inn** along Oahu's vaunted North Shore. The central building provides hostel-style rooms and features a TV lounge and kitchen. There's also a back house with private rooms that share a kitchen and bath. Like a hostel, it's budget-priced. Across the street, and directly on the beach, there's a house with private apartments that include their own kitchen and bathroom and are moderately priced. In addition, there are nine restored plantation houses with shared kitchens and baths set on a landscaped acre. The Vacation Inn has laundry facilities and barbecue areas for guests. They also sponsor daily activities and provide excellent opportunities for meeting other travelers. ~ 59-788 Kamehameha Highway, Haleiwa; 808-638-7838, fax 808-638-7515; www.backpackers-hawaii.com. BUDGET TO DELUXE.

Offering houses right on the beach, **Ke Iki Hale** is located between the Banzai Pipeline and Waimea Bay. You'll find moderate- and deluxe-priced duplexes and an ultra-deluxe-priced cottage on an acre-and-a-half of palm-shaded property. They are basic woodframe buildings with plain furnishings. The complex includes barbecue facilities, hammocks, a volleyball court and a wide beach. Accommodations are great for families. ~ 59-579 Ke Iki Road, Haleiwa; phone/fax 808-638-8229. MODERATE TO ULTRA-DELUXE.

DINING

Appropriately enough, you'll find the **Country Kitchen** out in the country (and not far from the old Kahuku Sugar Mill). The menu includes Hawaiian plate lunches as well as shrimp, seafood and steak dishes. Open for breakfast and lunch daily and dinner Friday through Sunday, it's plain and informal. ~ 55-565 Kamehameha Highway, Kahuku; 808-293-2110. BUDGET.

Just down the way is **Giovanni's Aloha Shrimp Truck**, serving gourmet plate lunches that the locals claim are the best on Oahu. There's a choice of scampi, grilled shrimp or hot and spicy shrimp, and, like all plate lunches, they come with two scoops of rice. Eleven picnic tables sit under an awning for this rain-or-shine outdoor eating spot. ~ Beside The Mill, Kamehameha Highway, Kahuku, 808-293-1839; www.giosauces.com. MODERATE.

The **Hilton Turtle Bay Golf and Tennis Resort** features one family restaurant and one poolside snack shop. At the **Palm Terrace**, overlooking the hotel's lovely grounds, you'll encounter moderate-priced dining in an attractive environment. The restaurant, serving three buffet meals, offers everything from burgers to *saimin* and teriyaki to linguine. Children's prices are available. At the **Orchid Snackshop**, munch on a hamburger or taco salad while lounging in the sun. ~ 57-091 Kamehameha Highway, Kahuku; 808-293-8811, fax 808-293-9147; www.turtlebayresort. hilton.com. MODERATE TO DELUXE.

Otherwise, the best places to chow down are in Haleiwa, the main town on the North Shore. The **Sunset Diner** packs local crowds into its awning-covered picnic tables, with plate lunches of barbecue chicken, *kalbi*, teri-beef, pork, as well as chili, ham-

KUA AINA IS DA KINE

Surfers pour into **Kua Aina Sandwich**, where they order hamburgers, french fries and mahimahi sandwiches at the counter, then kick back at one of the roadside tables. Great for light meals, the place is a scene and a half. ~ 66-214 Kamehameha Highway, Haleiwa; 808-637-6067. BUDGET.

burgers and a selection of fruit smoothies. Closed Monday. ~ 59-176 Kamehameha Highway, Haleiwa; 808-638-7660. BUDGET.

For relaxed sunset dining overlooking the ocean, try **Jameson's By the Sea**. This split-level establishment features a patio downstairs and a formal dining room upstairs. For lunch there are sandwiches, chowders and fresh fish dishes; at dinner they specialize in seafood. Fine dinner dining Wednesday through Sunday. Pub dinners Monday and Tuesday. Breakfast on the weekend. ~ 62-540 Kamehameha Highway, Haleiwa; 808-637-4336, fax 808-637-3225. MODERATE TO ULTRA-DELUXE.

Haleiwa Beach Grill, a small café in the center of Haleiwa, is as colorful as coral. Matter of fact, the tropic-hued walls are adorned with a wide range of vintage albums from the '60s and '70s. Read the menu and you'll discover charbroiled chicken, grilled sandwiches, burritos and "islander plates." There are *kalbi* ribs, teriyaki chicken and a mixed grill dish that includes mahi-mahi. ~ 66-079 Kamehameha Highway, Haleiwa; 808-637-3394. BUDGET.

At **Café Haleiwa** surfers swear by the huevos rancheros, pancakes and "the Barrel"—a blend of eggs, potatoes, green salsa and cheese wrapped in a tortilla. Sandwiches and burgers round out the menu. Located in a century-old building featuring local artwork, surfboards and surfing memorabilia, this local favorite also serves an excellent quesadilla. No dinner. ~ 66-460 Kamehameha Highway, Haleiwa; 808-637-5516. BUDGET TO MODERATE.

Paradise Found Café has a juice bar and vegetarian restaurant serving sandwiches, soups and salads. ~ Inside Celestial Natural Foods, 66-443 Kamehameha Highway, Haleiwa; 808-637-4540. BUDGET.

Meg's Drive-In is a small eatery serving local-style plate lunches and daily specials such as fried noodles with teriyaki beef. You can take your meal to-go or dine on the adjoining lanai. Closed Sunday. ~ 743 Waiakamilo Road, Haleiwa; 808-845-3943. BUDGET.

HIDDEN ► Years ago Haleiwa was home to Da Cuppa Kope, a great café and gathering place. Today it's been supplanted by an even better coffeehouse, the **Coffee Gallery**. In addition to the best cappuccino on the island, this homespun restaurant, decorated with coffee sacks, serves pastries, bagels, homemade soups and a variety of sandwiches. ~ North Shore Marketplace, 66-250 Kamehameha Highway, Haleiwa; 808-637-5355. BUDGET.

Mexican restaurants in Hawaii are different from their counterparts elsewhere in one respect—fish tacos. True to the islands, **Rosie's Cantina** offers them, rounding out a menu filled with the culinary features found in every south-of-the-border eatery. The breakfast menu features American standbys like pancakes and omelettes, while the dinner menu ranges from tacos and enchiladas to steaks and seafood. To complement the fare Rosie's stocks the largest selection of premium tequilas in Hawaii. ~ Haleiwa Shopping Plaza, 66-165 Kamehameha Highway, Haleiwa; 808-637-3538, fax 808-637-7615. BUDGET TO DELUXE.

Appropriately enough, **Portofino** captures an air of the Mediterranean with its cream-colored pastel walls, blond-wood furniture, overhead fans and breezy ambience. This Italian restaurant prepares rosemary chicken, penne *capricciosa* (with eggplant and shrimp) and a catch-of-the-day dish. So sink onto one of the upholstered banquettes or sidle over to the granite bar. ~ 66-250 Kamehameha Highway, Haleiwa; 808-637-7678, fax 808-637-2785. MODERATE TO DELUXE.

While Sunset Beach is actually only a single surfing spot, the name has become synonymous with a two-mile-long corridor that includes Banzai Beach and the adjacent Pipeline.

For an unexpected crowd that includes a big contingent of bikers, drop by the **Sugar Bar & Pizza Garden** in the ex-plantation town of Waialua, just a couple of miles from Haleiwa. Housed in what was once the town bank, it's a high-energy place with an abundance of local color, perfect for a late afternoon drink and a casual dinner. ~ 67-069 Kealohanui Street, Waialua; 808-637-6989, fax 808-637-7774 (Sugar Bar), 808-637-4212 (Pizza Garden). BUDGET.

◄ *HIDDEN*

Haleiwa Supermarket, one of the few large markets on the entire North Shore, is the best place to shop. ~ 66-197 Kamehameha Highway, Haleiwa; 808-637-5004. Out by Sunset Beach you'll find a **Foodland Super Market**. ~ 59-720 Kamehameha Highway, Haleiwa; 808-638-8081. There's also **Sunset Beach Store**, which has a small stock but is home to a modest bakery; it's conveniently located near Sunset Beach. ~ 59-024 Kamehameha Highway, Haleiwa; 808-638-8207.

GROCERIES

Celestial Natural Foods has an ample supply of health foods and fresh produce. ~ 66-443 Kamehameha Highway, Haleiwa; 808-637-6729.

Calling itself **The Only Show In Town** is a slight (very slight) exaggeration, but claiming to be "Kahuku's largest antique and vintage collectible shop" is definitely warranted. Some store specialties include Japanese glass fishing floats, ivory and Coca-Cola memorabilia. Fittingly, this wonderful antique store is located in the old Tanaka Plantation Store, an early-20th-century wood-frame building. ~ 56-931 Kamehameha Highway, Kahuku; 808-293-1295, fax 808-293-8585.

SHOPPING

Trendy shoppers head for the burgeoning town of Haleiwa. During the past several years boutiques and galleries have mushroomed throughout this once somnolent town. Since Haleiwa is a center for surfers, it's a good place to buy sportswear and aquatic equipment.

Iwa Gallery features a unique collection of artwork by a number of local island artists. ~ 66-119 Kamehameha Highway, Haleiwa; 808-637-4865.

Sunset Hawaii carries Hawaiian wear, bathing suits, accessories, handmade books, dolls, toys and stuffed animals. ~ 66-226 Kamehameha Highway, Haleiwa; 808-637-4782.

Oogenesis Boutique has a creative selection of women's fashions. ~ 66-249 Kamehameha Highway, Haleiwa; 808-637-4580.

Silver Moon Emporium offers women's wear and jewelry. ~ 66-250 Kamehameha Highway, in the North Shore Marketplace, Haleiwa; 808-637-7710.

Strong Current stocks everything imaginable that's related to surfing. They even have a small "surfing museum," consisting of memorabilia from the sport's early days. Then there are the books, videos, posters, boards and other appurtenances, all relating to a single theme. ~ North Shore Marketplace, 66-250 Kamehameha Highway, Haleiwa; 808-637-3406.

NIGHTLIFE   Entertainment is a rare commodity on the North Shore, but you will find contemporary Hawaiian music at the Turtle Bay Hilton's **Bay View**; on Saturday they feature disco music. ~ 57-091 Kamehameha Highway, Kahuku; 808-293-8811.

To mix with the locals, head to the **Sugarbar**, where you'll find live rock, rhythm-and-blues or Hawaiian music Wednesday, Friday and Sunday. ~ 67-069 Kealohanui Street, Waialua; 808-637-6989, fax 808-637-7774.

BEACHES & PARKS   **SUNSET BEACH** As far as surfing goes, this is the place! I think the best way to do Sunset is by starting from **Ehukai Beach Park**. From here you can go left to the "Banzai Pipeline," where crushing waves build along a shallow coral reef to create tube-like formations. To the right lies "Sunset," with equally spectacular surfing waves. Throughout the area the swimming is fair in summer; however, in winter it is extremely dangerous. From September to April, high waves and strong currents prevail. Be careful! Snorkeling here is poor; but some of the island's best snorkeling is at Pupukea Beach Park, a marine reserve on Kamehameha Highway six miles northeast of Haleiwa. This 80-acre park, fringed by rocky shoreline, divides into several section. Foremost is "Shark's Cove," located on the north side of the fire station, which contains spectacular tidepools and dive sites. Game fish caught around Sunset include *papio*, *menpachi* and *ulua*. Ehukai Beach Park has picnic areas, restrooms and shower. ~ Ehukai Beach Park is off Kamehameha Highway (Route 83) about seven miles northeast of Haleiwa.

WAIMEA BAY BEACH PARK 🏊 🦑 🎣 ⚓ If Sunset is *one* of the most famous surfing spots in the world, Waimea is *the* most famous. The biggest surfable waves in the world (40 feet in winter!) roll into this pretty blue bay. There's a wide white-sand beach and a pleasant park with a tree-studded lawn. It's a marvelous place for picnicking and sunbathing. During the winter crowds often line the beach watching top-notch surfers challenge the curl; in summer the sea is flat and safe for swimming; you can also bodysurf in the shorebreak and snorkel when the bay is calm. *Papio, menpachi* and *ulua* are common catches. Facilities include a picnic area, restrooms, showers and a lifeguard. ~ On Kamehameha Highway (Route 83) about five miles northeast of Haleiwa.

HALEIWA BEACH PARK 🏊 🦑 ⚓ This is an excellent refuge from the North Shore's pounding surf. Set in Waialua Bay, the beach is safe for swimming almost all year. You can snorkel, although it's only fair. Surfing in not possible here but "Haleiwa" breaks are located across Waialua Bay at Alii Beach Park. Facilities include a picnic area, restrooms, showers, a snack bar, a ball field, a basketball court, volleyball courts and a playground. The primary catches at Haleiwa are *papio, menpachi* and *ulua*. ~ On Kamehameha Highway (Route 83) in Haleiwa.

At Mokuleia, watch for skydivers and hang gliders, who often use the beach for their landings.

KAIAKA RECREATION AREA 🏊 🦑 ⚓ The setting at this peninsular park is beautiful. There's a secluded area with a tree-shaded lawn and a short strip of sandy beach. A rocky shoreline borders most of the park, so it's more for picnics than water sports. You *can* swim and snorkel but there's a rocky bottom. Fishing is good for *papio, menpachi* and *ulua.* The facilities here include a picnic area, showers and restrooms. ~ Located on Haleiwa Road just outside Haleiwa.

⚓ Permitted; a county permit is required.

MOKULEIA BEACH PARK AND MOKULEIA BEACH 🏊 🦑 🎣 ⚓ ◀ HIDDEN

The 12-acre park contains a sandy beach and large unshaded lawn. An exposed coral reef detracts from the swimming, but on either side of the park lie beaches with sandy ocean bottoms. If you do swim, exercise caution, especially in the winter months; there's no lifeguard. There's good snorkeling and in winter the surf breaks up to ten feet near Dillingham Airfield. Anglers try for *papio, menpachi* and *ulua.* Whatever your activity of choice, you'll have to contend with the noise of small planes from nearby Dillingham Airfield. The park is also an excellent starting point for exploring the unpopulated sections of Mokuleia Beach. Facilities include picnic areas, restrooms and showers. ~ On Farrington Highway (Route 930) about seven miles west of

Haleiwa. To the west of the park, this beach stretches for miles along a secluded coast. You can hike down the beach or reach its hidden realms by driving farther west along Farrington Highway (Route 930), then turning off onto any of the numerous dirt side roads.

▲ Tent and trailer camping are allowed with a county permit. Unofficial camping along the undeveloped beachfront is common.

▼▼▼▼▼▼▼▼▼▼▼▼
Leeward Coast

Out along the west coast of Oahu, less than 30 miles from the sands of Waikiki, Hawaiian culture is making a last stand. Here on the tableland that separates the Waianae Range from the ocean, the old ways still prevail. Unlike the cool rainforests of the Windward Coast or the rain-spattered area around Honolulu, this is a region of stark beauty, resembling the American Southwest, with rocky crags and cactus-studded hills.

Hawaiian and Samoan farmers populate the place. Since much of the rest of Oahu has been developed, the Leeward Coast has become the keeper of the old ways. Residents here jealously guard the customs and traditions that they see slipping away in the rest of Hawaii.

Few tourists pass this way and few tourist amenities line the roadway. The scenery consists of farmyards with chicken-wire pens, dusty houses and sunblasted churches. Sideroads off the main highway often turn to dirt and climb past truck farms and old homesteads. For entertainment there are family luaus, cockfights and slack-key guitarists.

Travelers who do venture out here have sometimes been hassled by local residents seeking to keep the *malihinis* in Honolulu. But if you are considerate and careful, you should do just fine. This is one of those places that really should be seen, and seen soon, for it, too, is falling to the forces of change. In the southwest corner of the island the ultra-modern Ihilani Resort & Spa in the Koolina area is only the beginning of the inevitable encroachment along this side of the island.

SIGHTS

From Honolulu you can visit the region by traveling west on Route H-1 or Route 90. If you want to tour a prime sugar-growing area, take Route 90 past Pearl Harbor, then turn left on Fort Weaver Road (Route 760). This country lane leads to the plantation town of **Ewa**. With its busy sugar mill and trim houses, Ewa is an enchanting throwback to the days when sugar was king. This town is a slow, simple place, perfect for wandering and exploring.

Near Oahu's southwest corner, Routes H-1 and 90 converge to become the Farrington Highway (Route 93). From here, follow the signs to **Hawaiian Waters Adventure Park**, perfect for those who are afraid of getting a little sand in their pants but love to ride waves or splash in the water. There are inner-tube slides, a 60-foot water slide, artificial waves and much more, spread over 29 acres. A hefty admission. ~ 400 Farrington Highway, Kapolei; 808-945-3928; www.hawaiianwaters.com, e-mail questions@ hawaiianwaters.com.

If you turn up Mailiilii Street in **Waianae**, you will pass placid Hawaiian homesteads and farmlands. This side road also provides sweeping views of the Waianae Range.

Makaha Beach, one of Hawaii's most famous surfing spots, is the site of an international surfing championship every year. The

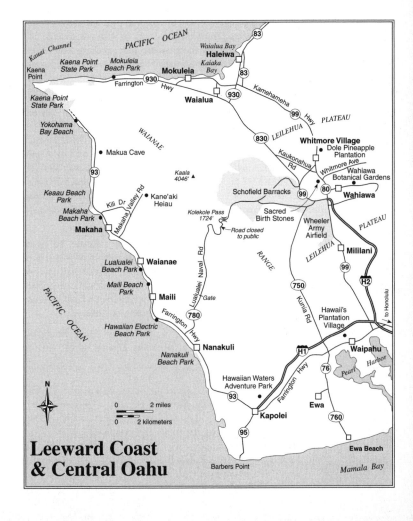

Leeward Coast & Central Oahu

Central Oahu

The 1000-foot-high Leilehua Plateau, a bountiful agricultural region planted with sugar and pineapple, extends from the North Shore to the southern reaches of Oahu. Situated in the middle of the island between the Waianae and Koolau ranges, this tableland has become a vital military headquarters. Wheeler Air Force Base, Schofield Barracks and several other installations occupy large plots of land here. Wahiawa, a small, grimy city, is the region's commercial hub. "Second City," a major development already being built near the town of Ewa, will eventually add thousands of houses to the area. From Haleiwa south to Wahiawa you can take Route 803, Kaukoahuna Road, a pretty thoroughfare with excellent views of the Waianaes, or follow Route 99, the Kamehameha Highway, which passes through verdant pineapple fields.

DOLE PINEAPPLE PLANTATION   Located about ten minutes south of Haleiwa along **Route 99**, the Dole Pineapple Plantation, often crowded with tourists, sells (who would have guessed) pineapple products. They offer a self-guided tour and the World's Largest Maze, a 1.7-mile labyrinth made from over 11,000 Hawaiian plants that covers two acres. Admission for maze. ~ 64-1550 Kamehameha Highway, Wahiawa; 808-621-8408, 888-611-6747, fax 808-621-1926; www.dole-plantation.com, e-mail sales@dole-plantation.com. The **Pineapple Variety Garden** displays many different types of the fruit in a garden museum. ~ Kamehameha Highway and Kamananui Road, Wahiawa.

KUKANILOHO   The east fork of Route 99 becomes **Route 80**, which passes near Kukaniloho, a cluster of sacred stones marking the place where Hawaiian royalty gave birth accompanied by chants, drums and offerings. Studded with eucalyptus trees, this spot has held an important place in Hawaiian mythology and religion for centuries. ~ Follow the dirt road across from Whitmore Avenue just north of Wahiawa.

WAHIAWA BOTANICAL GARDENS   Farther south along Route 80, Wahiawa Botanical Gardens is a handsome 27-acre retreat studded

Makaha Valley, extending from the ocean up into the Waianae Mountains, is home to the **Kane'aki Heiau**, a 15th-century temple dedicated to the god Lono. Closed Monday and when raining. ~ Take Manunaolu Street; phone/fax 808-695-9430.

The highway continues along the coastline past several beaches and parks. Across from Kaena Point State Park you'll come upon **Makua Cave**, a lava cavern large enough for exploring and snorwith tropical vegetation. Plants include orchids, ferns, cacti and bromeliads, as well as Heliconias, palms and gingers. ~ 1396 California Avenue, Wahiawa; 808-621-7321, fax 808-522-7050.

KOLEKOLE PASS   For a scenic and historic detour from Route 80, follow Route 80 until it links with Route 99. Take Route 99 west, pull up to the sentry station at **Schofield Barracks** and ask directions to Kolekole Pass. On that "day of infamy," December 7, 1941, Japanese bombers buzzed through this notch in the Waianae Range. You'll be directed through Schofield up into the Waianaes. When you reach Kolekole Pass, there's another sentry gate. Ask the guard to let you continue a short distance farther to the observation point. From here the Waianaes fall away precipitously to a plain that rolls gently to the sea. There's an astonishing view of Oahu's west coast. If you are denied permission to pass the sentry point, then take the footpath that begins just before the gate, leading up the hill. From near the cross at the top, you will have a partial view of both the Waianaes' western face and the central plateau region.

HAWAII'S PLANTATION VILLAGE   Back at Wahiawa, Route H-2 provides the fastest means back to Honolulu; the most interesting course is along **Route 750**, Kunia Road, which skirts the Waianaes, passing sugar cane fields and stands of pine. Along the way you can take in Hawaii's Plantation Village, a partially re-created and partially restored village that spreads across three acres of Waipahu Cultural Park in Waipahu. Comprised of over two dozen buildings, it includes a Japanese Shinto shrine, a company store and a Chinese Society building. Hawaii's many ethnic groups are represented in the houses, which span several architectural periods of the 19th and 20th centuries. Together they provide visitors with a window into traditional life on a plantation. Closed Sunday. Admission. ~ 94-695 Waipahu Street, Waipahu; 808-677-0110, fax 808-676-6727. From here, Honolulu is about 15 miles east along Route H-1, or you can take Route 750 south to Ewa.

keling. Beyond that, where the paved road turns to dirt, lies **Yokohama Bay**, with its curving sand beach and inviting turquoise waters.

The road past Yokohama is partially passable by auto, but it's very rough. If you want to explore **Kaena Point** from this side of the island, you'll have to hike. It's about two miles to the northwest corner of Oahu, past tidepools teeming with marine life. On a clear day you can see Kauai from this point. (Don't leave valuables in your car in this area.)

LODGING

While the premise of "hidden Hawaii" is that you'll save money by uncovering secluded places, sometimes the remote comes with a hefty price tag. Take the **JW Marriott Ihilani Resort & Spa**. Backed by the Waianaes and facing a curved expanse of ocean, this 387-room hideaway is part of the 640-acre Koolina Resort. There's a golf course, six tennis courts, four restaurants and a sophisticated spa facility. More important, you'll find a string of four lagoons, each with a crescent beach and a cluster of islets that protects the mouth of the lagoon. All this material and natural splendor lies way out in the southwestern corner of Oahu. The entire complex is quite beautiful, from the trim green grounds to the atrium lobby to the spacious and elegant rooms. ~ 92-1001 Olani Street, Kapolei; 808-679-0079, 800-626-4446, fax 808-679-0295; www.ihilani.com. ULTRA-DELUXE.

Schofield Barracks, made famous in *From Here to Eternity*, is the largest permanent Army post in the U.S.

Makaha Shores, a six-story resort condo complex, overlooks pretty Makaha Beach County Park, one of Hawaii's top surfing beaches. There are studios and one- and two-bedroom units, each individually decorated by their owners. The minimum stay is one week, and the units are handled by different agents. Hawaii Hatfields (phone/fax 808-696-7121) handles most of them. ~ 84-265 Farrington Highway, Makaha. MODERATE.

Makaha Valley Towers is a highrise set along the slopes of Makaha Valley. Units range from studios to two-bedrooms, with nightly, weekly and monthly stays available. Rates vary and accommodations are handled by local realtors. ~ End of Kili Drive, Makaha; 808-695-9568.

DINING

By way of resort restaurants, **JW Marriott Ihilani Resort & Spa** at Koolina has several deluxe- and ultra-deluxe-priced dining rooms. Foremost is **Azul**, where the lamb chops come with couscous, the lobster is served in *pistou* and the ideas are Mediterranean. **Ushiotei** is the ultimate in Japanese cuisine. And **Naupaka**, a poolside terrace serving cross-cultural dishes, is the Ihilani's answer to informality and easy elegance. Hours for all three vary with the season. Reservations are recommended. ~ 92-1001 Olani Street, Kapolei; 808-679-0079, fax 808-679-0080. MODERATE TO ULTRA-DELUXE.

This sparsely populated strip of shoreline has several other dining spots. All are located on Farrington Highway, the main road, and most are in the town of Waianae. **Cathay Inn Chop Suey** is a good choice for Chinese food. ~ 86-066 Farrington Highway, Waianae; 808-696-9477. BUDGET TO MODERATE.

Close by is **Hannara Restaurant** offering Korean and Hawaiian cuisines. Breakfast and lunch daily, no dinner Sunday. ~ 86-078 Farrington Highway, Waianae; 808-696-6137. BUDGET TO MODERATE.

Out at the Makaha Resort Golf Club, the **19th Hole** is an open-air café overlooking the golf course, where you can pick up ready-made sandwiches or muffins, or you can sit down to *saimin*, hot dogs and blue-plate specials. ~ 84-626 Makaha Valley Road, Makaha; 808-695-7525. BUDGET.

Sack 'n Save Foods is the prime market in this area. ~ 87-2070 **GROCERIES** Farrington Highway, Waianae; 808-668-1277.

Naupaka Terrace at the Ihilani Resort features nightly live en- **NIGHTLIFE** tertainment. The Ihilani is also home to the **Hokulea**, a nightspot that often has live music. Hours vary with season. ~ JW Marriott Ihilani Resort & Spa, 92-1001 Olani Street, Kapolei; 808-679-0079.

NANAKULI BEACH PARK 🏊 🤿 🎣 🛶 This park is so large **BEACHES** that a housing tract divides it into two parts. The main section **& PARKS** features a white-sand beach, *kiawe*-studded camping area and a recreation complex. It's simply a park with everything, unfortunately including weekend crowds. Needless to say, the swimming and snorkeling are good; lifeguard on duty. There are winter breaks with right and left slides. Fishing often rewards with *papio*, *ulua*, *moano* and *menpachi*. Facilities include picnic areas, restrooms, showers, a ball field, a basketball court and a playground. ~ 89-269 Farrington Highway (Route 93) about five miles south of Waianae; 808-668-1137.

▲ Tent and trailer camping are allowed, but a county permit is required.

HAWAIIAN ELECTRIC BEACH PARK 🏊 🤿 🎣 🛶 This once privately owned park, across the highway from a monstrous power plant, is now run by the county. There's a rolling lawn with palm and *kiawe* trees, plus a white-sand beach and coral reef. You can swim, snorkel, surf year-round and fish for *papio*, *ulua*, *moano* and *menpachi*. The drawbacks are the lack of facilities (there are restrooms and a picnic area) and the park's proximity to the electric company. ~ Located on Farrington Highway (Route 93) about seven miles south of Waianae.

▲ Not allowed here; but tent and trailer camping are okay at nearby Kahe Point Beach Park, with a county permit.

MAILI BEACH PARK 🏊 🤿 🎣 🛶 A long winding stretch of white sand is the high point of this otherwise unimpressive facility. The swimming is good in the summer; reef snorkeling is only fair.

Be aware of the reef's steep dropoff. There are winter surf breaks with a right slide. The principal game fish caught here are *papio*, *ulua*, *menpachi* and *moano*. The park contains shade trees and a spotty lawn. There are restrooms and showers. ~ 87-021 Farrington Highway (Route 93) in Maili a few miles south of Waianae.

▲ Not permitted here, but tent camping, with a county permit, is allowed in the summer at nearby **Lualualei Beach Park**.

MAKAHA BEACH PARK Some of the finest surfing in the world takes place right offshore here. This is the site of international competitions, drawing championship surfers from all across the Pacific. For more relaxed sports, there's a white-sand beach to sunbathe on and some good places to skindive. Swimming and snorkeling are both good when the sea is calm; otherwise, exercise extreme caution. Check with a lifeguard about water conditions. Anglers try for *papio*, *ulua*, *moano* and *menpachi*. The precipitous Waianae Mountains loom behind the park. There are picnic tables, restrooms and showers. ~ 84-369 Farrington Highway (Route 93) in Makaha, two miles north of Waianae.

KEAAU BEACH PARK Except for the absence of a sandy beach, this is the prettiest park on the west coast. It's a long, narrow grassy plot spotted with trees and backdropped by the Waianaes. Sunsets are spectacular here, and on a clear day you can see all the way to Kauai. There's a sandy beach just west of the park. Unfortunately, a coral reef rises right to the water's edge, making entry into the water difficult. But once you're in there's great snorkeling, swimming and bodysurfing. In summer there are good surf breaks with a left slide. People fish for *papio*, *ulua*, *moano* and *menpachi*. There are picnic areas, restrooms and showers. ~ Located on Farrington Highway (Route 93) about five miles north of Waianae.

Kaena Point, a great place to spot porpoises, is the legendary home of Nanue the Shark Man.

▲ Tent and trailer allowed. County permit required.

KAENA POINT STATE PARK (YOKOHAMA BAY) This curving stretch of white sand is the last beach along Oahu's northwest coast. With the Waianae Range in the background and coral reefs offshore, it's a particularly lovely spot. Though officially a state park, the area is largely undeveloped. You can walk from Yokohama Bay past miles of tidepools to Oahu's northwest corner at Kaena Point. Keep an eye out for porpoises. Yokohama Bay is a prime region for beach lovers and explorers both. When the sea is calm the swimming is good and the snorkeling is excellent but exercise extreme caution if the surf is up. There are summer breaks up to 15 feet over a shallow reef (left slide). Fish caught in this area include *papio*, *ulua*, *moano* and *menpachi*. Restrooms and showers are the only facilities. ~

Located at the end of the paved section of Farrington Highway (Route 93), about nine miles north of the town of Waianae.

Outdoor Adventures

Along with its traffic and crowds, Oahu has numerous parks. Unfortunately, these disparate elements overlap, and you may sometimes find you've escaped from Honolulu's urban jungle and landed in a swamp of weekend beachgoers. So it's best to plan outdoor adventures far in advance and to schedule them for weekdays if possible.

CAMPING

Camping at **county parks** requires a permit. Tent camping is permitted every night except Wednesday and Thursday; there are no trailer hookups. The free permits can be obtained from the Department of Parks and Recreation. ~ Honolulu Municipal Building, 650 South King Street, Honolulu, HI 96813; 808-523-4525, fax 808-523-4079. They are also available at any of the "satellite city halls" around the island.

State parks allow camping up to five days, depending on the park. It's first-come, first-served on the first day, but after that visitors may reserve spaces. The Division of State Parks issues the permits (which are also issued from island park offices). ~ 1151 Punchbowl Street, Room 130, Honolulu, HI 96813; 808-587-0300, fax 808-587-0311. You can also write in advance for permits.

Remember when planning your trip, rainfall is heaviest on the Windward Coast, a little lighter on the North Shore and lightest of all on the Leeward Coast.

In Honolulu **The Bike Shop** rents backpacks and two-person tents and has for sale a comprehensive line of camping equipment, from clothing and sleeping bags to tents and stoves. ~ 1149 South King Street; 808-596-0588. **McCully Bicycle and Sporting Goods** has a somewhat limited selection of camping equipment. ~ 2124 South King Street; 808-955-6329. For rentals and sales in Central Oahu try **Omar the Tent Man**. Closed Sunday. ~ 94-158 Leole Street, Waipahu; 808-677-8785.

DIVING

One of the great myths about Hawaii is that you need to go far off the beaten track to discover its secret treasures. The fact is that within half an hour of Waikiki are excellent snorkeling and diving opportunities. Only an hour away are excellent reefs easily reached by dive boats. Although the most popular snorkeling locale on the island is **Hanauma Bay,** and most people go there, other possible spots are **Shark Cove** on the North Shore and **Electric Beach** on Kahe Point on the northwest Coast. Or you can snorkel at **Makua Beach**, located between Makaha and Yokohama Bay on the Leeward Coast, and swim with the dolphins. Because conditions vary, I strongly recommend seeking instruction and advice from local diving experts before setting out.

Depending on the season, the **Haleiwa Surf Center** teaches such sports as snorkeling, surfing, swimming, lifesaving, windsurfing and sailing. This county agency is also an excellent source of information on island water sports and facilities. ~ Haleiwa-Alii Beach Park, Haleiwa; 808-637-5051.

In addition, many shops rent and sell diving equipment and offer underwater tours. **Prime Time Sports** rents equipment and offers a beginner's course in diving. ~ Fort DeRussy beachfront, Waikiki; 808-949-8952. **South Seas Aquatics** features dives off a custom 38-foot dive boat. They also sell diving equipment. ~ 2155 Kalakaua Avenue, Suite 112, Honolulu, HI 96815; 808-922-0852.

Hawaii Sea Adventures heads to the west side of Oahu and dives the *Mahi* shipwreck. They feature lessons as well as half- and full-day trips and charters. ~ 98-718 Moanalua Road, Pearl City; 808-487-7515.

Aloha Dive Shop runs day trips for certified divers and lesson packages for students at Maunalua Bay in the southeast corner of the island. ~ Hawaii Kai Shopping Center, Hawaii Kai; 808-395-5922. **Windward Dive Center** offers classes and does a few trips. ~ 789 Kailua Road, Kailua; 808-263-2311. At **Aaron's Dive Shop** you can choose between beach and boat dives, as well as special night trips. Celebrities like Tom Selleck have learned to dive at this five-star PADI facility. They've been in business for 30 years. ~ 602 Kailua Road, Kailua; 808-261-1211, 888-847-2822.

Up in the North Shore town of Haleiwa, check out **Surf N' Sea**. They offer half-day beach and boat dives on the North Shore and Leeward Coast including the *Mahi* shipwreck. ~ 62-595 Kamehameha Highway; 808-637-9887.

When all the fish start to look the same, it's time for something new. **Captain Bruce's Scuba Charters** will take you on excursions to explore World War II shipwrecks and a crashed fighter plane. ~ P.O. Box 240451, Honolulu, HI 96824; 808-373-3590; www.captainbruce.com; as will **Aqua Zone** on the North Shore. ~ Sheraton Waikiki, Waikiki Beach; 808-366-7573; www.aqua zone.net.

STAYING DRY WHILE EXPLORING THE DEPTHS

If you are not interested in Snuba or scuba diving but do want to see what's down under, try one of the two submarine adventures in Waikiki, **Atlantis Submarine** (808-973-9811, 800-548-6262; www.goatlantis.com) or **Voyager** (808-539-9495). You'll descend to 100 feet in air-conditioned hi-tech subs and explore an artificial reef complete with sunken ships and airplanes, created to bring back marine life to the area. It's not cheap though.

Somewhere between snorkeling and scuba diving is Snuba, a relatively new watersport that's catching on in resort areas around the world. You don't need certification, and it's quite safe.

SNUBA

Snuba was created for those who would like to take snorkeling a step further but may not be quite ready for scuba diving. It's a shallow-water dive system that allows underwater breathing. Basically this is how it works. Swimmers wear a breathing device (the same one used in scuba diving) that is connected to a built-in scuba tank that floats on a raft. They also wear a weight belt, mask and fins. The air comes through a 20-foot tube connected to the raft, which follows the swimmer. Groups of six participants are taken out with a guide. They can dive up to 20 feet.

Snuba of Oahu offers Snuba tours at Hanauma Bay, Maunalua Bay and Koolina. The Koolina trip leaves from JW Marriott Ihilani Resort & Spa and involves a two-and-a-half-hour sail out to sea; lunch is included. Common sightings include an array of fish, eels, dolphins and turtles. The company will pick you up in Waikiki or you can meet the group at the Snuba site. ~ Koko Marina Shopping Center, 7192 Kalanianaole Highway, Hawaii Kai; 808-396-6163.

Snowboarders with the summertime blues gave rise to the newest craze in water sports: wakeboarding. If the thrill of waterskiing is a little *too* thrilling, wakeboarding may be the sport to try. A relatively easy-to-control board is pulled slowly (well, 20–35 mph) behind a boat, while the rider skims the wake. The equipment is much easier to maneuver than waterskis, and when your skills are up to par, you can venture into the fancy stuff: jumps, backrolls, zip-zags.

WAKE-BOARDING & WATER-SKIING

Waterskiing is more physically demanding than wakeboarding, using every muscle in your body, requiring a higher speed and employing narrower, less agile skis.

If you plan to attempt either of these activities for the first time, it's a good idea to take a few lessons. **Hawaii Sports** provides all the equipment you need for their classes in both wakeboarding and waterskiing. ~ Koko Marina Shopping Center, 7192 Kalanianaole Highway; 808-395-3773.

Surfing, a sport pioneered centuries ago by Hawaiian royalty, is synonymous with Oahu. Stars bring their boards from all over the world to join international competitions that take advantage of ideal surf and wind conditions. From the 30-foot winter rollers on the North Shore to beginner lessons off Waikiki, this is beach boy and girl territory. Windsurfing is equally popular in areas like Kailua Bay and along the North Shore.

SURFING & WIND-SURFING

WAIKIKI For everything "on the water, in the water and under the water" see **Prime Time Sports Beach Rentals** on Kalia Road near Fort DeRussy Beach. They offer beach accessories, equipment sales and rentals, lessons and plenty of friendly advice.

Private and group surfing lessons have a "stand and surf" guarantee. ~ 808-949-8952. At the **Aloha Beach Service** you can take lessons and rent a long board. ~ In front of the Sheraton Moana Surfrider Hotel; 808-922-3111.

Koa Board Sports is a friendly place to rent equipment or take lessons. And if you decide to buy a board, they'll gladly ship it home for you. ~ 2420 Koa Avenue; 808-923-0189.

> A good way to catch marlin, mahimahi, ahi and *ono* is to head out 20 to 30 miles off the Leeward Coast. There are also prime fishing grounds off the south coast of Oahu.

DOWNTOWN HONOLULU   A number of stores located in different parts of the island also rent boards and sails. Near downtown go to **Local Motion** for surf board rentals. Check out their variety of beachwear, boards, and equipment for sale. ~ 1958 Kalakaua Avenue, Honolulu; 808-979-7873.

GREATER HONOLULU   Surfers in the Diamond Head area can rent boards at **Downing Hawaii**. Closed Sunday. ~ 3021 Waialae Avenue, Honolulu; 808-737-9696.

WINDWARD COAST   **Kailua Sailboard and Kayak Company** will teach you the tricks of the trade or help you brush up on your technique. You can also rent sailboards, boogieboards, long boards and snorkeling equipment here. ~ 130 Kailua Road; 808-262-2555. In the same area, **Naish Hawaii** offers windsurfing lessons and rentals. This company manufactures its own boards and also operates a shop filled with the latest in sailboarding apparel and accessories as well as long boards. ~ 155-A Hamakua Drive; 808-261-6067.

NORTH SHORE   A resource for both the participatory and spectator aspects of surfing and windsurfing is the **Haleiwa Surf Center**. Surf lessons normally run September through early May and windsurfing is taught from May through early September. ~ Haleiwa-Alii Beach Park, Haleiwa; 808-637-5051. In the same area surfing lessons and rentals are also available from **Surf N' Sea**; lessons last from two to three hours and the price includes all gear. ~ 62-595 Kamehameha Highway, Haleiwa; 808-637-9887.

FISHING   From deep sea-fishing to trolling for freshwater bass, Oahu offers challenges to suit any angler. You can try game fishing out in the Pacific, head down to the beach for surf casting or try one of the island's popular lakes.

Most of the island's fishing fleet dock at **Kewalo Basin** (Fisherman's Wharf) on Ala Moana Drive between Waikiki and downtown Honolulu.

Kono Fish and Charters goes out for big-game fishing such as blue marlin, yellow fin tuna and mahimahi. Reservations are required, all equipment provided. ~ 141 Kaai Street, Honolulu; 808-593-8472. Or consider **Sport Fishing**, which runs the *Pacific Blue* and *Ilima* out of Kewalo Basin. Equipment provided. ~ 808-596-2087.

For freshwater angling head up into the Koolau Mountains to fish the **Nuuanu Reservoir** (open to the public by lottery). Another possibility is the **Wahiawa Public Fishing Area**, also known as Lake Wilson. Both of these reservoirs are good places to catch Chinese catfish. Call the Division of Aquatic Resources, Department of Land & Resources at 808-587-0100 for information on permits and seasons.

SAILING

One of the best ways to enjoy Oahu is aboard a sailboat. From brief cruises off Honolulu to a day-long charter along the North Shore, this is the perfect antidote to the tourist crowds. It's also surprisingly affordable.

Above Heaven's Gate operates charter group cruises to the Diamond Head reef area aboard a 56-foot teakwood pirate ship. Reverend/Captain Howie also performs weddings and vow renewals at sea and in exotic locations on land (including the Pukalani Falls). You can also take a guided Hobie-cat tour off the Windward Coast to undiscovered islands most tourists miss (by appointment only). Along the way you'll enjoy Waimanalo, Lanikai and Kailua Bay. You can also learn how to sail this swift 16-foot craft. ~ 41-1010 Laumilo Street, Waimanalo Bay; 808-259-5429, 800-800-2933, fax 888-463-6933, www.hawaiiweddings.com, e-mail howie@hawaiiweddings.com.

If you're eager to charter your own yacht, contact **The Yacht Connection**. The company charters all sizes of vessels ranging from fishing boats to luxury yachts. ~ 1750 Kalakaua Avenue, Suite 3138, Honolulu; 808-523-1383; www.hawaiiyachts.com.

KAYAKING

A sport well suited for Oahu, kayaking is an ideal way to explore the island's protected bays, islands and inland rivers. It seems that kayakers are popping up everywhere, particularly around the southeast coast of the island and up the Waimea River. To rent or purchase kayaks and equipment, or to sign up for lessons, consider **Go Bananas** just outside Waikiki. ~ 799 Kapahulu Avenue; 808-737-9514. For kayak rentals and lessons, contact **Kailua Sailboard and Kayak Company**. ~ 130 Kailua Road, Kailua; 808-262-2555.

If you'd like to go on a group kayak expedition, sign on with **Kayak Oahu Adventures** for one of its one- to one-and-a-half-hour Diamond Head paddling tours or two-hour snorkeling trips. You may want to try whitewater kayaking—it's kind of like surfing but in a kayak. The company also runs trips up the Waimea River on the North Shore. ~ New Otani Kaimana Beach Hotel,

2863 Kalakaua Avenue, Waikiki, 923-0539; 59-864 Kamehameha Highway, Haleiwa, 808-638-8189.

Twogood Kayaks Hawaii has an interesting option: they'll deliver your kayaks right to the beach, give you a lesson, then send you on your way to a "desert isle," where you can spend the day napping, exploring, fishing, swimming or snorkeling. They also offer guided day trips, if you'd prefer an expert along. ~ 345 Hahani Strett, Kailua; 808-262-5656; www.aloha.com/~twogood/rental.html.

RIDING STABLES

Located on the Windward Coast across from Chinaman's Hat, **Kualoa Activity Club and Secret Island** leads one- and one-and-a-half-hour weekend rides in Kaaawa Valley. They also offer many other activities including a trip to Secret Island and snorkeling tours. Don't forget your swimsuit. ~ 49-560 Kamehameha Highway, Kaaawa; 808-237-8515.

The **Turtle Bay Hilton** on the North Shore has riding programs for the general public. They offer 45-minute guided tours for beginning riders, as well as 30-minute rides for advanced equestrians. These, and a one-and-one-half-hour evening ride, all take place on the grounds of the hotel, with trails along the beach and through a lovely wooded area. ~ 57-091 Kamehameha Highway; 808-293-8811.

Happy Trails Ranch on the North Shore conducts one- to two-hour trail rides through a rainforest valley and pastureland. Riders stop at tropical orchards to sample whatever fruit is in season. The ranch also has peacocks, showbird chickens and six species of ducks. Children will love this place, and they can ride if they are six years or older. ~ P.O. Box 461, Kahuku, HI 96731; 808-638-7433.

GOLF

Oahu offers duffers numerous choices to tee off from. The weather is beautiful and the courses, planted with palm trees and tropical foliage, make for ideal settings.

DOWNTOWN HONOLULU For a round of golf in Honolulu, try the **Ala Wai Golf Course**, Hawaii's first municipal course. ~ 404 Kapahulu Avenue; 808-733-7387.

GREATER HONOLULU Hawaii Kai Golf Course is a popular spot with both tourists and *kamaainas*. It features two 18-hole courses, one for beginners and one championship. ~ 8902 Kalanianaole Highway; 808-395-2358.

SOUTHEAST OAHU The lush **Olomana Golf Park** has an 18-hole course. ~ 41-1801 Kalanianaole Highway, Waimanalo; 808-259-7926.

WINDWARD COAST For a cheap round of golf visit the **Bay View Golf Park**. ~ 45-285 Kaneohe Bay Drive, Kaneohe; 808-

247-0451. Located below the Nuuanu Pali Lookout, the **Pali Golf Course** affords sweeping views of the rugged Koolaus and the windward coastline. ~ 45-050 Kamehameha Highway, Kaneohe; 808-266-7612. If you want to play a casual game, try the nine-hole **Kahuku Golf Course**. ~ Kahuku; 808-293-5842.

NORTH SHORE On the North Shore, two courses—an 18-hole and a 9-hole course that can be played twice—are open to the public at the **Hilton Turtle Bay Golf and Tennis Resort**. ~ Kahuku; 808-293-8811. The 18-hole course was designed by golf professional Arnold Palmer.

CENTRAL OAHU Set amid fields of sugarcane and pineapple along the Leilehua Plateau in the center of Oahu, the **Hawaii Country Club** is a bit run-down, but offers some challenging holes on an 18-hole, par-72 course. ~ 94-1211 Kunia Road, Wahiawa; 808-622-1744. The **Mililani Golf Club**, though not particularly demanding, provides lovely views of the Koolau and Waianae ranges. ~ 95-176 Kuahelani Avenue, Mililani; 808-623-2254. The flat **Ted Makalena Golf Course** is not well maintained, but is still popular with local golfers. ~ 93-059 Waipio Point Access Road, Waipahu; 808-675-6052.

LEEWARD COAST Out toward the Leeward Coast, a series of lakes, brooks and waterfalls meanders through the 18 holes at **Koolina Golf Club**. ~ 92-1220 Aliinui Drive, Kapolei; 808-676-5309. Bounded by the Waianae Range, the beautiful **Makaha Resort Golf Club** is among Oahu's foremost courses. ~ 84-626 Makaha Valley Road, Makaha; 808-695-9544, 808-695-9511.

Many of Oahu resorts offer complete tennis facilities. But don't despair if your hotel lacks nets. There are dozens of public tennis courts located around the island. Following is a partial listing.

TENNIS

In the Waikiki area, try **Kapiolani Park**. ~ Kalakaua Avenue. **Diamond Head Tennis Center** is another option in the area. ~ Paki Avenue. There are courts across from Ala Moana Center at **Ala Moana Tennis Center**. ~ Ala Moana Regional Park, Ala Moana Boulevard.

SAILS IN THE SUNSET

Ever dream of sailing off into the sunset, wind blowing in your hair? Snorkeling trips, swimming in the ocean off Diamond Head, a sunset cruise or a whale-watching venture can all be arranged with **Honolulu Sailing Company**. You can even get married at sea by your licensed and uniformed captain. This personable outfit will sail to meet your needs. ~ 47-335 Lulani Street, Honolulu; 808-239-3900, fax 800-829-0114; www.honsail.com.

In Greater Honolulu you can serve and volley at **Keehi Lagoon**. ~ Off the Nimitz Highway, Honolulu. Or opt for a set in the lush Manoa Valley at **Manoa Valley District Park**. ~ 2721 Kaaipu Avenue, Manoa.

For your tennis needs on the Windward Coast, try **Kailua District Park**. ~ 21 South Kainalu Drive, Kailua. Or visit **Kaneohe District Park**. ~ 45-660 Keaahala Road, Kaneohe.

Sunset Beach Neighborhood Park, with two lighted courts, is an option on the North Shore. ~ 59-360 Kamehameha Highway, Haleiwa.

Lighted courts are also available at **Waianae District Park** on the Leeward Coast. ~ 85-601 Farrington Highway, Waianae.

Call the County Department of Parks and Recreation for more information on public courts. ~ 808-971-7150. The Hawaii Visitors & Convention Bureau has information on private courts. ~ 808-923-1811.

BIKING

Oahu is blessed with excellent roads, well-paved and usually flat, and cursed with heavy traffic. About three-quarters of Hawaii's population lives here, and it sometimes seems like every person owns a car.

Honolulu can be a cyclist's nightmare, but outside the city the traffic is somewhat lighter. And Oahu drivers, accustomed to tourists driving mopeds, are relatively conscious of bicyclists.

Keep in mind that the Windward Coast is the wet side, the North Shore is slightly drier and the south and west coasts are the driest of all. And remember, rip-offs are a frequent fact of life on Oahu. Leaving your bike unlocked is asking for a long walk back. (Trails are one way unless otherwise noted.)

Peacock Flats—an ironic name for this one—is an advanced trail. Beginning at Mokuleia Beach Park and continuing in a 13-mile loop, it provides gorgeous views and an initial three miles of pavement.

For easier riding try the **Maunawili Trail** (11 miles) on the Windward side of the island. You'll be sharing the trail with hikers, so keep an eye out.

If you're seeking technical riding, try the **Manana Trail** (7 miles), beginning on the top of Pacific Palisades in Central Oahu—known to be hilly and rutty.

ON WHEELS

If you'd like a little two-wheeled company, check out the **Hawaii Bicycling League**, which regularly sponsors weekend bike rides and free annual events. ~ P. O. Box 4403, Honolulu, HI 96812; phone/fax 808-735-5756; e-mail bicycle@pixi.com.

Bike Rentals   In Waikiki, **Coconut Cruisers** rents beach cruisers and mountain bikes. ~ 2301 Kalakaua Avenue; 808-924-1644. Also in Waikiki, **Adventure Rentals** rents mountain bikes from two locations. ~ 1946 Ala Moana Boulevard, 808-944-3131; and at 2002 Kalakaua Avenue, 808-941-2222. **Blue Sky Rentals** has mountain, road and tandem bikes. ~ 1920 Ala Moana Boulevard; 808-947-0101.

Bike Repairs   In addition to doing repair work, **Eki Cyclery** has sold accessories and mountain bikes for more than 80 years. ~ 1603 Dillingham Boulevard, Honolulu; 808-847-2005. With mountain, road and triathlon bikes for sale, **The Bike Shop** also does repair work. ~ 1149 South King Street, Honolulu; 808-596-0588.

There are numerous hiking trails within easy driving distance of Honolulu. I have listed these as well as trails in the Windward Coast and North Shore areas. Unfortunately, many Oahu treks require special permission from the state, the armed services or private owners. But the hikes suggested here, none of which require official sanction, should provide ample adventure.   **HIKING**

To hike with a group or to obtain further information on hiking Oahu, contact the **Sierra Club**. ~ P.O. Box 2577, Honolulu, HI 96803; 808-538-6616; www.hi.sierraclub.org. Another agency that also has regular weekend hikes is the **Hawaiian Trail and Mountain Club**. Check their web page—some hikes are for members only. ~ P.O. Box 2238, Honolulu, HI 96804; www.geocities.com/yosemite/trails/3660. The **Hawaii Nature Center** offers guided hikes two or three times a month. Call ahead to make a reservation. You can also get free maps and general trail information. ~ 2131 Makiki Heights Drive; 808-955-0100.

All distances listed for hiking trails are one way unless otherwise noted.

GREATER HONOLULU   If you're staying in Waikiki, the most easily accessible hike is the short jaunt up **Diamond Head** crater. There's a sweeping view of Honolulu from atop this famous landmark. The trail begins inside the crater, so take Diamond Head Road around to the inland side of Diamond Head, then follow the tunnel leading into the crater.

At the Ko Olau Summit above Diamond Head there is a trail that climbs almost 2000 feet and affords excellent panoramas of the Windward Coast. To get to the **Lanipo Trail** (3.5 miles), take Waialae Avenue off of Route H-1. Then turn up Wilhelmina Rise and follow until it reaches Maunalani Circle and the trailhead.

For spectacular vistas overlooking the lush Palolo and Manoa valleys, you can hike **Waahila Ridge Trail** (2.5 miles). To get there, start at Waahila Ridge State Recreation Area, take St. Louis Heights Drive (near the University of Hawaii campus) and then follow connecting roads up to Manao Valley Features.

The following trails can be combined for longer hikes. **Manoa Falls Trail** (1 mile) goes through Manoa Valley. This is a pleasant jaunt that follows Manoa Stream through a densely vegetated area to a charming waterfall. **Manoa Cliffs Trail** (3.4 miles) a pleasant family hike, follows a precipice along the west side of Manoa Valley. And **Puu Ohia Trail** (.75 mile), which crosses Manoa Cliffs Trail, provides splendid views of the Manoa and Nuuanu valleys. Both trails begin from Tantalus Drive in the hills above Honolulu. **Makiki Loop Trail** (3 miles roundtrip) begins near Tantalus Drive. Composed of three interlinking trails, this loop passes stands of eucalyptus and bamboo trees and offers some postcard views of Honolulu. Another loop trail, **Judd Memorial** (.75 mile), crosses Nuuanu Stream and traverses bamboo, eucalyptus and Norfolk pine groves en route to the Jackass Ginger Pool. To get there, take the Pali Highway (Route 61) several miles north from Honolulu. Turn onto Nuuanu Pali Drive and follow it about a mile to Reservoir Number Two spillway.

You can access a two-mile-long portion of the **Old Pali Road** directly to the right of the Pali Lookout. The narrow paved roadway provides easy hikes that are perfect for family excursions and reward with sweeping panoramas of the Windward Coast. For those with a more strenuous hike in mind, the **Koolaupoko Trail** (10 miles) departs from the Pali Lookout parking lot for magnificent rainforest, valley and ocean views. In places the trail is quite steep and occasionally demanding.

Another hike located in this general area, along **Waimano Trail** (7 miles), climbs 1600 feet to an astonishing vista point above Oahu's Windward Coast. There are swimming holes en route to the vista point. To get there, take Kamehameha Highway (Route 90) west to Waimano Home Road (Route 730). Turn right and go two-and-a-half miles to a point along the road where you'll see a building on the right and an irrigation ditch on the left. The trail follows the ditch.

SOUTHEAST OAHU   There are several excellent hikes along this shore. The first few are within ten miles of Waikiki, near **Hanauma Bay**. From the beach at Hanauma you can hike two miles along the coast and cliffs to the Halona Blowhole. This trek passes the Toilet Bowl, a unique tidepool with a hole in the bottom that causes it to fill and then flush with the wave action. Waves sometimes wash the rocks along this path, so be prepared to get wet (and be careful!).

At the intersection where the short road leading down toward Hanauma Bay branches from Kalanianaole Highway (Route 72), there are two other trails. **Koko Head Trail**, a one-mile hike to the top of a volcanic cone, starts on the ocean side of the highway. This trek features some startling views of Hanauma Bay, Diamond Head and the Koolau Range. Another one-mile hike, along **Koko Crater Trail,** leads from the highway up to a 1000-foot peak. The views from this crow's nest are equally spectacular.

WINDWARD COAST There are several other particularly pretty hikes much farther north, near the village of Hauula. **Sacred Falls Trail** (2.2 miles) gently ascends through a canyon and arrives at a waterfall and swimming hole. The trail and immediately surrounding area constitutes Sacred Falls State Park. The trailhead for this popular trek is near Kamehameha Highway (Route 83) just south of Hauula. At press time the trail was closed due to a rock slide that had killed several hikers at the trail's end. Check with State Parks for current status of the trail at 808-587-0300.

Then, in Hauula, if you turn off of Kamehameha Highway and head inland for about a quarter-mile up Hauula Homestead Road, you'll come to Maakua Road. Walk up Maakua Road, which leads into the woods. About 300 yards after entering the woods, the road forks. Maakua Gulch Trail branches to the left. If you continue straight ahead you'll be on Hauula Trail, but if you veer left onto Maakua Gulch Trail, you'll encounter yet another trail branching off to the left in about 150 yards. This is Papali Trail (also known as Maakua Trail).

Maakua Gulch Trail (3 miles), en route to a small waterfall, traverses a rugged canyon with extremely steep walls. Part of the trail lies along the stream bed, so be ready to get wet. **Hauula Trail** (2 miles) ascends along two ridges and provides fine vistas of the Koolau Range and the Windward Coast. **Papali Trail** (2 miles) drops into Papali Gulch, then climbs high along a ridge from which you can view the surrounding countryside.

NORTH SHORE AND LEEWARD COAST In the mountains above Pearl Harbor, at Keaiwa Heiau State Park, is the **Aiea Loop Trail** (2.5 miles). Set in a heavily forested area, this hike passes the wreckage of a World War II cargo plane. It provides an excellent chance to see some of the native Hawaiian trees—*lehua*, *ohia* and *koa*—used by local woodworkers. (For directions to Keaiwa Heiau State Park, see the "Leeward Coast" section in this chapter.)

In ancient times, Kaena Point was sacred land; it was believed the souls of the dead departed from Kaena to the afterworld, called *milu*.

You can approach the trail to **Kaena Point** either from the North Shore or the Leeward Coast. It's a dry, rock-strewn path that leads to Oahu's westernmost tip. There are tidepools and swimming spots en route, plus spectacular views of a rugged, uninhabited coastline. If you're lucky you may sight nesting albatross or rare Hawaiian Monk seals. Keep your distance as both are protected species and a portion of the point is a wildlife preserve. To get to the trailhead, drive to the end of the paved portion of Route 930 on the North Shore or Route 93 on the Leeward Coast. Then follow the trail out to Kaena Point. It's about two miles via the Leeward Coast, and a half-mile via the North Shore.

▼▼▼▼▼▼▼▼▼▼▼
Transportation

AIR

There's one airport on Oahu and it's a behemoth. **Honolulu International Airport** is a Pacific crossroads, an essential link between North America and Asia. Most visitors arriving from the mainland land here first, and find it a convenient jumping-off point for venturing farther to the various neighbor islands. (See Chapter One for airline information.) Aloha Airlines and Hawaiian Airlines provide regular jet service to the outer islands, while smaller outfits like Aloha Island Air and Mahalo Air fly prop planes.

Honolulu International includes all the comforts of a major airport. You can check your bags or rent a locker; fuel up at a restaurant, coffee shop or cocktail lounge; shop at several stores; or shower.

To cover the eight or so miles into Waikiki, it's possible to hire a cab for $20 to $25, plus a small charge for each bag. For $8 (roundtrip $13), **Trans-Hawaiian Services** will take you to your Waikiki hotel or condominium. ~ 808-566-7333, 800-533-8765. And city bus #19 or #20 travels through Downtown Honolulu and Waikiki. This is the cheapest transportation, but you're only allowed to carry on baggage that fits on your lap. So, unless you're traveling very light, you'll have to use another conveyance.

CAR RENTALS

Of all the islands, Oahu offers the most rental agencies. At the airport, **Avis Rent A Car** (808-834-5536, 800-321-3712), **Budget Rent A Car** (808-838-1111, 800-527-0700), **Dollar Rent A Car** (808-831-2330, 800-800-4000), **National Car Rental** (808-831-3800, 800-227-7368) and **Hertz** (808-831-3500, 800-654-3011) all have booths. Their convenient location helps to save time while minimizing the problem of picking up your car.

Though not at the airport, **Alamo Rent A Car** (808-833-4585, 800-327-9633) provides airport pick-up service, often at a lower rate.

◆◆

BEFORE TAKEOFF

If you have spare time, stop by the **Pacific Aerospace Museum**, a technology exhibition devoted to aviation and the islands. In one exhibit a six-inch-tall "holovision" pilot guides you around a 1930s-era prop plane, explaining how it flies. Or you can design your own plane, using a computer-assisted design monitor. Then take the flight simulator controls and "land" a plane at Honolulu International. There are also three theaters that recapture the dramatic history of aviation. ~ Honolulu International Airport, second floor; 808-839-0777, fax 808-836-3267; e-mail pacaero@lava.net.

There are many other Honolulu-based companies offering very low rates but providing limited pick-up service at the airport. I've never found the inconvenience worth the savings. There you are—newly arrived from the mainland, uncertain about your environment, anxious to check in at the hotel—and you're immediately confronted with the Catch-22 of getting to your car. Do you rent a vehicle in which to pick up your rental car? Take a bus? Hitchhike? What do you do with your bags meanwhile?

If your budget is important, consider **VIP Rentals**, a cheaper but less convenient outfit. ~ 234 Beachwalk; 808-922-4605.

If you prefer to go in high style, book a limousine from **Cloud Nine**. ~ 808-524-7999, 800-524-7999.

Adventure Rentals (808-944-3131) and **Dollar Rent A Car** (808-831-2331) provide jeeps. **VIP Car Rental** (808-922-4605) rents Suzuki Samurais.

JEEP RENTALS

In Waikiki, **Adventure Rentals** rents mopeds and motorcycles. ~ 1946 Ala Moana Boulevard; 808-944-3131. You can also try **Blue Sky Rentals**, located on the ground floor of the Inn On The Park Hotel. ~ 1920 Ala Moana Boulevard; 808-947-0101. In addition to mopeds, **Diamond Head Mopeds and Motorcycles** rents Harley Davidson motorcycles. ~ 408 Lewers Street; 808-921-2899.

MOPED RENTALS

Oahu has an excellent bus system that runs regularly to points all over the island and provides convenient service throughout Honolulu. Many of the beaches, hotels, restaurants and points of interest mentioned in this chapter are just a bus ride away. It's even possible to pop your money in the fare box and ride around the entire island.

PUBLIC TRANSIT

TheBus carries more than 260,000 people daily, loading them into 525 buses that rumble along city streets and country roads from 5 a.m. until 10 p.m. (though some lines run past midnight). There are also express buses traveling major highways at commuter times. Most buses are handicapped accessible and many have bike racks.

If you stay in Waikiki you'll inevitably be sardined into a #19 or #20 bus for the ride through Honolulu's tourist mecca. Many bus drivers are Hawaiian; I saw some hysterical scenes on this line when tourists waited anxiously for their stop to be called, only to realize they couldn't understand the driver's pidgin. Hysterical, that is, after those early days when *I* was the visitor with the furrowed brow.

But you're surely more interested in meeting local people than tourists, and you can easily do it on any of the buses outside Waikiki. They're less crowded and a lot more fun for people-watching.

For information on bus routes call **TheBus** at 808-848-5555; www.thebus.org. And remember, the only carry-on luggage permitted is baggage small enough to fit on your lap or under your seat.

WALKING TOURS

What better way to stroll through the past than with a company called **Honolulu TimeWalks**. Based in Honolulu and featuring master storyteller Glen Grant, they offer a number of walking tours. One of the most popular visits the haunted places (including Iolani Palace!) of Honolulu; another features the history of Moili-ili, a historic neighborhood. Fee. ~ 808-943-0371, fax 808-951-8878; e-mail timewalk@pixi.com.

The best way to visit Chinatown is on the Tuesday walking tour sponsored by the **Chinese Chamber of Commerce**. The tour will carry you past temples, specialty stores and other intriguing spots around this diverse neighborhood. Meet at the Chamber office by 9:30 a.m. Fee. ~ 42 North King Street; 808-533-3181, fax 808-533-6967.

Oahu Nature Tours offers four different eco-tours that provide an overview of native Hawaiian birds and plants. One focuses on Oahu's volcanic coast, beginning in Diamond Head Crater, continuing through a lagoon wildlife sanctuary, then heading out to the island's southeast corner. Another tour takes you into the Hawaiian rainforest at 2000-feet elevation in the Koolau Mountains. Equipment, transportation and water are provided. Fee. ~ P.O. Box 8059, Honolulu, HI 96830; 800-924-2473; www.oahu naturetours.com, e-mail waltherc001@hawaii.rr.com.

AERIAL TOURS

The quickest way to see all Oahu has to offer is by taking to the air. In minutes you can experience the island's hidden waterfalls, secluded beaches and volcanic landmarks. Tranquil gliders and hovering whirlybirds all fly low and slow to make sure you see what you missed on the trip over from the mainland. You can also take extended flights that include the outer islands.

Rainbow Pacific Helicopters Ltd. offers helicopter tours of Waikiki and Honolulu, Hanauma Bay, the Koolau Mountains, Chinaman's Hat, Sacred Falls, Kahana Rainforest and the North Shore. Outerisland tours are also available. They also take trips to the "Jurassic Park Valley," an area where parts of the movie were filmed. Every passenger is guaranteed a window seat. Call for reservations. ~ 110 Kapalulu Place, Honolulu; 808-834-1111, 800-289-6412, fax 808-833-7406; www.rainbowhelicopters.com.

To enjoy a one- or two-passenger glider trip, head out to **The Original Glider Ride** and talk to Mr. Bill. On your 20-minute trip you're likely to see fields of sugar cane, marine mammals, surfers working the North Shore and neighboring Kauai. You'll also enjoy peace and quiet while working your way down from 3000 feet.

A videotape of the ride and your reactions makes a memorable souvenir. ~ Dillingham Airfield, Mokuleia; 808-677-3404; www. honolulusoaring.com, e-mail mrbill@poi.net.

The open cockpit and optional aerobatics of a **Stearman Biplane ride** may not be relaxing, but the unobstructed view is breathtaking. ~ Stearman Biplane Rides, P.O. Box 936, Waialua, HI 96791; 808-637-4461; www.honolulusoaring.com/bi-plane. **Island Seaplane Service** re-creates the glamour of Pan Am's "flying boats" with 30- and 60-minute narrated tours. The longer trip combines the natural vistas of the first with cultural sights such as Pearl Harbor. ~ 85 Lagoon Drive, Honolulu; 808-836-6273.

Hawaii

The Big Island, they call it, and even that is an understatement. Hawaii, all 4030 square miles, is almost twice as large as all the other Hawaiian islands combined. Its twin volcanic peaks, Mauna Kea and Mauna Loa, dwarf most mountains. Mauna Kea, rising 13,796 feet, is the largest island-based mountain in the world. Mauna Loa, the world's largest active volcano, which last erupted in 1950, looms 13,677 feet above sea level. This is actually 32,000 feet from the ocean floor, making it, by one system of reckoning, the tallest mountain on earth, grander even than Everest. And in bulk it is the world's largest. The entire Sierra Nevada chain could fit within this single peak.

Kilauea, a third volcano whose seething firepit has been erupting with startling frequency, is one of the world's most active craters. Since its most recent series of eruptions began in 1983, the volcano has swallowed almost 200 houses. In 1990 it completely destroyed the town of Kalapana, burying a once lively village beneath tons of black lava; then in 1992 it destroyed the ancient Hawaiian village of Kamoamoa. There is little doubt that the Big Island is a place of geologic superlatives.

But size alone does not convey the Big Island's greatness. Its industry, too, is expansive. Despite the lava wasteland that covers large parts of its surface, and the volcanic gases that create a layer of "vog" during volcanic eruptions, the Big Island is the state's greatest producer of coffee, papayas, vegetables, anthuriums, macadamia nuts and cattle. Its orchid industry, based in rain-drenched Hilo, is the world's largest. Over 22,000 varieties grow in the nurseries here.

Across the island in sun-soaked Kona, one of the nation's only coffee industries operates. Just off this spectacular western coast lie some of the finest deep-sea fishing grounds in the world. Between Hilo and Kona, and surrounding Waimea, sits the Parker Ranch. Sprawling across 225,000 acres, it is one of the world's largest independently owned cattle ranches.

Yet many of these measurements are taken against island standards. Compared to the mainland, the Big Island is a tiny speck in the sea. Across its broad est reach it measures a scant 93 miles long and 76 miles wide, smaller than Connecticut. The road around the island totals only 300 miles, and can be driven in a day, though I'd recommend taking at least five. The island's 142,000 population comprises just 8 percent of the state's citizens. Its lone city, Hilo, has a population of only 42,133.

Rain or shine, you can get the weather report for the entire island at 808-961-5582, or just for Hilo at 808-935-8555.

But large or small, numbers cannot fully describe the Big Island, for there is a magic about the place that transcends statistics. Hawaii, also nicknamed the Orchid Island and Volcano Island, is the home of Pele, the goddess of volcanoes. Perhaps her fiery spirit is what infuses the Big Island with an unquantifiable quality. Or maybe the island's comparative youth is what makes the elements seem nearer, more alluring and strangely threatening here. It's still growing in size because of lava flows from Kilauea and Mauna Loa. In fact, recent activity has added nearly a square mile to the island. The Big Island is geologically the youngest spot on earth, one million years old. Whatever it might be, the Big Island has always been where I feel closest to the Polynesian spirit. Of all the Hawaiian islands, this one I love the most.

It was here, possibly as early as 400 A.D., that Polynesian explorers may have first landed when they discovered the island chain. Until the advent of the white man, it was generally the most important island, supporting a large population and occupying a vital place in Hawaii's rich mythology. Little wonder then that Kamehameha the Great, the chief who would become Hawaii's first king, was born here in 1753. He established the archipelago's first capital in Kailua and ruled there until his death in 1819.

Within a year of the great leader's passing, two events occurred in Kailua that jolted the entire chain far more than any earthquake. First the king's heir, Liholiho, uprooted the centuries-old taboo system upon which the native Hawaiian religion rested. Then, in the spring of 1820, the first American missionaries dropped anchor off the coast of Kailua-Kona. It was also near here that Captain James Cook, history's greatest discoverer, was slain in 1779 by the same people who had earlier welcomed him as a god. Across the island another deity, Pele, was defied in 1824 when the high chieftess Kapiolani, a Christian, ate *kapu* (forbidden) fruit on the rim of an active lava lake at Kilauea, and suffered no ill consequence.

As stirring as the Big Island's story might be, much of its drama still awaits the visitor. For the land—the volcanoes, beaches and valleys—is as vital and intriguing today as in the days of demigods and kings. This is a place for the adventurer to spend a lifetime.

On the east coast, buffeted by trade winds, lies Hilo, a lush tropical town that soaks up 140 inches of rain annually. Here anthuriums and orchids are cultivated in a number of spectacular nurseries. Just to the south—smoking, heaving and sometimes erupting—sits Hawaii Volcanoes National Park.

The Puna District that straddles the coast between the volcanoes and Hilo has been the site of dramatic eruptions during the past decade. This lush rainforest is also the scene of a major political debate that has pitted environmentalists against developers of a geothermal power plant.

In the north, from the Hamakua Coast to the Kohala Peninsula, heavy erosion has cut through the volcano to form spectacular canyons such as the Waipio Valley. All along the Hamakua plateau, sugar plantations, fed by waters from Mauna Kea, stretch from the mountains to the surf.

In startling contrast to these verdant mountains is the desert-like Kau district at the southern tip of the island (and, for that matter, the southernmost point in the United States). Along the west coast stretches the Kona district, a vacationer's paradise. Suntan weather, sandy beaches and coral reefs teeming with tropical fish make this an ideal area to just kick back and enjoy. The island's central tourist area is located here in Kailua-Kona, where Hawaiian royalty settled in the 19th century.

And for something unique to the Big Island, there's Waimea with its rolling grasslands, range animals and *paniolos*, or Hawaiian-style cowboys. In fact, one of the biggest Hereford cattle herds is located here in the center of the island.

It's an island I don't think you should miss, an island that's beginning to change rapidly with the creation of a string of resorts along the Kohala coast, but one that still retains its original charm. To geologists the Big Island is a natural laboratory in which the mysteries of volcanic activity are a fact of everyday life; to many Hawaiians it is the most sacred of all the islands. To everyone who visits it, Hawaii is a place of startling contrasts and unspeakable beauty, an alluring and exotic tropical island.

Hilo

There's one thing you'll rarely miss in this tropical city—rain. Hilo gets about 140 inches a year. The Chamber of Commerce will claim it rains mostly at night, but don't be deceived. It's almost as likely to be dark and wet at midday. There is a good side to all this bothersome moisture—it transforms Hilo into an exotic city crowded with tropical foliage, the orchid capital of the United States.

Hilo is the closest you will approach in all Hawaii to a Somerset Maugham–style South Seas port town. With its turn-of-the-20th-century stores, many badly needing a paint job, and old Chinese shops, it's a throwback to an era when tourists were few and Hawaii was a territory. Sections of town, especially around Waianuenue Avenue, have been refurbished and dabbed with 1990s flash, but much of the downtown is still a collection of ethnic eateries, swap shops and Japanese groceries. The gutters are rusty, the rain awnings have sagged, and an enduring sense of character overhangs the place with the certainty and finality of the next downpour.

SIGHTS   Hilo is a tropical wonderland, a rainforest with hotels, shops and great places to visit. A visit to one of the city's many flower nurseries is an absolute must. These gardens grow orchids, anthuriums and countless other flowers. There are two that I highly recommend. **Orchids of Hawaii** specializes in *vanda* orchids, birds of paradise and anthurium leis and corsages. Closed Saturday and Sunday. ~ 2801 Kilauea Avenue; 808-959-3581, 800-323-

1449, fax 808-959-4497; www.alohaorchids.com, e-mail orchidhi @gte.net. **Nani Mau Gardens** is a 20-acre visual feast that houses a wide variety of tropical flowers and plants. It has a gift shop and a botanical museum. Admission. ~ Several miles south of Hilo near Route 11 at 421 Makalika; 808-959-3541, fax 808-959-3152; www.nanimau.com.

Banyan Drive is another green thumb's delight. Sweeping past Hilo's nicest hotels, this waterfront road is shaded with rows of

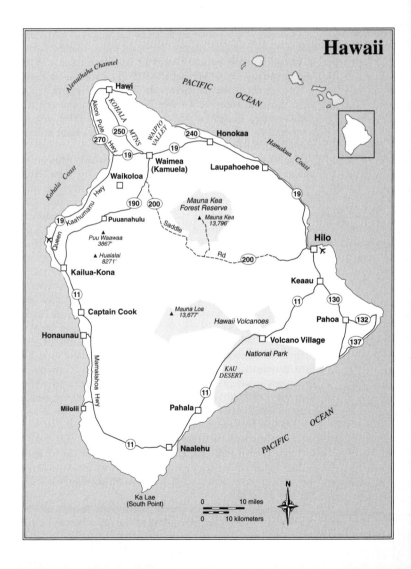

Hawaii

Alenuihaha Channel

PACIFIC OCEAN

Hawi

KOHALA MTNS

Akoni Pule Hwy

250

270

WAIPIO VALLEY

240

Honokaa

Hamakua Coast

19

19

Waimea (Kamuela)

Laupahoehoe

Kohala Coast

Waikoloa

190 200

Mauna Kea Forest Reserve

▲ Mauna Kea 13,796'

19

Kaahumanu Hwy

Puuanahulu

Saddle

Puu Waawaa 3867'

Rd

200

Hilo

Queen

▲ Hualalai 8271'

19

Kailua-Kona

Keaau

11 130

Captain Cook

▲ Mauna Loa 13,677'

Hawaii Volcanoes

Pahoa 132

Honaunau

Mamalahoa Hwy

Volcano Village

137

National Park

KAU DESERT

11

Miloli'i

Pahala

PACIFIC OCEAN

11

Naalehu

Ka Lae (South Point)

0   10 miles
0   10 kilometers

N

giant banyan trees. Plaques proclaim the dignitaries who planted them, including Franklin D. Roosevelt, Babe Ruth and Amelia Earhart. Next to this verdant arcade are the **Liliuokalani Gardens**, 19 acres exploding with color. These Japanese gardens, featuring both Hawaiian and Asian trees, are dotted with pagodas and arched bridges. ~ Banyan Drive and Lihiwai Street.

From Banyan Drive, a short footbridge crosses to **Coconut Island**, a palm-studded islet in Hilo Bay. This old Hawaiian sanctuary presents a dramatic view of Hilo Bay and, on a clear day, of Mauna Kea and Mauna Loa as well.

HIDDEN ►   A stone's skip across from the island, at **Suisan Fish Market**, fishing boats land their catches. Try to get there around 7 in the morning for a lively fish auction and a dose of local color. ~ 93 Lihiwai Street; 808-935-9349, fax 808-935-2115; www.suisan.com.

It's not far to **Wailoa River State Park**, where grassy picnic areas surround beautiful **Waiakea Fishpond**. Across one of the pond's arching bridges, at Wailoa Visitors Center, there are cultural exhibits and an information desk. ~ Off Kamehameha Avenue; 808-933-0416.

In downtown Hilo, the **Lyman House Memorial Museum** is a fascinating example of a 19th-century missionary home. Built in 1839, the house is furnished with elegant period pieces that create a sense of this bygone era (the house is open to guided tours only). Also on the property is a Hawaiian history museum focusing on Hawaiian culture and the islands' many ethnic groups, and an excellent collection of rocks and minerals. Among the museum's highlights is a 3-D map of the entire Hawaiian chain, from ocean floor to mountain top. Admission. ~ 276 Haili Street; 808-935-5021, fax 808-969-7685; e-mail lymanwks@interpac.net.

The **Pacific Tsunami Museum** recaptures in photos, videos and interactive displays the tidal waves that periodically wreak havoc on Hilo. Most notorious was the 1946 tsunami, which swept a half-mile inland and killed 94 people on the Big Island. Computers lead visitors through the history and physics of these infamous phenomena and survivors present first-hand accounts in the museum's videotaped oral histories. ~ 130 Kamehameha Avenue; 808-935-0926, fax 808-935-0842; www.tsunami.org, e-mail tsunami@aloha.net.

The **East Hawaii Cultural Center Gallery** displays the work of local and international artists in a series of exhibits that change monthly. The building itself, an old police station that has achieved historic landmark status, is a work of art. Closed Sunday and the last week of every month. ~ 141 Kalakaua Street; 808-961-5711, fax 808-935-9085.

Fronting the library on nearby Waianuenue Avenue are the **Naha** and **Pinao Stones**. According to legend, whoever moved

Five-day Itinerary Big Island

Day 1 • Arrive in **Kailua-Kona** (pages 198–211) and check into a condominium or hotel in Kailua-Kona or along the Kohala Coast.

• In the afternoon explore the **Kohala Coast** (pages 186–88) along Route 270, the Akoni Pule Highway, up to the **Pololu Valley Lookout** (page 188).

• Take Route 250 back through **Waimea** (pages 183–86) and plan to have dinner before heading back.

Day 2 • Spend the day snorkeling, swimming, horseback riding, sportfishing, or reading a book.

Day 3 • Drive around South Point with stops at **Kealakekua Bay** (page 212) on Route 160 and **Puuhonua o Honaunau National Historical Park** (Allow 1.5 hours) (page 212).

• Continue on Route 11 to **Hawaii Volcanoes National Park** (pages 224–28) and spend the night at **Volcano House** (page 228) or a local bed and breakfast.

Day 4 • Explore **Hawaii Volcanoes National Park** (pages 224–28).

• After lunch head up the **Hamakua Coast** (pages 178–83) to the **Waipio Valley** (page 179), then backtrack and spend the night in **Hilo** (pages 166–68, 170–78).

Day 5 • Drive back to Kailua-Kona via **Saddle Road** (Route 200) (pages 226–27).

the massive Naha Stone would rule all the islands. Kamehameha overturned the boulder while still a youth, then grew to become Hawaii's first king.

Continue up Waianuenue Avenue to **Rainbow Falls**, a foaming cascade in Wailuku River State Park. Here, particularly in the morning, spray from the falls shimmers in spectral hues. It's another two miles to **Boiling Pots**, where a series of falls pours turbulently into circular lava pools. The rushing water, spilling down from Mauna Kea, bubbles up through the lava and boils over into the next pool.

> If you tire of being herded around by guides, strike out on your own armed with a self-guided tour from the Hilo Mainstreet Program Office, which leads you to 17 sites of historic and architectural significance. ~ 252 Kamehameha Avenue; 808-935-8850.

Kaumana Drive, branching off Waianuenue Avenue, leads five miles out of town to **Kaumana Caves**. A stone stairway leads from the roadside down to two fern-choked lava tubes, formed during Mauna Loa's devastating 1881 eruption. Explore the lower tube, but avoid the other—it's dangerous.

HIDDEN ► Also be sure to visit the **Panaewa Rainforest Zoo**. Located in a lush region that receives over 125 inches of rain annually, this modest facility houses numerous rainforest animals as well as other species. There are water buffaloes and tigers, plus an array of exotic birds that include crowned cranes, macaws, parrots, Hawaiian coots, laysan ducks and nenes. ~ One mile off the Mamalahoa Highway several miles south of town; 808-959-7224, fax 808-961-8411; e-mail cohzoo@interpac.net.

LODGING   The main hotel district in this rain-plagued city sits astride the bay along Banyan Drive. Most hotels offer moderately priced accommodations, while a few are designed to fit the contours of a more slender purse.

Near the far end of beautiful Banyan Drive lies the **Hilo Seaside Hotel**. This charming place is actually on a side street fronting Reed's Bay, an arm of Hilo Bay. Owned by the Kimis, a Hawaiian family, it has the same friendly ambience that pervades their other hotels. There's a large lobby decorated with tile, *koa* wood and bamboo. A carp pond complete with footbridges dominates the grounds. The rooms are small and plainly decorated. Most are wallpapered and equipped with telephone, television and a combination shower-tub (perfect for soaking away a rainy day). The lanais overlook lush gardens and the hotel swimming pool. All in all, for friendly ambience and a lovely setting, the Seaside is a prime choice. ~ 126 Banyan Way; 808-935-0821, 800-367-7000, fax 808-969-9195; www.hiloseasidehotel.com, e-mail sand sea@aloha.net. MODERATE TO DELUXE.

Hilo Bay Hotel is another economical oceanfront establishment. The theme here is Polynesian, and proprietor "Uncle Billy"

Downtown Hilo

Hilo

POINTS OF INTEREST
- A Boiling Pots
- B County Library
- C East Hawaii Cultural Center Gallery
- D Liliuokalani Gardens
- E Lyman House Memorial Museum
- F Naha & Pinao Stones
- G Nani Mau Gardens
- H Orchids of Hawaii
- I Pacific Tsunami Museum
- J Suisan Fish Market
- K Wailoa Information Center

carries it off with flair: wicker furniture, thatch and *tapa* in the lobby, a restaurant/cocktail lounge, a bayside swimming pool and several carp ponds dotted about the tropical gardens. Standard rooms have wall-to-wall carpeting, televisions, telephones and air conditioning. The rooms are plainly furnished, located away from the water and rent for a moderate price. Superior rooms (which overlook the gardens, are larger, more attractive and come with ocean views) can be reserved for slightly more. Oceanfront rooms are also available and rent for deluxe prices. ~ 87 Banyan Drive; 808-935-0861, 800-367-5102, fax 808-935-7903; www. unclebilly.com, e-mail resv@unclebilly.com. MODERATE TO DELUXE.

For luxurious living my favorite Hilo hostelry is the **Hawaii Naniloa Hotel**, a highrise affair located right on the water. Rooms are comfortably furnished and nicely adorned. Restaurants, bars, a lounge and a spa are among the many amenities here, but the most alluring feature is the landscape—the tree-studded lawn is fringed with tidepools and volcanic rock. Add outdoor swimming pools, a spacious lobby and friendly staff and you have Hilo's premier hotel. Guests also have access to the Naniloa Country Club's nine-hole golf course across the street. ~ 93 Banyan Drive; 808-969-3333, 800-367-5360, fax 969-6622; www.naniloa.com, e-mail hinan@aloha.net. MODERATE TO DELUXE.

On a tree-lined residential street just across the Wailuku River sits the **Dolphin Bay Hotel**. This comfortable two-story establishment has 18 units, all equipped with kitchenettes. There are studios, one bedroom apartments, which can accommodate up to four, and a two-bedroom unit, which houses as many as six. Rooms upstairs have exposed-beam ceilings; all units have cinderblock walls, but personal touches like fresh flowers and fruit, and a garden with a running spring, make this a good choice. ~ 333 Iliahi Street; 808-935-1466, fax 808-935-1523; www.dolphin bayhotel.com, e-mail johnhilo@gte.net. MODERATE.

Not far away at the **Wild Ginger Inn** you'll find inexpensive guest rooms, which are carpeted wall-to-wall, attractively furnished and feature ceiling fans. There's a laundry room, a large garden, a spacious lobby and a full continental breakfast every morning. This vintage-1940s Hawaiian-style inn is surrounded by flowering trees and trimly manicured grounds. It also features an open-air lobby that's tastefully tiled and equipped with a very inviting hammock. ~ 100 Puueo Street; 808-935-5556, 800-882-1887, fax 808-969-1225; www.wildgingerinn.com, e-mail info@ wildgingerinn.com. BUDGET.

Arnott's Lodge is a clean, bright attractive hostel. Just one block from the waterfront, it is on the outskirts of Hilo in a low-key residential area. There are dormitory rooms available as well as private singles and doubles. Group activities such as hiking

Author Picks

CHAPTER FAVORITES

When I want to soak in the beauty of ancient Hawaii, I journey deep into lush **Waipio Valley**, favorite spot of the gods—I figure if it's good enough for Wakea, Zeus of the islands, it's certainly good enough for a mere mortal. *page 179*

I never fail to gape in amazement at the **Cape Kumukahi Lighthouse**, where a lava flow once destroyed everything in its path but left this beacon standing. *page 230*

When I need a change from beachfront ambience, I book a room at the **Kilauea Lodge**, unwind in front of

the fireplace and enjoy a cozy night of "mountain inn" atmosphere in the midst of the tropical islands. *page 228*

Decisions, decisions: Do I crave steak or seafood tonight? When these tough questions threaten to disrupt my vacation, I simply head to **Merriman's** and indulge in both. *page 186*

I love live music, to the dismay of my kids. Luckily, in addition to great live jazz the **Honu Bar** has a pool table and other games, so I can tune in to the sounds while the kids while away the hours. *page 193*

and snorkeling trips are frequently arranged, and there is a communal barbecue Wednesday and Saturday nights. With low-cost prices, and full kitchen and laundry facilities provided, it's one of the area's best bargains. ~ 98 Apapane Road; 808-969-7097, 800-368-8752, fax 808-961-9638; www.arnottslodge.com, e-mail arnott@aloha.net. BUDGET.

DINING

Scattered throughout Hilo are numerous cafés, lunch counters and chain restaurants serving low-cost meals.

Try the lunch menu at **Restaurant Kiku**, near the edge of hotel row, which consists of sandwiches (many at low, low cost) as well as Asian and American platters. The menu's limited and the atmosphere nonexistent, but Gwen's place isn't bad for a quick lunch or breakfast. ~ 96 Kalanianaole Avenue; 808-961-2044. BUDGET.

Ken's House of Pancakes has to top the list for all-American fare. If you've ever been to a Denny's or Howard Johnson's, you've been in Ken's. Endless rows of naugahyde booths, a long counter next to the kitchen, uniformed waitresses—the classic roadside America motif. The cuisine is on par with the decor, but it's a great place to join locals for breakfast and it's a good late-night option—open 24 hours. ~ 1730 Kamehameha Avenue; 808-935-8711, fax 808-961-5124. BUDGET TO MODERATE.

Uncle Billy's Fish and Steakhouse at the Hilo Bay Hotel sports a Hawaiian decor. In addition to its rattan furnishings, this cozy club hosts Polynesian dinner shows nightly. The menu is filled with surf-and-turf dishes priced reasonably. There's no lunch here, but they do offer breakfast and dinner daily. ~ 87 Banyan Drive; 808-935-0861; e-mail resv@unclebilly.com. MODERATE TO DELUXE.

At **Big Island Bistro** you can enjoy lunch or dinner while overlooking a lovely bonsai garden. The dining room offers a selection of traditional American dishes. In addition to pork chops and baby back ribs, the chefs prepare steak, seafood and prime rib. After dining, stroll past the pagodas and arched bridges that ornament the garden. No lunch on Saturday and Sunday. ~ 1550 Kamehameha Avenue; 808-934-8337. MODERATE TO DELUXE.

A local favorite that specializes in fresh, nutritious food is **Happy Cat's Cafe**. Their lunches include deli sandwiches, vegetarian meals, salads and burritos. Don't expect more than a take-out counter and a few picnic tables. Breakfast and lunch served. Closed Sunday. ~ 55 Mamo Street; 808-935-0595, fax 808-933-1882. BUDGET.

For breakfast or lunch in downtown Hilo consider **Canoes Café**. This informal patio-style dining area serves waffles and French toast in the morning and offers a "sandwich board" and fresh soups at lunch. ~ 308 Kamehameha Avenue; 808-935-4070; e-mail canoescafe@webtv.net. BUDGET.

There are more than three dozen dishes on the menu at **Reuben's Mexican Food**, numbered one to thirty-seven, and they cover the entire territory. Whether you're searching for enchiladas, *camarones empanizado*, beef tostadas, carne asada or huevos rancheros, you'll find it here. ~ 336 Kamehameha Avenue; 808-961-2552. BUDGET TO MODERATE.

Elsie's Fountain should be listed under sightseeing attractions. A classic soda fountain complete with red swivel seats and formica counter, it hasn't changed since the 1950s. Even the signs picturing the food are period pieces. Hamburgers cost $1.15! Tuna sandwiches are $.95! But a root beer float will set you back $1.50. I am not making this up. Stop by and see for yourself. No dinner served, sorry. ~ 339 Keawe Street; 808-935-8681. BUDGET.

The Old World oil paintings and red velvet upholstery at **Pescatore** seem out of place in tropical Hilo, but Italian food lovers won't debate the cuisine. They offer a *fra diavolo* dish with shrimp, mussel and calamari; saltimbocca; lasagna; cioppino; and lamb chops marinated in olive oil. Lunch and dinner every day; breakfast on weekends. ~ 235 Keawe Street; 808-969-9090, fax 808-969-7591; e-mail gmurphy@gte.net. DELUXE.

Don's Grill is one of those All-American places where dinner   ◀ *HIDDEN* comes with soup or salad, hot vegetables, fresh roll and your choice of mashed potatoes or fries. In this case it's Hawaiian All-American, so the menu switches from pork chops to teriyaki beef, rotisserie chicken to tofu stir fry, and barbecued ribs to breaded calamari. Very popular with the local folk. Closed Monday. ~ 485 Hinano Street; 808-935-9099, fax 808-961-0162. BUDGET TO MODERATE.

You can dine or take out at **Café Pesto**, an appealing eatery located in the historic S. Hata Building. This downtown Hilo gathering place serves wood-fired pizza, calzone, risotto dishes and salads. ~ 308 Kamehameha Avenue; 808-969-6640, fax 808-882-1459; www.cafepesto.com. MODERATE TO DELUXE.

Forget five-star restaurants and gourmet cuisine; Hilo is the place for ethnic eating on a budget.

For Chinese and Filipino food, **Mun Cheong Lau Chop Suey Restaurant** is the Orient's answer to the greasy spoon (greasy chopstick?) café. The place is as big as a barn and gaudily decorated with magenta walls and plastic lanterns. If you can get past the interior devastation, there's an ample menu listing numerous seafood, fowl, pork and rice dishes at chop suey prices. And in case of late-evening munchie attacks, Mun Cheong stays open until 9:30 p.m. Closed Tuesday. ~ 172 Kilauea Avenue; 808-935-3040. BUDGET.

Tsunami Grill and Tempura, a small café downtown, serves Japanese meals. Several *donburi, udon* and tempura dishes are on tap as well as special seafood dishes. Open for lunch and dinner. Closed Sunday. ~ 250 Keawe Street; 808-961-6789. BUDGET.

Thailand is represented by **Royal Siam**, an excellent eatery   ◀ *HIDDEN* with a warm ambience, friendly staff, local crowd and exceptional cuisine. Serving *phad thai* and traditional curries, it's open for lunch and dinner. Closed Sunday. ~ 70 Mamo Street; 808-961-6100. BUDGET TO MODERATE.

Hilo's foremost steak-and-seafood restaurant is **Harrington's**, a waterfront dining room that is particularly popular with locals. Here you can dine in a congenial atmosphere to the strains of Hawaiian music in the background. Harrington's also has a relaxing bar scene and can be counted on for good food with a view. No lunch on weekends. ~ 135 Kalanianaole Street; 808-961-4966, fax 808-961-4975. MODERATE TO DELUXE.

The island's largest city, Hilo has several supermarkets. Foremost   **GROCERIES** is **Sack-N-Save**. ~ 250 Kinoome Street; 808-935-3113.

Hilo hosts an excellent natural food outlet—**Abundant Life Wholefoods & Deli**. It contains healthy supplies of vitamins and juices, as well as a deli and fresh organic fruits and vegetables. ~ 292 Kamehameha Avenue; 808-935-7411.

Holsum/Oroweat Bakery Thrift Store offers fresh and day-old baked goods at unbeatable prices. Closed Sunday. ~ 302 Kamehameha Avenue; 808-935-2164.

SHOPPING   The most convenient way to shop in Hilo is at **Prince Kuhio Plaza**, a full-facility complex with everything from small crafts shops to swank boutiques to a sprawling department store. The Big Island's largest mall, it's a gathering place for local shoppers and a convenient spot for visitors. But bargains and locally crafted products are probably what you're after. So it's a good idea to window-shop through the centers, checking out prices, then do your buying at smaller shops. ~ 111 East Puainako Street; 808-959-3555.

The Most Irresistible Shop in Hilo doesn't quite live up to its bold name but does create a strong attraction with jewelry, clothing, ceramics, books and toys. They also feature works by local artists. ~ 256 Kamehameha Avenue; 808-935-9644.

For beach-reading materials, try The Book Gallery. This well-stocked shop has many popular titles. ~ 111 East Puainako Street, Prince Kuhio Plaza; 808-959-7744. If maps, guidebooks and volumes on Hawaiiana sound more inviting, **Basically Books** is an excellent choice. ~ 160 Kamehameha Avenue; 808-961-0144; www.readbook@interpac.net.

Mauna Kea Galleries specializes in Hawaiian and Polynesian art, antiques and artifacts. They have a selective but fascinating collection of ceramics, hula dolls, graphics and quilts. ~ 276 Keawe Street; 808-969-1184; www.maunakeagalleries.com.

Following a similar theme, **Hana Hou Encore** is a shop filled with "vintage and contemporary island treasures." Among those keepsakes are old Hawaiian song sheets, Matson menus and aloha shirts. Closed Sunday. ~ 164 Kamehameha Avenue; 808-935-4555; e-mail hanahou@ilhawaii.com.

Scene of a lively auction every morning, Suisan Company Limited is a great place to buy fresh fish. ~ 93 Lihiwai Street; 808-935-9349.

Specializing in "distinct island wearables, bedding and gifts," **Sig Zane Designs** has its own designer line of island dresses and aloha shirts. ~ 122 Kamehameha Avenue; 808-935-7077.

If it's fine *koa* wood pieces you're after, **Big Island Woodworks Gallery** is waiting for you. They have a finely honed collection of bowls and decorative pieces. ~ 206 Kamehameha Avenue; 808-961-0400; www.volcanogallery.com.

Another great spot for original woodwork is south of Hilo about 12 miles on Route 11 at **Dan DeLuz Woods**. The beautiful pieces are fashioned from banyan, sandalwood, *koa* and *milo*, all priced reasonably. The DeLuzes, the craftspeople who own the shop, do all their carving in a separate workshop. If you'd like a description of how the bowls are made, they're happy to provide an informal tour. ~ Mile marker 12, Route 11; 808-968-6607, fax 808-968-6019.

The main scene centers around the big hotels along Banyan Drive. By far the best place is the Hawaii Naniloa Hotel. This luxury hotel has a nicely appointed nightclub, **The Crown Room**. The lounge usually books local groups, but every once in a while it imports a mainland band for special events. There's usually a cover charge and two-drink minimum. Then there is **Joji's Lounge**, which sometimes provides piano tunes in the evening. ~ 93 Banyan Drive; 808-969-3333; e-mail hinan@aloha.net.

NIGHTLIFE

Harrington's hosts a Hawaiian guitarist on weekends. ~ 135 Kalanianaole Avenue; 808-961-4966.

The **Waioli Lounge** at the Hilo Hawaiian Hotel has live music on the weekend. Usually it's a contemporary duo. ~ 71 Banyan Drive; 808-935-9361.

KALAKAUA PARK Located on the corner of busy Kinoole Street and Waianuenue Avenue, this pretty little park has a grand old banyan tree and a pleasant picnic area.

BEACHES & PARKS

REED'S BAY BEACH PARK Reed's Bay, a banyan-lined cove is a marvelous picnic spot. The bay is actually an arm of Hilo Bay, but unlike the larger body of water, Reed's Bay offers excellent swimming in smooth water (though an underwater spring keeps the water cold). There is also an adjacent body of water popular with the locals. They call it "ice pond" due to its cold waters. Facilities include picnic areas, drinking water, showers and restrooms. ~ Located at the end of Banyan Drive.

ONEKAHAKAHA, KEALOHA AND LELEIWI COUNTY PARKS None of these three parks have sand beaches, but all possess lava pools or other shallow places for swimming. They also have grassy plots and picnic areas, plus restrooms and showers. If you fish along these shores, chances are good you'll net *papio*, threadfin, mountain bass, mullet, big-eyed scad, mackerel scad, milkfish, bonefish, or goatfish. Kealoha Park offers good snorkeling, surfing, spear-fishing and throw-netting. ~ All three parks are located within five miles of Hilo, east along Kalanianaole Avenue.

RICHARDSON'S OCEAN PARK This black-sand beach, south of Hilo Bay, is without doubt the finest beach in the area. From there you can see Mauna Kea hulking in the background. Coconut palms and ironwood trees fringe the beach, while a lava outcropping somewhat protects swimmers. The protected areas also make for good snorkeling. This is one of the best spots around Hilo for surfing as well as bodysurfing and

◄ *HIDDEN*

bodyboarding. Winter break with right slides. Mornings and evenings are the prime times, but at all times beware of currents, riptides and sharp reefs. Park officials warn beginners to learn the sport at a less treacherous location. Lifeguards are on duty every day. Anglers try for *papio*, mountain bass, mullet, big-eyed scad, mackerel scad, milkfish, bonefish and goatfish. Facilities here include restrooms and outdoor showers. ~ Take Kalanianaole Avenue to within a quarter-mile of where the paved road ends; watch for the sign to Richardson Ocean Park. The beach is behind and to the right of the center; 808-961-8695, fax 808-961-8696.

Hamakua Coast

Route 19, the Mamalahoa Highway, leads north from Hilo along the rainy, windswept Hamakua Coast. Planted with papaya, macadamia nuts, taro and ginger root, among other crops and teeming with exotic plant life, this elevated coastline is as lushly overgrown as Hilo.

A softly rolling plateau that edges from the slopes of Mauna Kea to the sea, the region is cut by sharp canyons and deep gulches. Waterfalls cascade down emerald walls and tumbling streams lead to lava-rock beaches. Beautiful is too tame a term for this enchanting countryside. There are stands of eucalyptus, shadowy forests and misty fields of sugar cane. Plantation towns, filled with pastel-painted houses and adorned with flower gardens, lie along the route.

SIGHTS

Several miles outside Hilo, follow the signs to the **Scenic Drive**. This old coast road winds past cane fields and shantytowns before rejoining the main highway. Alexander palms line the road. Watch for Onomea Bay: There you'll see a V-shaped rock formation where a sea arch collapsed in 1956.

You can also take in **Hawaii Tropical Botanical Garden**, an exotic nature preserve with streams, waterfalls, rugged coastline and over 2000 plant species. This jungle garden, edged by the Pacific and inhabited by shore birds and giant sea turtles, is a place of uncommon beauty. Admission. ~ On the Four Mile Scenic Route, seven miles north of Hilo; 808-964-5233, fax 808-964-1338; www.hawaiigarden.com, e-mail htbg@ilhawaii.net.

Back on the main road, you'll soon come to a turnoff heading inland to **Akaka Falls State Park**. Don't bypass it! A short nature trail leads past bamboo groves, ferns, ti and orchids to Akaka Falls, which slide 442 feet down a sheer cliff face, and Kahuna Falls, 400 feet high. This 66-acre preserve is covered in a canopy of rainforest vegetation. There are birds of paradise, azaleas and giant philodendrons whose leaves measure as much as two feet.

Countless gulches ribbon the landscape between Hilo and Honokaa. For a unique tour, take the road from Hakalau that winds down to **Hakalau Gulch**. Literally choked with vegetation, this gorge extends to a small beach. Towering above the gulch is the highway bridge.   ◀ HIDDEN

Another side road several miles north corkscrews down to **Laupahoehoe Point,** a hauntingly beautiful peninsula from which 24 students and teachers were swept by the 1946 tidal wave. Here gently curving palm trees and spreading lawns contrast with the lash of the surf.   ◀ HIDDEN

It's a jungle out there. But at **World Botanical Gardens** they're trying to make a tropical paradise out of it. Among the features under development are a 300-acre botanical garden, a pathway through a dense and very beautiful rainforest, and a vista point overlooking a triple-tiered waterfall. Be sure to put on the complimentary insect repellent. Admission. ~ Located near mile-marker 16 on Route 19 in Umauma; 808-963-5427, fax 808-964-5530; www.wbgi.com, e-mail wbgi@hotmail.com.

The plantation town of **Paauilo** offers a glimpse of vintage Hawaii: decaying storefronts and tinroof cottages. Then it's on to **Honokaa**, a village caught in a lazy-paced time warp and the world center of macadamia nut growing.   ◀ HIDDEN

Head out Route 240 to **Waipio Valley**, the island's largest valley. One mile wide and almost six miles long, this luxurious

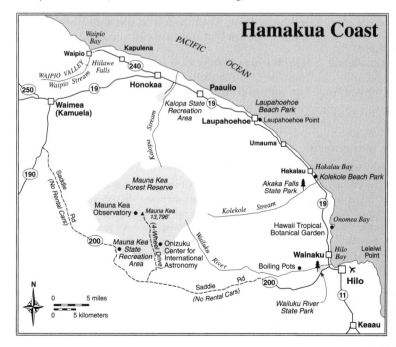

canyon, sparsely populated today, once supported thousands of Hawaiians. Agriculturally bountiful, Waipio is also rich in history. Here in 1780 Kamehameha the Great acknowledged the war god who would propel him to victory. At that time the valley, which has been inhabited for over 1000 years, supported a population of about 4000 Hawaiians. It also looms large in island mythology. Wakea, the Zeus of Hawaii, loved the valley, as did two other members of the Polynesian pantheon, Kane and Kanaloa. The god Lono came here seeking a wife and Maui himself is said to have died in the Waipio Valley.

Taro patches and tumbledown cottages still dot the valley. From the lookout point at road's end, a jeep trail drops sharply into Waipio. Explorers can hike down or take an hour-and-a-half four-wheel-drive tour with the **Waipio Valley Shuttle and Tours**. ~ 808-775-7121. Another agency with tours is **Waipio Valley Wagon Tour**. Its tour is part four-wheel-drive, part mule-drawn, GM shock-equipped wagon. ~ 808-775-9518. Both tours travel several miles up into the valley for eye-boggling views of 1200-foot Hiilawe Falls. Both are closed Sunday.

Eden for explorers, the valley territory and the rainforest is a riot of tropical colors. The homes of a few dozen dedicated residents dot the area and there are abandoned buildings, swimming holes and cascades to be discovered. (If you don't have time to explore the valley, be sure to at least take in the vista from the **Waipio Valley Lookout** at the end of Route 240.)

LODGING

HIDDEN ▶

Hotel Honokaa Club, perched on a hillside above the Hamakua Coast, has a boardinghouse atmosphere. The rooms upstairs are kept thoroughly scrubbed and freshly painted; they're quite adequate. A modest price buys a splendid ocean view, color television plus a tiny private bathroom. Or trade the cable TV away

◆◆

HIGHRISE HOTEL

The **Waipio Treehouse** really does have a treehouse. Smaller than the two cottages on the property, this unique lodging experience will take you 30 feet off the ground. The two guesthouses are nestled amid the lush foliage and dramatic waterfalls of the remote Waipio Valley and enjoy spectacular views. Each is equipped with kitchen facilities (bring your own food, this retreat is *very* secluded). Guests immerse themselves in Japanese hot tubs and then (with prior arrangement) fall prey to the hands of the massage therapist. Guided hiking and horseback eco-tours add to the adventure. ~ P.O. Box 5086, Honokaa; 808-775-7160; www.waipio.com. ULTRA-DELUXE.

and you can have a small cubicle with community bathroom at even less cost. These rooms are smaller and lack the view, but they're just as clean as the upstairs rooms. Dorm-style hostel accommodations are also available. A continental breakfast is included. ~ Route 240, Honokaa; phone/fax 808-775-0678, 800-808-0678; www.home1gte.net/honokaac, e-mail honokaac@gte.net. BUDGET TO MODERATE.

Built in 1921 as a plantation manager's house and now registered as an historic landmark, the **Paauhau Plantation House** is an extraordinary place to hang your hat. It rests on an elegantly landscaped plot and looks out on a sea of sugar cane that extends to the ocean itself. The interior could be a museum, filled as it is with fine antiques, *koa* furnishings and photos from old plantation days. Within the five-acre grounds are several cottages that feature full kitchens and offer complete privacy. They rent in the moderate range; rooms in the main house are deluxe in price. ~ Kalopa Road, off Mamalahoa Highway, Honokaa; 808-775-7222, 800-789-7614, fax 808-775-7223. MODERATE TO DELUXE.

◄ HIDDEN

DINING

Honokaa offers a convenient stop for those making a day-trip between Hilo and Kona. The Hotel Honokaa Club has a restaurant called **Paniolo Plantation Inn,** which serves steak, pizza and Mexican food. It's in a banquet-sized dining room that's large enough to play hockey on so don't expect a cozy hideaway. At least the food is hot, and priced well, too. On alternating Friday evenings, there is line dancing or live music. Another attraction is the monkey-pod-wood bar, which stretches 20 feet. Lunch and dinner daily; dinner only on Sunday. ~ Route 240, Honokaa; 808-775-9298. MODERATE.

Jolene's Kau Kau Korner has plate lunches, burgers and sandwiches during daylight hours. At dinner, they move on to mahimahi, shrimp and vegetable tempura, stir-fry beef and grilled chicken with pineapple. It's a simple café but reasonably priced. ~ 45-3625 Mamane Street, Honokaa; 808-775-9498. BUDGET TO DELUXE.

GROCERIES

First you can check out **Jan's Store.** Located in Honomu on the road to Akaka Falls, it has a limited stock, but you may find what you need. ~ 808-963-6062. Also try **Ti Kaneshiro Supermarket,** a small-town super across from the post office in Honokaa. ~ 808-775-0631.

SHOPPING

On the road to Akaka Falls in Honomu, you'll happen upon the **Ohana Gallery.** Here is a wide array of work by local artists and craftspeople. Of particular note are photographs of a volcano erupting on the Big Island. The Gallery also serves as an area information center. ~ 808-963-5467.

Kamaaina Woods in Honokaa has a splendid assortment of handmade bowls and decorations. With items fashioned from *milo*, mango and *koa*, this shop is practically a museum. And if you are interested in learning more about these woods, you can view the factory through the window. ~ Lehua Street; 808-775-7722.

The falsefront town of Honokaa also has **Bamboo Gallery**, a light, spacious studio filled with artworks crafted from bamboo. This charming shop also has paintings, jewelry and carvings by local and Japanese artists. ~ Mamane Street; 808-775-0933.

The **Waipio Valley Artworks**, located near the Waipio Valley Lookout, is also cluttered with woodcarvings. Made from several different woods, some of these creations are extremely beautiful. This shop also features paintings, ceramics and other locally crafted items. ~ Route 240; 808-775-0958.

BEACHES & PARKS

KOLEKOLE BEACH PARK Located at the mouth of a wide gulch lush with tropical vegetation, this comfortable park has a large and pleasant grassy area. A stream and waterfall tumble through the park down to the rocky, surf-torn shore. The sandy beach and natural beauty of the place make it very popular among local residents. You can swim in the stream but the ocean here is forbiddingly rough. Threadfin, *menpachi*, *papio* and *ulua* are the common catches. Facilities consist of a picnic area, restrooms and electricity; there is no drinking water, but spring water is available for cooking and showers. It's one mile to markets and restaurants in Honomu. ~ Located just off Mamalahoa Highway (Route 19) about 12 miles northwest of Hilo.

▲ Tent and trailer; $3 per night. County permit required.

LAUPAHOEHOE BEACH PARK Set on a low-lying peninsula that was inundated by the 1946 tidal wave, this hauntingly beautiful park is still lashed by heavy surf. A precipitous *pali* and lava-strewn shoreline surround the area. Swimming, snorkeling and surfing are good at times, but usually very dangerous. You can fish for *ulua*, *papio*, *menpachi* and *moi*. Facilities include a picnic area, restrooms, showers and electricity. It's at least 15 miles to restaurants or markets in Honokaa, so bring a lunch. ~ One mile off Route 19 down a well-marked twisting road, about 27 miles northwest of Hilo.

▲ Tent and trailer camping permitted; $3 per night. County permit required.

KALOPA STATE RECREATION AREA A wooded retreat set in the mountains above the Hamakua Coast, this 100-acre park has both untouched expanses ripe for exploring and several beautifully landscaped acres. Ranging from 2000 to 2500 feet elevation, it's a great place for hiking or just for escaping. There are picnic areas, restrooms, showers and cabins. ~ Take Route 19 southeast from Honokaa for about three miles. A well-marked paved road leads from the highway another two miles to the park.

▲ Tent camping is permitted and cabins are also available; call 808-974-6200 for reservations.

Just 15 miles from the tablelands of Honokaa and ten miles from the Kohala Coast, at an elevation of 2670 feet, sits Waimea. Covered with rolling grassland and bounded by towering mountains, Waimea (also called Kamuela) is cowboy country. Here *paniolos*, Hawaiian cowboys, ride the range on one of the world's largest independently owned cattle ranches. Founded by John Palmer Parker, an adventurous sailor who jumped ship in 1809, Parker Ranch extends from sea level to over 9000 feet. More than 55,000 cattle roam this sprawling 225,000-acre domain.

Waimea

This cool rustic countryside, rare in a tropical retreat like Hawaii, is dotted with carpenter's Gothic houses and adorned with stables and picket fences. There are Victorian buildings and deep green trees, cattle grazing in the meadows and horses edging along the fence line.

The museum at **Parker Ranch Visitors Center** presents a history of the Parker family that will carry you back 140 years with its displays of Victorian-era furniture and clothing. In addition to the artifacts and family momentos, there is a movie that tells the story of the Parker family from its earliest days to the present. Admission. ~ 808-885-7655, fax 808-885-7561; www.parkerranch.com.

SIGHTS

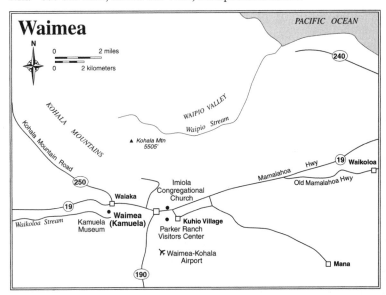

And at the **Historic Parker Ranch Homes** you can view the family's original 1840s-era ranch house and an adjoining century-old home (which doubles as a museum filled with extraordinary French Impressionist artwork). While the original home was built of *koa* and contains a collection of antique calabashes, the latter-day estate boasts lofty ceilings, glass chandeliers and walls decorated with the work of Pissarro and Corot, among others. ~ Mamalahoa Highway, one-half mile west of town; 808-885-5433, fax 808-885-5602; www.parkerranch.com, e-mail dquitiquit@parkerranch.com.

Another fine display is at the **Kamuela Museum.** Founded by J. P. Parker's great-great-granddaughter, this private collection of everything from Royal Hawaiian artifacts to moon-flight relics is fascinating, if poorly organized. Admission. ~ Junction of Kawai-hae Road and Kohala Mountain Road (junction of Highway 19 and 250); 808-885-4724.

For a splendid example of *koa* woodworking, visit **Imiola Congregational Church** on the east side of town. Built in 1832, this clapboard church has an interior fashioned entirely from the native timber. ~ Mamalahoa Highway; 808-885-4987.

LODGING   Set amid the Kohala Mountains in the cowboy town of Waimea are two hotels, both within walking distance of local markets and restaurants. **Waimea Country Lodge,** a modern multi-unit motel. Guest rooms are large, carpeted and equipped with telephones, shower-tub combinations and color televisions; some have small kitchenettes. The ceilings are exposed beam; the furniture is knotty pine. ~ 65-1210 Lindsey Road; 808-885-4100, 800-367-5004, fax 808-885-6711; www.castleresorts.com. MODERATE.

Kamuela Inn, a neighbor just down the street, has modest one- and two-room units, and suites in the new wing. These are clean and bright with private baths. All of the 31 units are equipped with cable TV and some have refrigerators. Guests are served a

FEELING AT HOME

Combining style with personalized service, **Hawaii's Best Bed & Breakfasts** specializes in small, upscale bed-and-breakfast, private cottage and small inn accommodations statewide. With more than 100 places to choose from, it places guests in privately owned facilities; most are deluxe in price. The unit I saw was a woodframe cottage that shared over an acre of land with the owner's house. Set in Waimea beside a stream and surrounded by trees and lofty green hills, it included a kitchen and sitting area. ~ P.O. Box 563, Kamuela, HI 96743; 808-885-4550, 800-262-9912, fax 808-885-0559; www.bestbnb.com, e-mail bestbnb@aloha.net. MODERATE TO ULTRA-DELUXE.

continental breakfast. ~ Kawaihae Road; 808-885-4243, 800-555-8968, fax 808-885-8857. MODERATE.

With all the fine-dining possibilities here, Waimea is short on short-order restaurants. There is not much in the way of inexpensive ethnic restaurants. You will find two in Waimea Center (Mamalahoa Highway): **Great Wall Chopsui** has steam-tray Chinese food for lunch and dinner but serves an American breakfast. ~ 808-885-7252. BUDGET. **Yong's Kalbi** serves Korean dishes. Closed Sunday. ~ 808-885-8440. BUDGET TO MODERATE.

DINING

There's a booth that seats 14 people at **Hawaiian Style Cafe**, but you'll probably be more comfortable at the U-shaped counter or a small table. You can settle in for a hearty island breakfast or a lunch that varies from sautéed mahimahi to tripe stew. There are hamburgers and sandwiches plus a few Asian dishes like *kalbi* and teriyaki steak. Dinner served Wednesday through Saturday. ~ Mamaloa Highway; 808-885-4295. BUDGET.

Aioli's is where you'll find local folks, not tourists. It's a comfortable place offering home-style cooking. Brunch only is served on Sunday; it's the only day any breakfast is served. The ever-changing menu can be described as "eclectic-American," always including vegetarian and fresh fish dishes. Closed Monday and for two weeks after Labor Day. ~ Opelo Plaza, Kawaihae Road; 808-885-6325, fax 808-882-7382. MODERATE TO DELUXE.

◄ HIDDEN

If you're hankering for a steak up here in cowboy country, then ride on in to **Paniolo Country Inn**. There are branding irons on the walls and sirloins on the skillet. The booths are made of knotty pine and dishes have names like "Lone Ranger" and "bucking bronco." You can order barbecued chicken, baby back ribs or a "south of the border" special. ~ 651214 Lindsey Road; 808-885-4377, fax 808-775-9543. MODERATE.

Koa House Grill takes its name from the walls—dark koa panels accented with cowboy gear and photos of paniolos. The cuisine is steak and seafood with a few additional pasta dishes for good measure. ~ 65-1144 Mamalahoa Highway; 808-885-2088, fax 808-885-5590. MODERATE TO ULTRA-DELUXE.

One of my favorite Waimea dining spots is the **Edelweiss** restaurant, a cozy club with a knockout interior design. The entire place was fashioned by a master carpenter who inlaid *sugi* pine, *koa* and silver oak with the precision of a jeweler. Run by a German chef who gained his knowledge at prestigious addresses like Maui's plush Kapalua Bay Hotel, Edelweiss is a gourmet's delight. The dinner menu includes wienerschnitzel, roast duck and a house specialty—sautéed veal, lamb, beef and bacon with *pfifferling*. For lunch there is bratwurst, sauerkraut and sandwiches. Closed Sunday and Monday and closed during September. ~ Kawaihae Road; 808-885-6800. DELUXE TO ULTRA-DELUXE.

Waimea's contribution to Hawaii regional cuisine is **Merriman's**, a very highly regarded restaurant that has received national attention. The interior follows a neo-tropical theme and the menu is tailored to what is fresh and local. Since the locale is not simply Hawaii, but upcountry Hawaii, the cuisine combines the seashore and the cattle ranch. You might find fresh fish with spicy *lilikoi* sauce or steak with *kiawe*-smoked tomato sauce; gourmet vegetarian dishes round out the fare. Highly recommended. No lunch Saturday and Sunday. ~ Opelo Plaza, Kawaihae Road; 808-885-6822; e-mail goodfood@lava.net. MODERATE TO ULTRA-DELUXE.

GROCERIES   The one supermarket along this route is **K.T.A. Super Store**, open daily from 6:30 a.m. to 11 p.m. ~ Mamalahoa Highway, Waimea; 808-885-8866.

Kona Healthways has a large supply of vitamins, baked goods, cosmetics and so on. ~ Waimea Center, Waimea; 808-885-6775.

SHOPPING   **Waimea Center** is *the* shopping complex in Waimea's cattle country. This modern center features boutiques, knickknack shops and more. You'll find the mall located in the center of Waimea.

The Quilted Horse has quilts (without the horse) and decorative items for the home like candles, woodcarvings and wall-hangings. ~ Kawaihae Road.

Parker Square specializes in "distinguished shops." Particularly recommended here is the **Gallery of Great Things**, a store that fulfills the promise of its name. Look for locally made arts and crafts, contemporary and tribal art and work representing Polynesia, Indonesia and the Pacific Rim. ~ Waimea; 808-885-7706.

Bentley's, in the same complex, offers everything from clothing to greeting cards. ~ Kawaihae Road; 808-885-5565.

Dan Deluz's Woods has beautifully handcrafted bowls, boxes and carvings. The owner, in the business for decades, is a master of his trade. ~ 64-1013 Mamalahoa Highway; 808-885-5856.

NIGHTLIFE   The 480-seat **Kahilu Theatre** offers dance performances, concerts, plays and current movies. ~ Parker Ranch Center; 808-885-6017.

▼▼▼▼▼▼▼▼▼▼
Kohala Coast   Stretching from the northern boundary of Kona to the northwestern tip of the Big Island are the districts of South and North Kohala. During the past two decades South Kohala, which includes some of the island's prettiest beaches, has seen the building of one upscale resort after another. Farther north, where Kohala Mountain forms a 5000-foot-high spine, the territory remains much as it has for decades. As the Kaahumanu Highway (Route 19) gives way to the northerly Akoni Pule Highway (Route 270), the landscape eventually changes from dry and barren to tropical and luxurious.

Exploring this region from Kailua-Kona you will find that Kaahumanu Highway cuts across a broad swath of lava-crusted country. There are views of Maui to the north, Mauna Kea to the east and Hualalai to the south.

For evidence of Kohala's historic significance you need look no further than Waikoloa, located between Honokaa and Waimea. While the area is now heavily developed with tourist resorts, it is also the site of the **Waikoloa Petroglyph Field**. Here you can wander amidst a forbidding lava field etched with ancient symbols. The contrast, with a modern golf course on one side and primitive rock carvings on the other, is ironic to say the least. The path to the petroglyphs is .3-mile in length and begins at the Kings' Shops Mall in Waikoloa. This rough lava course is part of the King's Trail, a mid-19th century trail built for horseback riders making the 32-mile trip from Kailua to Puako.

SIGHTS

From Puako, the highway moves north past the luxurious **Mauna Kea Beach Hotel**. Built by Laurence Rockefeller, it was the first of the five-star resorts to mushroom along the Kohala coastline.

The harbor of Kawaihae, one of the island's busiest ports, is the locale of two major *heiaus*, Mailekini and Puukohola, which have been dedicated as the **Puukohola National Historic Site**. Kamehameha built the impressive triple-tiered Puukohola in 1791 after a prophet related that doing so would ensure his victory over rival islands. At the temple dedication, the ambitious chief aided the prophecy by treacherously slaying his principal enemy. Measuring 224 feet by 100 feet, it was built of lava rocks and boulders that were fitted together using no mortar.

Just 12 miles to the north along Akoni Pule Highway (Route 270) is **Lapakahi State Historical Park**, where a preserved village provides a unique glimpse into ancient Hawaiian ways. This is definitely worth a leisurely look-see. Dating back 600 years, this unique site includes fishing shrines, canoe sheds, house sites and burial plots. Open daily. ~ 808-882-6207.

A POWERFUL SPIRIT

Geologically, the Kohala Coast was the section of the island that first rose from the sea. Later, as the volcanoes that formed Kohala Mountain became extinct, the region evolved into a center of historical importance. Kamehameha I was born and raised along this wind-blasted coastline and it was here that he initially consolidated his power base. The region is filled with ancient *heiaus* as well as more recent cemeteries that date to the era when sugar plantations dominated the local economy.

HIDDEN ►
If time permits, take the turnoff to Upolu Airport (just west of Hawi) to reach **Mookini Heiau**, one of the island's most important temples. This holy place—dating to 480 A.D. and measuring 250 feet by 130 feet—is reached by taking a left at the airfield, then following the dirt road for a mile-and-a-half. The **Birthplace of Kamehameha I**, marked with a plaque, lies one-third mile (and two gates) farther west along the same road. The boulders here are reputed to be the original birthstones.

The old plantation town of **Hawi**, with its trim houses and freshly painted storefronts, harkens back to an earlier era. Back in the 1980s, when the sugar cane industry was in decline, the town looked rather forlorn. But by the beginning of this century it had been completely restored by artists and entrepreneurs. Like neighboring **Kapaau**, it shows its new face in the form of small galleries and local shops. Both are charming enclaves adorned with small churches and relics from the days when sugar was king.

Pride of Kapaau is the original **Kamehameha Statue**, a nine-ton creation cast in bronze. The more famous Honolulu monument is actually only a replica of this gilt figure. Crafted in Florence around 1879 by an American sculptor, the original disappeared at sea on its way to Hawaii but was later recovered and installed here.

Along this lush, rainy side of the peninsula are taro patches and pandanus forests. Past the **Kamehameha Rock** (a large boulder that the mighty conqueror reputedly carried from the sea), the road ends at **Pololu Valley Lookout**. The view here overlooking Pololu Valley extends along the monumental cliffs that guard Hawaii's north coast. A half-mile trail leads down to a lovely beach, but watch out for the treacherous riptides.

HIDDEN ►
From this cul-de-sac you must backtrack to Hawi, where you can climb the back of **Kohala Mountain** along Route 250 (Kohala Mountain Road), completing a loop tour of North Kohala. Rising to 3564 feet, the road rolls through cactus-studded range country and offers startling views down steep volcanic slopes to the sea. En route are cattle ranches, stands of Norfolk pine and eucalyptus, and curving countryside covered with sweet grasses and wildflowers.

LODGING   In the small rustic town of Hawi near Hawaii's northwestern tip, the **Kohala Village Inn** and an adjacent restaurant are the hottest spots around. But there's still privacy and quiet aplenty out back in the sleeping quarters. Rooms in this refurbished establishment feature tinroofs and handsome hardwood floors, and face a small courtyard. The place is tidy, if less than elegant. There are also rooms in an adjacent building. ~ 55-514 Hawi Road, Hawi; 808-889-0419; e-mail marter@aloha.net. BUDGET TO MODERATE.

Waikoloa Villa is a collection of over 100 condos on the lower slopes of Mauna Kea. Located inland from the South Kohala coast, Waikoloa is a self-contained village with store, post office, pool, restaurant, tennis courts, golf course and riding stables. ~ For condominium rentals, call 883-9144, 800-535-0085, fax 808-883-8740; www.wkv@aloha.net, e-mail marc@aloha.net. DELUXE.

For years the Kohala district was a placid region strewn with lava and dotted by several pearly beaches. A single resort stood along its virgin coastline. Today it's one of the fastest developing spots in Hawaii. The **Outrigger Waikoloan Beach**, a sprawling

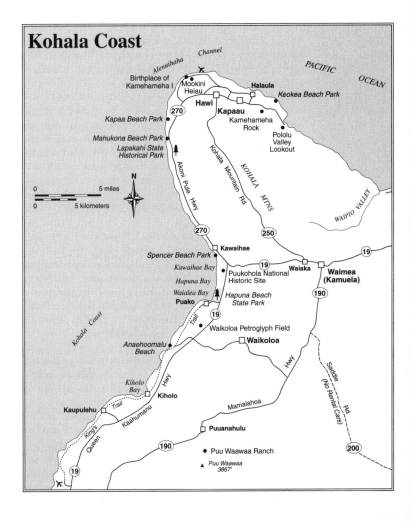

Kohala Coast

545-unit resort, stands along Anaehoomalu Beach. ~ Kaa-humanu Highway, Waikoloa; 808-886-6789, 800-462-6262, fax 808-886-7852; www.outrigger.com. DE-LUXE TO ULTRA-DELUXE.

All along the Kaahumanu Highway, there's a type of graffiti unique to the Big Island. Setting white coral atop black lava, and vice versa, ingenious residents and visitors have spelled out their names and messages.

Several miles north, the **Mauna Lani Bay Hotel and Bungalows**, a 3200-acre resort, rests on another white-sand beach. Designed in the shape of an arrowhead and boasting 350 rooms, this luxurious facility offers two golf courses, ten tennis courts and five restaurants, several of which are award-winners. With brilliant green gardens set against black lava, the landscape combines curving lawns and palm-ringed fishponds. Each guest room is spaciously laid out and designed in a pastel motif. ~ 68-1400 Mauna Lani Drive, Kawaihae; 808-885-6622, 800-367-2323, fax 808-885-1484; www. maunalani. com. ULTRA-DELUXE.

One way to avoid the high cost of the five-star Kohala Coast resorts is to rent a condominium in one of the many complexes. **Mauna Lani Point** is a collection of villa-style condominiums spread across 19 oceanfront acres, close to a white-sand beach. Luxuriously appointed, the condos have access to Mauna Lani's beaches, jogging trails, a 27-acre historic preserve and an early Hawaiian fishpond. Some of the units can fit up to four people; prices range from $260-$475 a night. ~ 68-1050 Mauna Lani Point Drive, Kohala Coast; 800-642-6284, fax 808-661-1025; e-mail info@classicresorts.com.

The sprawling **Westin Hapuna Beach Prince Hotel** is the sister resort of the illustrious Mauna Kea Beach Hotel. The posh Hapuna features the same beautifully landscaped grounds and also offers a golf course, tennis courts and its own white-sand beach. The 350 rooms are decorated in shades of peach and beige, and all have large lanais and ocean views. ~ 62-100 Kaunaoa Drive, Kohala Coast; 808-880-1111, 800-882-6060, fax 808-880-4162; www.hapunabeachprincehotel.com. ULTRA-DELUXE.

DINING

Outside the expensive resorts, you'll find very few restaurants along Hawaii's northwestern shore. Sailors say that any port is good in a storm, and on such a sparsely settled coast any restaurant is probably worth heading for.

If you cast anchor in the town of Kawaihae, consider **Café Pesto**. Pizza is the specialty at this simple café. But you'll also find linguini marinara, salmon alfredo and fresh fish. ~ Kawaihae Center, Suite 101; 808-882-1071, fax 808-882-1459; www.cafepesto. com, e-mail palmer@interpac.net. MODERATE TO ULTRA-DELUXE.

The food is Mexican but the theme is surfing at **Tres Hombres Beach Grill**, located in the same complex. There is a great display of surfing memorabilia and some of the bar counters are even fashioned from surfboards. ~ Kawaihae Center; 808-882-1031. MODERATE.

The **Blue Dolphin Restaurant** has a comfortable dining pavilion in back. They are open for dinner only, and feature occasional live music. Days of operation vary seasonally. ~ Across from Kawaihae Harbor; phone/fax 808-882-7771. MODERATE TO DELUXE.

Up near Kohala's northern tip, in the well-preserved historic town of Hawi, is the **Bamboo Restaurant**. Located in the 1920s-era general store, this restaurant is decorated with tropical plants and deep wicker chairs. The menu offers a mix of Pacific regional and "local style" cuisine and includes such items as coconut clam chowder, Thai broiled prawns and grilled fresh island fish in a variety of preparations. All meats and produce served are locally grown. There's Hawaiian music Friday and Saturday nights. Reservations required. Closed Sunday night and Monday. ~ Akoni Pule Highway; 808-889-5555; www.bamboorestaurant.com, e-mail bamboo@interpac.net. BUDGET TO MODERATE.

For a taste of funky, traditional Hawaii there's **The Soda Fountain**. Set in a tinroof plantation building with bare walls and plastic tablecloths, it serves breakfast, lunch and dinner at super low prices. ~ Just off Akoni Pule Highway about one mile east of Hawi; 808-889-0208. BUDGET. ◄ HIDDEN

In the center of Hawi is the **Kohala Coffee Mill**, a café that serves coffee and pastries, but especially Tropical Dreams Ice Cream. Created locally, Tropical Dreams whips up exotic flavors like mango and lychee. ~ Akoni Pule Highway, Hawi; 808-889-5577, fax 808-889-5062. BUDGET.

Generally, in outlying areas like the Kohala Peninsula, you will find that although the restaurants are few and simple, they have a homey atmosphere about them that can never be captured in crowded urban areas. As I'm sure you're well aware, this fact sometimes makes dining in the outback almost as grand an adventure as hiking or camping.

With all the development that occurred along the Kohala Coast, it seems inevitable that gourmet restaurants would become an important part of the landscape. Thus far few independent dining rooms have opened; most are connected with one of the several resorts now dotting the shoreline.

For Continental cuisine with a touch of Provence, try **The Batik** at the Mauna Kea Beach Hotel. This hotel, built on the Kohala coast by Laurence Rockefeller, is famous for its fabulous feasts. For American-style dishes plus spectacular ocean views, there's also the **Pavilion**. ~ Mauna Kea Beach Hotel, Kaahumanu Highway, Kawaihae; 808-882-7222. DELUXE.

The Mauna Lani Bay Hotel hosts some well-known, formal and very expensive restaurants. The **Bay Terrace** features an ever-changing menu. The offerings may include fresh grilled salmon in an asparagus sauce or mahimahi with feta cheese. Beef dishes include prime rib with a spicy horseradish sauce and Black Angus steak. Dinner only. ~ Mauna Lani Bay Hotel, 68-1400 Mauna Lani Drive, Kawaihae; 808-885-6622, fax 808-885-1478. DELUXE TO ULTRA-DELUXE.

Also located at the Mauna Lani Bay Hotel is the **Canoe House**, one of the Big Island's most highly regarded dining rooms. Specializing in Pacific Rim cuisine and offering spectacular sunsets as an appetizer, it delivers fine food and a fine time. The menu, which changes frequently, is a creative mix of island and Asian dishes. Dinner only. ~ 808-885-6622, fax 808-885-1478. ULTRA-DELUXE.

Roussels, a French/Creole restaurant founded by two brothers, made its reputation in Hilo then moved to the Waikoloa Village Golf Course. Decorated with New Orleans posters and furnished with bentwood pieces, it has a plate-glass view of the course. Start with escargot or pecan-crusted shrimp, then choose from Cajun prime rib, soft-shelled crab, duck in hunters sauce and shrimp creole. No dinner Sunday and Monday. ~ Waikoloa Village; 808-883-9644, fax 808-883-6298. DELUXE.

GROCERIES   On the western side of the island, there are several stores on the Kohala peninsula. Between Kawaihae and Kailua is one store in Puako, **Puako General Store**, with a small collection of groceries and dry goods. ~ 7 Puako Beach Drive; 808-882-7500.

K. Takata Store is an old market with an ample stock of groceries. It's the best place to shop north of Kailua. Closed Sunday afternoon. ~ Route 27, between Hawi and Kapaau; 808-889-5261.

MAKE A WISH

You may not associate Hawaii with stargazing, but the vast open spaces and crystal clear air make it a prime nocturnal viewing spot. **Mauna Kea Summit Adventures** offers a truly unique excursion: they'll pick you up and take you to the mountain while providing an informative narrative on the astronomy, geology and geography of Hawaii. After you've witnessed an indescribably beautiful sunset they'll take you mid-mountain where the highlight of the evening begins: stargazing through their portable telescope with narration provided by their knowledgeable experts. The evening concludes with hot chocolate and the peace of the night skies while you snuggle into the warm parka they've provided. ~ P.O. Box 9027, Kailua-Kona, HI 96745; 808- 322-2366, 888-322-2366, fax 808 - 322-6507; www.maunakea.com, e-mail info@maunakea.com.

A. Arakaki Store is conveniently located for campers and picnickers headed out to Pololu Valley. ~ Route 270, Halaula; 808-889-5262.

Whaler's General Store is a moderate-sized grocery market located in the Waikoloa mall complex. ~ Waikoloa Beach Drive, Waikoloa; 808-886-7057.

Up the mountain several miles above Waikoloa, you'll find **Waikoloa Village Market** in the Waikoloa Highlands Center. ~ 808-883-1088.

SHOPPING

Shopping in Kohala was once a matter of uncovering family-owned crafts shops in tiny towns. Now that it has become a major resort area, you can also browse at designer stores in several top-flight hotels. Simply drive along Akoni Pule Highway between Kailua and the Kohala Peninsula; you'll encounter, from south to north, the **Royal Waikoloan, Hilton Waikoloa Village, Mauna Lani Bay Hotel** and the **Mauna Kea Beach Hotel**. Each of these large resort complexes features an array of boutiques, knickknack shops, jewelers, sundries and other outlets.

Also consider the **Kings' Shops** in Waikoloa. Set on the road leading in to the Waikoloa resort complex, this mall contains clothing stores, a sundries shop and several other promising enterprises.

On the other hand, the diminutive town of Hawi, another of the island's clapboard plantation towns, hosts several artist shops. **Kohala Koa Gallery** has a marvelous little collection of island clothes, keepsakes and knickknacks. ~ Akoni Pule Highway; 808-889-0055. Another lunar landing place just down the road, **Sugar Moon** is a ceramics shop with beautifully crafted works in clay. ~ Akoni Pule Highway; 808-889-0994.

Farther along Akoni Pule Highway, in the falsefront town of Kapaau, you'll find **Ackerman Galleries**. Divided into two different stores on opposite sides of the street, Ackerman's features fine art in one location and crafts items in the other. ~ 808-889-5971; www.ackermangalleries.com.

NIGHTLIFE

Night owls along the Kohala Coast roost at one of four resort hotels. The Mauna Kea Beach Hotel has a Hawaiian band at **The Terrace** and features a solo guitarist or a jazz duo in the **Batik Room**. ~ Kaahumanu Highway, Kawaihae; 808-882-7222.

The **Honu Bar** at the Mauna Lani Bay Hotel is one of several places in this spacious resort to dance, listen to Hawaiian music, or imbibe. It swings to life Thursday through Saturday with a live jazz band. Some guests, however, may prefer a game of chess, pool or backgammon. ~ 68-1400 Mauna Lani Drive, Kawaihae; 808-885-6622.

Also in Kawaihae, there is the **Tres Hombres Beach Grill**, where you can enjoy the original collection of surfing memorabilia that decorates the place. ~ Kawaihae Center, Kawaihae; 808-882-1031.

Paradise Safaris' Mauna Kea Sunset Stargazing Trips takes you to the Mauna Kea summit for a telescopic adventure with astronomer Pat Wright. ~ Kailua; 808-322-2366.

The night scene at the **Royal Waikoloan** centers around a watering hole called the **Clipper Lounge** that offers a variety of diversions ranging from live bands to Polynesian revues. ~ Kaahumanu Highway, Waikoloa; 808-886-6789.

The **Paniolo Lounge** at the Orchid at Mauna Lani hosts a classical guitarist Monday and Tuesday, and a pianist and vocalist Wednesday through Saturday. ~ 1 North Kaniku Drive; 808-885-2000.

For Hawaiian music, try the **Bamboo Restaurant** on Friday and Saturday nights. Reservations required. ~ Akoni Pule Highway, Hawi; 808-889-5555.

BEACHES & PARKS

ANAEHOOMALU BEACH   An enchanting area, this is one of the island's most beautiful beaches. There are palm trees, two ancient fish ponds filled with barracuda, and a long crescent of white sand. Turn from the sea and take in the gorgeous mountain scenery. Or explore the nearby petroglyph field and archaeological ruins. This beach is very popular and often crowded since it's fronted by a major resort complex. Swimming is excellent along this partially protected shore; there is no lifeguard on duty. Snorkeling is good for beginners but it lacks the scenic diversity elsewhere. Mullet, threadfin, big-eyed scad, bonefish and *papio* are among the usual catches here. Facilities include picnic tables, restrooms and an outdoor shower; there are restaurants in the adjacent Royal Waikoloan. ~ Located a half-mile off Kaahumanu Highway, about 25 miles north of Kailua near the 76-mile marker.

HIDDEN ►   **"69" BEACH OR WAIALEA BAY**   No, it's not what you might think. This lovely beach is named for a numbered utility pole at the road turn-off rather than for licentious beach parties. The white-sand shoreline extends several hundred yards along a rocky cove. Despite houses nearby, the spot is fairly secluded; fallen *kiawe* trees along the beachfront provide tiny hideaways. It's a good place to swim but exercise caution. When the water is calm it's also a good spot for snorkeling. Surfers paddle out to the breaks near the southwest end of the bay and off the northwest point. There are no facilities here. ~ Located near the entrance to Hapuna Beach Park, about five miles south of Kawaihae. From Kaahumanu Highway, turn into the park entrance. Then take the paved road that runs southwest from the park (between the beach and the A-frames). Go about six-tenths of a mile on this road and then turn right on a dirt road (the road at the very bottom of the hill). When the road forks, after about one-tenth mile, go left. Follow this road another one-tenth mile around to the beach.

HAPUNA BEACH STATE PARK Here's one of the state's prettiest parks. A well-tended lawn—studded with *hala*, coconut and *kiawe* trees—rolls down to a wide corridor of white sand that extends for one-half mile, with points of lava at either end. Maui's Haleakala crater looms across the water. This is a popular and generally very crowded place. Unfortunately, a major resort hotel was built at one end of the beach. Swimming is excellent at the north end of the beach but beware of dangerous currents when the surf is high; lifeguards on duty. Snorkelers enjoy the coral and fish near the rocks and cliffs at the end of the beach. *Papio*, red bigeye, mullet, threadfin and *menpachi* are often caught here. Facilities include picnic areas, restrooms and showers. ~ Located on Kaahumanu Highway, three miles south of Kawaihae.

▲ No tent or trailer camping is allowed. However, screened A-frame shelters, located on a rise above the beach, can be rented. These cottages, which cost $20 per night, are equipped with a table, sleeping platforms and electricity; they sleep up to four people. Bring your own bedding and cooking utensils. Toilet and kitchen facilities are shared among all six A-frames. For reservations, contact Hawaii State Parks. ~ 808-882-7995.

SPENCER BEACH PARK Lacking the uncommon beauty of Anaehoomalu or Hapuna, this spacious park is still lovely. There's a wide swath of white sand, backed by a lawn and edged with *kiawe* and coconut trees. Swimming is excellent here and snorkeling will satisfy beginners and experts alike. Anglers try for *papio*, red bigeye, mullet, threadfin and *menpachi*. There are plenty of facilities: picnic area, restrooms, showers, a large pavilion, volleyball and basketball courts and electricity. This is the only county park with a nighttime security patrol. Also, the gates close you in from 11 p.m. to 6 a.m. ~ The park is located off Kawaihae Road about one mile south of Kawaihae.

▲ Both tent and trailer camping are allowed; $3 per night. County permit and reservations are required. This is a very popular place to camp so reserve early—capacity is limited.

MAHUKONA BEACH PARK This now-abandoned harbor village and boat landing lies along a rocky, windswept shore. The lawn is shaded with *kiawe* trees; there's no sandy beach here at all. Nicer areas lie to the south, but if you seek a site far from the frenzied crowd, this is a good retreat. The rocks make for poor access for swimming but snorkeling is good. Frequent catches include threadfin, mullet, *menpachi*, *papio* and red bigeye. Facilities include a picnic area, restrooms, showers and electricity.

Text continued on page 198.

Snorkeling & Scuba Diving the Gold Coast

Simply stated, Hawaii's Kona Coast offers some of the world's most spectacular diving. All along this western shoreline lie magnificent submerged caves, lava flows, cliffs and colorful coral reefs.

Protected from prevailing trade winds by Mauna Kea and Mauna Loa, Kona enjoys the gentlest conditions. Usually the weather is sunny, the surf mild and the water clear (visibility is usually in the 100-foot range). Locals claim they get about 345 ideal diving days a year. It's small wonder, then, that adventurers travel from all over the world to explore Kona's underwater world.

What will you see if you join them? The Kona Coast has over 650 species of reef fish including the brightly colored yellow tang, the aptly named raccoon butterflyfish, the trumpetfish, the coronetfish, the cow-eyed porcupine pufferfish, and the black, yellow and white moorish idol. Large marine animals abound as well, including green sea turtles, hawksbill turtles, manta rays, spotted eagle rays, pilot whales, pygmy killer whales and humpback whales.

When looking for marine life, swim over the coral, looking in, under and around all the corners, caves and crevices. Many spectacular sea creatures await discovery in these hiding spots. Keep in mind that while coral looks like rock, it is a living creature that can be easily killed. Standing on it, touching it, kicking it with your fin or even kicking sand onto it from the ocean floor can damage the coral. So gently drift over the reef and you will be rewarded with new discoveries and close encounters with beautiful tropical fish.

Following are brief descriptions of the best snorkeling and diving spots, as well as shops that provide equipment and tours. For specific information on a particular dive sight, drop by one of these shops. I also recommend you buy waterproof fish identification cards. You can take them into the water and use them to identify these magnificently colored fish.

KOHALA COAST SPOTS Anaehoomalu Beach is good for beginners, but it lacks the scenic diversity of other areas. There's good diving at the end of the road leading to Puako, but it's rocky. "69" Beach (or Waialea Bay) features good underwater opportunities when the surf is mild. Hapuna Beach State Park has an area that abounds in coral and fish near the rocks and cliffs at the end of the beach. Spencer Beach Park is filled with coral and suits beginners and experts alike.

Mahukona Beach Park is an old shipping area littered with underwater refuse that makes for great exploring. **Kapaa Beach Park** offers good diving, but it has a rocky entrance and tricky currents. **Keokea Beach Park**, an excellent spearfishing area, is often plagued by wind and high surf.

KAILUA-KONA AREA SPOTS   Kamakahonu Beach, the sand patch next to Kailua's King Kamehameha Kona Beach Hotel, is a crowded but convenient snorkel site. There are corals and many species of fish here, but watch out for heavy boat traffic along the wharf. On the south side of the pier, at the small beach where the Ironman Triathlon swim begins, is good snorkeling.

Old Airport Beach, just a stone's skip north of town, affords excellent diving on either side. The entry is rocky, but once in, you'll find the waters spectacular. Some glass-bottom boats tour this area.

Honokohau Beach has some good spots south of the small-boat harbor. **Kaloko Park**, north of Honokohau Harbor, has a trail that leads to an excellent beach and snorkeling site. Sometimes nudists are on the beach.

Kahaluu Beach Park, with its easy entry to the water and complete beach services including restrooms, lifeguard, picnic tables and showers, is the best spot for beginners. The waters here are too shallow for great scuba diving, which means they're all the better for snorkeling.

SOUTH KONA SPOTS   Across from Napoopoo Beach Park, at the Captain Cook Monument, is an excellent diving spot—so good, in fact, that it draws diving tours and glass-bottom boats. The best diving is across Keala-kekua Bay near the Captain Cook Monument.

Keei Beach features a lot of coral and, reportedly, a sea grotto. At **Puuho-nua o Honaunau Park**, also known as the City of Refuge, there are two natural steps carved into the rocky shoreline that allow for easy entry directly into swarms of reef fish. Because of the abundance of colorful marine life, the accessible location, the easy entry and the variety of depths, this is one of the coast's best spots for snorkelers and scuba divers alike. **Hookena Beach Park** offers good dive spots near the cliffs south of the beach. **Milolii** has excellent diving areas as well as fascinating tidepools.

DIVING TOURS AND EQUIPMENT   **Jack's Diving Locker** has detailed information and equipment rentals. They also have three dive boats and offer guided trips for snorkelers and scuba divers to offshore reefs. ~ Coconut Grove Market Place, 75-5819 Alii Drive, Kailua; 808-329-7585, 800-345-4807; www.jacksdivinglocker.com. **Fair Wind** offers guided snorkeling, snuba, and scuba trips and supplies you with equipment. The doubledecker *Fair Wind II* picks up excursionists at Keauhou Bay and goes to Kealakekua Bay. ~ 78-7130 Kaleopapa Road, Keauhou Bay; 808-322-2788; www.fair-wind.com.

There's no drinking water. ~ Located off Akoni Pule Highway about 13 miles north of Kawaihae.

▲ Tent and trailer; $3 per night. County permit required.

KAPAA BEACH PARK 🏊 🎣 ⚓ Besides a spectacular view of Maui, this rocky, wind-plagued park has little to offer. It does have a miniature cove bounded by *kiawe* trees, but lacks any sand, which is sometimes nice to have on a beach. Swimming is difficult because of the rocks. Kapaa offers good diving but the entrance is rocky and the currents are tricky. Fishing is probably your best bet here since you can stand on the rocks and try for threadfin, mullet, red bigeye, *papio* and *menpachi*. Picnic areas and restrooms are the only facilities. There's no drinking water. ~ Located off Akoni Pule Highway about 14 miles north of Kawaihae.

▲ Tents and trailers are allowed, but the terrain is very rocky for tent camping; $3 per night. County permit required.

KEOKEA BEACH PARK 🏊 ⚓ Seclusion is the password to this beautiful little park with its cliff-rimmed cove and tiered lawn fringed by *hala* and palm trees. Set way out on the Kohala peninsula, this retreat receives very heavy rainfall. You can swim here but only with extreme caution. It's an excellent area for spearfishing but is often plagued by high wind and high surf. Mullet, *papio*, red bigeye, threadfin and *menpachi* are the main catches here. There are picnic areas, drinking water, restrooms and showers. ~ Take Akoni Pule Highway about six miles past Hawi. Turn at the sign and follow the winding road one mile.

▲ Tent and trailer; $3 per night. County permit required.

The good news: The Kohala Coast is home to the island's best beaches. The bad news: Since the 1980s, they've all been developed.

Kailua-Kona Area

At the center of the tourist scene on the Kona Coast is the contemporary town of Kailua. Here, extending for five miles along Alii Drive from the King Kamehameha Hotel to Keauhou Bay, is a string of hotels, restaurants, condominiums and shopping malls. Like a little Waikiki, Kailua-Kona is the commercial focus for this entire side of the island.

SIGHTS

Despite the tinsel and tourist trappings, this old fishing village and former haunt of Hawaiian royalty still retains some of its charm. If you tour **Kailua wharf** around 4 p.m., the fishing boats may be hauling freshly caught marlin onto the docks. Some of the finest marlin grounds in the world lie off this shoreline and the region is renowned for other deep-sea fish. The wharf itself is a departure point not only for fishing charters but for snorkeling tours and glass-bottom boat cruises as well. It's also a favorite place for viewing Kona's fabled sunsets. ~ Alii Drive.

On the grounds of the nearby King Kamehameha's Kona Beach Hotel rests **Ahuena Heiau**, an important historical site that has been reconstructed. Unfortunately, a hotel luau facility was built immediately next to the site. This compound represents the royal grounds used by Kamehameha I for several years during the early 19th century. Tours of the hotel grounds are offered Monday through Friday at 1:30 p.m. ~ 75-5660 Palani Road; 808-329-2911, fax 808-329-4602; www.konabeachhotel.com, e-mail reservations@hthcorp.com.

Hulihee Palace, a small but elegant estate built in 1838, sits on Alii Drive in the middle of town. Today it's a museum housing royal Hawaiian relics. It seems that this two-story estate was built by the brother-in-law of Kamehameha I and later used by King Kalakaua as a summer palace during the 1880s. Among the fine furnishings are many handcrafted from native *koa*. Admission. ~ Alii Drive; 808-329-1877, fax 808-329-1321.

Mokuaikaua Church, directly across the street, is the oldest church in the islands. The first missionaries anchored offshore in 1820 after sailing over 18,000 miles around Cape Horn from Boston. They built the imposing lava-and-coral structure in 1836. By the way, that churchyard tree with the weird salami-shaped fruit is a sausage tree from West Africa.

Contrasting with these venerable sites is **Atlantis Adventures**, an impressive 80-ton submarine. Diving to depths of 120 feet, this 48-passenger sub explores tropical reefs. During the hour-long voyage, passengers view the underwater world through large viewing ports. Admission. ~ 808-329-6626, 800-548-6262, fax 808-329-1153; www.atlantisadventures.com.

Almost everything in Kailua sits astride Alii Drive, the waterfront street that extends south from town to Keauhou Bay. Several miles from Kailua, this road passes **Disappearing Sands Beach** (or Magic Sands Beach). The lovely white sand here is often washed away by heavy winter surf and then redeposited when the big waves subside.

Farther along, on the rocky shore of Kahaluu Bay, is **St. Peter's Catholic Church**. This blue-and-white clapboard chapel, precariously perched on a lava foundation, is reputedly the world's second-smallest church.

Located just across the bay are several interesting historical sites: two *heiaus* and the **King's Pool**. You can continue on to Keauhou Bay, where a monument marks the **Birthplace of Kamehameha III**.

Patey's Place in Paradise, a hostel in the center of Kailua, is small, clean and—remarkable for this area—conveniently priced. There are dormitory-style accommodations for 20 people as well as

LODGING

four private rooms that sleep two. Kitchen facilities, a television room and airport pickup are provided. ~ 75-195 Ala Ona Ona Street; 808-326-7018, 800-972-7408, fax 808-326-7640. BUDGET.

Kona Seaside Hotel is a sprawling 225-room complex set in the heart of Kailua. Located across the street from the ocean, this multi-faceted facility features the Tower Wing; the Garden Wing, where the rooms come with mini-kitchenettes; and the Pool Wing, where the rooms are smaller and less fashionable but are conveniently placed around one of the hotel's two swimming pools. While the more expensive rooms add lanais and wall-to-wall carpeting, all the accommodations are tastefully done. A lounge and restaurant are adjacent. ~ 75-5646 Palani Road; 808-329-2455, 800-367-7000, fax 808-922-0052; www.sand-seaside.com. DELUXE.

Kona Bay Hotel is part of the old Kona Inn, the rest of which fell to Kailua developers, who have perversely transformed it into yet another shopping mall. What remains is a four-story semi-circular structure with a pool, bar, restaurant and lounge in the center. The rooms are large, tastefully furnished and quiet. Some have lava walls that provide a pleasant backdrop plus excellent soundproofing. The staff is friendly, and the atmosphere is very appealing. I once spent a relaxing month here and highly recommend the place. ~ 75-5739 Alii Drive; 808-329-1393, 800-367-5102, fax 808-935-7903; www.unclebilly.com/kb.html, e-mail resv@unclebilly.com. MODERATE.

Kona Tiki Hotel, a mile down the road, is a quaint hotel neatly situated on the ocean. The rooms are bright and clean. Despite the contrasting decorative themes and the noise from Alii Drive, I recommend this 15-unit establishment for its oceanview lanais, oceanfront pool, barbecue, garden and complimentary continental breakfast. Some of the rooms are equipped with mini-kitchenettes (sink, refrigerator and two-burner stove crowded into one unit). ~ 75-5968 Alii Drive; 808-329-1425, fax 808-327-9402. BUDGET TO MODERATE.

Kona Islander Inn occupies several three-story buildings spread across a lush swath of land. Set between Alii Drive and Route 11 on Kailua's outskirts, this hotel has a large lobby and an oval pool flanked by MacArthur palms. All rooms have small lanais, cable televisions, microwaves, refrigerators, carpets and air conditioning. Tastefully appointed, but lacking a good ocean view. ~ 75-5776 Kuakini Highway; 808-329-3333, 800-622-5348, fax 808-326-4137; www.konahawaii.com, e-mail konahawaii@hotmail.com. BUDGET TO MODERATE.

Kona White Sands Apartment Hotel, located just across the street from Disappearing Sands Beach (the nicest beach along Alii Drive), is a ten-unit hotel of one-bedroom apartments. Each comes with a kitchenette and ceiling fans. The cinderblock and plasterboard walls are pretty plain, but who needs fancy interior decoration with that knockout ocean view? Rooms are cross-ventilated, and the cooling breeze will probably bring along noise from cars and sun revelers. That's the extra price for living this close to the Kona Coast. Many people are willing to pay it, so you'll have to reserve a room far in advance. ~ 77-6467 Alii Drive. For reservations here and at Kona Islander Inn, contact the Hawaii Resorts Management for reservations, 75-5776 Kuakini Highway, Suite 105-C, Kailua-Kona, HI 96740; 808-329-9393, 800-553-5035, fax 808-326-4137; www.konahawaii.com. MODERATE TO DELUXE.

Anchoring one end of Kailua Bay is the town's most historic hotel. The **King Kamehameha Kona Beach Hotel** is deserving of

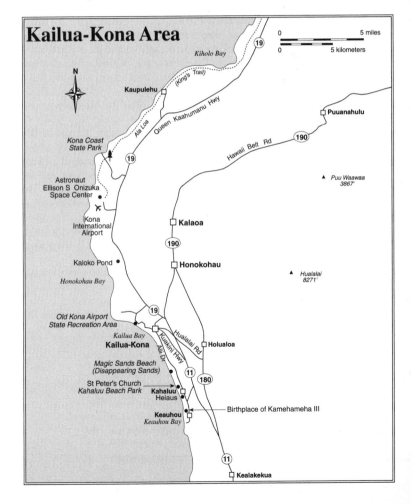

Kailua-Kona Area

note. The lobby alone is worth the price of admission: It's a wood-paneled affair along which you can trace the history of ancient Hawaii. For its guests, the "King Kam" has a pool, tennis courts and jacuzzi, plus a host of other amenities ranging from an activities desk to room service. The rooms themselves are quite spacious, fashionably decorated and equipped with positively everything. You will find plush carpeting, color televisions, air-conditioning, refrigerators and lanais with spectacular views of the ocean or mountains. ~ 75-5660 Palani Road; 808-329-2911, 800-367-2111, fax 808-329-4602; www.konabeachhotel.com, e-mail hthcorp@worldnet.att.net. MODERATE TO DELUXE.

Situated on a lava-rock beach just outside Kailua is the **Kailua Plantation House**. This contemporary two-story, plantation-style bed and breakfast has five rooms, all with private baths and lanais. Three of the rooms also feature oceanfront views. There's a jacuzzi and tiny pool along the oceanfront and a comfortable sitting room for guests. The entire place, painted white with oak trim, is light, bright and airy. Island art adorns the walls and a sense of easy elegance pervades the place. ~ 75-5948 Alii Drive; 808-329-3727, 888-357-4262, fax 808-326-7323; www.tales. com/kph. DELUXE TO ULTRA-DELUXE.

Aston Keauhou Beach Resort is a true sleeper. A large, blocky, seven-story hotel from the outside, it hardly seems like it could possess the Hawaiian spirit. But the beautifully landscaped grounds include an ancient *heiau* and other archaeological sites, and the waterfront boasts magnificent tidepools that extend for acres. The airy Hawaiian-style lobby overlooks an oceanfront swimming pool, a restaurant and the poolside Makai Bar. Spacious guest rooms look out over the ocean or gardens. ~ 78-6740 Alii Drive; 808-332-3441, 800-367-6025, fax 808-322-3117; www.aston hotels.com. MODERATE TO ULTRA-DELUXE.

HIDDEN ▶   Of course, when money is no object the place to stay is **Kona Village Resort**, a very plush, very private colony located 12 miles north of Kailua. Favored by movie stars and other celebrities seeking escape from autograph hounds and aggressive agents, this

A TIP OF THE HAT TO THE *CHALLENGER*

You can pay your respects to the crew of the space shuttle *Challenger* at the **Astronaut Ellison S. Onizuka Space Center**. Located eight miles north of Kailua at Kona International Airport, this interactive learning center is a tribute to Onizuka, who lived in Hawaii, and the other astronauts who died in the 1986 tragedy. Videos and interactive displays trace the astronauts' lives and the development of the space program. Admission. ~ 808-329-3441, fax 808-326-9751; www.onizukaspacecenter.org.

regal retreat is set along a white-sand cove in an ancient Hawaiian fishing village. The individual guest cottages are thatched-roof structures (*hales*), variously designed to represent the traditional houses of Hawaiian, Tahitian, Fijian, Samoan and other Polynesian groups. There are no TVs, telephones, radios, clocks or air-conditioners in the rooms, but you will find serenity, solitude and a well-heeled version of hidden Hawaii, not to mention a fitness center, tennis courts, sailboats, outrigger canoes and glass-bottom excursion boats. Prices are in the stratosphere and are based on the American plan. ~ P.O. Box 1299, Kaupulehu-Kona, HI 96745; 808-325-5555, 800-367-5290, fax 808-325-5124; www.kona village.com. ULTRA-DELUXE.

CONDOS

One-bedroom, two-bath apartments at **Kona Alii** run from $119 double (and from $99 during the off-season, April 1 to December 15). This seven-story building is just across the street from the ocean. ~ 75-5782 Alii Drive. Reserve through Hawaii Resorts Management. Contact the Hawaii Resorts Management for reservations, 75-5776 Kuakini Highway, Suite 105-C, Kailua-Kona, HI 96740; 808-329-9393, 800-553-5035, fax 808-326-4137; www.kona hawaii.com.

The Sea Village offers one-bedroom garden view units starting at $90 single or double; two bedrooms, two baths are $130 for one to four people. There's a swimming pool and tennis courts. Oceanfront, but no beach. ~ 75-6002 Alii Drive, about one mile south of Kailua. Reserve through Sun Quest Vacations, 808-329-6488, 800-367-5168; www.sunquest-hawaii.com, e-mail sqvac@sun quest-hawaii.com.

Kona Riviera Villa is a relatively small condo on a lava-rock beach outside Kailua. It's attractively landscaped, has a pool and rents one-bedroom units for $85 to $110 ($75 to $100 from April 15 to December 14). Three-day minimum. ~ 75-6124 Alii Drive; 808-329-1996. For reservations, contact Knutson and Associates, 75-6082 Alii Drive, Suite 8, Kailua-Kona, HI 96740; 800-800-6202, fax 808-326-2178; www.konahawaiirentals.com, e-mail knutson@aloha.net.

Apartments at **Kona Bali Kai** can be rented from Hawaii Resorts Management. Amenities include a jacuzzi and pool. It's just one mile from Disappearing Sands Beach. ~ 76-6246 Alii Drive; 800-553-5035.

Kona Magic Sands has a studio apartment renting for $75 without air conditioning, $85 with, year-round, single or double. It's located on the ocean, next to Disappearing Sands Beach. ~ 77-6452 Alii Drive. Contact the Hawaii Resorts Management for reservations, 75-5776 Kuakini Highway, Suite 105-C, Kailua-Kona, HI 96740; 808-329-9393, 800-553-5035, fax 808-326-4137; www. konahawaii.com.

Aston Kona By The Sea is a large, trimly landscaped complex on a lava-rock beach. The suites are one- and two-bedroom; all have two baths and a lanai; there's a pool and jacuzzi. Rates start at $235. ~ 75-6106 Alii Drive; 808-327-2300, 800-321-2558, fax 808-327-2333; www.aston-hotels.com.

DINING

Kona Coast Shopping Center, located at 74-5588 Palani Road, houses several short-order joints. **Betty's Chinese Kitchen** serves tasty, nutritious, inexpensive meals at its cafeteria-style emporium. ~ 808-329-3770. BUDGET.

Kamuela Deli is a plate-lunch place next door. You can dine on hot and cold sandwiches as well as an array of full meals. Of special interest are *shoyu* chicken and pork with cabbage plates, not to mention the fried rice with Spam. ~ 808-334-0017. BUDGET.

If this doesn't intrigue you, head downhill to the North Kona Shopping Center. There you'll find the **Sushi Shop**, a take-out window with a patio and tables. ~ 808-987-8490. BUDGET TO ULTRA-DELUXE.

In the King Kamehameha Mall, between the King Kamehameha Hotel and the Kona Industrial Area, is **Ocean Seafood Chinese Restaurant**. In traditional Chinese-restaurant style, the menu is divided into 13 sections ("A" through "M") with about 15 dishes for each category. So I won't even begin to tell you what they have. Suffice it to say that it's all there. ~ 75-5626 Kuakini Highway; 808-329-3055. BUDGET TO ULTRA-DELUXE.

Sibu Café prepares Indonesian and Southeast Asian dishes daily for lunch and dinner. Among the tangy favorites at this outdoor café are beef *saté*, tofu and vegetable stir-fry and Balinese chicken (which is marinated, cooked over an open flame, then served with peanut sauce). ~ Banyan Court, Alii Drive; 808-329-1112, fax 808-328-7308. MODERATE.

The **Oceanview Inn**, a large, informal dining room opposite Kailua Bay, has a voluminous menu. Chinese, American, Hawaiian, fresh fish and meat dishes, served all day, comprise only part of the selection. There's also a complete breakfast menu. Closed Monday. ~ Alii Drive; 808-329-9998. BUDGET TO MODERATE.

Next door is **Stan's Restaurant**, where you can order from a unique menu that lists dinners by price. Here you'll find numerous steak, seafood and chicken concoctions. This open-air establishment overlooking Kailua Bay has rattan-style furnishings and a windswept waiting area. Lunch isn't served, but breakfast features papaya, pineapple or banana hotcakes. ~ 75-5687 Alii Drive; 808-329-4500, fax 808-329-6157. MODERATE.

Basil's Restaurant, a hole-in-the-wall bistro punched into a storefront along Alii Drive, has reasonably priced Italian food. The menu is pretty standard as is the red-checkered oilcloth interior. ~ 75-5707 Alii Drive; 808-326-7836. BUDGET TO DELUXE.

A sport synonymous with Hawaii, surfing was pioneered by the Hawaiian royal family and was once reserved for their exclusive enjoyment. Today, it is a sport for everyone.

Above: Oheo Gulch (Seven Sacred Pools), located in the shadow of Haleakala, features a series of waterfalls and rock-bound pools, perfect for a fresh-water dip.

Below: The winding Hana Highway rewards drivers with secluded grottoes and lush vegetation.

Not all of Oahu's beaches are crowded. Leave Waikiki and within a few miles you'll discover places like Halona Cove Beach.

Top: Horseback trails above Hanalei offer stunning views of the Hanalei Valley.

Above left: Kayakers navigate Kauai's lovely Hanalei Bay.

Above right: Cyclists cruise by the Big Island's Parker Ranch, one of the world's largest independently owned cattle ranches.

Right: Ocean breezes at Diamond Head Beach Park provide perfect conditions for Oahu windsurfers.

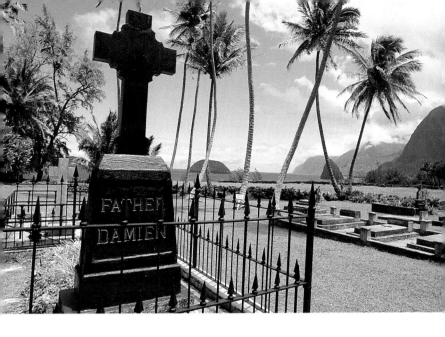

Above: Father Damien's grave at Philomena Ranch in Kalaupapa, Molokai. Known as the "Martyr of Molokai," the Belgian priest worked and lived with the lepers exiled to Molokai's lonely, windswept north shore.

Below: Sunrise and sunset on Lanai are the best times to experience the dramatic formation at the Garden of the Gods.

Above: Steam clouds rise from the ever-changing shoreline of the Big Island as hot lava pours into the sea.

Below: Haleakala Crater, home to Hawaiian legends, rises over 10,000 feet on Maui.

Left: A Native Hawaiian weaves baskets at Kawakiu Beach on Molokai.

Below left: The Big Island is home to numerous anthurium farms.

Below right: A silversword in Haleakala Crater on Maui. Each plant blooms once and then dies.

The northeast coast of Kauai is dotted with secluded beaches.

Flashbacks Bar and Grill, on the same waterfront drive, specializes in '50s Americana cuisine. Here you'll dine out on a lanai overlooking Kailua Bay or in one of several open-air rooms attractively paneled in *lauhala* and bamboo. This restaurant offers blue-plate specials, roast pork and beef, burgers, seafood, pasta and floats for dessert. ~ 75-5669 Alii Drive; 808-326-2840, fax 808-329-3612. MODERATE.

You not only can dine inexpensively at **Aki's Cafe**, you can dine under an umbrella overlooking the water. They may not live up to their motto of "fine Japanese and American food," but the cuisine is passable. They offer hamburgers, fish and chips and spaghetti on the American side of the menu, with sushi, stir-fry, yakitori and curry dishes on the other. For dinner, there's steak, chicken teriyaki and fish *misoyaki*. ~ 75-5699 Alii Drive; 808-329-0090. BUDGET.

If you care for Mediterranean, **Cassandra's Greek Tavern** has tables out on the patio as well as in a cozy little dining room.

Kailua

0   .5 mile
0   .5 kilometer

N

Queen Kaahumanu Hwy   19
Palani Rd   190
Luhia St
Alapa St
Eho St
Kaiwi St
Kopiko St
Pawai Pl
Kuakini Rd   11
Ololi
Ala Onaona
Kalani
Alakai
Lamaokaola
Alahou
Kalawa
Alanoe
Sarona
Kakina
Hualalai
Hawaii Belt Rd
182
Hualalai Rd
Alii Dr
Kahakai St
Walua Rd
Kuakini Hwy
Lunapule St
Hualalai Rd
Alii Dr
11

POINTS OF INTEREST
- **A**   Ahuena Heiau
- **B**   Atlantis Adventures
- **C**   Hale Halawai
- **D**   Hawaii Visitors Bureau
- **E**   Hulihee Palace
- **F**   Mokuaikaua Church
- **G**   Old Kona Airport State Recreation Area

Souvlaki, kebobs, moussaka and dolmas dominate the menu, but they also prepare steak and seafood dishes. No lunch Saturday and Sunday. ~ 75-5719 Alii Drive; 808-334-1066. MODERATE TO ULTRA-DELUXE.

Don't let the strip mall setting dissuade you from easing on over to **Oodles of Noodles**. Focus on the fine local art and stellar menu instead. The cuisine varies from Japanese to Thai to Vietnamese to Italian with a single common denominator—everything is prepared with noodles. It's also a showcase for one of Hawaii's finest chefs—Amy Ferguson Ota. If you try the duck noodle salad, you may be back every day you're on the island. ~ 75-1027 Henry Street #102; 808-329-9222, fax 808-329-0123. MODERATE TO DELUXE.

Drop in at the **Kona Ranch House** or the adjoining Plantation Lanai facility and you'll find an inventory of entrées ranging from ribs to chicken and from New York steak to fresh fish. There are also inexpensive sandwiches and appetizer plates. At breakfast Kona Ranch House offers an array of egg dishes. No dinner. ~ 75-5653 Ololi Street; 808-329-7061, fax 808-329-2166. BUDGET TO MODERATE.

The commemorative sign at the **Kona Inn** tells the tale of the old inn—how it was built back in the steamship era when Kona was gaining fame as a marlin fishing ground. The bad news is that the original hotel was converted into a shopping mall—of which this contemporary namesake is a part. The good news is that the restaurant is quite attractive—an open-air, oceanfront affair with two separate dining facilities. The Kona Inn Restaurant serves grilled appetizers and sandwiches in its café/grill. The dining room has a separate menu with several fresh fish dishes daily as well as prime rib and Hawaiian-style chicken. ~ 75-5744 Alii Drive; 808-329-4455, fax 808-327-9358. MODERATE TO DELUXE.

Set on a second-story terrace overlooking the ocean, **Lulu's** is one of Kailua's pleasingly windswept addresses. You can lean against the tile bar or sink into a booth, then order from a straight-

MEXICAN STANDOFF

For Mexican food along Alii Drive, you have two choices. At **Tres Hombres Beach Grill** you'll get a good, filling Mexican meal in a comfortable restaurant. ~ Alii Drive and Walua Road; 808-329-2173, fax 808-331-2850. BUDGET. If you're seeking a tropical drink and a tropical sunset over the water, then **Pancho & Lefty's Cantina & Restaurante** is the place. Similar food, different ambience. ~ 75-5719 Alii Drive; 808-326-2171. MODERATE TO DELUXE.

forward sandwiches-salads-and-hamburgers menu. ~ 75-5819 Alii Drive; 808-331-2633, fax 808-329-6766. MODERATE.

Durty Jake's Café and Bar serves an "American Continental" menu in an open air, casual setting, with fresh seafood and pizza as well as the normal fare. Full bar. Open for breakfast, lunch and dinner. ~ 75-5819 Alii Drive; 808-329-7366; www.durtyjakes. com. MODERATE.

Don't be deceived by the formica tables and cafeteria atmosphere, or the fact that it's located in an industrial park. **Sam Choy's Restaurant**, established by one of the islands' premier chefs, is a gourmet ghetto. Here you can enjoy oversized platters of Oriental lamb chops, Chinese-style honey duck, sautéed pork loin or seafood laulau. Or stop by for breakfast when they serve fried poke omelettes, pork chops and eggs, and Spam with Portuguese sausage. No dinner on Sunday or Monday. ~ 73-5576 Kauhola Street, Kaloko Light Industrial Park; located off Kaahumanu Highway four miles north of Kailua; 808-326-1545, fax 808-334-1230. MODERATE TO DELUXE.

Jameson's By the Sea is a lovely waterfront restaurant with an emphasis on fresh local seafood dishes. Tucked unpretentiously into the corner of a large condominium, Jameson's conveys a modest sense of elegance: bentwood furniture, potted palms, a seascape from the lanai or through plate-glass windows and good service. Choose from an enticing menu of fresh local catches, steaks, chicken dishes and other gourmet delights. Lunch and dinner weekdays, dinner only on weekends. ~ 77-6452 Alii Drive near Disappearing Sands Beach; 808-329-3195, fax 808-329-0780. MODERATE TO DELUXE.

For Continental cuisine in a fashionable setting, consider **La Bourgogne French Restaurant**. This French country dining room features New York steak with peppercorn sauce, roast saddle of lamb, veal sweetbreads with Madeira sauce, coquilles St. Jacques and fresh fish selections. For appetizers there are escargots, baked brie and lobster cocktail. Round off the meal with cherries jubilee or chocolate mousse and you have a French feast right here in tropical Hawaii. Reservations are highly recommended. Dinner only. Closed Sunday and Monday. ~ Kuakini Plaza on Kuakini Highway, four miles south of Kailua; 808-329-6711; e-mail burgundy@gte.net. DELUXE TO ULTRA-DELUXE.

GROCERIES

The best place to shop anywhere along the Kona Coast is in the town of Kailua. This commercial center features several supermarkets as well as a number of specialty shops. One of the first choices among supermarkets is **Sack 'n Save** in the center of Kailua. It has everything you could possibly need. ~ 75-5595 Palani Road, Lanihau Shopping Center; 808-326-2729.

If you'd prefer another supermarket with a similar selection, try **K.T.A. Super Store**. It's open every day from 5 a.m. to midnight, and is another of the Kailua-Kona area's most convenient and accessible shopping facilities. ~ Kona Coast Shopping Center; 808-329-1677.

Kona Natural Foods has an ample stock of vitamins, bathing supplies, grains, fruits and vegetables. By the simple fact that it is the only store of its kind in the area, it wins my recommendation. ~ Crossroads Shopping Center; 808-329-2296.

SHOPPING   You might remember that song about how "L.A. is a great big freeway." Well, the Hawaiian version could easily be "Kailua is a great big mall." I have never seen so many shopping arcades squeezed into so small a space. Here are goldsmiths, boutiques, jewelers galore, travel agencies, sandal-makers, knickknack shops, sundries, T-shirt shops and much, much more, all crowded onto Alii Drive.

Personally, I think most items sold along this strip are tacky or overpriced, and in some cases, both. One place I do recommend, however, is **Middle Earth Bookshoppe**. Here you'll find a good selection of Hawaiian books, as well as paperbacks and current bestsellers. ~ Kona Plaza Shopping Arcade, 75-5719 Alii Drive; 808-329-2123.

The **Kona Inn Shopping Village**, which parallels the waterfront, features dozens of shops. Because of its convenient location and variety of stores, it is the center of the visitor shopping scene. ~ Alii Drive.

While here be sure to stop by **Hula Heaven**. This retro Hawaiian shop has old movie posters, antique ukuleles, hula girl knickknacks and reproduction dresses and aloha shirts. ~ 75-5744 Alii Drive; 808-329-7885.

Kona Marketplace across the street is another prime shopping destination. Within this complex is the **Kim Taylor Reece Gallery**, which specializes in artistic photographs of classic hula dancers. ~ 75-5729 C Alii Drive; 808-331-2433.

One of the newer and more tastefully designed malls is **Waterfront Row**, a raw-wood-and-plank-floor shopping complex with perhaps a dozen stores and restaurants. ~ 75-5770 Alii Drive.

The **Hulihee Palace Gift Shop**, a small store located behind the palace, specializes in Hawaiian handicrafts and literature. ~ Alii Drive; 808-329-1877.

In addition to the centers located along Alii Drive, there are three large shopping malls a couple blocks up from the water. **Kona Coast Shopping Center** and **Lanihau Center** sit on either side of Palani Road near the Kaahumanu Highway intersection.

Just south, where the highway intersects with Henry Street, is the **Crossroads Shopping Center**. Across the highway is a **Borders** bookstore. ~ Queen Kaahumanu Highway; 808-331-1668.

The **King Kamehameha Kona Beach Hotel** has a cluster of shops. Several decades back, before the luxury hotels mushroomed along the Kohala Coast, this hotel was a prime stop for shoppers and sojourners alike. Today its glory has faded, but it still sports several interesting stores. ~ 75-5660 Palani Road; 808-329-2911.

Right next door, between the hotel and the Kona Industrial Area, is the **King Kamehameha Mall**, a small, modern complex with perhaps a dozen shops. ~ 75-5626 Kuakini Highway.

Kailua Village Farmers Market, where local growers gather under plastic tarps to sell their wares, is a good place to pick up home-grown fruits and vegetables. ~ Alii Drive, just south of Hualalai Road.

Toward the end of Alii Drive, several miles south of Kailua, stands the **Keauhou Shopping Center**. With several dozen stores, it is one of the largest complexes on the island (though granted, *Big* Island does not mean big shopping malls). ~ Alii Highway and Kamehameha III Road.

What action there is here is near the shorefront on Alii Drive. **NIGHTLIFE** Both of the following places have stunning ocean views and are usually packed to the gills. **Huggo's** features karaoke and various live bands every evening. ~ Alii Drive and Kakakai Road; 808-329-1493.

The **Billfish Bar**, located poolside at the King Kamehameha Kona Beach Hotel, has live Hawaiian contemporary music on weekends. ~ 75-5660 Palani Road; 808-329-2911.

Several of the waterfront nightspots in Kailua shine spotlights in the water so you can watch manta rays gliding along the shore.

For an evening of slow rhythms and dancing cheek-to-cheek, there's the **Windjammer Lounge** at the Royal Kona Resort, which has live music and entertainment on weekends. ~ 75-5852 Alii Drive; 808-329-3111.

To sample Hawaii's own designer beers, check out the **Kona Brewing Company**, a brew pub serving an exotic array of local flavors. ~ Kona Shopping Center, Kuakini Highway and Palani Road; 808-334-2739.

Another good bet is the **Big Island Comedy Club**, an ever-moving event that's staged at popular nightspots in Kailua and elsewhere along the coast. ~ 808-329-4368.

Catering to both a gay and straight clientele, **The Other Side** offers pool tables, dart boards and recorded sounds. ~ 74-5484 Kaiwi Street; 808-329-7226.

BEACHES & PARKS

HALE HALAWAI This small oceanfront park, fringed with coconut trees, has an activities pavilion but no beach. Its central location in Kailua does make the park a perfect place to watch the sunset, though. ~ Located near the intersection of Alii Drive and Hualalai Road in Kailua.

HIDDEN ►

OLD KONA AIRPORT STATE RECREATION AREA This white-sand beach parallels Kailua's former landing strip, extending for a half-mile along a lava-crusted shore. Very popular with Kailuans, this is a conveniently located spot for catching some rays. The water is shallow, with a rocky bottom. There are a few sand channels for entering the water; and there is a sandy inlet good for kids just north of the lighthouse. This area offers excellent diving; lifeguards on duty. Principal catches are threadfin, big-eyed scad, bonefish, *papio* and especially mullet. Facilities include a picnic area, restrooms and showers. ~ Located about one-half mile northwest of the King Kamehameha Kona Beach Hotel on Kuakini Highway in Kailua. The park gate is closed every evening at 8 p.m.

HIDDEN ►

HONOKOHAU BEACH This was once Kailua's nude beach, but prohibitions are in effect. Folks come for miles to soak up the sun on this long narrow strand. Bordered by a lagoon, backdropped by distant mountains, protected by a shallow reef and highly recommended for the adventurous. Since the water is well protected, it's good for swimming, although a bit shallow. There are recommended spots for skindiving south of the small-boat harbor but stay away from the harbor itself since sharks are frequent. Surfers enjoy Honokohau's waves. Rather than fish here try Kaloko Pond about one-half mile north. There are no facilities here. ~ Take Kaahumanu Highway a couple miles north from Kailua. Turn onto the road to Honokohau Small Boat Harbor. From the north side of the harbor, walk about 600 yards farther north to the beach.

KONA COAST STATE PARK Set at the end of a bumpy lava-bed road, this beach park is certainly secluded. You'll drive in a mile-and-a-half from the highway to a sand-and-coral beach that is bordered by a small lagoon and young palm trees. You can swim, although the bottom is rocky and the surf is often high—that's when the surfers come out. Anglers also frequent this beach. The only facilities are picnic tables and portable toilets. ~ Located one and a half miles off Kaahumanu Highway, about ten miles north of Kailua near the 91-mile marker.

DISAPPEARING SANDS BEACH A small strand studded with volcanic rocks, this spot is also called Magic Sands. It seems that the white sand periodically washes away, exposing a lava shoreline. When still carpeted with sand, this is a very popular and crowded place. This is a favorite area for swimming and bodysurfing. Kona's best surfing spot is just north of here at "Banyans," with breaks year-round over a shallow reef. There are right and left slides. The major catches include mullet, threadfin, big-eyed scad, bonefish and *papio*. Restrooms and showers are the only facilities. ~ Located on Alii Drive four miles south of Kailua.

KAHALUU BEACH PARK Set along the south shore of Kahaluu Bay, this county park is fringed with palm trees. The salt-and-pepper beach is small and often crowded. Swimming is excellent here since the cove is partially protected by outlying rocks. Tropical fish abound, making this a recommended place for snorkeling, especially for beginners. Surfing is good near the reef during periods of high surf. Anglers fish for mullet, threadfin, big-eyed scad, bonefish and *papio*. The bay is also a good spot for throw-netting and surround-netting. Facilities include picnic areas, pavilions, showers and restrooms. ~ Located on Alii Drive five miles south of Kailua.

One element that comes as a visual shock to many first-time visitors to the Kona Coast is the endless stretch of black lava that blankets this dry terrain. Backdropped by 8271-foot Hualalai and standing in the windshadow of both Mauna Loa and Mauna Kea, Kailua and the entire Kona region project the bald unreality of a moonscape.

Kona/Kau District

But the ragged shoreline has been trimmed with stands of palm trees and sections along the roadways are splashed with bougainvillea. Even in this land of lava you don't need to venture far to discover soft foliage and tropical colors.

SIGHTS

Along the lower slopes of Hualalai just above Kailua lies **Kona coffee country**. This 20-mile-long belt, located between the 1000- and 2000-foot elevation and reaching south to Honaunau, is an unending succession of plantations glistening with the shiny green leaves and red berries of coffee orchards. If you prefer your

◄ HIDDEN

SUNBATHE IN THE SHADOW OF HISTORY

Puuhonua o Honaunau Park, part of the Puuhonua o Honaunau National Historical Park (City of Refuge), is an excellent picnic spot when you're sightseeing. Besides the picnic tables and other facilities, enjoy the sandy sunbathing area. There's no beach, but the tidepools along the lava shoreline are fascinating. ~ Off Route 160 just south of the National Historical Park displays.

vegetation decaffeinated, there are mango trees, banana fronds, macadamia nut orchards and sunbursts of wildflowers. To make sure you remember that even amid all the black lava you *are* still in the tropics, old coffee shacks and tinroof general stores dot the countryside.

So rather than heading directly south from Kailua, make sure you take in the full sweep of Kona's coffee country. Just take Palani Road (Route 190) uphill from Kailua, then turn right onto Route 180. This winding road cuts through old Kona in the heart of the growing region—watch for orchards of the small trees. Before the coast road was built, this was the main route. Today it's somewhat off the beaten track, passing through funky old country towns like Holualoa before joining the Mamalahoa Highway (Route 11) in Honalo.

Once on this latter highway, you'll encounter the old Greenwell Store, a stone building that dates to 1867, and a perfect place to combine shopping with museum browsing. The **Kona Historical Society Museum** has taken over this former general store. Today it's filled with artifacts from Kona's early days plus contemporary postcards, calendars and other items. Of particular interest are the marvelous collections of photos and antique bottles. Closed Saturday and Sunday. ~ Mamalahoa Highway, Kealakekua; 808-323-3222, fax 808-323-2398; e-mail khs@ilhawaii.net.

This main route continues south along the western slopes of **Hualalai**. Near the town of Captain Cook, Napoopoo Road leads down to Kealakekua Bay. First it passes the **UCC Hawaii Coffee Factory Outlet**. I don't know about you, but I'm a confirmed "caffiend," happily addicted to java for years. So it was mighty interesting to watch how the potent stuff goes from berry to bean to bag, with a few stops between. If you haven't tried Kona coffee, one of the few brews grown in the United States, this is the time. ~ 160 Napoopoo Road; 808-322-3789, fax 808-324-1528; www.ucc-hawaii.com, e-mail info@ucc-hawaii.com.

Kealakekua Bay is a marine reserve and outstanding snorkeling spot with technicolor coral reefs and an array of tropical fish species. Spinner dolphins swim close to shore in this area. Here you can also check out the reconstructed temple, **Hikiau Heiau**, where Captain James Cook once performed a Christian burial service for one of his crewmen. Captain Cook himself had little time left to live. Shortly after the ceremony, he was killed and possibly eaten by natives who had originally welcomed him as a god. A white obelisk, the **Captain Cook Monument**, rises across the bay where the famous mariner fell in 1779.

Puuhonua o Honaunau National Historical Park sits four miles south of Kealakekua Bay on Route 160. This ancient holy ground, also known as the City of Refuge, was one of the few places to which *kapu* breakers and refugees could flee for sanctuary. Once

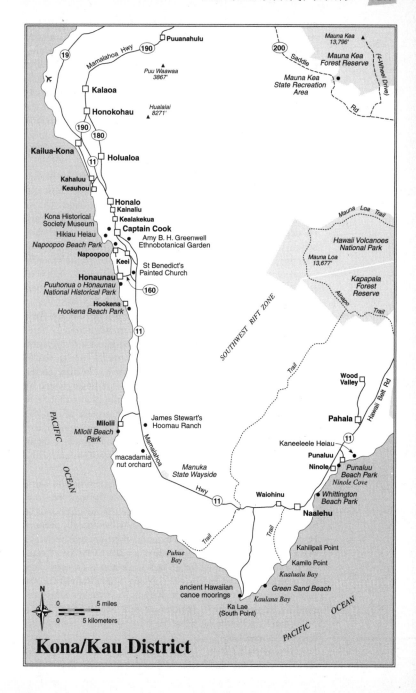

Kona/Kau District

inside the Great Wall, a lava barricade ten feet high and 17 feet wide, they were safe from pursuers. Free booklets are available for self-guided tours to the royal grounds, *heiaus* and menacing wooden images of Native Hawaiian gods that made this beach-front refuge one of Hawaii's most sacred spots. The *heiaus*, dating back to the 16th and 17th centuries, are among the finest examples of ancient architecture on the Big Island. Also explore the house models, built to traditional specifications, the royal fishpond and the displays of ancient arts and crafts. (There's also great snorkeling here in the area just offshore from the boat ramp.) Admission. ~ 808-328-2288, fax 808-328-8251.

St. Benedict's, my favorite church in all the islands, lies just up the hill. An imaginative Belgian priest, hoping to add color and imagery to the mass, transformed this rickety wooden chapel into a **Painted Church** by covering the interior walls with murals. He depicted several religious scenes and painted a vaulted nave behind the altar to give this tiny church the appearance of a great European cathedral. The charming exterior is carpenter's Gothic in style with a dramatic spire. Stop by and take a look, then proceed back to Mamalahoa Highway in Captain Cook. ~ 84-1540 Painted Church Road; 808-328-2227, fax 808-328-8482.

HIDDEN ►   Located on an ancient Hawaiian agricultural site, the **Amy B. H. Greenwell Ethnobotanical Garden** spreads across 12 acres of upland countryside. The land is divided into four vegetation zones, varying from seaside plants to mountain forests, and is planted with hundreds of Polynesian and native Hawaiian species. On a self-guided tour, you can wander through fields cleared by Hawaiians in pre-contact days and view the plants that were vital to early island civilizations. Guided tours are offered the second Saturday of every month at 10 a.m. or by appointment. Closed Saturday and Sunday. ~ Off Mamalahoa Highway, Captain Cook; 808-323-3318, fax 808-323-2394; www.bishopmuseum.org/bishop/greenwell.

At **Bay View Farm** you can tour a mill that produces Kona coffee. The trees here, like those you'll see along the roadside, grow to six or eight feet. Each will produce about 10 to 12 pounds of berries, which, after being picked by hand, will eventually produce two pounds of beans. Like peas in a pod, there are two beans per berry. A pulping machine squeezes them out of the berry skin. Next, the beans are dried for up to a week and are turned every hour, 24 hours a day. Finally, the skin layers are removed and the beans are graded and bagged for shipping. ~ Located on the same road as Painted Church, Honaunau; 808-328-9658, 800-662-5880, fax 808-328-8693; www.bayviewfarmcoffees.com, e-mail bayview@aloha.net.

There is little except you, alternating bands of greenery and dark lava, and the black macadam of the Mamalahoa Highway as you proceed toward the southern extremities of the Big Island. Here along the lower slopes of Mauna Loa, lifeless lava fingers cut across lush areas teeming with tropical colors. The contrast is overwhelming: Rounding a bend, the road travels from an overgrown land of poinsettias and blossoming trees to a bleak area torn by upheaval, resembling the moon's surface. Once past the lava flows that have ravaged the countryside, you'll discover a terrain that, though dry and windblown, is planted with macadamia nut orchards and fields of cattle-range grasses.

About 30 miles south of Kailua, take the turnoff to the quaint Hawaiian fishing village at **Milolii** (see the "Beaches & Parks" section below). This is a vintage South Seas scene that should not be missed.

Continuing south, the highway passes the late **James Stewart's Hoomau Ranch** (87-mile marker), then a sprawling **macadamia nut orchard**.

Eventually, the road arrives at the **South Point** turnoff. South Point Road leads through 11 miles of rolling grassland to the nation's southernmost point. En route you'll pass a cluster of windmills that draw energy from the trades that blow with ferocity through this region. Fishermen have built **platforms** along the sea cliff here to haul their catches up from the boats that troll these prime fishing grounds.

There are also **ancient Hawaiian canoe moorings** in the rocks below, and the remains of a *heiau* near the light tower. Some archaeologists believe that South Point was one of the places where Polynesian discoverers first settled. Another local feature, **Green Sand Beach**, is a two-mile hike along the waterfront from the Kaulana boat ramp. Olivine eroding from an adjacent cinder cone has created a beach with a decidedly greenish hue.

Buddhist services are performed in Tibetan every morning and evening at Wood Valley Temple.

Continue on to **Naalehu**, the nation's southernmost town, and then on to **Punaluu Beach Park**. With its palm trees and enchanting lagoon, Punaluu's black-sand beach is simply gorgeous. The tourist complex detracts from the natural beauty, but to escape the madding mobs the explorer need wander only a couple of hundred yards east to the rocky remains of **Kaneeleele Heiau**. Or venture about one-third mile south to **Ninole Cove**. Although there's a condominium complex nearby, this spot is a bit more secluded. Many of the stones along Ninole's pebbly beach are filled with holes containing "baby" stones that are said to multiply.

From Punaluu to Volcanoes National Park, the highway passes through largely uninhabited grassland, forests and lava fields. **Pahala**, the only town along this stretch, is a plantation colony. For an interesting side trip, go through Pahala to **Wood Valley Temple**, where a Tibetan Buddhist lama and his followers

◄ HIDDEN

have taken over an old Japanese temple. Situated on 25 acres, the temple was dedicated in 1980 by the Dalai Lama and visited by him again in 1994. A tranquil but dynamic place, it is painted in floral colors and adorned with a gilded statue of the Buddha. Since the small staff here has many responsibilities, call ahead for permission to visit and directions to the temple. ~ P.O. Box 250, Pahala, HI 96777; 808-928-8539, fax 808-928-6271; www.nechung.org, e-mail nechung@aloha.net.

To see the valley for which the temple is named, go right onto Pikake Street at the first stop sign in Pahala. When it forks after a little more than four miles, go left and proceed along the road **HIDDEN ▶** as it continues up into luxuriant **Wood Valley**, the scene of a devastating 1868 earthquake and mudslide.

LODGING   For a funky country place high in the mountains overlooking the Kona Coast, try the **Kona Hotel**. Catering primarily to workers, this 11-unit hotel remains a real sleeper. It might be difficult to book a room during the week, but on weekends, the lunchpail crowd heads home and you can rent a small place at an unbelievably low rate. Shared bathroom facilities. It's five miles to the beaches and action around Kailua, but if you're after an inexpensive retreat, this is the place. ~ Route 180, Holualoa; 324-1155. BUDGET.

Down the road, **Teshima's Inn** has small, cozy rooms at similar rates. These are set in an L-shaped structure fronting a small garden. The rooms have linoleum floors and wood-paneled walls decorated with Japanese art. Here you're 1300 feet above sea level and seven miles from Kailua. This charming inn is run by Mrs. Teshima, a delightful Japanese woman who has operated the establishment for years. ~ Mamalahoa Highway, Honalo; 808-322-9140. BUDGET.

SLEEP UNDER THE BIG TOP

If camping is your idea of vacation fun, check out **Margo's Corner**. Margo's guests are generally bicyclists looking for refuge from high-rise hotels and staid inns. Hot showers, breakfast and dinner are provided, and sleeping quarters consist of a number of tent sites situated in a large yard filled with pine trees and organic gardens. Some visitors sleep out in the open under the canopy of trees. For the less adventurous, a guest cottage with a queen-size bed, a private bath and a view of the garden is available, or try the "Adobe Suite" that sleeps six and includes a sauna. Also on the premises are a health food store and a community room filled with books and maps. Ask about the art retreats. No smoking. ~ P.O. Box 447; Naalehu, HI 96772; phone/fax 808-929-9614; e-mail margos.corner@mailcity.com. BUDGET TO MODERATE.

One of the more unique places to stay on the Big Island is **The Dragonfly Ranch**. Spread across two acres, the Dragonfly is billed by the owner, Barbara Moore, as a "healing-arts retreat." The grounds are as thick and luxurious as a well-tended jungle and the atmosphere is decidedly New Age. The "honeymoon suite" has an outdoor bed complete with canopy, a sunken bath and shower. Each of the four units have partial kitchen facilities, or, in exchange for preparation help, you can participate in the family-style dinner. Don't expect phones and air-conditioning, but do prepare yourself for an experience. ~ Route 160, Honaunau; 808-328-2159, 800-487-2159, fax 808-328-9570; www.dragon-flyranch.com, e-mail dfly@aloha.net. MODERATE TO ULTRA-DELUXE.

With manicured grounds leading to a tiled-roof villa, **Keala-kekua Bay Bed and Breakfast** combines picture-perfect views of Kealakekua Bay with equally impeccable accommodations. Three light and airy suites are available. The Alii includes a jacuzzi tub to relax in, but all rooms flaunt private entrances, private baths and refrigerators. Native Hawaiian prints, wicker furniture and ceiling fans adorn each room, including the lounge and dining room. For larger groups or just to be indulgent, you can rent the Ohana Kai cottage. With two bedrooms, two-and-a-half baths, a kitchen, laundry, cable TV with VCR, stereo and private lanai and garden, up to eight of you can enjoy your own private Hawaii. ~ P.O. Box 1412, Kealakekua 96750; 808-328-8150, 800-328-8150, fax 808-328-8866; www.keala.com, e-mail kbaybb@aloha.net. MODERATE TO DELUXE.

At **H. Manago Hotel**, you'll have a varied choice of accommodations. Rooms in the creaky old section have communal baths. The battered furniture, torn linoleum floors and annoying street noise make for rather funky living here. Rooms in the newer section rise in price as you ascend the stairs. First-floor accommodations are the least expensive and rooms on the ethereal third floor are the most expensive, but all reside in the budget range. The only advantage for the extra cost is a better view. All these rooms are small and tastelessly furnished—somehow orange carpets don't make it with naugahyde chairs. But you'll find visual relief in the marvelous views of mountain and sea from the tiny lanais. There's also a restaurant and television room in the old section. ~ Mamalahoa Highway, Captain Cook; 808-323-2642, fax 808-323-3451. BUDGET.

Shirakawa Motel, the country's southernmost hotel, sits on stunningly beautiful grounds. Once when I stopped by, a rainbow lay arched across the landscape and birds were loudly rioting in the nearby hills. Located 1000 feet above sea level, this corrugated-roof, 12-room hostelry offers quaint rooms with faded furniture and functional kitchenettes. Without cooking facilities, the bill is

◄ HIDDEN

even less. ~ Mamalahoa Highway, Waiohinu; phone/fax 808-929-7462; e-mail shirak@hialoha.net. You can also write P.O. Box 467, Naalehu, HI 96772 for reservations. BUDGET.

Wood Valley Temple, a Buddhist retreat, has dormitory-style and private rooms. Set on 25 landscaped acres, it provides a serene resting place. The guest rooms are pretty basic but have been pleasantly decorated and are quite comfortable. Baths are shared and guests have access to the ample kitchen facilities. Call for reservations; two-night minimum. They encourage small group bookings for programs or workshops. ~ Four miles outside Pahala; 808-928-8539, fax 808-928-6271; www.nechung.org, e-mail nechung@aloha.net. BUDGET.

Sea Mountain at Punaluu is a welcome contradiction in terms— a secluded condominium. Situated in the arid Kau District south of Hawaii Volcanoes National Park, it rests between volcanic headlands and a spectacular black-sand beach. A green oasis surrounded by lava rock and tropical vegetation, the complex contains a golf course, pool, tennis courts and jacuzzi. The several dozen condos are multi-unit cottages (moderate to deluxe). The condos are well decorated and include a bedroom, sitting room, kitchen and lanai; slightly larger units are available (deluxe to ultra-deluxe). ~ Off Mamalahoa Highway, Punaluu; 808-928-8301, 800-488-8301, fax 808-928-8008; www.seamtnhawaii.com. MODERATE TO ULTRA-DELUXE.

DINING

From Kailua south, the Mamalahoa Highway heads up *mauka* into the mountains above the Kona Coast. There are numerous restaurants in the little towns that dot the first 15 miles. All sit right on the highway.

Teshima's is a pleasant restaurant modestly decorated with lanterns and Oriental paintings. It's a good place to enjoy a Japanese meal or a drink at the bar. This café is very busy at lunch. Dinner features several Japanese and American delicacies. Breakfast is also served. ~ Mamalahoa Highway, Honalo; 808-322-9140. MODERATE.

There's a different mood entirely at the **Aloha Café**. Here in the lobby of the town's capacious movie house, a young crew serves delicious breakfasts as well as sandwiches and Mexican dishes during lunch and dinner. So if for some bizarre reason you've always longed to dine in the lobby of a movie theater . . . . If not, you can eat out on the oceanview lanai. Dinner on Thursday, Friday and Saturday. ~ Mamalahoa Highway, Kainaliu; 808-322-3383; www.alohacafe.com, e-mail alohacafe@nethawaii.net. MODERATE TO DELUXE.

Manago Hotel has a full-size dining room. Primarily intended for the hotel guests, the menu is limited and the hours restricted to "meal times" (7 to 9 a.m., 11 a.m. to 2 p.m., and 5 to 7:30

p.m. Tuesday through Sunday). Lunch and dinner platters consist of a few daily specials. Sandwiches are also available. Closed Monday. ~ Mamalahoa Highway, Captain Cook; 808-323-2642; www.managohotel.com, e-mail manago@lava.net. BUDGET.

In Kealakekua Ranch Center, a shopping center on Mamalahoa Highway in Captain Cook, there is one low-priced eatery, **Hong Kong Chop Suey**. It is one of those Chinese restaurants that have (literally) over 100 items on the menu. Closed Tuesday. ~ 808-323-3373. BUDGET TO MODERATE.

Canaan Deli comes recommended by several readers, who like the hoagies and the pastrami sandwiches and their specialty, Philly cheesesteak sandwiches. They also have pizzas and hamburgers at this friendly stopping place, as well as a breakfast menu. Personally, I go for the bagels with cream cheese and lox. ~ Mamalahoa Highway, Kealakekua; 808-322-6607. BUDGET.

On the road down to Puuhonua O Honaunau, there's a great lunch stop—**Wakefield Gardens & Restaurant**. You can wander the tropical preserve, then dine on a papaya boat, sandwiches, fresh garden salad, braised tofu or a "healthy burger" (made with natural grains), then try a slice of homemade pie. Lunch only. ~ Route 160, Honaunau; 808-328-9930. BUDGET TO MODERATE.

In the Kau district, **Cafe Ohia** serves Mexican food and a few local favorites at breakfast, lunch and dinner. No dinner on Sunday. Closed Monday. ~ Mile marker 77, Mamalahoa Highway; 808-929-8086. BUDGET.

For something more comfortable, try **Mister Bill's**. At this small dining room, the menu includes steak, prawns and coconut ginger chicken. In an area lacking in full-service dining facilities, this restaurant is a welcome oasis. Breakfast but no dinner on Sunday. ~ Mile marker 78, Mamalahoa Highway; phone/fax 808-929-7447. MODERATE TO DELUXE.

Down in Naalehu, the nation's southernmost town, you'll find the **Shaka Restaurant**. There are full-course breakfasts; at lunch they serve sandwiches, plate lunches and salads; the dinner menu has beef, seafood and chicken dishes. Closed Monday. ~ Mamalahoa Highway Noalehu; 808-929-7404. BUDGET TO MODERATE.

STILL LIFE WITH GALLERIES

Holualoa is a center for artists and art galleries. Within the ambit of this one-street town you'll find the **Kona Arts Center**, housed in an old coffee mill on Route 180, plus several private galleries nearby. Among the most noteworthy is **Studio 7 Gallery**, a beautifully designed multi-room showplace that displays pottery, paintings and prints. Closed Sunday and Monday. ~ Phone/fax 808-324-1335.

Along the lengthy stretch from Naalehu to Hawaii Volcanoes National Park, one of the few dining spots you'll encounter is the **Seamountain Golf Course & Lounge** in Punaluu. Situated a short distance from the black-sand beach, this restaurant serves a lunch consisting of cold sandwiches only. Topping the cuisine are the views, which range across the links out to the distant volcanic slopes. ~ Punaluu; 808-928-6222, fax 808-928-6111. BUDGET.

GROCERIES Strung along Mamalahoa Highway south of Kailua is a series of small towns that contain tiny markets.

The only real supermarket en route is **Choice Mart**. ~ Kealakekua Ranch Center (upper level), 82-6066 Mamalahoa Highway, Captain Cook; 808-323-3994.

Pineapple Park, about ten miles south of Kailua, has fresh fruits and vegetables. ~ Mamalahoa Highway, Captain Cook; 808-323-2224.

Down the road, in the Mango Court shopping center, **Evie's Natural Foods** has a large selection of organic produce, as well as an herb shop and deli. ~ Mamalahoa Highway, Kainaliu; 808-989-8862.

Kahuku Country Market, in the Kau district, has an ample inventory of groceries and drugstore items. ~ Mile marker 78, Mamalahoa Highway; 808-929-9011.

Down at the southern end of the island, the **Naalehu Island Market** is the prime place to stock up. ~ Mamalahoa Highway, Naalehu. ~ 808-929-7527.

SHOPPING After escaping the tourist traps in Kailua, you can start seriously shopping in South Kona. Since numerous shops dot the Mamalahoa Highway as it travels south, I'll list the most interesting ones in the order they appear.

For hats and baskets woven from pandanus and bamboo, and sold at phenomenally low prices, turn off the main road onto Route 18 (Hualalai Road) and check out **Kimura Lauhala Shop**. ~ Mamalahoa Highway, Holualoa; 808-324-0053.

Blue Ginger Gallery displays an impressive array of crafts items produced by local artisans. There are ceramics, custom glass pieces, woodwork and hand-painted silk scarves. ~ Mamalahoa Highway, Kainaliu; 808-322-3898.

Another recommended store is **Paradise Found**, which features contemporary and Hawaiian-style clothes. ~ Mamalahoa Highway, Kainaliu; 808-322-2111. **Antiques, Art and ?** is the place for things old and aging. ~ Mamalahoa Highway, Kealakekua; 808-323-2239.

HIDDEN ►   **Kahanahou Hawaiian Foundation**, an apprentice school teaching Hawaiians native arts, sells hand-wrought hula drums and other instruments, as well as masks and other crafts. It also serves as an introduction to Hawaiian music as you view bamboo nose flutes, musical bows, dancing sticks and ceremonial drums. ~ Mamalahoa Highway, Kealakekua; 808-322-3901.

One of my favorite shops is **Kealakekua's Grass Shack**. This place is crowded with Hawaiiana, not just from native Polynesians, but from the island's late arrivals as well—Americans, Chinese, Japanese, Portuguese. As a former owner once explained, "We go all the way from poi to tofu." There are *milo* and *koa* wood pieces, handwoven baskets and much more. Most interesting of all, to me at least, are the antique tools and handicrafts. Ask for a tour of the mini-museum. It'll be an education in things Hawaiian. ~ Konwena Junction, Kealakekua; 808-323-2877.

Not to be bypassed is **Wood Works**, a shop specializing in *koa* and other exotic hardwoods. The shop was born when two local woodworkers, alienated by the high prices demanded for their pieces by galleries, decided to go into business for themselves. The result is a shop where the work is not only exquisite but also financially accessible to all. Among the many items, you'll find bowls and boxes, as well as larger, more elaborate creations. Closed Sunday. ~ 82-6156 Mamalahoa Highway, beside the Manago Hotel, Captain Cook; 808-323-2247, fax 808-323-3495.

During the last two centuries, Big Island volcanoes have covered 200,000 acres with black lava, destroying almost everything in their path.

Omodt Art Designs sells jewelry and decorative pieces fashioned from a unique polymer clay technique. The process begins with cylinders of clay that have multiple colors and designs running their length; the cylinder is then sliced like a sushi roll, each segment revealing the same design. If this doesn't make sense to you, check it out for yourself. The studio does not keep specific hours; call ahead for an appointment. ~ 84-5222 Mamalahoa Highway, Honaunau; 808-328-8076; www.omodtart.com.

NIGHTLIFE

The **Kona Association for the Performing Arts** produces an ongoing series of theatrical performances. In addition to plays, it periodically schedules concerts. ~ 808-322-9924.

BEACHES & PARKS

NAPOOPOO BEACH PARK Many small boats moor at this black-rock beach on Kealakekua Bay. Set amidst cliffs that rim the harbor, it's a charming spot. Unfortunately, it draws caravans of tour buses on their way to the nearby Hikiau Heiau and Captain Cook Monument. Kealakekua Bay, one mile wide and filled with marine life, is an underwater preserve that attracts snorkelers and glass-bottom boats. In the bay there are good-sized summer breaks. Just north, at "Ins and Outs," the surf breaks year-round. Mullet, *moi*, bonefish, *papio* and big-eyed scad are the common catches. A picnic area, showers and restrooms are the only facilities. There's a soda stand just up from the beach. ~ In the town of Captain Cook, take Napoopoo Road, which leads four miles down to Kealakekua Bay; turn right at the end of the road.

HIDDEN ►   **KEEI BEACH** This salt-and-pepper beach extends for a quarter-mile along a lava-studded shoreline. Situated next to the creaky village of Keei, this otherwise mediocre beach offers marvelous views of Kealakekua Bay. It is far enough from the tourist area, however, that you'll probably encounter only local people along this hidden beach. What a pity! The very shallow water makes swimming safe, but limited. Try the north end. Plenty of coral makes for good snorkeling. Mullet, threadfin, bonefish, *papio* and big-eyed scad are common catches here. There are no facilities. ~ Take the Mamalahoa Highway to Captain Cook, then follow Napoopoo Road down to Kealakekua Bay. At the bottom of the hill, go left toward the Puuhonua o Honaunau National Historical Park. Take this road a half-mile, then turn right onto a lava-bed road. Now follow this extremely rough road another half-mile to the beach.

The cliffs looming behind the Captain Cook marker in Kealakekua Bay are honeycombed with Hawaiian burial caves.

HOOKENA BEACH PARK Popular with adventurous travelers, this is a wide, black-sand beach, bordered by sheer rock walls. Coconut trees abound along this lovely strand, and there's a great view of the South Kona coast. This is a recommended beach for swimming. Near the cliffs south of the beach are some good dive spots. Mullet, threadfin, bonefish, *papio* and big-eyed scad are among the most common catches. A picnic area and restrooms are the only facilities. There is no drinking water, but cooking and bathing water is available. ~ Take the Mamalahoa Highway south from Kailua for about 21 miles to Hookena. Turn onto the paved road at the marker and follow it four miles to the park.

▲ Tent camping is allowed; county permit required.

HIDDEN ►   **MILOLII BEACH PARK** Even if you don't feel like a character from Somerset Maugham, you may think you're amid the setting for one of his tropical stories. This still-thriving fishing village is vintage South Seas, from tumbledown shacks to fishing nets drying in the sun. Unfortunately, however, new houses have been springing up in the last few years. There are patches of beach near the village, but the most splendid resources are the tidepools, some of the most beautiful I've ever seen. This area is fringed with reefs that create safe but shallow areas for swimming, and great spots for snorkeling. Exercise extreme caution if you go beyond the reefs. This beach is a prime area for mullet, bonefish, *papio*, threadfin and big-eyed scad. Facilities include restrooms, picnic area and a volleyball court. There's no running water. ~ Take the Mamalahoa Highway south from Kailua for about 33 miles. Turn off onto a well-marked, winding, one-lane, macadam road leading five miles down to the village.

▲ Permitted only in the seaside parking lot. Get there early and you can park a tent beneath the ironwood trees with the sea washing in just below. County permit required.

MANUKA STATE WAYSIDE This lovely botanic park, almost 2000 feet above sea level, has a beautiful ocean view. The rolling terrain is planted with both native and imported trees and carpeted with grass. The only facilities are restrooms and a picnic area. ~ On Mamalahoa Highway, 19 miles west of Naalehu.

▲ No tent and trailers are allowed here, but you can park your sleeping bag in the pavilion. No electricity. A state permit is required.

WHITTINGTON BEACH PARK 🏊 🎣 🏕 🛶 This pretty little park features a small patch of lawn dotted with coconut, *hala* and ironwood trees. It's set on a lava-rimmed shoreline near the cement skeleton of a former sugar wharf. There are some marvelous tidepools here. Access to the water over the sharp lava rocks is pretty rough on the feet. But once you're in the snorkeling is very good and there's a good surf break in summer with a left slide. Mullet, *menpachi*, red bigeye, *ulua* and *papio* are the most frequent species caught. Facilities consist of picnic area, restrooms and electricity. ~ Across from the abandoned sugar mill on Mamalahoa Highway, three miles north of Naalehu.

▲ Tent and trailer camping are allowed; a county permit is required.

PUNALUU BEACH PARK 🏊 🎣 🏕 🛶 A black-sand beach fringed with palms and bordered by a breathtaking lagoon, this area, unfortunately, is regularly assaulted by tour buses. Still, it's a place of awesome beauty, one I would not recommend bypassing. One reason for the hubbub is the appearance of the endangered green sea turtles, which should not be disturbed. For more privacy, you can always check out **Ninole Cove**, a short walk from Punaluu. This attractive area has a tiny beach, grassy area and lagoon, which is a good swimming spot for children in calm conditions. Exercise caution when swimming outside the lagoon. Facilities include a picnic area, restrooms, showers and electricity. The snorkeling is only mediocre. Surfers attempt the short ride over a shallow reef (right slide). Principal catches are red bigeye, *menpachi*, *ulua* and *papio*. ~ Located about a mile off Mamalahoa Highway, eight miles north of Naalehu.

▲ Tents and trailers are allowed; county permit required.

▼▼▼▼▼▼▼▼▼▼▼▼▼▼
**Hawaii Volcanoes
National Park**

Covering 344 square miles and extending from the Puna shoreline to 4090-foot Kilauea to 13,677-foot Mauna Loa, this incredible park (admission) is deservedly the most popular feature on the Big Island. Its two live volcanoes, among the most active in the world, make the region as elemental and unpredictable as the next eruption.

Unlike Washington's Mt. St. Helens and Mt. Pinatubo in the Philippines, eruptions here are not usually explosive. So even Kilauea, which has destroyed almost two hundred homes and devoured an entire town during the last decade, has gained a reputation as a "drive-in volcano" where you can stand shoulder to shoulder with geologists and journalists watching Pele vent her wrath and create new earth.

SIGHTS

Also contained within this singular park are rainforests, black-sand beaches, rare species of flora and fauna, and jungles of ferns. If you approach the park from the southwest, traveling up the Mamalahoa Highway (Route 11), the points of interest begin within a mile of the park boundary. Here at the trailhead for **Kau Desert Trail**, you can follow a two-mile-long path that leads to the area where, according to legend, Halemaumau's hellish eruption overwhelmed a Hawaiian army in 1790. The troops, off to battle Kamehameha for control of the island, left the impressions of their dying steps in molten lava or so the story goes. According to Park officials, the tracks were left in hot mud by travelers, not warriors. Either way, the tracks can still occasionally be seen in the very fragile hardened ash layers.

Continuing along the highway, turn up Mauna Loa Road to the **Tree Molds**. Lava flowing through a Koa forest created these amazing fossils. The molten rock ignited the trees and then cooled, leaving deep pits in the shape of the incinerated tree trunks. It's a little farther to **Kipuka Puaulu** or **Bird Park**, a mile-long nature trail leading through a densely forested bird sanctuary. *Kipuka* means an "island" surrounded by lava and this one is filled with more than 30 species of Hawaiian trees, including koa, *kolea* and *ohia*. If the weather's clear, you can continue along this narrow, winding road for about ten miles to a **lookout** perched 6662 feet high on the side of Mauna Loa.

Back on the main road, continue east a few miles to **Kilauea Visitor Center**, which contains a museum, a film on recent eruptions, bookstore and information desk. ~ 808-985-6000, fax 808-985-6004; www.nps.gov/havo.

Across the road at **Volcano House**, there's a hotel and restaurant. An earlier Volcano House, built in 1877, currently houses the **Volcano Art Center**, right next to the visitor complex.

From here you can pick up Crater Rim Drive, one of the islands' most spectacular scenic routes. This 11-mile loop passes lava

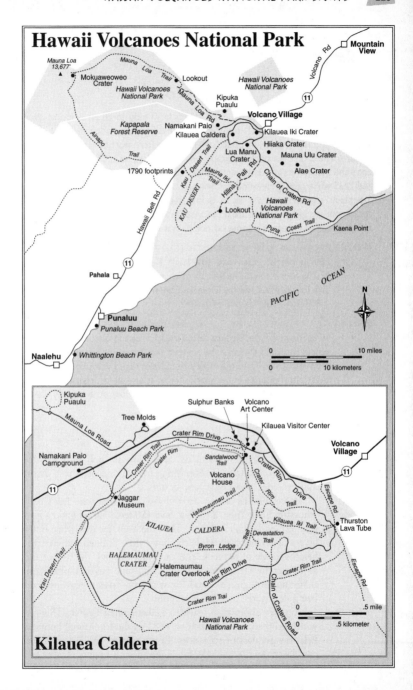

Hawaii Volcanoes National Park

Mountain View

Mauna Loa 13,677'

Mauna Loa Trail

Mokuaweoweo Crater

Lookout

Hawaii Volcanoes National Park

Hawaii Volcanoes National Park

Volcano Rd

11

Kipuka Puaulu

Mauna Loa Rd

Volcano Village

Kapapala Forest Reserve

Namakani Paio

Kilauea Iki Crater

Kilauea Caldera

Hiiaka Crater

Ainapo

Lua Manu Crater

Mauna Ulu Crater

Trail

Alae Crater

Kau Desert Trail

1790 footprints

Mauna Iki Trail

KAU DESERT

Hilina Pali Rd

Chain of Craters Rd

Hawaii Belt Rd

Lookout

Hawaii Volcanoes National Park

Puna Coast Trail

Kaena Point

11

Pahala

OCEAN

PACIFIC

N

Punaluu

Punaluu Beach Park

Naalehu

Whittington Beach Park

0   10 miles

0   10 kilometers

Kipuka Puaulu

Sulphur Banks

Volcano Art Center

Tree Molds

Crater Rim Drive

Kilauea Visitor Center

Mauna Loa Road

Crater Rim Trail

Crater Rim

Volcano Village

Namakani Paio Campground

Sandalwood Trail

Crater Rim

11

Volcano House

Crater Rim Drive

11

Jaggar Museum

Halemaumau Trail

Trail

Escape Rd

Kilauea Iki Trail

Thurston Lava Tube

KILAUEA   CALDERA

Devastation Trail

Byron Ledge

Kau Desert Trail

HALEMAUMAU CRATER

Halemaumau Crater Overlook

Crater Rim Drive

Crater Rim Trail

Chain of Craters Road

Escape Rd

Crater Rim Trai

Hawaii Volcanoes National Park

0   .5 mile

0   .5 kilometer

Kilauea Caldera

DRIVING TOUR
Saddle Road

Cutting across the island, Saddle Road climbs from Hilo to an elevation of over 6500 feet (bring a sweater!). The eastern section is heavily wooded with *ohia* trees and ferns and is often fog shrouded, while the western portion traverses rolling pastures. The Saddle is a stark landscape, a mosaic of decades-old flows from Mauna Loa's and Mauna Kea's grass-covered cinder cones. You cross lava flows from 1855 and 1935 while gaining elevation that will provide you with the finest view of these mountains anywhere on the island. Before setting out, pack warm clothing and check your gas gauge—there are no service stations or stores en route. And consult your car rental agency: Some do not permit driving on Saddle Road.

ONIZUKA CENTER FOR INTERNATIONAL ASTRONOMY   Near the 28-mile marker, the road to Mauna Kea leads 13 miles up to the 13,796-foot summit. The first six miles are passable by passenger car and take in a lookout and the Onizuka Center for International Astronomy. ~ 808-961-2180, fax 808-969-4892.

MAUNA KEA OBSERVATORY   Beyond this point you will need a four-wheel drive vehicle. Be sure to call ahead since the visitor station at the center sponsors tours of the summit and star-gazing opportunities. At the summit you'll find the Mauna Kea Observatory complex, one of the finest observatories in the world, but be prepared for freezing temperatures. You'll also be treated to some of the most otherworldly views imaginable.

flows and steam vents in its circuit around and into **Kilauea Caldera**. It also takes in everything from a rainforest to a desert and provides views of several craters.

Proceeding clockwise around the crater, the road leads near **Thurston Lava Tube,** a well-lit cave 450 feet long set amid a lush tree-fern and *ohia* rainforest. The tube itself, created when outer layers of lava cooled while the inner flow drained out, reaches heights inside of ten feet. You can walk through the tunnel and along nearby **Devastation Trail**, a half-mile paved asphalt trail that cuts through a skeletal forest of *ohia* trees regrowing after being devastated in a 1959 eruption.

Another short path leads to **Halemaumau Crater**. This pit, which erupted most recently in 1982, is the traditional home of Pele, the goddess of volcanoes. Even today steam and sulfurous gas blast from this hellhole, filling the air with a pungent odor and

MAUNA KEA STATE RECREATION AREA   Mauna Kea State Recreation Area, with cabins and recreation area, lies about midway along the Saddle Road. Situated on the tableland between Mauna Kea and Mauna Loa at 6500-feet elevation, this is an excellent base camp for climbing either mountain. The cabins here are also convenient for skiers headed up to Mauna Kea. With its stunning mountain views, sparse vegetation and chilly weather, this rarefied playground hardly seems like Hawaii. For remoteness and seclusion, you can't choose a better spot. A picnic area and restrooms are the only facilities. No tents or trailers are allowed. The cabins can be rented from the Division of State Parks, 75 Aupuni Street, Hilo, Hawaii, HI 96721; 808-974-6200. The individual cabins, each accommodating up to six people, have two bedrooms, bath, kitchenette and an electric heater. Cabins have loads of cooking utensils and sufficient bedding. Rates are $45 for four people and $5 for each additional person. There are also four-plex cabinettes that rent for $55 for eight people and $5 for each additional person. These aren't nearly as nice as the individual cabins. They are one-bedroom units crowded with eight bunks; cooking is done in a community dining and recreation area next door. ~ On the Saddle Road about 35 miles west of Hilo.

PANIOLO COUNTRY   The road continues past a United States military base, then descends through stands of eucalyptus windbreaks into Waimea cattle country. Here you can pick up the Mamalahoa Highway (Route 190) southwest to Kailua, only 87 miles from Hilo. Passing through sparsely populated range country over 2000 feet in elevation, this road has sensational views of the Kona Coast and Maui.

adding a sickly yellow-green luster to the cliffs. Halemaumau is actually a crater within a crater, its entire bulk contained in Kilauea's gaping maw. (People with sulfur sensitivity, heart or breathing problems should probably avoid this site as should infants, children and pregnant women.)

Around the southern and western edges of the caldera, the road passes part of the **Kau Desert**, a landscape so barren that astronauts bound for the moon were brought here to train for their lunar landing. At the **Jaggar Museum**, adjacent to the U.S.G.S. park observatory, you can catch an eagle-eye glimpse into Halemaumau Crater and take in a series of state-of-the-art displays on volcanology. Then the road continues on to a succession of steam vents from which hot mists rise continually.

The highway zips into Hilo from the Kilauea Crater area. Until several years ago you could take a more interesting and leisurely route by following **Chain of Craters Road** down to the Puna district. At present a lava flow several miles wide has closed part of the road. The 20-mile-long section that is still open skirts several pit craters, traverses miles of decades-old lava flows, and descends 4000 feet to the coast. Near the sea, a two-mile trail leads to an excellent collection of petroglyphs at Puuloa. The Chain of Craters Road then hugs the cliffs of the shoreline until it abruptly ends, buried for ten miles under lava flows as much as 75-feet deep.

LODGING   **Volcano House,** a 42-room hotel, perches 4000 feet above sea level on the rim of Kilauea Crater. Situated near the entrance to Hawaii Volcanoes National Park, this hotel provides a unique resting place. You can watch the steam rise from Halemaumau Crater or study the rugged contours of slumbering Kilauea. Standard rooms are unfortunately located in a separate building behind the main hotel. For a view of Kilauea, ask for a "crater view," from a superior or deluxe room on the volcano side. The rooms are small and decorated in an ever tidy and cozy fashion. There's wall-to-wall carpeting but no TV or radio. And you certainly won't need an air-conditioner at these breathless heights. ~ Near the entrance to Hawaii Volcanoes National Park; 808-967-7321, fax 808-967-8429. MODERATE TO ULTRA-DELUXE.

The Eruption Update, a 24-hour recorded message, provides information on the latest eruptions. ~ 808-985-6000.

Kilauea Lodge does not rest on the lip of the crater, but that doesn't prevent it from being the finest place in the area to stay. Set on tropically wooded grounds, this hideaway nevertheless conveys a mountain atmosphere. Some guest rooms have fireplaces; all have private baths. This coziness carries over into an inviting common room shared by guests and furnished with rocking chairs and a tile fireplace. The lodge, built in 1938 as a YMCA camp, rests at the 3700-foot elevation and combines the best features of a Hawaiian plantation house and an alpine ski lodge. It also provides a memorable contrast to the ocean-oriented places that you'll probably be staying in during the rest of your visit. ~ Old Volcano Road, Volcano Village; 808-967-7366, fax 808-967-7367; www.kilauealodge.com. MODERATE TO DELUXE.

There are also some small, privately run bed-and-breakfast inns around the volcano area. For information, contact **Volcano Accommodations,** a central agency that can help book reservations. ~ 808-967-8662, 800-733-3839, fax 808-985-7028; www.hawaii-volcano.net, e-mail info@hawaii-volcano.net.

DINING   If you're looking for a vista, **Volcano House Restaurant**—perched on the rim of Kilauea Crater—affords extraordinary views. Located at the 4000-foot elevation in Hawaii Volcanoes National

Park, this spacious dining room looks out on sheer lava walls and angry steam vents, and on a clear day, the imposing bulk of Mauna Loa. If you can tear yourself away from the stunning scenery, there's buffet-style breakfast and lunch, and an ample dinner menu highlighted by fresh fish, prime rib, linguini marinara and a variety of seafood dishes. ~ 808-967-7321. DELUXE.

In L.A. there's the Hard Rock Café; in Volcano Village, it's the **Lava Rock Café**. Breakfast, lunch and dinner feature "magma mini meals," but only at dinner can you get a "full eruption." The lasagna, T-bones, and fajitas are, presumably, burning hot. The Lava Rock also serves as an Internet café for you e-mail junkies. ~ Old Volcano Road, Volcano Village; 808-967-8526, fax 808-967-8090; www.volcanovillage.com. BUDGET TO DELUXE

He surfs, he cooks, heee's Surt! **Surt's** leans to Amer-Euro-Asian cuisine, with its line-up of pastas, curries and surf-n-turf. The restaurant's namesake is one of the owners, a man with a reputation as a chef and a wave rider. ~ Old Volcano Road, Volcano Village; 808-967-8511. DELUXE

And for those languorous evenings when time is irrelevant and budgets forgotten, there is **Kilauea Lodge**. You can sit beside a grand fireplace in an atmosphere that mixes tropical artwork with alpine sensibility. The exposed-beam ceiling and elegant hardwood tables comfortably contrast with a menu that features "prawns Mauna Loa," catch of the day and chicken Milanese. Dinner only. ~ Old Volcano Road, Volcano Village; 808-967-7366; www.kilauealodge.com, e-mail stay@kilauealodge.com. DELUXE.

GROCERIES **The Volcano Store**, located just outside the National Park, has a limited stock of groceries and dry goods. ~ Old Volcano Road, Volcano Village; 808-967-7210.

BEACHES & PARKS **NAMAKANI PAIO** Situated in a lovely eucalyptus and koa grove in the middle of Volcanoes National Park, this campground offers both outdoor and cabin camping. There is a picnic area and restrooms. Three miles away is a hotel restaurant and the Kilauea Visitor Center. ~ On Mamalahoa Highway (Route 11) about three miles west of park headquarters and 31 miles southwest of Hilo.

▲ Tent and trailer camping. No permit required, but, as always, campers should note that there is a seven-day limit.

Cabins are rented from the Volcano House (808-967-7321). Each cabin has one double and two single beds, plus an outdoor grill. No firewood or cooking utensils are provided. The units rent for $40 a day for two people, $8 for each additional person up to four. Sheets, blankets and towels are provided, but it's recommended that you bring a sleeping bag. Showers are not available for campers.

▼▼▼▼▼▼▼▼▼▼
Puna District

That bulging triangle in the southeast corner of the Big Island is the Puna District, a kind of living geology lab where lush rainforest is cut by frequent lava flows from the East Rift Zone of Kilauea. Here at the state's easternmost point, black-sand beaches, formed when hot lava meets the ocean and explodes into crystals, combine with anthurium farms and papaya orchards to create a region both luxurious and unpredictable. There are lava tubes, arches and caves galore, all formed by the lava that flows inexorably down from the rift zones of Kilauea.

SIGHTS

Now that Chain of Craters Road is covered in a layer of black lava, the only way to visit the area is by following Route 130, which will carry you through the tumbledown plantation town of **Keaau** and near the artistic little community of **Pahoa**, or along Route 137, an enchanting country road that hugs the coast.

In 1990, **lava flows** poured through Kalapana, severing Routes 130 and 137 (which have since been reconnected) and covering many houses. Kalapana, once home to more than 400 people, was largely destroyed. Today, a few isolated houses form oases in a desert of black lava. Just above the town, where the roadway comes to an abrupt halt, you can see how the lava crossed the road.

What you will not see here is the original black-sand beach at Kaimu, which was covered by lava. The ancient canoe ramp is also buried beneath black rock and the **Star of the Sea Painted Church**—a tiny 1920s-era chapel painted in imaginative fashion to make it resemble a grand cathedral—has been moved to a permanent location near the end of Route 130 on Ahia Road near the intersection with Route 137.

After exploring the area of recent volcanic action, you can backtrack along the coast via Route 137, which proceeds northeast through jungly undergrowth and past dazzling seascapes to the tiny villages of **Opihikao** and **Pohoiki**.

At the intersection of Route 137 and Route 132, take a right onto the dirt road and follow it seaward toward the site of a truly eerie occurrence. When the 1960 lava flow swept down to destroy this entire region, it spared the **Cape Kumukahi Lighthouse** on the state's easternmost point. Today you can see where the wall of lava parted, flowed around the beacon, then closed again as it continued to the sea. In the process, it added about 500 yards of land to the point—an awesome demonstration of how young this Big Island really is.

HIDDEN ▶

Now return to Route 132 and head west back toward Pahoa. The road passes more of the **1960 lava flow**, which covered almost 2000 acres and totally leveled the small village of Kapoho.

An earlier eruption, circa 1790, caused the grotesque formations down the road at **Lava Tree State Park**. Here the molten rock swamped a grove of *ohia* trees, then hardened around the skeletons to create a fossil forest. When fissures in the earth drained the molten lava, these petrified trees were left as a lonely legacy. In strange and exotic fashion, these giant skeletons, mixed with fresh growth, loom above huge cracks in the landscape.

LODGING

◀ *HIDDEN*

In the beautiful Puna District, a volcanic region fringed with black-sand beaches, there's a marvelous place called the **Kailani Eco-Resort and Adventures**. Situated on Route 137, 13 minutes from Pahoa, it sits just above the ocean on 113 acres. In addition to lodging, this New Age resort provides a lifestyle. There are weekly classes in hula, weaving and lei making; lectures on the history and culture of Hawaii; plus programs in dance, aerobics, yoga and massage. The facilities include a Japanese health spa with two jacuzzis and a sauna, a swimming pool and volleyball and tennis courts. Guests stay in multi-unit lodges, sharing a spacious living room, or in private cottages. Sleeping accommodations are basic but appealing, with pine walls; the room decorations are crafted at the center. Campsites are available at budget prices. Meals are $27 a day per person, or you can cook for yourself. ~ RR 2, Box 4500, Pahoa, HI 96778; 808-965-7828, 800-800-6886, fax 808-965-0527; www.kalani.com, e-mail kalani@kalani.com. MODERATE TO ULTRA-DELUXE.

GAY LODGING   After a long day traversing the dense growth of tropical flowers and macadamia and fruit trees, women guests are grateful for a soak in a hot tub, a stint in the steam house or a minute with the masseuse. All this and more are obtainable at the **Butterfly Inn,** an all-women bed and breakfast located between Hilo and the village of Volcano. Rooms are cozily decorated, and in the morning a breakfast of assorted fruits, juices and breads may be taken onto the enclosed deck. ~ P.O. Box 6010, Kurtistown, HI 96760; 808-966-7936, 800-546-2442; www.the butterflyinn.com, e-mail hiwomen@ilhawaii.net. MODERATE.

DINING   In the rustic town of Pahoa, there's **Luquin's Mexican Restaurant,** a friendly Mexican eatery serving a variety of dishes from south of the border. Breakfast, lunch and dinner daily. ~ Old Government Road, Pahoa; 808-965-9990. BUDGET.

An open-air design accented with overhead fans and bamboo panels gives **Sawasdee Thai Cuisine** an easy, friendly ambience of the East. Serving a full array of curry, rice and noodle dishes, this cozy restaurant is a comfortable fit for lunch or dinner. Closed Tuesday. ~ Old Government Road, Pahoa; 808-965-8186. BUDGET.

For more traditional fare consider **Black Rock Cafe.** This booth-lined shrimp-and-steak eatery offers a half-dozen different beef dishes as well as spaghetti, baby back ribs and a catch-of-the-day fish entrée. ~ Old Government Road, Pahoa; 808-965-1177. MODERATE.

GROCERIES   A farmers' market in the clapboard town of Pahoa convenes every Sunday morning. Otherwise, there are a few small markets. The junction town of Keaau has a **Sure Save.** ~ Old Volcano Road and Keaau–Pahoa Road; 808-966-9316.

BLACK HEAT

Since the latest series of volcanic eruptions began on the Big Island in 1983, the Puna District has been in constant turmoil. During one phase, an average of 650,000 tons of lava a day was spewing from the earth. In all, it has covered 40 square miles of the Big Island, creating new land masses along the ocean, destroying about 200 houses and fashioning several new black-sand beaches.

Also in Pahoa, there's **Da Store**. ~ Route 130; 808-965-9411. For health foods, consider **Pahoa Natural Groceries**. ~ Government Main Road off Route 130, Pahoa; 808-965-8322.

Out in the volcano region, on the road down to the Puna District, you'll pass through the tiny town of **Pahoa**. Either side of Route 130, the main drag, is lined with falsefront buildings. Each one seems to contain yet another ingenious craft shop run by a local resident.

SHOPPING

ISAAC HALE BEACH PARK 🏊 🎣 🛶 This small park on the Puna coast is pretty but run-down. There's a patch of black sand here and some hot springs nearby. A boat landing ramp makes this a popular park with local folks. Swimming is okay when the sea is calm. There are both summer and winter breaks in the center of the bay. The most common catches here are *papio*, *moi*, mountain bass, *menpachi*, red bigeye, *ulua* and goatfish. A picnic area and restrooms are the only facilities. ~ On Route 137 about two miles northeast of MacKenzie State Recreation Area.

BEACHES & PARKS

▲ Tent and trailer camping. County permit required. I much prefer nearby MacKenzie State Recreation Area for overnighting.

MACKENZIE STATE RECREATION AREA 🛶 This beautiful 13-acre park lies in an ironwood grove along a rocky coastline. King's Highway, an ancient Hawaiian trail, bisects the area. There is no swimming, snorkeling or surfing because a sea cliff borders the park. However, there's good shore fishing from rock ledges. Picnic area and pit toilets are the only facilities. There's no drinking water. ~ On Route 132, 9 miles northeast of Kaimu.

▲ Tent camping; a state permit is required.

There are few activities on the Big Island more pleasurable than camping. Beautiful state and county parks dot the island, while enticing hiking trails lead to remote mountain and coastal areas.

▼▼▼▼▼▼▼▼▼▼▼▼▼▼

Outdoor Adventures

CAMPING

No matter what you plan to do on the island, keep in mind that the Kona side is generally dry, while the Hilo side receives considerable rain. Also remember that the mountains can be quite cold and usually call for extra clothing and gear.

Camping at **county parks** requires a permit. These cost $3 per person per day ($1 for ages 13 through 17, 50¢ for children). Although trailer camping is allowed in many county parks, no special parking or electrical hook-ups are provided. Pick up permits from the County Department of Parks and Recreation. ~ 25 Aupuni Street, Hilo, Hawaii, HI 96720; 808-961-8311. Permits are also available at the South Kona Recreation Office. ~ P.O. Box 314, Captain Cook, Hawaii, HI 96740; 808-323-3060. The main county parks and recreation office for the west side of the island is the Hale Hawawai office in Kailua Kona. ~ 808-327-3560. County permits are issued for both tent and trailer camping, and can be obtained for up to two weeks at each park (one week during the summer).

Free **state parks** permits can be obtained through the State Department of Land and Natural Resources, Division of State Parks. ~ 75 Aupuni Street, Hilo, Hawaii, HI 96720; 808-974-6200. Maximum stay at each park is five days. For information on cabin rentals and camping in Volcanoes National Park, see the individual listings in the "Beaches & Parks" sections in this chapter.

Hilo Hawaii Sales and Surplus sells sleeping bags, backpacks, tents, stoves and the like. ~ 148 Mamo Street, Hilo; 808-935-6398. **Pacific Rent-All** rents family-size tents, sleeping bags, stoves, coolers and other camping equipment. ~ 1080 Kilauea Avenue, Hilo; 808-935-2974.

DIVING

The Big Island's coastal waters offer some of the most enticing dive sites in Hawaii. Good visibility, lava and coral formations and, of course, an intriguing variety of marine life assure plenty of fun. Whether you choose a beach or boat dive, you'll find the waters relatively uncrowded. Snorkelers will be attracted to beautiful Kealakekua Bay where Captain Cook met his maker.

HILO   **Nautilus Dive Center** operates one- and two-tank shore dives off the Hilo coast. You'll see a variety of marine life, including sea turtles, as well as coral formations and caves. Closed Sunday. ~ 382 Kamehameha Avenue, Hilo; 808-935-6939.

KOHALA COAST   **Kohala Divers** is a full-service diving center providing scuba and snorkeling lessons as well as gear rental. There is a two-tank boat dive available, or go out on their 36-foot custom dive boat. Closed Monday. ~ Kawaihae Shopping Center, Kawaihae; 808-882-7774.

KAILUA–KONA AREA   **Sandwich Isle Divers** is a full-service dive shop that offers repairs and instruction, and has two boats for

EELS, CORAL AND A SAIL

Bring your sunscreen, towel and hat for a wonderful half-day of snorkeling and sailing. Rather than heading out to Molikini with all the other folks, **Kamanu Charters** takes you to a hidden cove that teems with fish and otherworldly coral formations. You're bound to see a slinky eel, needle-nose fish and tons of parrot fish. If you're lucky, spinner dolphins cavort alongside the boat as you make your way back to the marina. A lively crew makes the day even more special. ~ P.O. Box 2021, Kailua-Kona, HI 96745; 808-329-2021, 800-348-3091, fax 808-329-7590; www.kamanu.com, e-mail jay@kamanu.com.

dive trips. Trip destinations include Turtle Pinnacles, Pine Trees, Golden Arches, Kaiwi Point and Kaloko Arches and more locations along the Kona Coast and beyond. They also conduct a night manta ray dive. ~ Kona Marketplace, Kailua; 808-329-9188.

Sea Paradise Scuba leads trips to lava tubes, caverns, caves and other fascinating formations at 25 locations south of Kailua. ~ 71-7128 Kaleopapa Street, Keauhou; 808-322-2500. **Big Island Dives** offers daytime and night dives along the Kona Coast. ~ 75-5467 Kaiwi Street, in the Kaahumanu Plaza, Kailua; 808-329-6068.

(Also see the "Snorkeling and Scuba Diving the Gold Coast" section in this chapter.)

SURFING & WIND- SURFING

For surfing U.S.A., consider the dynamic Kona Coast as well as Hilo Bay. Winter is peak season for surfing popular spots such as Lyman's and Banyan's. Also popular is Pohiki in the Puna area near the Kilauea volcano.

Windsurfing is good year-round. Try Anaehoomalu Beach on the Kona Coast or the South Point area.

Ocean Sports Hawaii rents sailboards and offers lessons. ~ Royal Waikoloan, Waikoloa; 808-886-6666 ext. 1.

At the Kona Inn Shopping Village, **Honolua Surf Company** sells surfboards and boogieboards and recommends the best locations. ~ 75-5744 Alii Drive; 808-329-1001.

Pacific Vibrations will outfit you for a day of surfing and the friendly staff is a great resource for info about local outdoor activities. ~ 75-5702 Alii Drive; 808-329-4140.

FISHING

The waters off the Kona Coast are among the Pacific's finest fishing grounds, particularly for marlin. Many charter boats operate out of Kailua; check the phone book for names or simply walk along the pier and inquire.

Kona Charter Skippers Association represents one of the larger outfits. They sponsor daily charters for marlin, yellowfin tuna, *ono*, mahimahi and other gamefish. Using boats 26 to 54 feet in length, they take out up to six passengers per boat for half- and full-day trips. Private charters are also available. ~ 74-857 Iwalani Place, Kailua-Kona; 808-329-3600, 800-762-7546; www.kona biggamefishing.com.

The **Sea Wife**, with Captain Jim Cox at the helm, sets out Monday through Saturday from Honokohau Harbor in pursuit of marlin, mahimahi or whatever else is running. ~ P.O. Box 2645, Kailua 96745; 808-329-1806.

Head up to the tuna tower to survey the fishing scene aboard **Pamela**, a 38-foot Bertram that focuses on marlin, short-nosed spearfish, mahimahi, yellowfin and wahoo. ~ Honokohau Harbor; 808-329-3600.

Another company offering similar service is the charter desk in the **Kona Fuel and Marine** building. ~ Honokohau Harbor, Kailua; 808-329-5735.

Jack's Kona Charters offers full- and half-day charters as well as overnight trips. ~ Honokohau Harbor, Kailua; 808-325-7558.

SAILING & PARA-SAILING

One of the authentic pleasures of a Big Island visit is a sail along the Kona or Kohala coast. Choose from a pleasure sail or take an adventure trip that includes a snorkeling excursion.

Among the popular operators is **Kamanu Charters**, which offers half-day trips with snorkeling at Pawai Bay. ~ Gentry's Complex in the Honokohau Harbor, Kailua; 808-329-2021. The **Maile Gulf Star** is a 50-foot sailboat available for a variety of trips around the Big Island. ~ Kawaihae Harbor; 808-326-5174.

Another popular sport in Hawaii is parasailing, in which you are strapped to a parachute that is towed aloft by a motorboat. For information, contact UFO **Parasail**. ~ Kailua; 808-325-5836.

KAYAKING

Kona Boy offers guided tours on the island's west side. Rentals of dive, surf, racing or touring kayaks are also available. Kona Boy is a resource for maps, information and advice on sea kayaking the big island. ~ Mamalahoa Highway near Mile marker 113; 808-322-3600.

The Big Island's only Hawaiian-owned and -operated kayak company is **Aloha Kayak Co.** These knowledgeable natives will rent you equipment and take you on exciting tours that include cliff-jumping, snorkeling and even swimming through lava tubes. ~ 79-7428 Kealakekua Highway, Honalo; 808-322-2868; www. alohakayak.com.

WHALE WATCHING & BOAT TOURS

Between November and May, when about 400 humpback whales inhabit Hawaiian waters, a popular spectator sport is spotting whales in the channels around the islands.

Captain Zodiac leads four-hour trips twice daily along the Kona Coast. You may see whales, dolphins, sea turtles and other marine life as you journey along the coast and visit sea caves and lava tubes. There's a stop at Kealakekua Bay for snorkeling. ~ Honokohau Harbor; 808-329-3199.

Captain Dan McSweeney's Whale Watching Adventures operates three-hour cruises. If you don't see whales, the company will give you another trip at no charge. ~ Honokohau Harbor, Kailua; 808-322-0028.

GOLF

Some of the best golfing in the country is found on the Big Island. From stunning links on the Kohala Coast to community courses in the Hilo area, this island has everything you need for a golf-oriented vacation. Sunny conditions on the Kona side mean you generally don't need to worry about taking a rain check. Throw in views of the lava landscape, verdant shorelines and swaying banyan trees, and you've created a duffer's view of paradise.

HILO Naniloa Country Club is a nine-hole, par-35 course overlooking Hilo Bay. This narrow course may look easy but don't be deceived: Water hazards and trees along the fairways create plenty of challenges. ~ 120 Banyan Drive, Hilo; 808-935-3000.

Hilo Municipal Golf Course is one of the best bargains on the islands. This 18-hole course has great views of the water and the mountains. Be sure to reserve tee times on the weekends. You can sharpen your skills on the driving range and practice greens. ~ 340 Haihai Street, Hilo; 808-959-7711.

HAMAKUA COAST Hamakua Country Club is another inexpensive choice. Located on the north shore about 40 miles from Hilo, this nine-hole course bans power carts. While it lacks the amenities of the resort links, Hamakua has a nice neighborhood feel. ~ Honokaa; 808-775-7244.

KOHALA COAST Creating a great golf course is easy if you just dip into Laurence Rockefeller's deep pockets, hire Robert Trent Jones Sr. and buy some lava-strewn oceanfront terrain. What you'll end up with is the 18-hole **Mauna Kea Beach Golf Course**. ~ Near Kawaihae; 808-882-7222. Quite a challenge, the original links have been complemented by the 18-hole **Hapuna Golf Course** created by Arnold Palmer. ~ 808-880-3000.

Waikoloa Village Golf Course is an 18-hole, par-72 layout that also includes a driving range and practice greens. This windy course, designed by Robert Trent Jones Jr., has great views of Mauna Kea and Mauna Loa. ~ Waikoloa; 808-883-9621. Nearby the **Waikoloa Beach Resort Golf Course** was also designed by Robert Trent Jones, Jr. ~ Waikoloa; 808-886-6060. The adjacent **Waikoloa Kings' Golf Club** has another popular course. ~ Waikoloa; 808-885-4647. Convenient to the Hyatt Regency Waikoloa

FLUMIN DA DITCH

Remember when you used to sneak into the neighbor's swimming pool at night? Well, in Hawaii, forbidden childhood adventures involved "Flumin da ditch": grabbing anything that would float and navigating the tunnels, flumes, waterfalls and underground springs of Hawaii's historic irrigation system. You can now participate in the fun (legally) with **Flumin Da Ditch**, a company that will provide everything you need to slip through the twists and turns of a three-and-a-half-mile portion of the system. Reservations are required. ~ 808-889-6922, 877-449-6922, fax 808-889-6944; www.flumindaditch.com.

and the Royal Waikoloan, each course has unique features. The beach course heads through petroglyph fields while the Kings Golf Club also has beautiful lava hazards.

Mauna Lani Golf Course has two 18-hole links built across rugged lava beds. If you miss the fairway, don't expect to find your ball out there in the volcanic landscape. There's also a driving range and practice greens. ~ Kohala Coast; 808-885-6655.

At the **Kona Country Club**, a pair of 18-hole golf courses are ideal for those who want to bunker down. Bring along your camera to capture memorable views of the ocean course. Or head uphill to fully enjoy the challenging Mauka course. If you're looking for over-water holes and hidden hazards, you've come to the right place. ~ 78-7000 Alii Drive, Kailua; 808-322-2595.

KONA/KAU DISTRICT   **Sea Mountain Golf Course** is a popular 18-hole course south of Kilauea volcano. It's beautifully landscaped with coconut and banyan trees. ~ Punaluu; 808-928-6222.

HAWAII VOLCANOES NATIONAL PARK   **Volcano Golf and Country Club** is the only course I know located in the vicinity of an erupting volcano. The high elevation (4200 feet) will give your ball an extra lift on this 18-hole course. ~ Volcanoes National Park; 808-967-7331.

TENNIS

Public tennis courts are convenient to all of the Big Island's popular resort destinations. In Hilo, you can play at the courts at Kalanikoa and Piilani streets or Kilauea and Ponahawai streets.

In Waimea, try Waimea Park on Lindsey Road off Route 19. In the Kailua area head for Kailua Park (Old Airport Road), Higashihara Park (Mamalahoa Highway, Keauhou), or the courts at the intersection of Palani and Kuakini roads.

Call the **County Department of Parks and Recreation** for information on public courts. ~ 808-961-8311. Or contact the **Hawaii Visitors & Convention Bureau** for information concerning public courts. ~ 808-961-5797, 808-329-7787.

BIKING

Hawaii offers very good roads and many unpopulated stretches that make it ideal for bikers. Much of the island is mountainous with some fairly steep grades in the interior. Saddle Road, the roads to Waimea, and the road from Hilo up to Volcanoes National Park will all make a heavy breather of you, but the coast roads are generally flat or gently rolling. Most roads have shoulders and light traffic. Keep in mind that the northeast side of the island receives heavy rainfall, while the Kona side is almost always sunny. But wet side or dry, the scenery is spectacular throughout.

Bike Rentals   In Kailua, try **Dave's Bike and Triathlon Shop.** They rent mountain and cross-training bikes—with shuttles to

Ski
Hawaii

During your island tour you'll inevitably pull up behind some joker with a bumper sticker reading "Think Snow." Around you trade winds may be bending the palm trees, sunbronzed crowds will be heading to the beach, and the thermometer will be approaching 80°. Snow will be the furthest thing from your mind.

But up on the 13,796-foot slopes of Mauna Kea, you're liable to see a bikini-clad skier schussing across a mantle of newly fallen snow! Any time from December until April or May, there may be enough dry snow to create ski runs several miles long and fill bowls a half-mile wide and almost a mile long. The slopes range from beginner to expert: Some have a vertical drop of 4500 feet. This is some of the world's highest skiing available.

Situated above the clouds about 80 percent of the time, this snow lover's oasis is baked by a tropical sun many times more powerful than at the beach. So it's easy to tan and easier yet to burn.

Ski Guides Hawaii offers all-day downhill skiing and snowboarding tours on Mauna Kea and cross-country skiing on Mauna Loa. The ski season lasts from December until April or May. This is not an inexpensive trip—but then again, skiing never is. ~ P.O. Box 1954, Kamuela, HI 96743; 808-885-4188; www.skihawaii.com.

Combined with the thin air and winds up to 100 miles per hour, Hawaii's ski slopes are not for the faint-hearted or fair-skinned. But if you're seeking an incredible adventure and want a view of the Hawaiian islands from a 13,000-foot crow's nest, the heights of Mauna Kea await. There are no lifts and no groomed trails; beneath the snow is hard lava rock and cinder. A four-wheel-drive vehicle is required to get you there. It's the same road used to get to the observatories.

and from hotels—and do repairs. If you want, you can ship your bike and Dave's will have it assembled before you arrive. ~ 75-5669 Alii Drive, 808-329-4522. **B & L Bike & Sports** rents Cannondales. ~ 75-5699 Kopiko Place, Kailua-Kona; 808-329-3309. **Hawaiian Pedals** also rents bikes. ~ Kona Inn Shopping Village, Kailua; 808-329-2294.

Bike Repairs   The folks at **Mid-Pacific Wheels** will do repair work or sell you bike accessories. ~ 1133-C Manono Street, Hilo; 808-935-6211. **B & L Bike & Sports** also does repairs. ~ 75-5699 Kopiko Place, Kailua-Kona; 808-329-3309.

RIDING STABLES

In Waimea, **Mauna Kea Beach Resort Stables** offer one- and two-hour guided trips on Parker Ranch, passing horse and cow herds and many historical sites. ~ Puukalani Road, Waimea; 808-885-4288.

Kings' Trail Rides O' Kona offers a riding/snorkeling combo. Riders descend the Kaawaloa Trail to Kealakekua Bay. Lunch is included, and children over seven with riding experience can participate. ~ Kealakekua; 808-323-2388; www.konacowboy.com, e-mail sales@konacowboy.com.

In Waipio Valley, **Naalapa Trail Rides** will take you on a two-hour ride through taro patches and waterfalls and (it goes without saying) past magnificent views. ~ Waipio Valley Artworks, Kukuihaele Village Roads, Kukuihaele; 808-775-0419.

Dahana Ranch operates a gorgeous spread. Besides offering packages of paniolo entertainment and a chance to "brand, rope and pen," they also have rides for the less dedicated. Their one-and-a-half-hour tour takes in views of the working ranch as well as the surrounding valley and mountains. The two-and-a-half-hour option includes participation in an authentic cattle drive. ~ P.O. Box 1293, Kamuela, HI 96743; 808-885-0057, 888-399-0057; www.dahanaranch.com.

HIKING

Of all the islands in the chain, Hawaii has the finest hiking trails. The reason? Quite simply, it's the Big Island's size. Larger than all the other islands combined and boasting the highest peaks, Hawaii offers the greatest diversity to explorers.

Mauna Loa and Mauna Kea, each rising over 13,000 feet, provide rugged mountain climbing. To the north, the Kohala Mountains feature trails through dense tropical terrain and along awesome cliffs. In Volcanoes National Park, hikers can experience the challenge of walking through a lava wasteland and into the belly of an active volcano.

Along much of Hawaii's shoreline lies a network of trails that have recently been under study by the Department of the Interior. Originally a series of access trails for the Hawaiians, they were paid for by local farmers to tax collectors. In 1823, William Ellis, a missionary, tried to follow them to circumnavigate the island. In more recent times, a group of journalists recreated—to the best of their ability—his route.

The plantations in the northeast destroyed any trails in that corner of the island. The sections that remain on the rest of Hawaii contain archaeological sites that should be left unmolested. Some people have proposed National Trail status for the network, but until then you'll need a topographic map, respect for private property and archaeology, and a yen for adventure to tackle the trails that the Hawaiians once tread.

Hawaii's official hiking trails run through three areas: Volcanoes National Park, Kau Desert and the Kohala Mountains. These are popular and well-defined trails, many of which are described below. Permits are required for any overnight backcountry camping within the boundaries of Hawaii Volcanoes National Park, which includes the Kau Desert. Apply the morning of your trip at the Kilauea Visitor Center. Permits are free, but first-come, first-served. All distances listed for hiking trails are one way unless otherwise noted.

HAMAKUA COAST **Waipio Valley Trail** begins from Waipio Valley lookout at the end of Route 24. Waipio is a broad, lush, awesomely beautiful valley ribboned with waterfalls and rich in history. From the trailhead, a jeep trail drops steeply for one mile to the valley floor. Here the trail joins one road leading up into the valley and another heading to the beach. The high road goes toward 1200-foot Hiilawe Falls and to an abandoned Peace Corps training camp.

Waipio Valley is ripe for exploring, but if you want to leave civilization completely behind, continue instead along the **Waimanu Valley Trail** (9 miles). This track begins at the base of the cliff that marks Waipio's northwest border. It climbs sharply up the

◆◆

WHERE THE WILD THINGS ARE

Hawaii Forest and Trail is an eco-tourism organization dedicated to the idea that education is fundamental to conservation. Their tours take small groups on explorations through limited-access wildlife refuges and other rarely visited areas. By providing an extensive look at the natural history of Hawaii and the threat to endangered plant and wildlife, the company leads you on more than a pretty hike. ~ 74-5035B Queen Kaahumanu Highway, Kailua-Kona; 808-331-8505, 800-464-1993, fax 808-331-8704; www.hawaii-forest.com, e-mail info@hawaii-forest.com.

1200-foot rock face in a series of switchbacks, then continues up and down across numerous gulches, and finally descends into Waimanu Valley. This exotic place, half the size of Waipio Valley, is equally as lush. Here, in addition to wild pigs, mountain apple trees and ancient ruins, you'll find naturally running water (requiring purification) and great spots for beachfront picnics. This is a challenging one-day hike, so you may want to camp. You may never want to leave.

KOHALA COAST   Stretching along Kohala peninsula's northeast coast is a series of sheer cliffs and wide valleys rivaling Kauai's Na Pali Coast in beauty. At either end of this rainswept *pali* are lush, still valleys that can only be reached by hiking trails. To camp legally in this area can be a challenge, since you need a permit or permission wherever you go, and the land could be State, corporate or owned by one of the dozens of property holders. If you want to camp, start by asking questions at the State Department of Land and Natural Resources; 808-587-0300.

Pololu Valley Trail (0.5 mile) descends from the Pololu Valley lookout at the end of Akoni Pule Highway to the valley floor 400 feet below. There you'll find a secluded beach (beware of the riptides) and a series of trails that lead up through the Kohala Mountains.

KONA/KAU AREA   From Volcanoes National Park's southern section several trails lead into the hot, arid Kau Desert. All are long, dusty trails offering solitude to the adventurous hiker.

Kau Desert Trail (3.5 miles) branches off Crater Rim Trail and drops 2000 feet en route to the lookout at the end of Hilina Pali Road. The shelter along the way, at Kipuka Pepeiau, provides a welcome resting place on this lengthy trek.

Mauna Iki Trail (3.6 miles) leads from Mamalahoa Highway (Route 11) to Hilina Pali Road. The trail passes near Footprints

◆◆

HUMDINGER

In the mountains of Hawi you'll discover that sports utility vehicles provide more than fashion. The Hummer, originally designed for the military, can pretty much go anywhere, perfect for a tour through the Hawaiian rainforest. **Hummer Safari** in Hawi takes groups of two-to-eight through the Kohala Mountains, which have recently been opened to the public. Waterfalls, local fauna and untouched riverbeds give visitors a glimpse into the beauty of ancient Hawaii before tourism (and Hummers). ~ 808-889-6922, 877-449-6922, fax 808-889-6944; www.kohala kayaks.com.

Trail, where a sudden volcanic eruption in 1790 engulfed a Hawaiian army at war with Kamehameha.

HAWAII VOLCANOES NATIONAL PARK The most interesting and easily accessible trails lead through the **Kilauea Caldera** area. The caldera, three miles long and 4000 feet above sea level, can be explored either by hiking along one extended trail or over several shorter connecting trails.

Crater Rim Trail (11.6-mile loop) begins near the park headquarters and encircles Kilauea Caldera. An excellent introduction to the volcanoes, this lengthy loop trail passes steam vents, the Kau Desert, the fractured Southwest Rift area and a fascinating fern forest. The views from along the rim are spectacular.

Sulphur Banks Trail (0.3 mile) begins at park headquarters and parallels Crater Rim Drive past steam vents and sulphur deposits.

Halemaumau Trail (3.5 miles) starts near Volcano House, then descends into Kilauea Caldera. The trail crosses the crater floor and affords astonishing views down into steaming Halemaumau crater, then climbs back up to join Crater Rim Trail. This has got to be one of the park's finest hikes.

Kilauea Iki Trail (5 miles) loops from the Thurston Lava Tube parking lot down into Kilauea Iki crater and returns via Crater Rim Trail. Crossing the crater floor, the trail passes over a lava crust beneath which lies a pool of hot rock. Rainwater percolates through the crust, reaches the hot rock, and emerges as steam. Step lightly.

Sandalwood Trail (1.5-mile loop) loops from near the Volcano House past sandalwood and *ohia* trees and then along the side of Kilauea Caldera.

Byron Ledge Trail (4 miles) branches off Halemaumau Trail, crosses the Kilauea caldera floor, and then climbs along Byron Ledge before rejoining Halemaumau. This makes an excellent connecting trail.

Starting within the Kapapala Forest Reserve at 5650 feet, the **Ainapo Trail** (3.5 miles) takes hikers on a moderately challenging trek past mesic *koa* and *ohia* trees. On the way up to the Ainapo Trail Shelter at Halewai, you'll catch sight of mountain goats and sheep. More experienced hikers can climb the rest of the fog-covered trail (7.5 miles) and will be rewarded with views from the rim of the Mokuaweoweo Caldera in Hawaii Volcanoes National Park. The trailhead begins at the cattleguard between the 40- and 41-mile markers on the Mamalahoa Highway between Volcano and Pahala. This hike requires permits from the National Park *and* the Division of Forestry and Wildlife in Hilo (808-974-4221). Reservations for the shelter can be made up to 30 days in advance.

Volcanoes National Park's premier hike is along **Mauna Loa Trail**. This tough 18-mile trek, requiring at least three days, leads to the top of the world's largest shield volcano. Cold-weather equipment and a sturdy constitution are absolute necessities for this challenging adventure. Permits are required for this hike.

Climbers usually hike seven miles the first day from the trailhead at the end of Mauna Loa Strip Road up to Red Hill (Pu'u 'Ula'ula). At this 10,035-foot way station, there is a rudimentary cabin with eight bunks with mattresses, but no provisions. A hearty 11-mile trek the second day leads to the rim of Mauna Loa's summit caldera, and to the Mokuaweoweo cabin (located on the rim). The return trip takes one or two days, depending on how fast you want to come down.

Beware of altitude sickness and hypothermia, and be sure to register for a permit at park headquarters before and after hiking. Purification tablets for the water and white gas for the stoves are also essential. Don't treat this as a casual jaunt; it's a real trek. Good planning will ensure your safety and enjoyment.

A single-lane paved road climbs from Saddle Road to an area near Mauna Loa summit. This alternative hiking route lacks the adventure but reduces the time needed to ascend Mauna Loa. This road is not open to rental cars.

▼▼▼▼▼▼▼▼▼▼▼
Transportation

AIR

Four airports serve the Big Island—Hilo International Airport (General Lyman Field) near Hilo, Kona International Airport, Upolu Airport on the Kohala peninsula and Waimea Kohala Airport near Waimea.

The main landing facility is **Kona International Airport**. Many mainland visitors fly here rather than to Honolulu to avoid Oahu's crowds. United Airlines, which provides the most frequent service to Hawaii, is the only carrier flying from the mainland directly to Kailua-Kona.

This facility has snack bars, cocktail lounges, duty-free shops, a restaurant and souvenir shops, but no lockers or bus service. A ten-mile cab ride into town costs about $30.

Passengers flying between the islands use Aloha Airlines or Hawaiian Airlines. They provide frequent jet service from Oahu and the other islands.

Hilo International Airport (General Lyman Field), once the island's main jetport, is now more like a small city airport. It is served by the same inter-island carriers as Keahole Airport. Here you'll find a cafeteria-style restaurant, cocktail lounge, gift shop, newsstand and lockers, but no bus service. Covering the two miles into town means renting a car, hailing a cab, hitching or hoofing.

Upolu Airport is a desolate landing strip on the Kohala peninsula along the island's northwest coast. There are no facilities whatever and only prop planes land here. No commercial flights operate regularly (or irregularly) from here.

Kamuela Airport is located two miles outside the cowboy town of Waimea. There are waiting rooms, but no shops of any kind here. Airline offices are often closed unless a flight is scheduled. No commercial flights operate from here.

CAR RENTALS

When choosing a rental agency, check whether they permit driving on the Saddle Road across the island and on South Point Road, both good paved roads with few potholes and many points of interest. I think it's quite unfair, even irrational, that some rental companies revoke insurance coverage if you drive these thoroughfares. But my protests will be of little benefit in case of an accident. So check first or be prepared to take your chances! It's wise to remember that you will be driving farther on Hawaii, sometimes through quite rural areas; it may sound obvious, but remember to watch your gas gauge.

Several other companies have franchises at the Hilo and Kailua-Kona airports. Among these are **Avis** (808-935-1290, 808-327-3001, 800-331-1212), **Budget Rent A Car** (808-935-6878, 808-329-8511, 800-527-0700), **Dollar Rent A Car** (808-961-6059, 808-329-2744, 800-800-4000), **Hertz Rent A Car** (808-935-2896, 808-329-3566, 800-654-3011) and **National Car Rental** (808-935-0891, 808-329-1674, 800-227-7368).

Many outfits located outside the Hilo International Airport and Keahole Airport feature competitive rates and free service to and from the airport.

JEEP RENTALS

Budget Rent A Car rents four-wheel drives. ~ 808-935-6878, 808-329-8511, 800-527-0700.

MOPED RENTALS

Motorcycles and scooters are available for rent at **DJ's Rentals**. ~ 75-5663-A Palani Road, Kailua-Kona; 808-329-1700.

PUBLIC TRANSIT

The **Hele-On Bus** provides cross-island service Monday through Saturday between Hilo and Kailua-Kona. There are also limited intra-city buses serving Hilo. Other buses drive to the Kona and Kau coasts. The Hele-On runs Monday through Saturday; fares range from 75¢ for short rides to $6 for the Hilo–Kailua cross-island run.

The Hilo bus terminal is on Kamehameha Avenue at Mamo Street. You'll see few bus stops indicated on the island. The official stops are generally unmarked, and you can hail a bus anywhere along its route. Just wave your hand. When it's time to get off, the driver will stop anywhere you wish.

For information and schedules, phone the **County Hawaiian Transit**. ~ 808-961-8343.

HITCHING   Thumbing is popular in Hawaii. Like any place, your luck will vary here, depending on your location, looks, the time, the tides, whatever. Generally, populated areas and tourist attractions are good spots for a ride. If you venture from these beaten paths, remember that the Big Island has long stretches with nothing but macadam and lava. Be sure to bring along water with you.

Check the Hele-On bus schedule before setting out just in case you get stranded. If your luck fails, you can hail a bus from anywhere along the roadside.

AERIAL TOURS   Thanks to the Kilauea eruption, the Big Island offers a wide variety of flightseeing options. In addition to the lava flows, you'll see remote coastlines, the slopes of Mauna Kea and coffee plantations. Bring your camera because the lava flow is one of Hawaii's greatest sightseeing opportunities.

Volcano Helitours offers a narrated 45-minute tour of all active eruptions. ~ Hilo International Airport; 808-967-7578.

At **Mauna Kea Helicopters** you have a choice of two flights lasting up to two hours. Passengers view the valleys and waterfalls on the island's northern end, as well as volcanic activity at Kilauea. ~ Mamalahoa Highway at the Waimea Airport, Waimea; 808-885-6400, 800-400-4354.

Safari Helicopters offers two tours on the Big Island that fly passengers past volcanoes and waterfalls. ~ Kona International Airport; 808-329-4655.

Big Island Air takes passengers on a circle island tour featuring Kilauea and the north end valleys and waterfalls. Flights last about 1 hour and 45 minutes. ~ Kona Airport; 808-329-4868.

SIX

Maui

Residents of Maui, Hawaii's second-largest island, proudly describe their Valley Isle by explaining that "Maui *no ka oi.*" Maui is the greatest. During the last decade, few of the island's visitors have disputed the claim. They return each year, lured by the enchantment of a place possessing 33 miles of public beaches, one of the world's largest dormant volcanoes, beautiful people, a breeding ground for rare humpback whales and a climate that varies from subtropic to subarctic.

Named after one of the most important demigods in the Polynesian pantheon, Maui has retained its mythic aura. The island is famous as a chic retreat and jet-set landing ground. To many people, Maui *is* Hawaii.

But to others, who have watched the rapid changes during the past several decades, Maui is no longer the greatest. They point to the 2.4 million tourists (second only to Oahu) who visited during a recent year, to the condominiums and resort hotels now lining the prettiest beaches and to the increasing traffic over once-rural roads. And they have a new slogan. "Maui is *pau.*" Maui is finished. Over-touristed. Overpopulated. Overdeveloped.

Today, among the island's 103,600 population, it seems like every other person is in the real estate business. On a land mass measuring 729 square miles, just half the size of Long Island, their goods are in short supply. During the 1970s and 1980s, land prices shot up faster than practically anywhere else in the country, although the 1990s saw prices decline.

Yet over 75 percent of the island remains unpopulated. Despite pressures from land speculation and a mondo-condo mentality, Maui still offers exotic, untouched expanses for the explorer. Most development is concentrated along the south and west coasts in Kihei, Wailea and Kaanapali. The rest of the island, though more populated than neighboring islands, is an adventurer's oasis.

The second-youngest island in the chain, Maui was created between one and two million years ago by two volcanoes. Haleakala, the larger, rises over 10,000 feet, and offers excellent hiking and camping within its summit caldera, the largest such dormant volcanic crater in the world. The earlier of the two firepits created the West Maui Mountains, 5788 feet at their highest elevation. Because of their relative age, and the fact they receive 400 inches of rainfall a year, they are more heavily eroded than the smooth surfaces of Haleakala. Between the two heights lies Central Maui, an isthmus formed when the lava from each volcano flowed together.

The twin cities of Kahului and Wailuku, Maui's commercial and civic centers, respectively, sit in this saddle. Until the 1990s, most of the island was planted in sugar, which became king in Maui after the decline of whaling in the 1860s. Today, a road through what remains of the cane fields leads south to the sun-splashed resorts and beaches of Kihei, Maalaea, Wailea and Makena.

Another road loops around the West Maui Mountains. It passes prime whale-watching areas along the south coast and bisects Lahaina, an old whaling town that is now the island's sightseeing capital. Next to this timeworn harbor is the resort area of Kaanapali, a two-mile stretch of beach backed by hotels, condominiums and a full range of resort facilities. Beyond Kaanapali lies eight miles of coast lined with crescent beaches and lava rock promontories with another collection of hotels, condos and homes at Honokawai, Kahana and Napili. Past Napili the Kapalua Resort adds an upscale alternative, with several hotels and condos and three of Hawaii's best golf courses. Head past Kapalua and the landscape becomes wilder, with the blue-green of pineapple mixing with a series of deep wilderness valleys and grassy headlands that offer magnificently wild coastal views. You'll want to take a break in rustic Kahakuloa, where taro is still grown and the lifestyle is reminiscent of old Hawaii. From Kahakuloa, the road continues around West Maui, returning you to Wailuku and Kahului.

The road girdling Haleakala's lower slopes passes equally beautiful areas. Along the rainswept northeast coast are sheer rock faces ribboned with waterfalls and gorges choked with tropic vegetation. The lush, somnolent town of Hana gives way along the southeast shore to a dry, unpopulated expanse that is always ripe for exploration.

On the middle slopes of Haleakala, in Maui's Upcountry region, small farms dot the landscape. Here, in addition to guavas, avocados and lychee nuts, grow the sweet Kula onions for which the Valley Isle is famous.

Because of its strategic location between Oahu and Hawaii, Maui has played a vital role in Hawaiian history. Kahekili, Maui's last king, gained control of all the islands except Hawaii before being overwhelmed by Kamehameha in 1790. Lahaina, long a vacation spot for island rulers, became a political center under Hawaii's first three kings and an important commercial center soon after Captain Cook sighted the island in 1778. It served as a supply depot for ships, then as a port for sandalwood exports. By the 1840s, Lahaina was the world capital of whaling. Now, together with the other equally beautiful sections of the Valley Isle, it is a mecca for vacationers.

Maui's magic has cast a spell upon travelers all over the world, making the island a vacation paradise. Like most modern paradises, it is being steadily gilded in plastic and concrete. Yet much of the old charm remains. Some people even claim that the sun shines longer on the Valley Isle than any other place on earth.

Maui

PACIFIC OCEAN

Honokohau

Kahana

Kaanapali

Lahaina

West Maui Forest Reserve

Eke Crater 4480'

Puu Kukui 5788'

Iao Valley State Monument

Kahekili Hwy

340

30

Wailuku

380

Waikapu

30

Olowalu

Honoapiilani Hwy

Auau Channel

Kahului

Puunene

311

Kihei

Kihei Rd

Piilani Hwy

31

Wailea

Makena

Molokini

Alalakeiki Channel

Kahoolawe

Kealaikahiki Channel

Kuau Hwy

Haleakala Hwy

37

Pukalani

377

Kula Hwy

Keokea

37

Ulupalakua Ranch

Pauwela

Paia

36

365

Makawao

Kailua

360

Hana Hwy

Kula Forest Reserve

Koolau Forest Reserve

Haleakala 8205'

Kahikinui Forest Reserve

Haleakala National Park

Wailua

360

Hana Hwy

Hana Forest Reserve

Hana

Kipahulu Forest Reserve

Piilani Hwy

Kaupo

(4-Wheel Drive Recommended)

Kaapahu Bay

Alenuihaha Channel

Hamakua Coast

N

0 5 miles

0 5 kilometers

They point to the legend of the demigod Maui who created his own daylight savings by weaving a rope from his sister's pubic hair and lassoing the sun by its genitals. And many hope he has one last trick to perform, one that will slow the course of development just as he slowed the track of the sun.

Lahaina

Maui's top tourist destination is a waterfront enclave that stretches for over two miles along a natural harbor, but measures only a couple of blocks deep. Simultaneously chic and funky, Lahaina has gained an international reputation for its art galleries, falsefront stores and waterfront restaurants.

It also happens to be one of Hawaii's most historic towns. A royal seat since the 16th century, Lahaina was long a playground for the *alii*. The royal surfing grounds lay just south of today's town center, and in 1802, Kamehameha I established his headquarters here, taking up residence in the Brick Palace, the first Western-style building in Hawaii.

It was in Lahaina that the first high school and first printing press west of the Rockies were established in 1831. From Lahaina, Kamehameha III promulgated Hawaii's first constitution in 1840, and established a legislative body that met in town until the capital was eventually moved to Honolulu.

During the 1820s, this quaint port also became a vital watering place for whaling ships and evolved into the whaling capital of the world. At its peak in the mid-1840s, the whaling trade brought over 400 ships a year into the harbor.

To the raffish sailors who favored it for its superb anchorage, grog shops and uninhibited women, Lahaina was heaven itself. To the stiff-collared missionaries who arrived in 1823, the town was a hellhole—a place of sin, abomination and vile degradation. Some of Lahaina's most colorful history was written when the Congregationalists prevented naked women from swimming out to meet the whalers. Their belligerent brethren anchored in the harbor replied by cannonballing mission homes and rioting along the waterfront.

The town declined with the loss of the whaling trade in the 1860s, and was transformed into a quiet sugar plantation town, serving the Pioneer Sugar Mill that opened during the same decade. Not until developers began building resorts in nearby Kaanapali a century later did it fully revive. During the 1960s, Lahaina was designated a national historic landmark and restoration of many important sites was begun. By the 1970s, the place was a gathering spot not only for the jet set but the ultra hip as well. Clubs like the Blue Max made Lahaina a hot nightspot where famous musicians came to vacation and jam.

Today, Lahaina retains a gentrified charm with shops, galleries, clubs and restaurants lining Front Street, an oceanside "Main

Hawaiian Getaway

Maui Five-Day Itinerary

Day 1
- Fly into Kahului, rent a car and drive to the Lahaina–Kaanapali area.
- Check into your condo or hotel and spend the afternoon relaxing on the beach.

Day 2
- Drive up to **Haleakala** (pages 325–28). (For the adventurous, arrive for sunrise, which means you have to leave around 4 a.m.—be sure to check weather conditions before you do this.)
- On the way down from the summit, explore the **Upcountry** (pages 319–24), including the town of Makawao and one of the loop tours, Route 390 or Route 365.
- Plan to spend the afternoon wandering through **Lahaina** (pages 250, 252–66), where you can shop and then have an early-bird dinner.

Day 3
- If it's whale-watching season, take an **excursion** from one of the many whale-watching outfits offered in the book. If it's not whale-watching season, you can still view other sea life up close and personal by **kayaking** along Maui's south shore or hopping aboard one of the numerous **snorkeling** adventures to Molokini.

Day 4
- Spend the day driving the heavenly **Hana Highway** (pages 302–309).
- Don't miss watching the wind- and kitesurfers at **Hookipa Beach Park** (page 302) and be sure to stop along the way to hike to a waterfall or picnic at **Kaumahina State Wayside** (page 304) or **Puaakaa State Wayside** (page 305).
- Check into a Hana bed and breakfast or hotel. (You should have made reservations.) Have dinner at the **Hotel Hana-Maui** (page 314).

Day 5
- Return to Kahului via the **backroad from Hana** (pages 308–309) if it is open (check weather conditions), stopping at **Oheo Gulch** (page 308) (also known as the "Seven Sacred Pools") and **Charles Lindbergh's grave** (page 309). If the backroad is closed, turn around at Lindbergh's grave and backtrack to Kahului.

Street." Most points of interest lie within a half-mile of the old sea wall that protects this narrow thoroughfare from the ocean, so the best way to explore the town is on foot.

Start at **Lahaina Harbor**, located on Wharf Street, and take a stroll along the docks. In addition to tour boats, pleasure craft from around the world put in here or cast anchor in the Lahaina Roads just offshore. During the heyday of the whaling industry in the 1840s, the Auau Channel between Lahaina and Lanai was a forest of masts.

Carthaginian II, the steel-hulled brig at dock's end, preserves those days in a shipboard museum. Actually a turn-of-the-20th-century brig that was converted into a replica of an old square-rigged sailing ship, this floating display case features videotapes on whales and intriguing artifacts from days of yore. Admission. ~ 808-661-8527.

Across Wharf Street sits the **Pioneer Inn**, a rambling hostelry built in 1901. With its second-story veranda and landscaped garden, this aging woodframe hotel is a great place to bend an elbow and breathe in the salt air. ~ 658 Wharf Street; 808-661-3636, fax 808-667-9366; www.pioneerinnmaui.com, e-mail info@pioneerinnmaui.com.

Just north of here a Hawaii Visitors Bureau sign points out the chair-shaped **Hauola Stone**, a source of healing power for ancient Hawaiians, who sat in the natural formation and let the waves wash over them.

There is nothing left of the **Brick Palace**, the two-story structure commissioned in 1798 by Kamehameha I. Located just inshore from the Hauola Stone and built by an English convict, the palace was used by the king in 1802 and 1803 (although some say he preferred to stay in his grass shack next door). Today the original foundation has been outlined with brick paving.

To the south, a 125-year-old **banyan tree**, among the oldest and largest in the islands, extends its rooting branches across almost an entire acre. Planted in 1873 to mark the advent of Protestant missionaries in Maui 50 years earlier, this shady canopy is a resting place for tourists and mynah birds alike. ~ Front and Hotel streets.

The sprawling giant presses up against the **Old Courthouse**, constructed in 1859 from coral blocks taken from the home built for King Kamehameha III. The historic building is home to the **Lahaina Visitors Center** (808-667-9193), where you can pick up maps and brochures, including one that provides all the details needed for a self-guided walking tour of Lahaina. The **Lahaina Art Society** (808-661-0111), a non-profit association of local artists, is also located in the courthouse. Art shows are presented under the banyan tree by the Art Society every other weekend. On alternate weekends Hawaiian crafts are the theme.

Those stone ruins on either side of the courthouse are the remains of the **Old Fort,** built during the 1830s to protect Lahaina from the sins and cannonballs of lawless sailors. The original structure was torn down two decades later to build a jail, but during its heyday the fortress guarded the waterfront with 47 cannons.

Across Front Street is the **Baldwin Home,** Lahaina's oldest building. Constructed of coral and stone in the early 1830s, the place sheltered the family of Reverend Dwight Baldwin, a medical missionary. Today the house contains period pieces and family heirlooms, including some of the good doctor's rather fiendish-looking medical implements. Beneath the hand-hewn ceiling beams rests the Baldwin's Steinway piano; the dining room includes the family's china, a fragile cargo that made the voyage around Cape Horn; and in the master bedroom stands a four-poster bed fashioned from native *koa*. Admission. ~ 808-661-3362, fax 808-661-9309; www.lahainarestoration.org, e-mail info @maui.net.

Lahaina–Kaanapali Area

The **Master's Reading Room** next door, an 1834 storehouse and library, is home to the Lahaina Restoration Foundation and not open to the public.

A Chinese gathering place that dates to 1912, the **Wo Hing Museum** has been lovingly restored. While the temple has been converted into a small museum, the old cookhouse adjacent is used to show films of the islands made by Thomas Edison in 1898 and 1903 during the early days of motion pictures. ~ 858 Front Street; 808-661-5553, fax 808-661-9309.

The **Holy Innocents' Episcopal Church** is a small structure dating from 1927. Very simple in design, the sanctuary is filled with beautiful paintings. The Hawaiian madonna on the altar and the tropical themes of the paintings are noteworthy features. Services are Sunday at 7 a.m. and 10 a.m. ~ 561 Front Street; 808-661-4202, fax 808-661-8667; e-mail ccannon@aloha.net.

Several other historic spots lie along Wainee Street, which parallels Front Street. **Waiola Cemetery**, with its overgrown lawn and eroded tombstones, contains graves dating to 1829. Queen Keopuolani, the wife of Kamehameha I and the mother of Hawaii's next two kings, is buried here. So is her daughter, Princess Nahienaena, and Governor Hoapali, who ruled Hawaii from 1823 to 1840. Surrounded by blossoming plumeria trees, there are also the graves of early missionaries and Hawaiian commoners.

Maui's first Christian services were performed in 1823 on the grounds of **Waiola Church** next door. Today's chapel, built in 1953, occupies the spot where the Wainee church was constructed in 1832. The earlier structure, Hawaii's first stone church, seated 3000 parishioners and played a vital role in the conversion of the local population to Christianity and Western ways. ~ 535 Wainee Street; 808-661-4349, fax 808-661-1734.

A little farther north on Wainee Street sits the **Lahaina Hongwanji Temple** with its three distinctive turrets. The building dates from 1927, but the Buddhist Hongwanji sect has been meeting at this site since 1910.

On the corner of Prison and Wainee streets rise the menacing walls of old **Hale Paahao**, a prison built by convicts in 1854 and used to house rowdy sailors as well as more hardened types. The coral blocks used to build this local hoosegow were taken from the Old Fort on Front Street.

Just north of the jail along Wainee Street sits the **Episcopal Cemetery** and **Hale Aloha**. Walter Murray Gibson, a controversial figure in 19th-century Hawaii politics who eventually became an adviser to King David Kalakaua, is buried here. Hale Aloha, completed in 1858 and restored several years ago, served as a church meetinghouse.

Nearby is **Maria Lanakila Church**, a lovely white-washed building with interior pillars that was built in 1928 to replace a

Author Picks

CHAPTER FAVORITES

I don't think there's anything quite like standing at the rim of **Haleakala crater** watching the sun rise over a moon-like landscape. *pages 325–26*

I get goosebumps when I come face-to-face with a wizened old sea turtle while kayaking in the **Ahihi–Kinau Natural Area Reserve**. *page 282*

When I really want to indulge my taste buds with Japanese cuisine, I head to the Japanese buffet at **Hakone** and fill my plate (a number of times) with their tempting selections. *page 289*

Camping at **Waianapanapa State Park** satisfies my need to get away from it all while relaxing in a lush landscape accessible to good snorkeling and swimming. *page 316*

When I want to spend the night in the lap of luxury, I check into the **Hotel Hana-Maui**, a world-class resting place down the street from Waianapanapa. *page 311*

Watching humpback whales or spinner dolphins cavorting in the Pacific is also on my short list of favorite things to do. *pages 333–34*

19th-century chapel. Adjacent is the **Seamen's Cemetery**, a poorly maintained ground where early sailors were laid to rest. ~ Wainee and Dickenson streets.

The **Lahaina Shingon Mission**, a simple plantation-era structure with an ornately gilded altar, was built in 1902 by a Japanese monk and his followers. It now represents another gathering place for Maui's Buddhists. ~ 682 Luakini Street between Hale and Dickenson streets; phone/fax 808-661-0466.

The proverbial kids-from-eight-to-eighty set will love the **Sugar Cane Train,** a reconstructed 1890-era steam train. Operating near the West Maui resort area, the Lahaina–Kaanapali & Pacific Railroad engine and passenger cars chug along a six-mile route midway between the mountains and ocean. Various package tours are available with the train rides, including a ride on a semisubmersible vessel in Lahaina, helicopter tours, bicycle trips down the slopes of a volcano, and a viewing of the film *Hawaii: Islands of the Gods,* shown on the 180-degree screen at the Omni Theatre. Admission. ~ The main station is off Hinau Street in Lahaina; 808-661-0089, 800-499-2307, fax 808-661-8389; www.sugarcanetrain.com.

Oceanic adventurers should take an opportunity to stop in at **Atlantis Submarines** and reserve an underwater tour. The voyage takes you aboard a 48-passenger submersible down to depths of

150 feet. En route you may see close-up views of technicolor coral reefs and outlandish lava formations. A trip to the depths requires deep pockets; these two-hour excursions aren't cheap. ~ 665 Front Street, in the Pioneer Inn; 808-667-2224, fax 808-667-5747; www.goatlantis.com.

And don't miss **Lahaina Jodo Mission**, a Buddhist enclave one-half mile north of Lahaina on Ala Moana Street. There's a temple and a three-tiered pagoda here, as well as the largest ceremonial bell in Hawaii. The giant bronze Buddha, with the West Maui Mountains in the background, is a sight to behold. It rests amid stone walkways and flowering oleander bushes in a park-like setting. ~ 12 Ala Moana Street; 808-661-4304, fax 808-661-0939.

For a splendid view of Lahaina, turn off Route 30 onto Lahainaluna Road, pass the now-closed, century-old Pioneer Mill, and head *mauka* (toward the mountains) to **Lahainaluna School**. Established by missionaries in 1831, it is one of the country's oldest high schools. Today this historic facility serves as a public high school for the Lahaina area. ~ 808-662-3997, fax 808-662-3997.

Hale Pai, its printing house dating to 1837, printed Hawaii's first money and many of the first bibles, religious tracts and primers produced in the islands. Hale Pai is open as a museum and research library. It houses a working reproduction of the original printing press. Closed Saturday and Sunday. ~ Phone/fax 808-667-7040; e-mail halepai@maui.net.

LODGING   To fully capture the spirit of Lahaina, there's only one place to stay—the **Best Western Pioneer Inn**. Located smack on Lahaina's waterfront, this wooden hostelry is the center of the area's action. On one side, sloops, ketches and glass-bottom boats are berthed; on the other side lies bustling Front Street with its falsefront shops. The Inn is noisy, vibrant and crowded with tenants and tourists. On the ground floor, you can hunker down over a glass of grog at the saloon, or stroll through the Inn's lushly planted courtyard. You can no longer book a room above the bar, but there are accommodations in the section overlooking the courtyard. These are small and plainly decorated, with telephones, overhead fans, air conditioning and lanais. A swimming pool completes the picture. ~ 658 Wharf Street; 808-661-3636, 800-457-5457, fax 808-667-5708; www.pioneerinnmaui.com, e-mail info@pioneerinnmaui.com. DELUXE.

While the building is actually quite modern, the **Plantation Inn** possesses the look and ambience of an early-20th-century hostelry. Modeled after the plantation architecture of an earlier era, it features 19 rooms individually decorated in period furniture. Most are adorned with either poster, brass or canopy bed, stained-glass windows and tile bathrooms. Combining the atmosphere of the past with the amenities of the present, guest rooms also

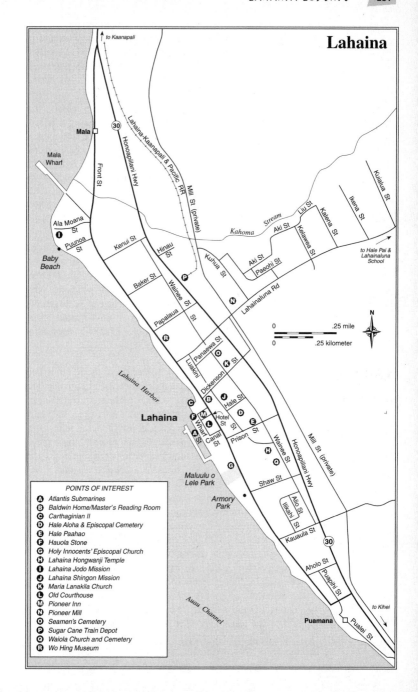

Lahaina

to Kaanapali

Mala

Mala Wharf

Ala Moana St

Baby Beach

Lahaina Harbor

Lahaina

Maluulu o Lele Park

Armory Park

Auau Channel

Puamana

to Kihei

to Hale Pai & Lahainaluna School

Kahoma Stream

to Kaanapali

Honoapiilani Hwy

Lahaina-Kaanapali & Pacific RR

Front St

Mill St (private)

Kuialua St

Ikena St

Liu St

Aki St

Kelawea St

Kalena St

Aki St

Paeohi St

Lahainaluna Rd

Kenui St

Hinau St

Kuhua St

Baker St

Wainee St

Papalaua St

Panaewa St

Luakini

Dickenson

Hale St

Hotel St

Wharf St

Canal St

Prison St

Wainee St

Honoapiilani Hwy

Mill St (private)

Shaw St

Ailo St

Ilikahi St

Kauaula St

Aholo St

Puaphi St

Pualei St

0   .25 mile
0   .25 kilometer

N

POINTS OF INTEREST

- **A** Atlantis Submarines
- **B** Baldwin Home/Master's Reading Room
- **C** Carthaginian II
- **D** Hale Aloha & Episcopal Cemetery
- **E** Hale Paahao
- **F** Hauola Stone
- **G** Holy Innocents' Episcopal Church
- **H** Lahaina Hongwanji Temple
- **I** Lahaina Jodo Mission
- **J** Lahaina Shingon Mission
- **K** Maria Lanakila Church
- **L** Old Courthouse
- **M** Pioneer Inn
- **N** Pioneer Mill
- **O** Seamen's Cemetery
- **P** Sugar Cane Train Depot
- **Q** Waiola Church and Cemetery
- **R** Wo Hing Museum

feature televisions, refrigerators and air conditioning, as well as VCRs on request. There's a pool with a shaded pavilion and jacuzzi on the premises. Continental breakfast. ~ 174 Lahainaluna Road; 808-667-9225, 800-433-6815, fax 808-667-9293; www.theplantationinn.com, e-mail info@theplantationinn.com. DELUXE TO ULTRA-DELUXE.

The Oscar for most original inn goes to the **Lahaina Inn**. Constructed earlier this century, this 12-room beauty was fully restored and appointed in Gay Nineties finery. Each room is wall to ceiling with gorgeous antiques—leaded glass lamps, mirrored armoires, original oil paintings, cast-iron beds and brass locks. Attention to detail is a way of life: the place simply exudes the aura of another era. If you don't stay here, stop by and visit. ~ 127 Lahainaluna Road; 808-661-0577, 800-808-669-3444, fax 808-667-9480; www.lahainainn.com, e-mail inntown@lahainainn.com. MODERATE TO DELUXE.

The **Aston Maui Islander Hotel** is a warren of woodframe buildings spread across lushly landscaped grounds. The ambience is an odd combination of tropical retreat and motel atmosphere. It features 360 trimly decorated rooms, some of which are small studios (with kitchens) and one-bedroom efficiencies. Swimming pool, laundry, tennis court, picnic area. ~ 660 Wainee Street; 808-667-9766, 800-367-5226, fax 808-661-3733; www.aston hotels.com. MODERATE TO ULTRA-DELUXE.

CONDOS

HIDDEN ▶

Perhaps the nicest place to stay on this side of the island is **Puamana**, a 28-acre retreat about a mile southeast of Lahaina. This townhouse complex, a 1920s-era sugar plantation, rests along a rock-strewn beach. The oceanfront clubhouse, open to guests, was once the plantation manager's house, and the landscaped grounds are still given over to mango, plumeria and torch ginger trees. Guests stay in low-slung plantation-style buildings that sport shake-shingle roofs and house from two to six units. Prices begin in the deluxe range for one-bedroom facilities that contain kitchens and sleep up to four people, and end in the ultra-deluxe range for two- and three-bedroom efficiencies that sleep up to six and eight, respectively. To round out the amenities there are three pools and a tennis court. There's a three-night minimum that increases to seven nights during the Christmas season. ~ 34 Pualima Place; 808-667-2551. Reservations through Klahani Resorts: 800-628-6731, fax 808-661-5875; www.klahani.com, e-mail klahani@hotmail.com. DELUXE TO ULTRA-DELUXE.

Though it's more expensive than many others, **Lahaina Shores Hotel** has the advantage of a beachfront location in Lahaina. This sprawling condominium complex offers studio apartments beginning at $140, while one-bedroom units start at $175. With a swimming pool, jacuzzi and the nearby beach, it's quite convenient. ~ 475 Front Street; 808-661-4835, 800-628-6699, fax 808-667-1145; www.lahaina-shores.com, e-mail info@classic resorts.com. DELUXE TO ULTRA-DELUXE.

DINING

One of my favorite light-food stops is a devil-may-care place called the **Sunrise Café**. Set in a tiny clapboard building with a fresh, airy look, it serves salads, sandwiches and espresso, plus such entrées as smoked *kalua* pork, grilled chicken breast and mango barbecue chicken. The café serves breakfast, lunch and an "early-bird" dinner (they close at 6:30 p.m.). ~ Located around back at 693 Front Street; 808-661-8558. BUDGET.

In keeping with the old hostelry upstairs, the **Pioneer Inn Restaurant** brings back the Lahaina of old. The main dining room is a cozy anchorage dotted with nautical fixtures and specializing in regional fare. The emphasis is on the "bounty of Hawaii"; in other words, fresh fish, upcountry produce and local herbs. Select one of the day's fresh fish specials and you can't go wrong. Breakfast begins at 6 a.m. ~ 658 Wharf Street; 808-661-3636, fax 808-667-9366. DELUXE.

Across the lobby from the Pioneer Inn Restaurant, the **Pioneer Grill and Bar** offers similar but less formal fare and boasts a view of Lahaina Harbor. Portuguese bean soup is a specialty of both eateries and both fire their dishes on a *kiawe* grill. No dinner served. ~ 658 Wharf Street; 808-661-3636, fax 808-667-9366. MODERATE TO DELUXE.

I can't say much for the nomenclature, but the prices are worth note at **Cheeseburger in Paradise**. This is a rare catch indeed—an inexpensive restaurant smack on the Lahaina waterfront that serves three meals a day and features live nightly rock-and-roll music. Granted, you won't find much on the menu other than hamburgers, salads and sandwiches. But if some couples can live on love, why can't the rest of us live on ocean views? ~ 811 Front Street; 808-661-4855, fax 808-661-9508. BUDGET TO MODERATE.

The surf-and-turf menu at **Woody's Oceanfront Grill** features blackened ahi, barbecued ribs, grilled *ono* and New York strip. Familiar appetizers are prepared with an island twist such as onion

ROYAL HAWAIIAN HOLIDAYS

Although the Hawaiian capital moved to Honolulu in 1850, Lahaina remained a favorite vacation spot for several kings, including Kamehameha III, IV and V, and Queen Liliuokalani. All had second homes in the area and returned often to indulge in those favorite Hawaiian pastimes—rest and relaxation.

rings with mango ketchup and grilled tiger shrimp served with a fresh mint and papaya relish. Dining is on two decks overlooking the water. ~ 839 Front Street; 808-661-8788; e-mail woodys@ mauigateway.com. MODERATE TO DELUXE.

If you've seen one **Hard Rock Café**, you know about the line for the T-shirt window, the line for a table and the line for the bar. What a formula: just get yourself a show car from the '50s, a few surfboards, guitars and Buddy Holly posters, throw in an exposed-beam ceiling and circular bar and you've got the Maui branch of this popular empire. The menu runs from beef and veggie burgers to lime barbecue chicken, marinated T-bones and fajitas. ~ Lahaina Center, 900 Front Street; 808-667-7400, fax 808-667-5929; www.hardrock.com. MODERATE.

Light, bright and airy, **Compadres** is a great place to sip a margarita or enjoy a Mexican meal with an island flair. The tropical ambience is as appealing as the steaming dishes served here. Especially popular are the fajitas and pork carnitas, but the menu also offers burgers, salads and vegetarian dishes. Breakfast, lunch and dinner—they open at 8 a.m. ~ Lahaina Cannery Mall, 1221 Honoapiilani Highway; 808-661-7189, e-mail compadresmaui@ hi.freei.net. MODERATE TO DELUXE.

The preferred style of dining in Lahaina is steak and seafood at one of the waterfront restaurants along Front Street. And the common denominator is the ever-popular, usually crowded **Kimo's**, where you can enjoy all the tropical amenities while dining on seafood fettuccine, lobster or prime rib. Most days a week they have live Hawaiian music. ~ 845 Front Street; 808-661-4811, www.hulapie.com, e-mail tskimos@aol.com. MODERATE TO DELUXE.

The **Bubba Gump Shrimp Co.** pays homage to the movie *Forrest Gump*. Featuring "shrimp any way you can think of eating it," and other American-style food, it is also filled with *Gump* memorabilia. ~ 889 Front Street; 808-661-3111, fax 808-667-6650; www.bubbagump.com. MODERATE TO DELUXE.

Slightly (I said *slightly*) off the tourist track is the **Old Lahaina Luau**. Dinner here is based on the traditional luau—from the grass hut buildings to the menu of roast pork, kalua pig, sweet potato, mahimahi and poi. Reserve early, show up on time and be prepared to make an evening of it. ~ 1251 Front Street, behind the Lahaina Cannery Mall; 808-667-1998, 800-248-5828; www. oldlahainaluau.com, e-mail kim@oldlahainaluau.com. DELUXE.

At **Longhi's**, a European-style café that specializes in Mediterranean dishes, informality is the password. The menu changes daily and is never written down; the waiter simply tells you the day's offerings. Usually there'll be several pasta dishes, sautéed vegetables, salads, a shellfish creation, steak, a wine-soaked chicken or veal dish and perhaps eggplant parmigiana. Longhi's prepares all of its own bread and pasta, buys Maui-grown produce and imports many cheeses from New York. The dinners reflect this diligence. Breakfasts and lunches are cooked with the same care. Definitely recommended, especially for vegetarians, who can choose from many of the dishes offered. ~ 888 Front Street; 808-667-2288; e-mail longhi@maui.net. DELUXE TO ULTRA-DELUXE.

David Paul's Lahaina Grill, headlining Pacific Rim cuisine, is an intimate dining room with a personalized touch. According to chef David Paul Johnson, the menu represents "a gathering of technique, flavors and skills from around the world, utilizing local ingredients to translate each dish into an exceptional dining experience." Currently you can order the tequila shrimp with firecracker rice, soft-shell crabs, Kona coffee–roasted rack of lamb or macadamia-smoked tenderloin, but the menu changes regularly. Decide for yourself whether he carries it off. Dinner only. ~ 127 Lahainaluna Road; 808-667-5117, 800-360-2606; www.lahainagrill.com, e-mail lahainagrill@aol.com. ULTRA-DELUXE.

Hawaii's first phone line was installed from Lahaina to Haiku in 1877.

A defining experience in Lahaina dining is **Gerard's Restaurant**. Here you'll encounter a French restaurant in a Victorian setting with tropical surroundings. Housed in the Plantation Inn, a bed and breakfast reminiscent of early New Orleans, Gerard's provides a chandelier-and-pattern-wallpaper dining room as well as a veranda complete with overhead fans and whitewashed balustrade. The chef prepares fresh fish, rack of lamb, *confit* of duck and puff pastry with shiitake mushrooms. Of course, that is after having started off with ahi steak tartar or crab bisque. Dinner only. ~ 174 Lahainaluna Road; 808-661-8939; e-mail gerard@maui.net. ULTRA-DELUXE.

Near the top of the cognoscenti's list of gourmet establishments is an unlikely looking French restaurant in Olowalu called **Chez Paul**. The place is several miles outside Lahaina in a renovated building that also houses Olowalu's funky general store. But for years this little hideaway has had a reputation far transcending its surroundings. You'll probably drive right past the place at first, but when you do find it, you'll discover a menu featuring such delicacies as homemade duck pâté with mustard seed, grilled rack of lamb with mango chutney, island fish poached in champagne and several other tempting entrées. While the tab is ethereal, the rave reviews this prim dining room receives make it worth every franc. Closed Sunday in summer. ~ Honoapiilani Highway, Olowalu; 808-661-3843, fax 808-667-5692; e-mail lucien@aloha.net. ULTRA-DELUXE.

◄ HIDDEN

Foodland is open daily from 6 a.m. to midnight. ~ Old Lahaina Center, Wainee Street; 808-661-0975.

GROCERIES

For health-food items, stop by **Westside Natural Food**. Open from 7:30 a.m. to 9 p.m. Monday to Saturday and 8:30 a.m. to 8 p.m. on Sunday. ~ 193 Lahainaluna Road; 808-667-2855.

South of Lahaina, the **Olowalu General Store** has a limited supply of grocery items. ~ Honoapiilani Highway, Olowalu; 808-661-3774.

SHOPPING Lahaina's a great place to combine shopping with sightseeing. Most shops are right on Front Street in the historic wooden buildings facing the water. For a walking tour of the stores and waterfront, start from the Pioneer Inn at the south end of the strip and walk north on the *makai* or ocean side. Then come back along the *mauka*, or mountain, side of the street.

One of the first shops you will encounter on this consumer's tour of Lahaina will be **The Gecko Store**. The only shop I've seen with a sand floor, it stocks inexpensive beachwear as well as T-shirts and toys. ~ 703 Front Street; 808-661-1078.

The **Endangered Species Store**, which features a multitude of conservation-minded items, is a worthy stop. Among other things, you will find chimes, statues and a healthy supply of T-shirts and stuffed animals. ~ 707 Front Street; 808-661-0208.

Past the sea wall, in an overgrown cottage set back from the street, lie several shops including **Pacific Vision**, with its hand-etched glass, hand-painted clothing, and bedding. ~ 819 Front Street; 808-661-0188.

Sgt. Leisure Resort Patrol has an array of imaginative T-shirts. ~ 855B Front Street; 808-667-0661.

There are just a few more street numbers before this shopper's promenade ends. Then if you cross the road and walk back in the opposite direction, with the sea to your right, you'll pass **South Seas Trading Post**, where you can barter greenbacks for Nepali wedding necklaces, Chinese porcelain opium pillows or New Guinea masks. ~ 780 Front Street; 808-661-3168.

Célébrités is a trendy showcase for the artistic work of several musicians and actors, including John Lennon, Miles Davis, the Rolling Stones' Ronnie Wood, Anthony Quinn and Charles Bronson. They also have album cover art and pieces signed by the Beatles and the Stones. ~ 764 Front Street; 808-667-0727.

Lahaina Galleries is of special note not only for the contemporary artworks but also because of the imaginative ways in which they're displayed. Even if you're not just dying to write that five-figure check, stop by for a viewing. ~ 728 Front Street; 808-667-2152, 800-228-2006; www.lahainagalleries.com.

The **Wharf Cinema Center** is a multilevel complex of shops and restaurants. Most interesting is **Island Coin & Stamps** (808-667-6155), where all sorts of Hawaiiana and other collectibles make tempting souvenirs. The theater is small, but the movies are first run if you're in the mood for a film while you're on Maui.

If you have children in tow, take a break and head to the **Fun Factory** (808-667-1922). There's enough video games and other electronic attractions to keep them busy for hours. While they're being entertained, you can enjoy a drink at the **Blue Lagoon Tropical Bar and Grill** (808-661-8141) in the adjacent courtyard. ~ 658 Front Street; 808-661-8748.

Contemporary Village Gallery features paintings by modern Hawaiian artists. Amid the tourist schlock is some brilliant artwork. ~ 180 Dickenson Street; 808-661-5559.

Also stop in at the Lahaina Art Society's **Banyan Tree Gallery**. This is a great place if you're in the market for local artwork; on display are pieces by a number of Maui artists. ~ 648 Wharf Street, first floor of the Old Courthouse; 808-661-0111.

The **Lahaina Cannery Mall**, a massive complex of stores housed in an old canning factory, is the area's most ambitious project. **Lahaina Printsellers** (808-667-7843), one of my favorite Maui shops, has an astounding collection of ancient maps and engravings from Polynesia and other parts of the world. **Kite Fantasy** (808-661-4766; www.kitefantasy.com) is the place to pick up stunt and sport kites including diamond, box and bird designs. Here you'll also find wind socks, kaleidoscopes, games and a wide array of toys. Complete flying instructions, including tips on where to launch your kite, are provided by the helpful staff. ~ 1221 Honoapiilani Highway.

If it's Friday, you can browse the art galleries of Lahaina, which sponsor a special Art Night every week.

Those are just a couple ideas to provide you with a jump start. Propel yourself through this place and you'll find a dozen more reasons that make it a favorite among Lahaina residents.

On the corner of Front and Papalana streets, **Lahaina Center** is another shopping mall, a sprawling complex of theaters, stores and restaurants. Among the shops here is **Just Mauied**, which caters to honeymooners, featuring frames made of *tapa*, a local tree bark, mugs and other cutesy items (808-661-5883). **Hilo Hattie Fashion Center** (808-667-7911) specializes in the tackiest alohawear imaginable. ~ 900 Front Street.

Front Street's the strip in Lahaina—a dilapidated row of buildings from which stream some of the freshest sounds around.

NIGHTLIFE

At the **Pioneer Grill and Bar**, there is no music, but it's worth a drop-in anyway. Tucked into a corner of the Best Western Pioneer Inn, this spot features a seagoing motif complete with harpoons, figureheads and other historical nautical decor. Usually packed to the bulkheads with a lively crew, it's a great place to enjoy a tall cold one. ~ 658 Wharf Street; 808-661-3636.

Moose McGillycuddy's is a hot club offering a large dance-floor and a variety of live music acts. The house is congenial and the drinks imaginatively mixed; for contemporary sounds with dinner, arrive before 9 p.m. Cover on Wednesday. ~ 844 Front Street; 808-667-7758.

Since it's named after Jimmy Buffett's famous lyric, it's only appropriate that **Cheeseburger in Paradise** should have live music. With a variety of performers, they have "fun" tunes from 4:30 'til close—around 10 p.m. every night. There is no dancefloor, however. ~ 811 Front Street; 808-661-4855.

Lahaina's favorite pastime is watching the sun set over the ocean while sipping a tropical concoction at a waterfront watering place. A prime place for this very rewarding activity is **Kimo's**, which features traditional Hawaiian music Monday through Thursday, and rock-and-roll on Friday and Saturday. ~ 845 Front Street; 808-661-4811.

The oldest American school west of the Rockies is Lahainaluna School, founded by missionaries in Lahaina in 1831.

The Bubba Gump Shrimp Co. hosts musicians nightly who play music that is—you guessed it—the sort featured in *Forrest Gump*. For those who didn't see the movie, that means classic '60s and '70s tunes. ~ 889 Front Street; 808-661-3111.

If you want to sample Maui and Hawaii microbrews, head to **Maui Brews**. With over 16 micros on tap, a full bistro menu and live music (cover), who could not enjoy themselves? Sit under the thatch at the bar or hang out at the ocean-view lanai. ~ Lahaina Center, 900 Front Street; 808-667-7794.

If it's Friday in Lahaina, you can also browse the town's art galleries, which sponsor a special **Art Night** every week. This is a great opportunity to meet some of the artists who have made Lahaina an international art scene. The artists, who welcome visitors at galleries where their work is displayed, talk story and add a unique personal touch to a night on the town.

For an awe-inspiring glimpse into Hawaii's past, watch the 40-minute film at the **Omni Theatre/Hawaii Experience**. Offering a three-dimensional perspective of the state's cultural and natural history, this film is shown on a huge domed 180-degree screen. Admission. ~ 824 Front Street; 808-661-8314.

BEACHES & PARKS

PAPALAUA WAYSIDE PARK   *Kiawe* trees and scrub vegetation spread right to the shoreline along Papalaua Wayside Park. There are sandy patches between the trees large enough to spread a towel, but I prefer sunbathing at beaches closer to Lahaina. Bounded on one side by Honoapiilani Highway, this narrow beach extends for a mile to join a nicer, lawn-fringed park; then it stretches on toward Olowalu for several more miles. If you want to be alone, just head down the shore. Swimming is good, snorkeling is okay out past the surf break and surfing is excellent at Thousand Peaks breaks and also very good several miles east in Maalaea Bay. There's an outhouse and picnic area at the county wayside. ~ Located about ten miles south of Lahaina on Honoapiilani Highway.

OLOWALU BEACHES To the north and south of Olowalu General Store lie narrow corridors of white sand. This is an excellent area to hunt for Maui diamonds. Swimming is very good, and south of the general store, where road and water meet, you'll find an excellent coral reef for snorkeling. There is also a growing green sea turtle population that can be seen by snorkelers at the 14-mile marker. Surfers will find good breaks with right and left slides about a half-mile north of the general store. *Ulua* are often caught from Olowalu landing. There are no facilities, but there is a market nearby. ~ Go south from Lahaina on Honoapiilani Highway for about six miles.

LAUNIUPOKO WAYSIDE PARK There is a seaside lawn shaded by palm trees and a sandy beach. A rock seawall slopes gently for entering swimmers, but offers little to sunbathers. It's located near the West Maui Mountains, with great views of Kahoolawe and Lanai. When the tide is high, it's a good place to take children to swim safely and comfortably in the tidal pool on the other side of the seawall. Otherwise, swimming and snorkeling are mediocre. There is good surf-casting from the seawall and south for three miles. The park has a picnic area, restrooms and showers. ~ Located three miles south of Lahaina on Honoapiilani Highway.

PUAMANA COUNTY WAYSIDE PARK A narrow beach and grass-covered strip wedged between Honoapiilani Highway and the ocean, Puamana Park is dotted with ironwood trees. The excellent views make this a choice spot for an enjoyable picnic. Facilities include restrooms and showers. ~ Located about two miles south of Lahaina on Honoapiilani Highway.

ARMORY PARK The one thing going for this park is its convenient location in Lahaina. Otherwise, it's heavily littered, shadowed by a mall and sometimes crowded. If you do stop by, try to forget all that and concentrate on the sandy beach, lawn and truly startling view of Lanai directly across the Auau Channel. Swimming is okay, snorkeling good past the reef and, for surfing, there are breaks in the summer near the seawall in Lahaina Harbor. This surfing spot is not for beginners! Threadfin and *ulua* are common catches here. Restrooms and tennis courts are across the street at Maluulu o Lele Park near the playing field. ~ Located on Front Street next to the 505 Front Street mall.

BABY BEACH 🏊 🦀 🏄 This curving stretch of white sand is the best beach in Lahaina. It lacks privacy but certainly not beauty. From here you can look back to Lahaina town and the West Maui Mountains or out over the ocean to Kahoolawe, Lanai and Molokai. Or just close your eyes and soak up the sun. Swimming is good and well protected, if shallow. Snorkeling is only fair. In summer there are breaks nearby at Mala Wharf; left slide. Threadfin is often caught. ~ Take Front Street north from Lahaina for about a half-mile. Turn left on Puunoa Place and follow it to the beach.

WAHIKULI WAYSIDE PARK 🏊 🦀 🏄 This narrow stretch of beach and lawn, just off the road between Lahaina and Kaanapali, faces Lanai and Molokai. There are facilities aplenty, which might be why this pretty spot is so popular and crowded. Swimming is very good, but snorkeling is only fair. (There's a better spot just north of here near the Lahaina Canoe Club.) The most common catches here are *ulua* and threadfin. Facilities include picnic areas and restrooms; there are tennis courts up the street at the Civic Center. ~ Located between Lahaina and Kaanapali on Honoapiilani Highway.

HANAKAOO BEACH PARK 🏊 🦀 🤽 🏄 Conveniently located beside Kaanapali Beach Resort, this long and narrow park features a white-sand beach and grassy picnic ground, and is referred to by locals as Canoe Beach. On Saturday during summer season, this is the place to watch Hawaiian canoe racing. The road is nearby, but the views of Lanai are outstanding. Swimming is good, snorkeling fair, but surfing poor. Common catches include *ulua* and threadfin. There are picnic areas, restrooms and showers. ~ Located between Lahaina and Kaanapali on Honoapiilani Highway.

Kaanapali–Kapalua Area

Even in the case of Maui's notorious land developers, there is method to the madness. The stretch of coastline extending for six miles along Maui's western shore, crowded to the extreme with hotels and condominiums, is anchored by two planned resorts. Like handsome bookends supporting an uneven array of dog-eared paperbacks, Kaanapali and Kapalua add class to the arrangement.

SIGHTS   Supporting the south end, **Kaanapali** is a 500-acre enclave that extends along three miles of sandy beach and includes six hotels, a half-dozen condominiums, two golf courses and an attractive shopping mall. Back in the 19th century it was a dry and barren segment of the sugar plantation that operated from Lahaina. Raw sugar was hauled by train from the mill out to Black Rock, a dramatic outcropping along Kaanapali Beach, where the produce was loaded onto waiting ships.

In 1963, Kaanapali's first resort opened near Black Rock and development soon spread in both directions. Important to developers, who built the Sheraton Maui hotel around it, **Black Rock** (Puu Kekaa) is a volcanic cinder cone from which ancient Hawaiians believed that the dead departed the earth in their journey to the spirit world. According to legend, the great 18th-century Maui chief Kahekili proved his bravery by leaping from the rock to the ocean below.

Kaanapali's modern-day contribution to Pacific culture is the **Whalers Village Museum**. This facility comprises an outdoor pavilion and a museum that details Lahaina's history of whaling. Outdoors, you'll find a 30-foot-long whale skeleton and a whaling longboat on display. The "golden era of whaling" is also portrayed in scrimshaw exhibits, a scale-model whaling ship, harpoons and other artifacts from the days when Lahaina was one of the world's great whaling ports. Self-guided tours are available. There's a wonderful shop on site, with a selection of fossilized whale ivory scrimshaw in addition to Victorian-era antiques. ~ Whalers Village, 2435 Kaanapali Parkway; 808-661-5992, fax 808-661-8584.

An earlier chief, Piilani, built a road through the area in the 16th century and gave his name to modern-day Route 30, the Honoapiilani Highway. Translated as "the bays of Piilani," the road passes several inlets located north of Kaanapali that have been developed in haphazard fashion. Honokowai, Kahana and Napili form a continuous wall of condominiums that sprawls north to Kapalua Bay and offers West Maui's best lodging bargains.

Kapalua, the bookend holding the north side in place, is a former pineapple plantation that was converted into a luxurious 1500-acre resort. Here two major hotels, three golf courses and several villa-style communities blanket the hillside from the white sands of Kapalua Bay to the deep green foothills of the West Maui Mountains. Like the entire strip along Maui's western flank, Kapalua enjoys otherworldly sunsets and dramatic views of Lanai and Molokai.

LODGING

In the Kaanapali area the modestly priced hotel is not an endangered species, it's totally extinct! So prepare yourself for steep tariffs. The **Kaanapali Beach Hotel** is a 430-room hostelry that sits right on the beach and sports four restaurants and a large lobby. Guest rooms enjoy private lanais and guests lounge around a grassy courtyard and a swimming pool. ~ 2525 Kaanapali Parkway, Lahaina; 808-661-0011, 800-262-8450, fax 808-667-5978; www.kaanapalibeachhotel.com, e-mail info@kaanapalibeach hotel.com. DELUXE TO ULTRA-DELUXE.

Or check out, and check in to, the **Royal Lahaina Resort**. Spreading across 27 acres, it encompasses 542 rooms, 11 tennis courts, 3 swimming pools, 3 restaurants, a coffee shop and a white-sand beach that extends for a half-mile. Rooms in the high-rise hotel price in the ultra-deluxe category, while the prices for the nicest accommodations, the multiplex cottages that dot the landscaped grounds, head for the sky. ~ 2780 Kekaa Drive, Kaanapali Beach; 808-661-3611, 800-447-6925, fax 808-494-3960; www.2maui.com. ULTRA-DELUXE.

In the realm of luxury hotels, the **Hyatt Regency Maui** is one of the better addresses in Hawaii. Built in 1980, its atrium lobby, Asian artwork and freeform swimming pool set the standard for resorts ever since. Unlike more recent hotels, in which the size of guest rooms is sacrificed for the sake of lavish grounds, the Hyatt Regency maintains an ideal balance between public and private areas. If you're seeking beautiful surroundings, friendly service and beachfront location, this 815-room extravaganza is the ticket. ~ 200 Nohea Kai Drive, Kaanapali; 808-661-1234, 800-233-1234, fax 808-667-4499; www.maui.hyatt.com, e-mail hrmsales@maui.net. ULTRA-DELUXE.

A subtle architectural style gives the **Kapalua Bay Hotel** a low profile. But don't be misled. Part of a 23,000-acre plantation, this relatively small hotel, with 196 rooms and suites, is the hub of one of Maui's most appealing and romantic resorts. A hillside setting overlooking a white-sand crescent beach means that nearly all the rooms have spectacular ocean views. The accommodations are luxurious and tasteful and include rattan- and wicker-furnished sitting areas, baths with sunken tubs, a jacuzzi and vanity areas. Floor-to-ceiling french doors open onto spacious lanais. Rock-lined ponds, tropical gardens, three golf courses, restaurants, shops and two tennis facilities add to Kapalua's charm. ~ 1 Bay Drive, Kapalua; 808-669-5656, 800-325-3589, fax 808-669-4690; www.kapaluabayhotel.com. ULTRA-DELUXE.

CONDOS   Most condominiums in this area are on the beach or just across the road from it. They are ideally situated for swimming or sunbathing; the major drawback, ironically, is that there are so many other condos around.

Kaanapali Alii ranks as one of Maui's better buys. Here the immense 1500- to 1900-square-foot suites can easily be shared by two couples or a family. All 210 condo units have large living and dining rooms, full kitchens, sitting areas and two baths. Fully carpeted and furnished with rattan, contemporary artwork and potted palms, these units start at $265 and top out at $750. The contemporary highrise facility rests along the beach and has a pool and tennis court. ~ 50 Nohea Kai Drive, Kaanapali; 808-

667-1400, 800-642-6284, fax 808-667-1145; www.classicresorts. com/unit-kalii, e-mail info@classicresorts.com.

Aston Kaanapali Shores has hotel room–style accommodations for $165 including a refrigerator; studios from $195 double with a balcony and full kitchen; and one-bedroom units with a garden view and full kitchen for $260. ~ 3445 Lower Honoapiilani Road; 808-667-2211, 800-922-7866, fax 808-661-0836; www.astonhotels.com.

The lava rock–walled units at **Papakea Resort** provide a pleasant retreat. Ranging from $160 studios to $250 two-bedroom units, all 130 condominiums come with spacious lanais. ~ 3543 Lower Honoapiilani Road; 808-669-4848, 800-922-7866, fax 808-665-0662; www.astonhotels.com.

One-bedroom apartments at the beachfront **Maui Sands** begin at $90 single or double; two bedrooms run from $125 for one to four people. There is a seven-night minimum. ~ 3600 Lower Honoapiilani Road, Honokowai; 808-669-1902, 800-367-5037, fax 808-669-8790; www.mauigetaway.com.

One-bedroom apartments at the oceanfront **Paki Maui** start at $215, depending on the view, and sleep one to four people; two-bedroom units start at $323, accommodating up to six people. Swimming pool with jet spa. ~ 3615 Lower Honoapiilani Road, Honokowai; 808-669-8235, 800-535-0085, fax 808-669-7987; www.marcresorts.com.

Located across the street from the beach, **Castle Maui Park** has studios from $135 ($109 from April 1 to December 21). ~ 3626 Lower Honoapiilani Road, Honokowai; 808-669-6622, 800-367-5004, fax 808-669-9647.

The one-bedroom apartments at **Honokowai Palms** have a lanai; they run $75 double and sleep up to four people. Two-bedroom units without lanai are $85 for one to six people. It's located right across the street from the ocean. ~ 3666 Lower Honoapiilani Road, Honokowai; 808-667-2712, 800-808-669-6284, fax 808-661-5875; www.klahani.com, e-mail klahani@hotmail.com.

The first sugar plantation laborers on Maui began to arrive from China in 1852.

On the waterfront, **Hale Maui** has one-bedroom condos from $75 double. The drawback to this budget rate is that there is no pool—but you won't miss it with the beach in your backyard. ~ 3711 Lower Honoapiilani Road, Honokowai; 808-669-6312, 888-621-1736, fax 808-669-1302; e-mail halemaui@maui.net.

The one-bedroom apartments at the oceanfront **Kaleialoha** are $105 double; $10 each additional person. ~ 3785 Lower Honoapiilani Road, Honokowai; 808-669-8197, 800-222-8688, fax 808-669-2502; e-mail kal@maui.net.

Hale Ono Loa offers one-bedroom units from $95 for up to four people. The condos are oceanfront but there's no beach access. ~ 3823 Lower Honoapiilani Road, Honokowai; 808-667-2712, 800-669-6284, fax 808-661-5875; www.klahani.com, e-mail klahani@hotmail.com.

Polynesian Shores has one-bedroom apartments that start at $110 double; two-bedroom units, $125 double; three-bedroom apartments, $200 double. All units have ocean views. ~ 3975 Lower Honoapiilani Road, Honokowai; 808-669-6065, 800-433-6284, fax 808-669-0909; www.polynesianshores.com.

Mahina Surf features one-bedroom units that start at $125 double ($110–$145 from April 15 to December 14); two-bedroom accommodations range from $155 to $190. There are oceanfront views with a lava-rock beach. There's a three-night minimum stay. ~ 4057 Lower Honoapiilani Road, Kahana; 808-669-6068, 800-367-6086, fax 808-669-4534; www.mahinasurf.com, e-mail mahainasf@maui.net.

Kahana Reef All Oceanfront has one-bedroom apartments for $110—$140 single or double. As the name suggests, all units are oceanfront; they require a four-night minimum stay. ~ 4471

Lower Honoapiilani Road, Kahana; 808-669-6491, 800-822-4409, fax 808-669-2192; www.astonhotels.com.

One-bedroom condos at **Napili Point Resort** are $189 for up to four people (from May 1 to June 30 and September 1 to December 21). Here sliding doors lead out to ocean-view patios. Located on a lava rock coastline, the resort is a short walk from sandy Napili Bay beach. ~ 5295 Lower Honoapiilani Road, Napili; 808-669-9222, 800-808-669-6252, fax 808-669-7984; www.napili.com.

Outrigger's Napili Shores Resort is a beautifully landscaped low-rise resort with studios and one-bedrooms running from $160 to $210. The units are appointed with rattan and oak pieces and the complex is graced by gardens of plumeria and hibiscus. The pool and beach areas are idyllic. ~ 5315 Lower Honoapiilani Road, Napili; 808-669-8061, 800-688-7444, fax 808-669-5407; www.outrigger.com, e-mail napilishores@outrigger.com.

Studio apartments at **The Napili Bay** are $105 double for oceanfront views. ~ 33 Hui Road, Napili; 808-661-5200, 888-808-661-7200, fax 808-661-2649; www.mauibeachfront.com, e-mail beachfront@maui.net.

The **Napili Kai Beach Resort** has 162 units—studios, one-bedroom and two-bedroom affairs—that range in price from $185 to $635. Most come with kitchens. All are fully carpeted and have private lanais, rattan furniture, picture windows and direct access to an impressive beach. ~ 5900 Honoapiilani Road, Napili; 808-669-6271, 800-367-5030, fax 808-669-0086; www.napilikai.com, e-mail stay@napilikai.com.

DINING

Luigi's Pasta & Pizzeria is located near the entrance to Kaanapali Beach Resort. A patio restaurant overlooking a golf course, it's a pretty place to dine on pizza, pasta and other Italian favorites. The restaurant features a menu that includes veal marsala, chicken parmesan and shrimp scampi. ~ 2991 Kaanapali Parkway; 808-661-3160, fax 808-661-5254. MODERATE.

The **Kaanapali Mixed Plate Restaurant** serves an all-you-can-eat buffet at a price that is surprisingly out of place for this expensive hotel. A complete breakfast is offered; lunch and dinner include a few entrées, a salad bar, soup and dessert buffets. Meat-eaters will revel in the dinner buffets all-you-can-eat prime rib. ~ Kaanapali Beach Hotel, 2525 Kaanapali Parkway; 808-661-0011, fax 808-667-5978. BUDGET TO MODERATE.

Another way to eat at a reasonable price is by stopping at the takeout stands on the lower level of Whalers Village. There are tables inside or out in the courtyard. **Village Korean Barbeque** has Korean dishes. ~ 808-661-9798. At **Pizza Paradiso** they serve an assortment of pies (including by the slice) plus spaghetti and meatballs and salads. For breakfast you can order a "breakfast pizza," bagel or coffee. ~ 808-667-0333. **Kawara Sobe Takase Restaurant** has noodle dishes, *onigiri* (rice balls wrapped with seaweed) and tempura. ~ 2435 Kaanapali Parkway; 808-667-0815. BUDGET.

Spats Trattoria is an elegant Italian restaurant featuring regional cuisine. Candlelit tables, antique armchairs and brass chandeliers are augmented by a menu of decadent dishes such as lobster on ribbon pasta covered with an herb cream sauce. Dinner only. ~ Hyatt Regency Maui, Kaanapali Beach Resort; 808-661-1234. DELUXE TO ULTRA-DELUXE.

The sunsets are otherworldly at **Leilani's On The Beach**, a breezy veranda-style dining room. Trimmed in dark woods and lava rock, the upstairs dining room is dominated by an outrigger canoe that hangs suspended from the ceiling. On the menu you'll find Malaysian shrimp, Cajun-style fresh fish, ginger chicken and teriyaki steak. At the end of the day this is sunset territory, a place to relax and take in the scene from the umbrella shade of the downstairs **Beachside Grill**, where cocktails accompany burgers, sandwiches and salads. Frequently there is live rock-and-roll in the afternoon. Touristy but appealing. ~ Whalers Village; 808-661-4495, fax 808-667-9027. MODERATE TO DELUXE.

From the ship's rigging, captain's chairs and marlin trophies, you could never guess what they serve at **Erik's Seafood Grotto**. What a surprise to discover a menu filled with crabmeat-stuffed prawns, lobster-stuffed chicken breast, salmon and wahoo. Early-bird specials. ~ 4242 Lower Honoapiilani Road, Kahana; 808-669-4806, fax 808-669-3997. MODERATE TO DELUXE.

Dollie's Pub and Café offers fettuccine alfredo, pizza and sandwiches. This is a sports-on-the-television bar with a small kitchen and adjacent dining room. ~ 4310 Lower Honoapiilani Road, Kahana; 808-669-0266, fax 808-665-0614. BUDGET TO MODERATE.

One of Maui's leading restaurants, **Roy's Kahana Bar and Grill** eschews the waterfalls, swans, tinkling pianists and other accoutrements of the island's top dining rooms. Instead, this spacious second-story establishment looks like a gallery with its exposed-beam ceiling, track lighting and paintings. The open kitchen serves up such creations as fresh seared lemongrass *shutome* with Thai basil peanut sauce, kiawe-grilled filet mignon with garlic mashed potatoes and Chinese barbecue cabernet, grilled ginger chicken with shoyu glaze and garlic chive rice and blackened ahi with soy-mustard butter. Reservations are a must! ~ Kahana Gateway Shopping Center, 4405 Honoapiilani Highway, Kahana; 808-669-5000, fax 808-669-6909. DELUXE TO ULTRA-DELUXE.

For Mongolian beef, Peking duck or hot Szechuan bean curd, try **China Boat**. At this family-style restaurant, you can ease into a lacquered seat and take in the Japanese *ukiyoe* prints that adorn the place. Adding to the ambience are lava walls that showcase beautiful Chinese ceramic pieces. Patio dining is also available. ~ 4474 Lower Honoapiilani Road, Kahana; 808-669-5089, fax 808-669-6132. MODERATE.

In addition to its namesake, **Maui Tacos** has chimichangas, tostadas, burritos, quesadillas and enchiladas. Nothing fancy, just a few formica booths and tables with molded plastic chairs. But the salsa's fresh daily, the beans are prepared without lard and the chips are made with cholesterol-free vegetable oil. Egg burritos and huevos rancheros are served for breakfast. Frozen yogurt and fruit smoothies are also available. ~ Napili Plaza, 5095 Napilihau Street, Napili; 808-665-0222, 888-628-4822; www. mauitacos.com, e-mail eatmaui@maui.net. BUDGET.

The **Orient Express** features a variety of Thai and Chinese dishes including shrimp saté, clay-pot seafood dishes, sour shrimp soup, red-curry beef and Thai noodles stir-fried with pork, egg and crushed peanuts. Part of the Napili Shores Resort, this lava-walled restaurant has a shocking-pink-and-purple color scheme. Dinner only. ~ 5315 Lower Honoapiilani Road, Napili; 808-669-8077. MODERATE.

Maui aficionados agree that **The Plantation House Restaurant** is among the island's best. Capturing their accolades is a spacious establishment with panoramic views of the Kapalua region and a decor that mixes mahogany and wicker with orchids and a roaring fire. Not to be upstaged by the surroundings, the chef prepares fresh island fish seven different ways. The most popular is the "taste of the rich forest"—the fish is pressed with wild mushrooms and roasted, then served on spinach with garlic mashed potatoes and Maui onion meunière sauce. For lighter appetites there are salads, pastas, honey guava scallops, and for lunch a wide range of soups and sandwiches. Breakfast is also served. ~ 2000 Plantation Club Drive, Kapalua; 808-669-6299, fax 808-669-1222; www.theplantationhouse.com. DELUXE TO ULTRA-DELUXE.

THE BIG ISLAND COMES TO MAUI

Peter Merriman, the chef extraordinaire who earned his reputation with a restaurant on the Big Island, transported his brand of Hawaii regional cuisine across the Alenuihaha Channel to open **Hula Grill** on the beach in Kaanapali. Specializing in seafood, this 1930s-era beach house has wok-charred ahi, seafood dim sum dishes and an array of entrées that includes Hawaiian seafood gumbo, *opakapaka* in parchment, firecracker mahimahi and teriyaki ahi. For landlubbers there's New York steak, Thai beef curry and goat cheese pizza. ~ Whalers Village; 808-667-6636, fax 808-661-1148. DELUXE.

There's little doubt that Hawaii's finest sunsets occur off the southwest coast of Maui. One of the best spots to catch the spectacle is **The Bay Club** at the Kapalua Bay Hotel, an oceanfront dining room that looks out on Molokai and Lanai. More than just a feast for the eyes, this open-air restaurant offers a gourmet menu at lunch and dinner. You can watch the sky melt from deep blue to flaming red while dining on fresh fish, seared sea scallops, Brazilian lobster tail, rack of lamb or New York steak. A rough life indeed. Evening dress code: no shorts, jeans, open-toed shoes or T-shirts. Dinner only. ~ 1 Bay Drive, Kapalua; 808-669-5656, fax 808-669-4694. ULTRA-DELUXE.

GROCERIES Out in the Kaanapali area, the best place to shop is **Star Market**, a good-sized supermarket that's open from 5 a.m. to 2 a.m. every day. ~ 3350 Lower Honoapiilani Road, Kaanapali; 808-667-9590.

Toward Kapalua, try the **Napili Market**, a well-stocked supermarket that's open from 6:30 a.m. to 11 p.m. every day. ~ Napili Plaza, 5095 Napilihau Street, Napili; 808-669-1600.

SHOPPING Worthy of mention is **Whalers Village** in the Kaanapali Beach Resort. This sprawling complex combines a shopping mall with a museum. Numbered among the stores you'll find gift emporia featuring coral and shells, a shirt store with wild island designs, other stores offering fine men's and women's fashions.

Several shops in this split-level complex should not be missed. **Lahaina Printsellers Ltd.** (808-667-7617) purveys "fine antique maps and prints." At **Blue Ginger Designs** (808-667-5793) original styles in women's and children's clothing are featured. For women's and children's swimwear and sportswear, head to **Maui Waterwear** (808-661-3916). Another store worth visiting here is **Endangered Species** (808-661-1139), a preservationist shop selling photos, sculptures and paintings of sharks, whales and rainforests. Through the sales of these products it also helps support many environmental causes. The **Ka Honu Gift Gallery** (808-661-0173) showcases locally produced goods including ornaments, dolls, lotions, soaps and jewelry. Handcrafted Hawaiian coral jewelry is the specialty of **Maui Divers of Hawaii** (808-661-1097). The **Dolphin Gallery** (808-661-5115) is a place to look for sculpture, art and jewelry. ~ 2435 Kaanapali Parkway.

Perhaps the best place in Whalers Village to discover the whaling tradition is **Lahaina Scrimshaw**. During their long journeys, sailors once whiled away the hours by etching and engraving on ivory, creating beautiful articles of scrimshaw. The sale of ivory from animals taken by hunters is banned, but the fossilized remains of ancient mammoths and walruses have kept this art alive. Using ivory that is thousands of years old, artists create a wide array of functional and decorative pieces, many of which are traded by aficionados of this art form. ~ 808-661-4034.

With the continuing influx of wealthy tourists, the upper tier of Whalers Village has gone stratospheric with several high-fashion boutiques. Among the shops representing this shift to the chic is **Chanel Boutique**, which displays fine jewelry, cosmetics and designer threads. Chanel also has a line of handbags and other fashion accoutrements guaranteed to put a hole in your wallet. ~ 2435 Kaanapali Parkway; 808-661-1555.

And then, to make shopping the grand adventure it should be, there are the displays. Within this mazework mall you'll discover blunderbusses, intricate scrimshaw pieces, the skeletal remains of leviathans and whaling boats with iron harpoons splayed from the bow. Practically everything, in fact, that a whaler (or a cruising shopper) could desire.

For serious shoppers, ready to spend money or be damned, there is nothing to compare with the neighboring hotels. Set like gems within this tourist cluster are several world-class hotels, each hosting numerous elegant shops.

Foremost is the **Hyatt Regency Maui**, along whose wood-paneled lobby are stores that might well be deemed mini-museums. One, called **Elephant Walk**, displays *koa* wood products, baskets and Niihau shell ornaments. There are art galleries, a fabric shop, clothing stores, jewelry stores and more—set in an open-air lobby that is filled with rare statuary and exotic birds. ~ 210 Nohea Kai Drive, Kaanapali; 808-667-2848.

Another favorite Hyatt Regency shop is **Hawaii Quilt Company**, where you'll find wallhangings, Thai silk pillows and needlepoint supplies as well as an array of quilts. Many of the quilts are designed by local artists. ~ 210 Nohea Kai Drive, Kaanapali; 808-661-1234.

The **Kapalua Bay Hotel** sports another upscale shopping annex. Among the temptations is **Mandalay** (808-669-6170), specializing in silks and cottons from Asia. There are blouses and jackets for women as well as a small collection of artfully crafted jew-

NEED A BREAK FROM THE KIDDIES?

Tired of building sandcastles? If you're staying in a condo or hotel without children's programs (and you're tearing your hair out) you can check your kids into day camps at the Ritz Carlton Kapalua's **Ritz Kids** (808-669-6200) or the **Keiki Kamp** (808-667-2525) at the Westin Maui Resort in Kaanapali, even if you're not a guest.

elry. Also stop by **South Seas of Kapalua** (808-669-1249), which carries native masks from New Guinea and other artwork from Oceania. If you're traveling with young ones or looking for a souvenir for those you left behind, stop by **Kapalua Kids** (808-669-0033). Here you can buy children's books on Hawaii as well as soft toys and an array of clothing. ~ 1 Bay Drive.

At the **Plantation Course Golf Shop** you'll find an impressive collection of jackets, shirts, sweaters, sweatshirts and shorts, many with a tropical flair. This is also a good place to look for the work of signature designers. ~ 2000 Plantation Club Drive, Kapalua; 808-669-8877.

NIGHTLIFE   Possibly the prettiest place in these parts to enjoy a drink 'neath the tropic moon is the bar at **Hula Grill**. Located in the Whalers Village mall, this beach house–style gathering place is decorated with original Hawaiian outrigger canoes. It features live Hawaiian music and hula nightly until nine o'clock. The place is located right on the water, so you can listen to a slow set, then stroll the beach. ~ 2435 Kaanapali Parkway; 808-667-6636; www.hulapie.com.

Hawaiian musicians perform nightly at the Hyatt Regency Maui in the elegant waterfront **Swan Court**. For contemporary music, head over to the **Weeping Banyan**, an open-air lounge. **Spats Trattoria** (cover) also offers entertainment nightly. ~ 200 Nohea Kai Drive; 808-661-1234, 800-233-1234, fax 808-667-4498.

There's music and Hawaiian entertainment at the Westin Maui in the **'Ono Surf Bar & Grill** and **Koala Seafood and Barbeque Buffet**. ~ 2365 Kaanapali Parkway; 808-667-2525.

At the Maui Marriott, the **Makai Bar** cooks every night with a solo or duo performing Hawaiian and pop numbers. ~ 100 Nohea Kai Drive; 808-667-1200.

PUEONE O HONOKAHUA

The Kapalua area includes one of Maui's most important cultural zones, Pueone o Honokahua. This 14-acre preserve, near the Ritz-Carlton Kapalua, was the site of fishing shrines and *heiaus* where the ancient Hawaiians worshipped their gods and made astronomical observations. Today you can see a burial ground dating back to 950 A.D. and portions of the King's Highway, a 16th-century stone road around Maui. Also extant are the outlines of terraced taro patches farmed by early inhabitants. Although this land has been claimed in turn by King Kamehameha III, the sugar king H. P. Baldwin, and lastly the Maui Land and Pineapple Company, the state now protects and preserves it as a native Hawaiian sanctuary. The Ritz-Carlton conducts a free tour called "A Sense of Place" at the preserve every Friday from 10 a.m. to 12 p.m. (808-669-6200).

The Sheraton Maui is a prime nightspot both early and later in the evening. Just before sunset you can watch the torchlighting and cliff-diving ceremony from the **Lagoon Bar**. ~ 2605 Kaanapali Parkway, Kaanapali; 808-661-0031.

There's occasional Hawaiian-style entertainment at the **Royal Ocean Terrace Lounge**, a beachfront watering hole on the grounds of the Royal Lahaina Resort. Arrive early and you can watch the sunset between Lanai and Molokai, followed by the ubiquitous torch-lighting ceremony. ~ 2780 Kekaa Drive; 808-661-3611.

For soft entertainment in a relaxed setting, try the **Bay Club** at the Kapalua Bay Hotel. This open-air lounge with nightly pianist is set in a lovely restaurant overlooking the water. The melodies are as serene and relaxing as the views of neighboring Molokai. ~ 1 Bay Drive; 808-669-8008.

At **The Lehua**, in the lobby of the Kapalua Bay Hotel, you can enjoy piano music nightly over cocktails and great views of the Pacific. ~ 1 Bay Drive; 808-669-5656.

A Hawaiian duo plays in the evenings at **The Lobby Lounge and Library** at the Ritz-Carlton Kapalua. At the **Anuenue Lounge** you can enjoy a pianist. ~ 1 Ritz-Carlton Drive, Kapalua; 808-669-6200.

BEACHES & PARKS

KAANAPALI RESORT BEACHES 🦀 🐟 The sprawling complex of Kaanapali hotels sits astride a beautiful white-sand beach that extends for three miles. Looking out on Lanai and Molokai, this is a classic palm-fringed strand. The entire area is heavily developed and crowded with tourists glistening in coconut oil. But it is an extraordinarily fine beach where the swimming is very good and the skindiving excellent around Black Rock at the Sheraton Maui. The beach has no facilities, but most of the resorts have public restrooms and there are restaurants nearby. ~ Take the public right-of-way to the beach from any of the Kaanapali resort hotels.

HONOKOWAI BEACH PARK 🦀 🐟 Compared to the beaches fronting Kaanapali's nearby resorts, this is a bit disappointing. The large lawn is pleasant enough, but the beach itself is small, with a reef that projects right to the shoreline. On the other hand, the view of Molokai is awesome. In the shallow reef waters the swimming and snorkeling are fair; surfing is nonexistent. *Ulua* and threadfin are among the most frequent catches. Picnic tables, restrooms and showers are available. ~ Located north of Kaanapali in Honokowai on Lower Honoapiilani Road (which is the oceanfront section of Route 30).

NAPILI BAY 🦀 🐟 You'll find wall-to-wall condominiums along the small cove. There's a crowded but beautiful white-sand beach studded with palm trees and looking out on Molokai.

Swimming and snorkeling are delightful and the surfing here is particularly good for beginners. ~ Located several miles north of Kaanapali, with rights-of-way to the beach from Lower Honoapiilani Road via Napili Place or Hui Drive.

KAPALUA BEACH 🏊 🤿 This is the next cove over from Napili Bay. It's equally beautiful, but not as heavily developed. The crescent of white sand that lines Kapalua Bay is bounded on either end by rocky points and backdropped by a line of coconut trees and the Kapalua Bay Hotel. Swimming and snorkeling are excellent. ~ There's a right-of-way to the beach from Lower Honoapiilani Road near the Napili Kai Beach Club.

D. T. FLEMING PARK 🏊 🤿 🛶 One of Maui's nicest beach parks, D. T. Fleming has a spacious white-sand beach and a rolling lawn shaded with palm and ironwood trees. There's a nice view of Molokai's rugged East End. Unfortunately, a major resort resides just uphill from the beach. Sometimes windy, the park is plagued by rough and dangerous surf during the winter. Use caution! You'll find good swimming and bodysurfing and fair snorkeling during the summer. There are also good breaks nearby at Little Makaha, named after the famous Oahu beach. For anglers the prime catches are *ulua* and *papio*. There are restrooms, a picnic area and showers. ~ Located about seven miles north of Kaanapali just off Honoapiilani Highway.

Northwest Maui

To escape from the crowds and commotion of the Kaanapali–Kapalua area and travel north on the Honoapiilani Highway is to journey from the ridiculous to the sublime. As you curve along the edge of the West Maui Mountains, en route around the side of the island to Kahului and Wailuku, you'll pass several hidden beaches that lie along an exotic and undeveloped shore. This is a region of the Valley Isle rarely ever seen by visitors.

SIGHTS

Near the rocky beach and lush valley at **Honokohau Bay**, the Honoapiilani Highway (Route 30) becomes the Kahekili Highway (Route 340). This macadam track snakes high above the ocean, hugging the coastline. From the highway rises a series of multihued **sandstone cliffs** that seems alien to this volcanic region and creates a picturesque backdrop to the rocky shore.

As the road continues, the scenery is some of the most magnificent on Maui. Down a dirt side road sits the rustic village of

HIDDEN ►

Kahakuloa. Nestled in an overgrown valley beside a deep blue bay, the community is protected by a solitary headland rising directly from the sea. Woodframe houses and churches, which appear ready to fall to the next gusting wind, are spotted throughout this enchanting area. Kahakuloa is cattle country, and you'll find that the villagers live and farm much as their forefathers did back when most of Maui was unclaimed terrain.

The road ascends again outside Kahakuloa. Opening below you, one valley after another falls seaward in a series of spine-backed ridges. Above the road, the mountain range rises toward its 5788-foot summit at Puu Kukui.

Six miles beyond Kahakuloa, you'll stumble upon **Aina Anuhea**   ◄HIDDEN **Tropical Gardens,** which in this heavenly environment represents a further ascent into the ethereal. Its six acres of curving paths lead along a mountain stream, through a Japanese garden, past a waterfall and up to a solitary gazebo perched high above the world. Along the way you can take in the ginger and heliconia, the maile and lokelani. A new volcano area is embraced by indigenous Hawaiian flora. Admission. ~ Kahekili Highway, between Kahakuloa and Waihee; 808-242-4592; e-mail ainanuhea @aol.com.

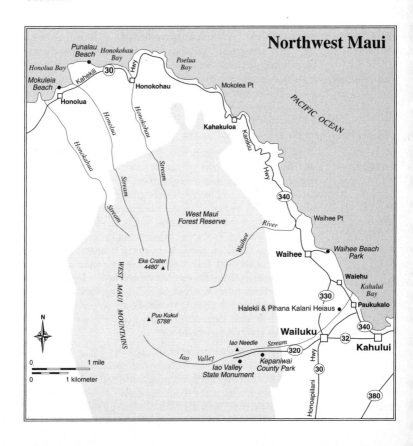

There are lush gulches farther along as the road descends into the plantation town of **Waihee**. Here rolling countryside, dotted with small farm houses, slopes from the roadside up to the foothills of the West Maui Mountains.

It was from the shoreline near Kahakuloa that the Polynesian canoe Hokulea *left on its famous voyage.*

You're still on the Kahekili Highway, but now once again it really is a highway, a well-traveled road that leads toward Kahului. Located just northwest of town, a side road leads to two sacred spots. The first, **Halekii Heiau**, overlooking Kahului Bay and Iao Stream, dates from the 1700s. Today this temple, once as large as a football field, is little more than a stone heap. **Pihana Kalani Heiau**, a short distance away, was once a sacrificial temple.

Before driving this route, as well as the back road from Hana to Ulupalakua, remember that the car rental agencies will not insure you over these winding tracks. Many cover the roads anyway, and I highly recommend that you explore them both if weather permits.

BEACHES & PARKS

MOKULEIA BEACH OR SLAUGHTERHOUSE BEACH 🏊 🐟
🏄 This lovely patch of white sand is bounded by cliffs and looks out on Molokai. Set at the end of a shallow cove, the beach
HIDDEN ► is partially protected. Swimming, snorkeling and surfing are all good. This is part of a marine sanctuary so fishing is not permitted. There are no facilities here. ~ Take Honoapiilani Highway for exactly eight-tenths of a mile past D. T. Fleming Park. Park on the highway and take the steep path down about 100 yards to the beach.

HIDDEN ► **HONOLUA BAY** 🏊 🐟 🏄 ⛵ A rocky beach makes this cliff-rimmed bay unappealing for sunbathers, but there are rich coral deposits offshore and beautiful trees growing near the water. In winter you're likely to find crowds along the top of the cliff watching surfers work some of the finest breaks in all Hawaii: perfect tubes up to 15 feet. Swimming is good, but the bottom is rocky. Snorkeling is excellent, particularly on the west side of the bay. No fishing is allowed; this is part of a marine sanctuary. There are no facilities (and usually very few people) here. ~ Located about one-and-a-third miles north of D. T. Fleming Park on Honoapiilani Highway. The dirt road to the beach is open only to cars with boats in tow. Park with the other cars along the highway and follow the paths to the beach.

HIDDEN ► **PUNALAU OR WINDMILL BEACH** 🏊 🐟 🏄 ⛵ A very secluded white-sand beach studded with rocks, Punalau is surrounded by cliffs and intriguing rock formations. The swimming is okay and when the water is calm snorkeling is excellent. A fascinating reef extends along the coast all through this area. Surfing is fine, peaking in winter; there are left and right slides. Leatherback, *papio*, milkfish, *moano* and big-eyed scad are the primary catches for anglers. No facilities. Day-use fee, $5. ~ Located three-and-a-half miles north of D. T. Fleming Park on Honoapiilani Highway. Turn left onto the dirt road and follow it a short distance to the beach.

▲ A permit is required from Maui Pineapple Co., Honolua Division, 4900 Honoapiilani Highway, Lahaina (808-669-6201, fax 808-669-7089; www.pineapplehawaii.com) and must be obtained in person. There is a three-day maximum stay.

HONOKOHAU BAY This rocky beach is surrounded by cliffs. To the interior, a lush valley rises steadily into the folds of the West Maui Mountains. When the water is calm, swimming and snorkeling are good. The surf offers rugged, two- to twelve-foot breaks. Keep in mind the changeable nature of this wave action, since it can vary quickly from the gentle to the dangerous. Milkfish, *papio*, leatherback, *moano* and big-eyed scad are the principal species caught in these waters. ~ Located about six miles north of D. T. Fleming Park on Honoapiilani Highway.

▲ Camping is allowed here, but the place is very rocky, and there are no facilities.

Kihei–Wailea–Makena Area

Stretching from Maalaea Bay to Makena is a near continuous succession of beautiful beaches that make Kihei and Wailea favored resort destinations. Second only to the Lahaina–Kaanapali area in popularity, this seaside enclave rests in the rainshadow of Haleakala, which looms in the background. Maui's southeastern shore receives only ten inches of rain a year, making it the driest, sunniest spot on the island. It also experiences heavy winds, particularly in the afternoon, which sweep across the island's isthmus.

Since the 1970s, this long, lean stretch of coast has become a developer's playground. Kihei in particular, lacking a master plan, has grown by accretion from a small local community into a haphazard collection of condominiums and mini-malls. It's an unattractive, six-mile strip lined by a golden beach.

Situated strategically along this beachfront are cement **pillboxes**, reminders of World War II's threatened Japanese invasion. Placed along Kihei Road just north of town, they are not far from **Kealia Pond Bird Sanctuary**, a 300-acre reserve frequented by migratory waterfowl as well as Hawaiian stilts and Hawaiian coots. You can take a nature walk here on an elevated boardwalk.

SIGHTS

◄ *HIDDEN*

To the south lies **Wailea**, an urbane answer to the random growth patterns of its scruffy neighbor. Wailea is a planned resort, all 1450 manicured acres of it. Here scrubland has been transformed into a flowering oasis that is home to five top-class hotels and six condos, as well as the required retinue of golf courses, tennis courts and overpriced shops. Like Kihei, it is blessed with beautiful beaches.

Home to some of Maui's most luxurious resorts, Wailea is the place to find Picasso originals, 50,000-square-foot spas and villas designed to keep a smile on the face of a high roller. Plantation- and Mediterranean-style architecture, accented by polished lime- stone tile and granite boulders imported from Mount Fuji, make this swank resort area an international retreat.

Connected by a mile-and-a-half-long ocean walk, and lining five crescent beaches, the resort's luxury properties comprise a self- contained retreat. Covering an area three times the size of Wai- kiki, Wailea has matured from a series of five crescent beaches separated by lava rock promontories into an elegant mix of hotels, condominiums, golf courses (there are three 18-hole champi- onship links and two clubhouses), tennis court and water sports facilities. The Shops of Wailea, set to open in 2001, is the latest addition to the resort's upscale infrastructure.

Adjacent to Wailea, the **Makena** area is a quiet, low-density destination resort with a single hotel (the Maui Prince) and several small condominiums sharing a full range of resort facilities, in- cluding two 18-hole golf courses. The setting, dominated by the upcountry slopes of Haleakala and the dry mix of *kiawe* and cactus that provide ground cover, is highlighted by the wide and luxuri- ous sands of **Makena Beach**, which I highly recommend visiting. Makena remains one of Maui's finest strands. A hippie hangout in the 1960s and early 1970s, it still retains a freewheeling at- mosphere, especially at nearby "**Little Makena**," Maui's most fa- mous nude beach. ~ Located along Makena Alanui about four miles beyond Wailea

HIDDEN ▶   Past here the road gets rough as it presses south to **Ahihi– Kinau Natural Area Reserve**. Encompassing over 2000 acres of land and ocean bottom, this preserve harbors an amazing array of marine life and contains the remains of an early Hawaiian fishing village. Almost 100 larval fish species and about two dozen species of stony coral have been found in this ecologically rich reserve. You can hike on a restored portion of the stone-lined Royal Road that in pre-contact times circled the island. The landscape of lava-scarred lowlands is dominated by the green upcountry pastures of Haleakala's mid-level slopes. This was the route of the annual Makahiki procession, when chiefs and their tax col- lectors made the rounds of the royal dominions, collecting praise and tribute.

The road continues on, bisecting the **1790 lava flow**, which resulted from Haleakala's last eruption. The flow created Cape

Kinau, a thumb-shaped peninsula dividing Ahihi Bay and **La Perouse Bay**. When I drove this route in a compact rental car, I reached La Perouse Bay before being forced by poor road conditions to turn back. The bay is named for the ill-starred French navigator, Jean-François de la Pérouse, who anchored here in 1786, the first Westerner to visit Maui. After a brief sojourn in this enchanting spot, he sailed off and was later lost at sea.

◄ HIDDEN

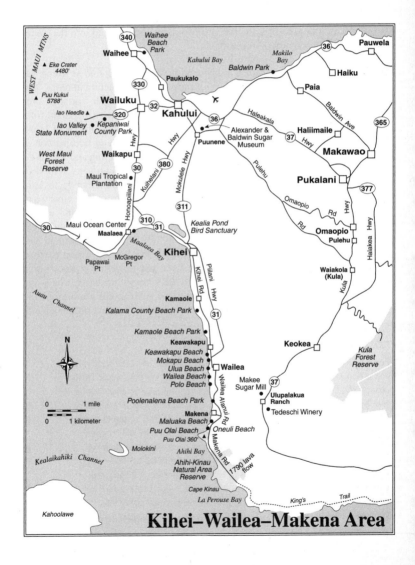

Kihei–Wailea–Makena Area

Anywhere along this coastline you can gaze out at **Molokini**, a crescent-shaped islet that is a favorite spot among snorkelers. Resting in the Alalakeihi Channel three miles west of Maui, it measures a scant 19 acres in area and rises 165 feet above sea level. The island is actually a tuff cone created by volcanic eruptions deep underwater that solidified into a hard substance called tuff. Black coral divers harvested the surrounding waters until the 1970s. According to Hawaiian legend, Molokini was created when the volcano goddess Pele cut a rival lover—a lizard—in two, turning the tail into Molokini and the head into the cinder cone near Makena Beach.

LODGING   Hotels are rare in Kihei. And in Wailea, a hotel in anything less than an ultra-deluxe price range is a contradiction in terms. The **Nona Lani Cottages**, with eight quaint wooden cottages, provides a little relief. They're situated across busy Kihei Road from a white-sand beach. Each is a one-bedroom unit with lanai, all-electric kitchen and a living room capable of housing one or two extra sleepers. There's wall-to-wall carpeting and a shower-tub combination, plus television and air conditioners in all bedrooms, but no phone. There is a four-night minimum from April 16 to December 15; seven-night minimum from December 16 to April 15. Rooms without kitchens also available for $63, all seasons, two-night minimum. ~ 455 South Kihei Road, Kihei; 808-879-2497, 800-733-2688, fax 808-891-0273. MODERATE.

Spread across 28 acres, the **Aston Maui Lu Resort** is tropically landscaped with palm trees and flowering plants. Within the grounds, which are across the street from a beach, you'll find a pool and two tennis courts. The guest rooms are furnished in standard fashion and located in a series of interconnecting build-

POLLYMAKENA

For a special retreat, check in to **PollyMakena**, a pair of oceanfront villas just a hop, skip and a jump from Makena Beach. Ideal for families or small groups, the larger villa has three bedrooms and a loft; the smaller unit has two bedrooms and sleeps up to five people. Beautifully appointed, they're filled with a fascinating assortment of treasures collected by the charming owner, Parks Hay. A hot tub and hammock surrounded by tiki torches adorn the front yard and create a small island of relaxation; a teeming tidepool fronts one of the complexes. PollyMakena is set on "Wedding Cove," so you're bound to witness at least one ceremony during your stay, adding to the romance of this special place. ~ For reservations contact Tropical Villa Vacations, 2050 Kanoe Street, Suite 208, Kihei, Maui; 888-875-2818, fax 877-875-8828. DELUXE TO ULTRA-DELUXE.

ings with some accommodations on the beach. ~ 575 South Kihei Road, Kihei; 808-879-5881, 800-922-7866, fax 808-879-4627; www.astonhotels.com. MODERATE TO DELUXE.

The **Maui Coast Hotel** is a 265-room facility across the street from the beach. It's light, airy, modern and has a pool, outdoor jacuzzis, tennis courts and a cluster of nearby restaurants. There's poolside Hawaiian entertainment nightly. ~ 2259 South Kihei Road, Kihei; 808-874-6284, 800-426-0670, fax 808-875-4731; www.westcoasthotels.com, e-mail mch@maui.net. DELUXE TO ULTRA-DELUXE.

Down the road at the **Maui Oceanfront Inn** you'll find a series of six buildings designed in mock-Hawaiian style and sandwiched between the highway and a white-sand beach. The rooms are tiny but attractively decorated with carpeting, air conditioning, television and refrigerator. ~ 2980 South Kihei Road, Kihei; 808-879-7744, 800-537-8483, fax 808-874-0145; www.mauiocean frontinn.com. DELUXE TO ULTRA-DELUXE.

The lushly landscaped **Four Seasons Resort Maui at Wailea** is the ultimate among ultimate destinations. The only Maui resort we know to feature a trompe l'oeil artwork in the lobby, it's a windswept, Hawaiian palace–style complex set on a luxurious beach. Furnished with wicker and rattan, most of the 380 plantation-style guest rooms offer ocean views. Casablanca fans, tropical plants and marbletop vanities add to the comfort. Louvered doors open onto spacious lanais. Reflecting pools, waterfalls and fountains give the public areas an elegant tropical air. ~ 3900 Wailea Alanui, Wailea; 808-874-8000, 800-334-6284, fax 808-874-2244; www.fourseasons.com. ULTRA-DELUXE.

Its remote location makes the **Westin Maui Prince Hotel** an unusual find. Built around a courtyard adorned with lush tropical gardens and lily ponds, the 310-room establishment rewards those willing to drive a few extra minutes to Maui's southernmost retreat. Here you're likely to be lulled to sleep by the sound of the surf. Decorated with heliconia and bougainvillea, the rooms and suites open onto lanais. This V-shaped hotel is next door to two of Maui's top golf courses. ~ 5400 Makena Alanui, Makena; 808-874-1111, 800-321-6284, fax 808-879-8763; www.prince hawaii.com. ULTRA-DELUXE.

CONDOS

Leilani Kai is a cozy eight-unit apartment hotel located right on the beach. Studio apartments are $60 double; one-bedroom units are $70 or $80 double; two bedrooms will run you $90 for one to four people. ~ 1226 Uluniu Street, Kihei; 808-879-2606, fax 808-879-0241.

Oceanside one-bedroom apartments at **Kihei Kai** are $90 to $110 double ($80 to $100 from mid-April to mid-December).

Each has television, phone, full kitchen and lanai. ~ 61 North Kihei Road, Kihei; 808-879-2357, 800-735-2357; e-mail kihei kai@maui.net.

Sunseeker Resort is a small, personalized place where studios with kitchenettes go for $60 double and one-bedrooms for $70 double. Add $6 for each additional person. Two-bedrooms with full kitchens go for $125. ~ 551 South Kihei Road, Kihei; 808-879-1261, 800-532-6284; e-mail sunseeker@maui.net.

A highrise condo, **Mana Kai Maui Resort** has "hotel units" that consist of the extra bedroom and bath from a two-bedroom apartment, renting from $235 to $290, depending on the month. One-bedroom units with kitchens are $200-$235, once again depending on the month. The condo has a beachfront location, as well as an adjoining restaurant and bar. ~ 2960 South Kihei Road, Kihei; 808-879-1561, 800-367-5242, fax 808-879-7825; www.crhmaui.com.

Lihi Kai has nine beach cottages with full kitchens, all renting for $69 single or double. Rates are lower for a seven-night stay. To be sure of getting a cottage, it's best to make reservations far in advance. There is a three-night minimum. ~ 2121 Iliili Road, Kihei; 808-879-2335, 800-544-4524.

Across the street from a beach park, **Kamaole Beach Royale** is a seven-story condo with one-bedroom apartments for $105 double; two-bedroom units, $85 to $90 double. From December to April, the rates increase to $120 and $125, respectively. No credit cards. ~ 2385 South Kihei Road, Kihei; 808-879-3131, 800-421-3661, fax 808-879-9163.

Kapulanikai can be described as a cozy place with only 12 apartments, all of which overlook the ocean and a grassy, park-like setting. One-bedroom apartments are $80 single or double ($65 from April to mid-December). ~ 73 Kapu Place, Kihei; phone/fax 808-879-1607; www.bellomaui.com/html/kapulani_kai.html.

For gay-friendly accommodations, you can either stay at **Jack & Tom's Condos or Cottage** or they can direct you to any of the other facilities they manage. Most condos have air conditioning; all have cable TV, ceiling fans and kitchen and laundry facilities. Prices range roughly from $50 to $175. ~ Maui Suncoast Realty, 3134 Hoomua, Kihei, HI 96753; 808-874-1048, 800-800-8608, fax 808-879-6932; www.mauisuncoast.com, e-mail mauijack@aol.com.

DINING   Ever since condominiums mushroomed from its white sands, Kihei has no longer qualified as a poor person's paradise. Yet there are still several short-order griddles like **Suda's Store and Snack Shop**, whose griddle is only open from 6 a.m. to 12:30 p.m. The "famous" chow-fun is $2.75 a bowl. Closed Sunday. ~ 61 South Kihei Road, Kihei; 808-879-2668. BUDGET.

Azeka's Market Snack Shop runs a take-out window. For atmosphere there's a parking lot, but for food there's a fair choice, with hamburgers and plate lunches priced low. Breakfast and lunch only. ~ One Azeka Place, 1280 South Kihei Road, Kihei; 808-879-0611. BUDGET.

Surfside Spirits and Deli has a takeout delicatessen serving sandwiches, salads and slaw. Breakfast too! ~ 1993 South Kihei Road, Kihei; 808-879-1385. BUDGET.

At **Canton Chef** the cuisine ranges from roast duck to beef with oyster sauce. This traditional Chinese restaurant offers almost 100 different choices including a selection of spicy Szechuan dishes. ~ Kamaole Shopping Center, 2463 South Kihei Road, Kihei; 808-879-1988. BUDGET TO MODERATE.

Margarita's Beach Cantina is one of those big brassy Mexican restaurants that are ever more present along the beaches— the kind that have live sports on big-screen television and a buzzing night scene. What sells this place is the oceanside dining and happy-hour margarita specials. The menu covers lunch and dinner, featuring carnitas, tacos and chimichangas, as well as hamburgers, chicken sandwiches and a Tuesday- and Saturday-night lobster special. ~ 101 North Kihei Road, Kihei; 808-879-5311. MODERATE.

For inexpensive Korean and local food, there's **The Kal Bi House**. Squeezed into a corner of Kihei Center (next to Longs Drugs) and furnished with plastic seats, it's not much on atmosphere. But it's hard to beat their cheap barbecued ribs, grilled chicken and beef marinated in Korean sauce, *katsu* chicken or Korean soups. A good place for a takeout meal. ~ 1215 South Kihei Road, Kihei; 808-874-8454. BUDGET.

◆◆◆

A TASTE OF THE PACIFIC

The tab at **A Pacific Café Maui** will fluctuate dramatically depending on whether you order an inexpensive pizza or one of the dishes specially prepared on the wood-burning grill. A sister to the famous gourmet restaurant on Kauai, the Maui sibling is beautifully designed with a bolted-beam ceiling, bright pastel walls and a heart-shaped bar. From that smoky grill they serve up ahi steak, Chilean sea bass and Mongolian rack of lamb. Or how about roast duck with garlic mashed potatoes or scallops in polenta crust? Highly recommended. Dinner only. ~ Azeka Place II, 1279 South Kihei Road, Kihei; 808-879-0069, fax 808-879-0325. DELUXE TO ULTRA-DELUXE.

Parked in the same complex is **Stella Blues Café & Delicatessen**, where you can dine indoors or outside beneath a sidewalk umbrella. The bill of fare includes vegetarian dishes, pastas and sandwiches. Breakfast, lunch and dinner. ~ 1215 South Kihei Road, Kihei; 808-874-3779. MODERATE.

Hapa's Restaurant features four house-brewed lagers, Italian food, a sushi bar, and nightly entertainment. ~ Lipoa Center, 41 East Lipoa Street, Kihei; 808-879-9001. MODERATE.

If you'd like something from Southeast Asia, **Royal Thai Cuisine** sits across the street in the original Azeka Place. Here the chairs are wood and the menu includes *dozens* of selections such as crab legs, chili shrimp, cashew chicken or seafood combinations. No lunch on weekends. ~ Azeka Place Shopping Center, 1280 South Kihei Road, Kihei; 808-874-0813. BUDGET TO MODERATE.

Did you say Greek? No problem. Located nearby is the **Greek Bistro** with a full selection of Mediterranean dishes such as moussaka, souvlaki, lamb kebabs and dolmas. Dinner only. ~ Kai Nani Village, 2511 South Kihei Road, Kihei; 808-879-9330. MODERATE.

Back in the days of California's gold rush, Maui found its own underground nuggets in potatoes: Countless bushels were grown in this area and shipped to a hungry San Francisco market. Today the crop is used to prepare Maui potato chips.

Or forget the ethnic food and head next door to the **Kihei Prime Rib and Seafood House**. A reliable if undistinguished dining room, it offers a good salad bar, early-bird specials and numerous beef and fresh fish dishes. There are views across the road overlooking the ocean. Dinner only. ~ Kai Nani Village, 2511 South Kihei Road, Kihei; 808-879-1954. DELUXE TO ULTRA-DELUXE.

Why do celebrities such as Richard Dreyfuss, Cuba Gooding, Jr., Halle Berry and Debra Winger book reservations at **Carelli's On The Beach**? Perhaps it's the imaginative Italian menu at this Keawakapu Beach establishment. Specialties include steamed clams in garlic, interesting pastas and fire-roasted rack of lamb. The open-air dining room, with its murals of Venice and Naples, adds to the allure. Dinner only. ~ 2980 South Kihei Road, Kihei; 808-875-0001, fax 808-874-7571. DELUXE.

Bentwood chairs, brass fixtures and plastic tablecloths create a comfortable although uncreative atmosphere at **Sandcastle Restaurant and Lounge**. The menu consists of middle-of-the-road American entrées with pizzas, pastas and fresh fish to round things off. ~ Kamaole Shopping Center, Kihei; 808-879-0606; www.sandcastlemaui.com, e-mail trg@maui.net. MODERATE.

From the day his ship docked in 1924 until his death four decades later, the writer Don Blanding lured visitors to the islands with more than a dozen books. An exhibition of this haole poet laureate's work is found at the Outrigger Wailea Resort restaurant named for one of his best-known volumes, **Hula Moons**.

The establishment is like a small museum appointed with art pieces, ceramic plates and aloha shirts that Blanding designed, as well as his books, poems and sheet music. The menu includes Australian lamb chops, macadamia nut–crusted mahimahi and vegetarian entrées. Berry cheesecake tart highlights the dessert list. ~ 3700 Wailea Alanui, Wailea; 808-879-1922, fax 808-891-0324. DELUXE TO ULTRA-DELUXE.

At **Hana Gion** you can choose between tableside *teppanyaki* cooking or a private booth. Built in Japan, broken down and shipped to Maui for reassembly, this beautiful restaurant in the Renaissance Wailea Beach Resort was created with the guidance of one of Kyoto's leading restaurant-owning families. Specialties such as tempura, *shabu-shabu* and sukiyaki are served by kimono-clad waitresses. There's also a popular sushi bar on the premises. It's a good idea to call before going. Dinner only. Closed Thursday. ~ 3550 Wailea Alanui, Wailea; 808-879-4900, fax 808-874-5370. ULTRA-DELUXE.

Seasons, the signature restaurant at the Four Seasons Resort Wailea, gained a vaunted reputation soon after it opened in 1990. Marble trim and knockout ocean views create the suitable ambience. But the cuisine is what the dining room is particularly known for. Specializing in fresh fish and locally grown produce prepared in a contemporary American style, it's one of Maui's top restaurants. Dinner only. Closed Sunday and Monday. ~ 3900 Wailea Alanui, Wailea; 808-874-8000, fax 808-874-5370. ULTRA-DELUXE.

Consider the *kiawe*-grilled hamburgers, the giant onion rings, the pupus or the salads at the Kea Lani Hotel's **Polo Beach Grille and Bar**. This poolside dining spot is also a great place for a cool drink. Open 11 a.m. to 6 p.m. daily. ~ 4100 Wailea Alanui, Wailea; 808-875-4100, fax 808-875-1200. MODERATE TO DELUXE.

Hakone is the kind of restaurant you'd expect to find at any self-respecting Japanese-owned resort. The shoji screens, Japanese fans and a sushi bar are authentic; the ocean views are entirely Hawaiian. Start with tempura or miso soup. Entrées include sashimi, *sukiyaki* and New York steak. Better yet, go on Monday night when they have the Japanese buffet and try a little bit of everything. Outstanding. Reservations are required. Dinner only. Closed Sunday. ~ Maui Prince Hotel, 5400 Makena Alanui, Makena; 808-874-1111, fax 808-879-8763. DELUXE TO ULTRA-DELUXE.

Foodland is a large supermarket open 24 hours a day. ~ Kihei Town Center, South Kihei Road; 808-879-9350.   **GROCERIES**

Star Market, open all day except between 2 a.m. and 5 a.m., has a large selection of groceries. ~ 1310 South Kihei Road; 808-879-5871.

Azeka's Snack Shop up the road is often price-competitive. Open from 7:30 a.m. to 5 p.m. ~ Azeka Place Shopping Center, 1280 South Kihei Road; 808-879-0611.

For healthful items, try Hawaiian Moons Natural Foods, which also has a salad bar. Open 8 a.m. to 9 p.m. Monday through Saturday and 8 a.m. to 7 p.m. on Sunday. ~ 2411 South Kihei Road, Kihei; 808-875-4356.

SHOPPING Shopping in Kihei is centered in the malls and doesn't hold a lot of promise. You'll find swimwear shops and an assortment of other clothing outlets, but nothing with style and panache. Foremost among the malls is Azeka Place Shopping Center, which stretches along the 1200 South block of Kihei Road.

Kukui Mall just down the road has that most wonderful of inventions—a bookstore: a Waldenbooks bookstore to be exact. ~ 1819 South Kihei Road, Kihei; 808-874-3688.

You're likely to find a bargain or two at The Maui Clothing Company's Outlet Store if resortwear and Maui logowear are your thing. There's plenty to choose from. ~ Kihei Gateway Plaza, 362 Huku Li'i Place #106, Kihei; 808-879-0374.

Kalama Village Shopping Center, an open-air market with about 20 vendors, is a funky counterpoint to Kihei's other shopping spots. Here you'll find T-shirts, shells, jewelry and souvenirs sold at cut-rate prices by local people. If you're a Kona coffee fan, check out the Bad Ass Coffee Company (808-879-1950). There are flavorful blends, pure mild Kona and hearty roasts. ~ 1941 South Kihei Road, Kihei.

If you don't find what you're searching for at any of these addresses, there are countless other strip malls along Kihei Road.

Or, if you prefer more sophisticated shops, continue on to Wailea. The Shops at Wailea, currently undergoing a major facelift, hosts a variety of upscale shops including Black Pearl Gallery, Louis Vuitton, Tiffany & Co. and Lahaina Galleries. One of the more unique shops is White House/Black Market, two boutiques in one—one carrying only white clothing and accessories, the other only black-hued merchandise. Maui's premier shopping center. ~ 3750 Wailea Ala Nui Drive; 808-891-6770.

Much of the $30 million art collection in the Grand Wailea Resort and Spa comes from the personal holdings of the owner, Takeshi Sekiguchi. At the hotel's Napua Gallery, you can see his original Warhol paintings and some of his best Picasso lithographs, including *Les Deux Femmes Nues*. This series focuses on Picasso's longtime companion, Françoise Gilot, and demonstrates the artist's personal evolution. Available for purchase are paintings, mixed-media works and sculpture by leading contemporary artists. ~ 3850 Wailea Alanui, Wailea; 808-875-1234.

At **Mandalay Imports** you'll find Thai silk, designer dresses, lacquer chests, Chinese opera coats, beaded belts and Balinese art. This shop in the Four Seasons Resort Wailea also sells innovative necklaces and ceramic vases. ~ 3900 Wailea Alanui, Wailea; 808-874-5111.

A Pacific Café Maui is the hot spot for live music and a lively crowd. ~ Azeka Place II, 1279 South Kihei Road.

NIGHTLIFE

At night, **Hapa's Restaurant** hosts an upbeat and occasionally flamboyant gay scene with risque revues and music. Cover on Monday and Wednesday through Saturday. ~ 41 East Lipoa Street, Kihei; 808-879-9001.

The **Sunset Terrace Lounge** is a pleasant spot to see live Hawaiian entertainment when day turns to night. It's located at the Renaissance Wailea Beach Resort. ~ 3550 Wailea Alanui, Wailea; 808-879-4900.

Live Hawaiian entertainment is a nightly feature at the Aston Wailea Resort in **Kumu Bar and Grill**. Come for dinner or have a drink poolside as you enjoy an appealing island show. ~ 3700 Wailea Alanui, Wailea; 808-879-1922.

Leave it to the Grand Wailea Resort Hotel and Spa—the accent's on Grand—to have Maui's most elaborate high-tech nightclub. **Tsunami** cost $4 million to build and has 20 video monitors and a 14-foot-wide karaoke screen. Cover. ~ 3850 Wailea Alanui, Wailea; 808-875-1234.

A venue at the Four Seasons Resort Wailea is **Ferraros**, where live Italian music is perfectly timed for enjoying a sunset drink. ~ 3900 Wailea Alanui, Wailea; 808-874-8000.

Morning is the best time to go to the beach in Wailea and especially in Kihei. Later in the day, the wind picks up.

There is Hawaiian entertainment nightly at the **Molokini Lounge**. ~ Maui Prince Hotel, 5400 Makena Alanui, Makena; 808-874-1111.

KIHEI BEACH This narrow, palm-fringed beach that runs from Maalaea Bay to Kihei can be seen from several points along Kihei Road and is accessible from the highway. The entire stretch is dotted with small parks and picnic areas and doesn't actually go by a specific name. There are buildings and numerous condominiums along this strip, but few large crowds on the beach. Beach joggers take note: You can run for miles along this unbroken strand, but watch for heavy winds in the afternoon. Shallow weed-ridden waters make for poor swimming and only fair snorkeling (you'll find better at Kamaole beaches). For those anglers in the crowd, bonefish, *papio*, mullet, goatfish, *ulua, moano* and mountain bass are all caught here. There are

BEACHES & PARKS

picnic tables and restrooms at Kihei Memorial Park, which is midway along the beach.

KALAMA COUNTY BEACH PARK This is a long, broad park (36 acres) that has an ample lawn but very little beach. Rather than lapping along the sand, waves wash up against a stone seawall. Backdropped by Haleakala, Kalama has stunning views of West Maui, Lanai and Kahoolawe. A new attraction is the in-line skating rink, which features a view so compelling you could easily lose concentration and run into a fellow skater. This park is an excellent place for a picnic but, before you pack your lunch, remember that it, like all Kihei's beaches, is swept by afternoon winds. For surfers there are summer breaks over a coral reef; left and right slides. Snorkeling and fishing are fair; swimming is poor. There are picnic areas, restrooms, a shower and tennis courts. ~ Located on South Kihei Road, across from Kihei Town Center.

KAMAOLE BEACH PARKS (I, II AND III) Strung like beads along the Kihei shore are these three beautiful beaches. Their white sands are fringed with grass and studded with trees. With Haleakala in the background, they all offer magnificent views of the West Maui Mountains, Lanai and Kahoolawe—and all are windswept in the afternoon. Each has picnic areas, restrooms, lifeguard and showers. Kamaole III also has a playground. Swimming is very good on all three beaches. The best snorkeling is near the rocks ringing Kamaole III. Goatfish is the main catch. ~ Located on South Kihei Road near Kihei Town Center.

KEAWAKAPU BEACH Ho hum, yet another beautiful white-sand beach . . . Like other nearby parks, Keawakapu has marvelous views of the West Maui Mountains and Lanai, but is plagued by afternoon winds. The half-mile-long beach is bordered on both ends by lava points. The swimming is good, but Keawakapu is not as well protected as the Kamaole beaches.

MAKENA LANDING

Now a peaceful cove, Makena Landing, located on Makena Road, was once a port as busy as Lahaina. During the California gold rush, prevailing winds prompted many San Francisco–bound ships coming up from Cape Horn to resupply here. Fresh fruits and vegetables, badly needed by the would-be miners, were traded in abundance. Later local ranchers delivered their cattle to market by tethering them to longboats and swimming the animals out to steamers waiting just offshore from Makena Landing.

Snorkelers explore the area around the rocks. The fishing is excellent. There are no facilities except showers. ~ Located on South Kihei Road between Kihei and Wailea.

MOKAPU AND ULUA These are two crescent-shaped beaches fringed with palms and looking out toward Lanai and Kahoolawe. Much of their natural beauty has been spoiled by the nearby hotels and condominiums The beaches have landscaped miniparks and are popular with bodysurfers. Swimming and snorkeling are both good; restrooms and a shower are available. ~ Located in Wailea on Makena Alanui Road, adjacent to the Renaissance Wailea Beach Resort.

WAILEA BEACH Another lovely white-sand strip, once fringed with *kiawe* trees, is now dominated by two very large, very upscale resorts, part of the ultramodern Wailea development here. Swimming is good (the beach is popular with bodysurfers) and so is snorkeling. Restrooms and showers are available. ~ Located on Makena Alanui Road in Wailea between the Grand Wailea Resort and the Four Seasons Wailea Resort.

POLO BEACH Though not quite as attractive as Wailea Beach, it still has a lot to offer. There's a bountiful stretch of white sand and great views of Kahoolawe and Molokini. The beach, popular with bodysurfers, has a landscaped minipark with picnic tables, restrooms and showers. Swimming is also good here and the snorkeling is excellent. ~ Located off Makena Alanui Road on Kaukahi Road in Wailea, adjacent to the Kea Lani Hotel.

POOLENALENA (OR PAIPU) BEACH PARK Once known by locals as Chang's Beach, this is a lovely white-sand beach that has been transformed into an attractive facility frequented by people from throughout the area. The beach has showers, restrooms, picnic tables and a wonderful shaded lawn; unfortunately it also has as its neighbor the Maui Prince Hotel. Swimming is good, snorkeling fair and fishing very good—many species are caught here. ~ Located on Makena Alanui Road about one-and-one-fifth mile before (north of) the Maui Prince Hotel.

BLACK SANDS BEACH OR ONEULI BEACH This is ◀ HIDDEN a long, narrow, salt-and-pepper beach located just north of Red Hill, a shoreline cinder cone. Fringed with *kiawe* trees, this stretch of beach is less attractive but more secluded than Makena. Facilities are nonexistent. Swimming and snorkeling are both fair, but the fishing is very good, many species being caught here. ~ Located on Makena Alanui Road four-fifths mile past the Maui Prince Hotel. Turn right on the dirt road at the north end of Red Hill, then bear right and go one-third mile to the beach.

▲ There is unofficial camping but it's illegal and not recommended.

MAKENA STATE BEACH 🏊🐟 Much more than a beach, Makena is an institution. For over a decade, it's been a counter-cultural gathering place. There are even stories about rock stars jamming here during Makena's heyday in the early 1970s. Once a hideaway for hippies, the beach today is increasingly popular with mainstream tourists. So far this long, wide corridor of white sand curving south from Red Hill is still the most beautiful beach on Maui. There are pit toilets. ~ From Wailea Shopping Village, go about four-and-one-half miles south on Makena Alanui. Turn right into the parking lot.

HIDDEN ▶   **LITTLE BEACH (PUU OLAI BEACH)** 🏊🐟 This pretty stretch of white sand next to Makena Beach, just across Red Hill, is a nude beach. It's also popular with the island's gay crowd. But if you go nude here or at Makena, watch out for police; they regularly bust nudists. Swimming is good (bodysurfing is especially good at Little Makena) and you can snorkel near the rocks at the north end of the beach. The fishing is fair. There are no facilities. ~ Follow Makena Alanui for about four-and-one-half miles south from Wailea Shopping Village. Watch for Red Hill, the large cinder cone on your right. Just past Red Hill, turn right into the parking lot for Makena Beach. From here a path leads over Red Hill to Little Beach.

▲ Camping, though unofficial, is very popular here, but beware of thieves.

▼▼▼▼▼▼▼▼▼▼▼▼▼▼▼▼
Kahului–Wailuku Area

The island's commercial, civic, and population centers are located in the adjoining towns of Kahului and Wailuku. With no clear dividing place, these two municipalities seem at first glance to be "twin towns." They drift into one another as you climb uphill from Kahului Harbor toward the mountains. Kahului is significantly younger than its neighbor, however, and focuses its daily life around commerce. Maui's main airport is here, together with a skein of shopping malls and a few hotels that line a blue-collar waterfront. Wailuku presents a more rolling terrain and is the seat of government for Maui County.

SIGHTS   **Kahului**, with its bustling harbor and busy shopping complexes, offers little to the sightseer. The piers along the waterfront, lined with container-cargo ships and weekly cruise ships, are the embarkation point for Maui's sugar and pineapple crops. Established as a sugar town more than a century ago, Kahului has a commercial feel about it.

Coming from the airport along Kaahumanu Avenue (Route 32), you can wander through **Kanaha Pond Wildlife Sanctuary**. Once a royal fishpond, this is now an important bird refuge, especially for the rare Hawaiian stilt and Hawaiian coot.

The highway leads uphill to **Wailuku**, Maui's administrative center. Older and more interesting than Kahului, Wailuku sits astride the foothills of the West Maui Mountains at the entrance to Iao Valley. A mix of woodframe plantation houses and suburban homes, it even boasts a multi-story civic building. For a short tour of the aging woodfront quarter, take a right on Market Street and follow it several blocks to **Happy Valley**. This former red-light district still retains the charm, if not the action, of a bygone era. Here you'll discover narrow streets and tinroof houses framed by the sharply rising, deeply creased face of the West Maui Mountains.

The county government buildings reside along High Street. Just across the road rests picturesque **Kaahumanu Congregational Church**. Queen Kaahumanu attended services here in 1832 when the church was a grass shack, and requested that the first permanent church be named after her. Now Maui's oldest church, this grand stone-and-plaster structure was constructed in 1876, and has been kept in excellent condition for its many visitors. With a lofty white spire, it is the area's most dramatic manmade landmark. ~ 808-244-5189.

Iao Valley, Maui's Valley of the Kings, is one of Hawaii's most sacred spots.

Nearby you'll find the **Bailey House Museum**, run by the Maui Historical Society. Lodged in the dwelling of a former missionary, the displays include 19th-century Hawaiian artifacts, remnants from the early sugar cane industry and period pieces from the missionary years. This stone-and-plaster house (completed in 1850) has walls 20 inches thick and beams fashioned from hand-hewn sandalwood. Together with an adjoining seminary building, it harkens back to Wailuku's days as an early center of western culture. Admission. ~ 2375-A Main Street; 808-244-3326; www.mauimuseum.org.

The **Hawaii Nature Center**, situated on the edge of Iao Valley,   ◄ HIDDEN
off the gateway to Iao Valley State Park, features an Interactive Science Arcade designed for adults as well as children. The Nature Center also hosts hikes Monday through Friday into the Iao Valley, complete with environmental educators. Admission. ~ 875 Iao Valley Road; 808-244-6500.

Bounded on both sides by the sharp walls of Iao Valley, **Tropical Gardens of Maui** encompasses four densely planted acres of fruit trees, orchids and flowering plants. Iao Stream rushes through the property, which offers garden paths and a lily pond. Admission. ~ 200 Iao Road, 808-244-3085; www.tropicalgardensofmaui.com.

Up the road at **Kepaniwai County Park and Heritage Gardens**, there's an outdoor cultural showcase to discover. Backdropped by Iao Valley's adze-like peaks, this adult playground features lovely Japanese and Chinese monuments as well as a taro patch. There are arched bridges, a swimming pool and an Oriental garden. The houses of Hawaii's many cultural groups are represented by a Hawaiian grass hut, New England saltbox (complete with white picket fence), Filipino bamboo house and a Portuguese villa. On this site in 1790 Kamehameha's forces overwhelmed the army of a Maui chief in a battle so terrible that the corpses blocking Iao Stream gave Kepaniwai ("damming of the waters") and Wailuku ("bloody river") their names.

HIDDEN ► Uphill at the **John F. Kennedy Profile** you'll see Hawaii's answer to Mt. Rushmore, chiseled by nature. Ironically, this geologic formation, which bears an uncanny resemblance to the former president, was never noticed until after his assassination.

Iao Valley State Monument, surrounded by those same moss-mantled cliffs, provides an excellent view of **Iao Needle,** a single spire that rises to a point 1200 feet above the valley (and 2250 feet above sea level). With the possible exception of Haleakala Crater, this awesome peak is Maui's most famous landmark. A basalt core that has withstood the ravages of erosion, the "Needle" and mist-filled valley have long been a place of pilgrimage for Hawaiians. (Be sure to explore the paths from the parking lot that lead across Iao Stream and up to a vista point.)

LODGING The hotel strip in the harbor town of Kahului lies along the beach on Kahului Bay.

The **Maui Seaside Hotel** consists of two separate complexes sitting beside each other along Kaahumanu Avenue (Route 32). There is a pool, restaurant and lounge. Rooms in the older poolside wing are a bit less expensive: clean, but lacking in decorative flair, the surroundings are quite adequate. Just a few well-spent dollars more places you in a larger, more attractive room in the newer complex, which has more upscale appointments. Both facilities feature phones, TVs, refrigerators and air conditioning. Some include kitchenettes. Ask about discounts. ~ 100 West Kaahumanu Avenue, Kahului; 808-877-3311, 800-560-5552, fax 808-877-4618; www.sand-seaside.com. MODERATE TO DELUXE.

The nearby **Maui Beach Hotel** incorporates the old Maui Palms Hotel as its Palms wing, where rooms are about as inexpensive as things get on Maui. Rooms in the Palms wing are comfortable, although decor and facilities are a bit dated; some units include air conditioners and refrigerators. The main wing is more contemporary, with larger rooms that translate into higher rates. While conveniently located in Kahului, it is not your made-in-paradise setting, with "oceanfront" meaning the waters of Kahu-

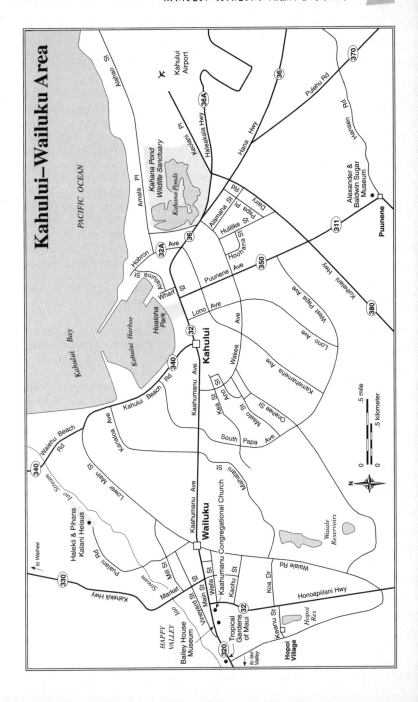

lui Harbor. The grounds are appealingly studded with palms, and there is a pleasant pool area with a small adjacent beach, plus two restaurants and a sundries shop. The attitude is island-style friendly. ~ 170 Kaahumanu Avenue, Kahului; 808-877-0051, 888-649-3222, fax 808-871-5797. MODERATE TO DELUXE.

The **Banana Bungalow** is a kind of resort for low-budget travelers. This hotel/hostel caters to windsurfers, surfers and adventurers. It offers a jacuzzi, garden and fruit trees, a sand volleyball court and cable TV and movies. The folks here conduct their own tours and have a free airport drop-off. There are laundry facilities and a community kitchen and, of course, hammocks. ~ 310 North Market Street, Wailuku; 808-244-5090, 800-846-7835, fax 808-244-3678; www.mauihostel.com. BUDGET.

Northshore Inn is another clean, trim hostel-cum-hotel with shared rooms and private singles or doubles. The lobby/television room is decorated with surfboards, flags and modern art, and the place has an easy, windswept air about it. There are laundry and kitchen facilities; baths are shared. Every room has a refrigerator and overhead fan. Your seventh night is free. ~ 2080 Vineyard Street, Wailuku; 808-242-8999, 800-647-6284, fax 808-244-5004; www.hostelhawaii.com. BUDGET.

DINING   The best place in Kahului for a quick, inexpensive meal is at one of several shopping arcades along Kaahumanu Avenue (Route 32). For common fare, head over to the Maui Mall. Here you can drop in at **Restaurant Matsu** (808-871-0822), a short-order eatery that features such Japanese selections as tempura, bento plates, sushi and *saimin*. Next door at **Siu's Chinese Kitchen** (808-871-0828), they serve three meals a day. To round off the calorie count, you can try a cup of *guri guri* sherbet at **Tasaka Guri Guri Shop** (808-871-4513). ~ Maui Mall, Kahului. BUDGET.

HIDDEN ►   The white booths and black-tile tables are an appealing touch at **Marco's Grill & Deli**. So is the attention to detail at this family-operated Italian restaurant. They blend their own coffee and grind their own meat for sausages and meatballs. The result is a menu that ranges from chocolate cinnamon French toast at breakfast to submarine sandwiches and vodka rigatoni later in the day. In addition to pasta entrées, they serve seafood dishes. ~ 444 Hana Highway, Kahului; 808-877-4446, fax 808-874-7032. MODERATE.

If you're staying at one of Kahului's bayfront hotels, you might try **Vi's Restaurant** in the Maui Seaside Hotel. This open-air Polynesian-style establishment has steak with fish or shrimp and other assorted dinners. The ambience here is pleasant, and the staff congenial, but in the past the service has sometimes been slow. Vi doesn't serve lunch, but at breakfast (7 to 9 a.m.) the specials might include banana hot cakes. Dinner is from 6 to 8 p.m. ~ 100 West Kaahumanu Avenue; 808-871-6494. MODERATE.

The **Rainbow Dining Room** lies along Kaahumanu Avenue in the Maui Beach Hotel. Overlooking the pool, this spacious open-air restaurant serves a Japanese buffet most of the week, and at lunch and breakfast features American cuisine. The former includes shrimp tempura, scallops, mixed vegetables, yakitori chicken, teriyaki steak, many different types of Japanese salad and a host of other dishes. Open 7 a.m. to 9 p.m. ~ 170 Kaahumanu Avenue, Kahului; 808-877-0051, fax 808-871-5797. DELUXE.

Up the road apiece in Wailuku there are numerous ethnic restaurants guaranteed to please both the palate and the purse. **Sam Sato's** features local noodle dishes. Open for breakfast and   ◀ HIDDEN lunch, it specializes in *manju* (a bean cake pastry), dry *mein* (a noodle dish) and the ubiquitous *saimin*. Closed Sunday. ~ 1750 Wili Pa Loop; 808-244-7124. BUDGET.

The nearby **Fujiya** stirs up similar money belt–tightening Japanese meals. Well worth a visit. There's also a sushi bar. No lunch on Saturday. Closed Sunday. ~ 133 Market Street, Wailuku; 808-244-0206. BUDGET.

A local favorite, **Siam Thai Cuisine** is always a good choice   ◀ HIDDEN for Southeast Asian fare. Attractively decorated with posters and artwork from Thailand, this restaurant features a complete menu that includes dozens of delicious dishes. Try the chicken-coconut soup, *tom-yum goong*, Siam chicken, or the *pod-pet,* beef or pork or chicken sautéed with ginger and bamboo shoots. No lunch on Saturday and Sunday. ~ 123 North Market Street, Wailuku; 808-244-3817. BUDGET.

> Kahului, then Maui's largest town, was deliberately destroyed by fire in 1890 to kill rats that were spreading an epidemic of bubonic plague.

Saeng's Thai Cuisine sits in a beautifully designed building embellished with fine woodwork and adorned with Asian accoutrements. The menu, which lists three pages of dishes from Thailand, is like an encyclopedia of fine dining. Meals, which are served in the dining room or out on a windswept veranda, begin with *sateh* and spring rolls, venture on to dishes like the "evil prince" and "tofu delight," and end over tea and tapioca pudding. No lunch Saturday and Sunday. ~ 2119 Vineyard Street, Wailuku; 808-244-1567. BUDGET TO MODERATE.

A Saigon Café doesn't advertise itself with even a sign on the   ◀ HIDDEN outside, but business still flourishes. You'll find a small space inside, but a big menu that includes vegetarian, clay pot, seafood and even steak entrées. ~ 1792 Main Street, Wailuku; 808-243-9560, fax 808-243-9566. BUDGET TO DELUXE.

Ramon's is the region's entry in the Mexican food category. This split-level eatery features entertainment and patio seating. The varied menu is spelled out with tacos, tamales, a sushi bar, local food items, seafood, fajitas and chile rellenos. ~ 2102 Vineyard Street, Wailuku; 808-244-7243. BUDGET TO MODERATE.

Wailuku's low-rent district lies along Lower Main Street, where ethnic restaurants cater almost exclusively to locals. These are informal, family-owned, formica-and-naugahyde-chair cafés that serve good food at down-to-earth prices. You'll find Japanese food at **Tokyo Tei**. No lunch on Sunday. ~ 1063-E Lower Main Street; 808-242-9630. BUDGET.

Southeast Asia is represented by **Cali Café**. Their menu features Vietnamese food like stir-fried vegetables, curried chicken rice plates, shrimp in clay pot and beef noodle dishes. Closed Sunday. ~ 1246 Lower Main Street, Wailuku; 808-244-2167. BUDGET.

GROCERIES Kahului features two sprawling supermarkets. **Foodland** is open daily from 6 a.m. to 11 p.m. ~ Kaahumanu Center, Kaahumanu Avenue; 808-877-2808. **Star Super Market** is open daily from 6 a.m. to 10 p.m. ~ Maui Mall, Kaahumanu Avenue; 808-877-3341.

Down to Earth Natural Foods in Wailuku has a complete line of health food items and fresh produce. Add to that a healthy stock of herbs and you have what amounts to a natural food supermarket. This gets my dollar for being the best place on Maui to shop for natural foods. ~ 305 Dairy Road; 808-877-2661.

There is also **Ah Fook's Super Market** in the Kahului Shopping Center. ~ Kaahumanu Avenue; 808-877-3308.

Wakamatsu Fish Market has fresh fish every day but Sunday, when they are closed. ~ 145 Market Street, Wailuku; 808-244-4111.

Love's Bakery Thrift Shop sells day-old baked goods at old-fashioned prices. ~ 340 Ano Street, Kahului; 808-877-3160. In Wailuku, **Holsum/Oroweat Thrift Shop** is another place for baked goods. ~ 350 Hoohana Street, Kahului; 808-877-5445.

SHOPPING For everyday shopping needs, you should find the Kahului malls very convenient. Three sprawling centers are strung along Kaahumanu Avenue (Route 32).

Kaahumanu Center is Maui's finest and most contemporary shopping mall, with **Liberty House** (808-877-3361) and **Sears**

MAUI'S FAMOUS POTATO CHIPS

Always a favorite with locals, Maui potato chips have by now become a worldwide phenomenon. One of the most popular brands is "Kitch'n Cook'd," made at the family-owned and operated **Maui Potato Chip Factory**. This place has been around since the 1950s, annually increasing in popularity, and it now brings in orders from around the globe. These chips are hard to find in mainland stores, but you can stock up on them here where they're freshly made. No tours. Closed Saturday and Sunday. ~ 295 Lalo Place, off Route 360, Kahului; 808-877-3652.

(808-877-2221), a photo studio, **Waldenbooks** (808-871-6112), boutiques, shoe stores, candy stores, a sundries shop and a jeweler. For Japanese foods, try **Shirokiya** (808-877-5551). ~ 275 Kaahumanu Avenue.

Nearby **Maui Mall** has a smaller inventory of shops. **Mom's** (808-877-3711) stocks a connoisseur's selection of tobaccos and coffees, and even has a coffee bar and vegetarian deli. ~ 180 East Wakea Avenue.

You might also try **Kahului Shopping Center**, though I prefer the other, more convenient malls. ~ Kaahumanu Avenue.

Summerhouse Boutique might be called a chic dress shop. But they sell everything from jewelry to porcelain dolls and natural fiber garments. ~ 395 Dairy Road, Kahului; 808-871-1320.

Up in Wailuku, a tumbledown town with a friendly face, you'll find the little shops and solicitous merchants that we have come to associate with small-town America. Along North Market Street are several imaginative shops operated by low-key entrepreneurs.

Brown & Kobayashi, another nearby antique store, specializes in rare pieces from the Orient. ~ 160-A North Market Street, Wailuku; 808-242-0804.

Some of the island's most reasonably priced souvenirs are found at the **Maui Historical Society Museum Gift Shop**. Here you'll find an outstanding collection of local history books and art prints. Quilts and *koa* bookmarks are also popular. ~ 2375-A Main Street, Wailuku; 808-244-3326.

NIGHTLIFE

Nightly music and dancing attract a local crowd at **Sal's Place**, an Italian restaurant where the beat ranges from reggae to disco to Hawaiian. The music is live on select weekends. Otherwise it's DJ-selected. Cover. ~ 162 Alamaha Street, Kahului; 808-893-0609.

The crowd's also mostly local at the **Ale House,** which has karaoke Sunday through Wednesday, with live music and dancing until 2 a.m. from Thursday through Saturday. ~ 355 East Kamehameha Avenue, Kahului; 808-877-9001.

BEACHES & PARKS

HOALOHA PARK   Located next to the Kahului hotels, this is Kahului's only beach, but unfortunately the nearby harbor facilities detract from the natural beauty of its white sands. What with heavy boat traffic on one side and several hotels on the other, the place is not recommended. There are much better beaches in other areas of the island. Swimming and snorkeling are poor; surfers will find good breaks (two to six feet, with a left slide) off the jetty mouth near the north shore of Kahului Harbor. It is, however, a good spot to beachcomb, particularly for Maui diamonds. Picnic tables are available. Goatfish, *papio* and triggerfish can be hooked from the pier; *ulua* and *papio* are often caught along the shore. ~ Located on Kaahumanu Avenue (Route 32).

KEPANIWAI COUNTY PARK AND HERITAGE GARDENS 🏊
This beautiful park is carefully landscaped and surrounded by sheer cliffs. You'll discover paths over arched bridges and through Japanese gardens, plus pagodas, a thatch-roofed hut, a taro patch and banana, papaya and coconut trees. An ideal and romantic spot for picnicking, it has picnic pavilions, restrooms and a swimming pool. ~ Located in Wailuku on the road to Iao Valley.

WAIHEE BEACH PARK 🏊 🐟 🎣 This park is used almost exclusively by local residents. Bordered by a golf course and shaded with ironwood trees and *naupaka* bushes, it has a sandy beach and one of Maui's longest and widest reefs. There's a grassy area perfect for picnicking, established picnic areas and restrooms with showers. Beachcombing, *limu* gathering and fishing are all good. Swimming and snorkeling are okay, though the reef is rather shallow. ~ Located outside Wailuku on the rural road that circles the West Maui Mountains. To get there from Route 340 in Waiehu, turn right on Halewaiu Road and then take the beach access road from Waiehu Golf Course.

▼▼▼▼▼▼▼▼▼▼▼
Hana Highway

The Hana Highway (Route 360), a smooth, narrow road running between Kahului and Hana, is one of the most beautiful drives in all Hawaii. Following the path of an ancient Hawaiian trail, it may in fact be one of the prettiest drives in the world. The road courses through a rainforest, a luxurious jungle crowded with ferns and African tulip trees, and leads to black sand beaches and rain-drenched hamlets. The vegetation is so thick it seems to be spilling out from the mountainside in a cascade of greenery. You'll be traveling the windward side of Haleakala, hugging its lower slopes en route to a small Hawaiian town that receives 70 inches of rain a year.

There are over 600 twists and turns and 56 one-lane bridges along this adequately maintained paved road. It'll take at least three hours to drive the 51 miles to Hana. To make the entire circuit around the south coast, plan to sleep in Hana or to leave very early and drive much of the day. If you can, take your time—there's a lot to see.

SIGHTS
About seven miles east of Kahului, you'll pass the quaint, weather-beaten town of **Paia**. This old sugar plantation town, now a burgeoning artist colony and windsurfing mecca, has been painted in nursery colors. Along either of Paia's two streets, plantation-era buildings have been freshly refurbished.

On the eastern side of town is the **Mantokuji Buddhist Temple**, which celebrates sunset every day by sounding its huge gong.

Hookipa Beach Park, one of the world's premier windsurfing spots, lies about three miles east of town. Brilliantly colored sails

Hana Highway

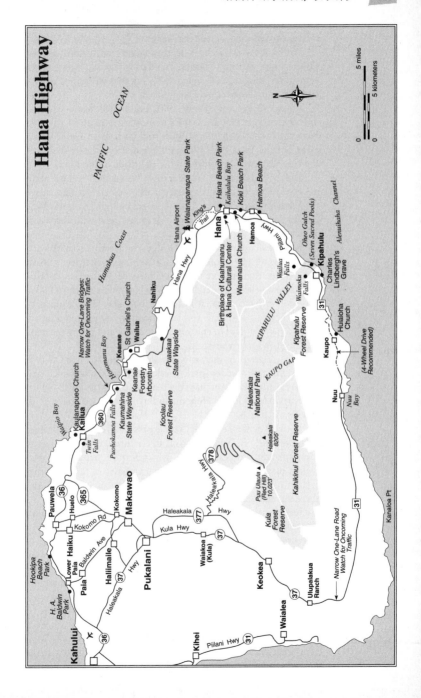

PACIFIC   OCEAN

N

0   5 miles
0   5 kilometers

Hamakua Coast

Wailua Bay

Twin Falls

Puohokamoa Falls

Kaumahina State Wayside

Kaulanapueo Church

Narrow One-Lane Bridges; Watch for Oncoming Traffic

Honomanu Bay

St Gabriel's Church

Keanae

Wailua

Keanae Forestry Arboretum

Puaakaa State Wayside

Nahiku

Koolau Forest Reserve

Hana Hwy

Hana Airport

King's Trail

Waianapanapa State Park

Hana Beach Park

Hana

Kaihalulu Bay

Koki Beach Park

Birthplace of Kaahumanu & Hana Cultural Center

Wananalua Church

Hamoa

Hamoa Beach

KIPAHULU VALLEY

Wailua Falls

Waimoku Falls

Oheo Gulch (Seven Sacred Pools)

Piilani Hwy

Kipahulu

Charles Lindbergh's Grave

Kipahulu Forest Reserve

Haleakala National Park

KAUPO GAP

Kahikinui Forest Reserve

Kula Forest Reserve

Alenuihaha Channel

Kaupo

31

Hualoha Church

(4-Wheel Drive Recommended)

Nuu

Nuu Bay

Kanaloa Pt

Haleakala 8205'

Puu Ulaula (Red Hill) 10,023'

378

Haleakala Hwy

Makawao

Haleakala 37 Hwy

Kula Hwy

37

Pauwela

Huelo

36

365

Kokomo

Kokomo Rd

Waiakoa (Kula)

Keokea

Kailua

360

Lower Haiku

Baldwin Ave

Paia

Hookipa Beach Park

H.A. Baldwin Park

Haliimaile

37

Pukalani

Haleakala Hwy

Kahului

36

37

Waialea

Ulupalakua Ranch

Narrow One-Lane Road Watch for Oncoming Traffic

31

Kihei

Piilani Hwy   31

race along the horizon as windsurfers perform amazing acrobatic stunts, cartwheeling across the waves.

Within the next ten miles the roadway is transformed, as your slow, winding adventure begins. You'll drive past sugar cane fields, across verdant gorges, through valleys dotted with tumbledown cottages and along fern-cloaked hillsides.

Route 36 becomes Route 360, beginning a new series of mileage markers that are helpful in locating sites along the way. Near the two-mile marker, a short trail leads to an idyllic swimming hole at **Twin Falls** (the path begins from the west side of the Hoolawa Stream bridge on the right side of the road).

Nearby Huelo, a tiny "rooster town" (so named because nothing ever seems to be stirring except the roosters), is known for the **Kaulanapueo Church**. A coral chapel built in 1853, this New England–style sanctuary strikes a dramatic pose with the sea as a backdrop.

Farther along, on **Waikamoi Ridge**, you'll see picnic areas and a nature trail. Here you can visit a bamboo forest, learn about native vegetation and explore the countryside. Remember to bring mosquito repellent, especially if you're planning a rainforest hike.

Another picnic area, at **Puohokamoa Falls** (11-mile marker), nestles beside a waterfall and large pool. If you packed a lunch, this is a perfect place to enjoy it. Trails above and below the main pool lead to other waterfalls.

A few zigzags farther, at **Kaumahina State Wayside** (12-mile marker), a tree-studded park overlooks Honomanu Gulch and Keanae Peninsula. From here the road descends the gulch, where a side road leads left to **Honomanu Bay** (14-mile marker) and its black sand beach.

Above Keanae Peninsula, you'll pass the **Keanae Arboretum** (16-mile marker). You can stroll freely through paved trails in these splendid tropical gardens, which feature many native Hawaiian plants including several dozen varieties of taro. Another section of the gardens is devoted to exotic tropical plants and there is a mile-long trail that leads into a natural rainforest.

Just past the arboretum, turn left onto the road to the **Keanae Peninsula** (17-mile marker). This rocky, windswept point offers stunning views of Haleakala. You'll pass rustic houses, a patchwork of garden plots and a coral-and-stone church built around 1860. A picture of serenity and rural perfection, Keanae is inhabited by native Hawaiians who still grow taro and pound poi. Their home is a lush rainforest—a quiltwork of taro plots, banana trees, palms—that runs to the rim of a ragged coastline.

Another side road descends to **Wailua** (18-mile marker), a Hawaiian agricultural and fishing village. Here is another luxurious checkerboard where taro gardens alternate with banana patches and the landscape is adorned with clapboard houses.

The town is known for **St. Gabriel's Church**, a simple structure made completely of sand and coral, dating from 1870.

Back on the main road, there's yet another picnic area and waterfall at **Puaakaa State Wayside** (22-mile marker). The cascade tumbles into a natural pool in a setting framed by eucalyptus and banana trees. Puaakaa means, by the way, "plenty of pigs."

Past here, another side road bumps three miles through picturesque **Nahiku** (25-mile marker) to a bluff overlooking the sea.   ◄ *HIDDEN* The view spreads across three bays all the way back to Wailua. Directly below, the ocean pounds against rock outcroppings, spraying salt mist across a stunning vista. Set in one of the wettest spots along the entire coast, Nahiku village is inundated by rainforest and graced by yet another 19th-century church.

Several miles before Hana, be sure to stop at **Waianapanapa State Park**. Here you will find a black-sand beach and two lava tubes, **Waianapanapa** and **Waiomao caves**. Hawaiian mythology tells of a Hawaiian princess who hid from her cruel husband here, only to be discovered by him and slain. Now every spring the waters hereabouts are said to run red with her blood. Offshore you will also see several sea arches and nearby a blowhole that spouts periodically.

Just before the town of Hana, on the right, is **Helani Farm and Gardens**, a sprawling oasis of tropical plant life. Only a section of the gardens is currently open to the public, but it's worth a stop as there's a wealth of flowering plants, trees and vines. You'll also find fruit trees, baobab trees, papyrus, ginger plants and even a carp pond. Visits by appointment only. Admission. ~ Hana Highway; phone/fax 808-248-8274, 800-385-5241; e-mail bj4flowers@aol.com.

Hana's three police officers report that the region's number one crime is driving without a seatbelt.

For a cultural treat, turn off Route 360 at Ulaino Road following the signs to the **Kahanu Garden**, part of the National Tropical Botanical Gardens. The focus here is on native Hawaiian plants and culture. A highlight of the 90-minute tour is a look at the massive Piilanihale *heiau*, which overlooks a moody stretch of coast. The football field–sized platform, built of moss- and algae-covered lava rocks, is the largest of the ancient *heiau* sites remaining in Hawaii. The power of the past can be felt here, especially with the soulful expertise that tour guides impart on a visit. The sense of authenticity makes this a true encounter with Polynesian Hawaii. You can only visit the garden on a guided tour, which runs twice daily. Closed Saturday and Sunday. Admission. ~ 808-248-8912.

To reach the secluded hamlet of **Hana**, you can take the old Hawaiian shoreline trail (see the "Hiking" section at the end of this chapter) or continue on along the highway. This Eden-like town, carpeted with pandanus, taro and banana trees, sits above

DRIVING TOUR
Central Maui

Central Maui is defined not by what it is but by what lies to the east and west of it. On one side Haleakala lifts into the clouds; on the other hand loom the West Maui mountains, a folded landscape over 5000 feet in elevation. Between them, at the center of the island, sits an isthmus, some areas planted in sugar cane and pineapple. Never rising more than a few hundred feet above sea level, it houses Kahului along its northern edge and serves as the gateway to both the Lahaina–Kaanapali and Kihei–Wailea areas. Three highways cross the isthmus separating West Maui from the slopes of Haleakala. From Kahului, Mokulele Highway (Route 350) tracks south to Kihei through this rich agricultural area. The Kuihelani Highway (Route 380), running diagonally across sugar cane fields and through open stretches, joins the Honoapiilani Highway (Route 30) in its course from Wailuku along the West Maui Mountains. The low-lying area that supports this network of roadways was formed by lava flows from Haleakala and the West Maui Mountains.

ALEXANDER & BALDWIN SUGAR MUSEUM The Alexander & Baldwin Sugar Museum, an award-winning nonprofit organization, is across from the largest operating sugar plantation in Hawaii. It provides a brief introduction to Hawaii's main crop. Tracing the history of sugar cultivation in the islands, its displays portray everything from early life in the cane fields, the multi-ethnic plantation life, to contemporary methods for producing refined sugar. Closed Sunday except in July and August. Admission. ~ Puunene Avenue and Hansen Road, Puunene; 808-871-8058.

MAUI TROPICAL PLANTATION The Maui Tropical Plantation is a 60-acre enclave complete with orchards and groves displaying dozens of island fruit plants. Here you'll see avocados, papayas, bananas, pineapples, mangoes, coffee and macadamia nuts growing in lush profusion. There's a tropical nursery and a tram that will carry you through this ersatz plantation. Admission for the tram. ~ 1670 Honoapiilani Highway; 808-244-7643.

an inviting bay. Known as "heavenly Hana," it's a ranch town inhabited primarily by part-Hawaiians. Because of its remote location it has changed little over the years. The rain that continually buffets Hana makes it a prime agricultural area and adds to the luxuriant, unsettling beauty of the place.

Because of its strategic location directly across from the Big Island, Hana was an early battleground in the wars between the chiefs of Maui and the Big Island, who conquered, lost and regained the region in a succession of bloody struggles. During the

MAUI OCEAN CENTER   In Maalaea, you can visit the Maui Ocean Center. Facilities include a reef exhibit, touch pool, and a clear tunnel that runs through a giant tank filled with Hawaiian underwater distillers. Maui Ocean Center's parent company, Coral World International, researches ways to rebuild coral reefs. The results of their study can be seen in action in the Ocean Center's displays. ~ Maalaea Road, Maalaea; 808-270-7000.

MAALAEA BAY   Past the small boat harbor at Maalaea Bay, the highway hugs the southwest coast. There are excellent lookout points along this elevated roadway, especially near the lighthouse at **McGregor Point**. During whale season you might spy a leviathan from this landlocked crow's nest. Just offshore there are prime whale breeding areas.

OFFSHORE ISLANDS   Down the road from McGregor Point, you'll see three islands anchored offshore. As you look seaward, the portside islet is **Molokini**, the crescent-shaped remains of a volcanic crater. **Kahoolawe**, a barren, desiccated island once used for naval target practice, sits in the center. Located seven miles off Maui's south coast, it is a bald, windblasted place, hot, arid and home to feral goats. Hawaiian activists long demanded an end to the bombing of this sacred isle by the U.S. Navy. After years of demonstrations, their demands were finally acknowledged in 1994 when the island was turned over to the state of Hawaii. The humpbacked island to starboard is **Lanai**. Lying eight miles across the Kealaikahiki Channel, it is a pear-shaped island boasting a 3370-foot peak and a population of about 3200 people. As you continue toward Kaanapali, **Molokai** sails into view. Known as the "Friendly Isle," it covers 260 square miles and contains the highest per capita concentration of native Hawaiians of any of the main islands. With a population of about 7000 people, it's a sleepy destination ideal for a Maui getaway excursion.

19th century it became a sugar plantation, employing different ethnic groups who were brought in to work the fields. Then, in 1946, Paul Fagan, a San Francisco industrialist, bought 14,000 acres and created the Hana Ranch, turning the area into grazing land for Hereford cattle and opening the exclusive Hotel Hana-Maui.

Head down to **Hana Bay**. Here you can stroll the beach, explore the wharf and take a short path along the water to a plaque that marks the **Birthplace of Kaahumanu**, King Kamehameha I's favorite wife and a key player in the 1819 overthrow of the ancestral Hawaiian religious system. To reach this sacred spot, pick up the trail leading from the boat landing on the right side of the bay. It leads along the base of **Kauiki Hill**, a cinder cone covered with ironwood trees that was the scene of fierce battles between Kahekili, the renowned Maui chief, and the Big Island chief Kalaniopuu.

HIDDEN ▶

Near the Hotel Hana-Maui (where you can request a key to open the gate), you can drive or hike up a short road to **Mount Lyons** (that camel-humped hill with the cross on top). From this aerie, a memorial to Paul Fagan, there's a fine view of Hana Bay and the surrounding coastline.

The **Hana Cultural Center**, an enticing little museum, displays such artifacts from Hana's past as primitive stone tools, rare shells and Hawaiian games. There are antique photographs and elaborately stitched quilts. ~ 4974 Uakea Street; 808-248-8622.

The honor system is alive and well at the untended self-serve coconut stand near Hana Highway's 48-mile marker.

Also on the grounds, the old **Court House**, built in 1871, is a modest but appealing structure containing five small benches and the original desk for the judge.

Wananalua Church, a lovely chapel built from coral blocks during the mid-19th century, has been beautifully refurbished. Today, services are conducted in English and Hawaiian. Located atop an ancient *heiau*, stately and imposing in appearance, it is a perfect expression of the days when Christianity was crushing the old Hawaiian beliefs. ~ Hauoli Street and Hana Highway.

FROM HANA TO ULUPALAKUA The backroad from Hana around the southeast side of Maui is one of the island's great adventures. It leads along the side of Haleakala past dense rainforest and tumbling waterfalls to an arid expanse covered by lava flows, and then opens onto Maui's vaunted Upcountry region. Since a five-mile stretch is unpaved and other sections are punctuated with potholes, car rental companies generally do not permit driving on parts of this route; so check with them in advance or be prepared to take your chances. Also check on road conditions: The road is sometimes closed during periods of heavy rain.

Past Hana, the road, now designated the Piilani Highway and renumbered as Route 31 (with mileage markers that descend in sequence), worsens as it winds toward an overgrown ravine where **Wailua Falls** (45-mile marker) and another waterfall pour down sharp cliff faces.

At **Oheo Gulch** (known to some as Seven Sacred Pools) in the Kipahulu District of the Haleakala National Park (42-mile marker), a series of waterfalls tumbles into two dozen pools before reaching the sea. The pools are rock-bound, some are bordered by cliffs, and several provide excellent swimming holes. This is an eerie and beautiful place from which you can see up and down the rugged coastline. Used centuries ago by early Hawaiians, they still offer a cool, refreshing experience.

Every tourist to Maui dreams of visiting the "Seven Sacred Pools." In fact, says Mark Tanaka-Sanders, a ranger who helps manage a coastal section of Haleakala National Park, "there are 24 pools in the area." Who's responsible for the miscount? "Blame it on the tourist industry," he says. "It's also important to know that the Hawaiian people do not consider these pools sacred." They refer to them as the pools at Oheo.

Another special spot, **Charles Lindbergh's grave** (41-mile   ◄ HIDDEN
marker), rests on a promontory overlooking the ocean. The great aviator spent his last days here and lies buried beside Palapala Hoomau Church. The whitewashed chapel and surrounding shade trees create a place of serenity and remarkable beauty. (To find the grave, continue 1.2 miles past Oheo Gulch. Watch for the church through the trees on the left. Turn left onto an unpaved road and drive several hundred yards, paralleling a stone fence. Turn left into the churchyard.)

Not far from here, in **Kipahulu**, the paved road gives way to dirt. It's five miles to the nearest pavement, so your car should have good shock absorbers; sometimes the weather makes it impassable. The road rises along seaside cliffs, some of which are so steep they jut out to overhang the road. This is wild, uninhabited country, ripe for exploration.

Huialoha Church, built in 1859, rests below the road on a   ◄ HIDDEN
wind-wracked peninsula. The last time I visited this aging worship hall, horses were grazing in the churchyard. Nearby you'll encounter the tinroof town of **Kaupo**, with its funky general store. Located directly above the town is **Kaupo Gap**, through which billowing clouds pour into Haleakala Crater.

The road bumps inland, then returns seaward to **Nuu Bay's** rocky beach. From here the rustic route climbs into a desolate area scarred by lava and inhabited with scrub vegetation. The sea views are magnificent as the road bisects the **1790 lava flow**. This was the last volcanic eruption on Maui; it left its mark in a torn and terrible landscape that slopes for miles to the sea.

It's several miles farther until you reach **Ulupalakua Ranch**, a lush counterpoint to the lava wasteland behind. With its grassy acres and curving rangeland, the ranch provides a perfect introduction to Maui's Upcountry region.

Along the Hana Highway out in Paia, about seven miles from   **LODGING**
Kahului, sits **Nalu Kai Lodge**. Tucked behind the Wine Corner Liquor Store near the town hub, this seven-unit resting place is

a real sleeper. The rooms are often occupied by long-term renters. But if you snag one of the vacant rooms, you'll check into a small, plain cubicle with no carpeting and little decoration. And only one of the rooms has a double bed. Sound unappealing? Well, even bare walls sometimes look good at the right price. ~ Nalu Lane, off Hana Highway; 808-579-8009. BUDGET.

A very convenient accommodation located on the Hana Highway in Keanae is the Maui YMCA's **Camp Keanae**. For just $15 a night, both men and women are welcome to roll out their sleeping bags on bunks in the dormitory or one of five cabins. The camp overlooks the sea, and comes with hot showers, laundry facilities, full-size gym, kitchen and outdoor cooking area. Sorry, the maximum stay here is three nights. Guests must make reservations and provide their own bedding. ~ Hana Highway; 808-242-9007, 808-248-8355, fax 808-244-6713; e-mail ymcacamp keanae@aol.com. BUDGET.

HIDDEN ▶   **Aloha Cottages**, perched on a hillside above Hana Bay, has two-bedroom cottages and one three-bedroom cottage that are situated among banana trees and feature hardwood floors and redwood walls. The decor is simple, the kitchens are all-electric and many of the furnishings are rattan. Representing one of Hana's best bargains, the cottages have been recommended many times over the years by readers and friends. There are only five units at this small complex, so advance reservations are a good idea. ~ 73 Keawa Place; 808-248-8420. MODERATE.

You can also consider heading down toward the water to the **Hana Kai Maui Resort**. Located smack on a rocky beach, this pair of two-story buildings sits amid lush surroundings. The ornamental pool is a freshwater affair fed by toe-dipping spring water. The location and exotic grounds rate a big plus. Both studio apartments and one-bedroom condominiums are available. ~ 1533 Ukea Road; 808-248-8426, 800-346-2772, fax 808-248-7482; www.hanakaimaui.com. DELUXE TO ULTRA-DELUXE.

HIDDEN ▶   Speaking of scenery, **Heavenly Hana Inn** is blessed indeed. Located in Hana Town, this hostelry offers three suites and is entered through a Japanese gate. On either side, stone lions guard a luxuriant garden. The interior mirrors this elegance. Each suite is decorated in a Japanese style with futon beds, shoji screens and tiled bathrooms with soaking tubs. Continental breakfast, picnic lunches, tea and early dinner are provided for a fee. ~ Hana Highway; phone/fax 808-248-8442; e-mail hanainn@maui.net. ULTRA-DELUXE.

Hana Accommodations and Plantation Houses has cottages and studios. Scattered throughout the Hana area are homes with either mountain or ocean views; each unit is fully equipped with (or has access to) a kitchen. Many of the accommodations are decorated with tapa-cloth designs and Hawaiian paintings. Most are cooled with ceiling fans and all have outdoor grills perfect for a private feast. Some facilities are within walking distance of the beach and ancient Hawaiian fishponds. Gay-friendly. ~ Locations throughout Hana; 808-248-7868, 800-228-4262, fax 808-248-8240; www.hana-maui.com. MODERATE TO DELUXE.

Hana Alii Holidays offers a similar selection of accommodations—including studios and homes—in several price ranges. Here you can settle into a place on Hana Bay or on an idyllic hillside. Some units sit atop lava-rock bluffs overlooking the ocean, others are found in secluded five-acre settings. Most accommodations come with lanais, outdoor barbecues and full kitchens. ~ 103 Keawa Place; 808-248-7742, 800-548-0478, fax 808-248-8595; www.hanaalii.com, e-mail info@hanaalii.com. MODERATE TO ULTRA-DELUXE.

One of Hawaii's finest resting places is the **Hotel Hana-Maui**, a luxurious retreat on a hillside above the bay. From ocean views to tropical landscape to rolling lawn, this friendly inn is a unique, world-class resort. Spread across the 66-acre grounds are 76 cottages, all elegantly designed and devoid of clocks, radios and TVs. The hotel's health and fitness complex sponsors a variety of hiking excursions and nature walks. The adjacent 25-meter pool, landscaped with lava walls and monkeypod trees, enjoys a spectacular setting. The staff has been here for generations, lending a sense of home to an enchanting locale. Rates for this getaway of getaways are stratospheric, but I highly recommend the Hotel Hana-Maui. ~ P.O. Box 9, Hana, HI 96713; 808-248-8211, 800-321-4262, fax 808-248-7202; www.hotelhanamaui.com. ULTRA-DELUXE.

Don't forget the cabins at **Waianapanapa State Park** (for information, refer to the "Beaches & Parks" section later in this chapter).

GAY LODGING   The road to Hana is also home to several bed and breakfasts that cater to a gay, lesbian and straight clientele. **Golden Bamboo Ranch** has three suites and a cottage amid seven acres of gardens. There are views of the ocean through a horse pasture. ~ 422 Kaupakalua Road, Haiku; 808-572-7824, phone/fax 800-344-1238; www.goldenbamboo.com. MODERATE.

◆◆

SPRING TRAINING, HANA STYLE

In 1946, Hana hosted the only mainland American baseball team ever to conduct spring training in Hawaii. That was the year that financier Paul Fagan brought the Pacific Coast League's San Francisco Seals to the islands. Arriving with the players was a squadron of sportswriters who sent back glowing dispatches on "Heavenly Hana," helping to promote the destination and the Hotel Hana-Maui, owned of course by Paul Fagan.

Halfway to Hana House is a private and secluded studio with a mini-kitchen overlooking the ocean. Guests enjoy a great sunrise view. Stay seven nights or longer and you'll get a 10 percent discount. ~ P.O. Box 675, Haiku, HI 96708; 808-572-1176, fax 808-572-3609; www.halfwaytohana.com, e-mail gailp@maui.net. MODERATE.

The **Huelo Point Lookout** is set on two acres and bounded by the ocean on three sides. There's lodging in three cottages—the Rainbow, Start and Haleakala, each with a full kitchen. Also available is a lookout house, a two-story home complete with a full kitchen, dining room, and space for up to eight people. You can also enjoy the hot tub and pool. Gay-friendly. ~ P.O. Box 117, Paia, HI 96779; 808-573-0914, 800-808-871-8645, fax 808-573-0227; www.mauivacationcottages.com, e-mail dreamers@maui.net. DELUXE TO ULTRA-DELUXE.

Napulani O'Hana offers spacious accommodations within a few miles of Hana. It's a ranch-style house set on four acres. Enjoy the pineapples and papaya served in season. ~ P.O. Box 118, Hana, HI 96713; 808-248-8935, 800-628-7092, fax 808-248-7494. BUDGET TO MODERATE.

DINING

Paia, an artsy little town located just a few miles out on the Hana Highway, has several restaurants to choose from. If you don't select any of them, however, be forewarned—there are no pit stops between here and Hana.

HIDDEN ►

At **Jacques Bistro**, the look is decidedly young and attractive, making it upbeat and easy when ordering a meal you'll undoubtedly rate as delicious. The Pacific Rim menu of chef Jacques Pauvert hints of French and Italian origins. The fresh fish means a variety of things, depending on the catches of the day. Rich-sauced pastas like chicken farfalle are hard to resist. This is a top spot for people watching, Maui-style. Reasonable prices make Jacques a find for value as well as taste. If you're headed back to the coast after a Haleakala sunset, stop here for dinner. You won't regret it. ~ 89 Hana Highway, Paia; 808-579-6255. MODERATE TO DELUXE.

FISHING FOR FOOD

If you're craving a tasty fish sandwich, the **Paia Fish Market** is the place to go. When you're not in the mood for seafood, this eatery also offers hamburgers, pasta and Mexican dishes such as fajitas. It's is a casual place with plenty of greenery, and prints of water sports on the walls. ~ Corner of Baldwin Avenue and Hana Highway; 808-579-8030. BUDGET TO MODERATE.

For box lunches, drop in at **Picnics**. Open for breakfast, lunch and dinner, this light and airy café serves a variety of items including spinach-nut burger and mahimahi sandwiches. The menu also offers patrons basic breakfast selections, deli sandwiches, vegetarian options and plain old burgers. ~ 30 Baldwin Avenue, Paia; 808-579-8021; e-mail picnics@aloha.net. BUDGET.

The Vegan Restaurant is the prime address hereabouts for vegetarian food. Place your order at the counter—there are salads, sandwiches and hot entrées that include Thai specialties. ~ 115 Baldwin Avenue, Paia; 808-579-9144. BUDGET.

Bangkok Cuisine promises "authentic Thai food." They certainly sport an authentically attractive dining room decorated with tiles and pastel walls. There's also a patio where you can dine alfresco beneath an umbrella of palm trees. Oh, and the menu—Cornish game hen in a sauce of garlic and black pepper, eggplant beef and evil prince shrimp. Dinner only Saturday and Sunday. ~ 120 Hana Highway, Paia; 808-579-8979. BUDGET TO MODERATE.

You can also try **Mama's Fish House** outside Paia. This oceanfront nook is simply decorated: shell leis, an old Hawaiian photo here, a painting there, plus potted plants. During lunch, the varied menu includes Hawaiian seafood sandwiches and salads as well as fresh fish specialties. Other than a few steak and poultry dishes, the dinner menu is entirely seafood. Evening entrées include bouillabaisse, seafood provençal and fresh Hawaiian lobster. There are always at least four varieties of fresh fish, prepared ten different ways. ~ Hana Highway; 808-579-8488, 800-860-4852, fax 808-579-8594. DELUXE TO ULTRA-DELUXE.

If you plan to stay in Hana for any length of time, pack some groceries in with the raingear. You'll find only four restaurants along the entire eastern stretch of the island. Luckily, they cover the gamut from budget to ultra-deluxe.

Tutu's At Hana Bay, within whistling distance of the water,   ◄ HIDDEN
whips up French toast and *loco moco* (rice, hamburger and an egg smothered with gravy) for breakfast and plate lunches, sandwiches and burgers for lunch. ~ Hana Bay; 808-248-8224. BUDGET.

Hana Ranch Restaurant is a small, spiffy establishment decorated with blond wood and providing great ocean views. There's a flagstone lanai for outdoor dining. Open daily for lunch, they serve steak and seafood for dinner every Friday and Saturday. On Wednesday night they serve pizza. Lunch is buffet style or à la carte; in the evening they offer fresh fish, steak and baby-back ribs. ~ Hana Highway; 808-248-8255. DELUXE TO ULTRA-DELUXE.

There's also a **takeout stand** serving breakfast and lunch, with picnic tables overlooking the ocean. ~ Hana Bay. BUDGET.

Hana's premier restaurant is the dining room of the **Hotel Hana-Maui**. This extraordinary resort, perched on a hillside overlooking the ocean, provides three gourmet meals a day to its guests and the public alike. The evening menu features pan-seared veal chops, bamboo-steamed seafood and baked Hunan-style lamb. The menu changes seasonally. Dinner only. ~ Hana Highway; 808-248-8211, fax 808-248-7202. DELUXE TO ULTRA-DELUXE.

GROCERIES There are few restaurants and even fewer stores in this remote region, so stock up where you can. On the Hana Highway in Paia, **Nagata Store** has a small supply of groceries. It's open Monday through Friday 6 a.m. to 7 p.m., Saturday from 6 a.m. to 6 p.m., and Sunday from 6 a.m. to 1 p.m. ~ 808-579-9252. If you can't find what you need here, check the **H&P Market & Seafood**, which keeps the same hours as the Nagata Store. ~ In the Nagata Store, Hana Highway; 808-579-8362. You can also try the **Paia General Store**. It's open from 6 a.m. to 9 p.m. during the week, and from 7 a.m. to 9 p.m. on weekends. ~ Hana Highway, Paia; 808-579-9514.

Hawaiians called Maui's Isthmus *Kula o ka Mao Mao*, "the land of mirages."

Mana Foods has a complete range of health foods and organic produce. Open from 8 a.m. to 8 p.m. every day. ~ 49 Baldwin Avenue, Paia; 808-579-8078.

With a limited stock of grocery items are **Hana Ranch Store**, open daily from 7 a.m. to 7 p.m. ~ Mill Street, Hana; 808-248-8261; and **Hasegawa General Store**, open Monday through Saturday from 7 a.m. to 7 p.m., and Sunday from 8 a.m. to 6 p.m. ~ 5165 Hana Highway, Hana; 808-248-8231.

HIDDEN ► Clear across the island, along the back road from Hana, there's a sleeper called **Kaupo General Store** that's open from 9:30 a.m. to 5:30 p.m. "most of the time." You'll find it tucked away in the southeast corner of the island. Selling a limited range of food, drinks and wares, this store, founded in 1925, fills the gaps on the shelves with curios from its illustrious history. Closed Sunday. ~ Base of Kaupo Gap; 808-248-8054; e-mail kaupostore@yahoo.com.

SHOPPING Paia, just seven miles outside Kahului, is my favorite place to shop on Maui. Many fine artisans live in the Upcountry area and come down to sell their wares at the small shops lining the Hana Highway. The town itself is a work of art, with old wooden buildings that provide a welcome respite from the crowded shores of Kaanapali and Kihei. I'll mention just the shops I like most. Browse through town to see for yourself. If you discover places I missed, please let me know.

On display at the **Maui Crafts Guild** is a range of handmade items all by local artists. Here you'll find anything from pressed hibiscus flowers to sculptures. There are also fabrics, ceramics, jewelry, baskets, woodwork and other Maui-made items. ~ 43 Hana Highway, Paia; 808-579-9697.

Paia Trading Company has a few interesting antiques and a lot of junk. Among the more noteworthy items: turquoise and silver jewelry, wooden washboards, apothecary jars and antique glassware. Closed Sunday. ~ 106 Hana Highway, Paia; 808-579-9472.

Around the corner on Baldwin Avenue lies another shop worth browsing. **Maui Girl and Co.** features a fine selection of women's beachwear. ~ 12 Baldwin Avenue, Paia; 808-579-9266.

One of my favorite shops in Hana is the **Hana Coast Gallery**, located in the Hotel Hana-Maui. It features native Hawaiian art and artifacts and fine paintings by Hawaiian artists, as well as pieces by the novelist Henry Miller. Also here are beautiful serigraphs, model racing canoes in *koa*, ceremonial objects, feathered art, fiber collages and painted tapa cloth. ~ Hana Highway; 808-248-8636.

Also on the grounds of Hotel Hana-Maui is **Susan Marie**, a shop specializing in linen clothing, hand-painted items and handmade jewelry. Closed Sunday. ~ Hana Highway; 808-248-7231.

For everything you could possibly want or need, drop by the **Hasegawa General Store**. This store stocks everything from groceries, clothing, sandals and hardware to placemats, movie rentals, film, cards and gas. The original Hasegawa's burned down years ago, but the name is still famous. ~ 5165 Hana Highway; 808-248-8231.

NIGHTLIFE

In the early evening, you can enjoy a duo singing Hawaiian music at the Hotel Hana-Maui's **Paniolo Bar**. As relaxed as Hana itself, this low-key establishment is always inviting. ~ Hana Highway; 808-248-8211.

BEACHES & PARKS

H. A. BALDWIN PARK This spacious county park is bordered by a playing field on one side and a crescent-shaped beach on the other. Palm and ironwood trees dot the half-mile-long beach. There's good shell collecting and a great view of West Maui. The swimming is good, as is the bodysurfing, but beware of currents; the snorkeling cannot be recommended. For surfing there are winter breaks, with a right slide. Fishing for threadfin, mountain bass, goatfish and *ulua* is good. Facilities include a picnic area with large pavilion, showers and restrooms. ~ Located about seven miles east of Kahului on the Hana Highway.

HOOKIPA BEACH PARK For serious surfers, kitesurfers and windsurfers this is one of the best spots on Maui. The beach itself is little more than a narrow rectangle of sand paralleled by a rocky shelf. Offshore, top-ranked windsurfers or kitesurfers may be performing airborne stunts. On any day you're likely to see a hundred sails with boards attached skimming the whitecaps. The swimming is good only when the surf is low. There are picnic areas, restrooms and showers. ~ Located just off the Hana Highway about three miles east of Paia near Mama's Fish House.

HIDDEN ►   **HONOMANU BAY** 🏄 A tranquil black-sand-and-rock beach surrounded by pandanus-covered hills and bisected by a stream, Honomanu Bay is a beautiful and secluded spot. There are no facilities, and the water is often too rough for swimming, but it's a favorite with surfers. ~ Located off the Hana Highway, about 30 miles east of Kahului. Turn off onto the dirt road located east of Kaumahina State Wayside; follow it to the beach.

WAIANAPANAPA STATE PARK 🏊 🎣 🛶 Set in a heavenly seaside locale, this park is one of Hawaii's prettiest public facilities and is a very popular spot. The entire area is lush with tropical foliage and especially palmy pandanus trees. There's a black-sand beach, sea arches, a blowhole and two legendary caves. But pack your parkas; wind and rain are frequent. Swimming and snorkeling are good—when the water is calm—and the fishing is good. Facilities here include a picnic area, restrooms and showers. ~ Located just off the Hana Highway about four miles north of the town of Hana.

▲ There are sites for up to 60 people on a grass-covered bluff overlooking the sea. There are also plain but attractive accommodations renting for $45 for up to four people. Two additional people are allowed at $5 each. Each cabin contains a small bedroom with two bunk beds, plus a living room that can double as an extra bedroom. All cabins are equipped with bedding and complete kitchen facilities, and some have ocean views. A state permit is required. The cabins are rented through the Division of State Parks. ~ 54 South High Street, Suite 101, Wailuku, Maui, HI 96793; 808-984-8109.

HANA BEACH PARK 🏊 🎣 🏄 🛶 Tucked in a well-protected corner of Hana Bay, this park has a large pavilion and a curving stretch of sandy beach. It's a great place to meet local people. Swimming is fine; snorkeling is good near the lighthouse; and beginning surfers will find both summer and winter breaks on the north side of the bay (left slide). Some days are very calm, however. Bonefish, *ulua* and *papio* are routinely taken here and *moilii* run in the months of June and July. As well as the picnic area, there are restrooms and showers and there is a snack bar across the street. ~ Located off the Hana Highway at Hana Bay.

HIDDEN ►   **RED SAND BEACH** 🚶 🏊 🎣 🛶 Known to the Hawaiians as Kaihalulu ("roaring sea") Beach, this is one of the most exotic

Shell Hunting

With over 1500 varieties of shells washing up on its beaches, Hawaii has some of the world's finest shelling. The miles of sandy beach along Maui's south shore are a prime area for handpicking free souvenirs. Along the shores are countless shell specimens with names like horned helmet, Hebrew cone, Hawaiian olive and Episcopal miter. Or you might find glass balls from Japan and sunbleached driftwood.

Beachcombing is the easiest method of shell gathering. Take along a small container and stroll through the backwash of the waves, watching for ripples from shells lying under the sand. You can also dive in shallow water where the ocean's surge will uncover shells.

It's tempting to walk along the top of coral reefs seeking shells and other marine souvenirs, but these living formations maintain a delicate ecological balance. Reefs in Hawaii and all over the planet are dying because of such plunder. In order to protect this underwater world, collect only shells and souvenirs that are adrift on the beach and no longer necessary to the marine ecology.

The best shelling spots along Maui's south shore are Makena, Kihei beaches, Maalaea Bay, Olowalu, the sandy stretch from Kaanapali to Napili Bay, D. T. Fleming Park and Honolua Bay. On the north coast, the stretch from Waiehu to Waihee (west of Kahului) and the beaches around Hana are the choicest hunting grounds.

After heavy rainfall, watch near stream mouths for Hawaiian olivines and in stream beds for Maui diamonds. Olivines are small, semiprecious stones of an olive hue. Maui diamonds are quartz stones and make beautiful jewelry. The best places to go diamond hunting are near the Kahului Bay hotel strip and in Olowalu Stream.

and truly secluded beaches in all Hawaii. It is protected by lofty cliffs and can be reached only over a precarious trail. A volcanic cinder beach, the sand is reddish in hue and coarse underfoot. Most dramatic of all is the lava barrier that crosses the mouth of this natural amphitheater, protecting the beach and creating an inshore pool. This beach is popular with nudists. Swimming, snorkeling and fishing are all good. Technically, visiting this beach is illegal. There are no facilities. ~ This is one place where getting to the beach becomes a grand adventure. It is located on the far side of Kauiki Hill in Hana. Follow Uakea Road to its southern terminus. There is a grassy plot on the left between Hana School and the parking lot for the Hotel Hana-Maui's sea ranch cottages. Here you will find a trail leading into the undergrowth. It traverses an overgrown Japanese cemetery and curves around Kauiki Hill, then descends precipitously to the beach. Be careful!

HAMOA BEACH Located at the head of Mokae Cove, this stretch of salt-and-pepper sand with rock outcroppings at each end is a pretty place. Unfortunately, the Hotel Hana-Maui uses the beach as a semiprivate preserve. There are restrooms for guests and separate facilities for everybody else and a dining pavilion that is available only to guests, so a sense of segregation pervades the beach. ~ Follow the Hana Highway south from Hana for a little over a mile. Turn left on Haneoo Road and follow it for a mile to Hamoa.

KOKI BEACH PARK A sandy plot paralleled by a grassy park, this beach is more welcoming than Hamoa. Backdropped by lofty red cinder cliffs, Koki can be very windy and is plagued by currents. With a small island and sea arch offshore, it is also very pretty. Swimmers should exercise caution. ~ Located half a mile back up the Haenoo Road toward the highway.

▲ Primitive beach camping is allowed.

OHEO GULCH The stream that tumbles down Haleakala through the Oheo Gulch forms several large pools and numerous small ones. The main pools descend from above the Hana Highway to the sea. This is a truly enchanting area swept by frequent wind and rain, and shadowed by Haleakala. It overlooks Maui's rugged eastern shore. You can swim in the chilly waters and camp nearby. There are picnic facilities and outhouses; bring your own drinking water. ~ Located in the National Park's Kipahulu section (about ten miles south of Hana).

▲ Primitive, meadow-style camping is available on a bluff above the sea. No permit is required and there are no restrictions on the number of occupants but there is a three-day limit.

Maui's Upcountry is a verdant mountainous belt that encircles Haleakala along its middle slopes. Situated between coastline and crater rim, it's a region of ample rainfall and a sparse but growing population that is ideal for camping, hiking or just wandering. Here the flat fields of sugar cane and pineapples that blanket central Maui give way to open ranchland where curving hills are filled with grazing horses.

Upcountry

Farmers plant tomatoes, cabbages, carrots and the region's famous Maui onions. Proteas, those delicate flowers native to Australia and South Africa, grow in colorful profusion. Hibiscus, jacarandas, silver oak and other wildflowers sweep along the hillsides like a rainstorm. And on the region's two ranches—35,000-acre Haleakala Ranch and 35,000-acre Ulupalakua Ranch—Angus, Hereford and Brangus cattle complete a picture far removed from Hawaii's tropical beaches. Brangus cattle, by the way, are a Brahma–Angus hybrid.

Home to *paniolos*, Hawaii's version of the Western cowboy, the Upcountry region lies along the highways that lead to the crest of Haleakala. Route 37, Haleakala Highway, becomes the Kula Highway as it ascends to the Kula uplands.

SIGHTS

It's impossible to tell from the road the beauty within at the **Enchanting Floral Garden**. This eight-acre floral fantasy, however, is in spectacular bloom much of the year, thanks to dedicated owners Kazuo and Kazuko Taketa, who have spent nearly a decade planting and nurturing an amazing array of flowers. They drip from vines and trees in great swaths of vibrant color with the Maui lowlands for a backdrop. Admission. ~ Route 37, 10-mile marker, Kula; 808-878-2531; www.qpg.com/e/enchanting.

> Those cute little baby whales born in Maui waters weigh about 2000 pounds. They end up weighing close to 40 tons as adults— quite a weight gain!

The **Church of the Holy Ghost** (12-mile marker), a unique octagonal chapel, was built here in 1897 for Portuguese immigrants working on Maui's ranches and farms.

This roadway angles southwest through Ulupalakua Ranch to the ruins of the **Makee Sugar Mill**, a once flourishing enterprise built in 1878. A currently flourishing business, **Tedeschi Vineyards**, which produces a pineapple wine called Maui Blanc, sits just across the road. The tasting room is located in a building that served as a retreat for King Kalakaua, also known as "The Merry Monarch" because of his passion for composing hula music. Here at Hawaii's oldest winery you can stop for a taster's tour. ~ 808-878-6058; www.maui.net/~winery.

You can also turn up Route 377 to **Kula Botanical Gardens**. An excellent place for picnicking, the landscaped slopes contain an aviary, a pond and a "Taboo Garden" with poisonous plants and over 60 varieties of protea, the flowering shrub that grows so beautifully in this region. Admission. ~ Kula; 808-878-1715.

Several farms, including **Sunrise Protea Farm**, devoted primarily to proteas, are located nearby. ~ Haleakala Crater Road; 808-876-0200; www.sunriseprotea.com.

If you make a right from Route 377 onto the road marked for Polipoli before you get to Kula Botanical Gardens, you'll eventually reach **Polipoli Spring State Recreation Area**. This recreation area is the starting point for uncrowded, easy hikes on Haleakala's upper slopes. Head to Polipoli in the morning and you'll likely catch sight of hang gliders taking off on flights to the lowlands below. Note: The final half of the road to Polipoli is extremely rough; a four-wheel-drive vehicle is recommended. For more information on trails, see "Hiking" detailed at the end of the chapter.

Another intriguing place is the tiny town of **Makawao**, where battered buildings and falsefront stores create an Old West atmosphere. This is the capital of Maui's cowboy country, similar to Waimea on the Big Island, with a rodeo every Fourth of July.

HIDDEN ►

From Makawao the possibilities for exploring the Upcountry area are many. There are two **loop tours** I particularly recommend. The first climbs from town along Olinda Road (Route 390) past **Pookela Church**, a coral sanctuary built in 1843.

It continues through a frequently rain-drenched region to the **Tree Growth Research Area**, jointly sponsored by state and federal forestry services. You can circle back down toward Makawao on Piiholo Road past the **University of Hawaii Agricultural Station**, where you will see more of the area's richly planted acreage.

The second loop leads down Route 365 to the Hana Highway. Turn left on the highway for several miles to Haiku Road, then head left along this country lane, which leads into overgrown areas, across one-lane bridges, past banana patches and

HIDDEN ►

through the tinroof town of **Haiku**.

LODGING

A mountain lodge on the road to the summit of Haleakala offers a cold-air retreat that is well-situated for anyone who wants to catch the summit sunrise. For years, **Kula Lodge** has rented five chalets, some with fireplaces, sleeping lofts and sweeping ocean and mountain views. The individual chalets are carpeted wall-to-wall and trimmed with stained-wood paneling. The central lodge features a cheery restaurant, bar and stone fireplace. An appealing mountain hideaway. ~ Haleakala Highway, Kula; 808-878-1535, 800-233-1535, fax 808-878-2518; www.kulalodge.com. DELUXE.

HIDDEN ►

What more could an urban cowpoke ask for than a bed and breakfast with trail rides that begin in the front yard? That's the scene up at **Silver Cloud Ranch**, a nine-acre spread located at 3000-feet elevation on the slopes of Haleakala. In addition to a

Upcountry

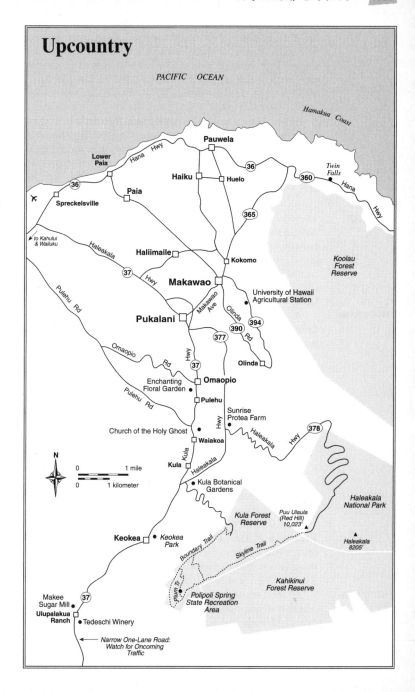

PACIFIC   OCEAN

Hamakua Coast

Pauwela

Lower Paia

Hana Hwy

Twin Falls

36

360

Hana Hwy

Haiku

Huelo

36

Paia

Spreckelsville

365

to Kahului & Wailuku

Haleakala

Haliimaile

Kokomo

Koolau Forest Reserve

37

Hwy

Makawao

University of Hawaii Agricultural Station

Makawao Ave

Olinda Rd

Pulehu Rd

Pukalani

394

390

377

Omaopio

Rd

Hwy

37

Olinda

Enchanting Floral Garden

Omaopio

Pulehu Rd

Pulehu

Sunrise Protea Farm

378

Haleakala Hwy

Church of the Holy Ghost

Hwy

Waiakoa

N

0   1 mile

0   1 kilometer

Kula

Kula

Haleakala

Kula Botanical Gardens

Haleakala National Park

Kula Forest Reserve

Puu Ulaula (Red Hill) 10,023'

Keokea

Keokea Park

Boundary Trail

Skyline Trail

Haleakala 8205'

Kahikinui Forest Reserve

Makee Sugar Mill

Ulupalakua Ranch

37

Plum Tr.

Polipoli Spring State Recreation Area

Tedeschi Winery

← Narrow One-Lane Road: Watch for Oncoming Traffic

broad swath of cattle country, the ranch looks out over several neighboring islands. Accommodations include six bedrooms in a big ranch house, a bunkhouse with five studio units and a private cottage. Full breakfast, pardner. There's a $15 surcharge for one-night stays. ~ R.R. 2, Box 201, Kula, HI 96790; 808-878-6101, 800-532-1111, fax 808-878-2132; www.silvercloudranch.com. MODERATE TO DELUXE.

Kailua Maui Gardens, a gay-owned, mixed-clientele guest house, has everything from a one-room cottage to a three-bedroom house with a pool. It's set in a tropical garden with shaded paths and bridges plus a spa. Two-night minimum; rates drop with length of stay. ~ S.R. 1 Box 9, Haiku, HI 96708; 808-572-9726, 800-258-8588; www.maui.net/~kmg. MODERATE.

DINING

There are several good dining spots in Pukalani Terrace Center. Among them is **Nick's Place**, a breakfast-and-lunch-only cafeteria serving Japanese-Chinese-American fare. Choose from such à la carte items as *chow fun*, tempura, Portuguese sausage, stew or corned-beef hash; together they make a hearty meal. At breakfast, try the eggs with Portuguese sausage. ~ Pukalani Terrace Center, Haleakala Highway, Pukalani; 808-572-8258. BUDGET.

HIDDEN ►

A good local restaurant for breakfast or lunch is the **Up Country Café**. The theme here is bovine all the way, with the restaurant decked out in everything from cow bells to cow salt-and-pepper shakers. Breakfast is pretty predictable; lunch includes a half-dozen entrées such as teriyaki beef and New York steak, as well as such nonbovine fare as chicken curry with fresh country vegetables, sautéed mahimahi and vegetarian lasagna. Also open for dinner Monday through Saturday. ~ Haleakala Highway and Aewa Place, Pukalani; 808-572-2395. BUDGET TO MODERATE.

For something a step more upscale, consider the **Makawao Steak House**. Knotty pine walls and a comfortable lounge lend the place an air of refined rusticity. The popular menu serves a mix of surf-and-turf dishes; unfortunately there are no vegetarian dishes. Dinner only. ~ 3612 Baldwin Avenue, Makawao; 808-572-8711. DELUXE.

In Makawao, you can go Mediterranean at **Casanova Italian Restaurant & Deli**, a stylish bistro that serves Italian-style seafood, pasta dishes, and pizza. For something faster, cheaper and more casual, you can try the adjacent deli. ~ 1188 Makawao Avenue; 808-572-0220. MODERATE TO DELUXE.

HIDDEN ►

Or head across the street to **Polli's Restaurant**. This sombreros-on-the-wall-and-oilcloth-on-the-tables eatery offers a full selection of Mexican dishes for three meals a day. A local gathering place popular with residents throughout Maui's Upcountry region, Polli's has become an institution over the years. It will inevitably be crowded with natives dining on tacos, burritos and tamales, as well as burgers, sandwiches and ribs. ~ 1202 Makawao Avenue, Makawao; 808-572-7808. BUDGET TO MODERATE.

On the lower slope of Haleakala, **Kula Lodge Restaurant** enjoys a panoramic view of the island. Through picture windows you can gaze out on a landscape that rolls for miles to the sea. The exposed-beam ceiling and stone fireplace lend a homey feel, as do the homemade pastries. Specialties include rack of lamb, pasta dishes and vegetarian entrées. ~ Haleakala Highway, Kula; 808-878-1535, 800-233-1535; e-mail info@kulalodge.com. MODERATE TO DELUXE.

GROCERIES

Along the Haleakala Highway there's a **Foodland**, open from 5 a.m. to midnight. ~ Pukalani Terrace Center; 808-572-0674.

You can also count on **Down to Earth Natural Foods** for health foods and New Age supplies. Open from 8 a.m. to 8 p.m. ~ 1169 Makawao Avenue, Makawao; 808-572-1488.

SHOPPING

Baldwin Avenue in the western-style town of Makawao has developed over the years into a prime arts-and-crafts center. Housed in the falsefront stores that line the street you'll find galleries galore and a few boutiques besides.

The Courtyard is an attractive woodframe mall that contains **Hot Island Glass** (808-572-4527), with a museum-quality collection of handblown glass pieces made in the store. Also here is **Viewpoints Gallery** (808-572-5979), which puts many of the higher-priced Lahaina galleries to shame. ~ 3260 Baldwin Avenue.

Gecko Trading Company is a small boutique that features contemporary fashions at reasonable prices, as well as other gift items. ~ 3621 Baldwin Avenue; 808-572-0249.

The kids will love **Maui Child Toys & Books** for its puppets, art supplies, wooden toys and music tapes. ~ 3643 Baldwin Avenue, Makawao; 808-572-2765.

Check out **Goodie's** for gift items: crystal mobiles, locally made jewelry, picture frames. There are also women's fashions, men's shirts and handmade Hawaiian baskets. ~ 3633 Baldwin Avenue, Makawao; 808-572-0288.

FIVE-STAR GENERAL STORE

Upcountry's contribution to Hawaii Regional Cuisine is **Haliimaile General Store**. A former plantation store that has been converted into a chic gathering place, it puts a creative spin on contemporary cuisine and serves roast duckling, fresh island fish and beef from the Big Island. No lunch on Saturday and Sunday. ~ 900 Haliimaile Road, Haliimaile; 808-572-2666. DELUXE.

HIDDEN ▶

On the outskirts of Makawao, the 1917 Mediterranean-style Baldwin mansion is home to the **Hui Noeau Visual Arts Center**. Here you can view rotating educational exhibits, purchase works by Maui artists or take the plunge yourself at one of the regular workshops on painting, printmaking, pottery, sculpture and much, much more. Closed Monday. ~ 2841 Baldwin Avenue; 808-572-6560; e-mail hui@maui.net.

In the Kula Lodge complex, the **Curtis Wilson Cost Gallery** sells prints, limited editions and originals by Curtis Wilson Cost. The emphasis is on local landscapes and ocean scenery. ~ Haleakala Highway, Kula; 808-878-6544.

Proteas of Hawaii specializes in gift boxes, Proteas and tropical floral arrangements. They also sell orchids. ~ 210 Mauna Place, Kula; 808-878-2533.

NIGHTLIFE   There are live bands on Friday and Saturday nights and deejay music Wednesday and Thursday at **Casanova Italian Restaurant**. One of Upcountry's only nightspots, it features a range of live acts—from local Mauian to internationally known. Cover. ~ 1188 Makawao Avenue, Makawao; 808-572-0220.

BEACHES & PARKS   **POLIPOLI SPRING STATE RECREATION AREA** 🏃 Located at 6200-foot elevation on the slopes of Haleakala, this densely forested area is an ideal mountain retreat. Monterey and sugi pine, eucalyptus and Monterey cypress grow in stately profusion; not far from the campground there's a grove of redwoods. From Polipoli's ethereal heights you can look out over Central and West Maui, as well as the islands of Lanai, Molokai and Kahoolawe. Miles of trails, some leading up to the volcano summit, crisscross the park. Polipoli has a picnic area, restrooms and running water. ~ From Kahului, take Haleakala Highway (Route 37) through Pukalani and past Waiakoa to Route 377. Turn left on 377 and follow it a short distance to the road marked for Polipoli. About half of this ten-mile road to the park is paved. The second half of the track is extremely rough and often muddy. It is advisable to take a four-wheel-drive vehicle.

In Maui's Upcountry, you may spot axis deer, Hawaiian owls and pheasants.

▲ There is meadow-style camping (a state permit is required) for up to 20 people; the cabin houses up to ten people and rents on a sliding scale from $10 single and $14 double up to $50 for ten people. The spacious cabin (three bedrooms) is sparsely furnished and lacks electricity. It does have a wood heating stove, gas cooking stove, gas lanterns, kitchen utensils and bedding. It can be rented from the Division of State Parks. It's recommended to bring in drinking water.

KEOKEA PARK This is a pleasant picnic spot on Route 37 in Keokea. There's a rolling lawn with picnic tables and restrooms.

It seems only fitting that the approach to
the summit of Haleakala is along one of   # Haleakala National Park
the world's fastest-climbing roads. From
Kahului to the summit rim—a distance of 40 miles along Routes
37, 377 and 378—the macadam road rises from sea level to over
10,000 feet, and the silence is broken only by the sound of ears
popping from the ascent.

At the volcano summit, 10,023-feet in elevation, you look
out over an awesome expanse—seven miles long, over two miles
wide, 21 miles around. This dormant volcano, which last erupted
around 1790, is the central feature of a 28,808-665-acre national
park that extends all the way through the Kipahulu Valley to the
sea. The crater floor, 3000 feet below the rim, is a multihued
wasteland filled with cinder cones, lava flows and mini-craters.
It's a legendary place, with a mythic tradition that's as vital as its
geologic history. It was from Haleakala ("House of the Sun")
that the demigod Maui lassoed the sun and slowed its track across
the sky to give his mother more daylight to dry her tapa cloth.

Technically, by the way, this area is an "erosional depression," not a crater. The converging headwaters of eroding valleys
met at the top of the mountain and scooped out the seven-mile
by two-mile bowl. Later eruptions studded the floor with cinder
cones and lava flows. "Erosional depression" is cumbersome compared to "crater," so if you are like me and still say crater, you
can at least claim to know the difference.

In the afternoon the volcano's colors are most vivid, but during the morning the crater is more likely to be free of clouds.
Before going up Haleakala, call 808-871-5054 for a weather report. Then you can decide what time of day will be best for your
explorations. Remember that it takes an hour-and-a half to two
hours to reach the summit from Kahului, longer from the
Kaanapali– Kapalua area. Be sure to bring warm clothes since
the temperature drop from sea level to 10,000 feet can be 30° or
more, which means the temperature may even be below freezing.

On the way up to the summit you'll pass **Hosmer's Grove** (6800-   **SIGHTS**
feet), a picnic area and campground surrounded by eucalyptus,
spruce, juniper and cedar trees.

National Park Headquarters, located at the 7030-foot elevation, contains an information desk and maps, and makes a good
starting point. You may be lucky enough to see the Hawaiian state
bird, the nene, which frequents the area around headquarters. Be
sure to keep your distance during nesting season. ~ 808-572-4400.

The first crater view comes at **Leleiwi Overlook**, an 8800-
foot perch from where you'll be able to see all the way from Hana
across the island to Kihei. Here at sunrise and sunset, under correct
meteorological conditions, you can see your shadow projected

on the clouds and haloed by a rainbow. To experience this "Specter of the Brocken," stand atop the volcano rim looking toward the cloud-filled crater with the setting sun at your back.

Up the hill, a side road leads to **Kalahaku Overlook**, a 9324-foot aerie that offers a unique view of several cinder cones within the volcano. Just below the parking lot are numerous **silverswords**. Related to sunflowers, these spike-leaved plants grow only on Maui and the Big Island. They remain low bristling plants for 20 years or more before blooming into a flowering stalk. Each plant blossoms once, sometime between May and November, and then dies.

The best view of the wilderness area is farther up the road at the **Haleakala Visitors Center**, 9745-feet elevation, where you'll find an information desk, as well as a series of exhibits about the volcano. From this vantage point you can gaze out toward Koolau Gap to the north and Kaupo Gap to the south. Several peaks located along the volcano loom out of the clouds; cinder cones, including 600-foot Puu o Maui, rise up from the crater floor.

From the visitors center a short trail heads up to **White Hill**. Composed of andesite lava and named for its characteristic light color, this mound is dotted with stone windbreaks once used as sleeping places by Hawaiians who periodically visited the summit of Haleakala.

It's a short drive to the summit at **Puu Ulaula Overlook**. From the plate-glass lookout you can view the Big Island, Molokai, Lanai, West Maui and wilderness area itself. On an extremely clear day this 360° panorama may even include a view of Oahu, 130 miles away.

Perched high above atmospheric haze and the lights of civilization, Haleakala is also an excellent spot for stargazing. If you can continue to the end of Skyline Drive, past the **Haleakala Observatory**, you'll see that it is also an important center for satellite tracking and television communications.

While the views along the volcano rim are awesome, the best way to see Haleakala is from the inside looking out. With 36 miles of hiking trails, two campsites and three cabins, the wilderness provides a tremendous opportunity for explorers. Within the belly of this monstrous volcano, you'll see such geologic features as cinder cones, lava tubes and spatter vents. The Hawaiians marked their passing with stone altars, shelters and adze quarries. You may also spy the rare nene (a Hawaiian relative of the Canada goose), as well as chukar partridges and pheasants.

HIDDEN ▶   The **volcano floor** is a unique environment, one of constant change and unpredictable weather. Rainfall varies from 12 inches annually in the southwestern corner to 200 inches at Paliku. Temperatures, usually hovering between 55° and 75° during daylight, may fall below freezing at night. Campers should come prepared with warm clothing and sleeping gear, a tent, poncho,

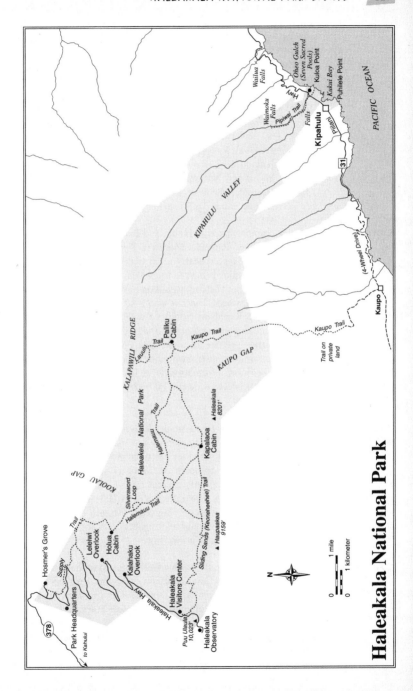

Haleakala National Park

PACIFIC OCEAN

Oheo Gulch (Seven Sacred Pools)
Kuloa Point
Kukui Bay
Puhilele Point

Wailua Falls

Waimoku Falls

Pipiwai Trail

Hana Hwy

Falls

Kipahulu

Piilani

31

KIPAHULU VALLEY

(4-Wheel Drive)

Kaupo

Kaupo Trail

Trail on private land

Kaupo Trail

Paliku Cabin

Lauulu Trail

KALAPAWILI RIDGE

Haleakala National Park

KAUPO GAP

▲Haleakala 8201'

Halemauu Trail

Kapalaoa Cabin

Silversword Loop

KOOLAU GAP

Sliding Sands (Keoneheehee) Trail

▲Haupaakea 9159

Halemauu Trail

Supply Trail

Hosmer's Grove

Leleiwi Overlook

Holua Cabin

Kalahaku Overlook

Haleakala Visitors Center

Haleakala Hwy

Puu Ulaula 10,023

Haleakala Observatory

Park Headquarters

378

to Kahului

N

0   1 mile
0   1 kilometer

lantern and stove (no open fires are permitted). Don't forget the sunblock, as the elevation on the bottom averages 6700 feet and the ultraviolet radiation is intense.

Within the wilderness area you can explore three main trails. **Sliding Sands Trail**, a steep cinder and ash path, begins near the Haleakala Visitors Center. It descends from the rim along the south wall to Kapalaoa cabin, then on to Paliku cabin. In the course of this ten-mile trek, the trail drops over 3000 feet. From Paliku, the **Kaupo Trail** leaves the crater through Kaupo Gap and descends to the tiny town of Kaupo, eight miles away on Maui's southeast coast. **Halemauu Trail** (8 miles) begins from the road three-and-a-half miles beyond National Park Headquarters and descends 1400 feet to the crater floor. It passes Holua cabin and eventually joins Sliding Sands Trail near the Paliku cabin.

LODGING   There are campgrounds at **Holua** and **Paliku** that require a permit from National Park Headquarters. Permits are given out on a first-come, first-served basis (not available in advance), so plan accordingly. Camping is limited to two days at one site and three days total at both. The campgrounds have pit toilets and nonpotable running water. There is also a 12-person cabin at each campsite and at **Kapalaoa**. Equipped with wood and gas stoves, pit toilets, cooking utensils, bunks and limited nonpotable water, these primitive facilities are extremely popular. So popular, in fact, that guests are chosen by a monthly lottery three months in advance. ~ For more information, write Haleakala National Park, P.O. Box 369, Makawao, Maui, HI 96768, attention: cabins; or call 808-572-4400.

Outdoor Adventures

The opportunities for adventuring on the Valley Isle are numerous and the conditions for several activities are outstanding. Whale watching, for example, is top-notch on Maui as humpbacks return each year to the waters off Lahaina to give birth. For cyclists, there are thrilling rides down the slopes of Haleakala and challenging courses on Hana's curving coast. Maui is also home to several of the world's premier windsurfing spots including Hookipa Beach on the island's north shore.

CAMPING   Though extremely popular with adventurers, Maui has very few official campsites. The laws restricting camping here are more strictly enforced than on other islands. The emphasis on this boom island favors condominiums and resort hotels rather than outdoor living, but you can still escape the concrete congestion at several parks and unofficial campsites (including one of the most spectacular tenting areas in all Hawaii—Haleakala Wilderness Area).

Camping at **county parks** requires a permit. These are issued for a maximum of three consecutive nights at each campsite, and cost $3 per person per night, children 50¢. Permits can be obtained at War Memorial Gym adjacent to Baldwin High School, Route 32, Wailuku, or by writing the Department of Parks and Recreation Permit Department, 1580 Kaahumanu Avenue, Wailuku, Maui, HI 96793; 808-270-7389.

State park permits are free and allow camping for five days. They can be obtained at the Division of State Parks in the State Building, High Street, Wailuku, or by writing the Division of State Parks. ~ 54 South High Street, Room 101, Wailuku, Maui, HI 96793. You can also rent cabins at Waianapanapa and Polipoli state parks through this office.

If you plan on camping in the Haleakala Wilderness Area, you must obtain a permit on the day you are camping. You can do so at Haleakala National Park headquarters, located on the way to the valley. These permits are allocated on a first-come, first-served basis.

Remember, rainfall is heavy along the northeast shore around Hana, but infrequent on the south coast. Also, Haleakala gets quite cold; you'll need heavy clothing and sleeping gear.

It is best to bring along your own camping gear, but in a pinch check **Gaspro Inc.** ~ 365 Hanakai Street, Kahului; 808-877-0056. **Sears** at Kahului's Kaahumanu Center also carries camping gear. ~ 275 Kaahumanu Avenue, Kahului; 808-877-2206.

More and more adventure tours are becoming eco-tours. **ECO-TOURS** Combining the usual tourist activities with a dose of conservation, eco-tours are a lovely way to soak up the beauty and culture of Hawaii while "leaving only footprints."

Mango Mitch Tropical Ecotours, a pioneer of Hawaiian nature tours, will tailor their tours to you but they won't take groups of more than five—the better to keep it personal. They have snorkeling, whale watching and various rainforest excur-

ABOVE MAUI

High above Maui looms Haleakala, the island's 10,023-foot shield volcano. According to legend, it was here that the hero Maui lassoed the sun and forced it to crawl slower across the skies, thus providing more light for his people. One of the benefits of driving to this remote spot is the rapid change in topography and weather along the way. Be sure to dress warmly (it's been known to snow), stay hydrated and rest frequently as you adjust to the change in climate. But when you reach the top, there's no way to prepare for the sight that awaits.

sions. ~ 220 Ulana Street, Makawao; 808-573-1848; www.maui gateway.com/~mangos.

The flora and fauna of Maui, as well as traces of the ancient Polynesians, are the focus of **Paths in Paradise**. The company's owner/operator is an environmentalist who will lead you on hikes to explore Hawaii's endangered nature. They have seven- and fourteen-day trips that include accommodations, hiking, snorkeling and a luau show. Shorter trips are also available, as are cultural trips to a hula school. ~ P.O. Box 667, Makawao, HI 96768; 808-573-0094; www.mauibirdhikes.com

An excellent educational opportunity awaits you at the **Ocean Project**, a marine research center studying the coral reefs of Maui. They have extensive knowledge and will build their events around your interests. At the beach, they'll give you a "class" in the subject of your choice (for example, identification of fish and coral species or the behavior of giant green sea turtles), and then take you snorkeling for an up-close look at what you just learned. The sessions are about two to three hours long and will change the way you view those pretty-colored fish. ~ Lahaina; 808-661-6706.

DIVING   Maui offers a wide variety of snorkeling and diving opportunities ranging from Black Rock off Kaanapali to Honolua Bay not to mention Olowalu, Ahihi–Kinau Natural Area Reserve and Ulua Beach. While most of the dive operators are located near the island's south coast resorts, there are also good diving and snorkeling opportunities on the north shore at Paia's Baldwin Beach Park, as well as Hana's Waianapanapa State Park. From Maui it's also easy to reach neighboring destinations such as the Molokini Crater Marine Preserve and reefs off Lanai.

Molokini, a crescent-shaped crater off Maui's southern coast, offers one of the island's great snorkeling adventures. Every day dozens of boatloads of people pull up to dive the remarkably clear waters. Visibility typically ranges between 80 and 150 feet, conditions so clear you can spot fish before even entering the

LATE SLEEPERS, TAKE NOTE

One of Maui's favorite rituals is a predawn trip to the top of Haleakala to watch the sun rise. Unfortunately, the weather can be foggy and cold. Besides that, getting up early is probably the last thing you want to do on vacation. If so, consider the alternative: Sleep late, take your time getting to the top and arrive in time for sunset. But, then again, you'll miss a dazzling, almost religious experience. In any case, call 808-871-5054 to check on the weather before making the trip up!

水。During winter months, you're also likely to see the humpback whales cavorting nearby.

LAHAINA **Extended Horizons** offers half-day excursions to the Molokini crater and Lanai's west coast. Dive through caverns and lava tubes in search of dolphins, turtles and whales. ~ Mala Wharf, Lahaina; 808-667-0611, 888-348-3628; www.scubadive maui.com.

Ocean Riders Adventure Rafting specializes in snorkeling trips; set out from Maui to Lanai or Molokai on full-day snorkel trips accompanied by schools of tropical fish and topped with a continental breakfast and lunch. ~ Mala Wharf, Lahaina; 808-661-3586.

Lahaina Divers Inc. is another well-liked dive operator. Their retail store provides equipment and accessories. Scuba classes and trips are available year round depending on the weather. Equipment repair and service are also available. ~ 143 Dickenson Street, Lahaina; 808-667-7496.

KIHEI–WAILEA–MAKENA AREA **Molokini Divers** features scuba and snorkeling trips to this popular islet. Visibility of 150 feet makes this marine preserve a favorite place to splash down. ~ Kihei Boat Harbor, Kihei.

Maui Classic Charters offers half-day dives into the Molokini crater along with schooner excursions. ~ 1215 South Kihei Road, Kihei; 808-879-8188; www.mauicharters.com.

Another recommended tour operator that also rents snorkel and scuba equipment is **Maui Dive Shop**, which has six locations in Maui. ~ 1455 South Kihei Road, Kihei, 808-879-1175, 800-542-3483; www.mauidiveshop.com.

Well-known by underwater photographers, **Mike Severns Diving** runs trips for certified divers to Molokini and Makena. His dives focus on the southwest rift of Haleakala, a fascinating place to study marine life. Led by informative biologists, these trips are an excellent way to see Maui's hidden marine life. ~ Kihei Boat Ramp, Kihei; 808-879-6596; www.mikesevernsdiving.com.

Maui Sun Divers provides all gear and offers everything from beginner trips to certification classes to night dives. A true part of "Hidden Hawaii," you won't find them on land. They will take you anywhere around the island, weather permitting. ~ Kihei; 877-879-3337; www.mauisundivers.com.

Experienced divers should sign on with **Ed Robinson's Diving Adventures**. A prominent oceanic photographer, Robinson leads half-day scuba excursions aboard the *Seadiver II* and *Sea Spirit* to the Lanai Cathedrals, Molokini and other favored dive sites. ~ Kihei; 808-879-3584; www.mauiscuba.com.

Makena Boat Partners operates the 46-foot *Kai Kanani*, which departs from Makena Beach, and goes closer to the largely sub-

331

merged volcano than other touring vessels. Prices include all equipment, food and drink. ~ 808-879-7218.

KITE-SURFING, SURFING & WIND-SURFING

If you must go down to the sea again, why not do it on a board? For surfing, Maalaea, Honolua Bay and Hookipa are consistent world-class spots. La Perouse is an expert's heaven.

Pro windsurfers and kitesurfers (a relatively new sport, this one is just what it sounds like) will want to head to Hookipa. Pros at other things should confine their windsurfing and kitesurfing to Kanaha, Kihei and Spreckelsville.

LAHAINA Goofy Fool has a portable surfing site they'll outfit you from; they also give beginner- to advanced-level lessons and lead surf safaris. ~ 505 French Street, Lahaina; 808-244-9283.

KAANAPALI–KAPALUA AREA Maui Ocean Activities offers surfing and windsurfing lessons on the adjacent beach. Ninety-minute windsurfing lessons come with a guarantee of success. Four-person surfing classes are also offered, weather permitting. Rentals are available. ~ Whalers Village, Kaanapali; Maui Ocean Activities reservations 808-667-2001, fax 808-667-5164; www.mauiwatersports.com, e-mail beaches@maui.net.

KAHULUI–WAILUKU AREA Maui Windsurf Company can help work windsurfing into your visit, either with a car rack and sails or with lessons. Instruction is held in the calmer waters at Kanaha, near the airport. Hookipa's more powerful winds are recommended only for experts. ~ 22 Hana Highway, Kahului; 808-877-4816; 800-872-0999; www.mauiwindsurf.com.

At **Second Wind Sail Surf & Kite**, you can get everything you need for a day (or longer) of surfing, windsurfing or kitesurfing. They offer equipment rental and sales, extensive instruction and even car rentals. ~ 111 Hana Highway, Kahului; 808-877-7467; www.secondwindmaui.com

You can buy surfing gear at **Lightning Bolt**, the oldest surf shop on Maui. ~ 55 Kaahumanu Avenue, Kahului; 808-877-3484.

HANA AREA Kai Nalu Surf Tours will take you on a four-day excursion to lesser-known Maui and Oahu surfing spots. ~ 536 Kahua Place, Paia; 808-579-9937.

FISHING

The deep blue sea around Maui can be nirvana for sportfishing enthusiasts. Choose between party boats, diesel cruisers and yachts custom-designed for trolling. All outfits provide equipment and bait. Just bring your own food and drinks and you're in business. Occasionally, your skipper may head for the productive game fishing waters between Maui and the Big Island. It's a treacherous channel, however, so you're more likely to fish the leeward side of the island or off neighboring Lanai.

There is also good fishing from the shore in many places. For information on the best spots, ask at local fishing stores, or try the following beaches: Hoaloha Park, Launiupoko State Wayside Park, Honokowai Beach Park, D. T. Fleming Park, Honokohau Beach, Keawakapu Beach, Poolenalena Beach Park, Black Sands Beach, Little Beach and Waianapanapa State Park.

LAHAINA Ideal for groups up to four, **Robalo-One** is a stable 23-foot vessel that hits speeds up to 40 miles per hour in pursuit of bottomfish. You'll catch snapper, wrasse, barracuda or jack crevalle on half-day trips. ~ 645 Lahaina Harbor; 808-661-0480.

Luckey Strike Charters fishes for marlin, mahimahi, wahoo and tuna with light and medium tackle. Light-tackle bottom fishing is also available. ~ Lahaina Harbor; 808-661-4606; www. luckeystrike.com.

Hinatea is a sportfishing boat that offers trips into coastal waters. On half- and full-day trips you'll fish for marlin, tuna, mahimahi, wahoo and shark. ~ Lahaina Harbor; 808-667-7548.

KIHEI–WAILEA–MAKENA AREA In the Kihei area, contact **Carol Ann Charters** for four-, six- and eight-hour fishing trips great for catching marlin, tuna, mahimahi and *ono*. She runs a 33-foot Bertrum. ~ Maalaea Harbor; 808-877-2181.

Rascal Charters fishes for ahi, *ono*, mahimahi and marlin. They also run four-, six- and eight-hour trips aboard a Bertrum, only Rascal's is 31 feet. Trips can include game or bottom fishing. ~ Maalaea Harbor; 808-874-8633.

From mid-December until the middle of May, it is prime whale-watching season on Maui. Humpback whales, measuring about 40 feet and weighing over 40 tons, migrate as many as 4000 miles from their summer home in Alaska. On the journey south, they consume tons of krill and tiny fish, then fast while in Hawaii. It is in the waters off Maui that they give birth to their young, babies that can weigh as much as three tons and gain up to 100 pounds a day.

SAILING & WHALE WATCHING

BE A CONTENDER

Imagine the thrill of big-time yacht racing when you sail aboard **America II**, a 65-foot America's Cup contender. There are morning whale-watching excursions from December 15 through April and afternoon tradewind and sunset sails the rest of the year. The trips last two hours and include soft drinks and snacks. ~ Lahaina Harbor; 808-677-2195.

Eager to protect the whales who winter in these waters, local officials have forced power craft to keep their distance from these cetaceans. But these restrictions are not so severe as to unduly interfere with the many sailing vessels that offer whale-watching opportunities off the Maui coast. You can also enjoy dive trips or pure performance rides on these beautiful vessels.

A prime area for whale watching lies along Honoapiilani Highway between Maalaea Bay and Lahaina, particularly at McGregor Point. So while you're visiting Maui, always keep an eye peeled seaward for vaporous spume and a rolling hump. The place you're standing might suddenly become an ideal crow's-nest.

Between 2000 and 3000 of the world's 10,000 humpbacks make the annual migration to Maui's southwestern coast each year. Today they are an endangered species, protected by federal law from whalers. Several local organizations study these leviathans and serve as excellent information sources.

The **Pacific Whale Foundation** issues daily reports over local radio stations during whale season. This same organization conducts "eco-adventure cruises," the profits from which help fund their whale protection projects. They have snorkeling tours to Molokini and whale-watching cruises, both led by marine naturalists. Most interesting is their dolphin adventure, where you snorkel Lanai's untouched coral reefs and see spinner and bottlenose dolphins in one of the island's many hidden coves. ~ 101 North Kihei Road, Kihei; 808-879-8860. Whale hotline: 800-942-5311.

LAHAINA Trilogy Excursions specializes in half- and full-day sailing adventures. They also offer whale-watching trips aboard a 41-foot sloop, as well as snorkeling excursions, scuba trips, in-

SPELUNKING

Lava tubes form when surface lava hardens and the flowing lava continues to drain downslope through a tube. **Hana Cave Tours** offers excursions through a two-mile-long lava tube that winds its way 30 to 40 feet below the surface. You'll be fully outfitted with a hard hat, gloves, a fanny pack with water, and a powerful flashlight that illuminates even the largest caverns in this long, linear cave. There are one- and two-hour tours, each taking in more of the cave system, all with plenty of interesting detail about what you're passing through. Snacks or meals are provided. Turn toward the ocean when you hit Ulaino Road, which is just before the Hana Airport Road. ~ P.O. Box 40, Hana, HI 96713; 808-248-7308; www.mauicave.com.

struction and joysailing. Special trips include Molokini crater and Lanai. Trilogy receives high praise from repeat clients who climb aboard the 50-foot catamaran for excursions to Lanai. Once on the nearby island, they can swim and snorkel Hulopoe Bay Marine Reserve, enjoy a Hawaiian barbecue and tour Lanai City. Trips depart from Lahaina, Maalaea harbors and Kaanapali Resort beach. ~ Lahaina Harbor; 808-661-4743.

Scotch Mist Sailing Charters offers half-day snorkeling trips to Lanai. Whale watching, sailing and champagne-and-chocolate sunset sails are also available. ~ Lahaina Harbor; 808-661-0386.

Windjammer Cruises has a 70-foot, three-masted schooner ideal for whale watching in addition to brunch and sunset dinner sails. You can dine on island cuisine, enjoy traditional Polynesian entertainment and take in the vistas of Kahoolawe, Molokai and Lanai. Sunset dinner cruises daily, brunch cruises on Friday and Sunday. ~ Lahaina Harbor; 808-661-8600, 800-732-4852.

Or, for a more intimate experience, try the six-passenger **Cinderella**, a 50-foot luxury sailboat. ~ Maalaea Harbor; 808-244-0009.

Operating out of Maalaea Bay, which boasts some of the best sailing in the world, **Hawaiian Charters Inc.** has several options. You can take a morning sail/snorkel intended for all levels (although they specialize in beginners), an afternoon sail/whale watch or a sunset sail. ~ P.O. Box 959, Kihei, HI 96753; 808-244-6655; www.mauisailing.net.

Island Marine Activities offers whale-spotting cruises from mid-December to May. They also have fine-dining sunset dinner cruises, Molokini Crater snorkel tours, and four package tours to Molokai, from a walking tour to a car rental package. ~ 113 Prison Street, Lahaina; 808-661-8397.

KAANAPALI–KAPALUA AREA   **Kapalua Kai** is a popular catamaran offering picnic-and-snorkeling and sunset sails. It sails Maui's most scenic waters and features whale-watching excursions in winter months. Scuba trips also available. ~ Kaanapali; 808-667-5980; www.sailingmaui.com.

Lahaina and Kaanapali Beach are perfect places to become airborne. Wonderful views of Maui's west side and neighboring Molokai add to the fun. The typical parasailing trip includes 30 to 45 minutes shuttling out and back to the launch point and eight to ten minutes in the air.

Parasail Kaanapali riders rise as high as 900 feet, single or tandem. Closed mid-December to mid-May. ~ Mala Wharf, Lahaina; 808-669-6555. UFO **Parasail** lets you ascend up to 800 feet and also fly with a companion. Open mid-May to mid-December. ~ Whalers Village, Kaanapali; 808-661-7836.

PARA-SAILING & HANG GLIDING

For hang gliding from some of the most beautiful spots on the island, try **Hang Gliding Maui**. They also operate motorized hanggliding out of Hana Airport. Reservations required. ~ Makawao; 808-572-6557; www.hangglidingmaui.com.

KAYAKING   A sport that's grown tremendously in popularity, kayaking is an up-close way to explore Maui's waters.

KAANAPALI–KAPALUA AREA   Kayaks are available from **Kaanapali Windsurfing School**. Trips are offered through the Hyatt Regency. ~ Whalers Village, Kaanapali; Maui Ocean Activities reservations 808-667-1964.

KIHEI–WAILEA–MAKENA AREA   Kayak rentals and tours can also be arranged through **South Pacific Kayaks**. Their naturalist-guided trips include snorkeling, and you're likely to see whales, sea turtles and dolphins, depending on the season. ~ 2439 South Kihei Road, Kihei; 808-875-4848; www.mauikayak.com, e-mail seakayaks@maui.net.

KAHULUI–WAILUKU AREA   In Central Maui, **Maui Sea Kayaking** offers day trips to Maui and Lanai and full-moon trips to Molokini. Or they'll lead you on an overnight "romance" retreat, for which a guide will arrange a seaside campsite that is off the beaten track and inaccessible by car. In the morning, the guide will return to prepare your breakfast and lead the way back to civilization. They also lead kayak and wave-ski surfers to beaches good for surfing. Maximum four people. ~ Puunene; 808-572-6299; www.maui.net/~kayaking.

RAFTING   Rafting trips are the adventurous way to enjoy the Maui coast. Easily combined with dive and whale-watching trips, these sturdy craft are a great way to reach hidden coves and beaches.

LAHAINA   **Hawaiian Rafting Adventures** operates half- and full-day trips to Lanai and Lanai dive trips. Whale-watching ex-

---

KAYAK CAREENING

An easy-going kayaking excursion along the Makena–La Perouse area can be had with **Kelii's Kayak Tours**. Rising early in the morning, you get a quick lesson on ocean kayaking, and then venture off the shoreline in search of Maui's sea life. Those lazy-looking sea turtles bobbing alongside you don't have to work as hard as you do. The trip concludes with a dip in the sea for an up-close-and-personal snorkeling adventure. Kelii's also offers north shore tour excursions in the Honolua Bay/Honokohau area. ~158 Lanakila Place, Kihei; 808-874-7652, 888-874-7652; e-mail kelii@maui.net.

cursions are great fun in the winter months. ~ 1223 Front Street, Lahaina; 808-661-7333; www.thesupersites.com/hirafting.

Ocean Riders Adventure Rafting will take you out to Lanai and, weather permitting, Molokai, for a glorious day of snorkeling, as well as whale watching during whale season. All trips are aboard rigid-hull inflatable boats. ~ Mala Wharf, Lahaina; 808-661-3586; www.mauioceanriders.com.

Another company offering tours is **Captain Steve's Rafting Excursions**, which heads out regularly in search of tropical fish, dolphins and exotic birdlife. One trip not to miss circumnavigates Lanai. ~ Mala Wharf, Lahaina; 808-667-5565; e-mail office@captainsteves.com.

Full- and half-day trips are offered aboard **Hawaii Ocean Rafting**'s vessel, a motorized raft that takes you to a variety of different snorkeling spots while spinner dolphins leap picturesquely in your wake. ~ P.O. Box 381, Lahaina, HI 96767; 808-667-2191.

KIHEI–WAILEA–MAKENA AREA   **Blue Water Rafting** offers both rafting and snorkeling trips to Molokini. ~ Kihei Boat Ramp, Kihei; 808-879-7238; www.bluewaterrafting.com.

Maui's volcanic landscape, beaches and sculptured valleys are choice sites for equestrian excursions. A variety of rides are available across the island—from the shoreline of Hana to the slopes of Haleakala, you can count on seeing wildlife, lava fields and those famous Maui sunsets.

RIDING STABLES

KIHEI–WAILEA–MAKENA AREA   **Makena Stables** leads trail rides across the scenic 20,000-acre Ulupalakua Ranch on the south slope of Haleakala. Mountain trails cross a 200-year-old lava flow. Choose among two-hour, three-hour and all-day rides. Possibilities include visiting La Perouse Bay or Kalua Olapa, which is an old, inactive volcanic vent, and sunset rides. ~ 8299 South Makena Road, Makena; 808-879-0244; www.makenastables.com.

HANA HIGHWAY   **Oheo Stables** offers outings up the back slope of Haleakala. Trips ascend through a tropical rainforest and include views of waterfalls and the Kipahulu Valley. Highlights include the view from Pipiwai lookout above Oheo Gulch. Six riders maximum. ~ Hana Highway, one mile south of National Park Headquarters at Pools of Ohea; 808-667-2222.

UPCOUNTRY AND HALEAKALA   Hit the trail on Maui's north shore with **Adventures on Horseback** and you will ride along 300-foot cliffs, see lush rainforests and take a break to swim in waterfall-fed pools. Six riders maximum. ~ Makawao; 808-242-7445.

Ironwood Ranch in Napili offers some easy, scenic excursions including a jaunt through a pineapple plantation and a sunset view from horseback. Most of the trips are three-and-a-half hours. ~ Lahaina; 808-669-4991.

At **Thompson Ranch and Riding Stables** ride through pastureland on short day and sunset trips that offer views of the other islands. Trips are suitable for children. ~ Thompson Road, Kula; 808-878-1910.

For tours of Haleakala National Park, contact **Pony Express Tours**, which leads half- and full-day horseback trips to the crater. Rides in the Haleakala Ranch are available, as is a one-hour introduction to horse riding. Closed Sunday. ~ 808-667-2200; www.ponyexpresstours.com. On the weekends **Charlie's Trail Rides and Pack Trips** provides overnight horseback trips from Kaupo through Haleakala. There is a six-person maximum on overnight trips. Two- and four-hour trips outside the Park are also available. Meals are included in the travel package. ~ 808-248-8209.

GOLF

With more than a dozen public and private courses, Maui is golf heaven. Choices on the Valley Isle range from country club links to inexpensive community courses. Also, several resorts offer a choice of championship courses ideal for golfers looking for a change of pace. These are open to the public for a hefty fee. Consider reserving tee-times before your visit, especially during the high season. Some courses allow you to book up to a month in advance.

KAANAPALI–KAPALUA AREA   The **Kaanapali Golf Courses** are among the island's finest. The championship par-71 North Course, designed by golf course architect Robert Trent Jones, Sr., has a slight incline. The easier South Course is intersected by Maui's popular sugar cane train. ~ Kaanapali Beach Resort, Kaanapali; 808-661-3691; www.kaanapali-golf.com.

With three courses, the **Kapalua Golf Club** is one of the best places to golf on Maui. For a real challenge, try the par-73 Plantation Course built in the heart of pineapple country. The oceanfront Bay Course, and the Village Course, which ascends into the foothills, were created by Arnold Palmer himself. ~ 300 Kapalua Drive, Kapalua; 808-669-8044.

KIHEI–WAILEA–MAKENA AREA   The **Wailea Golf Club**, located in the heart of the Wailea Resort complex, offers three courses, all with ocean views. The 18-hole "blue course" heads uphill along the slopes of Haleakala. The least-challenging "emerald course" is also the shortest. The "gold course" is the longest and most challenging, with 93 bunkers. There are two clubhouses on the premises. ~ 100 Wailea Golf Club Drive; 808-879-2966.

Located next to the Maui Prince Resort, **Makena Golf Club** has two 18-hole courses. Designed by Robert Trent Jones, Jr., the "North" and "South" courses are intended to blend into the natural Hawaiian landscape while offering high-challenge golf. Rolling terrain and beautiful views of the neighbor islands make these links a treat. ~ 5415 Makena Alanui, south of Wailea; 808-879-3344; www.makenagolf.com.

KAHULUI-WAILUKU AREA   **Waiehu Municipal Golf Course** is the island's only publicly owned course. With a front nine on the shoreline and a challenging back nine along the mountains, this course offers plenty of variety. Other amenities include a driving range and practice green. ~ Kahekili High-way, Waiehu; 808-244-5934.

The somewhat hilly, par-72 **Sandalwood** was designed by Nelson and Wright. Three holes have lakes or ponds. There's a restaurant and pro shop on the premises, as well as a prac-tice range, a chipping green and two putting greens. ~ 2500 Honoapiilani Highway, Waikapu; 808-242-7090.

If you're planning to explore Haleakala volcano, be sure to bring cold-weather gear; tem-peratures are much lower than at sea level and the summit occasionally receives snow. Also, the air is very thin, so plan to pace yourself.

HANA HIGHWAY   The **Maui Country Club** is a rel-atively easy nine-hole course open to the public on Mondays. ~ 48 Nonohe Place, Paia; 808-877-7893.

UPCOUNTRY AND HALEAKALA   The upcountry **Pukalani Country Club**, on the slopes of Haleakala, is an 18-hole public course. Bring a jacket or sweater because these links can get cool. Boasting the highest elevation of all Maui's courses, this one is a sleeper (with great views). ~ 360 Pukalani Street; 808-572-1314.

TENNIS

If you're an avid tennis fan, or just in the mood to whack a few balls, you're in luck. Public tennis courts are easily found through-out the island. Almost all are lighted and convenient to major re-sort destinations.

LAHAINA   In the Lahaina area, you'll enjoy the courts at the **Lahaina Civic Center** ~ 1840 Honoapiilani Highway; or at **Malu-ulu-olele Park** ~ Front and Shaw streets. For more infor-mation call the Parks and Recreation Department in Lahaina. ~ 808-661-4685.

KAANAPALI-KAPALUA AREA   There are several resorts in the area that open their courts to the public for a fee. One is the **Hyatt Regency Maui** ~ 200 Nohea Kai Drive, Kaanapali; 808-661-1234. Another is the **Maui Marriott**. ~ 100 Nohea Kai Drive, Kaanapali; 808-667-1200.

The **Kapalua Tennis Garden** offers ten courts. Fee. ~ 100 Kapalua Drive, Kapalua; 808-669-5677.

KIHEI-WAILEA-MAKENA AREA   There are public courts at **Kalama Park** on Kihei Road and **Maui Sunset Condominiums** on Waipulani Road. ~ 808-879-4364.

Makena Resort Tennis Club is a favorite resort that lets the public use its courts. Fee. ~ Makena Resort, 5400 Makena Ala-nui, Makena; 808-879-8777.

Wailea Tennis Club has 11 courts. Fee. ~ 131 Wailea Iki Place, Wailea; 808-879-1958.

KAHULUI–WAILUKU AREA   In the Kahului area, try the courts at the **Kahului Community Center** on Onehee and Uhu streets and the **Maui Community College** on Kaahumanu and Wakea avenues. In Wailuku, try **Wailuku War Memorial** at 1580 Kaahumanu Avenue, or the public courts at Wells and Market streets. ~ 808-270-7389.

HANA HIGHWAY   In the Hana area try the **Hana Ball Park**.

UPCOUNTRY AND HALEAKALA   Popular Upcountry courts are found at the **Eddie Tam Memorial Center** in Makawao and the **Pukalani Community Center** in Pukalani. ~ 808-572-8122.

BIKING   If you've ever wanted to zip down a mountainside or go off-road in volcanic highlands, you've come to the right place. While Maui is best known for its downhill cycling trips, there are also many other challenging adventures. For example, you can enjoy the remote route from Hana to Ulupalakua or head from Kapalua to Wailuku via Kahakuloa.

For a friendly cruise down Haleakala on single-gear beach cruisers, contact **Maui Mountain Cruisers.** They serve breakfast or lunch on sunrise or midday rides, stopping for lunch at the Sunrise Market and Protea Farm. ~ 15 South Wakea Street, Kahului; 808-871-6014, 800-232-6284.

Chris' Adventures runs such intriguing trips as the Haleakala Wine Trek, a tour of the mountain's remote backside and a trip along the island's hidden northwest coast, complete with off-road biking. Unlike other bike tours, this company lets riders bicycle at their own pace. Other tour options include boat-bike tours to Molokai and a "volcano bike" trip. ~ Kula; 808-871-2453.

Aloha Bicycle Tours is a family-run operation that bills itself as a ride-at-your-own-pace tour company. Sounds like an especially good idea along these gorgeous routes. The volcano tour, for example, swings through Haleakala National Park, stops at a flower farm and Keokea (a.k.a. China Town) and descends to a winery. Minimum age is 14. ~ Kula; 808-249-0911, 800-749-1564.

At **Maui Downhill,** you'll enjoy sunrise day-trips and mid-morning runs on Haleakala. The sunrise run is a beautiful 38-mile trip from the crater to sea level. The longer trips include a meal; helmets, windbreakers, suits and insulated gloves are provided for all rides. ~ 199 Dairy Road, Kahului; 808-871-2155, 888-661-6887; www.alohafrommaui.com/mauidownhill.html.

Family-owned and -operated, **Cruiser Phil's Volcano Rides** also runs Haleakala downhill tours. Phil's has custom-built low-rider, single-gear cruisers and included with the uniform of safety gear are Kevlar motorcycle jackets. ~ 552 Keolani Place, Kahului; 808-893-2332.

Many people complain that Maui is overdeveloped. The wall-to-wall condominiums lining the Kaanapali and Kihei beachfront can be pretty depressing to the outdoors lover. But happily there is a way to escape. Hike right out of it.

The Valley Isle has many fine trails that lead through Hana's rainforest, Haleakala's magnificent valley, up to West Maui's peaks and across the south shore's arid lava flows. Any of them will carry you far from the madding crowd. It's quite simple on Maui to trade the tourist enclaves for virgin mountains, untrammeled beaches and eerie volcanic terrain.

One note: A number of trails pass preserved cultural or historical sites. Please do not disturb these in any way.

For more information, contact the Division of Forestry and Wildlife, Na Ala Hele Trails and Access Program. ~ 54 South High Street, Room 101, Wailuku, HI 96793; 808-984-8100, 808-873-3509, fax 808-984-8111.

You might want to obtain hiking maps; they are available on Oahu from **Hawaii Geographic Maps & Books**. They also sell informational guides and books useful for hiking. ~ P.O. Box 1698, Honolulu, HI 96806; 808-538-3952, 800-538-3950.

If you're uncomfortable about exploring solo, you might consider an organized tour. The **National Park Service** provides information to hikers interested in exploring Haleakala or other sections of the island. What follows is a basic guide to most of Maui's major trails. ~ Haleakala National Park, P.O. Box 369, Makawao, Maui, HI 96768; 808-572-4400, fax 808-572-1304.

All distances listed for hiking trails are one way unless otherwise noted.

KAHULUI–WAILUKU AREA   The main hiking trails in this region lie in Iao Valley, Kahului and along Kakekili Highway (Route 340).

Iao Stream Trail (1 mile) leads from the Iao Valley State Monument parking lot for half a mile along the stream. The second half of the trek involves wading through the stream or hop-

MORE THAN A WALK

Hike Maui has been offering hiking tours longer than anyone else on the island. They emphasize natural history, and their affection for their subject matter shows. One of the hikes wanders through Kipahula Valley, on the track of waterfalls and streams. You can swim through clear pools past ferns and hanging vines, then lunch at the top of a 200-foot waterfall. They also have volcano and coastline hikes. ~ P.O. Box 330969, Kahului, HI 96733; 808-879-5270.

ping across the shoreline rocks. But your efforts will be rewarded with some excellent swimming holes en route. You might want to plan your time so you can relax and swim.

Not far from Kahului Airport on Route 360, birders will be delighted to find a trail meandering through the **Kanaha Pond Wildlife Sanctuary** (2 miles). This jaunt follows two loop roads, each one mile long, and passes the natural habitat of the rare Hawaiian stilt, the Hawaiian duck (a species re-introduced to Maui in 1991) and the Hawaiian coot. The trails in the Kanaha Pond area are closed during bird-breeding season (April–August). The pond-kiosk area, which has a short observation "peninsula," is open year-round, but to hike on the trail, you'll need a permit from the State Division of Forestry. ~ 808-984-8100.

Northwest of Kahului, along the Kahekili Highway, are two trails well worth exploring, the **Waihee Ridge Trail** and **Kahakuloa Valley Trail**.

Waihee Ridge Trail (3 miles) begins just below Maluhia Boy Scout Camp outside the town of Waihee. The trail passes through a guava thicket and scrub forest and climbs 1500 feet en route to a peak overlooking West and Central Maui. The trail summit is equipped with a picnic table rest stop.

KIHEI–WAILEA–MAKENA AREA   King's Highway Coastal Trail (5.5 miles) follows an ancient Hawaiian route over the 1790 lava flow and is considered a desert region. The trail begins near La Perouse Bay at the end of the rugged road that connects La Perouse Bay with Makena Beach and Wailea. It heads inland through groves of *kiawe* trees, then skirts the coast and finally leads to Kanaloa Point. From this point the trail continues across private land. Because segments of the trail pass through the Ahihi-Kinau Natural Area Reserve, which has stricter regulations, call Na Ala Hele Trails and Access Program for more information. ~ 808-243-5352.

HANA HIGHWAY   Hana-Waianapanapa Coastal Trail (3 miles), part of the ancient King's Highway, skirts the coastline between Waianapanapa State Park and Hana Bay. Exercise extreme caution near the rocky shoreline and cliffs. The trail passes a *heiau*, sea arch, blowhole and numerous caves while winding through lush stands of *hala* trees.

Waimoku Falls Trail (2 miles) leads from the bridge at Oheo Gulch up to Waimoku Falls. On the way, it goes by four pools and traverses a bamboo forest. (Mosquito repellent advised.) Contact Haleakala National Park Headquarters for information on this trail.

UPCOUNTRY   The main trails in Maui's beautiful Upcountry lie on Haleakala's southern slopes. They branch out from Polipoli

Spring State Recreation Area through the Kula and Kahikinui Forest Reserves.

Redwood Trail (1.7 miles) descends from Polipoli's 6200-foot elevation through impressive stands of redwoods to the ranger's cabin at 5300 feet. There is a dilapidated public shelter in the old CCC camp at trail's end. A four-wheel drive is required to reach the trailhead.

Plum Trail (1.7 miles) begins at the CCC camp and climbs gently south to Haleakala Ridge Trail. The route passes plum trees as well as stands of ash, redwood and sugi pine. There are shelters at both ends of the trail.

> Brrrr... the lowest recorded temperature in the Hawaiian Islands was 11°F, in 1961, atop Haleakala!

Tie Trail (0.5 mile) descends 500 feet through cedar, ash and sugi pine groves to link Redwood and Plum Trails. There is a shelter at the Redwood junction.

Polipoli Trail (0.6 mile) cuts through cypress, cedars and pines en route from Polipoli Campground to Haleakala Ridge Trail.

Boundary Trail (4 miles) begins at the cattle guard marking the Kula Forest Reserve boundary along the road to Polipoli. It crosses numerous gulches planted in cedar, eucalyptus and pine. The trail terminates at the ranger's cabin.

Waiohuli Trail (1.4 miles) descends 800 feet from Polipoli Road to join Boundary Trail. Along the way it passes young pine and grasslands, then drops down through groves of cedar, redwood and ash. There is a shelter at the Boundary Trail junction.

Skyline Road (6.5 miles) begins at 9750 feet, near the top of Haleakala's southwest rift, and descends more than 3000 feet to the top of Haleakala Ridge Trail. The trail passes a rugged, treeless area resembling the moon's surface. Then it drops below timberline at 8600 feet and eventually into dense scrub. The unobstructed views of Maui and the neighboring islands are awesome. Bring your own water.

Haleakala Ridge Trail (1.6 miles) starts from Skyline Trail's terminus at 6550 feet and descends along Haleakala's southwest rift to 5600 feet. There are spectacular views in all directions and a shelter at trail's end.

Transportation

AIR

Three airports serve Maui—Kahului Airport, Kapalua–West Maui Airport and Hana Airport. The latter two are exclusively inter-island.

The **Kahului Airport** is the main landing facility and should be your destination if you're staying in the Central Maui region or on the southeast coast in the Kihei–Wailea–Makena area. American Airlines, Delta Air Lines, Hawaiian Airlines, United

Airlines, and a couple of charter companies offer nonstop service from the mainland.

If you land at the Kahului Airport, you will arrive at a bustling airport. I never realized how popular Maui was until I first pushed through the mobs of new arrivals here. In addition to the masses, you'll find a coffee shop and lounge, a newsstand, a gift shop, a lei stand, baggage service and an information booth (808-872-3893).

For weather forecasts on Maui, call 808-877-5111; marine conditions, 808-877-3477.

Kapalua–West Maui Airport serves the Lahaina–Kaanapali region. IslandAir flies into the facility.

Hana Airport, really only a short landing strip and a one-room terminal, sits near the ocean in Maui's lush northeastern corner. IslandAir lands in this isolated community. And don't expect very much ground transportation waiting for you. There is no bus service here, though there is a car rental agency.

BOAT

One of the few day-trip services in Hawaii is provided by **Sea Link of Hawaii.** Their 118-foot, air-conditioned power yacht, *Maui Princess,* provides trips several days a week between Maui and Molokai. The price is not cheap. ~ 808-667-6165.

Another ferry, **Expeditions** operates out of Maui and links Lahaina with Manele Bay on Lanai. There are five boats per day in each direction. The 45-minute trip provides a unique way to travel between the islands. ~ P.O. Box 10, Lahaina, HI 96767; 808-661-3756.

CAR RENTALS

If, like most visitors to Maui, you arrive at the airport in Kahului, you certainly won't want for car rental agencies. There are quite a few with booths right at the airport. A number of others are located around town. Most agencies require renters to be 25 years old.

In Kahului, the airport car-rental agencies are as follows: **Avis Rent A Car** (808-871-7575, 800-331-1212), **Budget Rent A Car** (808-871-8811, 800-527-0700), **Dollar Rent A Car** (808-877-2731, 800-800-4000), **Hertz Rent A Car** (808-877-5167, 800-654-3131) and **National Car Rental** (808-871-8851, 800-227-7368).

The rental agencies outside the airport include several companies that rent older model cars at very competitive rates. One of these is **Word of Mouth Rent A Used Car,** which strongly recommends reservations. ~ 808-877-2436, 800-533-5929; www.mauirentacar.com, e-mail word@maui.net.

If you find yourself in the Lahaina–Kaanapali area wanting to rent a car, try **Avis Rent A Car** (808-661-4588, 800-331-1212), **Budget Rent A Car** (808-661-8721, 800-527-0700), **Dollar Rent A Car** (808-667-2651, 800-800-4000), **Hertz Rent A Car** (808-

661-7735, 800-654-3131) or **National Car Rental** (808-667-9737, 800-227-7368). All of these agencies have courtesy phones at the Kapalua–West Maui Airport.

Dollar Rent A Car is the sole company in Hana. ~ 808-248-8237, 800-800-4000.

Kihei is served by **Avis Rent A Car**. ~ 808-874-4077, 800-331-1212. For a cheaper alternative, try **Kihei Rent A Car**. ~ 808-879-7257, 800-251-5288.

JEEP RENTALS

There are several companies on the island of Maui that rent four-wheel-drive vehicles. Some outfits offering jeeps are **Adventures Rent A Jeep** (190 Papa Place, Kahului; 808-877-6626, 800-701-5337) and **Budget Rent A Car** (808-871-8811, 808-661-8721, 800-527-0700).

MOPED RENTALS

A & B Moped Rental rents mopeds by the hour. These vehicles provide an exhilarating and economical way to explore the area. Though they are not intended for long trips or busy roadways, they're ideal for short jaunts to the beach. ~ 3481 Lower Honoapiilani Highway, Honokowai; 808-669-0027.

PUBLIC TRANSIT

There is almost no general transportation on Maui and the little that is provided lies concentrated in one small sector of the island. The **West Maui Shuttle** travels between Wailea, Lahaina, Kaanapali and Kapalua with stops at major resorts, Lahaina Harbor, the Sugar Cane Train and Whalers Village. ~ 808-877-7308. **Akina Bus Service** (808-879-2828) operates buses in the Wailea area.

Speedy Shuttle (808-875-8070) offers transportation from Kahului Airport to resorts on the west to the southside of the island. (It's recommended that you call at least a day in advance, though last-minute pickups are available.)

AERIAL TOURS

Much of Maui's best scenery is reached via serpentine roads or steep mountain drives. While the views are stunning, the best way to get a bird's-eye view is from the air. Helicopters, fixed-wing aircraft and gliders all make it easy to see the volcanic uplands, waterfall splashed cliffs and dreamy back-country beaches.

There's also a west Maui/Molokai flight highlighting the tallest waterfall in the state, Molokai's Kahiwa. **Hawaii Helicopters** offers tours ranging from 30 minutes to three hours. The longer tours stop in Hana for 45 minutes to three hours, offering a chance to explore this verdant area's beaches and waterfalls via limousine van. ~ Kahului Heliport; 808-877-3900.

Sunshine Helicopters offers tours that include whale watching when in season, waterfalls, island circumnavigation and private charters. ~ Kahului Heliport; 808-871-0722, 800-544-2520.

AlexAir, a Maui-based helicopter-tour company, offers pilot-to-passenger radio communication on all of its flights. They also offer choreographed CD music on the trips, and a free (two-for-one) sunset catamaran cruise. ~ Kahului Heliport; 808-871-0792, 888-418-8458.

Another option is **Blue Hawaiian Helicopters,** a company that has accumulated its share of accolades. They offer a standard roster of tours. ~ Kahului Heliport; 808-871-8844, 800-745-2583.

SEVEN

Lanai

Eight miles from Maui, across the historic whaling anchorage at Lahaina Roads, lies the pear-shaped island of Lanai. In profile the island, formed by an extinct volcano, resembles the humpback whales that frequent its waters. It rises in a curved ridge from the south, then gradually tapers to the north. The east side is cut by deep gulches, while the west is bounded by spectacular sea cliffs rising 1500 to 2000 feet. Lanaihale, the island's tallest peak, stands 3370 feet above sea level.

First discovered by Captain Cook's men in 1779, Lanai was long avoided by mariners, who feared its reef-shrouded shores and saw little future in the dry, barren landscape. You can still see testaments to their fear in the rotting hulks that lie off Shipwreck Beach.

Ancient Hawaiians believed Lanai was inhabited only by evil spirits until Kaululaau, son of the great Maui chief Kakaalaneo, killed the spirits. Kaululaau, a Hawaiian-style juvenile delinquent who chopped down fruit trees with the gay abandon of young George Washington, had been exiled to Lanai by his father for his destructive behavior. After the wild youth redeemed himself by making the island safe from malevolent spirits, Lanai was settled by Hawaiians and controlled by powerful Maui chiefs.

Most archaeologists doubt that the native population, which lived from taro cultivation and fishing along the eastern shore, ever exceeded 2500. Even periods of peak population were punctuated by long intervals when the island was all but deserted. Lying in Maui's wind shadow, Lanai's rainfall ranges from 40 inches along its northeast face to a meager 12 inches annually in the barren southwest corner.

Like Molokai, its neighbor to the north, Lanai for centuries was a satellite of Maui. (Even today it is part of Maui County.) Then in 1778 it was overwhelmed by the forces of Kalaniopuu, the king of the Big Island. Later in the century, an even more powerful monarch, Kamehameha the Great, set up a summer residence along the south coast in Kaunolu.

During the 19th century, Lanai was a ranchers' island with large sections of flat range land given over to grazing. Missionaries became active saving souls and securing property in 1835 and by the 1860s one of their number had gained control of Lanai's better acreage. This was Walter Murray Gibson, a Mormon maverick whose life story reads like a sleazy novel. Despite being excommunicated by the Mormon church, Gibson went on to become a formidable figure in Hawaiian politics.

Gibson was not the only man with a dream for Lanai. George Munro, a New Zealand naturalist, came to the island in 1911 as manager of a plantation complex that originally tried to grow sugar on the island and then turned to cattle raising. While his herds grazed the island's tablelands, Munro worked in the rugged highlands. He extended the native forest, planting countless trees to capture moisture and protect eroded hillsides. He restored areas ravaged by feral goats and imported the stately Norfolk pines that still lend a mountain ambience to Lanai City. And, most important, Munro introduced an ecological awareness that hopefully will continue to pervade this enchanting island.

The land that Gibson and Munro oversaw changed hands several times until James Dole in 1922. Dole, descended from missionaries, was possessed of a more earthly vision than his forebears. Pineapples. He converted the island to pineapple cultivation, built Lanai City, and changed the face of Lanai forever.

Filipinos, now about 50 percent of the island's population, were imported to work the fields. They bent to their labors all over Lanai, wearing goggles and gloves to protect against the sharp spines that bristled from the low-lying plants. Pineapples are cultivated through plastic sheets to conserve precious water and harvesting is done by hand. Up until the early 1990s, you could see hundreds of acres covered in plastic. Downtown Lanai would roll up the streets at 9 p.m., but the lights would burn bright in the pineapple fields as crews worked through the night loading the hefty fruits onto conveyor belts.

That was yesterday, back when Lanai retained something of an ambiguous reputation. Most tourists, hearing that Lanai was nothing but pineapples and possessed only 20 miles of paved roads and a single ten-room hotel, left the place to the antelopes and wild goats.

Now, however, the sleeping midget has awakened. You still rent your car in an old gas station with scuffed floors and deer trophies on the wall. And there are still only three paved roads on the island. But nothing else here is the same.

Stores have been renovated, old plantation homes have received fresh coats of paint, and two small clusters of homes have been constructed on the outskirts of town. Castle & Cooke, the conglomerate that now owns the island, has poured $350 million into the place, building two resorts and transforming little Lanai into luxurious Lanai. The Manele Bay Hotel, a 250-room oceanfront extravaganza, opened in 1991 just one year after the christening of The Lodge at Koele, a rustic but refined 102-room resort situated along Lanai's forested mountain slopes.

Meanwhile the days of pineapple cultivation are over. The output has dropped from a peak of about 16,000 acres to a mere 200 acres, sufficient to supply island needs and give visitors a glimpse at what life was like "back when." Fields are being converted to alfalfa and oats; cattle raising is being reintroduced; and the island's Filipino and Japanese population is quitting the plantation and going to work serving the visitors who make their way to Lanai to enjoy the two posh resort hotels and a plethora of outdoor activities like golf, tennis, biking and horseback riding.

In the midst of all the change, this lovely little isle retains its charm. Even now only a fraction of Lanai's 140 square miles is developed. The rest of the island is covered with a network of jeep and hiking trails guaranteed to keep the heartiest adventurer happy.

Here is an entire island that fits the description "hidden Hawaii." Almost all of Lanai's 3200 citizens live in rustic Lanai City at the island's center and most tourists are concentrated at the lodge at Keole one mile away or along Hulope Beach at the Manele Bay Resort. Just beyond these clusters lie mountains, rainforests, ranchlands and remote beaches—untouched realms ripe for exploration.

▼ ▼ ▼ ▼ ▼ ▼ ▼ ▼ ▼ ▼

Lanai City

Situated at 1645 feet, **Lanai City** is a trim community of corrugated-roof houses and small garden plots. Tourist brochures present the place as a quaint New England village, but until the Lodge at Koele was built the town was rather drab. Most of the houses were constructed around the 1920s in traditional company-town fashion. They are square boxes topped with tin roofs and tend to look alike. Norfolk pines break the monotony, and now that Lanai is much more self-conscious, many homes are freshly painted in a rainbow assortment of hues.

It is still a company town, but today the company is harvesting tourists instead of planting pineapples. Several housing developments and condominium complexes have been built on the outskirts to house hotel employees. With everything centered around the town square, Lanai City embraces almost the entire population of the island. Situated at the center of the island at an elevation midway between the beach and the mountain peaks, it is cool and breezy with a temperate climate.

Nevertheless, the really interesting places on Lanai lie outside town, and most require driving or hiking over jeep trails. It's advisable to get specific directions wherever you go, since the maze of pineapple roads can confuse even the most intrepid pathfinder. Where possible, I've included directions; otherwise, check with the jeep rental shop in Lanai City or at the hotels.

To be extra safe, ask about road conditions, too. The slightest rain can turn a dusty jeep road into a slick surface, and a downpour can transmogrify it into an impassable quagmire. I once dumped a jeep into a three-foot ditch when the trail to Polihua Beach collapsed. It had been raining steadily for three days and the soft shoulder couldn't support the weight of a vehicle. I was 11 miles from Lanai City with the wheels hopelessly embedded and an hour left until dark.

The way back led past pretty menacing country, heavily eroded and difficult to track through. Rain clouds brought the night on in a rush. I gathered up my poncho and canteen, convinced myself that the worst to come would be a cold and wet night outdoors, and began trekking back to civilization. Fortunately, after five miserable hours I made it. But the entire incident could have been avoided if I had first checked road conditions and had allowed at least several hours of daylight for my return.

This shouldn't discourage you, though. With the proper precautions, exploring Lanai can be a unique experience, challenging but safe. To make things easy, I'll start with a journey to the island's northeastern shore, part of which is over a paved road. Then I'll continue clockwise around the island.

LODGING

HIDDEN ►

Once the only inn on the entire island, the **Hotel Lanai** is a modest mountain retreat. Set 1600 feet above sea level and surrounded by Norfolk pines, it offers clean, medium-sized rooms equipped with private baths. The lodge was built in the '20s, as was most of Lanai City, but was refurbished several years ago. It features a restaurant and lounge, and is a local gathering place at dinnertime. A lot of folks hang out in the lobby here, making for a warm, friendly atmosphere, and the staff is congenial. Choose between small- and medium-sized standard accommodations and rooms with lanais. There's a cottage in the back and a U-shaped structure with only ten rooms, so reservations can be troublesome. It's advisable to arrange transportation with the hotel at the time of making reservations. ~ 828 Lanai Avenue; 808-565-7211, 800-795-7211, fax 808-565-6450; www.onlanai. com. MODERATE TO DELUXE.

The Lodge at Koele, a fashionable 102-room hideaway, is a study in style and decorum. The most noteworthy feature is the lobby, a vaulted-ceiling affair faced on either end with a stone fireplace that rises to the roofline. Etched-glass skylights extend the length of the room, illuminating the "great hall." The plantation-style guest rooms are done with four-poster beds, hand-stenciled walls, statuettes and decorative plates. To make sure you remember that even here amid the Cook pines you are still in Hawaii, an overhead fan beats the air in languid motions.

Backdropped by mountains and surrounded by miles of grasslands, the emphasis at The Lodge is on staying put. There are porches lined with wicker chairs, a croquet court, a swimming pool and two jacuzzis that look out on field and forest, and a congenial staff to take care of every request. Five-night minimum at Christmastime. ~ P.O. Box 630310, Lanai City, HI 96763; 808-565-7300, 800-321-4666, fax 808-565-3868; www.lanai resorts.com. ULTRA-DELUXE.

You can discover for yourself whether **Dreams Come True on Lanai**. That's what Michael and Susan Hunter, two local jewelry makers, claim can happen when you stay in the six-bedroom house they transformed into one of the island's only bed and breakfasts. Set in Lanai City and surrounded by fruit trees and flowering gardens, the house is decorated with hand-carved screens and furniture that the owners transported from Sri Lanka and Bali. There's a large living room for guests as well as a selection of single and double rooms, some with canopied four-poster beds. Swedish and Shiatsu massage available. ~ 547 12th Street, Lanai City; 808-565-6961, 800-566-6961, fax 808-565-7056; www.go-native.com/inns/0117.html, e-mail hunters@aloha.net. MODERATE.

DINING

HIDDEN ►

Henry Clay's Rotisserie at the Hotel Lanai offers wholesome dinners featuring an assortment of steak, seafood, pasta, ribs and other selections. Its knotty pine walls decorated with island photographs, this is a cozy place to share a meal. You can strike up a conversation with a local resident, sit back and enjoy the mountain air or bask in the glow of the restaurant's two fireplaces. Dinner only. ~ 828 Lanai Avenue; 808-565-7211, fax 808-565-6450. MODERATE TO ULTRA-DELUXE.

If the hotel restaurant is closed, Lanai City has two alternatives. The first is **S. T. Property**, a luncheonette that serves breakfast and lunch. ~ 417 7th Street; 808-565-6537. BUDGET.

HIDDEN ►

Your second alternative, the **Blue Ginger Café**, rests in an old plantation house and serves three solid meals a day. Traditional paintings and simple drawings of tropical fish adorn the place and the red paint on the cement floor has worn away almost completely. But the white walls shine and the dinners are served

*Author
     Picks*

CHAPTER FAVORITES

I had an eerie feeling when I arrived at Keahi Kawelo, the **Garden of the Gods**. It's like being on the moon, with geological formations that are otherworldly. *page 364*

For a drive on the wild side, I love to venture down to **Polihua Beach** at the end of the road that leads through the Garden of the Gods. One of the prettiest stretches of beach in Hawaii, it rarely shows the footprints of more than one or two other people. *page 364*

There's nothing quite like bouncing along in a jeep on the **Munro Trail**,

taking in views that extend down sharp canyons and out to neighboring islands. *page 355*

When I want to splurge, I check into the **Manele Bay Hotel**. It's a great place to begin a Hidden adventure—or would be if I could force myself to leave the hotel's pool, tropical gardens and white-sand beach. *page 360*

If I want to continue the splurge, I head over to the Lodge at Koele to dine at **The Formal Dining Room**, with its gourmet cuisine and views of the hotel's spectacular garden. *page 353*

piping hot. Breakfasts and plate lunches are pretty standard, but the evening meal is sophisticated enough to include New York steak, *kalbi* short ribs and mixed plates. ~ 409 7th Street; 808-565-6363, fax 808-565-6306; e-mail gabilay@aloha.com. BUDGET TO MODERATE.

On Lanai, isolation is the engine of ingenuity. Confronted with all that land and so few people, The Lodge at Koele transformed sections of the island into an organic garden, hog farm and cattle ranch. After adding a master chef, they had the ingredients for two gourmet restaurants that would be the pride not only of tiny Lanai but any island. Meals in The Terrace and The Formal Dining Room (jackets are required) are as enticing as the hotel's sumptuous surroundings.

The Terrace serves breakfast, lunch and dinner in a fairly casual atmosphere. Here the day begins with sweet rice waffles, breakfast bread pudding, or bacon and eggs fresh from the farm. By evening the chef progresses to oysters on the half shell and oven-braised lamb shank with herbed polenta, as well as vegetarian specialties. ~ The Lodge at Koele; 808-565-7300, fax 808-565-4561. DELUXE TO ULTRA-DELUXE.

The Formal Dining Room serves dinner only; feast on roasted rack of lamb or Lanai venison loin with mashed sweet potatoes. Both restaurants overlook the back of the lodge grounds, with views of the fishpond, fountain and orchid house. ~ The Lodge at Koele; 808-565-7300, fax 808-565-4561; www.lanairesorts. com. ULTRA-DELUXE.

GROCERIES   For standard food needs, try **Richard's Shopping Center**. This "shopping center" is really only a small grocery store with a dry goods department. Richard's is open Monday through Wednesday from 8:30 a.m. to noon and from 1:30 to 6:30 p.m., and Thursday through Saturday from 8:30 a.m. to 6:30 p.m. Closed Sunday. ~ 8th Street; 808-565-6047.

If, by some strange circumstance, you can't find what you're seeking here, head down the street to **Pine Isle Market**. Open Monday through Thursday from 8 a.m. to noon and 1:30 to 7 p.m., and Friday and Saturday from 8 a.m. to 7 p.m. Closed Sunday. ~ 356 8th Street; 808-565-6488.

SHOPPING   Granted, it doesn't have much competition (in fact it doesn't have any competition), but **Heart of Lanai Art Gallery** would be remarkable regardless of where it was located. Many of the paintings and sculptures were done by local artists and depict the plantation culture that was once Lanai's lifeblood but is now fast becoming its legacy. Call ahead. Closed Sunday. ~ 758 Queens Street (behind Hotel Lanai); 808-565-808-6678.

When James Dole bought Lanai in 1922, he paid $1.1 million for the entire island.

Don't miss **Gifts with Aloha** on the corner of 8th and Houston streets. This boutique, run by the genial Duprees, features Lanai and Hawaiian artists. Watercolor originals, pottery and wood pieces along with tempting jams, jellies and sauces, hats and casual resort wear round out the offerings at this Lanai-style (i.e., laidback) store. ~ 811B Houston Street; 808-565-6589.

Otherwise, you will have to seek out the gift shop at **The Lodge at Koele** (808-565-7300) or the **Hotel Lanai** (808-565-7211).

NIGHTLIFE   Visitors find this a great spot to get the sleep they missed in Lahaina or Honolulu. If rest isn't a problem, Lanai may be a good place to catch up on your reading or letter writing. One thing is certain—once the sun goes down, there'll be little to distract you. You can have a drink while listening to local gossip at the **Hotel Lanai** (808-565-7211) or while mixing with the gentry at **The Lodge at Koele** (808-565-7300), where the lounge possesses a kind of gentlemen's library atmosphere with an etched-glass-and-hardwood interior. But on an average evening, even these night owl's nests will be closed by midnight (*pupus* are served until 11 p.m.). In addition to its plush lounge, The Lodge at Koele fea-

Munro
Trail

Named for New Zealand naturalist George Munro, this seven-mile jeep trail climbs through rainforest and stands of conifers en route to Lanaihale, the highest point on Lanai. From this 3370-foot perch you can see every major Hawaiian island except Kauai.

On the way to Lanaihale, about two miles up the trail, you'll pass **Hookio Gulch.** The ridge beyond is carved with a defense work of protective notches made by warriors who tried futilely to defend Lanai against invaders from Hawaii in 1778.

A footpath leads to an overlook above 2000-foot deep **Hauola Gulch,** Lanai's deepest canyon. Here you may see axis deer clinging to the sharp rockfaces, seeming to defy gravity as they pick their way along the heights.

This knife-edge ridge, little more than 100 feet wide in places, is studded with ironwood and eucalyptus trees, as well as the stately Norfolk pines that New Zealand naturalist George Munro personally planted along the heights. From this aerie the slopes fall away to reveal the twin humps of Maui. The Big Island rests far below you, anchored in open ocean. The sea itself is a flat, shimmering expanse.

From Lanaihale you can either turn around or continue and descend through open fields to Hoike Road, which connects with Route 440. The Munro Trail begins in Koele off Route 430 (Keomuku Road) about a mile north of Lanai City. Be sure to check road conditions and try to go early in the morning before clouds gather along the ridgetop. While it's rough going at times, the trail affords such magnificent views from its windswept heights that it simply must not be ignored by the adventurous sightseer.

tures hula dancers on weekends at lunchtime or other live entertainment in the lobby (the "great hall") at night.

Northeast—Shipwreck Beach and Naha

From Lanai City, Route 430 (Keomuku Road) winds north through hot, arid country. The scrub growth and red soil in this barren area resemble a bleak southwestern landscape, but the sweeping views of Maui and Molokai could be found only in Hawaii.

By the way, those stones piled atop one another along the road are neither an expression of ancient Hawaiian culture nor proof of the latest UFO landing. They were placed there by imaginative hikers. Each one is an *ahu*, representative of a local tradition in which columns of three or so stones are built to help ensure good luck.

SIGHTS

Near the end of the macadam road you can turn left onto a dirt road. This track leads past colonies of intermittently inhabited squatters' shacks, many built from the hulks of vessels grounded on nearby **Shipwreck Beach**. The coral reef paralleling the beach has been a nemesis to sailors since whaling days. The rusting remains of a barge and a 1950s-era oil tanker still bear witness to the navigational hazards along this coast. Needless to say, this is one of the best areas in Hawaii for beachcombing. Look in particular for the Japanese glass fishing floats that are carried here on currents all the way from Asia.

HIDDEN ►

At the end of the dirt road, a path marked with white paint leads to clusters of ancient **petroglyphs** depicting simple island scenes. Those interested in extensively exploring the coast can hike all the way from Shipwreck eight miles west to Polihua Beach along jeep trails and shoreline.

Back on the main road (continuing straight ahead as if you had never made that left turn that led to Shipwreck Beach) you will discover that the macadam gives way to a dirt road that leads along the northeast shore for 12 teeth-clicking miles. It was along this now-deserted coast that the ancient Hawaiian population lived. Numbering perhaps 2000 in pre-Western times, they fished the coast and cultivated taro.

The ghost town of **Keomuku**, marked by a ramshackle church that's been partly refurbished, lies six miles down the road. It's another mile and a half to **Kahea Heiau**, a holy place that many claim is the reason Keomuku was deserted. It seems that stones from this temple were used to build the nearby Maunalei Sugar Company plantation despite warnings against disturbing the sacred rocks. So when the plantation failed in 1901 after its sweet water mysteriously turned brackish, the Hawaiians had a heavenly explanation. It was shortly after this incident that most of the rest of Lanai's populace moved up to Lanai City, leaving only spirits along the coast.

Several miles farther, past numerous salt-and-pepper-colored beaches, the road ends at the old Hawaiian village of **Naha**. Today nothing remains of this once prosperous colony.

SHIPWRECK BEACH 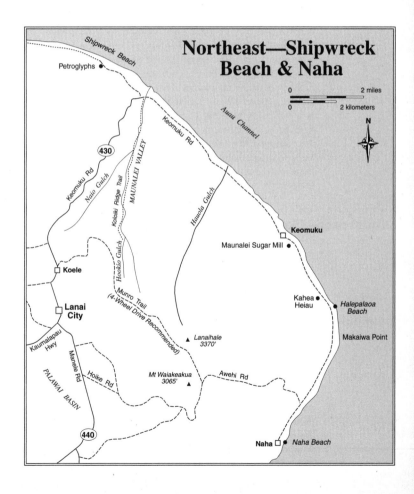 This strand is actually a string of small sandy patches that stretches for eight miles along the north coast, all the way to Polihua Beach. The glass fishing balls, driftwood and occasional nautilus shells on the beach make this a beachcomber's paradise. The remains of misguided ships

BEACHES & PARKS

Northeast—Shipwreck Beach & Naha

0 _____ 2 miles

0 _____ 2 kilometers

N

Shipwreck Beach

Petroglyphs

Auau Channel

Keomuku Rd

430

Keomuku Rd

Naio Gulch

Kolokī Ridge Trail

MAUNALEI VALLEY

Hookio Gulch

Hauola Gulch

Keomuku

Maunalei Sugar Mill

Koele

Munro Trail
(4-Wheel Drive Recommended)

Lanai City

Kaumalapau Hwy

Marele Rd

PALAWAI BASIN

Hoike Rd

Lanaihale
3370'

Mt Waiakeakua
3065'

Awehi Rd

Kahea
Heiau

Halepalaoa Beach

Makaiwa Point

440

Naha

Naha Beach

that gave the beach its name also add to the allure. It's often windy. You can swim here but the water is shallow and you must beware of sharp coral—a protecting reef is 200 yards offshore. Snorkeling is not advised because of sharks. There's good diving for lobsters, but again, be cautious! You'll find good fishing for *ulua*, *papio* and octopus in the area between the squatters' houses and the petroglyphs. There are no established facilities at the beach. ~ Ten miles north of Lanai City. Head north on Route 430 (Keomuku Road) and turn left at the end of the paved road. (See the "Northeast—Shipwreck Beach and Naha" section above for more details.)

HALEPALAOA BEACH AND NAHA BEACH 🏊 🛶 🎣 A string of salt-and-pepper-colored sand beaches lies along the 12-mile dirt road to Naha. While most are unattractive and crowded with shoals, they do offer great views of Molokai, Maui and Kahoolawe. The Naha road winds in and out along the seafront, with numerous access roads leading to the shore. The prettiest strand is Halepalaoa Beach, a mile-long white-sand corridor partially bordered by sand dunes. These are swimming beaches; most are well-protected by shoals, but the waters are shallow. Snorkeling is a possibility here but beware of currents. You can also fish here. Several beaches, including Naha, have small picnic areas. ~ Take Route 430 north from Lanai City and continue on after it turns southward and becomes a dirt road. The dirt road extends for about 12 miles, ending at Naha; Halepalaoa Beach is about seven miles out along the dirt road.

▼▼▼▼▼▼▼▼▼▼▼▼▼▼▼▼▼
Southeast—Manele Bay

Heading south from Lanai City on Route 440 (Manele Road), you'll be traveling through the Palawai Basin, the caldera of the extinct volcano that formed the island. This was also the heart of Lanai's once extensive pineapple plantation.

SIGHTS

HIDDEN ►

The explorer can detour off the main highway to the **Luahiwa petroglyphs**. Finding them requires obtaining explicit directions, then driving through a field, and finally climbing a short distance up a steep bluff. But the Luahiwa petroglyphs—portraying human figures, deer, paddles and turtles—are among the finest rock carvings in Hawaii and are definitely worth the search. As you approach each cluster of boulders, you'll see pictographic stories begin to unfold. One in particular depicts a large outrigger canoe, sails unfurled, being loaded Noah-style with livestock. Preparing, perhaps, for the ancient migration north to the Hawaiian Islands? To locate the petroglyphs, head south from Lanai City on Route 440. Turn left at the first dirt road. Follow the lower road as it curves along the bottom of the hillside. After passing below a watertank and pipeline, the road forks and you follow the left fork. The road goes into a horseshoe curve; when you come out of the curve there will be black boulders on the hillside above you to the left. Spread across a few acres, they contain the petroglyphs.

The main road leads through agricultural fields and winds down to the twin bays at **Manele Small Boat Harbor** and **Hulopoe Bay**, which together comprise a marine life conservation area. Just offshore from the cinder cone that separates these two harbors is a sea stack, **Puu Pehe**, known not only for its beauty but its legends as well. Puu Pehe was a lovely Maui girl kidnapped by a Lanai warrior who kept her hidden in a sea cave.

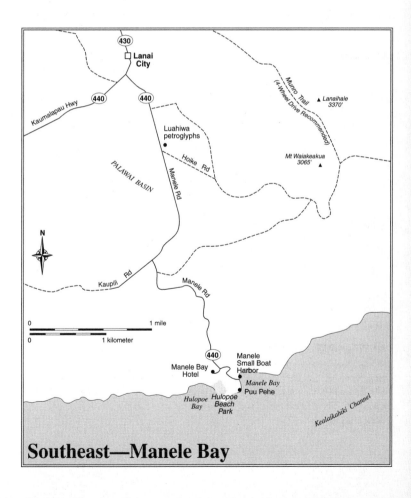

Southeast—Manele Bay

One day when he went off in search of water, a huge sea wave swept the girl to her death. Stricken with grief and remorse, the young warrior buried her on top of the rock island and then jumped to his death from its heights.

The small-boat harbor at Manele, rimmed by lava cliffs along the far shore, contains ruins of ancient Hawaiian houses. You'll also see an old wooden chute protruding from the rocks, a loading platform used years ago to lead cattle onto ships. Today this rock-rimmed anchorage is a mooring place for fishing boats and yachts. Hulopoe offers the island's finest beach, a crescent of white sand with gentle waves, crystalline waters and a fine park facility. You'll find the stone ruins of an ancient Hawaiian home and canoe house at the north end of the beach. Just above the beach, on the grounds in front of the plush Manele Bay Hotel, stands the remains of an *ahu* or traditional Hawaiian shrine.

LODGING   While The Lodge at Koele is situated at 1600-feet elevation in Lanai City, eight miles from the ocean, Lanai's other fashionable resting spot, the **Manele Bay Hotel**, is a traditional beachfront resort. Set on a bluff overlooking the best beach on the island, it is a 250-room extravaganza designed along both Asian and Mediterranean lines and surrounded by artistically planted gardens. Elegance here is in no way subdued: It speaks from the stone floors and white columns, the dark-paneled library and the recessed ceilings. The two-tiered lobby combines art deco windows with stylized Asian murals; the lower level is a terrace with glass doors that open onto ocean views.

Guest accommodations look out either on the beach or the grounds, which are sculpted into five different theme gardens—Japanese, Bromeliad, Hawaiian, Chinese and Kamaaina. Each room is spacious, done in pastel hues and decorated with Asian armoires and color sketches of Hawaiian flora. The four-poster beds are accented with quilts and upholstered throw pillows. Add a four-leaf-clover-shaped pool, six tennis courts, spa and workout room and you will realize that once-sleepy little Lanai has

HOME, HOME ON THE RANGE

While touring Lanai you're bound to meet more of the island's wildlife than its human citizenry. Asian Axis deer roam everywhere while the mouflon, which look like big horn sheep, tend to be found in the lower elevations of the island. Also keep an eye out for wild turkeys and ringneck pheasants.

joined the 21st century. ~ 1 Manele Bay Drive; 808-565-7700, 800-321-4666, fax 808-565-3868; www.lanairesorts.com. ULTRA-DELUXE.

Outside Lanai City the dining choices—a grand total of three—are concentrated at the Manele Bay Hotel. Here, ladies and gentlemen, lunch is served at the **Pool Grille** on a bougainvillea-covered terrace. Set poolside just above the beach, this patio dining facility features island salads, including a seasonal fruit offering. There is also a standard assortment of sandwiches, as well as grilled mahimahi on *nori* bread and other specialties. Lunch only. ~ 808-565-7700, fax 808-565-2483. MODERATE.

DINING

This spacious resort offers more formal dining in the **Hulopoe Court Restaurant**, a high-ceiling dining room equipped with glass doors that open onto a veranda overlooking the ocean. Island murals adorn the walls and pineapple-motif chandeliers dominate the room. The decor blends Asian and Polynesian styles while the menu features Hawaiian regional cuisine. Breakfast and dinner only. ~ 808-565-7700, fax 808-565-2483. ULTRA-DELUXE.

Sweeping views of Hulopoe Bay star at the **Ihilani Dining Room**. The menu features Mediterranean cuisine and specializes in lamb, bouillabaisse, and fresh fish dishes. The service is formal, and the wine list and cheese cart extensive. Jacket required. Dinner only. Closed Sunday and Monday. ~ 808-565-7700, 808-565-2996, fax 808-565-2483. ULTRA-DELUXE.

Down along Hulopoe Beach at the Manele Bay Hotel, the **Hale Ahe Ahe Lounge** combines several different settings, each equally inviting. The lounge itself has dark textured walls, a hardwood bar and a clubby ambience. It features piano or contemporary Hawaiian music Tuesday through Saturday. Out on the terrace you can settle into a comfortable armchair or lean against the rail and enjoy the ocean view. The adjacent **Holokai Room** is a game room complete with backgammon board and an air of relaxed elegance. ~ 808-565-2000, fax 808-565-2483.

NIGHTLIFE

HULOPOE BEACH PARK Lanai's finest beach also possesses the island's only fully developed park. Set in a half-moon inlet and fringed with *kiawe* trees, this white-sand beach is an excellent spot for all sorts of recreation. It is also the site of the 250-room Manele Bay Hotel, which rests on a bluff about 50 yards above the waterfront. Part of a marine life conservation area, Hulopoe has a lava terrace with outstanding tidepools along its eastern point. There is also a wading area for children at this end of the park. If you continue a short distance along this

BEACHES & PARKS

eastern shoreline you'll encounter **Puu Pehe Cove**, a small beach with abundant marine life that is excellent for swimming and snorkeling. Little wonder that Hulopoe is the island's favorite picnic spot. It's also recommended for surfing and fishing. Prime catches are threadfin, *ulua* and bonefish. This is the most accessible surf-casting beach on the island. There are restrooms and showers. ~ Take Route 440 (Manele Road) south from Lanai City for seven miles.

▲ This is it—the only campground on the island! There are campsites at the far end of the beach. Expect to pay a $5 registration fee plus a charge of $5 per camper per day. Permits are issued by the Lanai Company. ~ P.O. Box 310, Lanai City, Lanai, HI 96763; 808-565-3978, fax 808-565-3984.

MANELE BAY Primarily a small-boat harbor, this cliff-fringed inlet is populated by sailboats from across the Pacific. Carouse with the crews, walk along the jetty or scramble up the rocks for a knockout view of Haleakala on Maui. It's a very good place for swimming since the harbor is well protected, but you need to be wary of boat traffic. Because Manele Bay is part of a marine preserve the snorkeling is notable and the fishing is limited. Only pole fishing is allowed—no nets. There's a park for picnicking, and just around the corner at Hulopoe Beach are facilities for camping, swimming and other sports. ~ Located Route 440 south of Lanai City.

Southwest—Kaumalapau Harbor & Kaunolu

A southwesterly course along Route 440 (Kaumalapau Highway) will carry you steadily downhill for about six miles to **Kaumalapau Harbor**. This busy little harbor was built by pineapple interests and used primarily to ship the fruit on barges to Honolulu. During the heyday of Lanai's pineapple industry, more than a million pineapples a day were loaded onto waiting ships. On either side of Kaumalapau, you can see the *pali*, which rises straight up as high as 1000 feet, protecting Lanai's southwestern flank. These lofty sea cliffs are an ideal vantage point for watching the sunset.

The most interesting point along this route involves a detour near the airport and a journey down a *very* rugged jeep trail to

HIDDEN ►

Kaunolu Village. A summer retreat of Kamehameha the Great and now a national historic landmark, this ancient fishing community still contains the ruins of more than 80 houses as well as stone shelters, petroglyphs and graves. Pick your way through it carefully, lest you step on a ghost. Kamehameha's house, once perched on the eastern ridge, looked across to **Halulu Heiau** on the west side of Kaunolu Bay. Commanding a dominant view of the entire region, these rocky remains are bounded on three sides by cliffs that vault 1000 feet from the ocean.

From nearby **Kahekili's Leap,** warriors proved their courage by plunging more than 60 feet into the water below. If they cleared a 15-foot outcropping and survived the free fall into 12 feet of water, they were deemed noble soldiers worthy of their great king.

Just offshore from this daredevil launching pad lies **Shark Island,** a rock formation that bears an uncanny resemblance to a shark fin. Could it be that warriors skilled enough to survive Kahekili's Leap had then to confront the malevolent spirit of a shark?

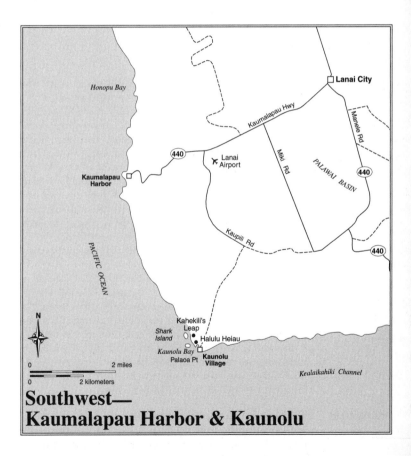

Southwest—
Kaumalapau Harbor & Kaunolu

▼▼▼▼▼▼▼▼▼▼▼▼
Northwest—
Polihua Beach

HIDDEN ▶

From Lanai City, a graded pineapple road passes through an eerie stand of iron-wood trees, then disintegrates into an ungraded dirt track that leads about seven miles to the **Garden of the Gods**. This heavily eroded area resembles the Dakota Badlands and features multihued boulders that change color dramatically during sunrise and sunset. A fantasy land of stone, the Garden of the Gods is planted with ancient lava flows tortured by the elements into as many suggestive shapes as the imagination can conjure. The colors here vibrate with psychedelic intensity and the rocks loom up around you as though they were the gods themselves—hard, cold, dark beings possessed of untold power and otherworldly beauty.

Past this surreal and sacred spot, Polihua Trail, a rugged jeep road, descends several miles to the ocean. **Polihua Beach**, stretching more than a mile and a half, is the longest and widest white-sand beach on the island. Once a prime nesting beach for green sea turtles, it is an excellent spot to watch whales as they pass close by the shoreline

**BEACHES
& PARKS**

HIDDEN ▶

POLIHUA BEACH   A wide white-sand beach situated along Lanai's northwest shore, this isolated strand, with a stunning view of Molokai, rivals Kauai's trackless beaches. Swimming is allowed here but exercise caution—strong winds and currents prevail throughout this region. The water here is sometimes muddy but when it's clear, and when the Fish and Game Division declares it "in season," you can dive for lobsters. According to local anglers, this is the best spot on the island for fishing. Common catches include *papio*, *ulua*, bonefish, threadfin and red snapper. There are no facilities here. ~ It's about 11 miles from Lanai City through pineapple fields and the Garden of the Gods. The last half of the drive is over a rugged jeep trail. For specific directions and road conditions, check with the jeep rental garages.

▼▼▼▼▼▼▼▼▼▼▼▼▼▼
Outdoor Adventures

CAMPING

With so much virgin territory, Lanai should be ideal for camping. But here, as on the other islands, landowners restrict outdoors lovers. The villain is the outfit that manages the island. It permits island residents to camp where they like, but herds visitors into one area on the south coast. This campsite is located at Hulopoe Beach; reservations are recommended; $5 for camping permit plus $5 per person per day. ~ Lanai Company, P.O. Box 310, Lanai City, HI 96763; 808-565-3978, fax 808-565-3984.

KAYAKING

Lanai EcoAdventure Centre features sea kayaking/snorkel combo trips. Explore the reef and the shipwreck on the island's east side or the volcanic history to the west. ~ Corner of 8th and Gay streets, Lanai City; 808-565-7737; www. kayakhawaii.com.

Although there are no establishments on the island that rent scuba or snorkeling gear, a number of outfitters that operate out of Maui provide everything you'll need (including refreshments) to test the waters off Lanai. One area—Cathedrals—is considered the best dive site in Hawaii. Expect to float among Hawaiian green turtles, butterfly fish, black sturgeons and eels. Departure times for the trips can vary by season.

DIVING

Trilogy Excursions conducts a snorkel/sail trip from Lahaina Harbor to Hulopoe Beach Park on Lanai. Guests enjoy a barbecue chicken lunch and an hour-long guided van tour around the island. When conditions are good, introductory scuba dives are an option for non-certified divers. Diving equipment is available but costs extra. ~ Lahaina Harbor, Maui; 808-661-4743, fax 808-667-7766.

Scotch Mist Sailing Charters offers half-day snorkeling trips to various locations, at the captain's discretion. ~ Lahaina Harbor, slip 2, Maui; 808-661-0386.

Catering to all levels of experience, **Dive Maui** explores over 30 locations, including the Cathedrals. ~ 900 Front Street, Lahaina, Maui; 808-667-2080; www.divemauiscuba.com.

Golfers won't be disappointed when they tee off in Lanai. The premier course on the island is one designed by Greg Norman and Ted Robinson, **The Experience at Koele**. Set against the backdrop of forested hills and steep gorges, it lies in the verdant central

GOLF

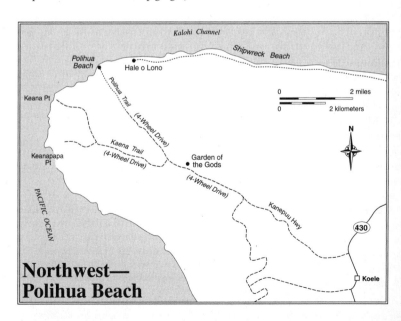

Northwest— Polihua Beach

highlands. Green 17 is completely surrounded by a lake. Reserve tee times up to 30 days in advance. ~ Lanai City; 808-565-7300.

The nine-hole **Cavendish Golf Course**—where the locals play—is open to the public as well. ~ Lanai City.

Or try **Challenge at Manele,** an 18-hole golf course at the Manele Bay Hotel. Designed by Jack Nichlaus, it lies on natural lava outcroppings and follows towering cliffs. The signature hole, number 12, demands a 200-yard tee shot across the ocean. Reserve tee times up to 30 days in advance. ~ 808-565-7700.

ARCHERY & SPORTING CLAYS

Ready to test your skills at a medieval sport? **Lanai Pine Archery** has a 12-target range for archers of all skills and ages. Instructors provide safety tips and pointers. If bows and arrows are too tame for you, try your luck at shooting clay targets **Lanai Pine Sporting Clays.** Games include skeet, wobble traps and compact sporting. Clays are launched to simulate running patterns of various animals and birds. The staff offers instruction. ~ Located one mile north of the Lodge at Koele on Keamoku Highway; 808-559-4600, fax 808-565-4808.

RIDING STABLES

The Lodge at Koele offers horseback riding and equestrian tours. Choose between five rides that take you on various trails around the lodge. The Koele Ride is an hour-long leisurely walking ride that follows a wooded trail and gives riders stunning views of Maui, Molokai and Lanai City. ~ 808-565-7300.

BIKING

There are a few nice rides from Lanai City, but all are steep in places and pass over pockmarked sections of road. One goes south eight miles to Manele Bay and the beach at Hulopoe, another diverts west to busy little Kaumalapau Harbor, and the last heads north 14 miles to Shipwreck Beach. The **Munro Trail** is perfect for those in good shape and into mountain biking.

Covered in scrub vegetation along much of its surface, Lanai still supports several rare endemic bird species.

Road and mountain bike tours and rentals are available through **Lanai EcoAdventure Center**. ~ Corner of Kaumala Pau Highway and Houston Street, Lanai City; 808-565-7373; www. kayakhawaii.com.

Lanai City Service Inc. is a good place to obtain information concerning Lanai roads. ~ 808-565-7227.

HIKING

Hikers on Lanai are granted much greater freedom than campers. Jeep trails and access roads are open to the public; the only restriction is that hikers cannot camp along trails. Since most of the trails lead either to beaches or points of interest, you'll find them described in the regional sightseeing and "Beaches & Parks" sections above. All distances for hiking trails are one way unless otherwise noted.

The **Koloiki Ridge Trail** (5 miles) leads through forest lands and the Cathedral of Pines (a group of pines resembling a gothic church) to a ridge that runs between Naio Gulch and Maunalei Valley. This moderately difficult hike provides views of Molokai and Maui.

Guided hikes, including overnight camping trips, are offered by **Lanai EcoAdventure Centre**. ~ Located at the corner of Kaumala Pau Highway and Houston Street, Lanai City; 808-565-7373; www.kayakhawaii.com.

Transportation

AIR

Planes to Lanai land at **Lanai Airport** amid an endless maze of grassland and tilled fields four miles from downtown Lanai City. This tiny landing strip has a small gift shop and a courtesy telephone for car rentals (you'll be picked up in a shuttle). There are no lockers or public transportation. A few rooms house airline offices. Hawaiian Airlines offers jet service to the islands; IslandAir flies propeller-driven planes and features competitive rates. ~ 808-565-6757.

If you're staying at any of the island hotels, they will provide transportation into town, as will any of the island's car rental agencies if you're renting a vehicle from them.

BOAT

A ferry service called **Expeditions** operates out of Maui and links Lahaina with Manele Bay on Lanai. There are five boats per day in each direction. The 45-minute crossing provides a unique way to arrive on the island and if you're lucky, a chance to spy spinner dolphins and flying fish. ~ P.O. Box 10, Lahaina, HI 96767; 808-661-3756.

CAR & JEEP RENTALS

Lanai City Service Inc., which is affiliated with Dollar Rent A Car, rents automatic compact cars with free mileage. But renting a car on Lanai is like carrying water wings to the desert: there's simply nowhere to go. Rental cars are restricted to pavement, while most of Lanai's roads are jeep trails: four-wheel drive is the only way to fly. ~ 1036 Lanai Avenue; 808-565-7227.

The first time I visited the island of Lanai, I rented a vintage 1942 jeep. The vehicle had bad brakes, no emergency brake, malfunctioning windshield wipers and no seat belts. It was, however, equipped with an efficient shock absorber—me. Today, Lanai City Services Inc., described above, rents new and reliable jeeps. (Be aware that the rental car collision insurance provided by most credit cards does not cover jeeps.)

BOAT TOURS

There are boat tours of Lanai offered by the Maui-based outfit **Trilogy Excursions**. They'll take you on a full-day excursion, leaving from Lahaina Harbor. Breakfast and lunch is provided, as well as snorkeling equipment and instruction. You'll also go on a one-hour van tour of the island. ~ 808-661-4743.

HITCHING   Officially, it's illegal, but actually it's common. The folks in these parts are pretty friendly, so rides are easy to get. The trick lies in finding someone who's going as far as you are—like all the way to Shipwreck Beach or out to the Garden of the Gods.

EIGHT

Molokai

Between the bustling islands of Oahu and Maui lies an isle which in shape resembles Manhattan, but which in spirit and rhythm is far more than an ocean away from the smog-shrouded shores of the Big Apple. Molokai, Hawaii's fifth-largest island, is 38 miles long and 10 miles wide. The slender isle was created by three volcanoes that mark its present geographic regions: one at West End where the arid Mauna Loa tableland rises to 1381 feet, another at East End where a rugged mountain range along the north coast is topped by 4970-foot Mount Kamakou, and the third, a geologic afterthought, which created the low, flat Kalaupapa Peninsula.

Considering that the island measures a modest 260 square miles, its geographic diversity is amazing. Arriving at Hoolehua Airport near the island's center, travelers feel as though they have touched down somewhere in the American Midwest. Red dust, dry heat and curving prairie surround the small landing strip and extend to the west end of Molokai. This natural pastureland gives way in the southcentral region to low-lying, relatively swampy ground and brown-sand beaches with murky water.

The prettiest strands lie along the western shore, where Papohaku Beach forms one of the largest white-sand beaches in the state, and at the east end around Halawa Valley, a region of heavy rainfall and lush tropic vegetation. To the north is the vaunted pali, which rises in a vertical wall 3000 feet from the surf, creating the tallest sea cliffs in the world. Here, too, is an awesome succession of sharp, narrow valleys cloaked in velvet green.

Kaunakakai, a sleepy port town on the south shore, is the island's hub. From here a road runs to the eastern and western coasts. Kalaupapa and the northern *pali* are accessible overland only by mule and hiking trails.

Even in a region of islands, Molokai has always been something of a backwater. To the early Hawaiians it appeared desiccated and inhospitable. The rich Halawa Valley was settled in the 7th century and the island developed a haunting reputation for sorcery and mystical occurrences. In ancient times it was also called *pule-oo,* or "powerful prayer," and was revered for the potency of its priests.

When Captain James Cook "discovered" the island in November 1778, he found it bleak and inhospitable. Not until 1786 did a Western navigator, Captain George Dixon, bother to land. When Kamehameha the Great took it in 1795, he was actually en route to the much grander prize of Oahu. His war canoes are said to have loomed along four miles of shoreline when he attacked the island at Pakuhiwa Battleground and slaughtered the island's outnumbered defenders.

The next wave of invaders arrived in 1832 when Protestant missionaries introduced the Polynesians to the marvels of Christianity. Around 1850 a German immigrant named Rudolph Meyer arrived in Molokai, married a Hawaiian chieftess, and began a reign as manager of the Molokai Ranch that lasted for almost a half-century.

Leprosy struck the Hawaiian Islands during the 19th century, and wind-plagued Kalaupapa Peninsula became the living hell to which the disease's victims were exiled. Beginning in 1866, lepers were torn from their families and literally cast to their fates along this stark shore. Here Father Damien de Veuster, a Belgian priest, the Martyr of Molokai, came to live, work and eventually die among the afflicted.

For years Molokai was labeled "The Lonely Isle" or "The Forgotten Isle." By 1910 a population that once totaled 10,000 had decreased to one-tenth the size. Then in 1921, Polynesians began settling homesteads under the Hawaiian Homes Act, which granted a 40-acre homestead to anyone with over 50 percent Hawaiian ancestry. Molokai eventually became "The Friendly Isle," with the largest proportion of native Hawaiians anywhere in the world (except for the island of Niihau, which is closed to outsiders). With them they brought a legacy from old Hawaii, the spirit of aloha, which still lives on this marvelous island. Young Hawaiians, sometimes hostile on the more crowded islands, are often outgoing and generous here.

During the 1920s, while Hawaiians were being granted the hardscrabble land that had not already been bought up on the island, Libby (which later sold out to Dole) and Del Monte began producing pineapples across the richer stretches of the island. The company towns of Maunaloa and Kualapuu sprang up and Molokai's rolling prairies became covered with fields of spike-topped fruits. Over the years competition from Asia became increasingly intense, forcing Dole to shut its operation in 1975 and Del Monte to pull out in 1982.

As elsewhere in Hawaii, the economic powers realized that if they couldn't grow crops they had better cultivate tourists. During the 1970s thousands of acres along the island's western end were allocated for resort and residential development and the sprawling Kaluakoi Resort was built. In 1996, vandals opposed to this sort of development destroyed five miles of water pipes on Molokai Ranch, which had earlier closed access to several beaches and evicted a number of former plantation workers from their homes.

Today the island's population numbers under 7000. There isn't a single traffic light here, and the weak economy has saved Molokai from the ravages of development that plagued the rest of Hawaii during the 1980s. Change is coming, but like everything on Molokai, it is arriving slowly. Time still remains to see Hawaii as it once was and to experience the trackless beaches, vaulting seacliffs, sweeping ranchlands and forested mountains that led ancient Hawaiians to believe in the mystical powers of Molokai.

Molokai

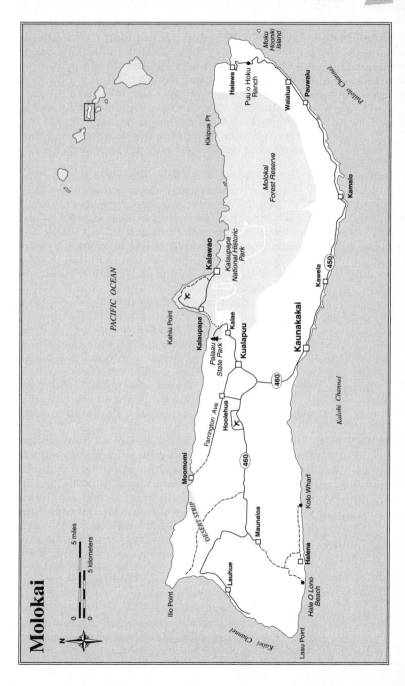

▼▼▼▼▼▼▼▼▼▼▼▼▼▼▼▼▼
Kaunakakai to East End

You don't need a scorecard, or even a map for that matter, to keep track of the sightseeing possibilities on Molokai. Across its brief expanse, the Friendly Isle offers several rewards to the curious, none of which are difficult to find.

First of course is the falsefront town of Kaunakakai, a commercial hub that more resembles a way station on the road to Dodge City. From here a simple two-lane road, Route 450 (Kamehameha V Highway), threads its way along the southern shore in search of the Halawa Valley at the far east end of the island.

SIGHTS

It is only too appropriate that **Kaunakakai** gained its greatest fame from someone who never existed. Known for a song written about "The Cock-eyed Mayor of Kaunakakai," the town has in fact had only one mayor—whether he was cock-eyed, no one will say. This somnolent village, with its falsefront buildings and tiny civic center, is administered from Maui. Poor but proud, it possesses a population of fewer than 3000, and has a main drag (Ala Malama Street) that extends a grand total of three blocks but still represents the hub of Molokai.

Nearby is the **wharf**, extending seaward almost a half-mile and offering a mooring place for a few fishing boats, charter outfits, and private sailboats. A good place to gaze out on the island of Lanai, it is also an ideal vantage from which to take in the green slopes that rise toward the ridgeline of Molokai. Kids love to swim off the Kaunakaki Wharf, where a roped off area keeps them safe from the boats. It's also a great place to meet local children.

Close to the pier landing rest the rocky remains of **Kamehameha V's Summer Home**, where Hawaii's king luxuriated during the late-19th century.

HIDDEN ▶

For birdwatching, you'll want to check out the **Wastewater Reclamation Facility**, where the nutrient-rich (read bug-infested) water is a year-round hit with endangered species such as the Hawaiian coot and stilt. In the winter, keep an eye out for the occasional shoveler, green-winged teal, wandering tattler and other migratory waterfowl. ~ Located off Maunaloa Highway on the ocean side just before Kaunakakai; 808-553-5341, fax 808-553-4251.

From Kaunakakai to Halawa Valley, a narrow macadam road leads past almost 30 miles of seascapes and historic sites. Route 450 runs straight along the south shore for about 20 miles, presenting views across the Kalohi and Pailolo channels to Lanai and Maui. Then the road snakes upward and curves inland before descending again into Halawa Valley.

Due to the calm, shallow waters along the southeastern shoreline, this area once supported one of the greatest concentrations of fishponds in Hawaii. Numbering as many as five dozen during the pre-Western period, these ancient aquaculture structures

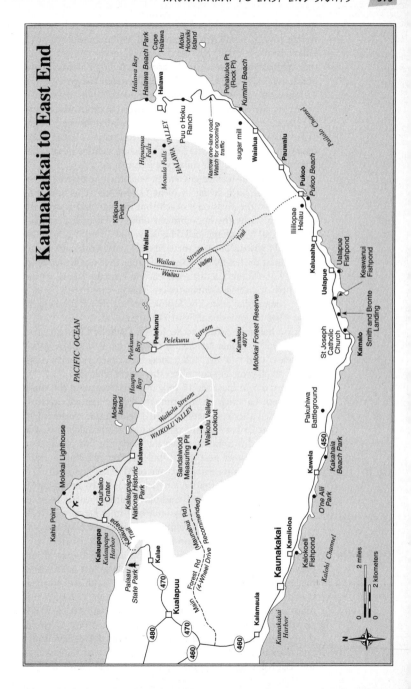

Kaunakakai to East End

PACIFIC OCEAN

Kahiu Point

Molokai Lighthouse

Kalaupapa
Kalaupapa Harbor

Kauhako Crater

Kalaupapa National Historic Park

Kalae

Palaau State Park

Kualapuu

Kalamaula

Kamiloloa

Kaunakakai
Kaunakakai Harbor

Kalokoeli Fishpond

Kalohi Channel

One Alii Park

Kawela

Kakahaia Beach Park

Pakuhiwa Battleground

Kamalo

St. Joseph Catholic Church

Smith and Bronte Landing

Ualapue
Keawanui Fishpond

Ualapue Fishpond

Kaluaaha

Iliiliopae Heiau

Pukoo
Pukoo Beach

Pauwalu

Waialua

sugar mill

Narrow one-lane road: Watch for oncoming traffic

Puu o Hoku Ranch

HALAWA VALLEY

Moaula Falls

Hipuapua Falls

Halawa
Halawa Bay
Halawa Beach Park
Cape Halawa

Moku Hooniki Island

Pohakuloa Pt (Rock Pt)
Kumimi Beach

Pailolo Channel

Kikipua Point

Wailau
Wailau Stream
Wailau Valley

Trail

Pelekunu
Pelekunu Bay
Pelekunu Stream

Haupu Bay

Mokapu Island

Kalawao

Kamakou 4970'

Molokai Forest Reserve

Waikolu Stream
WAIKOLU VALLEY
Waikolu Valley Lookout

Sandalwood Measuring Pit

Forest Rd (Maunahui Rd) Recommended
Forest Rd (4-Wheel Drive recommended)

Main

470
480
470
460
450

0   2 miles
0   2 kilometers

N

were built of lava and coral by commoners to raise fish for Hawaiian royalty. Small fish were trapped within these stone pens, fattened and eventually harvested. You will see the rebuilt remains of several as you drive along the coast, including **Kalokoeli Fishpond**, two miles east of Kaunakakai, **Keawanui Fishpond**, about 12 miles east of town, and **Ualapue Fishpond**, a mile farther east.

About five miles from town lies Kawela, once an ancient city of refuge, now known as the place where two battles were fought at **Pakuhiwa Battleground**. In his drive to become Hawaii's first monarch, Kamehameha the Great launched a canoe flotilla that reportedly extended four miles along this shore.

For a face-to-feather encounter with the endangered nene, Hawaii's state bird, swing by **Nene O Molokai**. This nonprofit facility raises the birds on a beachfront location and is open for educational visits (by appointment only). ~ Located past Mile Marker 4 off Kamehameha V Highway; 808-553-5992, fax 808-553-9029; www.aloha.net/~nene, e-mail nene@aloha.net.

Just past the ten-mile marker (indicating that you are ten miles east of Kaunakakai), a dirt road leads to **Kamalo Wharf**, an old pineapple and cattle shipping point. This natural harbor, once a major commercial center (by Molokai standards!), is now a gathering place for occasional fishermen and boats.

It's a half-mile farther to **St. Joseph Catholic Church**, a tiny chapel built by Father Damien in 1876. A statue of the bespectacled priest, clad in a cape and leaning on a cane, graces the property. A small cemetery completes this placid tableau.

A monument (past the 11-mile marker) designates the **Smith and Bronte Landing**, an inhospitable spot where two aviators crash-landed after completing the first civilian transpacific flight in 1927. The 25-hour flight from California, scheduled to land in Honolulu, ended abruptly when the plane ran out of gas. (An opening in the trees past the 12-mile marker reveals the aforementioned Keawanui Fishpond, one of Molokai's largest.)

Set back from the road in a clearing framed by mountains is **Our Lady of Seven Sorrows Catholic Church**, located 14 miles east of Kaunakakai. Originally built by Father Damien in 1874 and reconstructed almost a century later, it's a pretty chapel surrounded by coconut trees and flanked by a small cemetery.

HIDDEN ►   One of the largest temples in the islands, **Iliiliopae Heiau**, rests hidden in the underbrush on private land just inland from the highway. Measuring about 100 yards in length and 40 yards in width, it was once a center of sorcery and human sacrifice that today consists of a stone platform and adjoining terraces. This is also the trailhead for the Wailau Valley Trail. According to legend, the *heiau*'s stones were all transported from this distant valley and assembled in a single night. ~ 15 miles east of Kaunakakai; for permission and directions, call Pearl Petro at 808-558-8113.

The best way to visit this ancient site is on the **Molokai Wagon Ride,** a horse-drawn-wagon or horseback tour conducted by several delightful local fellows. ~ Mapulehu Mango Grove, about 15 miles east of Kaunakakai; 808-558-8132; e-mail wgnride@ aloha.net.

The Molokai Wagon Ride also visits the nearby **Mapulehu Mango Grove,** a stand of over 2000 fruit trees that were planted in 1926 and now represent one of the largest such groves in the world. The wagon ride winds up at a picturesque beach where guests enjoy a Molokai-style lunch on the beach complete with coconut husking and Hawaiian net throwing.

The ruins of the island's first **sugar mill** stand near Route 450's 20-mile marker. All that remains of this early factory, which burned down about a century ago, is a solitary stack.

Just beyond the 20-mile marker is Kumimi Beach, which presents your first view of **Moku Hooniki Island** as well as otherworldly vistas of Maui.

The road now begins a sinuous course along a string of pearl-white beaches, then climbs above a rocky coastline. As you curve upward into Molokai's tropical heights, the roadside flora becomes increasingly colorful and dense. First you encounter the open pastures and rolling ranchland of 14,000-acre **Puu o Hoku Ranch,** then dive into the tropical foliage of Molokai's windblown northeast coast.

As the road winds high above **Halawa Valley** it offers several vista points from which to view this V-shaped canyon bounded by green walls. Directly below, tropical greenery gives way to white surf and then aquamarine ocean. A river bisects this luxuriant region. At the far end, surrounded by sheer walls, two waterfalls—Hipuapua and Moaula—spill down the mountainside. Obviously East End has withheld its most spectacular scenery until the last.

Archaeologists believe that Molokai's first settlement was established here, possibly as early as the 7th century. The ancient Hawaiians terraced the surrounding slopes, planting taro and living off the largesse of the sea.

In 1946 (and again in 1957) a tidal wave swept through the valley, leveling buildings and leaving salt deposits that destroyed the agricultural industry. Today you can drive down into the valley, where you'll find a park, a lovely curve of sandy beach, freshwater Halawa Stream, an old church and several other structures. A hiking trail leads to 250-foot Moaula Falls and 500-foot Hipuapua Falls, which lie to the interior of this awesomely beautiful vale. Please note, however, that this trail has been closed by the landowner and is not open to the public. You may, however, embark on a guided tour of the area by contacting **Pilipo's Halawa Falls and Cultural Hike**. Closed Sunday. ~ 808-553-4355.

LODGING

Two miles east of Kaunakakai is the 45-room **Hotel Molokai**, a lowrise hotel with faux-Polynesian architectural details. The accommodations are small but comfortable, and have rattan furnishings, tropical prints, refrigerators and ceiling fans; some units also have kitchenettes. There is an oceanside pool and a pleasant lounge area with an adjacent restaurant and cocktail lounge. The hotel fronts a narrow beach, and shallows offshore are not suitable for ocean swimming, but they're great for fishing. The grounds are nicely landscaped with plenty of tall palms that provide a tropical feel. ~ Kamehameha Highway; 808-553-5347, 800-367-5004, fax 808-553-5047; www.hotelmolokai.com. MODERATE TO DELUXE.

If privacy is what you're after, you'll love **Kamalo Plantation Bed & Breakfast**. Set on five acres of orchards and tropical gardens, the secluded cottage lies in the middle of lush grounds. Screen windows let in the tropical smell of the flowering trees, and a private lanai is perfect for the breakfast of homemade bread and fresh fruit from the orchard. ~ HCO1 Box 300, Kaunakakai, HI 96748; phone/fax 808-558-8236; e-mail kamaloplantation@ aloha.net. MODERATE TO DELUXE.

CONDOS

If you're traveling with several folks or want kitchen facilities, there are also condominiums: **Marc Molokai Shores Suites** offers oceanfront accommodations with full kitchen, lanai and color television. A series of low-slung buildings that forms a U-shaped

Author Picks

CHAPTER FAVORITES

For me, the **Molokai Mule Ride** to Kalaupapa is like a pilgrimage. The three-mile trip down a steep trail culminates on a wind-swept peninsula, one of the most stunning in all the islands. *page 375*

I love to wander the beach in **Halawa Valley** and explore this luxurious agricultural region inhabited by Hawaiians for 1300 years. *pages 375–376*

Camping isn't quite the same at **Molokai Ranch.** Their oceanview tent camping and outdoor adventures make me think I'm a kid again, riding the range in cowboy movies—but this time with a Hawaiian paniolo theme. *page 385*

configuration around a landscaped lawn extending to the beach sits among palm trees, a swimming pool, shuffleboard and barbecue areas. Rates start at $144. ~ Phone/fax 808-553-5954, 800-535-0085; www.marcresorts.com.

DINING

A gourmet will starve on Molokai, but someone looking for a square meal at fair prices should depart well-fed. The budget restaurants are clustered along Ala Malama Street in Kaunakakai.

Outpost Natural Foods has a takeout counter at the back of its tiny health food store. Here you can fuel up with delicious sandwiches, salads and smoothies that are both nutritious and inexpensive. There are also burritos and daily specials. Open 10 a.m. to 3 p.m. No dinner. Closed Saturday. ~ 70 Makaena Place; 808-553-3377, fax 808-553-5857. BUDGET.

◄ *HIDDEN*

Molokai Pizza Cafe is an excellent neighborhood pizzeria located just outside of town. Clean and modern, this local hangout is a great place for a tasty lunch or a quick-and-easy dinner. On Wednesday, Mexican standards are featured, while on Sunday, prime rib is added to the menu. Try one of their homemade pies for dessert. ~ Kaunakakai Place; 808-553-3288, fax 808-553-5400. BUDGET TO MODERATE.

GROCERIES

The nearest Molokai approaches to a supermarket is **Misaki's,** a medium-sized grocery store on Kaunakakai's main drag, Ala Malama Street. The prices are higher and the selection smaller here than at the chain markets, so it's wise to bring a few provisions from the larger islands. Open 8:30 a.m. to 8:30 p.m., Sunday 9 a.m. to noon. ~ 78 Ala Malama Street; 808-553-5505, fax 808-531-6447.

Outpost Natural Foods, down the street and around the corner from Misaki's, offers a friendly atmosphere as well as juices, herbs, dried fruit, fresh local produce and other health food items. Closed Saturday. ~ 70 Makaena Place; 808-553-3377, fax 808-553-5857.

Try Kanemitsu's Bakery for delicious raspberry jelly, bread and pastries. ~ Ala Malama Street; 808-553-5855.

On the East End, Neighborhood Store 'n Counter has groceries and a stock of liquor. Open 8 a.m. to 6 p.m. daily. ~ Kamehameha Highway (near the 17-mile marker); 808-558-8498.

SHOPPING   You needn't worry about falling into the shop-till-you-drop syndrome on Molokai. Long before you have even begun to think about being tired you will have visited every store on the island. Shopping is still an adventure here, since the few stores operating are all owned by local people and provide a window into life on Molokai.

Ala Malama Street, Kaunakakai's main street, offers a modest row of shops. Molokai Island Creations specializes in clothing, jewelry, glassware and gift items made by Molokai artists. ~ 63 Ala Malama Street; 808-553-5926; www.molokai-aloha.com/fishdive.

In the same complex, Molokai Fish & Dive, "home of the original Molokai T-shirt designs," features its signature clothing and souvenirs as well as beach items and sporting equipment. ~ 63 Ala Malama Street, Kaunakakai; 808-553-5926; www.molokai-aloha.com/fishdive.

Imports Gift Shop features casual wear, cultured and mabe pearls, and Hawaiian heirloom jewelry. ~ 828 Ala Malama Street; 808-553-5734.

For surfwear you can try Molokai Surf. Closed Sunday. ~ 130 Kamehameha Highway, Suite 103; 808-553-5093.

BEACHES & PARKS   O'NE ALII PARK   This spacious park features a large grass-covered field and coconut trees plus a narrow beach with an excellent view of Lanai. A reef far offshore makes this

---

OVIEDO'S LUNCH COUNTER

If you're into Filipino fare, try Oviedo's Lunch Counter. This mom-and-pop restaurant serves up spicy steaming dishes at low prices. You'll find plank board walls surrounding a few plastic chairs and yellow formica tables. The steam-tray cuisine includes chicken papaya, pig's feet, turkey tail adobo and mango beans. Open for lunch and early dinner. ~ Ala Malama Street, Kaunakakai; 808-553-5014. BUDGET.

area very shallow and affords ample protection. It's excellent for children. Snorkeling, though, is only mediocre. As for surfing, all the action is far out on the reef and it's rarely any good. Surf-casting isn't bad here but it's even better farther to the east. The most common catches are *manini*, red and white goatfish, parrotfish, *papio*, *ulua*, milkfish and mullet. The facilities here include a picnic area, restrooms, showers and electricity at the pavilion. ~ Located four miles east of Kaunakakai on Route 450; 808-553-3204, fax 808-553-3206.

▲ Mainly tent camping; no hookups, $3 per person per night. Very popular and therefore sometimes crowded and noisy. County permit required.

KAKAHAIA BEACH PARK 🏃 🚣 This is a long, narrow park wedged tightly between the road and the ocean; it's the site of the Kakahaia National Wildlife Refuge. Since the water is both shallow and murky, swimming and snorkeling are not recommended. Picnicking, surfing and fishing are much the same as at O'ne Alii Park. Day use only. ~ Located six miles east of Kaunakakai on Route 450.

PUKOO BEACH 🏊 🤿 🚣 This crescent-shaped strand is mirrored by another curving beach just to the west. Maui lies directly across the channel and there are also marvelous views of Lanai. With a shallow, rocky bottom, this beach provides only mediocre swimming. However, it's very popular with anglers. There are no facilities. ~ The old Neighborhood Store 'n' Snack Bar, located on Route 450 near Mile Marker 16, is your landmark. Just past here, traveling east, turn into the second driveway on the right. This access road leads a short distance to the beach.

KUMIMI BEACH, POHAKULOA POINT AND OTHER EAST END BEACHES 🏊 🤿 🏃 🚣 Beginning near the 18-mile marker on Route 450, and extending for about four miles, lies this string of small sandy beaches. These are among the island's loveliest, featuring white sands and spectacular views of the islands of Maui and Lanai. The swimming is very good, but beware of heavy currents and high surf. Plentiful coral makes for great snorkeling and good lobster diving. There are numerous surfing breaks throughout this area. Pohakuloa Point (or Rock Point), located eight-tenths of a mile past the 20-mile marker, is one of Molokai's top surfing spots. Barracuda are sometimes caught in the deeper regions. Also bonefish, mountain bass, threadfin, *manini*, red and white goatfish, *ulua*, *papio*, parrotfish, milkfish, and mullet. There is a small market near Mile Marker 15. ~ These pocket beaches are located along Route 450 between the 18- and 22-mile markers.

HALAWA BEACH PARK 🏊 🤿 🏃 🚣 Set in lush Halawa Valley, one of Molokai's most splendid areas, the park is tucked neatly between mountains and sea on a grassy plot dotted with coconut palms and ironwood trees. Cliffs, waterfalls, two pocket beaches—altogether a heavenly spot, though sometimes rainy and almost always windy. This is an okay place to swim because it is partially protected by the bay, but exercise caution anyway. Snorkeling is good, though the water is sometimes murky. It's one of the very best spots on the island for surfing. Fishing is also notable; the reefs studding this area make it a prime locale for many of the species caught along East End Beaches. The park is a bit weatherbeaten and overgrown and although there are a picnic area and restrooms, the running water must be boiled or treated chemically. ~ Located 30 miles east of Kaunakakai on Route 450.

▲ Not permitted in the park, but people camp on the other side of Halawa Stream on property owned by Puu o Hoku Ranch (808-558-8109). You will have to park and carry your gear to where you want to camp.

Kaunakakai to West End

Generally, if you are not pointed east on Molokai, you are headed westerly. The thoroughfare that carries you across the prairie-like plains of west Molokai is Route 460, also called the Maunaloa Highway, another two-lane track. Along the way you can venture off in search of the plantation town of Kualapuu and the vista point overlooking Kalaupapa, but eventually you will arrive at road's end out in the woodframe town of Maunaloa. From this red-dust municipality it's a short jaunt to Papohaku Beach, Molokai's western shore.

SIGHTS   Just a mile west of the cock-eyed town of Kaunakakai on Route 460 is the **Kapuaiwa Coconut Grove**, planted in the 1860s by Kamehameha V. This magnificent stand of coconut palms, once 1000 in number, consists of particularly tall trees. The grove creates the sensation of being in a tropical dream sequence, with hundreds of palm trees flashing green and yellow fronds and extending to the lip of the ocean. Some appear to stand in columns, but others have bent so far to the wind they have fallen out of formation. Pay a visit toward sunset, when the palms are memorably silhouetted by tropic skies for a wonderful end-of-day setting. Watch out for falling coconuts: these trees are not the trimmed-back kind made safe for the unwary. Adjacent to the coconut grove is the **Kalanianaole Community Hall**, a unique early-20th-century cultural landmark that still serves the community. ~ Route 460.

Strung like rosary beads opposite the grove are seven tiny churches. This **Church Row** includes Protestant, Mormon, Jehovah's Witness and several other denominations. Like sentinels protecting the island from the devil, they too are gathered in rows. The most intriguing are the oldest, tiny woodframe structures

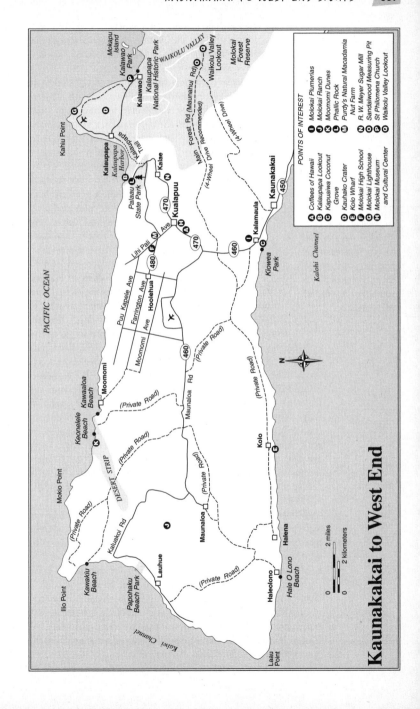

Kaunakakai to West End

POINTS OF INTEREST
- Coffees of Hawaii
- Kalaupapa Lookout
- Kapuaiwa Coconut Grove
- Kauhako Crater
- Kolo Wharf
- Molokai High School
- Molokai Lighthouse
- Molokai Museum and Cultural Center
- Molokai Plumerias
- Molokai Ranch
- Moomomi Dunes
- Phallic Rock
- Purdy's Natural Macadamia Nut Farm
- R. W. Meyer Sugar Mill
- Sandalwood Measuring Pit
- St Philomena Church
- Waikolu Valley Lookout

with modest steeples. These one-room chapels lack worldly frills like stained glass and are furnished with creaky wooden pews that seat a few dozen parishioners. Stop by and inquire about services; visitors are always welcome.

Molokai Plumerias is a family-run company that will take you on a tour of their one-acre plumeria farm. Plumeria, with the scent of heaven, are the primary flowers used in lei making. Your guide will teach you about the flower, allow you to pick your own and provide you with the necessary tools to create a lei. There are no regularly scheduled tours, so make reservations in advance. ~ Kalamaula, about two miles west of Kaunakakai; 808-553-3391.

A side trip along Route 470 leads past the tinroof town of **Kualapuu**. Filled with modest plantation houses, it hearkens back to an earlier era when Molokai cultivated pine-apples rather than tourists. Today its claim to fame is a 1.4-million-gallon reservoir that is reportedly the largest rubber-lined water tank in the world.

According to legend, Molokai was the child of the god Wakea and his mistress Hina, whose cave still lies along the southeastern edge of the island.

If you tire of Hawaii's relaxed pace and long for a jolt of java, arrange a tour at **Coffees of Hawaii**. Walking and mule-drawn wagon tours are offered here; you'll be led around the 500-acre coffee plantation to witness the roasting process "from seed to cup." The tour wraps up in the tasting room, where an espresso bar churns out samples. Reservations required. ~ P.O. Box 160, Kualapuu, HI 96757; 800-346-5051, fax 808-567-9270; coffeehawaii.com.

Farther up Route 470, Kalae is home to the R. W. Meyer Sugar Mill, which is the highlight of the **Molokai Museum and Cultural Center**. There is an 1878 steam-generated operation that has been restored in sparkling fashion. The mule-driven cane crusher, copper clarifiers and dependable old steam engine are ready and waiting for Molokai to return to its old ways. There are also well-presented displays and heirlooms of the German immigrant family that owned the mill, as well as native Molokai artifacts. Closed Sunday. Admission. ~ Route 470, Kalae; 808-567-6436.

Route 470 ends at the **Kalaupapa Lookout**. Here cliffs as green as Ireland fall away in dizzying fashion to reveal a softly sloping tableland 1600 feet below, the Kalaupapa Peninsula. Fringed by white-sand beaches, this geologic afterthought extends more than two miles out from the foot of the *pali*. A lighthouse and land-ing strip occupy the point of the peninsula. Nearer the cliffs, a cluster of houses comprises the famous leper colony; while neigh-boring Kauhako Crater, a nicely rounded circle far below you, represents a vestige of the volcano that created this appendage. Ringed by rock and water, protected by the tallest sea cliffs in the world, Kalaupapa Peninsula is a magnificent sight indeed.

A short hike from the lookout, **Phallic Rock** protrudes obscenely from the ground amid an ironwood stand as thick as pubic hair. This geologic formation, so realistic it almost seems sculpted, was said to represent the Hawaiian fertility god, who was turned to stone when his wife caught him admiring a beautiful young girl. Legend says that a woman offering gifts and spending the night here will return home pregnant.

Route 480 will take you into the town of Hoolehua, where you'll find **Purdy's Natural Macadamia Nut Farm**. Located right behind the island's only high school, this small grove of 70-year-old macadamia nut trees is open to the public for free tours and tastings. The owner will explain the growing cycles of the trees and demonstrate harvesting and cooking techniques. Visitors can taste the raw product and also sample the nut after it's been naturally roasted, a process that cuts down greatly on the fat and calories found in nuts sold in stores. Closed Sunday. ~ Lihipali Avenue, Hoolehua; phone/fax 808-567-6601.

Route 460 continues over dry rolling plains toward Molokai's West End. This arid plateau, windswept and covered by deep red, iron-rich soil, was once planted in pineapple. Today Molokai Ranch, which still owns much of the region, has turned to hay cultivation to feed cattle.

If nothing else, the West End is rich in myth and history. As Hawaiian storytellers recount, the region around Maunaloa, the volcano that formed this side of the island, was once a cultural focus of the Polynesians. It was here that the hula originated; from the slopes of Maunaloa the goddess Laka spread knowledge of the sensuous dance to all the other islands.

Like the pineapple industry itself, Route 460 ends in **Maunaloa**. With the departure of Dole's operations in 1975, this company town assumed the dusty, falsefront visage of the Wild West after the mines petered out and the saloons shut down. That's all begun to change in the past few years as the Molokai Ranch, which owns just about all of Maunaloa, has started a revitalization program that has seen the more ramshackle plantation houses replaced by contemporary homes, some of the town's more historic buildings upgraded, and several new buildings added, including a lovely 22-room lodge and Molokai's first movie theater. The old post office and general store provide links to Maunaloa's days as a pineapple town, and the overall feeling remains rustically charming, albeit with an increasingly gentrified air.

Any tour of West End should of course finish at the west end. **Papohaku Beach**, a sparkling three-mile long swath of white sand, would be a fitting finale to any tour. Reached by taking Kaluakoi Road from Route 460 and driving through the rolling hills of sprawling Kaluakoi Resort, Papohaku is one of the largest beaches

Molokai's Outback

For a splendid tour of Molokai's mountainous interior, take a drive or hike on the Main Forest Road (Maunahui Road), located four miles west of Kaunakakai. This bumpy dirt road requires four-wheel-drive vehicles along its ten-mile length. To reach the Main Forest Road, take Route 460 west from Kaunakakai. There is a white bridge a little more than three and a half miles from town, just before the four-mile marker. Take a right on the dirt road right before the bridge and you're on the Main Forest Road.

MOLOKAI FOREST RESERVE   Deer, quail, pheasant, doves and chukkar partridge populate the route. Numerous secondary roads and trails lead to the very edge of the mammoth Molokai Forest Reserve, through which the main road passes. These side roads offer excellent possibilities for adventurous hikers.

LUA MOKU ILIAHI   After nine miles, the main road passes Lua Moku Iliahi, known to the English-speaking world as the **Sandalwood Measuring**

in the state. During World War II troops practiced shore landings along this coast. But today you will have the beach and surrounding sand dunes almost entirely to yourself.

LODGING   Far from the madding crowd on the west end of Molokai, you will find a 6700-acre master-planned complex, the **Kaluakoi Resort**. Divided into the 116-room Kaluakoi Hotel & Golf Club, the cottage-like condos of Kaluakoi Villas, and two other condominium complexes, it is set near a luxurious three-mile-long beach. This is Molokai's premier resting spot, offering both seclusion and comfort. Here you'll find the essence of plush living: wasp-waisted pool, golf course, a view of Oahu across the channel, and an oceanfront lounge and restaurant. The hotel rooms are located in a two-story building and have all the necessities: lanai, color TV, tile bathroom, overhead fan, rattan furniture. For an ultra-deluxe price tag, you can buy a piece of that ocean view in a studio unit with a kitchenette. The villas are more spacious, also include a kitchenette and are priced deluxe. ~ Kaluakoi Hotel & Golf Club: 808-552-2555, 888-552-2550, fax 808-552-2821, www.kaluakai.com; Kaluakoi Villas: 808-552-2721, 800-367-5004, fax 808-552-2201; www.castle-group.com.

    Ke Nani Kai Resort, a 120-unit condominium, has one- and two-bedroom units starting at $149 per night. Over Christmas

Pit. This depression, dug into the earth to match the hull size of an old sailing vessel, was used by 19th-century Hawaiians to gauge the amount of sandalwood needed to fill a ship.

WAIKOLU VALLEY LOOKOUT   It's another mile to **Waikolu Picnic Grove**, a heavily wooded retreat ideal for lunching or camping. Here you'll find picnic facilities and an outhouse. (State permit required to camp.) Across the road, Waikolu Valley Lookout perches above Waikolu Valley, which descends precipitously 3000 feet to the sea.

KAMAKOU PRESERVE   Here you can also explore Kamakou Preserve, a 2774-acre sanctuary managed by The Nature Conservancy. Home to more than 200 plants that live only in Hawaii, the preserve is a lush rainforest and an important watershed for Molokai. There are several forest birds, including the *apapane* and *amakihi*. For information on visiting the reserve or to check the condition of the Main Forest Road (which may be closed in wet weather), call **808-553-5236**, fax **808-553-9870**; www.tnc-hawaii.com.

there's a two-night minimum. The complex includes a pool, tennis courts, a putting green and an outdoor party area with barbecues. ~ Kepuhi Place; 808-552-2761, 800-888-2791, fax 808-552-0045; www.kenanikai.com.

Nearby **Paniolo Hale**, has 22 units starting at $95 per night. These also include all the amenities and access to a pool, barbecue area and paddle tennis. Closed Sunday. ~ Kakaako Road; 808-552-2731, 800-367-2984, fax 808-552-2288; www.paniolo haleresort.com.

The two-story **Lodge at Molokai Ranch** in Maunaloa is the latest addition to Molokai's accommodations infrastructure. Designed and decorated with the town's plantation past in mind, the 22-room lodge exudes a sense of intimacy and charm, with rattan furnishings and '30s-style Hawaiian prints. Rooms are spacious and individually decorated with cheerful upcountry decor. All offer long, unobstructed views of West Molokai's rolling hills, with the ocean in the distance. The eight-acre property includes a day spa, swimming pool, game room and lounge. ~ P.O. Box 259, Maunaloa, HI 96770; 877-726-4656, fax 808-552-2773; www.molokai-ranch.com. ULTRA-DELUXE.

If there is such a thing as luxury camping, a stay at **The Camps at Molokai Ranch** would be it. Their idea of "roughing it" includes spacious wood-frame "tentalows," canvas-sided bungalows that come with queen-size beds, overhead fans, solar-heated bathrooms and private wooden decks for lounging about. Three hearty meals are served in the communal cookhouse at each of the three camp-sites. **Paniolo Camp** is located several miles from Maunaloa, while **Kaupoa** is adjacent to a private white sand beach. **Kolo Cliffs** also has an oceanside setting on a hillside overlooking the south coast. Equally appealing are the wide range of activities offered to guests: mountain biking, horseback riding, kayaking and cultural hikes. There are also unique options like The Ropes Challenge, an adventurous obstacle course; the Paniolo Roundup, where guests participate in a cattle roundup; and the Cattle Drive, where you'll join *paniolos* as they move cattle from one pasture to another. The staff couldn't be more friendly or helpful, and time flies as one beautiful day flows into the next. ~ P.O. Box 259, Maunaloa, HI 96770; 877-726-4656, fax 808-552-2773; www.molokai-ranch.com. ULTRA-DELUXE.

DINING   The **Maunaloa Village Grill** offers dining amidst a plantation-town setting with wood floors, a screened-in dining veranda, a wonderful old brass bar, Hawaii's first stonegrill, plus *paniolo* memorabilia to provide a sense of place. The ranch-style cuisine ranges from well-prepared standards like prime rib and fresh catch to burgers. ~ Maunaloa; 808-552-0012, fax 808-552-2413. MODERATE TO ULTRA-DELUXE.

The Kaluakoi Hotel, on the island's far west end, has a penny-saver **snack bar** with sandwiches. ~ BUDGET.

That's just light artillery to back up the hotel's big gun, the **Ohia Lodge**, Molokai's finest restaurant. This multilevel, handsomely appointed establishment (high-beamed ceiling, rattan furnishings) looks out on the distant lights of Oahu. You can order from an extensive surf-and-turf menu that includes orange-glazed almond chicken, seafood linguine, tenderloin of beef with bearnaise sauce and rack of lamb with black-bean beurre blanc. Seeking a place to splurge? This is it. Breakfast and dinner. Dinner reservations required. ~ 808-552-2555, fax 808-552-2821; www.kaluakai.com. MODERATE TO ULTRA-DELUXE.

GROCERIES   Out West End way, **Maunaloa General Store,** in Maunaloa a few miles away from Kaluakoi Resort, has a limited stock of grocery items. Open 8 a.m. to 6 p.m. Closed Sunday. ~ 200 Maunaloa Highway; 808-552-2346.

SHOPPING   Over on Molokai's West End in the red-dust town of Maunaloa you'll stumble upon two great shops that share the same building and the same telephone. **Big Wind Kite Factory** has an astonishing assortment of high flyers. There are diamond kites, dancer kites, windsocks and rainbow tail kites. You can even pick up flags and banners here. At **The Plantation Gallery** there are aloha shirts, batik sarongs, tribal art, shell necklaces and other original pieces by over 30 Molokai craftspeople. They also have the largest collection of books about Hawaii and Hawaiian culture on the island. ~ Maunaloa Highway; 808-552-2364.

The **Kaluakoi Hotel** has a sundries store. Also on the grounds is the **Laughing Gecko**, offering local artwork and handicrafts, as well as T-shirts, *lauhala* jewelry and bracelets. ~ 808-552-2320.

To step out in style, head west to Kaluakoi Hotel's **Ohia Lounge**. The rattan furnishings, carpets, overhead fans and marvelous view of Honolulu, not to mention a local musician on the weekends, make it *the* place. ~ 808-552-2555.

NIGHTLIFE

KIOWEA PARK Watch for falling coconuts in the beautiful Kapuaiwa Grove, which is the centerpiece of this beach park. Towering palm trees extend almost to the water, leaving little space for a beach. The swimming here is only okay; the water is well-protected by a distant reef, but the bottom is shallow and rocky, and the water is muddy. Beyond the reef, fishing yields mullet, *manini*, parrotfish, milkfish, and *papio*, plus red, white and striped goatfish; crabbing is good in the evening. (This park is generally restricted to homesteaders, but if you stop for a picnic you may be allowed by the locals to stay.) A nice place to visit, but I wouldn't want to fall asleep in the shade of a coconut tree. Facilities include picnic area, restrooms and pavilion. (Unfortunately, the park is closed until further notice.) ~ Located one mile west of Kaunakakai on Route 460; 808-567-6104, fax 808-560-6665.

BEACHES & PARKS

Molokai's West End was once a rich adze quarry. The rock, vital to a Stone Age society, was fashioned into tools that were in turn used to create weapons, canoes, bowls and other necessities.

▲ Camping is usually restricted to homesteaders. If the park is vacant however, the Hawaiian Homelands Department in Hoolehua will issue permits for $5; hours are Monday through Friday from 7:45 a.m. to 4:30 p.m.

PALAAU STATE PARK Set in a densely forested area, this 233-acre park is ideal for a mountain sojourn. Several short trails lead to petroglyphs, a startling phallic rock, and the awesome Kalaupapa Lookout. The trail down to Kalaupapa Peninsula is also nearby. There are picnic area, restrooms and pavilion. ~ Take Route 460 six miles west from Kaunakakai, then follow Route 470 (Kalae Highway) about six more miles to the end of the road; 808-567-6923.

▲ State permit required. Tent camping only.

Text continued on page 390.

Molokai Pilgrimage

The ultimate Molokai experience is the pilgrimage to the Kalaupapa leper colony located along the rugged north shore of the island. Isolated on a 12-square-mile lava tongue that protrudes from the north shore, this sacred and historic site can be reached only by foot, mule or plane.

Here about 68 victims of Hansen's Disease, a chronic infectious bacterial disease that causes sores and ulcers and destroys tissue, live in solitude. Doctors have controlled the affliction since 1946 with sulfone drugs, and all the patients are free to leave. But many are 60 to 90 years old, and have lived on this windswept peninsula most of their lives.

The story of the remaining residents goes back to 1866 when the Hawaiian government began exiling lepers to this lonely spot on Molokai's rain-plagued north coast. In those days Kalaupapa was a fishing village, and lepers were segregated in the old settlement at Kalawao on the windy eastern side of the peninsula. The place was treeless and barren—a wasteland haunted by slow death. Lepers were shipped along the coast and pushed overboard. Abandoned with insufficient provisions and no shelter, they struggled against both the elements and disease.

To this lawless realm came Joseph Damien de Veuster, Father Damien. The Belgian Catholic priest, arriving in 1873, brought a spirit and energy that gave the colony new life. He built a church, attended to the afflicted and died of leprosy 16 years later. In 1995, the Pope made Father Damien "The Blessed Father Damien." Perhaps it is the spirit of this "Martyr of Molokai" that even today marks the indescribable quality of Kalaupapa. There is something unique and inspiring about the place, something you will have to discover yourself.

To visit Kalaupapa, you can fly, hike or ride muleback; there are no roads leading to this remote destination. Once there you must take a guided tour; no independent exploring is permitted. And no children under 16 are allowed. Bus tours are organized by **Molokai Mule Ride**. ~ 808-567-6088, 800-567-7550; www.muleride.com. For flight information, check **Molokai Air Shuttle** from Honolulu. ~ 808-567-6847. **Paragon Air** (808-244-3356, 800-428-1231) and **Pacific Wings** (808-873-0877, 888-575-4546; www.pacificwings.com) fly from Maui.

As far as I'm concerned, the mule ride is the only way to go. The Molokai Mule Ride conducts tours daily, except Sunday when the park is closed, weather permitting. You saddle up near the Kalaupapa Lookout and descend a 1700-foot precipice, among the tallest sea cliffs in the world. Kalaupapa unfolds below you as you switchback through lush vegetation on a three-mile-long trail. The ride? Exhilarating, frightening, but safe. And the views are awesome.

On the tour you will learn that Kalaupapa has been designated a national historical park. Among the points of interest within this refuge are numerous windblasted structures, a volcanic crater and several monuments. You'll visit **St. Philomena Church**, built by Father Damien in the 1870s, and **Kalawao Park**, an exotically beautiful spot on the lush eastern side of the peninsula. Father Damien's grave is also located here.

Definitely visit Kalaupapa. Fly in and you'll undergo an unforgettable experience; hike and it will become a pilgrimage.

HIDDEN ►

MOOMOMI BEACH 🏃 ⛵ 🤿 🏊 🚣 A small, remote beach studded with rocks and frequented only by local people—what more could you ask? While Moomomi is a small pocket beach, many people use the name to refer to a three-mile length of coastline that extends west from the pocket beach and includes two other strands, Kawaaloa Beach and Keonelele Beach. Moomomi offers good swimming, but use caution because the bottom is rocky and the beach is only partially protected. The snorkeling is very good along reefs and rocks. As for surfing, there are fair breaks at the mouth of the inlet. There's good surf-casting from the rocky headland to the west; you must pay a $25 deposit (refundable) to the Nature Conservancy. Keonelele Beach forms the coastal border of the Moomomi Dunes, a unique series of massive sand dunes that extend as far as four miles inland, covering Molokai's northwestern corner. Also known as the Desert Strip, this unique ecosystem is overseen by the Nature Conservancy (808-553-5236, fax 808-553-9870; www.tnc-hawaii.com), which can provide information and tours. The preserve protects five endangered plant species and is a habitat for the endangered Hawaiian green sea turtle. You'll find no facilities. ~ Take Route 460 west from Kaunakakai to Hoolehua. Go right on Route 481 (Puupeelua Avenue), then left on Farrington Avenue. Farrington starts as a paved road, then turns to dirt. After 2.2 miles of dirt track, the road forks. Take the right fork and follow it a half-mile to the beach. A four-wheel drive vehicle may be required.

HIDDEN ►

HALENA AND OTHER SOUTH COAST BEACHES ⛵ 🤿 🏃 🛶 🚣 Don't tell anyone, but there's a dirt road running several miles along a string of trackless beaches on the south shore. (Note, however, that at last report this road was closed to the public.) The first one, **Halena**, is a very funky ghost camp complete with a dozen weatherbeaten shacks and a few primitive facilities. To the west lies **Hale O Lono Beach**, with its pleasant bay and lagoon. To the east is **Kolo Wharf** (an abandoned pier collapsing into the sea), plus numerous fishponds, coconut groves and small sand beaches. This is an excellent area to explore, camp, hike, fish (bass, threadfin, *enenue*, red goatfish) and commune with hidden Hawaii. The swimming is also good if you don't mind muddy water. It's wise to boil or chemically treat the water. *Note*: Only Hale O Lono Beach has a public-access road; the other two are located on Molokai Ranch and are open to guests only. ~ Take Route 460 to Maunaloa. As you first enter town (before the road curves into the main section), you'll see houses on the left and a dirt road extending perpendicularly to the right.

Now, to get to Halena, take a right at the fork, then a quick left (there are signs posted), then drive a few hundred yards to the end. The shore is nearby; simply walk west along the beach several hundred yards to the shacks.

To get to Hale O Lono Beach, walk about a mile west along the beach from Halena.

To get to Kolo Wharf and the other beaches, go straight where the road forks. Kolo is two miles east over an equally rugged road. Sand beaches, coconut groves and fishponds extend for another six miles past Kolo. Then the road turns inland, improving considerably, and continues for seven miles more until it meets the main road two miles west of Kaunakakai.

For current information about road access contact Molokai Ranch. ~ 808-552-2741.

KAWAKIU BEACH 🏃 🏖 🛶 🦀 This idyllic spot is my favorite ◄ HIDDEN
Molokai campground. Here a small inlet, tucked away in Molokai's northwest corner, is edged by a beautiful beach with a sandy bottom. Nearby is a shady grove of *kiawe* trees, fringed by the rocky coastline. On a clear night you can see the lights of Oahu across Kaiwi Channel. This is a very good place to swim because the inlet offers some protection, but exercise caution. Snorkeling is good in summer near the rocks when the surf is low. People fish here for mountain bass, threadfin, *enenue* and red goatfish. There are no facilities here. ~ Take Route 460 west from Kaunakakai. At the Kaluakoi Hotel Golf Course, head to the road near the back 9. Drive north until you hit the beach. It's a tricky route, so you may want to check in with the hotel staff for further details; they warn against making the trip without a four-wheel drive. ~ 808-552-2555, 888-552-2550.

▲ That shady grove is a perfect site to pitch a tent.

PAPOHAKU BEACH PARK 🏖 🏃 🦀 This splendid beach extends for three miles along Molokai's west coast; it's an excellent place to explore, collect puka shells, or just lie back and enjoy

MOLOKAI KA HULA PIKO

If you're in town in mid- to late-May, you'll want to experience **Molokai Ka Hula Piko**, an event that honors the tradition that claims the hula was first danced on Molokai. A mile-long hike to a sunrise ceremony on a hillside leads to where the dances were said to have originated. Cameras are not allowed and decorum is the rule at this spiritual rite. Later in the day beachfront festivities at Papohaku Beach Park include hula and general high spirits. It can be hard to find a room or car during the event, so plan accordingly. Call the Molokai Visitors Association (800-800-6367) for information and updates.

the view of Oahu. Backed by *kiawe* trees and low sand dunes, Papohaku is the largest beach on the island, averaging 100 yards in width. Swimming is excellent, but use caution; sit out on the beach and observe the wave action before jumping in. There's not much rock or coral here so the snorkeling is only mediocre. You'll find good breaks for surfing when the wind isn't blowing from the shore. Use caution, especially in the winter months. The beach is also popular with bodysurfers. The fishing is good, usually for mountain bass, threadfin, *enenue* and red goatfish. There are picnic areas, restrooms and showers. ~ Take Route 460 for about 14 miles from Kaunakakai. Turn right onto the road to the Kaluakoi Resort. Continue past the hotel (don't turn onto the hotel road) and down the hill. Follow this macadam track, Kaluakoi Road, as it parallels the beach. Side roads from Kaluakoi Road and Pohakuloa Road (an adjoining thoroughfare) lead to Papohaku and other beaches.

▲ Tent only. County permit required.

Pope John Paul II beatified Father Damien in recognition of his service to leprosy victims banished to Kalaupapa.

Outdoor Adventures

With so little development and such an expanse of untouched land, Molokai would seem a haven for campers. Unfortunately, large segments of the island are owned by Molokai Ranch and other private interests; with the exception of a few beaches on Molokai Ranch property, these tracts are closed off behind locked gates.

CAMPING

There are a few parks for camping. A county permit is required for Papohaku Beach and O'ne Alii Park. Permits are $3 per person a day (50 cents for children) and are obtained at the County Parks and Recreation office in Kaunakakai. Hours are 8 a.m. to 4 p.m., Monday through Friday, so get your permit in advance. ~ 808-553-3204, fax 808-553-3206.

Camping at Palaau State Park is free but requires a permit from the Department of Land and Natural Resources (808-984-8109) on Maui, or from the park ranger (808-567-6923).

Molokai Fish & Dive sells camping gear. ~ 63 Ala Malama Street, Kaunakakai; 808-553-5926.

DIVING

If you're not traveling with gear, the following outfitters can rent you snorkeling equipment. Several provide snorkeling trips to prime spots around the island, and you might check with them regarding other activities such as scuba diving, kayaking and sailing. The best place for snorkeling on Molokai is at the 20-mile marker on the east side of the island. Here you're likely to see sturgeon, trumpetfish and a few green turtles.

Check out **Molokai Fish & Dive** for masks, fins and snorkels. ~ 61 Ala Malama Street, Kaunakakai; 808-553-5926. **Bill Kapuni's Snorkel and Dive Adventure** rents snorkel equipment. He leads dives to spots where it's not uncommon to see tiger sharks, hammerhead sharks and countless green turtles. He also teaches PADI classes. ~ 808-553-9867. **Molokai Action Adventures** offers three- to four-hour snorkeling expeditions. ~ Kaunakakai; 808-558-8184.

KAYAKING

For a scenic paddling adventure, **Lani's Kayak** has full-day North Shore excursions that take in breathtaking sea cliffs and lush greenery. Its two-and-a-half-hour Southeast tour features turtles and waterfalls. ~ P.O. Box 826, Kaunakakai, HI 96748; 808-558-8563.

Molokai Action Adventures has half- and full-day kayaking trips. ~ Kaunakakai; 808-558-8184.

An exploration of the old Kolo wharf in an ocean kayak is offered by **Molokai Ranch**. Your guides will share their knowledge of the ancient Hawaiian fish ponds. ~ 888-729-0059.

One- and two-person kayak rentals are available at **Hotel Molokai's Outdoor Activities**. They also have car carriers for rent. ~ Kamehameha V Highway, Kaunakakai; 808-553-4477; www.hotelmolokai.com.

SAILING

Providing Molokai's only sailing adventure, **Molokai Charters** operates *Satan's Doll*, a 42-foot sloop that is docked on the wharf in Kaunakakai. Step aboard for sunset cruises, whale-watching tours and snorkeling excursions to Lanai. ~ 808-553-5852.

FISHING

Depending on the weather, deep-sea fishing charters will take you to various spots that are within ten to twenty miles of Molokai. Here you're likely to catch mahimahi, tuna, marlin and *ono*.

Alyce C Commercial and Sport Fishing offers half-, three-quarter, and full-day excursions—all equipment included. Bring your own food and drink. They also operate whale-watching tours from late November to late March. ~ Kaunakakai; 808-558-8377. **Molokai Action Adventures** provides all the equipment for half- or full-day charters. ~ Kaunakakai; 808-558-8184.

An expert in **netcasting** at **Molokai Horse and Wagon Ride** takes folks out by the reef for a half-day or full-day excursion. You can lay nets, cast fish or even learn how to throw net. ~ 808-558-8380.

RIDING STABLES

Molokai Wagon Ride sponsors wagon and saddle tours to scenic and historic sites at Mapulehu on eastern Molokai; this outfit also rents horses with guides. ~ Mapulehu Mango Grove, about 15 miles east of Kaunakakai; 808-558-8380; e-mail wgn ride@aloha.net. **Molokai Ranch** offers a variety of horseback rides including a paniolo round-up and a cattle trail drive. ~ 808-552-2741.

BIKING

Traffic is light and slow-moving, making Molokai an ideal place for two-wheeling adventurers. The roads are generally good, with some potholes out East End near Halawa Valley. The terrain is mostly flat or gently rolling, with a few steep ascents. Winds are strong and sometimes make for tough going.

For those in good shape and who like to climb, contact **Molokai Ranch** for their advanced mountain-bike tour on rugged terrain. Afternoon tours are for beginners and feature a single-track or ranch-road descent to Hale O Lono. All in all, the ranch features 100 miles of trails. ~ 888- 729-0059.

Molokai has the largest reef system in the United States and the highest bog in the world.

Bike Rentals   **Molokai Bicycle** sells, repairs and rents mountain and road bikes. Rentals include helmets, locks and maps. Closed Sunday, Monday and Friday. ~ 80 Mohala Street, Kaunakakai; 808-553-3931. **Hotel Molokai's Outdoor Activities** has bikes for younger children and buggies for tots. ~ Kamehameha V Highway, Kaunakakai; 808-553-4477; www.hotelmolokai.com.

HIKING

Molokai features some splendid country and numerous areas that seem prime for hiking, but few trails have been built or maintained and most private land is off-limits to visitors. Some excellent hiking possibilities, but no official trails, are offered along the beaches described above. Palaau State Park also has several short jaunts to points of interest.

The only lengthy treks lead to the island's rugged north coast. Four valleys—Halawa, Wailau, Pelekunu and Waikolu—cut through the sheer cliffs guarding this windswept shore.

The **Pelekunu Trail** begins several hundred yards beyond the Waikolu Valley Lookout (see the Driving Tour on "Molokai's Outback"). It is unmaintained and extremely difficult. Traversing Nature Conservancy property, the trail leads to a lookout point and then drops into the valley. This is one to avoid.

The **Wailau Trail** is another very difficult trail; it takes about 12 hours and passes through some muddy rainforest regions. The trailhead is off Route 450 about 15 miles east of Kaunakakai. The trail extends across nearly the entire island from south to north. Dangers include deep mud and wild boar. To hike it, you must obtain permission from Pearl Petro. Send a self-addressed stamped envelope with a letter of nonresponsibility. ~ P.O. Box 125, Kaunakakai, HI 96748; 808-558-8113.

The **Kalaupapa Trail** is the easiest and best-maintained trail descending the north *pali*. A trail description is given in the "Kalaupapa" section in this chapter. To hike here you must obtain permission and pay $40 for a mandatory tour of the leper colony. Bring food and water along for this four-hour tour. Call Damien Tours for permission and information. ~ 808-567-6171, fax 808-567-9018.

The only valley accessible by car is Halawa. The **Halawa Valley Trail,** one of Molokai's prettiest hikes, extends for two miles from the mouth of the valley to the base of Moaula Falls. This 250-foot cascade tumbles down a sheer cliff to a cold mountain pool perfect for swimming. Hipuapua Falls, a sister cascade just a third of a mile north, shoots 500 feet down the *pali*. The trail can be accessed only through a guided tour. Call **Pilipo's Halawa Falls and Cultural Hike.** ~ 808-553-4355.

Historical Hikes West Molokai offers hikes to Molokai's west end. Guides integrate *mo'olelo* (or storytelling) into the tour to share their knowledge of the area's cultural heritage. You'll explore old fishing villages, ancient *heiaus*, petroglyphs and sacred monuments. Lunch is provided on the intermediate and advanced hikes. ~ 808-553-9803, 800-274-9303; www.molokai-aloha. com/bikes.

Transportation

AIR

When your plane touches down at **Molokai Airport,** you'll realize what a one-canoe island you're visiting. There's a snack bar and adjoining lounge, which seem to open and close all day, plus a few car rental and airline offices. It's seven miles to the main town of Kaunakakai. There's no public transportation available. However, shuttle service can be arranged through some of the hotels, and taxis are available.

The airport is served by Hawaiian Airlines in turbo prop planes. Aloha Island Air and Molokai Air Shuttle fly small prop planes.

Pacific Wings, Molokai Air Shuttle and Paragon have daily flights from Maui and Oahu. To fly direct from Honolulu to Kalaupapa, try Aloha Island Air, which can always be relied upon for friendly service.

CAR RENTALS

The existing companies are **Dollar Rent A Car** (808-567-6156, 800-800-4000 from the mainland, 800-367-7006 in Hawaii) and **Budget Rent A Car** (808-567-6877, 800-283-4387 from the mainland, 800-451-3600 in Hawaii), and **Island Kine Auto Rentals** (808-553-5242).

JEEP RENTALS

Budget Rent A Car rents jeeps, but requires that you drive them only on paved roads! ~ 808-567-6877, 800-283-4387 from the mainland, 800-451-3600 in Hawaii. (Be aware that the rental car collision insurance provided by most credit cards does not cover jeeps.)

TOURS **Kukui Tours and Limousine Service** (808-553-5133) offers half- and full-day tours (and limo service, if you want to go in style). **Molokai Off-Road Tours** (808-553-3369) will take you to see the Coffees of Hawaii plantation, a macadamia nut farm, St. Joseph's Church and the fishponds.

Kauai

Seventy miles northwest of Oahu, across a storm-wracked channel that long protected against invaders, lies Kauai. If ever an island deserved to be called a jewel of the sea, this "Garden Isle" is the one. Across Kauai's brief 33-mile expanse lies a spectacular and wildly varied landscape.

Along the north shore is the Hanalei Valley, a lush patchwork of tropical agriculture, and the rugged Na Pali Coast with cliffs rising 2700 feet above the boiling surf. Spanning 14 miles of pristine coastline, the narrow valleys and sheer walls of Na Pali are so impenetrable that a road entirely encircling the island has never been built. Here, among razor-edged spires and flower-choked gorges, the producers of the movie *South Pacific* found their Bali Hai. To the east flows the fabled Wailua River, a sacred area to Hawaiians that today supports a sizable population in the blue-collar towns of Wailua and Kapaa.

Along the south coast stretch the matchless beaches of Poipu, with white sands and an emerald sea that seem drawn from a South Seas vision. It was here in November 1982 that Hurricane Iwa, packing 110-mile-an-hour winds and carrying devastating tidal waves, overwhelmed the island. Ironically, it was also this area that sustained some of the most severe damage when Hurricane Iniki struck in September 1992.

The tourist enclave of Poipu gives way to rustic Hanapepe, an agricultural town asleep since the turn of the 20th century, and Waimea, where in 1778 Captain James Cook became the first Westerner to tread Hawaiian soil. In Kauai's arid southwestern corner, where palm trees surrender to cactus plants, snow-white beaches sweep for miles along Barking Sands and Polihale.

In the island's center, Mount Waialeale rises 5148 feet (Mount Kawaikini at 5243 feet is the island's tallest peak) to trap a continuous stream of dark-bellied clouds that spill more than 450 inches of rain annually, making this gloomy peak the wettest spot on earth and creating the headwaters for the richest river system in all Hawaii—the Hanapepe, Hanalei, Wailua and Waimea rivers. Also draining Waialeale is the Alakai Swamp, a wilderness bog that covers 30 square miles of the island's interior. Yet to the west, just a thunderstorm away, lies a barren landscape seemingly borrowed from Arizona and featuring the 2857-foot-deep Waimea Canyon, the Grand Canyon of the Pacific.

From Lihue, Kauai's largest and most important city, Route 50 (Kaumualii Highway) travels to the south while Route 56 (Kuhio Highway) heads along the north shore. Another highway climbs past Waimea Canyon into the mountainous interior.

Papayas, taro and bananas grow in lush profusion along these roads, and marijuana is grown deep in the hills and narrow valleys, but sugar is still Kauai's most significant crop. Tourism has overtaken agriculture in the Kauai economy and is becoming increasingly vital to the island's 56,000 population.

It's sad to see the decline of the sugar industry, which is intensifying demands to replace agricultural income with tourist dollars. But the Garden Isle still offers hidden beaches and remote valleys to any traveler possessing a native's sensibility. And even though sugar is in retreat, some cane fields are still evident across most of the island. A number of years ago, Kauai provided a window on 19th-century life, when sugar was king. Deep-green stalks covered the landscape in every direction, edging from the lip of the ocean to the foot of the mountains. But two major hurricanes and a waning industry have led to many cane fields being left fallow or converted to coffee, sunflowers and corn.

Nevertheless, a few island sugar mills are still redolent with the cloyingly sweet smell of cane, and mammoth cane trucks, sugar stalks protruding like bristles from a wild boar, continue to charge down dusty roads. Depending on the phase of the growing cycle, visitors pass fields crowded with mature cane, tall as Midwest corn, or deep-red earth planted with rows of seedlings. In the evening, when harvested cane is set afire, black smoke billows from deep within the fields.

Historically, Kauai is Hawaii's premier island—the first to be created geologically and the first "discovered" by white men. It was here that Madame Pele, goddess of volcanoes, initially tried to make her home. Perhaps because of the island's moist, tropical climate, she failed to find a place dry enough to start her fire and left in frustration for the islands to the southeast.

Formed by a single volcano that became extinct about six million years ago, Kauai is believed by some anthropologists to be the original Hawaiian island populated by Polynesians. After Captain Cook arrived in 1778, explorers continued to visit the island periodically. Ten years later, settlers began to arrive, and in 1820 the first missionaries landed in the company of Prince George, son of Kauai's King Kaumualii. By 1835, the Koloa sugar plantation was founded, becoming the first successful sugar mill in Hawaii.

Kauai was the site not only of the original but the anomalous, as well. In 1817, George Scheffer, a Prussian adventurer representing Czar Nicholas of Russia, built a fort in Waimea. He soon lost the support of both the Czar and Kauai's King Kaumualii, but left as his legacy the stone ruins of Russia's imperialist effort.

Kauai was the only island not conquered by Kamehameha the Great when he established the Hawaiian kingdom. Thwarted twice in his attempts to land an attack force—once in 1796 when high seas prevented an invasion from Oahu and again in 1802 when his battle-ready army was suddenly ravaged by disease—he finally won over Kaumualii by diplomacy in 1810.

But Kauai's most fascinating history is told by mythmakers recounting tales of the *Menehunes*, the Hobbits of the Pacific. These miniature forest people labored like giants to create awesome structures. Mysterious ruins such as the Menehune Fishpond outside Lihue reputedly date back before the Polynesians and are attributed by the mythically inclined to an earlier, unknown race. Supernaturally strong and very industrious, the *Menehunes* worked only at night, completing each project by dawn or else leaving it forever unfinished. Several times they made so much noise in their strenuous laboring that they frightened birds as far away as Oahu.

They were a merry, gentle people with ugly red faces and big eyes set beneath long eyebrows. Two to three feet tall, each practiced a trade in which he was a master. They inhabited caves, hollow logs and banana-leaf huts, and eventually grew to a population of 500,000 adults.

Some say the *Menehunes* came from the lost continent of Mu, which stretched across Polynesia to Fiji before it was swallowed by floods. Where they finally traveled to is less certain. After the Polynesians settled Kauai, the *Menehune* king,

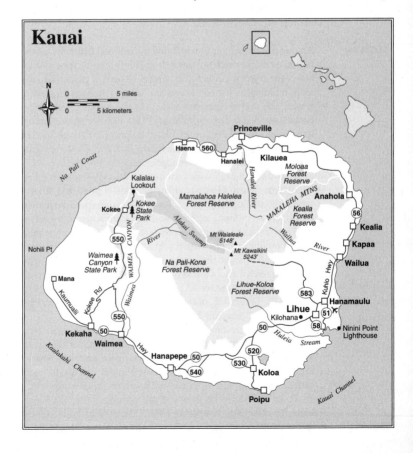

Kauai

concerned that his people were intermarrying with an alien race, ordered the *Menehunes* to leave the island. But many, unwilling to depart so luxurious a home, hid in the forests. There, near hiking trails and remote campsites, you may see them even today.

▼▼▼▼▼▼▼▼▼▼
Lihue Area

Unappealing in appearance, Lihue sits at the crossroads between the tropical regions of the north and the sunsplashed beaches to the south. So a visit to Lihue is inevitable. Commercial and civic center of the island, the town is an odd amalgam of contemporary Hawaii and traditional plantation life. The sugar mill at the edge of town, with its aging conveyor belts and twin smoke stacks, is still a vital element in the landscape. A portion of the 5500 population continues to live in woodframe plantation houses, and cane fields surround the town. But the airport here is an international landing strip that has grown considerably during the past two decades and Lihue possesses Kauai's main port, Nawiliwili Harbor.

SIGHTS

Among the attractions you will find is the **Kauai Museum**, a two-building complex rich in Hawaiiana. This is a prime spot to learn about the history, culture and natural history of the island. The main building focuses on Hawaiian heritage with its displays of feather leis and ancient calabashes. In the adjacent exhibition, Kauai's natural history unfolds and 19th-century plantation life is revealed in a collection of old photographs. Closed Sunday. Admission. ~ 4428 Rice Street, Lihue; 808-245-6931, fax 808-245-6864; e-mail museum@midpac.net.

Providing an even wider window on Kauai's sugar-cane heritage, **Grove Farm Homestead** is a beautifully preserved 80-acre spread. Founded in 1864 by the son of missionaries, the plantation is like an outdoor museum with the main house, farm office, workers' homes and a private cottage still intact. Surrounding these tinroof buildings are banana patches, gardens and pastures. Two-hour guided tours of this fascinating facility are available (Monday, Wednesday and Thursday at 10 a.m. and 1 p.m.) by reservation. Donation requested. ~ Call in advance or write to P.O. Box 1631, Lihue, HI 96766, and they will provide directions; 808-245-3202, fax 808-245-7988.

Another interesting side trip from Lihue is down Rice Street to busy **Nawiliwili Harbor**. This deep-water port, with its cruise ships and cargo vessels, is the island's major seaport. Nearby **Kalapaki Beach** is one of Kauai's most popular strands, both because of its proximity to Lihue and its pretty white sands.

From Nawiliwili Harbor, you can continue on to the **Menehune** (or **Alakoko**) **Fishpond**. This 900-foot-long pond, spread across a valley floor and backdropped by the Hoary Head Moun-

Three-Day Itinerary

Day 1
- Arrive at the airport in Lihue and drive to the Poipu area. Check in to your condominium or hotel and spend the afternoon relaxing on the beach.

- Have dinner in one of Poipu's many restaurants or venture up to Koloa Town to dine.

Day 2
- Drive out Route 50, stopping in **Hanapepe** (page 420) to peruse the local art galleries (page 427).

- Continue on Route 50, turning right on Route 550 out to what is called the Pacific's "Grand Canyon"—**Waimea Canyon** (page 424). Make sure to continue out to the end of the road to visit the **Kalalau Lookout,** which gives you an extraordinary view of the Kalalau Valley.

- If you want to continue out along Route 50 to the two-mile stretch of white sand at **Polihale State Park** (page 430)—you won't be disappointed.

Day 3
- This is the day to head up to the **North Shore** (assuming it's not raining there). First stop in Lihue at **Ma's Family Restaurant** (page 405) for a local-style breakfast.

- Drive on up to **Hanalei** (page 446) for a look around and to stock up on ice-cold water and other provisions. If you're adventurous, hike the first two miles of the **Kalalau Trail** (page 465) at the end of Route 560. If you're in a lazier mood, join the others relaxing at **Kee Beach** and snorkeling along the reef (page 447).

- Plan to have dinner in Hanalei or Kapaa before returning to Poipu.

tain Range, dates back well before the Polynesians. Or so the mythmakers would like you to believe. Legend has it that a line of leprechaun-like *Menehunes* 25 miles long passed rocks from hand to hand and built the pond in a single night. Their only request of the prince and princess for whom they built the structure was that these two mortals not watch them while they worked. When the *Menehunes* discovered that curiosity had overcome the two, who were watching the midget workers by the light of the moon, the *Menehunes* turned them into the pillars of stone you see on the mountainside above the fishpond. ~ Take Rice Street to Nawiliwili, then right on Route 58, a quick left on Niumalu Road and finally right on Hulemalu Road.

HIDDEN ►   Also visible from the vista overlooking the fishpond, and accessible to kayakers, is the adjoining **Huleia National Wildlife Refuge**, a 238-acre preserve that rises from the river basin up the wooded slopes of Huleia Valley. This estuary is home to 31 bird species including four different endangered species of waterbirds—the Hawaiian stilt, Hawaiian duck, Hawaiian gallinule and Hawaiian coot.

A short distance from Lihue, Kuhio Highway (Route 56), the main road to Kauai's north shore, descends into the rustic village of **Kapaia**. Sagging wood structures and a gulch choked with banana plants mark this valley. On the right, **Lihue Hongwanji Temple**, one of the island's oldest, smiles from beneath a modern-day facelift.

To the left, off Kuhio Highway, Maalo Road threads through three miles of sugar cane to **Wailua Falls**. These twin cascades tumble 80 feet into a heavenly pool fringed with *hala* trees. A steep, difficult trail leads down to the luxurious pool at the base of the falls; or if you're not that ambitious, a more easily accessible pool lies just a couple hundred yards past the falls.

Follow Kuhio Highway and you'll arrive in **Hanamaulu**, an old plantation town where falsefront stores and tinroof houses line the roadway.

Or you can head a mile-and-a-half southwest from Lihue on Kaumualii Highway (Route 50) to **Kilohana** for a view of the luxurious side of island life. This 16,000-square-foot Tudor mansion was once home to the Wilcoxes, one of the island's most prominent families. Today, the 1935 house serves as a center for arts-and-crafts shops and museum displays, and the 35 surrounding acres are devoted to a re-creation of traditional plantation life. Wander down the "coral path" and you'll pass a tropical garden and a succession of corrugated-roof houses. Papaya, banana and avocado trees line the route and roosters crow in the distance. Directly behind the plantation grounds, fields of sugar cane roll to the foothills of the mountains. Carriages pulled by Clydesdales tour the grounds and wagon tours lead out into the cane fields. There are weekly luaus. ~ Kaumualii Highway; 808-245-5608, fax 808-245-7818; e-mail kilohana@hawaiian.net.

If you are in search of budget-priced lodging facilities, there are few places in all Hawaii as inviting as Lihue. Three low-cost establishments are located just two miles from the airport and a block or two from downtown Lihue.

LODGING

Lihue Area

At the **Tip Top Motel** you'll find trim rooms with tile floors, stall showers and air conditioning. The sheer size of this two-story, two-building complex makes it impersonal by Kauai standards, but I found the management to be very warm. You'll have to eat meals in the adjoining restaurant or elsewhere, since none of the rooms have kitchenettes. ~ 3173 Akahi Street, Lihue; 808-245-2333, fax 808-246-8988. BUDGET.

The **Motel Lani**, three blocks from the Rice Shopping Center, has ten cozy rooms facing a small patio where guests can lounge about in lawn chairs. The units are clean and comfortable, though sparsely furnished. About half are air conditioned; all have fans and refrigerators. This place has a noisy lobby (with television) just off busy Rice Street. ~ 4240 Rice Street, Lihue; 808-245-2965. BUDGET.

On a back street less than a half-mile from downtown Lihue, there's a motel called **Hale Lihue**. Here the proprietor rents rooms without kitchenettes and others that are equipped both with kitchens and air conditioning. The rooms are simply furnished and well-kept. There's a lobby with television plus a tiny garden in the front yard. ~ 2931 Kalena Street, Lihue; 808-245-2751. BUDGET.

Conveniently situated across the street from Nawiliwili Park is the **Garden Island Inn**. You'll find it near the corner of Waapa Road and Wilcox Road, a short stroll from Kalapaki Beach. Each room is light and airy with comfortable furnishings, fresh flowers, attractive appointments and overhead fans. You'll hear occasional noise from passing trucks and planes. Children are welcome, and several of the large rooms are sufficiently spacious for families. All of the fully equipped units have refrigerators, wet bars and microwave ovens. Second- and third-story rooms have air conditioning. Beach gear, including boogieboards, is loaned free to guests. The grounds are trimly landscaped and highlighted by a koi pond in which several dozen carp flash their colors. ~ 3445 Wilcox Road, Lihue; 808-245-7227, 800-648-0154, fax 808-245-7603; www.gardenislandinn.com, e-mail info@gardenislandinn.com. MODERATE TO DELUXE.

Banyan Harbor Resort, a collection of woodframe buildings across a busy street from Nawiliwili Harbor, has one- and two-bedroom condominiums with ocean and garden views. Most of the 148 units here are leased by the month, but a handful rent by the night. ~ 3411 Wilcox Road, Lihue; 808-245-7333, 800-422-6926, fax 808-246-3687; www.vacation-kauai.com, e-mail banyan @aloha.net. MODERATE TO DELUXE.

DINING

HIDDEN ▶

For the money, the best breakfast spot on the island is **Ma's Family Restaurant**. This nondescript café makes up in clientele what it lacks in physical beauty. Early in the morning the place is crowded with locals on their way to the cane fields. In the world of breakfasts, this is the bargain basement. Or if you want to go Hawaiian at lunch, order a *laulau*, poi and *lomi* salmon dish. No dinner. ~ 4277 Halenani Street, Lihue; 808-245-3142. BUDGET.

What Ma's is to breakfast, **Hamura Saimin** is to lunch and dinner. It's just around the corner, so you're liable to see the same faces lining Hamura's curving counter. When I ate there the place was packed. I had the *"saimin* special," a combination of noodles, won tons, eggs, meat, onion, vegetables and fish cake in a delicious broth. ~ 2956 Kress Street, Lihue; 808-245-3271. BUDGET.

Oki Diner is open 24 hours a day. Ramen, wonton soup and various Asian dishes are among the offerings. ~ 3125 Kuhio Highway, Lihue; 808-245-5899. BUDGET TO MODERATE.

Want to go Japanese? Try **Restaurant Kiibo**, a contemporary-style restaurant with a tatami room. You'll find the menu filled with yakitori, tempura and tofu dishes, as well as sushi and sashimi. ~ 2991 Umi Street, Lihue; 808-245-2650. BUDGET TO DELUXE.

The **Lihue Barbeque Inn** offers Asian dishes as well as all-American meals. Breakfasts at this comfortable establishment are pretty standard; the lunch menu includes salads, soups, sandwiches, hamburgers and a daily special that often features teriyaki and Pacific Rim–influenced dishes; at dinner, there's steak, shrimp tempura and scampi. Closed Sunday. ~ 2982 Kress Street, Lihue; 808-245-2921. MODERATE TO DELUXE.

A favorite among tourists is the **Tip Top Café and Bakery**. Visitors can take their pick from any in a succession of booths in this large and impersonal eatery. Breakfasts are inexpensive (and the macadamia nut pancakes are delicious). Lunch entrées are not very imaginative and have received negative reviews from readers. The well-known bakery serves macadamia nut cookies, the house

FROM THE MENEHUNES TO INDIANA JONES

Board your kayak and head down the Huleia River, home to the legendary Menehune Fishpond. **Island Adventures,** an eco-friendly kayaking company, escorts you to the heart of the Huleia National Wildlife Refuge. Spottings of Koloa ducks, egrets, Hawaiian stilts and jumping fish are all part of the adventure. You can even play Indiana Jones at the rope swing used in *Raiders of the Lost Ark.* To complete the trip, you'll take a short hike through the wildlife refuge, where your local guide will point out Hawaiian medicinal plants and fruits as you squish along a muddy trail. A very enjoyable, laidback Hawaiian adventure. ~ Nawiliwili Small Boat Harbor, Lihue; 808-245-9662, fax 808-246-9661; www.kauaifun. com, e-mail funkauai@hawaiian.net.

specialty. No dinner. Closed Monday. ~ 3173 Akahi Street, Lihue; 808-245-2333, fax 808-246-8988. BUDGET.

If you're in Nawiliwili, check out **The Beach Hut**. They offer a full breakfast menu; for lunch and dinner, there are hamburgers, sandwiches and salads. Order at the window and dine upstairs on a deck overlooking the water. ~ 3474 Rice Street, Nawiliwili; 808-246-6330. BUDGET.

Nearby, the Pacific Ocean Plaza has two tasty options. The ever-popular **Kauai Chop Suey** (808-245-8790) features an ample Cantonese menu. Closed Monday. BUDGET TO MODERATE. **Café Portofino** (808-245-2121), a bright and attractive Italian restaurant, offers a partial ocean view. Comfortably furnished and nicely decorated, the café serves up several pasta dishes as well as house specialties like calamari, scampi, eggplant parmigiana and sautéed rabbit. There's also an espresso bar. MODERATE TO ULTRA-DELUXE. ~ 3501 Rice Street, Nawiliwili.

For good food at modest prices, Lihue is a prime spot. This is the center of most island business, so it contains numerous restaurants that cater largely to local folks.

J. J.'s Broiler is widely known for its "Slavonic steak," a tenderloin that's broiled, then sliced thin and basted with a wine, butter and garlic sauce. This family-style eatery offers standard steak dishes, seafood platters and a salad bar, and enjoys a waterfront location overlooking Kalapaki Beach. With its windswept terrace and open-air dining room, it has a sunny Southern California ambience. ~ 3416 Rice Street, Nawiliwili; 808-246-4422, fax 808-245-7019; e-mail jjsbroiler@altavista.com. DELUXE TO ULTRA-DELUXE.

If it's atmosphere and a taste of the Orient you're after, reserve a tea room at the **Hanamaulu Café**. My favorite is the garden room overlooking a rock-bound pond filled with carp. Lunch and dinner are the same here, with an excellent selection of Japanese and Chinese dishes. There's also a sushi bar at night. Children's portions are available. Closed Monday. ~ Kuhio Highway, Hanamaulu; 808-245-2511, fax 808-245-2497. MODERATE.

Take a plantation manor, add a flowering garden, and you have the setting for **Gaylord's**. Elevating patio dining to a high art, this alfresco restaurant looks out on the spacious lawns and spreading trees of Kilohana plantation. The menu features fresh island fish, pasta, farm-raised venison, baby back ribs, slow-roasted prime rib and chicken Kauai in addition to exotic daily specials and a well-rounded wine list. Or consider attending their luau Monday, Tuesday or Thursday. A rare combination of Old World elegance and tropical ambience; lunch, dinner and Sunday brunch. Reservations recommended. ~ At Kilohana on Kaumualii Highway, one-and-one-half miles southwest of Lihue; 808-245-9593, fax 808-246-1087; www.gaylordskauai.com, e-mail gylords @aloha.net. DELUXE TO ULTRA-DELUXE.

Lihue has by far the greatest number of grocery, health food and **GROCERIES** fresh fish stores on the island. This commercial center is an ideal place to stock up for a camping trip, a hike or a lengthy sojourn in an efficiency apartment.

The **Big Save Market** is one of Lihue's main grocery stores. Its doors are open from 7 a.m. to 11 p.m. every day. ~ Lihue Shopping Center, 4444 Rice Street, Lihue; 808-245-6571.

Vim & Vigor has an excellent line of vitamins, juices and bath supplies, plus natural foods and sandwiches. ~ Rice Shopping Center, 4300 block of Rice Street, Lihue; 808-245-9053.

If you hanker for fresh fish, be sure to check out **The Fish Express.** ~ 3343 Kuhio Highway, Lihue; 808-245-9918.

Don't miss the **Sunshine Market** every Friday afternoon in ◄ *HIDDEN* the parking lot of the town stadium. Local folks turn out to sell homegrown produce, "talk story," and generally have a good time. It's a great place to buy island fruits and vegetables at bargain prices, and an even better spot to meet Kauai's farmers. Early morning is the best time to arrive—before the best produce has disappeared. ~ Hoolako Street. For other market locations, check www.kauaivisitorsbureau.org.

Love's Bakery sells day-old products including delicious breads at a discount. ~ 4100 Rice Street, Nawiliwili; 808-245-6113.

For everyday needs and common items, try the local shopping **SHOPPING** centers. **Anchor Cove**, a beachside mall, stands along Rice Street near Kalapaki Beach in Nawiliwili. **Pacific Ocean Plaza**, a glass-and-stucco shopping center, rests nearby at 3501 Rice Street. Under renovation at press time, most of the shops plan to remain open.

The **Kauai Marriott Resort** has a selection of shops along its colonnaded walkways. ~ Kalapaki Beach, Lihue; 808-245-5050.

At the **Kapaia Stitchery** half the items are designed and stitched by local women. There's an array of T-shirts, aloha shirts, Hawaiian quilting kits and dresses, plus stunning patchwork quilts. This is an excellent place to buy Hawaiian fabrics. In addition to the handmade quality, the prices here are often lower than in larger stores. ~ Kuhio Highway, just north of the hamlet of Kapaia; 808-245-2281.

Kukui Grove Center is the island's largest shopping mall, an ultramodern complex. Here are department stores, bookshops, specialty stores and other establishments. Though lacking the intimacy of Kauai's independent handicraft outlets, the center provides such a concentration of goods that it's hard to bypass. ~ Kaumualii Highway, one-half mile southwest of Lihue; 808-245-7784.

If you can't find what you're after in Lihue, you've always got the rest of the island. Failing that, you'll just have to wait for that plane flight back to the Big Papaya, Honolulu.

NIGHTLIFE You'll find a lot of local color at the **Lihue Café**. The drinks are cheap, the tourists are few. ~ 2978 Umi Street, Lihue; 808-245-6471.

Duke's Canoe Club, an attractive watering hole overlooking the beach at the Kauai Marriott Resort, has live Hawaiian minstrels roaming nightly. ~ Kalapaki Beach, Lihue; 808-245-5050.

BEACHES & PARKS **KALAPAKI BEACH** 🏊 🚣 🏄 This wide strand stretches for a quarter-mile in front of the Marriott Kauai hotel. Popular with surfers since ancient Hawaiian times, Kalapaki is situated right on Nawiliwili Bay, an appealing but busy harbor. It is also one of the best swimming beaches on the island since the harbor protects it from heavy shorebreak. Out past the harbor, the Hoary Head mountains rise in the background. Beginner's surfing is best in the center of Nawiliwili Bay, where there is a right slide. More experienced surfers will find good breaks next to the rock wall near the lighthouse, where there's a left slide. There's also good surfing on the right side of the bay. Nicknamed "Hang Ten," these left slide breaks are a good place for nose-riding. Snorkeling is so-so at Kalapaki, but anglers should have better luck. Both off the pier and near the lighthouse are good spots for mullet, big-eyed scad, *papio*, bonefish and threadfin; sometimes *ulua*, *oama* and red bigeye can be caught here, too. Nawiliwili Park, next to the beach, has a picnic area and restrooms. ~ Take Rice Street from Lihue to Nawiliwili Park. Enter from the park.

NIUMALU BEACH PARK 🏕 🚣 🎣 This tree-lined park is tucked into a corner of Nawiliwili Harbor near a sugar-loading facility and a small-boat harbor. With neighbors like this and no swimming facilities, the park's key feature is its proximity to Lihue. It is popular nonetheless with picnickers and the adjacent Huleia River attracts kayakers, fishermen and crabbers. Facilities include a picnic area, restrooms and showers. ~ Take Rice Street to Nawiliwili, turn right on Route 58, then left on Niumalu Road.

▲ Camping allowed with county permit.

FROM SUGAR TO SHOPS

Kilohana is one of Hawaii's most beautiful complexes. Set in a grand sugar plantation house, it rests amid acres of manicured grounds. Many rooms in this museum-cum-mall are furnished in period style to recapture 1930s-era plantation life. The galleries, boutiques and crafts shops are equally enchanting. ~ Kaumualii Highway, one-and-one-half miles southwest of Lihue.

NININI BEACH 🏖 🐟 🏊 Hidden along a rocky coastline   ◄ HIDDEN
between Nawiliwili Bay and the lighthouse on Ninini Point are
two small sand beaches. Lying at the base of a sea cliff, these pocket
beaches are separated by a lava rock formation and are usually
protected from currents and winds. The smaller beach is about a
quarter-mile from Ninini Point and the larger is known as **Running
Waters Beach**, named for the numerous springs that bubble out
of the lava and percolate up into the sand. Both are excellent for
sunbathing and swimming. Snorkeling is very good, and bodysurfers frequent Running Waters Beach. Since both beaches are
pretty close to civilization, I don't recommend camping at either
beach. There are no facilities here. ~ Take the road leading through
the Marriott Kauai property in Nawiliwili. Follow this road to
the golf course clubhouse. Park and walk across the golf course
in a direction several degrees to the right of the lighthouse. The
smaller beach can be reached by walking from Running Water
Beach toward the lighthouse for about three-tenths of a mile.

HANAMAULU BEACH PARK 🏖 ⚓ Here's an idyllic park nestled in Hanamaulu Bay and crowded with ironwood and coconut
trees. The beach is a narrow corridor of sand at the head of
Hanamaulu Bay. The bay is well-protected, affording excellent
swimming, but the water is usually murky so there is not much
snorkeling. I found this a great place for picnicking and shell collecting. Anglers can expect to hook bonefish, mullet and big-eyed
scad. A picnic area, restrooms, showers and a playground are some
of the facilities here. ~ Take Kuhio Highway to Hanamaulu, then
turn down the road leading to the bay.

▲ Needles from the ironwood trees make a natural bed at
this lovely site. Tent and trailer camping; county permit required.

All during the 1980s and early 1990s, the Poipu Beach
region represented the fastest-growing tourist destination   **Poipu Area**
on Kauai. With the construction of new condominiums
and the opening of the Hyatt Regency Kauai in 1991, it was one
of the most popular spots in the entire state. However, Hurricane
Iniki slowed the pace of development, and has significantly
diminished Poipu's previous pattern of steady growth. Some of
the hotels along the beach are still boarded up years after Hurricane Iniki.

What you will find in this warm, dry, sunny southeastern corner is a prime example of everyone's favorite combination—the
old and the new. The traditional comes in the form of Koloa
town, site of Hawaii's first successful sugar mill, a 19th-century
plantation town that has been refurbished in tropical colors. For
the modern, you need look only a couple miles down the road to

Poipu, a series of scalloped beaches that has become action central for real estate developers.

Anchoring these enclaves to the east is Puuhi Mount, scene of the last volcanic eruption on Kauai. To the north rises the Hoary Head Range, a wall of wooded mountains that divides the district from the Huleia Valley and Lihue. Everywhere else you'll find fields lying fallow or acres that are still planted with sugar.

SIGHTS   Without doubt, you'll want to drive out from Lihue along Kaumualii Highway (Route 50) to explore the south coast. Along the way, if you possess a Rorshach-test imagination, you'll see **Queen Victoria's Profile** etched in the Hoary Head Range. (Need a helping eye? Watch for the Hawaii Visitors Bureau sign on the side of the highway.)

When you turn south toward Poipu on Maluhia Road (Route 520), you won't need a road sign to find what locals refer to as **Tree Tunnel**, an arcade of towering swamp mahogany trees that forms a shadowy tunnel en route to the timeworn town of **Koloa**. The remains of the original sugar plantation stand in an unassuming pile on the right side of the road as you enter town; a plaque near this old chimney commemorates the birth of Hawaii's sugar industry, a business that dominated life in the islands throughout most of the 19th century. A sugar mill continues to operate just outside town and Koloa still consists primarily of company-town houses and humble churches surrounded by fields of sugar cane. But the main street was gentrified during the 1980s as tropical-colored paints were added to the old woodframe and falsefront town center.

The tiny **Koloa History Center**, located in the Old Koloa Town Mall, provides a brief introduction to the history of the area in the form of artifacts from the old plantation days. ~ Koloa Road, Koloa.

If a one-word association test were applied to **Poipu**, the word would be "beach." There really is no town here, just a skein of hotels, condominiums and stores built along a series of white-sand beaches. Nevertheless, this is Kauai's premier playground, a sun-soaked realm that promises good weather and good times.

While civilization has encroached to the very side of the sea, nature continues to display some of its gentle wonders along the colorful reefs and pearly sands. Most remarkable of all is **Spouting Horn** (end of Lawai Road), an underwater lava tube with an opening along the shore. Surf crashing through the tube dramatically transforms this blowhole into a miniature Old Faithful. Try to time your visit with the high tide when the spumes from Spouting Horn reach their greatest heights. The mournful sounds issuing from the blowhole are said to be the plaintive cries of a legendary lizard or *moo*. It seems that he was returning from another island where he had been told of the death of his two sisters. Blinded by tears he missed his landing and was swept into the blowhole. (You should also look around at this intriguing coastline, which is covered by coral outcroppings and tidepools and is the location of several archaeological sites.)

LODGING

One place for people wanting to rough it or to establish a base camp is **Kahili Mountain Park,** run by the Seventh Day Adventist Church. Facing the Hoary Head Range and backdropped by Kahili Mountain, this 197-acre domain offers an easy compromise between hoteling and camping. The two-bedroom cabin comes equipped with lanai and private bathroom, plus a funky kitchenette; the other cabins are one-bedroom units. The facilities include cabinettes with shared baths as well as the cabins. Both types of facilities should be reserved several months in advance. Cooking utensils and bed linens are provided. Furnishings seem a bit spartan: The floors are uncarpeted and the sole decoration is the surrounding mountains. Thank God for nature. At this rustic resort you can rope-swing into the swimming pond or hike the nearby trails. Closed Saturday. ~ Write to Kahili Mountain Park, P.O. Box 298, Koloa, Kauai, HI 96756. The park is five miles from Koloa town and about one mile off Kaumualii Highway; phone/fax 808-742-9921; www.kahilipark.com, e-mail d-lh@juno.com. MODERATE TO DELUXE.

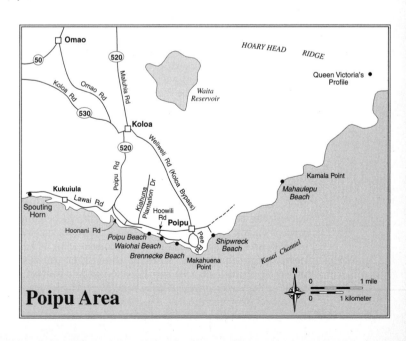

Poipu Area

HIDDEN ►   Located on a small bluff overlooking the ocean is **Garden Isle Cottages Oceanfront**. These pretty one-bedroom hideaways are decorated with artistic flair: Oil paintings and woven pieces adorn the walls, the furnishings are rattan and the kitchens are modern. The rooms, which are decorated with Asian, Polynesian and Indonesian themes, overlook Koloa Landing, site of the best snorkeling on the island. There is usually a two-night minimum stay. Closed Saturday and Sunday. ~ 2660 Puuholo Road, Koloa; 808-742-6717, 800-742-6711, fax 808-742-1933; www.oceancottages.com, e-mail vacation@oceancottages.com. DELUXE.

Similarly, **Koloa Landing Cottages** in Poipu offers a studio, a one-bedroom unit, and three cottages, one of which sleeps up to six. These are attractive facilities with kitchens. With a garden setting and family atmosphere, they evoke a comfortable sense of familiarity. Three-night minimum. ~ 2704-B Hoonani Road, Poipu; 808-742-1470, 800-779-8773, fax 808-332-9584; www.planet-hawaii.com/koloa, e-mail dolfin@aloha.net. MODERATE.

Poipu Bed & Breakfast Inn is a lovely woodframe house with four guest rooms. The decor is dominated by white wicker furniture and merry-go-round horses (there's one in the living room and in three of the bedrooms). You can also expect wall-to-wall carpeting and overhead fans. There are small porches in front and back plus a yard complete with garden and mango tree. ~ 2720 Hoonani Road, Poipu; 808-743-0100, 800-808-2330, fax 808-742-1794; www.poipu-inn.com, e-mail info@poipu-inn.com. DELUXE.

For a place located right on the water, there's **Gloria's Spouting Horn Bed & Breakfast**. This custom-designed beachhouse features three oceanfront guest rooms that feature canopy beds, handmade Hawaiian quilts and *koa* furniture. Open and airy, Gloria's is a place where you can relax on the lanai that sits just above the waves, lie in a hammock, swim in the pool, or go surfing outside your front door. Full breakfast served. ~ 4464 Lawai Beach Road, Poipu; phone/fax 808-742-6995; www.gloriasbedandbreakfast.com, e-mail glorbb@gte.net. ULTRA-DELUXE.

It would be an elastic stretch of the imagination to call the **Hyatt Regency Kauai Resort & Spa** a hidden destination. This *is*, after all, a Hyatt Regency—with over 600 guest rooms, several pools, six restaurants, six lounges and several acres of manmade lagoons. But before this luxury resort was built, the beach on which it sits was one of the great hidden locales on Kauai. Shipwreck Beach is still a magnificent crescent of white sand, and the Hyatt Regency Kauai Resort & Spa, backdropped by cane fields and deep-green mountains, enjoys some of the seclusion for which Keoneloa Bay was renowned. With its wood-paneled lobby, atrium garden and plush guest rooms, it is one of Hawaii's prettier hotels. ~ 1571 Poipu Road, Poipu; 808-742-1234, 800-554-9288, fax 808-742-1557; www.kauai-hyatt.com. ULTRA-DELUXE.

One of the most unique condos around is **Poipu Crater Resort.** Located just 600 yards from the beach, it's also one of the best deals. This entire 30-unit facility rests in the crater of an extinct volcano. The accommodations are contained in attractive wood-frame houses; all are two-bedroom condos and rent for about $100, depending on length of stay. There's a pool, tennis courts, a sauna and a barbecue area. ~ Hoohu Road, Poipu; 808-742-7400, 800-367-8020, fax 808-742-9121; www.suite-paradise.com, e-mail mail@suite-paradise.com.

CONDOS

◀ *HIDDEN*

A particularly well-known destination, **Kiahuna Plantation** is a 35-acre beachfront spread. This complex of resort condominiums is landscaped with lily ponds, lagoon and a spectacular cactus garden. The units are housed in attractive plantation-style structures, which dot the resort's rolling lawns. ~ 2253 Poipu Road, Poipu; 808-742-6411, 800-688-7444, fax 808-742-1698. ULTRA-DELUXE.

Poipu Kai Resort consists of a succession of separate buildings spread around a spacious lawn. There are six pools and nine tennis courts plus a restaurant, jacuzzi and barbecues. It's across the street from Brennecke Beach. One-bedroom condos start at around $125 ($110 from April 1 to December 21). ~ 1941 Poipu Road, Poipu; 808-742-7400, 800-367-8020, fax 808-742-9121; www. suite-paradise.com, e-mail mail@suite-paradise.com.

Poipu Shores is a small (39 unit) complex right on the ocean with a swimming pool so close to the water the waves seem poised to break across it. One-bedroom units start at $235 ($207 off-season). ~ 1775 Pee Road, Poipu; 808-742-7700, fax 808-742-9720; www.castle-group.com.

At **Sunset Kahili Condominiums** one-bedroom apartments are $103 to $143 double; two bedrooms will run $134 to $175 for one to four people. All units have ocean views. Two-night mini-

◆◆◆

OCEANFRONT LIVING

Neatly situated near the oceanfront just a short jaunt to the beach, **Poipu Kapili**, offers you a great place to unpack your bags. It's a 60-unit complex with a pool and tennis courts amid lush vegetation. Each condo, uniquely decorated by its owner, offers views (and sounds) of the blue Pacific. One-bedroom condos start at $235. ~ 2221 Kapili Road, Koloa; 808-742-6449, 800-443-7714, fax 808-742-9162; www.poipukapili.com, e-mail aloha@poipukapili.com.

mum. Closed Saturday and Sunday. ~ 1763 Pee Road, Poipu; 808-742-1691, 800-827-6478, fax 808-742-6058; www.sunsetkahili.com, e-mail info@sunsetkahili.com.

At **Kuhio Shores**, one-bedroom apartments are $110 for one to four people; two bedrooms, two baths, cost $225 for one to six people. On the shore, but lacking a beach. ~ 5050 Lawai Road, Poipu; 808-742-7555, 800-367-8022, fax 808-742-1559; www.r7r.com, e-mail randr@r7r.com

On the road to Spouting Horn, **Lawai Beach Resort**, a large timeshare complex located across the street from the ocean, has one-bedroom units starting at $175. Two-bedroom units start at $225. There are three pools and spas plus tennis courts. ~ 5017 Lawai Road, Koloa; 808-240-5100, fax 808-240-5187; www.lawaibeach.org, e-mail reservations@lawaibeach.org.

The best way to shop for value and location among Poipu condos is to contact one of the local rental agencies. They include **Poipu Beach Resort Association** at 2440 Hoonani Road in Koloa (808-742-7444, fax 808-742-7887; www.poipu-beach.org, e-mail info@poipu-beach.org.), **Grantham Resorts** at 3176 Poipu Road in Poipu (808-742-2000, 800-325-5701, fax 808-742-9093; www.grantham-resorts.com, e-mail info@grantham-resorts.com) and **R & R Realty & Rentals, Inc.** at 1661 Pee Road in Poipu (808-742-7555, 800-367-8022, fax 808-742-1559; www.r7r.com, e-mail randr@r7r.com). Talk to these agencies at length. Ask them about the best deals they have to offer in the season you're going. If interested, you can also ask about packages that include rental cars.

DINING   "Snack bar" comes closer to describing the low-priced dining facilities here than "restaurant." This lovely beach area hosts no full-sized budget restaurants. In Koloa town, two miles from Poipu, there's the **Kauai Kitchens**, a snack bar next to the Big Save Market. No dinner. ~ Koloa Road, Koloa; 808-742-1712. BUDGET.

South-of-the-border cuisine comes in the form of tamales, chile verde, enchiladas and tacos at **Mi Casita Mexican Restaurant**. With oilcloth on the tables and a desert-and-cactus mural covering an entire wall, this home-style eatery is a good bet for a filling meal. Lunch and dinner daily; dinner only on Sunday. ~ 5470 Koloa Road, Koloa; 808-742-2323. BUDGET TO MODERATE.

For patio dining stroll down the street to **Tom Kats Grill**. Situated in a small interior courtyard, this easy-going restaurant has filet mignon and barbecue pork ribs for "meat lovers," chicken marinara and garlic seafood for "pasta lovers" as well as sandwiches and hamburgers for "the kittens." ~ 5400 Koloa Road, Koloa; 808-742-8887. MODERATE.

Budget-priced cafés in Poipu are rare. In Poipu proper, the best place to look for a quick, inexpensive meal is in the Poipu

Author Picks

CHAPTER FAVORITES

I enjoy kayaking the **Huleia River**—passing by the Menehune Fishpond and exploring the Huleia Wildlife Preserve, then stopping at the rope swing for a splash in the river. *page 405*

I wouldn't miss the **Na Pali coastline**. There are lots of ways to see it—from kayak to power-motored catamaran—but it has to be seen. *page 459*

The **Kalalau Lookout** at Waimea Canyon is where I escape to when I want to contemplate the beauty of Kauai. *page 422*

A night tucked away in the **Kokee Lodge Cabins** is what I seek when I've had enough of the surf and sand of the islands. The wood-burning stove and surrounding forest create a totally different mind set. *page 424*

I can't leave Kauai without a meal at **A Pacific Café**. The prices are reasonable, the cuisine is delectable and the service is friendly. It's one of the best restaurants in the islands. *page 437*

On the other hand, when I want to get down with the locals, I visit **Ma's Family Restaurant** in Lihue and talk story over a bowl of saimin. *page 404*

Shopping Village on Poipu Road. Here you'll find takeout stands dispensing sub sandwiches and other nutritious items. The **Plantation House** offers patio dining and a complete menu. Entrées include teriyaki chicken, rum-marinated pork chops and mahimahi tempura. They also serve hamburgers, sandwiches and salads at lunch. ~ 2360 Kiahuna Plantation Drive, Koloa; 808-742-7373, fax 808-742-7477. DELUXE.

Keoki's Paradise, a beautiful patio-style restaurant centered around a tropical garden and pond, is also in the shopping village. They feature a steak-and-seafood menu. The setting alone makes it worth a visit. ~ 2360 Kiahuna Plantation Drive, Koloa; 808-742-7534, fax 808-742-7847. MODERATE TO ULTRA-DELUXE.

Or try **Pattaya Asian Cafe**, where you can settle back at a teak dining table. This small patio restaurant serves broccoli noodles, lemon chicken, fresh sweet basil beef, and numerous other Southeast Asian dishes. Worth a stop. ~ 2360 Kiahuna Plantation Drive, Koloa; 808-742-8818. MODERATE TO DELUXE.

Overlooking Poipu Beach is **Brennecke's Beach Broiler**. Downstairs at this two-level dining spot you'll find a budget-priced deli serving sandwiches. The upper deck is occupied by an open-air restaurant that serves appetizers and lunch from 11 a.m. to 4 p.m. daily, then stokes the *kiawe* broiler for dinner selections that include fresh fish dishes, steak, chicken and seafood kabob. There is also pasta. ~ Hoone Road, Koloa; 808-742-7588, 888-384-8810, fax 808-742-1321; www.brenneckes.com, e-mail bob@brenneckes. com. MODERATE TO ULTRA-DELUXE.

It seems like everywhere you go in Hawaii these days, Roy Yamaguchi has a restaurant. On Kauai it is **Roy's Poipu Bar & Grill**, an informal dining room with the kitchen behind a glass partition. The menu is a sample of what the staff call Euro-Asian Pacific cuisine. You can order steamed opakapaka, hibachi-style salmon, *kiawe*-grilled ribeye steak or an *imu*-baked pizza. Or at least that's what was on the ever-changing menu last time I was in. In any case, it's hard to go wrong. Reservations are recommended. Dinner only. ~ Poipu Shopping Village, 2360 Kiahuna Plantation Drive, Koloa; 808-742-5000, fax 808-742-5050. DELUXE TO ULTRA-DELUXE.

The House of Seafood is situated among a cluster of condominiums and overlooks a set of tennis courts. That should tell you something about this traditional, white-tablecloth dining room. And even more about the surf-and-turf cuisine, which includes ten fresh fish catches nightly. We're talking filet mignon and lobster, filet mignon and fish, filet mignon and scampi, filet mignon and crab legs. Or, if combinations are not your cup of tea, there's steak dijon, medallions cognac and bouillabaisse. For dessert, try a flambé. Dinner only. ~ 1941 Poipu Road, Poipu; 808-742-6433, fax 808-742-6314; e-mail iakai@aloha.net. DELUXE TO ULTRA-DELUXE.

The Hyatt Regency Kauai Resort ~ Spa is home to three recommended restaurants. The signature restaurant here is **Dondero's**, a fashionable Italian dining spot. Here you can begin with carpaccio or porcini mushroom crêpes, progress to minestrone or a pomodoro salad, then get serious with a list of entrées that includes cioppino, veal scallopine, veal osso buco, or *spiedini*, a seafood skewer with lobster, scallops and shrimp. Festive and

HOMEGROWN CHEF

The stars, the ocean and a **Beach House Restaurant** is a showcase for Honolulu-born chef Linda Yamada's island cuisine and for painter Jan Kasprzycki's land- and seascapes. Signature items include the "Ahi Taster," Kauai asparagus salad, lemongrass- and kaffir lime–crusted scallops, daily fresh fish and a coconut-butter mochi sundae. Not only is the food worth the splurge, the oceanfront location, on the road to Spouting Horn, is a perfect setting for watching the waves under the stars. Dinner only. ~ 5022 Lawai Road, Koloa; 808-742-1424, fax 808-742-1369; www.the-beach-house.com. DELUXE TO ULTRA-DELUXE.

original, it's a solid choice for a special meal. Dinner only ~ 1571 Poipu Road, Poipu; 808-742-1234. ULTRA-DELUXE.

You can dine beside a koi pond and listen to the tumble of waterfalls at the Hyatt Regency's **Ilima Terrace**. The decor is plantation style and nightly buffet themes include three Kauai Seafood nights and two Prime Rib nights. DELUXE TO ULTRA-DELUXE.

The Hyatt Regency Kauai Resort & Spa's most imaginative restaurant is without doubt **Tidepools**. The theme is grass-shack Polynesia, with each of the several dining rooms resembling a classic *hale pili*. Set in a quiet lagoon and graced with classic Hawaiian sunsets and ocean breezes, it's a great place to dine. The offerings include charred ahi sashimi and a mixed seafood grill with lobster, scallops, shrimp and fish. ~ 1571 Poipu Road, Poipu; 808-742-1234, fax 808-742-1557; www.kauai-hyatt.com. DELUXE TO ULTRA-DELUXE.

GROCERIES There's a **Big Save Market** which includes a dry goods section and is definitely the place to shop on the way to Poipu Beach. ~ Koloa Road, Koloa; 808-742-1614.

Also popular with local shoppers is **Sueoka Store**, a classic old grocery store right in the center of town. ~ Koloa Road, Koloa; 808-742-1611.

If you're already soaking up the sun at Poipu, you have two grocery options. **Brennecke's Mini-Deli** is conveniently situated across the street from Poipu Beach Park. This mom-and-pop business has liquor, cold drinks and a limited selection of groceries. ~ Hoone Road, Poipu; 808-742-1582.

To increase your choices and decrease your food bill, head up Poipu Road to **Kukuiula Store**. This market has prices that are nearly competitive with the nearby Big Save Market. ~ Poipu Road, Poipu; 808-742-1601.

SHOPPING On the way to Poipu, the former plantation town of Koloa supports a cluster of shops as well as a miniature mall. Several clothing stores line Koloa Road. The mall, called **Old Koloa Town** (even though it was totally overhauled in the 1980s), houses a string of small jewelry stores, a T-shirt shop and a photo studio. ~ Koloa Road, Koloa.

Atlantis Gallery & Frames has contemporary Hawaiian paintings and prints. ~ 5400 Koloa Road, Koloa; 808-742-2555.

Walk into **Island Soap & Candle Works** and get an education in how to make both. This amazing little shop has soaps made from coconut, guava, plumeria and every other island product imaginable. There are bath gels, botanical hand lotions and, oh yes, candles—dozens of different kinds. ~ Koloa Road, Koloa; 808-742-1945.

Poipu Shopping Village is a resort-style shopping complex with 27 businesses, including two fine dining restaurants, a store that sells only designer jewelry, a surf shop and a sundries shop. ~ Poipu Road, Poipu; 808-742-2831.

Foremost among them are the twin shops, Hale Mana and Hale Mana Fine Arts. The first offers a wonderful selection of designer island clothing, art prints, Chinese antiques, and "gifts for the spirited." Its sister store specializes in fine art and museum pieces. ~ 2360 Kiahuna Drive, Koloa; 808-742-1027.

You can also venture down to the Hyatt Regency Kauai. It's a spectacular property, well worth touring, and also offers nine sleek shops. ~ 1571 Poipu Road, Poipu; 808-742-1234.

NIGHTLIFE   To catch a local crowd, head down to Brennecke's Beach Broiler. There's no music, but the crowds are young and the views otherworldly. ~ Hoone Road, Koloa; 808-742-7588.

Keoki's Paradise in Poipu Shopping Village features contemporary Hawaiian music every Thursday and Friday night and Sunday during the day. You can sit outdoors in a garden setting and enjoy the sounds. ~ 2360 Kiahuna Plantation Drive, Koloa; 808-742-7534.

There's live Hawaiian and light contemporary music at The Point nightly from 8 to 11 p.m., and dancing on Sunday. The 225-degree view and wavefront location are an even stronger draw. Great at sunset. ~ Sheraton Kauai Resort, 2440 Hoonani Road, Poipu; 742-1661 ext. 52.

The Hyatt Regency Kauai, the lavish resort on Shipwreck Beach, hosts several top nightspots. My favorite is Stevenson's Library, a stately wood-paneled lounge that evokes a sense of colonial-era Polynesia. For a drink with a view of the beach, try the Tidepools Lounge. For music and entertainment, check out Sea View Terrace.

BEACHES & PARKS   **POIPU BEACH AND WAIOHAI BEACH** Extending along the main hotel area in Poipu are two adjacent white-sand beaches crowded with visitors. Popular with sunbathers, swimmers and water-sport aficionados, both are protected by a series of offshore reefs. At Poipu Beach there is good surfing for beginners near the beach, for intermediate surfers about 100 yards offshore and for expert surfers about a half-mile out at "First Break." This beach is also popular with windsurfers. Waiohai Beach has an offshore break near the reef known as "Waiohai." There's fishing from the nearby rocks (the beach area is usually crowded). ~ Located along Poipu Road near the closed Waiohai hotel.

POIPU BEACH PARK This has got to be one of the loveliest little parks around. There's a well-kept lawn for picnickers and finicky sunbathers, a crescent-shaped beach with protecting reef and the sunny skies of Poipu. Swimming is excellent, and the entire area has some of the best diving on the island. An offshore sandbar makes for good bodysurfing. Bonefish, rockfish and *papio* are common catches; there's also good spearfishing on the nearby reefs. You'll find a picnic area, restrooms, showers and lifeguards. ~ Located on Hoone Road in Poipu.

SHIPWRECK BEACH Back in the 1980s, this was one of the greatest of Kauai's hidden beaches. Then condominiums began crawling along the coast and eventually the Hyatt Regency Kauai was built right on the beach. Today, it's a sandy but rock-studded beach, quite beautiful but bordered by a major resort. Swimming is good when the surf is low. This is also an outstanding bodysurfing and windsurfing area (the best spot is at the east end of the beach). Fishing is good from nearby Makawehi Point. There is a full host of (expensive) facilities at the hotel. ~ From the Poipu Beach area, follow Poipu Road east and simply look for the Hyatt Regency Kauai, which borders the beach.

MAHAULEPU BEACH If you've come to Hawaii seeking that South Seas dream, head out to these lovely strands. Mahaulepu is a dreamy corridor of white sand winding for two miles along a reef-protected shoreline and including several strands and pocket beaches. In addition to being incredibly beautiful and ripe with potential for outdoor sports, Mahaulepu is important scientifically. Remains of extinct birds have been found here; flocks of seabirds inhabit the area; and petroglyphs have been discovered along the shoreline. If that's not enough, the beach boasts 100-foot-high sand dunes. There are well-protected sections of beach where you can swim. Snorkeling and surfing are also good at this beach. There are rocky areas along this stretch where you can fish. The beach has no facilities. ~ From the Poipu Beach area, follow Poipu Road east past the Hyatt Regency Kauai at Shipwreck Beach. Beyond Shipwreck, the pavement ends and the thoroughfare becomes a cane road. Continue on the main cane road (which is like a dirt road continuation of

◄ *HIDDEN*

BARTERING BESIDE THE BLOWHOLE

My favorite shopping spot around Poipu has always been at the **Spouting Horn**. Here, next to the parking lot that serves visitors to the blowhole, local merchants set up tables to sell their wares. You're liable to find coral and puka shell necklaces, trident shell trumpets, rare Niihau shell necklaces and some marvelous mother-of-pearl pieces. You are free to barter, of course, though the prices are pretty good to begin with. If you're interested in jewelry, and want to meet local artisans, this is an intriguing spot. ~ End of Lawai Road, Poipu.

Poipu Road). Follow this road for about two miles (even when it curves toward the mountains and away from the ocean). Numerous minor cane roads will intersect from the right and left: ignore them. Finally, you will come to a crossroads with a major cane road (along which a line of telephone poles runs). Turn right and follow this road for about a mile (you'll pass a quarry off in the distance to the right), then watch on the right for roads leading to the beach. You will encounter a guard shack at the turnoff where you are required to sign a waiver to continue onto the property. The beach entrance is closed from 7 p.m. to 7:30 a.m.

▼ ▼ ▼ ▼ ▼ ▼ ▼ ▼ ▼
Waimea Area

The Western world's relationship with Hawaii, a tumultuous affair dating back more than two centuries, began in southwest Kauai when Captain James Cook set anchor at Waimea Bay. Cook landed on the leeward side of the island, a hot, dry expanse rimmed by white-sand beaches and dominated to the interior by Waimea Canyon, the "Grand Canyon of the Pacific."

Like the district surrounding Poipu, this is sugar-cane country. Several small harbors dot the coast and the population is concentrated in company towns consisting of old plantation cottages and falsefront stores.

SIGHTS

One of the first plantation towns you'll encounter driving west on Kaumualii Highway (Route 50) is Kalaheo. Here, a left on Papalina Road will lead a mile up to **Kukuiolono Park**, a lightly visited Japanese garden complete with stone bridge, ornamental pool and florid landscaping. Take a stroll through this peaceful retreat and you'll also enjoy a stunning view that sweeps across a patchwork of cane fields to the sea.

En route from one tinroof town to the next, you'll pass the **Hanapepe Valley Lookout**, which offers a view of native plant life dramatically set in a gorge ringed by eroded cliffs.

HIDDEN ▶

Be sure to take the nearby fork into **Hanapepe**, a vintage village complete with wooden sidewalks and weather-beaten storefronts. During the 1924 sugar strike, 16 workers were killed here by police. Even today, the independent spirit of those martyrs pervades this proud little town. For a sense of Hanapepe during the plantation days, drive out Awawa Road. Precipitous red lava cliffs rim the roadside, while rickety cottages and intricately tilled fields carpet the valley below.

For a guided tour of one of Hawaii's few remaining sugar plantations, contact **Gay & Robinson Tours** on the eastern outskirts of Waimea. The tour office features a mini-museum and gift shop, and the tour itself leads through the canefields and factories of a classic Hawaiian plantation. ~ Near the 19-mile marker on Kau-

mualii Highway, Waimea; 808-335-2824; www.gandrtours-kauai.
com, e-mail toursgnr@aloha.net.

Russian Fort Elizabeth State Historical Park, just outside Waimea at the mouth of the Waimea River, is now just a rubble heap.
Historically, it represents a fruitless attempt by a maverick adventurer working for a Russian trading company to gain a foothold
in the islands in 1817. Designed in the shape of a six-pointed star,
the original fort bristled with guns and had walls 30 feet thick.

An earlier event, Captain James Cook's 1778 "discovery" of
Hawaii, is commemorated with a lava monolith near his landing
place in Waimea. Watch for roadside markers to **Cook's Monument.** ~ On the road to Lucy Wright Park.

Cook was not the only outsider to assume a role in Waimea's
history. It seems that those industrious leprechauns who built the
fishpond outside Lihue were also at work here constructing the
Menehune Ditch. This waterway, built with hand-hewn stones in   ◄ HIDDEN
a fashion unfamiliar to the Polynesians, has long puzzled archaeologists. ~ Outside town on Menehune Road.

You'll pass the town of Kekaha, home of a sugar mill and a
colony of plantation houses, before arriving at the next stop on
Kaumualii Highway's scenic itinerary—**Barking Sands Airfield.**
Actually, it's not the airfield but the sands that belong on your
itinerary. These lofty sand dunes, among the largest on the island,
make a woofing sound when ground underfoot. This, according
to scientists, is due to tiny cavities in each grain of sand that
cause them to resonate when rubbed together. (Similar sands are
found in Egypt's Sinai Desert, the Gobi Desert of Mongolia and
in Saudi Arabia.) If you have trouble making the sound, remember what one local wag told me: The hills actually got their name
from tourists becoming "dog-tired" after futilely trying to elicit
a growl from the mute sand. (Since the beach here at Major's Bay
is on a military reservation, call 808-335-4229 or fax 808-335-

FRESH ROASTED

Did you know that Hawaii produces over half of all the coffee grown in the
United States? If you're a coffee addict like I am, or are just interested in
seeing how it's grown and treated, stop by the **Kauai Coffee Visitor
Center.** Housed in a former plantation-worker's home, the center displays pictures from the area's sugar-plantation days, as well as information
about contemporary coffee production. Best of all, they have free tastings. Open daily from 9 a.m. to 5 p.m. ~ Route 50, near Kalaheo; 808-
335-0813, fax 808-335-3149; www.kauaicoffee.com, e-mail greensales
@kauaicoffee.com.

4429 to make sure the facility is open; also note its unusual weekday hours: 4 p.m. to 6 a.m.) There are also guided tours of the adjacent **Pacific Missile Range Facility**, an important launch area for military and meteorological rockets and the site of periodic war games. Tours are given the first and third Wednesday of each month. Reservations for the tours should be made a month in advance, and tours will not be conducted with fewer than six people; call 808-335-4740 for more information.

Having made a fool of yourself trying to get sand to bark, continue on past the deserted town of Mana (along a graded dirt road for the last five miles) to the endless sands of **Polihale State Park**. This very hot, very dry, very beautiful retreat represents the last stretch of a 15-mile-long sand beach, one of the longest in the state, that begins way back in Kekaha. The sand marathon ends at the foot of the Na Pali cliffs, in an area sacred to the Hawaiians. Here the ancients built **Polihale Heiau**, a temple whose ruins remain. And here the road ends, further passage made impossible by the sea cliffs that wrap around Kauai's northwest corner.

Another candidate in the contest for ultimate adventure—one that is free, doesn't require a helicopter and always lies open to exploration—is **Waimea Canyon**. Touring the "Grand Canyon of the Pacific" involves a side trip from either the town of Waimea or Kekaha. Waimea Canyon Drive leads from the former and Kokee Road climbs from the latter; they join about halfway up the mountain. For an overview of the entire region, go up along Waimea Canyon Drive, since it hugs the canyon rim and provides the best views, then follow Kokee Road down.

As the paved road snakes along the side of this 2857-foot-deep canyon, a staggering panorama opens. The red and orange hues of a barren southwestern landscape are splashed with tropic greens and yellows. Far below, the Waimea River, which carved this ten-mile-long chasm, cuts a sinuous course. Several vista points provide crow's-nest views of the territory, including one (Poohinahina Overlook at 3500-feet elevation) that provides views of the canyon to the east and Niihau in the west.

The road continues deep into Kauai's cool interior before arriving at **Kokee State Park**. Here you'll find a restaurant, cabins and the **Kokee Museum**, a small display space devoted to the flora, fauna and natural history of the area. This intriguing exhibit also features collections of shells and Hawaiian artifacts. ~ 808-335-9975, fax 808-335-6131; e-mail kokee@aloha.net.

It's a short drive onward and upward to the **Kalalau Lookout** where Kauai's other face is reflected in knife-edged cliffs and overgrown gorges that drop to the sea 4000 feet below. Another nearby overlook gazes out across the Alakai Swamp to Mount Waialeale. (Because of cloud cover in the valley, it's best to arrive at the overlook before 10 a.m. or after 4 p.m.) One more spectacular scene along the way, one more reason to bring you back to this magnificent island.

Accommodations on Kauai's southwest side include beachside cottages in Waimea and ethereal facilities in Kokee State Park.

Waimea Plantation Cottages is one of the most alluring and secluded facilities on the entire island. Here in a spectacular coconut grove, fronting a salt-and-pepper beach, is a cluster of charmingly rustic 1920s-era plantation cottages. Each has been carefully restored and many are furnished with rattan furniture. These one, two and multibedroom houses have full kitchens. Maid service is every third day. Like the rest of the complex, the swimming pool follows the style of an earlier era (most visitors swim here since the offshore waters are usually murky). The place is a little gem out on Kauai's remote westside. ~ Kaumualii Highway, Waimea; 808-338-1625, 800-992-7866, fax 808-338-2338; www.

LODGING

◄ *HIDDEN*

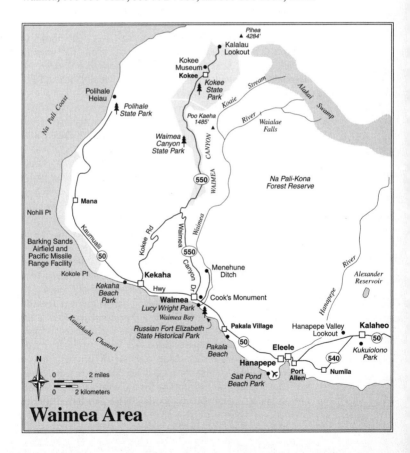

Waimea Area

waimea-plantation.com, e-mail waiple@aloha.net. DELUXE TO
ULTRA-DELUXE.

Nestled in secluded woods between Waimea Canyon and the
Kalalau Valley Lookout are the **Kokee Lodge Cabins**. Each of the
12 mountain cabins, varying in size from one large room to two-
bedroom complexes, comes with complete kitchen, wood-burning
stove and rustic furnishings. These cedar cabins, 3600 feet above
sea level, are a mountaineer's dream. With forest and hiking
trails all around, Kokee is ideal for the adventurer. It gets chilly,
so bring a jacket or sweater. Reservations are essential. Some
cabins sleep as many as six people. ~ 808-335-6061. BUDGET.

DINING

Traveling west toward Waimea Canyon and Barking Sands, you'll
find the watering places decrease as rapidly as the rainfall. Most
restaurants en route are cafés and takeout stands. If you're on a
budget, you're in luck; if you're looking for an exclusive, elegant
establishment, you'll find slim pickings out Waimea way.

At the **Kalaheo Steak House** you'll step into a comfortable
wood-paneled dining room. Pull up a chair, rest your elbows on
the table (it's permitted) and choose among sirloin, filet mignon,
scampi, Cornish hens and several other appealing entrées. No
reservations accepted. Dinner only. ~ 4444 Papalina Road, Kalaheo; 808-332-9780. MODERATE TO DELUXE.

HIDDEN ►

Camp House Grill is a trim little café with an island-style lunch
and dinner menu. Favored by nearby residents, they serve *huli
huli* chicken and pork ribs. ~ Kaumualii Highway, Kalaheo; 808-
332-9755. BUDGET TO MODERATE.

The best restaurant along this highway is Hanapepe's **Green
Garden Restaurant**. Dining is indoors, but the tropical plants
convey a genuine garden feeling. At breakfast you can enjoy eggs
and hot cakes along with a steaming cup of coffee. The lunch
menu features a broad selection of meat, seafood and Asian platters, all priced comfortably. And for dinner, the deliciously varied
menu ranges from pork chow mein to rock lobster tail. I particularly enjoyed the seafood special, a platter of mahimahi, shrimp,
oysters and scallops. Children's portions are available. Closed Tuesday. ~ Kaumualii Highway, Hanapepe; 808-335-5422. MODERATE.

Gourmet vegetarian with an Italian flair is the way they describe the food at **Hanapepe Cafe and Espresso**. Every Friday and
Saturday night you'll find them preparing such entrées as marinated eggplant lasagna, pasta primavera with portabello mushrooms or marinara dishes made with locally grown produce.
They're also open for breakfast and lunch Tuesday through Saturday. That's when you can stop by for a Caesar salad, a "health-
nut sandwich," pasta specials, garden burgers or baked frittata.
Reservations recommended. ~ 3830 Hanapepe Road, Hanapepe;

The Forbidden Island

There's little doubt that the most hidden place in "hidden Hawaii" is **Niihau**, Hawaii's westernmost inhabited island. About 250 native Hawaiians live on this privately owned island under conditions similar to those prevailing during the 19th century. Used as a cattle and sheep ranch and closed to the public, it is Hawaii's last unspoiled frontier.

The Robinsons, a Scottish family that came to Hawaii from New Zealand, purchased the island in the 1860s and have protected (some critics say segregated) its inhabitants from the rest of the world ever since. Residents of Niihau are free to come and go from the island as they please, and while the situation does have a company-town aura about it, the Robinsons have historically shown an abiding concern for the people and ecology of Hawaii.

While Niihau measures a mere 73 square miles and rises only 1281 feet above sea level at its highest point, the island lays claim to rich fishing grounds and is famous for its Niihau shell necklaces, fashioned from rare and tiny shells that wash up on the windward shore only a few times a year.

Until the 1980s, Niihau fully deserved its nickname, "The Forbidden Island." But today outsiders with a sense of adventure (and some extra cash) can climb aboard a **Niihau Helicopter** flight and tour a part of the island. You'll fly over most of the island, avoiding the village where the population is concentrated, and land on a remote beach for a short hike along the shore. You won't meet any Niihau residents, but you will have an experience that could prove to be your ultimate encounter with "hidden Hawaii." ~ Kaumaualii Highway; 808-335-3500.

If you'd rather explore the island by ground, **HoloHolo Charters** offers an interesting option. Leaving from Port Allen and including a continental breakfast, their "Supertour" first stops at the Na Pali Coast to view the natural wonders of the area. They then head to Niihau for a snorkeling visit, during which you'll receive instruction by the crew. A buffet-style lunch follows. During the meal, the crew discusses the people and history of Niihau. ~ 800-848-6130.

808-335-5011, fax 808-335-5018; www.hanapepecafe.com. MOD-
ERATE TO DELUXE.

Da Imu Hut Café has Hawaiian dishes, *saimin*, fried chicken,
teriyaki chicken, fried noodles and hamburgers at 1950s prices.
It's not much on looks, but it fills the belly. ~ Hanapepe Road,
Hanapepe; 808-335-0200. BUDGET.

In Waimea, there's **John's Place**, a short-order restaurant offering sandwiches, hamburgers, burritos and salads. They serve
breakfast and lunch. Closed Sunday. ~ 9875 Waimea Road, Waimea; 808-338-0330. BUDGET.

Steaks, naturally, are the order of the day at **Wranglers Steakhouse**. Here guests can choose to take their meals outside or indoors in a rustic dining room. Hardwood floors and galvanized
awnings contribute to the Western feel, as do the old wagon and
wooden horse. Also on the menu are sandwiches, hamburgers
and Mexican food. No lunch on Saturday. Closed Sunday. ~
9852 Kaumualii Highway, Waimea; 808-338-1218, fax 808-338-
1266. MODERATE TO DELUXE.

The only real sit-down establishment past Waimea is **Toi's Thai
Kitchen**. The lunch and dinner menu consists primarily of Thai
food, but fried chicken and mahimahi are also served. ~ Eleele
Shopping Center, 178 Hanapepe Bay; 808-335-3111. BUDGET TO
DELUXE.

When you're up in the heights above Waimea Canyon you'll
be mighty glad to discover **Kokee Lodge** in remote Kokee State
Park. From the dining room of this homey hideaway, you can
gaze out at the surrounding forest or enjoy the lava rock fireplace
and *koa* bar. The restaurant offers a light breakfast and lunch
menu. The emphasis is on fresh, healthy dishes and local specialties like lilikoi pie. For breakfast try the pastries, muffins or
cornbread, and for lunch choose from soups, sandwiches and
salads. ~ 808-335-6061. BUDGET.

GROCERIES   There are two **Big Save Markets** along Kaumualii Highway. Traveling west from Lihue, the first is in the Eleele Shopping Center.
~ 808-335-3127. The second is in the center of Waimea. ~ 808-
338-1621.

Also along the highway is the **Menehune Food Mart**, a convenience store in Kalaheo. ~ 808-332-7349. For groceries past
Waimea, try the **Menehune Food Mart** on Kekaha Road in Kekaha. ~ 808-337-1335.

SHOPPING   Head up to Eleele off of Route 50 near Kalaheo and you'll discover **Red Dirt Hawaii**, home of the "original Red Dirt shirt."
Made with dyes from the iron-rich soil of Kauai, these T-shirts
have become a cottage industry with workers all over the island
dyeing them. If your shirt starts fading, don't worry—just roll it

in the dirt or wash it with mud and it will look like new again! Closed weekends. ~ 4352 Waialo Road, Eleele; 808-335-5670, fax 808-335-3478; www.dirtshirt.com, e-mail reddirt@aloha.net.

Hanapepe, a turn-of-the-century town with a falsefront main street, is steadily developing into an art center. **The Village Gallery** showcases the work of several local artists, including some evocative and imaginative pieces. ~ 3890 Hanapepe Road, Hanapepe; 808-335-0343.

The entire **Lele Aka Studio Gallery** is dedicated to the futuristic portraits of a single artist. ~ 3876 Hanapepe Road, Hanapepe; 808-335-5267.

Similarly, the **Dawn M. Traina Gallery** has paintings, drawings and prints of native Hawaiian people created by the store's namesake. ~ 3840-B Hanapepe Road, Hanapepe; 808-335-3993.

Kim Starr Gallery displays the owner's oil paintings, pastels and serigraphs. ~ 3878 Hanapepe Road, Hanapepe; 808-335-0381.

This is also the home of **Kauai Fine Arts**, a singular gallery   ◄ *HIDDEN*
housing an outstanding collection of antique maps and prints. ~ 3905 Hanapepe Road, Hanapepe; 808-335-3778.

You can buy a hand-painted coconut (the kind you mail home) at **Giorgio's Gallery**. Better yet, consider one of Giorgio's tropical oil paintings or hand-painted surfboards. Or one of his brother's sculptures. ~ 1-3437 Kaumualii Highway, Hanapepe; 808-335-3949.

Collectibles & Fine Junque has an amazing collection of glassware, aloha shirts, dolls and old bottles. It's a good place to pick up antiques or knickknacks. ~ 9821 Kaumualii Highway, Waimea; 808-338-9855.

SALT POND BEACH PARK A pretty, crescent-   **BEACHES**
shaped beach with a protecting reef and numerous coconut trees,   **& PARKS**
this park is very popular with locals and may be crowded and noisy on weekends. It's a good place to collect shells, though. The road leading to the park passes salt ponds that date back hundreds of years and are still used today to evaporate sea water and produce salt. Swimming is good in this well-protected area. Snor-

KAUAI IS FOR THE BIRDS

Kauai offers a unique opportunity for spotting a wide variety of Hawaiian birds, such as the *akekee*, the *anianiau* and the *amakihi*. **Terran Tours** provides one- to three-day tours through the Alakai swamp. A professional guide will escort you. ~ P.O. Box 1018, Waimea, HI 96796; 808-335-3313, fax 808-335-5849; e-mail dkuhn@rare-dear.com.

keling is fair and there is diving near rocks and along the offshore reef. For surfing, there's a shore break by the mouth of the Hanapepe River nearby in Port Allen. Sandy and shallow with small waves, this area is safe for beginners. There are left and right slides. Along the outer harbor edge near Port Allen Airport runway there are summer breaks, for good surfers only, which involve climbing down a rocky shoreline. At Salt Pond there are occasional summer breaks (left and right slides) requiring a long paddle out. This is also a very popular windsurfing area. Rockfish and mullet are the most common catches here. Facilities include a picnic area, restrooms, showers and lifeguards. ~ Take Kaumualii Highway to Hanapepe. Turn onto Route 543 and follow it to the end.

▲ There's a grassy area near the beach for tent camping; a county permit is required.

HIDDEN ►

PAKALA BEACH 🏖 🐟 🛶 ⚓ This long narrow ribbon of sand is bounded by trees and set in perfectly lush surroundings. Surfers will probably be the only other people around. They may come out of the water long enough to watch the spectacular sunsets with you and to tell you of the fabled summer waves that reach heights of 10 to 12 feet. If this book were rating beaches by the star system, Pakala Beach would deserve a constellation. When the surf is low it's a good place to swim. You can also snorkel along the reef. This is one of Hawaii's top summer surfing spots. The incredibly long walls that form along a wide shallow reef allow you to hang ten seemingly forever. Hence the nickname for these breaks—"Infinity." The one drawback: It's a long paddle out. Fishing is good from the rock outcropping off to the left. There are no facilities here. ~ Located along Kaumualii Highway near the 21-mile marker (two miles east of Waimea) you'll see a concrete bridge crossing Aakukui stream with the name "Aakukui" chiseled in the cement. Go through the gate just below the bridge and follow the well-worn path a few hundred yards to the beach.

LUCY WRIGHT PARK 🏖 🐟 ⚓ This five-acre park at the Waimea River mouth is popular with locals and therefore sometimes a little crowded. Despite a sandy beach, the park is not as appealing as others nearby: The water is often murky from cane field spillage. If you're in need of a campground you might stop here, otherwise, I don't recommend the park. Swimming is fair, unless the water is muddy. Surfing varies from small breaks for beginners to extremely long walls that build four different breaks and is best near the river mouth. There's a left slide. In Waimea Bay, there are parrotfish, red goatfish, squirrelfish, *papio*, bonefish, bigeyed scad and threadfin. You can also fish from the pier a few hundred feet west of the park. Facilities include a picnic area, restrooms and showers. ~ Located in Waimea.

▲ Tent camping only. County permit required.

KEKAHA BEACH 🏃 This narrow beach parallels Kaumualii Highway for several miles along the eastern edge of Kekaha. Although close to the highway, the lovely white strand offers some marvelous picnic spots, but the rough surf and powerful currents make swimming dangerous. There are many surfing spots along here; the foremost, called "Davidson's," lies off Oomano Point.

KEKAHA BEACH PARK 🐾 🏃 🌊 Set on a beautiful ribbon of sand, this 20-acre park is a great place to kick back, picnic and catch the sun setting over the island of Niihau. Swimming is good when surf is down; otherwise it can be dangerous. For surfers, immediately west of the park are several breaks, including "Inters" (near Kaumualii Highway and Akialoa Street) and "First Ditch" and "Second Ditch," located in front of two drainage ditches. Anglers try for threadfin. There are picnic facilities and restrooms. ~ Located on Kaumualii Highway in Kekaha.

KOKOLE POINT 🐾 🏃 🌊 Out by an old landing strip/drag strip, a local dump and a rifle range, there is a wide sandy beach that stretches forever and offers unofficial camping and outrageous sunsets. Fishermen, joggers and beachcombers love the place, but those who hold it nearest their hearts are surfers. The breaks here go by such names as "Rifle Range," "Targets," and "Whispering Sands." Currents and high surf usually make swimming unadvisable. However, fishing is good. There are no facilities. ~ Take the road that leads off Kaumualii Highway one mile west of Kekaha (there's a sign directing traffic to the dump). Follow any of the dirt roads in as far as possible. These will lead either to the dump or to a nearby landing strip. Walk the last three-tenths of a mile to the beach.

◀ *HIDDEN*

Kauai has the most beaches per mile of shoreline of any of the chain's islands.

BARKING SANDS 🐾 🎣 🏃 ⛵ 🌊 The military installation at Major's Bay is bounded by very wide beaches that extend for miles. You'll see the Barking Sands dunes and magnificent sunsets and get some of the best views of Niihau anywhere on Kauai. The weather is hot and dry here: a great place to get thoroughly baked, but beware of sunburns. The Pacific Missile Range Facility is located here, and the area is sometimes used for war games. These beaches are usually open on weekends, holidays and nighttime hours only, and are sometimes closed for maneuvers. Swimming is good, but exercise caution. The coral reefs make for good snorkeling. Major's Bay is an excellent surfing spot with both summer and winter breaks. Other breaks include

"Rockets" near the rocket launch pad, "Kinkini" at the south end of the airfield runway and "Family Housing" just offshore from the base housing facility. Windsurfers also frequent Major's Bay and "Kinkini." A particularly good fishing spot is around Nohili Point; the most common catches are bonefish, threadfin and *ulua*. There are no facilities. ~ Take Kaumualii Highway several miles past Kekaha, then watch for signs to the Pacific Missile Range Facility. You can request a pass at the front gate.

▲ Check with the security guards (808-335-4221) at the front entrance. Camping only on weekends and holidays.

HIDDEN ▶ **POLIHALE STATE PARK** This 300-foot-wide beach blankets the coast for over two miles along Kauai's west end and is the United States' westernmost park. It borders the sea cliffs of the Na Pali Coast, covering 138 acres. The hot, dry weather is excellent for sunbathing, and prime for burning, so load up on sunscreen. You might even want to bring an umbrella or other form of shade. The afternoons bring great sunsets. This park has magnificent mountain surroundings: Niihau looms in the distance. Swimming is for experts only. The safest swimming is at Queen's Pond, an area that, depending on the year's weather conditions, floods and creates a protected lagoon along the beachfront near the middle of the park. Surfing is okay; there's a shore break with left and right slides. There's good windsurfing off Queen's Pond. This beach is also especially great for shell collecting. Bonefish, threadfin and *ulua* are the most common game fish. Facilities include a picnic area, restrooms and showers. ~ Take Kaumualii Highway until it ends, then follow the signs along dirt roads for about five miles.

▲ You can pitch a tent on the beach under a star-crowded sky, or find a shady tree (though they are rare in these parts) for protection against the blazing sun. This is a wonderful place to camp for a day or two. After that, the barren landscape becomes tiresome and monotonous. Tent camping allowed. A state permit is required.

KOKEE STATE PARK This spectacular park, high in the mountains above Waimea Canyon, is a mecca for hikers, campers and other outdoor enthusiasts. Sprawling across 4345 heavily wooded acres, this rugged country offers a unique perspective on the Garden Isle. In the rivers there's excellent freshwater angling for rainbow trout during August and September; a state license is required, though. Kokee has everything but a grocery store, so come well-stocked or plan to eat at the lodge restaurant. There is seasonal plum picking, and pig hunting is allowed in the public hunting area. The lodge also has a museum and gift shop. Nearby are cabins, restrooms, showers, a picnic area and hiking trails. See the "Hiking" section at the end of this chapter for trail descriptions. ~ Take Kaumualii Highway to Waimea, then pick up Waimea Canyon Drive from Waimea or Kokee Road from Kekaha. They eventually join and lead about 15 miles up to the park.

▲ An area at the north end of the park has been allocated for tent camping. There are also several wilderness camps along the hiking trails. A state permit is required for nonwilderness camping.

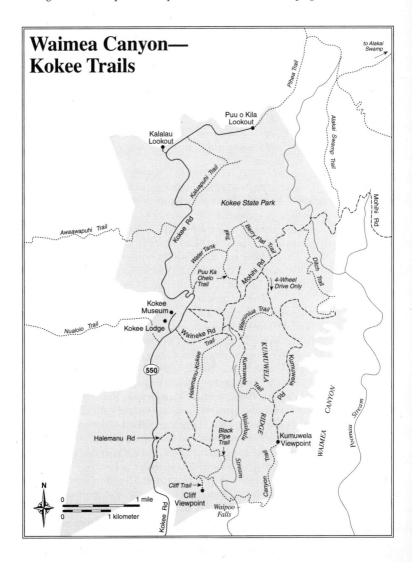

Waimea Canyon—
Kokee Trails

to Alakai Swamp

Pihea Trail

Alakai Swamp Trail

Puu o Kila Lookout

Kalalau Lookout

Kaluapuhi Trail

Mohihi Rd

Kokee State Park

Kokee Rd

Awaawapuhi Trail

Water Tank Trail

Berry Flat Trail

Ditch Trail

Puu Ka Ohelo Trail

Mohihi Rd

4-Wheel Drive Only

Kokee Museum

Wainiiniua Trail

Nualolo Trail

Kokee Lodge

Waineke Rd Trail

KUMUWELA

Halemanu-Kokee Trail

Kumuwela Trail

Kumuwela Rd

550

RIDGE

Kumuwela Viewpoint

WAIMEA CANYON

Poomau Stream

Black Pipe Trail

Waialohula Trail

Halemanu Rd

Canyon Trail

Stream

Cliff Trail

N

0   1 mile

0   1 kilometer

Kokee Rd

Cliff Viewpoint

Waipoo Falls

Wailua–Kapaa Area

If Lihue is the commercial center of Kauai, Wailua is the cultural heart of the island. Here along the Wailua River, the only navigable river in Hawaii, the *alii* built *heiaus* and perpetuated their princely lines.

There are broad surfing beaches here as well as cascades and grottoes up along the Wailua River. The Hawaiian nobility added fishponds and coconut groves to these natural features and forbade commoners from entering their domain.

The oral tradition they handed down tells of a Tahitian holy man named Puna, one of the first Polynesians to arrive in Hawaii, who chose this sacred spot to live. Other legends recount the lost tribe of Mu, a pre-Polynesian people, dwarfish and cruel, who inhabited caves far up the Wailua River.

Developed as a resort destination before Poipu and Princeville, this area has nevertheless avoided the overdevelopment that plagues other parts of the island. Wailua and Kapaa, while hosting a string of oceanfront condominiums, remain working-class towns, maintaining a contemporary version of the cultural pride of the ancient *alii*.

SIGHTS

Lydgate State Park, at the confluence of the Wailua River and the ocean, bears the rocky remains of the **Hauola Place of Refuge**. Here *kapu* breakers under sentence of death could flee; once inside its perimeter, their crimes were absolved. A stone retaining wall also marks the ancient **Hikina Heiau**. ~ Kuhio Highway, Wailua.

On the other side of the highway you can step from the sacred to the profane. Billing itself as "Kauai's best-kept secret," **Smith's Tropical Paradise** is actually the island's biggest tourist trap. Covering 30 riverside acres is a series of gardens and mock Pacific villages in the form of a tropical theme park. There are hibiscus, bamboo and Japanese gardens as well as re-creations of life in Polynesia, the Philippines and elsewhere. On Monday, Wednesday and Friday evenings, they stage a luau and show. Admission. ~ 174 Wailua Road, Wailua; 808-821-6895, fax 808-822-4520.

Fittingly, the adjacent marina is the departure point for boat trips up the Wailua River to **Fern Grotto**. The scenery along the way is magnificent as you pass along a tropical riverfront that is luxuriously overgrown. The grotto itself is a 40-foot cavern draped with feathery ferns, a place so beautiful and romantic that many people choose to be married here. But the boat ride is one of the most cloyingly commercial experiences in Hawaii, a 20-minute voyage during which you are crowded together with legions of tourists and led in chants by a narrator with an amplifier. Admission. ~ 808-821-6892, fax 808-822-4520.

Past Coco Palms Resort (which closed after Hurricane Iniki), the road courses through Kauai's most historic region, the domain of ancient Hawaiian royalty. Watch for Hawaii Visitors

Bureau signs pointing out the **Holo-Holo-Ku Heiau**, one of the oldest temples on the island, a place where human sacrifices were performed. A short distance uphill, you'll find a small but interesting Japanese cemetery. Ironically, this is also the site of **Pohaku-Ho-o-Hanau,** a sacred spot where royal women came to give birth.

As you continue up Route 580, the lush Wailua Valley opens to view. On the left along the hilltop rest the rocky remains of **Poliahu Heiau.** A short path leads down to the **Bell Stone,** which resounded when struck with a rock, loudly signaling the birth of royal infants. All these places, vital to Hawaiian myth, were located along the old King's Highway, a sacred thoroughfare used only by island rulers.

For some vivid mountain scenery, continue on Route 580 past **Opaekaa Falls** (a path along the highway brings you to a   ◄ *HIDDEN* great viewpoint). The road passes through **Wailua Homesteads,** a ranch and farm region filled with fruit orchards and macadamia

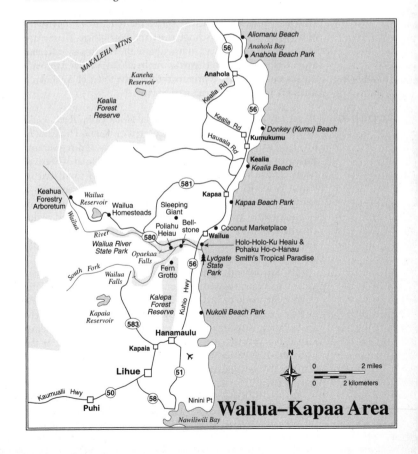

Wailua–Kapaa Area

nut trees. It ends at **Keahua Forestry Arboretum**, where hiking trails wind through groves of painted gum trees. The adjoining state forest climbs all the way to Waialeale, providing unique views of the world's wettest place.

As the road dips down into Kapaa, you'll be passing from one Hawaiian era to another. This 19th-century town, with its falsefront stores and second-story balconies, is home to everyday folks. This is where the local plumber, carpenter and fisherman live. The population is Japanese, Hawaiian, Caucasian, Filipino and Chinese. They reside in small plantation houses and attend the local churches that dot the surrounding countryside.

From Kapaa, there's an excellent view of the Sleeping Giant, a recumbent figure naturally hewn out of the nearby mountain range.

In its northerly course between Wailua and Kapaa, Kuhio Highway (Route 56) passes the **Coconut Marketplace** with its sprawling shopping mall and grove of royal palm trees.

Follow the highway and you'll arrive at a curving ribbon of sand known as Kealia Beach. Across the road, in various states of disrepair, are a local school, store and post office. These clapboard buildings represent in its entirety the tiny town of **Kealia**. From Kealia, the Kuhio Highway climbs and turns inland through sugar cane fields and continues through the town of **Anahola**, a small Hawaiian homestead settlement.

HIDDEN ▶

LODGING

To get any closer to the water than the **Hotel Coral Reef**, you'd have to pitch a tent in the sand. Located on Kuhio Highway in Kapaa, it's within strolling distance of markets and restaurants and is an excellent choice for the wanderer without wheels. A floral garden leads out to a comfortable strip of sand next to Kapaa Beach Park. In this beachfront building you can enjoy a touch of wood paneling, soft beds, refrigerator and a delightful seascape just beyond those sliding glass doors. A second building offers rooms with fans and ocean views. ~ 1516 Kuhio Highway, Kapaa; 808-822-4481, 800-843-4659, fax 808-822-7705. BUDGET TO MODERATE.

The **Kauai Sands Hotel** costs a little more, but it's still a bargain. This beachfront accommodation is part of the only hotel chain in the world owned by a Hawaiian family, the Kimis. You'll find a relaxed and spacious lobby, restaurant, two pools, a well-tended lawn, carpeting, lanai, imaginative decor and a touch of Hawaiiana. Ask about discounts. ~ 420 Papaloa Road near the Coconut Marketplace, Wailua; 808-822-4951, 800-560-5533, fax 808-822-0978; www.sand-seaside.com, e-mail info@sand-seaside.com. DELUXE.

The nearby **Kauai Coast Resort at the Beachboy**, a link in the Aston hotel chain, is another extremely appealing place. Located behind the Coconut Marketplace, it's popular with swimmers and shoppers alike. There's a pool, spa, fitness center and tennis courts amid the hotel's central grounds, plus a windswept lobby with adjoining shops and restaurant. For pleasant surroundings near the center of the action, it's definitely among the area's top choices. The rooms have been converted to one- and two-bedroom condominiums. They are air conditioned and include televisions, full kitchens, washer/dryers and lanais. The decor is quite taste-ful, and the rates, considering what the hotel provides, are rea-sonable. ~ 484 Kuhio Highway, Kapaa; 808-822-3441, 800-922-7866, fax 808-822-0843. MODERATE TO ULTRA-DELUXE.

The **Kauai International Hostel** has both dormitory and pri-vate rooms at low prices. Facilities, as you might expect, are spar-tan. There's a scruffy yard with two buildings; guests share a tele-vision room, kitchen, washer-dryer and a pool table. Like hostels everywhere, it's a good deal for the dollar. ~ 4532 Lehua Street, Kapaa; 808-823-6142. BUDGET.

Keapana Center Bed and Breakfast, set in the mountains out-side Kapaa, is a lush three-acre complex offering a restful environ-ment and otherworldly views. This hilltop B&B provides a unique escape that somehow seems perfectly suited to the slow rhythms of Kauai. There's also a separate yurt, situated away from the main building and equipped with a small outdoor bathroom and kitchen (breakfast not included). From the center, you can hike the surrounding mountains, drive to a nearby beach or relax in the jacuzzi or on the windswept lanai with its hammock and invit-ing armchairs. A rare retreat. Two-day minimum for the rooms; five-day minimum for the yurt or a secluded or garden cottage. ~ 5620 Keapana Road; 808-822-7968, 800-822-7968, fax 808-823-9013; e-mail keapana@aloha.net. BUDGET TO MODERATE.

◄ HIDDEN

GAY LODGING   There are four comfortable, airy guest rooms at the gay-friendly, clothing-optional bed and breakfast **Mohala Ke Ola**. It's situated right across the river from Opaekaa Falls and offers grand views of Mount Waialeale. Pool; jacuzzi; continental breakfast on the deck. ~ 5663 Ohelo Road, Kapaa; phone/fax 808-823-6398, 888-465-2824; www.waterfallbnb.com. MODERATE.

Looking like it has been lifted straight out of the Japanese countryside, **Mahina Kai Ocean Villa** has a Japanese garden and teahouse to match. Three suites and one single guest room are fitted with kimono quilts and shoji screen doors and share a kitchen; a cottage includes a full kitchen. There's an indoor pond and a pool as well as an ocean view from this two-acre property. ~ 4933 Aliomanu Road, Anahola; 808-822-9451, 800-337-1134, fax 808-822-9614; www.mahinakai.com. DELUXE TO ULTRA-DELUXE.

Wailua Bay View offers one-bedroom apartments, $100 for up to four people; three-night minimum stay. Ocean view. ~ 320 Pa-

CONDOS

paloa Road, Kapaa; 808-245-4711, 800-767-4707, fax 808-245-8115; www.prosserrealty.com, e-mail holiday@aloha.net.

Studio apartments at **Kapaa Sands Resort** are $95 single or double, $110 for an oceanfront unit. Two-bedroom apartments, $126 (one to four people); $143 for an oceanfront location. ~ 380 Papaloa Road, Kapaa; 808-822-4901, 800-222-4901, fax 808-822-1556; www.kapaasands.com, e-mail ksresort@gte.net.

Mokihana of Kauai has studio apartments that run $65 single or double. These units are supplied with a hotplate and small refrigerator. ~ 796 Kuhio Highway, Kapaa; 808-822-3971, fax 808-822-7387.

Kauai Kailani features two-bedroom apartments, $75 for up to four people; $7.50 for each extra person. This offers a lot of square footage for the money, but there's one catch—reservations are difficult to obtain and should be made a year in advance. Three-night minimum. ~ 856 Kuhio Highway, Kapaa; 808-822-3391, fax 808-822-7387.

DINING

Antique Japanese screens set the theme at **Restaurant Kintaro**, where you can dine at the sushi bar or enjoy *teppanyaki*-style cooking. If you decide on the latter, choose between filet mignon, shrimp, scallops, steak teriyaki or oysters sautéed with olive oil. They also prepare traditional tempura and yakitori dinners as well as *yose nabe* (Japanese bouillabaisse). Closed Sunday. ~ 4-370 Kuhio Highway, Wailua; 808-822-3341, fax 808-822-2153. DELUXE.

There are short-order stands galore at the Coconut Marketplace. **Harley's Ribs-'n-Chicken** delivers what its name promises. ~ 808-822-2505. TC's **Island Grill** features good old American food like hot dogs and hamburgers. ~ 808-823-9181. The **Fish Hut** lives up to its name. ~ 808-822-1712. You'll never guess what they serve at **Aloha Kauai Pizza**. ~ 808-822-4511. Any time from early morning until 8 or 9 p.m., several of these stands will be open. An interesting way to dine here is by going from one to the next, nibbling small portions along the way. ~ Kuhio Highway, Wailua. BUDGET.

Hidden (but certainly not hiding) in the wings at Coconut Marketplace is **Buzz's Steak & Lobster**. Dim lighting, potted palms, tropical paintings, overhead fans—all these spell Polynesia. There is a surf-and-broiler menu. ~ Kuhio Highway, Wailua; 808-822-0041. MODERATE TO DELUXE.

The **Waipouli Delicatessen and Restaurant** is a small Japanese-style luncheonette serving Asian and American food and owned by a delightful Asian woman. It's open for breakfast, lunch and dinner daily. ~ Kuhio Highway, Waipouli; 808-822-9311. MODERATE.

It's beef, beef and beef at **The Bull Shed**. We're talking about prime rib, beef kebab, top sirloin, garlic tenderloin and teriyaki steak. All this in a captain's-chair-and-fish-trophy restaurant that's so close to the surf your feet feel wet. Speaking of surf, they also serve lobster, broiled shrimp, Alaskan king crab and fresh fish. Dinner only. ~ 796 Kuhio Highway, Kapaa; 808-822-3791, fax 808-822-7387. MODERATE TO DELUXE.

For a light, healthful meal, you can cross the street to **Papaya's Natural Foods**. This takeout counter with outdoor tables has pasta, pizza, sandwiches, vegetable stir-fry, grilled fish and salads. Papaya's also caters to vegetarians and vegans. Closed Sunday. ~ Kauai Village Shopping Center, 4-831 Kuhio Highway, Kapaa; 808-823-0191, fax 808-823-0756; www.organic@hawaiian. net. BUDGET.

Kalua pig, lomi salmon and poi highlight the Hawaiian menu at the Aloha Diner. Closed Sunday. ~ Waipouli Complex, 971-F Kuhio Highway, Waipouli; 808-822-3851. MODERATE.

The best restaurant on the island, **A Pacific Café** serves beautifully presented Hawaii regional cuisine. The accent is on freshness, with an open-kitchen design and a menu that changes daily. The restaurant ranks high among local critics, who rave about the wok-charred mahimahi with garlic sesame crust and lime-ginger sauce and the potato-crusted *onaga* with cabernet-thyme butter. The decor is a simple mix of Asian and Hawaiian with paintings by local artists adorning the walls. Dinner only. ~ Kauai Village Shopping Center, 4-831 Kuhio Highway, Kapaa; 808-822-0013, fax 808-822-0054; www.pacificcafe.com. DELUXE TO ULTRA-DELUXE.

Up Kapaa way on Kuhio Highway in the center of town, there's a restaurant known to Mexican food aficionados for miles around. **Norberto's El Café** draws a hungry crowd of young locals for dinner. The owners raise a lot of their own vegetables, and they serve monstrous portions. If you're not hungry, order à la carte. If you are, choose from a solid menu ranging from enchiladas (including Hawaiian taro-leaf enchiladas) to burritos to chile rellenos. Children's portions are available and all meals can be converted to cater to vegetarians. Definitely worth checking out. Dinner only. Closed Sunday. ~ Kuhio Highway, Kapaa; 808-822-3362. MODERATE.

The local crowds attest to the quality and value at **Mermaid's Café**. Serving breakfast and lunch only, this tiny place offers vegan and vegetarian choices as well as wraps, burritos, and chicken satay and curry plates. ~ 4-1384 Kuhio Highway, Kapaa; 808-821-2026. BUDGET TO MODERATE.

One of the loveliest dining spots hereabouts is **Kapaa Fish & Chowder House**. Each room is trimly decorated, comfortably furnished and adorned with nautical items and an assortment of potted plants; the back room is a garden patio. They serve stir-fry fish dishes, shellfish, tiger prawns, calamari, New York steak and chicken. ~ 4-1639 Kuhio Highway, Kapaa; 808-822-7488, fax 808-822-2379. MODERATE TO DELUXE.

Given the popular bar scene, the café half of **Tropix Island Style Café and Bar** seems like an afterthought. But this is a great place to chow down on local cuisine. There's fresh fish, roast pork and saimin. Enjoy live Hawaiian contemporary music, Monday, Wednesday, Friday and Saturday. ~ 4-1330 Kuhio Highway, Kapaa; 808-822-7330. BUDGET TO MODERATE.

Some of the best hamburgers on the island are found at **Duane's Ono CharBurger**. ~ Kuhio Highway, Anahola; 808-822-9181. BUDGET.

GROCERIES There are two major grocery stores in the Wailua–Kapaa area. Try **Foodland** in the Waipouli Town Center. ~ Waipouli; 808-822-7271. Or shop at **Safeway**. ~ Kauai Village Shopping Center, Kapaa; 808-822-2464. There's a **Big Save Market** at the Kapaa Shopping Center. ~ 1105-F Kuhio Highway; 808-822-4971.

Ara's Sakana-Ya Fish House has a wide variety of fresh fish and seafood, as well as island *poke*. ~ 3-4301 Kuhio Highway, Suite 102, Hananaulu; 808-245-1707.

To the north is the **Whaler's General Store**. This well-stocked market is the largest store between Kapaa and Princeville. ~ Kuhio Highway, Anahola; 808-822-5818.

SHOPPING One of the top shopping spots on Kauai is the **Coconut Marketplace**. This theme mall consists of wooden stores designed to resemble little plantation houses. For decor you'll find the pipes, valves, gears and waterwheels characteristic of every tropical plantation. This is a good place for clothing, curios, jewelry, toys, Asian imports, T-shirts, luggage, plus leather goods, betters and bests. If you don't want to buy, you can always browse or have a snack at the many short-order stands here. In any case, it's worth a walk through. ~ Kuhio Highway, Wailua.

> What attracted Hawaiian royalty to Kauai's east coast was the weather along this windward shore, cooler in the summer than the baking sands of Poipu but not so moist as the tropical rainforests to the north.

Two galleries within the Marketplace are worthy of note. **Island Images** (808-822-3636) features premier Hawaiian artwork by artists such as George Sumner, Jan Parker, Pegge Hopper, Roy Tabora and Randy Puckett. Fine art prints, limited edition lithographs and *raku* pottery can be purchased at Island Images. Also consider **Ship Store Galleries** (808-822-7758), which highlights an eclectic group of artists. **Overboard** (808-822-1777), also in the Coconut Marketplace, has aloha shirts and other Hawaiian wear.

Kauai Village Shopping Center, a multi-store complex in the center of Kapaa, is another of Kauai's shopping destinations. Anchored by a grocery store, it features a string of small shops. **Kahn Fine Arts at Kauai Village** (808-822-4277) has original sculptures, paintings and lithographs by Hawaiian artists. There's a **Waldenbooks** (808-822-7749) in this complex that sells an array of local titles as well as national bestsellers. ~ Kuhio Highway, Kapaa.

Talk about unusual. **Island Hemp & Cotton** specializes in things made from the evil weed. There's a very attractive line of women's clothing here, not to mention soap, paper, body lotion and even coffee filters, all fabricated from hemp. ~ 1373 Kuhio Highway, Kapaa; 808-821-0225.

Tin Can Mailman specializes in new, used and rare books, particularly Pacific Island titles. It is also rich in stamps, maps and botanical prints. ~ 356 Kuhio Highway, Kapaa; 808-822-3009.

Check out the **Jolly Roger**. It's a karaoke bar with a lively crowd. ~ Coconut Marketplace, Kuhio Highway, Wailua; 808-822-3451.

NIGHTLIFE

The **Cascades Bar & Grill** at the Radisson Kauai Beach Resort has live Tahitian music and dancing as well as contemporary music nightly from 7 to 10 p.m. ~ 4331 Kauaui Beach Drive, Wailua; 808-245-1955.

Thursday is jazz night at **Kapaa Fish & Chowder House**. If you're in town that evening, you'll find them jamming between 8 and 11 p.m. ~ 4-1639 Kuhio Highway, Kapaa; 808-822-7488.

Comedies, dramas and musicals are all part of the bill of fare at the **Kauai International Theatre**. Wednesday is concert night, while plays are featured Thursday through Saturday. ~ Kauai Village, Kapaa; 808-821-1588.

NUKOLII BEACH PARK 🏖️ 🎣 🚣 🚿 Located adjacent to the Outrigger Kauai Hilton Hotel, this is a long narrow strand with a shallow bottom. From the park, the beach extends for several miles all the way to Lydgate Park in Wailua. One of the island's prettiest beaches, it provides an opportunity to use the park facilities or to escape to more secluded sections (adjacent to Wailua Golf Course). A dirt road parallels the beach north of the park for about a half-mile, but if you seek seclusion, just start hiking farther north along the shore. You'll find places galore for water sports. Swimming is good in well-protected and shallow waters. Snorkeling is good among reefs and there are good surf breaks on the shallow reef at "Graveyards." Fishing is best near reefs. ~ Located at the end of Kauai Beach Drive. To reach the more secluded sections, go north from Lihue on Kuhio Highway and take a right onto the road that runs along the southern end of the Wailua Golf Course. This paved road rapidly becomes a dirt strip studded with potholes. Driving slowly, proceed a quarter-mile, then take the first left turn. It's another quarter-mile to the beach; when the road forks, take either branch.

BEACHES & PARKS

◀ *HIDDEN*

LYDGATE STATE PARK 🏖️ 🎣 🏊 🚿 The awesome ironwood grove and long stretches of rugged coastline make this one of Kauai's loveliest parks. Near the Wailua River, it is also one of the most popular. Two large lava pools, one perfect for kids and the other protecting swimmers and snorkelers, make it a great place to spend the day. Swimming is very good. Surfers must take a long paddle out to breaks off the mouth of Wailua River. There's a right slide. This park is also popular with windsurfers. *Ulua* is the most common catch. You'll find a picnic area, showers, restrooms, playground and lifeguards. ~ From Kuhio Highway, turn toward the beach at Leho Drive, the road just south of the Wailua River.

Wailua River State Park, near Lydgate Park, features sacred historic sites and breathtaking views of river and mountains.

KAPAA BEACH PARK While it sports an attractive little beach, this 15-acre facility doesn't measure up to its neighbors. Located a block from the highway as the road passes through central Kapaa, the park is flanked by ramshackle houses and a local playing field. The area sports a picnic area and restrooms. Swimming and fishing are only fair, but there is good squidding and torchfishing. ~ Located a block from Kuhio Highway, Kapaa.

KEALIA BEACH This strand is one of those neighbors that makes Kapaa Beach the pimply kid next door: It's a wide, magnificent beach curving for about a half-mile along Kuhio Highway. The swimming is good, but requires caution. Good surfing and bodysurfing can be found at the north end of the beach. Fish here for *papio*, threadfin and *ulua*. There are no facilities. ~ Located on Kuhio Highway, Kealia.

HIDDEN ▶ **DONKEY BEACH OR KUMU BEACH** This broad, curving beach is flanked by a grassy meadow and towering ironwoods. Favored as a hideaway and nude beach by locals, it's a gem that should not be overlooked. Also note that the two-mile stretch from here north to Anahola is lined by low sea cliffs that open onto at least four pocket beaches. This entire area is popular with beachcombers, who sometimes find hand-blown Japanese glass fishing balls. (Several other hidden beaches are strung anonymously along cane roads paralleling the coast from Kealia to Anahola. Watch for them as you travel through this area.) Swimmers take care: currents here can be treacherous and the nearest lifeguard is a world away. Right off Donkey Beach there is good surfing and bodysurfing. Just north of the beach is "14 Crack," a popular left slide break. This is a popular spot for pole-fishing and throw-netting. There are no facilities here. ~ Follow Kuhio Highway north from Kealia. At the 11-mile marker the road begins to climb slowly, then descends. At the end of the descent, just before Mile Marker 12, there is a cane road on the right. Take this road; bear right and watch for Donkey's Beach on the left within a half-mile. (Since the road is presently chained, you'll have to hike in from Kuhio Highway.)

▲ Unofficial camping is common.

ANAHOLA BEACH PARK 🏊 🪝 🎣 🛶 A slender ribbon of ◀ *HIDDEN* sand curves along windswept Anahola Bay. At the south end, guarded by ironwood trees, lies this pretty little park. Very popular with neighborhood residents, this is a prime beachcombing spot where you may find Japanese glass fishing balls. There is a protecting reef here; but as elsewhere, use caution swimming because of the strong currents. Snorkeling is good behind the reef. Surfers have a long paddle out to summer and winter breaks along the reef (left and right slides). There is a break called "Unreals" offshore from the old landing. This is also a popular bodysurfing beach. There's good torchfishing for lobsters, and anglers often catch *papio*, rudderfish, *ulua*, threadfin, bonefish and big-eyed scad. Facilities include a picnic area, restrooms and showers. ~ Turn onto Anahola Road from Kuhio Highway in Anahola; follow it three-quarters of a mile, then turn onto a dirt road that forks left to the beach.

▲ You can pitch a tent on the grassy area near the beach; county permit required.

ALIOMANU BEACH 🏊 🛶 On the far side of Anahola Bay, sep- ◀ *HIDDEN* arated from the park by a lagoon, sits another sandy beach. Shady ironwood trees, several roadside houses and a picnic table dot this area, which is a favorite among locals. What makes Aliomanu particularly popular is the offshore reef, one of Kauai's longest and widest fringing reefs. This is an excellent area for gathering edible seaweed. Swimming is fairly safe in the lagoon but use caution seaside. Local residents spear octopus and go torchfishing here. ~ Turn off Kuhio Highway onto Aliomanu Road just past Anahola.

▼▼▼▼▼▼▼▼▼▼

North Shore

It is no accident that when it came time to choose a location for Bali Hai, the producers of *South Pacific* ended their search on the North Shore of Kauai. The most beautiful place in Hawaii, indeed one of the prettiest places on earth, this 30-mile stretch of lace-white surf and emerald-green mountains became Hollywood's version of paradise.

While the scenery is so spectacular as to seem mythic, there is nothing insubstantial about the North Shore. The tiny villages that dot the waterfront are populated by people with a strong sense of defending their environment. With development concentrated in the resort complex of Princeville, Hanalei remains a tiny town of taro fields and one-lane bridges. The village of Kilauea is still a sanctuary for a vast population of waterfowl and attempts to widen the North Shore's lone road have been fought with religious intensity.

Backdropping this thin line of civilization is the **Na Pali Coast**.   **SIGHTS** Here, sharp sea cliffs vault thousands of feet from the ocean, silver waterfalls streaming along their fluted surfaces. There are pocket beaches ringed by menacing rock formations and long, wide strands as inviting as a warm tub.

The North Shore is wet and tropical, drawing enough precipitation to dampen the enthusiasm of many tourists. It is suited for travelers who don't mind a little rain on their parade if it carries with it rainbows and seabirds and a touch of magic in the air.

Your civic introduction to this realm comes in **Kilauea**, a former sugar town with a cluster of stores and a couple noteworthy churches. The cottages that once housed plantation workers are freshly painted and decorated with flowering gardens and the place possesses an air of humble well-being.

But as everywhere along the North Shore, humankind is a bit player in the natural drama being presented here. To take in that scene, you need venture no farther than **Kilauea Point National Wildlife Refuge**. Here on Kilauea Point, a lofty peninsula that falls away into precipitous rockfaces, you'll have the same bird's-eye view of the Na Pali Coast as the boobies, tropicbirds, albatrosses and frigate birds, some of which nest in the cliffs. As you stand along this lonely point, gazing into the trees and along the cliffs, birds—graceful, sleek, exotic birds—swarm like bees. A vital rookery, the preserve is also home to Hawaiian monk seals and green turtles, as well as occasional whales and dolphins. Admission. ~ End of Kilauea Road, Kilauea; 808-828-1413, fax 808-828-6634.

HIDDEN ►

Counterpoint to this natural pageant is the **Kilauea Lighthouse**, a 52-foot-high beacon built in 1913 that bears the world's largest clamshell-shaped lens. Capable of casting its light almost 100 miles, it is the first sign of land seen by mariners venturing east from Asia. This old lighthouse, now replaced by a more modern beacon, sits on the northernmost point of Kauai. People gather at the point for interpretive talks of the bird life and natural history of the region.

Civilization stakes its claim once again at **Princeville**, a 11,000-acre planned resort community that combines private homes, condominiums and the elegant Princeville Hotel. Set along a luxurious plateau with scintillating views of the Na Pali Coast, it is a tastefully designed complex complete with golf courses and acres of open space.

Past Princeville, the road opens onto the **Hanalei Valley Lookout**, a vista point that transcends prose with its beauty. Below you spreads a patchwork of tropical vegetation, fields of broad-leafed taro that have been cultivated for over 1200 years. This green carpet, swaying and shimmering along the valley floor, is cut by the thin silver band of the Hanalei River. Framing this scene, as though a higher power had painted the entire tableau, are deep-green cliffs, fluted and sharp, that rise 3500 feet from the tilled fields.

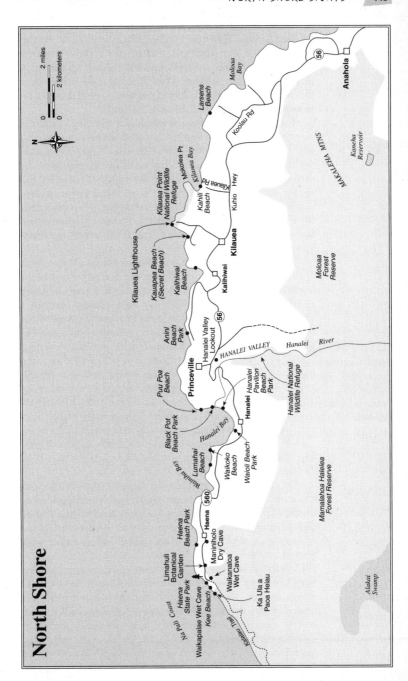

North Shore

Nā Pali Coast

Kalalau Trail

Waikapalae Wet Cave
Kee Beach
Ka Ula a
Paoa Heiau
Waikanaloa Wet Cave
Maniniholo
Dry Cave
Haena
Haena
Beach Park
Limahuli
Botanical
Garden
Haena State Park

560

Lumahai
Beach
Wainiha Bay
Black Pot
Beach Park
Puu Poa
Beach

Waikoko
Beach
Waioli Beach
Park
Hanalei Hanalei
Pavilion
Beach
Park
Hanalei Bay
Hanalei National
Wildlife Refuge

Princeville
Hanalei Valley
Lookout
HANALEI VALLEY   *Hanalei*   *River*

Anini
Beach
Park
56

Kilauea Lighthouse

Kauapea Beach
(Secret Beach)
Kalihiwai
Beach
Kilauea Point
National Wildlife
Refuge
Mokolea Pt
Kilauea Bay

Kahili
Beach
Kalihiwai
Kilauea Rd
Kilauea
Kuhio Hwy

56

*Moloaa Forest
Reserve*

*Larsens
Beach*
Koolau Rd
Moloaa Bay

Anahola

MAKALEHA MTNS

*Kaneha
Reservoir*

*Mamalahoa Halelea
Forest Reserve*

*Alakai
Swamp*

2 miles
2 kilometers
0
0

N

These taro patches and surrounding wetlands comprise the 917-acre **Hanalei National Wildlife Refuge**, home to the Hawaiian duck, Hawaiian stilt, the Hawaiian coot and the Hawaiian moorhen, all of which are endangered. For a close-up version of this panorama, turn left onto Ohiki Road near the old bridge at the bottom of the hill. It will lead you back several eras to a region of terraced fields and simple homesteads.

In town, a combination of ramshackle buildings, dramatic mountain views and curving beaches creates a mystique that can

HIDDEN ► only be described in a single word—Hanalei. It makes you wonder if heaven, in fact, is built of clapboard. The town is little more than a string of woodframe bungalows and falsefront stores lining the main road (the *only* road). On one side a half-moon bay, rimmed with white sand, curves out in two directions. Behind the town the *pali*, those awesome cliffs that fluctuate between dream and reality in the focus of the mind, form a frontier between Hanalei and the rest of the world.

It's almost superfluous that the **Waioli Mission House**, built in 1836, provides glimpses of a bygone era: The entire town seems a reflection of its former self. But this one-time home of Abner and Lucy Wilcox, missionaries from New England, extends a special invitation to step back into the 19th century. A small but stately house, shiplap in design with a second-story lanai, it sits amid palm and *hala* trees on a broad lawn. The rooms look undisturbed since the days when the Wilcoxes prayed and proselytized. The china rests in the cupboard and an old rocker sits in one room while the canopied bed and cradle still occupy a bedroom. The walls are decorated with paintings of the Wilcox family and knickknacks from their era are scattered about the entire house. Guided tours are led Tuesday, Thursday and Saturday between 9 a.m. and 3 p.m. ~ 808-245-3202, fax 808-245-7988.

All along the North Shore, numerous side roads lead from Kuhio Highway through fields and meadows to hidden beaches.

The road winds on from Hanalei past single-lane bridges and overgrown villages. The air seems moister and the real world more distant as you pass **Lumahai Beach**, a sandy scimitar where Mitzi Gaynor vowed to "wash that man right out of my hair" in the 1957 movie *South Pacific*. ~ Off Kuhio Highway about five miles west of Hanalei.

Several caves along this route were created eons ago when this entire area was underwater. The first is **Maniniholo Dry Cave**, which geologists claim is a lava tube but which legend insists was created by *Menehunes*. The **Waikapalae** and **Waikanaloa Wet Caves** nearby are said to be the work of Pele, the Hawaiian goddess of volcanoes, who sought fire in the earth but discovered only water.

A loop trail three-quarters of a mile long winds through the **Limahuli Botanical Garden**. Devoted to conservation of native and Polynesian-introduced plants, the valley is rich in history and contains several archeological sites. The path winds through ancient terraces with Hawaiian taro, into a forest supporting many endangered Hawaiian plants, and out to ocean and mountain views. Self-guided and guided tours are available. Closed Monday and Saturday. Admission. ~ 808-826-1053, fax 808-826-1394; www.ntbg.org.

The cinematic appears once more at **Kee Beach**, a lovely strand with protecting reef that was used to film some of the torrid love scenes in *The Thorn Birds*. This is the end of the road, beyond which the fabled Kalalau Trail winds along the Na Pali Coast.

Just above Kee Beach at the far west end of the strand rises **Ka Ulu a Paoa Heiau**. This grass-covered terrace was also the site ◄ **HIDDEN** of a hula platform and ceremonial hall; Hawaii's greatest hula masters once taught here. According to legend, the volcano goddess Pele departed Kauai from here, settling on the Big Island, where she still lives. ~ Follow the path on the top of the stone wall just above Kee Beach. About ten yards past the end of the beach, take the left fork in the path. Another 20 yards and you will be on the platform.

The North Shore is short on bargains, but at **Hanalei Inn** there **LODGING** are eight studio units, five with kitchens. They are attractive, well-maintained rooms with outdoor barbecues, hardwood floors, local art on the walls and fresh flowers. There's also a tiny budget-priced room for unfinicky backpackers looking for a place to crash for the night; it sleeps two. This intimate inn sits amid a garden 100 yards from the beach. ~ Kuhio Highway, Hanalei; 808-826-9333. BUDGET TO MODERATE.

At the YMCA's beachfront **Camp Naue**, there are dormitory accommodations in bunkhouses. Bring your own bedding. There is also an adjacent area for camping and a private cabin (sleeps up to four people) with private kitchen and bath. Reservations can only be made for large groups or for the cabin; otherwise, it is on a first-come, first-served basis. ~ Write to P.O. Box 1786, Lihue, Kauai, HI 96766. The camp is located off Kuhio Highway, Haena; 808-246-9090. BUDGET.

Hanalei Bay Resort, spectacularly perched on a hillside overlooking the coastline, provides full vacation facilities. The 22-acre property, which descends to a beach, contains a restaurant, lounge, tennis courts and a spacious swimming pool. The guest rooms are located in three-story buildings dotted around the grounds; some include kitchens. ~ 5380 Honoiki Road, Princeville; 808-826-6522, 800-922-7866, fax 808-826-6680; www.astonhotels.com. ULTRA-DELUXE.

The North Shore's premier resting place is a clifftop roost called the **Princeville Hotel and Resort**. Situated on a point and sporting one of the best views this side of paradise, it's a 252-room complex decorated in European style with a large touch of Hawaiiana. The hotel rises above a white-sand beach and features several restaurants and shops as well as a pool and jacuzzi. Trimmed in gold plating and marble, this is a concierge-and-doorman resort long on service. ~ Princeville; 808-826-9644, 800-826-1260, fax 808-826-1166; www.princeville.com. ULTRA-DELUXE.

CONDOS   In the Princeville resort complex, a few miles east of Hanalei, are several condos: **The Cliffs at Princeville** has condominiums from $155. ~ 808-826-6219, 800-367-8024, fax 808-826-2140. The **Pali Ke Kua** offers one- and two-bedroom apartments for $179 and up. ~ 808-826-9066, fax 808-826-4159. **Pahio at Kaeo Kai** has studios from $115. These are modern, fully equipped units with all the amenities. There is a swimming pool on each property. ~ 808-826-6549, fax 808-826-6715.

The **Hanalei Colony Resort** is the only oceanfront condo complex on the north shore and the most highly recommended. Two-bedroom apartments, $145 single or double; $175 ocean view; $265 oceanfront. There is a wedding coordination service available. Closed weekends. ~ Kuhio Highway, Hanalei; 808-826-6235, 800-628-3004, fax 808-826-9893; www.hcr.com, e-mail hcr@aloha.net.

For information on other condominiums, as well as cottages and houses, and to learn where the best deals are available during any particular time, check with **Hanalei Vacations**. You can also browse (virtually) through every one of their properties at their website. ~ P.O. Box 1109, Hanalei, HI 96714; 808-826-7288, 800-487-9833, fax 808-826-7280; www.800hawaii.com.

DINING   If you'd simply like a pizza, the little town of Kilauea contains **Pau Hana Pizza**, a combination kitchen and bakery that cooks up some delicious pies. ~ Kong Lung Center, Lighthouse Road, Kilauea; 808-828-2020. MODERATE TO DELUXE.

In the resort complex of Princeville, **Hale O'Java** offers a good brew and simple menu. Breakfast includes egg dishes and French toast; for lunch, there are sandwiches and pizza; dinner consists of a pizza menu. ~ Princeville Market; 808-826-7255. BUDGET TO MODERATE. Equally informal is **Paradise Bar & Grill**. It's located one tier up from Hale O'Java and serves sandwiches at lunch and steak and seafood every evening. ~ Princeville Market, Princeville; 808-826-1775. BUDGET TO DELUXE.

The prize for prettiest dining room on the North Shore goes to **La Cascata**, the Princeville Resort's signature restaurant. That is not even taking into account the edenic views of the Na Pali Coast or the soft breezes wafting in from the ocean. All we're counting is the tilework, the murals and the Mediterranean pastel colors. The bill of fare for this award winner is mostly Italian-influenced Mediterranean. It begins with potato crusted crab cake on black olive and artichoke salad; then it evolves into such entrées as fresh island ahi with Kailua corn cakes and charred summer vegetables and fire-roasted rack of lamb on soft porcini mushroom polenta with charred peppers and carmelized onions. ~ Princeville; 808-826-9644, fax 808-826-1166. ULTRA-DELUXE.

Any restaurant critic in the world would immediately award five stars to the view at **Bali Hai Restaurant**. Perched on a deck high above Hanalei Bay, it overlooks a broad sweep of mountains and sea. The menu features classic island fare, ranging from fresh catches to steak to pasta. Reservations are recommended. ~ Hanalei Bay Resort, 5380 Honoiki Road, Princeville; 808-826-6522, fax 808-826-6680. DELUXE.

As beautiful and popular as Hanalei happens to be, the area possesses only a few low-priced facilities. If you've ever tried to find a place to stay here, you know how tight things can be. And the budget restaurant situation is not a whole lot better.

The **Hanalei Wake-Up Cafe** is a low-key eatery offering omelettes and other egg dishes in the morning. There's a small dining room as well as a patio. ~ Aku Road, Hanalei; 808-826-5551. BUDGET.

There are several luncheonettes, including **Village Snack and Bakery**, which serves standard breakfast and lunch fare. ~ Ching Young Village, Kuhio Highway, Hanalei; 808-826-6841. BUDGET.

The atmosphere of **Hanalei Gourmet** is laid-back and local. To fit this feeling, the menu is solid but unpretentious. There are numerous salads, including a chicken salad boat and an ahi pasta salad. The sandwich selection features a shrimp sandwich and a

BEEN HERE BEFORE?

Does this place seem familiar? Are you on the set of *Jurassic Park*? Isn't that Bali Hai from *South Pacific*? Kauai's beauty and tropical ambiance have provided numerous backdrops for blockbuster movies and television shows. Kee Beach at the end of Route 56 is where Father de Bricassart (Richard Chamberlain) made love to Meggie Cleary (Rachel Ward) in the TV series *The Thorn Birds*. The Huleia River still sports the rope swing used in *Raiders of the Lost Ark*, and the Coco Palms Resort, abandoned after Hurricane Iniki in 1992, awaits Elvis' return to *Blue Hawaii*. **Hawaii Movie Tours** will take you to these sites and more while you watch the featured scenes in your "theater on wheels." ~ Kapaa; 808-822-1192, 800-628-8432, fax 808-822-1608; www.hawaiimovietour.com.

special concoction with eggplant and red peppers. Following this seafood and vegetable theme are the dinner entrées, which change nightly. The bar scene is lively, there's live entertainment nightly and the kitchen prepares good food at favorable prices. ~ 5-5161 Kuhio Highway, Hanalei; 808-826-2524, fax 808-826-6007. MODERATE TO DELUXE.

You can follow a similar culinary trail across the street to **Hanalei Mixed Plate**, a takeout stand that serves everything from buffalo burgers to veggie burgers as well as stir-fry, tofu, ginger chicken and kalua pig. ~ Located next to Ching Young Village, Kuhio Highway, Hanalei; 808-826-7888. BUDGET.

Or forget all this nonsense about good health and low cholesterol, step up to the window at **Bubba's**, and order a hot dog or a "Big Bubba" (a half-pound hamburger with three patties). ~ 5-5161 Kuhio Highway, Hanalei; 808-826-7839. BUDGET.

HIDDEN ► The **Tahiti Nui Restaurant** has a luau every Wednesday at 5 p.m. A refreshing alternative to the commercialized luaus of big hotels, this is a family affair. If you miss it, try offerings from the menu, which features steak, fresh fish, calamari, scampi, pasta and chicken dishes. And check out the bamboo-fringed lanai, or the lounge decorated with Pacific Island carvings and overhung with a thatch canopy. Best of all, strike up a conversation with Louise, the robust Tahitian who owns the place. Open for breakfast and lunch except on Wednesday. ~ 5-5134 Kuhio Highway, in the center of Hanalei; 808-826-6277. DELUXE.

With woven *lauhala* walls, bamboo bar and outrigger canoe, **Zelo's Beach House** certainly looks the part. It's airy and informal—a great spot to relax. When you're ready to order, you'll find an eclectic menu. The central focus is pasta: linguine and clams with toasted pine nuts, cajun chicken pasta and an all-you-can-eat spaghetti dish. But they also have steak, hamburgers, fresh seafood and fish tacos. ~ 5-5256 Kuhio Highway, Hanalei; 808-826-9700, fax 808-828-0638. DELUXE.

From the porthole windows to the Japanese fishing balls, the **Hanalei Dolphin Restaurant and Fish Market** presents an interesting aquatic decor. Built smack on the bank of the Hanalei River, this eatery offers a turf-and-surf menu that includes fresh fish,

LIGHTHOUSE CUISINE

A pleasant veranda-style dining room, **Lighthouse Bistro** features a regionally-based menu that ventures into such cross-cultural delights as Cajun barbecued jumbo shrimp, filet *au poivre* and veal piccata. The fresh fish comes broiled, blackened, sautéed or pan seared. ~ Kong Lung Center, Kilauea; 808-828-0480. MODERATE TO DELUXE.

shrimp dishes and New York steak. The restaurant, which is highly recommended, is open for lunch and dinner; no reservations are taken. The fish market at the back of the restaurant offers many of the same fish found on the menu to take home and cook yourself; it's open 11 a.m. to 8 p.m. ~ 5-5016 Kuhio Highway, Hanalei; 808-826-6113, fax 808-826-6699. MODERATE TO DELUXE.

Sushi Blues Grill, a Hanalei hotspot, combines industrial decor with live entertainment. The menu at this second-floor restaurant/club includes sizzling seafood stir fry, coconut shrimp, linguine and scallops, and of course a host of sushi selections. Dinner only. Closed Monday. ~ Ching Young Village, Hanalei; 808-826-9701. DELUXE.

GROCERIES The best place on the North Shore is **Foodland**. It's very well stocked and open from 6 a.m. to 11 p.m. ~ Princeville Shopping Center, off Kuhio Highway; 808-826-9880.

Hanalei supports one large grocery store on Kuhio Highway, **Big Save**. ~ Ching Young Village, Hanalei; 808-826-6652.

Hanalei Natural Foods has organic and health-related items. ~ Ching Young Village, Kuhio Highway, Hanalei; 808-826-6990.

Banana Joe's Tropical Fruit Farm has ripe, delicious fruits as well as smoothies and dried fruit. They can also arrange farm tours. ~ 5-2719 Kuhio Highway, Kilauea; 808-828-1092.

SHOPPING **Kong Lung Co.** in Kilauea has a marvelous assortment of Pacific and Asian treasures as well as a selection of Hawaiian books. Don't miss this one. ~ Kilauea Lighthouse Road; 808-828-1822.

Princeville is the closest you will come to a shopping center on the North Shore. The **Princeville Shopping Center** features a cluster of shops that represents the area's prime spot for window browsers. ~ Off Kuhio Highway; 808-826-3040.

Hanalei's **Ching Young Village** is a small shopping mall that contains a variety store, clothing shops and several other outlets. ~ Kuhio Highway, Hanalei.

Across the street you'll find the **Hanalei Center**, which houses several shops in the Old Hanalei School Building. ~ Kuhio Highway, Hanalei; 808-826-7677.

Kai Kane is an attractively decorated shop featuring fashions of their own design. It's a great place to shop for alohawear. ~ 5-5016 Kuhio Highway, Hanalei; 808-826-5594.

Yellowfish Trading Company has a marvelous collection of antiques and Hawaiian collectibles. ~ Hanalei Center, Kuhio Highway; 808-826-1227.

On the Road To Hanalei has tapa cloth, woodcarvings, jewelry, quilts and other locally and globally fashioned craft items. ~ Located next to Ching Young Village, Kuhio Highway, Hanalei; 808-826-7360.

If you're interested in homemade goods, you'll find a few more stores in other small towns along the North Shore.

NIGHTLIFE In all the world there are few entertainment spots with as grand a view as the Princeville Hotel's **Living Room Bar**. Overlooking Hanalei Bay, it also features a singer and pianist playing standards and contemporary music nightly. ~ Princeville Hotel, Princeville; 808-826-9644.

Hale O'Java in the Princeville Shopping Center offers live Hawaiian music on Sunday afternoon. ~ Princeville; 808-826-7255.

At nearby Hanalei Bay Resort's **Happy Talk Lounge,** you can enjoy the views of Hanalei Bay and relax with contemporary Hawaiian music or jazz daily. ~ 5380 Honoiki Road, Princeville; 808-826-6522.

Amelia's, located out at the Princeville Airport, has live music on weekends. ~ 5-3541 Kuhio Highway, Princeville; 808-826-9561.

For a tropical drink amid a tropical setting, place your order at **Tahiti Nui Restaurant**. ~ 5-5134 Kuhio Highway, Hanalei; 808-826-6277. Or try the **Hanalei Dolphin Restaurant**. ~ Kuhio Highway, Hanalei; 808-826-6113.

The **Hanalei Gourmet** has a guitarist/vocalist every night. ~ 5-5161 Kuhio Highway, Hanalei; 808-826-2524.

On most Wednesday through Sunday nights there's blues or jazz at the **Sushi Blues Grill**. Occasional cover on Friday and Saturday. ~ Ching Young Village, Hanalei; 808-826-9701.

Ola's showcases the work of over 100 craftspeople from Hawaii and the mainland. ~ Off Kuhio Highway, next to Hanalei Dolphin Restaurant; 808-826-6937.

BEACHES & PARKS

MOLOAA BEACH 🏊 🪶 ⛵ Nestled in Moloaa Bay, a small inlet surrounded by rolling hills, Moloaa Beach is relatively secluded, though there are homes nearby. A meandering stream divides the beach into two strands. You'll see a coral reef shadowing the shore. There is good beachcombing at the west end of the strand. Swim with caution. Snorkeling and fishing are good, as is lobster diving. There are no facilities. ~ Take Koolau Road where it branches off Kuhio Highway near the 16-mile marker. Go one-and-three-tenths miles, then turn onto Moloaa Road. Follow this to the end. All roads are paved.

HIDDEN ► **LARSENS BEACH** 🏊 🪶 ⛵ This narrow, sandy beach extends seemingly forever through a very secluded area. Rolling hills, covered with small trees and scrub, rim the strand. A protecting reef provides excellent swimming and snorkeling. Glass fishing balls and other collectibles wash ashore regularly, making this a prime beachcombing spot. It is also very popular for seaweed gathering and throw-netting. There are also good fishing spots. There are no facilities here. ~ It's hard to get to, but more than worth it when you arrive. Take Koolau Road as it branches off Kuhio Highway near the 16-mile marker. Go two-and-one-half miles to a cane road on the right, which switches back in the opposite direction. Get on this road, then take an immediate left onto another dirt road (lined on either side with barbed wire). Don't let the fences scare you—this is a public right of way. Follow it a mile to the end. Hike through the gate and down the road. This leads a half-mile down to the beach, which is on your left. (There is also an access road from Koolau Road that is located one-and-one-fifth miles from the intersection of Koolau Road and Kuhio Highway.)

KAHILI BEACH 🏊 🚶 🛶 Tucked away in Kilauea Bay, this ◀ *HIDDEN* beach is bordered by tree-covered hills and a rock quarry. It's a lovely, semi-secluded spot with a lagoon that represents one of Hawaii's most pristine estuaries. Kahili is also a prime beach-combing spot. For a spectacular view of windswept cliffs, follow the short quarry road that climbs steeply from the parking area. Swimming is good when the sea is calm. The favorite surf break is "Rock Quarry," located offshore from the stream. Fishing is rewarding, and the reef at the east end of the beach is also a favored net-throwing spot. There are no facilities. ~ Take Kilauea Road from its beginning for seven-tenths mile toward the lighthouse in Kilauea. You'll pass through town; on the outskirts of town, before the road veers up toward the lighthouse, turn right onto the narrow dirt road. This road leads one-and-one-half miles to the beach.

▲ Unofficial camping.

KAUAPEA BEACH OR SECRET BEACH 🏊 Inaccessibility ◀ *HIDDEN* means seclusion along this hidden strand. Ideal for birdwatching, swimming and unofficial camping, this half-mile-long beach lies just below Kilauea Lighthouse. Very wide and extremely beautiful, it is popular with nudists and adventurers alike. No facilities spoil this hideaway. ~ The beach can be seen from Kilauea Lighthouse, but getting there is another matter. From Kuhio Highway just west of Kilauea turn onto Kalihiwai Road (be sure to get on the eastern section of Kalihiwai Road, near Banana Joe's Tropical Fruit Farm). The road immediately curves to the left; go right onto the first dirt road; proceed three-tenths mile to a parking lot; from here follow the fenceline down into a ravine to Kauapea Beach.

KALIHIWAI BEACH 🏊 🚶 🛶 Bounded by sheer rock wall on ◀ *HIDDEN* one side and a rolling green hill on the other, this semi-secluded beach is crowded with ironwood trees. Behind the ironwoods, the Kalihiwai River has created a large, shallow lagoon across which stretches the skeleton of a bridge, a last grim relic of the devastating 1946 tidal wave. "Kalihiwai" is one of the top surfing breaks on the North Shore. It's also popular for bodysurfing. Swimmers should exercise caution. Bonefish and threadfin are the most common catches. This is also a great spot for surround-netting of akule. Facilities are limited to picnic tables. ~ Take heed—there are two Kalihiwai Roads branching off Kuhio Highway between Kilauea and Kalihiwai. (The washed-out bridge once connected them.) Take the one closest to Lihue. This bumpy macadam road leads a short distance directly to the beach.

▲ Unofficial camping under the ironwoods.

ANINI BEACH PARK Here a grass-covered park fronts a narrow ribbon of sand, while a protecting reef parallels the beach 200 yards offshore. I thought this an ideal place for kids: The ocean is glass smooth and the beachcombing is excellent. As a result, it's very popular and sometimes crowded. Swimming is excellent and very safe. Snorkeling is also topnotch. Surfers' note: There are winter breaks on very shallow reef (left and right slides). This is also a very popular windsurfing site. Bonefish, *papio* and *ulua* are regularly caught here. People also torchfish, throw-net, spear octopus and harvest seaweed at Anini. Facilities include a picnic area, restrooms and a shower. ~ Between Kilauea and Hanalei, turn off Kuhio Highway onto the second Kalihiwai Road (the one farthest from Lihue, on the Hanalei side of the Kalihiwai River). Then take Anini Road to the beach.

▲ Pleasant, but lacks privacy. A county permit is required. Tent camping only.

PRINCEVILLE BEACHES There are three beaches directly below the plateau on which the Princeville resort complex rests. The most popular is **Puu Poa Beach**, a long and wide strand located next to the Princeville Hotel and reached through the hotel. It offers good swimming and easy access to the hotel's (expensive) facilities but is often crowded. The other two are pocket beaches. **Sealodge Beach**, reached via a right of way behind Unit A of the Sealodge condominium, is a white-sand beach backdropped by cliffs. Offshore is a surfing break called "Little Grass Shacks." **Hideaways** consists of two mirror-image beaches, one below Pali Ke Kua condos and the other below Puu Poa condos. They are both good spots for swimming and snorkeling and feature a well-known surf break. ~ To reach Sealodge Beach, turn right from Kuhio Highway onto Kahaku Road and into the Princeville complex. Turn right on Kamehameha Road and follow it to the Sealodge condos. Access to Hideaways is located between Puu Poa condos and the Princeville Hotel near the end of Kahaku Road.

HANALEI BAY BEACHES 🐟 ⚓ ⛵ 🚣 A sandy, horseshoe-shaped strip of sand curves the full length of Hanalei Bay. Along this two-mile strand there are four beach parks. **Black Pot Beach Park**, a local gathering place, lies at the eastern end of the bay and is bounded on one side by the Hanalei River and on the other by a 300-foot-long pier (Hanalei Landing). With showers and lifeguard facilities available to beachgoers, it is very popular with watersport enthusiasts of all stripes—swimmers, surfers, bodysurfers, windsurfers, kayakers and anglers. It is located at the eastern end of Weke Road. **Hanalei Pavilion Beach Park**, located along Weke Road between Pilikoa and Aku roads, is a favorite picnic spot. **Waioli Beach Park**, a small facility set in an ironwood grove, is situated near the center of the half-moon-shaped bay. It can be reached from the end of either Hee Road or Amaama Road. Black Pot Beach Park, Hanalei Pavilion Beach Park and Waioli Beach Park all have lifeguards on duty. **Waikoko Beach** is a slender strand paralleled by a shallow reef. Popular with families who come here to swim and snorkel, it lies along Kuhio Highway on the western side of the bay.

> Anini Road snakes along the shoreline for several miles on either side of Anini Beach Park. Numerous dirt roads lead a short distance off the road to secluded beaches. These offer the same natural features as the park, plus privacy.

There are three major surf breaks here. "Impossible" breaks require a long paddle out from the pier; right slide. "Pine Tree" breaks, off Waioli Beach Park, are in the center of the bay. "Waikoko" breaks are on the shallow reef along the western side of the bay. All are winter breaks. Surfing in Hanalei is serious business, so be careful. Early morning and late afternoon are the best surfing times. The bay is also a popular bodysurfing area. Fish for squirrelfish, rockfish, red bigeye, *oama*, big-eyed scad, *ulua* and *papio*. There is crabbing off Hanalei Landing pier. All beaches have picnic areas, restrooms and marvelous ocean and mountain views. ~ Located in Hanalei just off Kuhio Highway.

🏕 Tent camping permitted on weekends and holidays at Black Pot Beach Park only. A county permit is required.

LUMAHAI BEACH 🐟 🚣 Many people know this strand as the Nurse's Beach in the movie *South Pacific*. Snuggled in a cove and surrounded by lush green hills, Lumahai extends for three-fourths of a mile. With white sand against black lava, it's a particularly pretty spot. Swim only when the sea is very calm and exercise extreme caution. You can try for *papio* and *ulua*. There are no facilities. ~ Watch for a vista point near the five-mile marker on Kuhio Highway. From here, a crooked footpath leads to the beach.

TUNNELS BEACH AND OTHER HAENA BEACHES

There are beach access roads all along Kuhio Highway near Haena. Taking any of these dirt roads will shortly lead you to secluded strands. Most popular of all is "Tunnels," a sandy beach with a great offshore reef. One of Kauai's best spots for water sports, this is where many of the boats headed along the Na Pali Coast are launched. According to divers, the name "Tunnels" derives from the underwater arches and tunnels in the reef; but surfers claim it's from the perfect tunnel-shaped waves. Windsurfers consider this one of the best sites on Kauai. You'll also find swimmers, snorkelers, sunbathers and beachcombers here. Kepuhi Point is one of the best fishing spots on the North Shore; Tunnels attracts fishermen with nets and poles. There are no facilities here. ~ These beaches are located along Kuhio Highway near Wainiha Bay and Kepuhi Point. Tunnels is two-fifths mile east of Maniniholo Dry Cave.

HAENA BEACH PARK

This grassy park, bounded by the sea on one side and a sheer lava cliff on the other, is right across the street from Maniniholo Dry Cave. It's very popular with young folks and provides good opportunities for beachcombing. There are very strong ocean currents here, which make swimming impossible. Surfing "Cannon's" breaks on a shallow reef in front of Maniniholo Dry Cave is for experts only (right slide). There is excellent surfcasting and torchfishing for red bigeye, squirrelfish, *papio* and *ulua*. Cardinal fish are sometimes caught on the reef at low tide during the full moon. A picnic area, restrooms and a shower are the facilities here. ~ Located on Kuhio Highway five miles west of Hanalei.

▲ It's an attractive campground, sometimes crowded, open to both tents and trailers, and requiring a county permit. There is also camping nearby at the YMCA's Camp Naue (808-246-9090).

HAENA STATE PARK AND KEE BEACH

At the end of Kuhio Highway, where the Kalalau trail begins, 6.7-acre Haena State Park encompasses a long stretch of white sand, with Kee Beach at its western end. This reef-shrouded beach is one of the most popular on the North Shore. When the surf is gentle, swimming is superb; lifeguards on duty. At such times, this is one of the best snorkeling beaches for beginners, with its protective coral reef brilliantly colored and crowded with tropical fish. There are also 4000-year-old sea caves to explore. The Haena shoreline is also one of the island's best shelling beaches. Surfing is good at "Cannons" and "Bobo's" breaks. This is also a prime windsurfing area. There is good fishing along the reef. There are restrooms and showers. ~ Located at the end of Kuhio Highway.

Hidden
Beaches and
Cane Roads

Strung like jewels along Kauai's shore lies a series of hidden beaches that are known only to local people. Among these are some of the loveliest beaches on the entire island, removed from tourist areas, uninhabited, some lacking so much as a footprint. For the wanderer, they are an uncharted domain, and to the camper they can be a secret retreat.

Over a dozen of these hideaways are described in the accompanying sections on Kauai's beaches. Some are located right alongside public thoroughfares; others require long hikes down little-used footpaths. Most can be reached only by private cane roads. These graded dirt roads are owned by sugar plantations and marked with menacing "No Trespassing" signs. Officially, the public is not permitted, and few tourists ever travel along them. But local people use cane roads all the time.

They do so with the greatest courtesy and discretion, realizing that they are treading on private property. They watch cautiously for approaching cane trucks, and yield to plantation traffic. Most important, they respect the awesome beauty of these areas by leaving the beaches as they found them. As one Hawaiian explained to me, the golden rule for visitors is this: "If you want to go native, act like one!"

▼ ▼ ▼ ▼ ▼ ▼ ▼ ▼ ▼ ▼ ▼ ▼ ▼

Outdoor Adventures

CAMPING

To visit Kauai without enjoying at least one camping trip is to miss a splendid opportunity. This lovely isle is dotted with county and state parks that feature ideal locations and complete facilities. There are also many hidden beaches where unofficial camping is common.

Camping at **county parks** requires a permit. These are issued for seven days. You are allowed to camp seven consecutive days at one county park and a total of 60 days per year at all county parks. Permits cost $3 per person per night; children under 18 are free. Permits can be obtained weekdays at the Division of Parks and Recreation. You can also buy permits from a ranger at the campsite for $5 per person per night. ~ 4444 Rice Street, Suite 150, Lihue; 808-274-3445.

State park permits are free. They allow camping five consecutive days at each park, and should be requested at least one month in advance for winter, at least a year in advance for summer reservations. These permits are issued by the Department of Land and Natural Resources. ~ 3060 Eiwa Street, Lihue, HI 96766; 808-274-3445.

The State Division of Forestry also maintains camping areas in the **forest reserves**. Currently, these are free (but call the Division of Forestry to see about new fees); permits are available at the State Division of Forestry. ~ 3060 Eiwa Street, Room 306, Lihue, HI 96766; 808-274-3433. Camping is limited at each site, and there's a four-night maximum on the Kukui Trail campsites near Waimea Canyon and a three-night limit at the Sugi Grove and Kawalkoi sites in the rainforest area at the top of Waimea Canyon.

Camping elsewhere on the island is officially prohibited but actually quite common. Local folks use discretion in selecting hidden beaches for camping, and so can you. By the way, an extra effort should be made to keep these areas clean. One of the best suggestions I've ever heard is to leave your campsite cleaner than when you arrived.

Rainfall is much heavier along the North Shore than along the south coast, but be prepared for showers anywhere. The Kokee area gets chilly, so pack accordingly. And remember, boil or chemically treat all water from Kauai's streams. Water from some of these streams can cause dysentery, and none of the waterways are certified safe by the Health Department.

DIVING

The Garden Isle offers snorkeling and scuba opportunities at such spots as Haena Beach, Tunnels Beach, Moloaa and Koloa Landing. In the Poipu area, Koloa Landing has a number of green sea turtles in its midst and is mainly for experienced snorkelers. The beach in front of Lawai Beach Resort is another popular spot for snorkelers. Brennecke's Beach is now completely restored from the damage wrought by Hurricane Iniki. Even if you have your own equipment, it's a good idea to stop by one of the local dive shops to pick up a map, as well as advice on local conditions.

POIPU AREA   To familiarize yourself with the region's treasures you may want to begin with a group tour. **Fathom Five Divers** rents diving and snorkeling equipment and takes groups to hot spots such as Sheraton Caverns and Brennecke's Ledge. Divers often spot fish unique to Kauai such as bandit angel fish, long-nosed hawk-fish and boarfish. Half-day dives leave every morning and afternoon. ~ Poipu Road, Koloa; 808-742-6991. **Seasport Divers** rents snorkeling and scuba equipment and offers lessons, tours, and day and night dives. ~ 2827 Poipu Road, Poipu; 808-742-9303.

Surfing on Kauai means summer breaks in the south and winter breaks in the north.

WAILUA–KAPAA AREA   **Snorkel Bob's Kauai** rents snorkeling equipment returnable at branches on all the other islands. The shop puts together a tip sheet of the best current snorkel spots (factoring in the weather, tides and so forth). They can also arrange helicopter tours, boat rides and luaus. ~ 4-734 Kuhio Highway, Kapaa, 808-823-9433; and also at 3236 Poipu Road, Koloa, 808-742-2206.

NORTH SHORE   **Hanalei Water Sports Inc.** offers certification classes. Beginners start right at Princeville Beach; more advanced divers may join small groups in exploring the lava tubes and caverns of Tunnels Beach. ~ Princeville Hotel, Princeville; 808-826-7509. Another good possibility for snorkeling rentals is **Hanalei Surf Company**. Check out their supply of boogieboards, wet suits and kids gear. ~ 5-5161 Kuhio Highway, Hanalei; 808-826-9000. **Pedal 'n Paddle** has snorkels, masks and fins as well as single and double kayaks for rent. ~ Ching Young Village, Hanalei; 808-826-9069.

Conditions at the Poipu beaches are usually gentler than on the other side of the island. But if you're qualified, you might want to take on challenging North Shore beaches like Hanalei. Keep in mind that conditions can be extremely dangerous during the winter months. Don't try this area unless you're an expert.

SURFING & WIND-SURFING

POIPU AREA   **Progressive Expressions** not only sells and rents surfboards; they make their own. Bodyboards and swim fins are also available. Surfers head for the Poipu coastline. ~ 5428 Koloa Road, Koloa; 808-742-6041. Surfing champion Margo Oberg offers beginner's surfing lessons at **Nukaumoi Beach and Surf Center** on Poipu Beach. Boogieboards, snorkel gear and accessories are for rent. ~ Next to Brennecke's Beach Broiler, Poipu; 808-742-8019.

If you're new to surfing, or just want a refresher course, sign up for a lesson with the **Kauai Surf School**. They give two-hour private and group lessons, mainly aimed at beginners although advanced classes are also available. Groups are limited to four so that everyone receives personalized instruction. ~ Poipu; 808-742-6331.

WAILUA–KAPAA AREA   The **Kauai Water Ski and Surf Company** rents surfboards and offers all levels of lessons, usually conducted on Wailua Beach. They also have a boat on Wailua River for knee boarding or wake boarding. Boards and accessories are also for sale. ~ 4-356 Kuhio Highway, Wailua; 808-822-3574.

NORTH SHORE   Both fiberglass and soft surfboards, boogieboards and swim fins can be rented at **Hanalei Surf Company**. ~ 5-5161 Kuhio Highway, Hanalei; 808-826-9000. Rentals and beginner-to-expert windsurfing lessons are offered at **Windsurf Kauai**. The North Shore's Anini Beach is often the setting for the lessons, with its reef-protected lagoon. ~ Hanalei; 808-828-6838. Both windsurfing and surfing lessons of all levels are conducted right on Anini Beach at **Anini Beach Windsurfing**. ~ 808-826-9463.

FISHING   Both saltwater and freshwater fishing opportunities make Kauai popular with anglers. Intriguing possibilities include overnight adventures off the Niihau coast, fishing for giant tuna and marlin. Keep a sharp eye out on your trip and you may spot spinner dolphins or breaching whales along the way.

Sea Lure Fishing Charters provides everything you need to fish for marlin, ahi, *ono* and *aku* on Kauai's south and east coasts. The four-hour charter accommodates up to six people; six- and eight-hour charters are also available. ~ Nawiliwili Harbor, Lihue; 808-822-5963.

Head inland to fish for bass on Kauai's reservoirs with **Cast and Catch Freshwater Bass Guides**. Half- and full-day trips are conducted at reservoirs all over the island. A 17-foot bass boat takes anglers out to try for large mouth, small mouth and peacock bass. Bait, tackle and beverages are included. ~ Koloa; 808-332-9707.

BOAT TOURS   The trade winds ensure excellent sailing in Kauai waters. From a catamaran trip along the southern shore to a thrilling trip along the rugged Na Pali Coast, these waters are ideal for cruising. Many of the cruises stop at isolated beaches and also offer excellent snorkeling opportunities.

LIHUE AREA   **True Blue Charters** has the only sailboat rentals on the island. One-hour rides tour Kalapaki Bay; more exclusive rides will take you to remote destinations of your choice. All levels of sailing lessons are offered, as well as kayak tours of Huleia River. Boogieboards and snorkel gear are also rented. ~ Kalapaki Beach, Lihue; 808-245-9662; www.kauaifun.com.

POIPU AREA For south coast sailing tours on the 55-foot-long *Spirit of Kauai* catamaran, weigh anchor with **Captain Andy's Sailing Adventures**. Along the way, you may spot humpback whales or giant green sea turtles. Sunset sails are among the intriguing possibilities. ~ Port Allen; 808-335-6833. **Blue Water Sailing** runs four-hour snorkel sails to Makua Reef. Two-hour sunset sails are also available. ~ Hanalei Bay from May to September; Port Allen Boat Harbor, October to April; 808-828-1142; www.sail-kauai.com.

WAIMEA AREA Expect more than a cruise along the extraordinary Kauai coastline when you board the **Na Pali Explorer**. In addition to providing descriptions of flora, fauna and Hawaiian culture that make the experience educational, the crew is always on the lookout for dolphins and sea turtles. They are attentive to your needs, ecologically oriented, and will lead you along one of the most beautiful coastlines in the world, past craggy cliffs and into remote sea caves. Then they'll take you snorkeling amid the region's colorful coral reefs. You can't miss with one of their trips. These five-hour expeditions run from May through September; snorkeling gear and light snacks are provided. ~ 9935 Kaumualli Highway, Waimea; 808-335-9909, 800-852-4183; www.napali-explorer.com.

The safest swimming along the North Shore is in the summer when the surf is relatively low.

Kauai Z-Tourz has a rafting trip that explores the entire Na Pali coast including the seacaves, and offers snorkeling at the Nualolo Kai reef. Lunch and equipment included. ~ P.O. Box 1082, Kalaheo, HI 96741; 808-742-6331; www.ztourz.com.

WAUILUA–KAPAA **Paradise Outdoor Adventures** leads tours and rents kayaks, ideal for exploring rivers and wildlife refuges. ~ 4-1596 Kuhio Highway, Kapaa, 808-822-1112, 800-662-6287.

NORTH SHORE **Captain Zodiac** offers rafting expeditions along the Na Pali Coast. Six-hour trips include visits to sea caves, beautiful reefs and an ancient fishing village. All trips include some snorkeling, and equipment is provided. Backpacker drop-offs and sunrise and sunset cruises, are offered in summer, while whale watching along the north shore in the winter months is also featured. ~ Hanalei; 808-826-9371, 800-422-7824.

Na Pali Eco-Adventures also serves the Na Pali Coast with motor-powered catamarans. Snorkeling equipment is provided on these narrated tours of historic Kauai, while from January through early April the focus is on whale watching. ~ Port Allen; 808-826-6804, 800-659-6804. Zodiac and catamaran tours of the Na Pali Coast are also offered by **Hanalei Sea Tours**. Half-day snorkeling tours take you to a landing on a secluded beach for first-rate snorkeling, while two-hour whale-watching tours are led by naturalists. ~ Hanalei; 808-826-7254, 800-733-7997.

KAYAKING   Kayaking is one of Kauai's fastest growing water sports. And why not? Choose from verdant river valleys or, if you like, go down to the sea again.

POIPU AREA   Outfitters Kauai offers paddling around Poipu. Bring your snorkel gear along, as there will be time to explore. ~ 2827-A Poipu Road, Poipu Beach; 808-742-9667.

WAILUA–KAPAA AREA   **Kayak Kauai Outfitters** rents kayaks and runs snorkel trips. They also sponsor river tours of waterfalls on the Wailua River, as well as day and overnight tours of the Na Pali Coast. More experienced kayakers can explore sea caves along the Na Pali Coast. This trip includes a lunch break at the ruins of an ancient Hawaiian fishing village. ~ Kapaa, 808-822-9179; Hanalei, 808-826-9844, 800-437-3507.

Kauai is the oldest populated island in the archipelago.

If you want to go out on your own, you can rent a kayak from **Kauai Water Ski and Surf Company**. Kayakers are provided with a map leading them to such Wailua River highlights as the Fern Grotto, a waterfall and a remote Hawaiian village. ~ 4-356 Kuhio Highway, Wailua; 808-822-3574.

Kayak Wailua has a similar self-guided adventure: they'll provide equipment and a laminated map to guide you two and a half miles up Wailua River. At a Hawaiian village along the way, you can secure your boats and continue on foot. Here you'll discover canyons, waterfalls, a swimming hole where ancient Hawaiian kings and high chiefs once bathed, as well as other natural treasures. They also have guided tours. ~ 808-822-3388.

NORTH SHORE   **Kayak Hanalei** will take you on a relaxing tour of the river, stopping to snorkel, eat and laze. Or, if you prefer, they'll introduce you to the rich history of Kauai on a narrated tour. All equipment is provided. ~ Kuhio Highway, Hanalei; 808-826-1881; www.kayakhanalei.com.

Guided Tours   **Kayak Kauai Outfitters** has two morning and afternoon trips. Take a sea kayak tour out to Na Pali Coast, or kayak the Wailua River and then hike to secret waterfalls. From the Kapaa location, tours lead through mountain terrain along the Sleeping Giant Trail to the Keahua Arboretum. ~ Hanalei, 808-826-9844, 800-437-3507; Kapaa, 808-822-9179; www.kayakkauai.com.

WATER-SKIING   If you've ever wondered what it feels like to waterski through paradise, why not head for the town of Wailua. The serene Wailua River is the perfect place to glide through verdant canyons graced by waterfalls. You can practice your slalom technique, try out a pair of trick skis or enjoy yourself on the hydroslide.

Kauai Water Ski and Surf Company offers trips for intermediate to advanced waterskiers. Hot doggers will want to try out the competition slalom course; half-hour or hour-long runs can be arranged. ~ 4-356 Kuhio Highway, Wailua; 808-822-3574.

From scenic coastal trail rides to journeys up the Hanalei Valley, Kauai is an equestrian's delight. Colorful Waimea Canyon offers another intriguing possibility.

RIDING STABLES

In the Poipu area, try CJM **Country Stables**. Possibilities include two-hour rides along the south shore to Mahaulepu and Haupu beaches. They also offer a three-hour "breakfast ride" departing at 8:30 a.m. and covering some of the best beaches in the Poipu area. You may be tempted to return later on foot to explore these hidden spots. (No rides on Sunday.) ~ At the end of Poipu Road; 808-742-6096.

Garden Island Ranch offers rides in the Waimea Canyon region, including the canyon rim. A best bet here is the sunset beach ride. Reservations recommended. ~ Kaumualii Highway, Waimea; 808-338-0052.

In the Hanalei area, contact **Princeville Ranch Stables** for three- or four-hour picnic rides to waterfalls (includes a moderately strenuous hike), as well as 90-minute country rides to the bluff overlooking Anini Reef. The ranch also leads an hour-and-a-half cattle drive every Wednesday morning. ~ Kuhio Highway, Princeville; 808-826-6777.

Some of the best golfing in Hawaii is found on the Garden Isle. In addition to outstanding resort courses at Princeville, the Marriott Kauai and the Hyatt Regency Kauai, you can enjoy several excellent public courses. Beautifully situated with dramatic ocean and mountain backdrops, all of these links will make your game a pleasure.

GOLF

LIHUE AREA   Kiele Course and the **Mokihana Course,** both created by Jack Nicklaus, are two of the island's best-known golfing spots. Both courses have 18 holes, full equipment rental, spectacular ocean views and guava mango forests. ~ Both are located at the Marriott Kauai, Nawiliwili; 808-241-6000, 800-634-6400.

POIPU AREA   Next door to the Hyatt Regency Kauai is the Robert Trent Jones, Jr.–designed 18-hole **Poipu Bay Resort Golf Course.** Full equipment rental is available at this course that was specifically designed to provide an ocean view from each hole. ~ 2250 Ainako Street, Koloa; 808-742-8711.

WAIMEA AREA   On the south side of the island, the 9-hole, semi-private **Kukuiolono Golf Course** is also popular. This 9-hole course offers club rentals only and views of ocean and Kalaheo mountains. ~ Kalaheo; 808-332-9151.

WAILUA–KAPAA AREA   If your idea of a public golf course is long lines and boring terrain, head for the 18-hole, oceanfront **Wailua Golf Course**. The golfing public is well served here and the low green fees make this course a best buy. ~ Wailua; 808-241-6666.

NORTH SHORE   With 27 holes, the **Princeville Makai Golf Course** was designed by Robert Trent Jones. Full equipment rental is available and the scenery is beautiful. ~ Princeville; 808-826-3580. It is complemented by the demanding 18-hole **Prince Country Club** course next door. There's also a driving range to help sharpen your skills. ~ Princeville; 808-826-5000.

BIKING

There are no bikeways on Kauai and most roads have very narrow shoulders, but the Garden Isle is still the most popular island for bicycling. Roads are good, and except for the steep 20-mile climb along Waimea Canyon, the terrain is either flat or gently rolling. The spectacular scenery and network of public parks make this a cyclist's dream.

A favorite local spot for biking is along **Route 56**. This is a narrow road with one-lane bridges that keep tour buses and large trucks out of the area but make it perfect for bikes.

For hearty mountain bikers, the **Powerline Trail** (15 miles) is an arduous but rewarding challenge. It follows a powerline that connects the North Shore with the east side of Kauai. The trail takes you into the interior of the island, offering views of Mt. Waialeale, one of the wettest spots on earth. Be sure to bring a U.S. Survey map (available at local camping stores), water and food with you. This journey is for experienced mountain bikers who are in the best of shape. ~ To get to the trailhead, turn inland at the corner of Princeville stables and continue beyond the row of houses.

Bike Rentals   In Poipu, head for **Outfitters Kauai**. A daily canyon-to-coast trip takes bikers to the top of Waimea Canyon to coast downhill to Kekaha Beach. Renters can tool around the

---

FLY LIKE AN EAGLE (OR A GOONIE BIRD)

What better way to see Kauai than to soar on high with the birds? Okay, so you don't have wings. How about trying a motorized hang glider, accompanied by a fully certified flight instructor from **Birds in Paradise**? Be assured, you'll get a briefing on the basics of flying in a "weight-shift aircraft," and you will always be in communication with the pilot through an intercom on your helmet. ~ Phone/fax 808-822-5309; www.birdsinparadise.com, e-mail birds@birdsinparadise.com.

roads alongside Poipu Beach. ~ 2827-A Poipu Road; 808-742-9667. In Hanalei, try **Pedal 'n Paddle**, where everything from mountain bikes to kids' BMX bikes are rented. Popular destinations from here include Princeville and the lagoon at Kee Beach. Car racks are also available. ~ Ching Young Village; 808-826-9069.

Bike Repairs   Bicycle John's Lihue location offers a full-service sales and repair shop. ~ 3215 Kuhio Highway, Lihue; 808-245-7579.

Hiking is among the finest, and certainly least expensive, ways of touring the Garden Isle. Kauai's trails are concentrated in the Na Pali Coast and Waimea Canyon–Kokee regions, with a few others near the Wailua River. Most are well maintained and carefully charted. For further information, contact the State Department of Land and Natural Resources. ~ 808-984-8100.

HIKING

All distances listed for hiking trails are one way unless otherwise noted.

WAILUA RIVER   While none of these hikes actually follow the Wailua, all begin near Route 580, which parallels the river.

Nounou Mountain Trail—East Side (1.75 miles long) begins off Haleilio Road at the parking lot in the Wailua Houselots and climbs 1250 feet to the Sleeping Giant's head at Mount Nounou summit. This trail is strenuous.

Nounou Mountain Trail—West Side (1.5 miles) begins off Route 581 and ascends with moderate difficulty 1000 feet to join the East Side trail. Moderate.

Keahua Arboretum Trail (0.5 mile) begins two miles past the University of Hawaii Wailua Experiment Station on Route 580. This easy nature trail is lined with foreign plants.

Kuilau Ridge Trail (1.2 miles) begins on Route 580 near the Keahua Arboretum. This moderate, scenic hike goes past several vista points and picnic areas.

WAIMEA CANYON–KOKEE   Kokee State Park has about 45 miles of hiking trails through rugged, beautiful country. Along the mountain paths listed here, you'll discover some of the finest hiking in all Hawaii.

Alakai Swamp Trail (3.5 miles) passes through bogs and scrub rainforests to the Kilohana Lookout. This moderate once-muddy trail is now partially covered with boardwalks. It begins off Mohihi (Camp 10) Road, but is also accessible by the Pihea Trail.

Awaawapuhi Trail (3.25 miles) starts on Route 550 midway between Kokee Museum and Kalalau Lookout. This physically challenging trail leads through a forest to a vista at 2500-feet elevation that overlooks sheer cliffs and the ocean. The trail then connects with Nualolo Trail for a 13-mile loop.

Berry Flat Trail (0.6 mile) and **Puu Ka Ohelo Trail** (0.5 mile) combine off Mohihi (Camp 10) Road to form an easy loop that passes an interesting assortment of trees, including California redwood, *ohia*, *sugi* pine and *koa*.

Black Pipe Trail (0.5 mile) links Canyon Trail with Halemanu Road. It follows a cliff past stands of the rare *iliau* plant, a relative of Maui's famous silversword.

Canyon Trail (1.8 miles) forks off Cliff Trail and follows a relatively easy path around Waimea Canyon's northern rim to a vista sweeping down the canyon to the sea.

Cliff Trail (0.1 mile) begins at the end of the right fork of Halemanu Road and offers a pleasant walk to a viewpoint above Waimea Canyon. Feral goats are often spotted.

Ditch Trail (1.7 miles) runs from Mohihi Road at one end to Waininiua Road at the other. It's a moderate trail with spectacular views of forest areas and the Poomau River.

Halemanu-Kokee Trail (1.2 miles) sets out from the old ranger station. Birdwatchers should especially enjoy this easy jaunt.

Iliau Nature Loop (0.3 mile roundtrip) starts along Route 550 on a short course past 20 local plant species, including the *iliau*, endemic only to the Garden Isle. This easy trail offers good views of both Waimea Canyon and Waialae Falls.

Kalupuhi Trail (1.6 miles) begins at Route 550 en route to a plum grove. The plums are in season every other year. In a good year, you can enjoy both plums and a pleasant hike.

Kawaikoi Stream Trail (1.7 miles), an easy loop trail, starts on Mohihi (Camp 10) Road across from Sugi Grove and follows near the stream through a manmade forest.

Koaie Canyon Trail (3 miles) branches off the Waimea Canyon trail near Poo Kaeha. It's a moderate hike that crosses the Waimea River and passes ancient terraces and rock walls en route to Lonomea camp, a wilderness campsite. Here you'll find a shelter and a stream chock-full of swimming holes.

Kumuwela Trail (1 mile) begins off Mohihi (Camp 10) Road and passes through a fern-choked gulch. Good for birdwatchers.

Nature Trail (0.1 mile) begins behind the Kokee Museum and passes through a *koa* forest.

Nualolo Trail (3.75 miles) starts near Park headquarters. Along the strenuous path you'll be able to see Nualolo Valley on the Na Pali Coast.

Pihea Trail (3.7 miles) offers excellent views of Kalalau Valley and the Alakai Swamp. This moderate trail also features a variety of birds and plant life. It begins at Puuokila Lookout.

Poomau Canyon Lookout Trail (0.3 mile) heads through a stand of Japanese *sugi* trees and a native rainforest. It begins from Mohihi (Camp 10) Road and ends at a vista overlooking Poomau and Waimea Canyons.

Waimea Canyon Trail (8 miles) can be reached from the Kukui Trail. Its very challenging path follows the Waimea River through the center of the canyon.

Hiking
Kalalau

Kauai's premier hike, one of the finest treks in all the islands, follows an 11-mile trail along the rugged Na Pali Coast. This ancient Hawaiian trail to Kalalau Valley descends into dense rainforests and climbs along windswept cliffs. Streams and mountain pools along the path provide refreshing swimming holes. Wild orchids, guavas, *kukui* nuts, mangoes and mountain apples grow in abundance.

The trail begins near Kee Beach at the end of Kuhio Highway. After a strenuous two-mile course the trail drops into Hanakapiai Valley. From here, it climbs through the valley and up to Hanakapiai Falls. Fringed by cliffs and possessing a marvelous sand beach, Hanakapiai makes an excellent rest point or final destination.

If you bypass the side trails and continue along the Kalalau Trail, you'll find that as it climbs out of Hanakapiai Valley, it becomes slightly rougher. Sharp grass presses close to the path as it leads through thick foliage, then along precipitous cliff faces. Four miles from Hanakapiai Valley, the trail arrives at Hanakoa Valley. There is an open-air shelter for public use here, as well as a steep one-third-mile trail that goes up to Hanakoa Falls.

The final trek to Kalalau, the most difficult section of the trail, passes scenery so spectacular as to seem unreal. Knife-point peaks, illuminated by shafts of sunlight, rise thousands of feet. Frigate birds hang poised against the trade winds. Wisps of cloud fringe the cliffs. The silence is ominous, almost tangible. A foot from the trail, the ledge falls away into another sheer wall, which plummets a thousand feet and more to the surf below.

The narrow, serpentine trail then winds down to Kalalau Valley. A well-fed stream rumbles through this two-mile-wide vale. If you must use the water here, be sure to boil or otherwise purify it. Farther along, a white-sand beach sweeps past a series of caves to the far end of the valley. You may want to stop awhile and explore the caves, but if you swim here or at Hanakapiai, exercise extreme caution. The undertow and riptides are wicked.

Kalalau has many fine campsites near the beach, but firewood is scarce and cutting trees is *kapu*, so you'd best bring a campstove. Camping at Hanakapiai, Hanakoa or Kalalau will necessitate a state permit. Anyone hiking beyond Hanakapiai also needs a permit. These are available from the State Parks office. ~ 3060 Eiwa Street, Lihue; 808-274-3434.

Waininiua Trail (0.6 mile) leads from the unpaved Kumuwela Road through a forest where ginger grows.

NORTH SHORE The **Powerline Trial** (15 miles) is a strenuous hike through Kauai's interior. Beginning in Princeville, it follows the Hanalei River, offering views of countless waterfalls and Mt. Waialiale, ending on the east side of the island near Kapaa. If you're feeling less adventurous, hike in a few miles and enjoy the waterfalls and lush vegetation before turning back the way you came. ~ To get to the trailhead, turn inland at the corner of Princeville stables and continue beyond the row of houses.

Hiking Tours Combine an education about the history, flora and fauna of Kauai's interior with a hiking/kayaking adventure. **Princeville Ranch Hiking Adventures** offers a number of options. Hikes include the "Hidden Hanalei" (a trek into the hills towards Mt. Namolokama to a perfect picture-taking spot) and the "Jungle Waterfall Kayak Adventure" (a combination kayaking/ hiking/inner-tubing experience). There is also a range of private excursions available, with length and destinations tailored to your interests. Children over five are welcome. ~ Princeville; 808-826-7669, 888-355-1669; www.kauai-hiking.com.

Kauai Nature Tours is a company that encourages "effective co-existence of earth's environment and its human inhabitants." To this end, all tours are led by local scientists and provide a detailed look into the natural wonders of Hawaii. The Waimea Canyon Explorer tour explores Kauai's geologic past. The Na Pali hiking adventure takes you along a scenic trail built by early Polynesian settlers. The Mahaulepu Coast hike shows you Kauai's limestone ledges and discusses the history of the coastline. This is a perfect way to learn to "take only pictures, leave only footprints." ~ Koloa; 808-742-8305, 888-233-8365; www.teok.com, e-mail teok@aloha.net.

▼▼▼▼▼▼▼▼▼▼▼▼

Transportation

AIR

Visiting Kauai means flying to the centrally located **Lihue Airport**. ~ 808-246-1448. Aloha Airlines, Hawaiian Airlines and United Airlines operate here.

The Lihue Airport has a restaurant, cocktail lounge, lockers, newsstand and flower shop. What you won't find are buses, far more useful to most travelers than cocktails and flowers. Transportation (it's two miles into town) requires reserving a seat on a shuttle, renting a car, hailing a cab, hitching or hoofing. Cabs generally charge about $6 to Lihue.

CAR RENTALS

Across the street from the terminal at Lihue Airport you'll find a series of booths containing car rental firms. These include **Alamo Rent A Car** (808-246-0645, 800-327-9633), **Avis Rent A Car** (808-245-3512, 800-331-1212), **Budget Rent A Car** (808-245-

9031), **Dollar Rent A Car** (808-245-3651, 800-800-4000) and **National Car Rental** (808-245-5636, 800-227-7368).

Budget Rent A Car has four-wheel-drives. However, most Kauai roads, including cane roads, are accessible by car so you probably won't need a jeep. ~ Lihue Airport; 808-245-9031, 800-527-0700.

JEEP RENTALS

Kauai Bus is a shuttle that travels between Lihue and Hanalei seven times a day from 6:45 a.m. to 6 p.m. It stops at about a dozen places, including the major shopping centers. ~ 808-241-6410.

PUBLIC TRANSIT

Kauai Mountain Tours has full-day, off-road four-wheel-drive tours into the mountains of Kokee State Park around Waimea Canyon. Bring comfortable walking shoes and binoculars, as the tours often include a hike on the Halemanu Trail, a mecca for bird-watchers. Lunch is included and usually takes place in the scenic Alakai Swamp area. ~ 808-245-7224.

JEEP TOURS

Whether you choose a whirlybird's-eye view from a helicopter or prefer the serenity of a glider, aerial sightseeing is one of Kauai's great thrills. From simple flyovers to thrilling acrobatic flights, you'll gain a unique perspective on the island's canyons and rainforests, hidden beaches and tropical retreats.

AERIAL TOURS

Island Helicopters offers a one hour tour of all the major scenic areas of the island, from the Na Pali Coast to the Mount Waialeale Crater. ~ Lihue Airport; 808-245-8588, 800-829-5999.

Ohana Helicopter Tours provides a 50-minute Makihana tour that hits all the major sights of Kauai—Waimea Canyon, Sleeping Giant, and the Na Pali Coast. The 65-minute Maile Tour offers a more extensive view of the Na Pali Coast, Alakai Swamp and Kaapoko. Shuttle service is available from southern resorts. ~ Lihue Airport; 808-245-3996, 800-222-6989.

Hawaii Helicopters, based in Princeville Airport, features unique glimpses of scenic treasures like Waialeale, the Na Pali Coast and Waimea Canyon. ~ 808-826-6591, 800-994-9099.

If you want an airplane tour, **Fly Kauai** will take you on a one-hour ride over the most beautiful parts of the island or on a three-island tour featuring Lehua and Niihau. ~ Lihue Airport; 808-246-9123.

Niihau Helicopters specializes in trips to the Forbidden Isle. Bring your own snorkeling equipment because the twin-engine helicopter will land on one of the island's remote beaches, ideal for exploring its pristine underwater environment. ~ Kaumualii Highway; 808-335-3500.

Recommended Reading

The Beaches of Oahu, by John R.K. Clark. University of Hawaii Press, 1977. This book, and companion volumes that cover the other islands, provides excellent background information on all the beaches.

Hawaii, by James Michener. Bantam Books, 1978. This lengthy historic novel skillfully blends fact and fiction, dramatically tracing the entire course of Hawaiian history.

Hawaii Pono, by Lawrence H. Fuchs. Harcourt Brace Jovanovich, 1961. A brilliant sociological study of 20th-century Hawaii that vividly portrays the islands' ethnic groups.

Hawaii: The Sugar-Coated Fortress, by Francine Du Plessix Gray. Random House, 1972. A hard-hitting analysis of modern-day Hawaii that details the tragic effect Western civilization has had on the Hawaiian people.

Hawaiian Antiquities, by David Malo. Bishop Museum Press, 1971. Written by a Hawaiian scholar in the 19th century, this study contains a wealth of information on pre-European Hawaiian culture.

Hawaiian Hiking Trails, by Craig Chisholm. Fernglen Press, 1986. The best single-volume hiking guide available, this handbook provides excellent descriptions of Hawaii's most popular treks.

The Legends and Myths of Hawaii, by David Kalakaua. Charles E. Tuttle Company, 1972. Written by Hawaii's last king, this fascinating collection includes fables of the great chiefs and priests who once ruled the islands.

Polynesian Researches: Hawaii, by William Ellis. Charles E. Tuttle Company, 1969. This missionary's journal originally appeared in the 1820s. Despite some tedious sermonizing, it poignantly portrays Hawaii at a historic crossroads and graphically describes volcanoes and other natural phenomena on the big island.

Shoal of Time, by Gavan Daws. University Press of Hawaii, 1974. The finest history written on Hawaii, this volume is not only informative but entertaining as well.

Shore Fishing in Hawaii, by Edward Y. Hosaka. Petroglyph Press, n.d. This how-to guide is filled with handy tips on surfcasting, fabricating your own equipment and identifying Hawaii's fish species.

Index

Abbreviations used for island names are (H) Hawaii, (K) Kauai, (L) Lanai, (M) Maui, (Mo) Molokai and (Oa) Oahu.

Adventure travel, 31
Aerial tours: (H) 246; (K) 425, 467; (M) 345–46; (Oa) 162–63
Ahihi–Kinau Natural Area Reserve (M), 282
Ahuena Heiau (H), 199
Aina Anuhea Tropical Gardens (M), 279
Air travel, 20; (H) 244–45; (K) 466; (L) 367; (M) 343–44; (Mo) 395; (Oa) 160
Akaka Falls State Park (H), 178
Ala Moana Regional Park (Oa), 103
Alakoko Fishpond (K), 400, 402
Alexander & Baldwin Sugar Museum (M), 306
Aliiolani Hale (Judiciary Building) (Oa), 88
Aliomanu Beach (K), 441
Aloha Tower (Oa), 91
Amy B. H. Greenwell Ethnobotanical Garden (H), 214
Anaehoomalu Beach (H), 194
Anahola (K): dining, 438; groceries, 438; lodging, 435; sights, 434
Anahola Beach Park (K), 441
Animals, 27–29. *See also specific animals*
Anini Beach Park (K), 452
Archery: (L) 366
Arizona Memorial (Oa), 108
Armory Park (M), 265
Astronaut Ellison S. Onizuka Space Center (H), 202
Atlantis Adventures: (H) 199; (Oa) 108
Atlantis Submarines (M), 255–56

Baby Beach (M), 266
Babysitters, 15
Bailey House Museum (M), 295
Baldwin Home (M), 253
Banyan tree (M), 252
Banzai Pipeline (Oa), 132
Barking Sands (K), 421–22, 429–30
Battleship *Missouri* Memorial (Oa), 108
Bay View Farm (H), 214
Bed-and-breakfast inns, 12. *See also* Lodging *in area and town entries; see also Lodging Index*
Bed-and-breakfast referral services. *See* Lodging/condo referral services

Bell Stone (K), 433
Bellows Field Beach Park (Oa), 120
Big Island. *See* Hawaii (island)
Biking: (H) 238, 240; (K) 462–63; (L) 366; (M) 340; (Mo) 394; (Oa) 156–57
Bird Park (Kipuka Puaulu) (H), 224
Birds, 28–29
Birthplace of Kaahumanu (M), 307–308
Birthplace of Kamehameha I (H), 188
Birthplace of Kamehameha III (H), 199
Bishop Museum (Oa), 98, 106–107; shopping, 112
Black Pot Beach Park (K), 453
Black Rock (Puu Kekaa) (M), 267
Black Sands Beach (Oneuli Beach) (M), 293–94
Boat tours: (H) 236; (K) 458–60; (L) 367–68
Boat travel. *See* Boat tours; Cruises; Ferries
Boats (inter-island), 16, 91; (L) 367; (M) 344
Boiling Pots (pools) (H), 170
Bowfin Submarine Museum (Oa), 108
Brick Palace (M), 252
Brigham Young University–Hawaii Campus (Oa), 122
Byodo-In Temple (Oa), 121

Cabins. *See* Lodging
Calendar of events, 5–9
Camping, 33–34; (H) 233–34; (K) 456; (L) 364; (M) 328–29; (Mo) 392; (Oa) 149. *See also* Camping *in area and town entries*
Cane roads (K), 455
Canoe's Surf (Oa), 66
Cape Kumukahi Lighthouse (H), 230
Capitol Building (Oa), 88, 90
Captain Cook (town) (H): dining, 218–19; groceries, 220; lodging, 217; shopping, 221; sights, 212, 214
Captain Cook Monument: (H) 212; (K) 420
Car rentals, 21; (H) 245; (K) 466–67; (L) 367; (M) 344–45; (Mo) 395; (Oa) 160–61

Carthaginian II (ship) (M), 252
Caving: (M), 334. *See also specific caves*
Central Maui (M), 306–307; sights, 306–307
Central Oahu (Oa), 144–45; map, 143; sights, 144–45
Chain of Craters Road (H), 228
Chang's Beach (Poolenalena Beach Park) (M), 293
Children, traveling with, 13–15
Chinaman's Hat (island), 124
Chinatown (Honolulu) (Oa): dining, 97–99; groceries, 100; lodging, 94; shopping, 101; sights, 92–93
Church of the Holy Ghost (M), 319
Church Row (Mo), 380, 382
City of Refuge (Puuhonua o Honaunau National Historical Park) (H), 211, 212, 214
Clothing to bring, 10–11
Coconut Island, 168
Coconut Marketplace (K), 434; shopping, 438
Coffees of Hawaii tour (Mo), 382
Condos, 12–13. *See also* Condos *in area and town entries; see also Lodging Index*
Contemporary Museum (Oa), 106
Cook's Monument: (H) 212; (K) 420
Coral Queen (boat) (Oa), 122
Coronation Pavilion (Oa), 88
Cottages. *See* Lodging
Crabbing, 30
Crouching Lion rock (Oa), 122
Cruises, 16, 91
Cuisine, 52–53
Cultural Plaza (Oa), 93
Culture, 49–58

D. T. Fleming Park (M), 278
Damien Museum (Oa), 66
Devastation Trail (H), 226
Diamond Head (Oa), 68–69
Diamond Head Beach Park (Oa), 109, 113
Diamond Head Lighthouse (Oa), 109
Dining, 13. *See also* Dining *in area and town entries; see also Dining Index*
Disabled travelers, 17
Disappearing Sands Beach (H), 199, 210–11
Diving: (H) 196–97, 234–35; (K) 456–57; (L) 365; (M) 330–32; (Mo) 392–93; (Oa) 149–50
Dole Pineapple Plantation (Oa), 144
Donkey Beach (Kumu Beach) (K), 440–41

East End area (Mo). *See* Kaunakakai to East End area
East End beaches (Mo), 379
East Hawaii Cultural Center Gallery (H), 168
East–West Center (Oa), 109
Eco-tours: (M) 329–30
Economy, 2, 4
Ehukai Beach Park (Oa), 132, 140
Eleele (K): groceries, 426
Enchanting Floral Garden (M), 319
Episcopal Cemetery (Lahaina) (M), 254
Eruption Update (phone hotline) (H), 228
Events, 5–9
Ewa (Oa): sights, 142

Falls of Clyde (ship) (Oa), 90
Fauna, 27–29
Fern Grotto (K), 432
Ferries: (L) 367; (M) 344
Fishing, 29–30; (H) 235–36; (K) 458; (M) 332–33; (Mo) 393; (Oa) 152–53. *See also* Beaches & parks *in area and town entries*
Flora, 23–27
Flowers, 24
Fong's Plantation and Gardens (Oa), 122
Foreign travelers, 18–19
Fort De Russy Beach (Oa), 65
Fort Street Mall (Oa), 91
Foster Botanical Garden (Oa), 92–93
Fruits and vegetables, 25–27

Garden of the Gods (L), 364
Gay and lesbian travelers, 16–17; (H) lodging, 232; nightlife, 209; (K) lodging, 435; (M) lodging, 286, 310–11, 322; (Oa) lodging, 74–75; nightlife, 86–87; shopping, 101
General Lyman Field (Hilo International Airport) (H), 244
Geology, 22–23
Glider rides: (Oa) 134. *See also* Aerial tours
Goat Island (Oa), 130–31
Golf: (H) 236–38; (K) 461–62; (L) 365–66; (M) 338–39; (Oa) 154–55
Green Sand Beach (H), 215
Greenwell Ethnobotanical Garden (H), 214
Grove Farm Homestead (K), 400

H. A. Baldwin Park (M), 315
Haena (K): lodging, 445
Haena Beach Park (K), 454
Haena beaches (K), 454
Haena State Park (K), 454

Haiku (M): lodging, 311–12, 322; sights, 320
Haiku Gardens (Oa), 121
Hakalau Gulch (H), 179
Halaula (H): groceries, 193
Halawa Beach Park (Mo), 379–80
Halawa Valley (Mo), 375–76
Hale Aloha (meetinghouse) (M), 254
Hale Halawai (park) (H), 210
Hale O Lono Beach (Mo), 390–91
Hale Paahao (prison) (M), 254
Hale Pai (museum) (M), 256
Haleakala National Park (M), 325–28; lodging, 328; map, 327; sights, 325–28; visitor information, 325, 326; weather, 326; weather information, 325
Haleakala Observatory (M), 326
Haleiwa (Oa): dining, 137–39; groceries, 139; lodging, 136–37; shopping, 139–40; sights, 134
Haleiwa Beach Park (Oa), 141
Halekii Heiau (M), 280
Halemaumau Crater (H), 226–27
Halemauu Trail (M), 328
Halena Beach (Mo), 390–91
Halepalaoa Beach (L), 358
Haliimaile (M): dining, 323
Halona Blowhole (Oa), 115–16
Halona Cove Beach (Oa), 118–19
Halulu Heiau (L), 362–63
Hamakua Coast (H), 178–83; beaches & parks, 182–83; camping, 182, 183; dining, 181; groceries, 181; lodging, 180–81; map, 179; shopping, 181–82; sights, 178–80
Hamoa Beach (M), 318
Hana (M). See Hana Highway area
Hana Airport (M), 344
Hana Bay (M), 307–308
Hana Beach Park (M), 316
Hana Cultural Center (M), 308
Hana Highway area (M), 302–18; beaches & parks, 315–16, 318; camping, 316, 318; dining, 312–14; groceries, 314; lodging, 309–12; map, 303; nightlife, 315; shopping, 314–15; sights, 302–309
Hanakaoo Beach Park (M), 266
Hanalei (K): condos, 446; dining, 446–49; groceries, 449; lodging, 445; nightlife, 450; shopping, 449; sights, 444
Hanalei Bay beaches (K), 453
Hanalei National Wildlife Refuge (K), 444
Hanalei Pavilion Beach Park (K), 453
Hanalei Valley Lookout (K), 442
Hanamaulu (K): dining, 406; sights, 402
Hanamaulu Beach Park (K), 409

Hananaulu (K): groceries, 438
Hanapepe (K): dining, 424, 426; shopping, 427; sights, 420
Hanapepe Valley Lookout (K), 420
Hanauma Bay Nature Preserve (Oa), 114–15, 118
Hang gliding: (M) 335–36
Happy Valley District (Wailuku) (M), 295
Hapuna Beach State Park (H), 195
Hauola Gulch (L), 355
Hauola Place of Refuge (K), 432
Hauola Stone (M), 252
Hauula (Oa): groceries, 127; sights, 122
Hauula Beach Park (Oa), 129
Hauula Congregational Christian Church (Oa), 122
Hauula Door of Faith Church (Oa), 122
Hawaii (island), 2, 164–246; events, 5–9; itinerary, suggested, 169; map, 167; outdoor adventures, 233–44; transportation, 244–46; weather information, 165. See also specific areas and towns
Hawaii Kai (Oa): dining, 117; groceries, 118
Hawaii Maritime Center (Oa), 90
Hawaii Nature Center (M), 295
Hawaii Theatre (Oa), 91
Hawaii Tropical Botanical Garden (H), 178
Hawaii Volcanoes National Park (H), 224–29; beaches & parks, 229; camping, 229; dining, 228–29; driving tour, 226–27; groceries, 229; lodging, 228; map, 225; sights, 224–28; visitor information, 224
Hawaii's Plantation Village (Oa), 145
Hawaiian cuisine, 52–53
Hawaiian culture, 49–58
Hawaiian Electric Beach Park (Oa), 147
Hawaiian Islands (overview): animals, 27–29; events, 5–9; cuisine, 52–53; culture, 49–58; economy, 2, 4; geology, 22–23; history, 35–49; islands, 2; language, 53–55; map, 3; outdoor adventures, 29–34; people, 51–52; plants, 23–27; time zone, 2; transportation, 19–21; visitor information, 10; weather, 4–5. See also specific islands
Hawaiian language, 53–55
Hawaiian people, 51–52
Hawaiian Waters Adventure Park (Oa), 142–43
Hawi (H): dining, 191; lodging, 188; nightlife, 194; shopping, 193; sights, 188
Heeia State Park (Oa), 99, 122
Helani Farm and Gardens (M), 305

Helicopter tours. *See* Aerial tours
Hideaways beaches (K), 452
Hikiau Heiau (H), 212
Hikina Heiau (K), 432
Hiking, 33–34; (H) 240–44; (K) 463–66;
   (L) 366–67; (M) 341–43; (Mo) 394–95;
   (Oa) 157–59
Hilo (H), 166–78; beaches & parks,
   177–78; dining, 173–75; groceries,
   175–76; lodging, 170, 172–73; map,
   171; nightlife, 177; shopping, 176–77;
   sights, 166–70; weather, 166
Hilo International Airport (General
   Lyman Field) (H), 244
Historic Parker Ranch Homes (H), 184
History, 35–49
Hitchhiking: (H) 246; (L) 368
Hoaloha Park (M), 301
Hokulea (canoe) (Oa), 90
Holo-Holo-Ku Heiau (K), 433
Holualoa (H): lodging, 216; shopping,
   219, 220
Holy Innocents Episcopal Church
   (Lahaina) (M), 254
Honalo (H): dining, 218; lodging, 216
Honaunau (H): dining, 219; lodging,
   217; shopping, 221; sights, 214
Honokaa (H): dining, 181; groceries,
   181; lodging, 180–81; shopping, 182;
   sights, 179
Honokohau Bay and Beach (M), 278,
   281
Honokohau Beach (H), 210
Honokowai (M): condos, 269–70
Honokowai Beach Park (M), 277
Honolua Bay Beach (M), 280
Honolulu. *See* Honolulu, downtown;
   Honolulu, greater; Waikiki
Honolulu Academy of Arts (Oa), 93
Honolulu, downtown (Oa), 87–103;
   beaches & parks, 103; camping, 103;
   dining, 94–99; groceries, 100; lodging,
   93–94; map, 89; nightlife, 101–103;
   shopping, 100–101; sights, 87–93
Honolulu, greater (Oa), 103–14; beaches
   & parks, 113–14; camping, 113; din-
   ing, 110–12; groceries, 112; lodging,
   109–10; map, 105; nightlife, 113; shop-
   ping, 112–13; sights, 104–109
Honolulu Hale (Honolulu City Hall)
   (Oa), 88
Honolulu International Airport (Oa), 160
Honolulu Memorial Park (Oa), 104
Honolulu Myohoji Temple (Oa), 104
Honolulu Zoo (Oa), 68
Honomanu Bay and Beach (M), 304, 316
Honomu (H): groceries, 181; shopping,
   181
Hookena Beach Park (H), 222

Hookio Gulch (L), 355
Hookipa Beach Park (M), 302, 304,
   315–16
Hoolehua (Mo): sights, 383
Hoomaluhia Botanical Garden (Oa),
   120–21
Horseback riding: (H) 240; (K) 461; (L)
   366; (M) 337–38; (Mo) 393-94; (Oa)
   154
Hosmer's Grove (M), 325
Hospitals, 14–15
Hostels: (H) 172–73, 199–200; (K) 435;
   (M) 298; (Oa) 69–71, 110
Hotels, 11–12. *See also* Lodging *in area
   and town entries; see also Lodging
   Index*
Huialoha Church (M), 309
Huilua Fishpond (Oa), 129–30
Hukilau Beach (Oa), 130
Hula, 57–58
Huleia National Wildlife Refuge (K), 402
Hulihee Palace (H), 199
Hulopoe Bay (L), 359
Hulopoe Beach Park (L), 361–62

Iao Needle (M), 296
Iao Valley State Monument (M), 296
Iliiliopae Heiau (Mo), 374
Imiola Congregational Church (H), 184
International travelers, 18–19
Iolani Palace and Barracks (Oa), 88, 98
Isaac Hale Beach Park (H), 233
Izumo Taishakyo Mission (Oa), 92

Jaggar Museum (H), 227
James Campbell National Wildlife Refuge
   (Oa), 125
James Stewart's Hoomau Ranch (H), 215
Jeep rentals, 21; (H) 245; (K) 467; (L)
   367; (M) 345; (Mo) 395–96; (Oa) 161
Jeep tours: (K) 467

Ka Ulu a Paoa Heiau (K), 445
Kaaawa (Oa): dining, 127; groceries, 127
Kaahumanu Congregational Church (M),
   295
Kaalawai Beach (Oa), 113–14
Kaanapali–Kapalua area (M), 266–78;
   beaches & parks, 277–78; condos,
   268–71; dining, 271–74; groceries, 274;
   lodging, 267–71; map, 269; nightlife,
   276–77; shopping, 274–76; sights,
   266–67
Kaanapali resort beaches (M), 277
Kaena Point (Oa), 136, 145–46
Kaena Point State Park (Oa), 148–49
Kahakuloa (M): sights, 278–79
Kahala Beach (Oa), 114
Kahala District (Honolulu) (Oa), 109

Kahaluu Beach Park (H), 211
Kahana (M): condos, 270–71; dining, 272–73
Kahana Bay (Oa), 122
Kahana Valley State Park (Oa), 129–30
Kahanamoku Beach (Oa), 65
Kahanu Garden (M), 305
Kahea Heiau (L), 356
Kahekili's Leap (L), 363
Kahili Beach (K), 451
Kahoolawe (island), 5, 307
Kahuku (Oa): dining, 137; lodging, 136; nightlife, 140; shopping, 139; sights, 124–25
Kahuku Golf Course Park (Oa), 131
Kahuku Sugar Mill (Oa), 124–25
Kahului Airport (M), 343–44
Kahului–Wailuku area (M), 294–302; beaches & parks, 301–302; dining, 298–300; groceries, 300; lodging, 296, 298; map, 297; nightlife, 301; shopping, 300–301; sights, 294–96
Kaiaka Recreation Area (Oa), 141
Kaihalulu Beach (Red Sand Beach) (M), 316, 318
Kailua (Oa): dining, 126–27; groceries, 127; lodging, 125; nightlife, 128; shopping, 128; sights, 120
Kailua Beach (Oa), 128
Kailua-Kona area (H), 198–211; beaches & parks, 210–11; condos, 203–204; dining, 204–207; groceries, 207–208; lodging, 199–204; map, 201; nightlife, 209; shopping, 208–209; sights, 198–99
Kailua wharf (H), 198
Kainaliu (H): dining, 218; groceries, 220; shopping, 220
Kakaako Waterfront Park (Oa), 103
Kakahaia Beach Park (Mo), 379
Kalae (Mo): sights, 382
Kalahaku Overlook (M), 326
Kalaheo (K): dining, 424; groceries, 426; sights, 421
Kalakaua Park (H), 177
Kalalau Lookout (K), 422–23
Kalama Beach County Park (Oa), 128
Kalama County Beach Park (M), 292
Kalapaki Beach (K), 400, 408
Kalaupapa Lookout (Mo), 382
Kalawao Park (Mo), 389
Kalihiwai Beach (K), 451–52
Kalokoeli Fishpond (Mo), 374
Kalopa State Recreation Area (H), 182–83
Kamakou Preserve (Mo), 385
Kamalo Wharf (Mo), 374
Kamaole Beach Parks (M), 292
Kamehameha Rock (H), 188

Kamehameha Statue: (H) 188; (Oa) 88, 98
Kamehameha V's Summer Home (Mo), 372
Kamuela (H). *See* Waimea
Kamuela Museum (H), 184
Kanaha Pond Wildlife Sanctuary (M), 295
Kane'aki Heiau (Oa), 144
Kaneeleele Heiau (H), 215
Kaneohe (Oa): dining, 127; groceries, 127; lodging, 125–26; shopping, 128; sights, 120–22
Kaneohe Bay (Oa), 122
Kapaa (K) area. *See* Wailua–Kapaa area
Kapaa Beach Park (H), 198
Kapaa Beach Park (K), 440
Kapaau (H): shopping, 193; sights, 188
Kapaia (K): shopping, 407; sights, 402
Kapalua area (M). *See* Kaanapali–Kapalua area
Kapalua Beach (M), 278
Kapalua–West Maui Airport (M), 344
Kapiolani Park (Oa), 66, 68
Kapolei (Oa): dining, 146; lodging, 146; nightlife, 147
Kapolei (Oa): sights, 142–43
Kapuaiwa Coconut Grove (Mo), 380
Kau Desert (H), 227
Kau Desert Trail (H), 224
Kau District (H). *See* Kona/Kau District
Kauai (island), 2, 397–467; events, 5–9; itinerary, suggested, 401; map, 399; outdoor adventures, 456–66; transportation, 466–67. *See also specific areas and towns*
Kauai Coffee Visitor Center (K), 421
Kauai Museum (K), 400
Kauapea Beach (Secret Beach) (K), 451
Kauiki Hill (M), 308
Kaulanapueo Church (M), 304
Kaumahina State Wayside (M), 304
Kaumalapau Harbor (L), 362
Kaumana Caves (H), 170
Kaunakakai to East End area (Mo), 372–80; beaches & parks, 378–80; camping, 379, 380; condos, 376–77; dining, 377; groceries, 377–78; lodging, 376–77; maps, 373, 375; shopping, 378; sights, 372–76
Kaunakakai to West End area (Mo), 380–92; beaches & parks, 387, 390–92; camping, 387, 392; dining, 386; driving tour, 384–85; groceries, 386; lodging, 384–86; map, 381; nightlife, 387; shopping, 386–87; sights, 380–84
Kaunakakai Wharf (Mo), 372
Kaunolu Village (L), 362

Kaupo (M): groceries, 314; sights, 309
Kaupo Gap (M), 309
Kaupo Trail (M), 328
Kaupulehu-Kona (H): lodging, 202–203
Kawaihae (H): dining, 190–92; lodging, 190; nightlife, 193–94; sights, 187
Kawaihao Church (Oa), 87–88
Kawakui Beach (Mo), 391
Kawela (Mo): sights, 374
Kayaking: (H) 236; (K) 460; (L) 364; (M) 336; (Mo) 393; (Oa) 153–54
Keaau (H): sights, 230
Keaau Beach Park (Oa), 148
Keahua Forestry Arboretum (K), 434
Keaiwa Heiau State Recreation Area (Oa), 113
Kealakekua (H): dining, 219; lodging, 217; shopping, 220–21; sights, 212
Kealakekua Bay (H), 212
Kealia (K): sights, 434
Kealia Beach (K), 440
Kealia Pond Bird Sanctuary (M), 281
Kealoha County Park (H), 177
Keanae (M): lodging, 310
Keanae Arboretum (M), 304
Keanae Peninsula (M), 304
Keawakapu Beach (M), 292–93
Keawanui Fishpond (Mo), 374
Kee Beach (K), 445, 454
Keei Beach (H), 222
Kekaha (K): groceries, 426; sights, 421–22
Kekaha Beach (K), 429
Kekaha Beach Park (K), 429
Kennedy Profile (M), 296
Keokea Beach Park (H), 198
Keokea Park (M), 324
Keomuku (L): sights, 356–57
Kepaniwai County Park and Heritage Gardens (M), 296, 302
Kewalo Boat Basin (Oa), 91
Kihei Beach (M), 291–92
Kihei–Wailea–Makena area (M), 281–94; beaches & parks, 291–94; camping, 294; condos, 285–86; dining, 286–89; groceries, 289–90; lodging, 284–86; map, 283; nightlife, 291; shopping, 290–91; sights, 281–84
Kilauea (K): dining, 446, 448; groceries, 449; shopping, 449; sights, 442
Kilauea Caldera (H), 226
Kilauea Lighthouse (K), 442
Kilauea Point National Wildlife Refuge (K), 442
Kilauea Visitor Center (H), 224
Kilohana (mansion) (K), 402–403
King's Pool (H), 199
Kiowea Park (Mo), 387
Kipahulu (M): sights, 309

Kipuka Puaulu (Bird Park) (H), 224
Kitesurfing: (M) 332
Kohala Coast (H), 186–95, 198; beaches & parks, 194–95, 198; camping, 195, 198; dining, 190–92; groceries, 192–93; lodging, 188–90; map, 189; nightlife, 193–94; shopping, 193; sights, 187–88
Kohala Mountain (H), 188
Kokee Museum (K), 422
Kokee State Park (K), 422, 430–31; dining, 426; lodging, 424; map, 431
Koki Beach Park (M), 318
Koko Crater (Oa), 114
Koko Crater Botanical Gardens (Oa), 116
Koko Head (Oa), 114
Kokole Point (K), 429
Kokololio Beach Park (Oa), 130
Kolekole Beach Park (H), 182
Kolekole Pass (Oa), 145
Kolo Wharf (Mo), 390–91
Koloa (K): condos, 413, 414; dining, 414–16; groceries, 417; lodging, 412, 413, 414; nightlife, 418; shopping, 417, 418; sights, 410
Koloa History Center (K), 410
Kona area (H). *See* Kailua-Kona area; Kona/Kau district
Kona Coast State Park (H), 210
Kona coffee country (H), 211–12
Kona Historical Society Museum (H), 212
Kona International Airport (H), 244
Kona/Kau district (H), 211–23; beaches & parks, 221–23; camping, 222, 223; dining, 218–220; groceries, 220; lodging, 216–18; map, 213; nightlife, 221; shopping, 219, 220–21; sights, 211–16
Koolau Range (Oa), 117
Kualapuu (Mo): sights, 382
Kualoa Beach Park (Oa), 129
Kuhio Beach Park (Oa), 66
Kuilei Cliffs Beach Park (Oa), 113–14
Kukaniloho (Oa), 144
Kukuiolono Park (K), 420
Kula (M): dining, 323; lodging, 320, 322; shopping, 324; sights, 319–20
Kula Botanical Gardens (M), 319–20
Kumimi Beach (Mo), 379
Kumu Beach (Donkey Beach) (K), 440–41
Kurtistown (H): lodging, 232
Kwan Yin Temple (Oa), 93

La Perouse Bay (M), 283
Lahaina (M), 250, 252–66; beaches & parks, 264–66; condos, 258–59; dining, 259–61; groceries, 261–62; lodging, 256, 258–59, 269; map, 253; nightlife,

263–64; shopping, 262–63; sights, 252–56; visitor information, 252
Lahaina Art Society (M), 252–53
Lahaina Harbor (M), 252
Lahaina Hongwanji Temple (M), 254
Lahaina Jodo Mission (M), 256
Lahaina Shingon Mission (M), 255
Lahainaluna School (M), 256
Laie (Oa): groceries, 128; lodging, 126; sights, 122, 124
Laie Point (Oa), 124
Lanai (island), 2, 307, 347–68; events, 5–9; map, 349; outdoor adventures, 364–67; transportation, 367–68. See also specific areas and towns
Lanai Airport (L), 367
Lanai City (L), 350–54, 356; dining, 352–54; groceries, 354; lodging, 350–52; map, 351; nightlife, 354, 356; shopping, 354
Language, 53–55
Lanikai Beach (Oa), 128–29
Lapakahi State Historical Park (H), 187
Larsens Beach (K), 450–51
Launiupoko Wayside Park (M), 265
Laupahoehoe Beach Park (H), 182
Laupahoehoe Point (H), 179
Lava flows: (H) 224, 226, 230; (M) 282–83, 309
Lava Tree State Park (H), 230–31
Leeward Coast (Oa), 142–49; beaches & parks, 147–49; camping, 147, 148; dining, 146–47; groceries, 147; lodging, 146; map, 143; nightlife, 147; sights, 142–46
Leleiwi County Park (H), 177
Leleiwi Overlook (M), 325–26
Leper colony (Mo), 388–89
Lesbian travelers. See Gay and lesbian travelers
Lihue Airport (K), 466
Lihue area (K), 400, 402–409; beaches & parks, 408–409; camping, 408, 409; dining, 404–406; groceries, 407; lodging, 403–404; map, 403; nightlife, 408; shopping, 407, 408; sights, 400, 402–403
Lihue Hongwanji Temple (K), 402
Liliuokalani Gardens (H), 168
Limahuli Botanical Garden (K), 444–45
Lindbergh (Charles) grave (M), 309
Little Beach (Puu Olai Beach) (M), 294
Little Grass Shack (Oa), 109
Little Makena Beach (M), 282
Lodging, 11–13. See also Lodging in area and town entries; see also Lodging Index
Lodging/condo referral services, 12; (H) 184, 228; (K) 414, 446; (Oa) 76, 77

Lua Moku Iliahi (Sandalwood Measuring Pit) (Mo), 384–85
Luahiwa petroglyphs (L), 358–59
Lualualei Beach Park (Oa), 148
Lucy Wright Park (K), 428–29
Lumahai Beach (K), 444, 453
Lydgate State Park (K), 432, 439–40
Lyman House Memorial Museum (H), 168
Lyon Arboretum (Oa), 109

Maalaea Bay (M), 307
Mackenzie State Recreation Area (H), 233
Magic Sands Beach (Disappearing Sands Beach) (H), 199, 210–11
Mahaulepu Beach (K), 419–20
Mahukona Beach Park (H), 195, 198
Mail, 19
Maili Beach Park (Oa), 147–48
Makaha (Oa): dining, 147; lodging, 146
Makaha Beach and Beach Park (Oa), 143–44, 148
Makapuu Beach Park (Oa), 116, 119
Makapuu Point (Oa), 116
Makapuu Point State Wayside (Oa), 119
Makawao (M): dining, 322–23; groceries, 323; nightlife, 324; shopping, 323–24; sights, 320
Makee Sugar Mill (M), 319
Makena (M): dining, 289; lodging, 285; nightlife, 291; sights, 282
Makena Landing (M), 292
Makena State Beach (Oneloa Beach) (M), 282, 294
Makua Cave (Oa), 144–45
Malaekahana State Recreation Area (Oa), 130–31
Manele Bay area (L), 358–62; beaches & parks, 361–62; camping, 362; dining, 361; lodging, 360–61; map, 359; nightlife, 361; sights, 358–60
Manele Small Boat Harbor (L), 359
Manoa Valley (Oa), 109
Mantokuji Buddhist Temple (M), 302
Manuka State Wayside (H), 223
Mapulehu Mango Grove (Mo), 375
Maria Lanakila Church (M), 254–55
Master's Reading Room (M), 254
Maui (island), 2, 247–346; events, 5–9; driving tour, 306–307; itinerary, suggested, 251; map, 249; outdoor adventures, 328–43; transportation, 343–46; weather information, 344. See also specific areas and towns
Maui Ocean Center (M), 307
Maui Tropical Plantation (M), 306

Mauna Kea Beach Hotel (H), 187; dining, 191; nightlife, 193
Mauna Kea Observatory (H), 226
Mauna Kea State Recreation Area (H), 227
Maunakea Marketplace (Oa), 92
Maunaloa (Mo): dining, 386; groceries, 386; lodging, 385–86; shopping, 386–87; sights, 383
McGregor Point (M), 307
Menehune (Alakoko) Fishpond (K), 400, 402
Menehune Ditch (K), 421
Menehunes, 121, 399–400
Merchant Street (Honolulu) (Oa), 91
Milolii (H): sights, 215
Milolii Beach Park (H), 222–23
Mission Houses Museum (Oa), 87
Mission Memorial Building (Oa), 88
Missouri Memorial (Oa), 108
Mokapu Beach (M), 293
Moku Hooniki Island, 375
Mokuaikaua Church (H), 199
Mokuleia Beach (Slaughterhouse Beach) (M), 280
Mokuleia Beach and Beach Park (Oa), 141–42
Moloaa Beach (K), 450
Molokai (island), 2, 307, 369–96; events, 5–9; driving tour, 384–85; events, outdoor adventures, 392–95; transportation, 395–96. *See also specific areas and towns*
Molokai Airport (Mo), 395
Molokai Forest Reserve (Mo), 384
Molokai Museum and Cultural Center (Mo), 382
Molokai Plumerias (Mo), 382
Molokai Wagon Ride (Mo), 375
Molokini (island), 284, 307
Mookini Heiau (H), 188
Moomomi Beach (Mo), 390
Moped rentals: (H) 245; (M) 345; (Oa) 161
Mormon Temple (Oa), 124
Mosquitoes, 34
Motels. *See* Lodging
Mount Lyons (M), 308
Munro Trail (L), 355
Music, 56–57

Na Pali Coast (K), 441–42
Naalehu (H): dining, 219; groceries, 220; lodging, 216; sights, 215
Naha (L), 357
Naha Beach (L), 358
Naha Stone (H), 168, 170
Nahiku (M): sights, 305

Namakani Paio (H), 229
Nanakuli Beach Park (Oa), 147
Nani Mau Gardens (H), 167
Napili (M): condos, 271; dining, 273; groceries, 274
Napili Bay Beach (M), 277–78
Napoopoo Beach Park (H), 221–22
Natatorium (Oa), 68
National Memorial Cemetery (Oa), 104, 106
Nawiliwili (K): dining, 406; groceries, 407; shopping, 407; sights, 400, 402
Nawiliwili Harbor (K), 400
Nene O Molokai (Mo), 374
Niihau (island), 5, 425
Ninini Beach (K), 409
Ninole Cove (H), 215
Niumalu Beach Park (K), 408
North Shore (K), 441–54; beaches & parks, 450–54; camping, 451, 452, 453, 454; condos, 446; dining, 446–49; groceries, 449; lodging, 445–46; map, 443; nightlife, 450; shopping, 449–50; sights, 441–45
North Shore (Oa), 131–42; beaches & parks, 140–42; camping, 141, 142; dining, 137–39; groceries, 139; lodging, 136–37; ; map, 133; nightlife, 140; shopping, 139–40; sights, 132–36
North Shore Surf and Cultural Museum (Oa), 134
Northeast Lanai (L), 356–58; beaches & parks, 357–58; map, 357; sights, 356–57
Northwest Lanai (L), 364; beaches & parks, 364; map, 364; sights, 364
Northwest Maui (M), 278–81; beaches & parks, 280–81; camping, 281; map, 279; sights, 278–80
Nukolii Beach Park (K), 439
Nuu Bay (M), 309
Nuuanu Avenue (Honolulu) (Oa), 104
Nuuanu Pali Drive and Lookout (Honolulu) (Oa), 99, 107

Oahu (island), 2, 59–163; events, 5–9; cultural tour, 98–99; driving tour, 144–45; itinerary, suggested, 62–63; map, 61; outdoor adventures, 149–59; transportation, 160–63. *See also specific areas and towns*
Ocean safety, 32–33
Oheo Gulch (M), 308–309, 318
Old Court House (Hana) (M), 308
Old Courthouse (Lahaina) (M), 252
Old Fort (Lahaina) (M), 253
Old Kona Airport State Recreation Area (H), 210

Old Sugar Mill (Oa), 122
Older travelers, 17
Olomana Peak (Oa), 117
Olowalu (M): dining, 261; groceries, 262
Olowalu Beaches (M), 265
O'ne Alii Park (Mo), 378–79
Onekahakaha County Park (H), 177
Oneuli Beach (Black Sands Beach) (M), 293–94
Onizuka Center for International Astronomy (H), 226
Onizuka Space Center (H), 202
Opaekaa Falls (K), 433
Opihikao (H): sights, 230
Orchids of Hawaii (garden) (H), 166–67
Original Glider Ride (Oa), 134
Our Lady of Seven Sorrows Catholic Church (Mo), 374
Outdoor adventures, 29–34. See also Outdoor adventures in island chapters
Outrigger canoes (Oa), 79

Paauilo (H): sights, 179
Pacific Aerospace Museum (Oa), 160
Pacific Missile Range Facility (K), 422
Pacific Tsunami Museum (H), 168
Package tours, 19–20
Packing, 10–11
Pahala (H): lodging, 218; sights, 215–16
Pahoa (H): dining, 232; groceries, 232–32; lodging, 231–32; shopping, 233; sights, 230
Paia (M): dining, 312–13; groceries, 314; lodging, 312; shopping, 314–15; sights, 302
Painted churches: (H) 214, 230
Paipu Beach Park (Poolenalena Beach Park) (M), 293
Pakala Beach (K), 428
Pakuhiwa Battleground (Mo), 374
Palaau State Park (Mo), 387
Panaewa Rainforest Zoo (H), 170
Paniolo country (H), 227
Papalaua Wayside Park (M), 264–65
Papohaku Beach Park (Mo), 383–84, 391–92
Parasailing: (H) 236; (M) 335–36
Parker Ranch (H), 183–84
Pearl Harbor (Oa), 107–108
Petroglyphs, 356, 358–59
Phallic Rock (Mo), 383
Pidgin language, 54–55
Pihana Kalani Heiau (M), 280
Pillboxes (World War II) (M), 281
Pinao Stone (H), 168, 170
Pineapple Variety Garden (Oa), 144
Pioneer Inn (M), 252; dining, 259; lodging, 256; nightlife, 263

Plants, 23–27
Pohaku-Ho-o-Hanau (K), 433
Pohakuloa Point (Rock Point) (Mo), 379
Pohoiki (H): sights, 230
Poipu area (K), 409–20; beaches & parks, 418–20; condos, 413–14; dining, 414–17; groceries, 417; lodging, 411–14; map, 411; nightlife, 418; shopping, 417–18; sights, 410–11
Poipu Beach (K), 418
Poipu Beach Park (K), 418–19
Poliahu Heiau (K), 433
Polihale Heiau (K), 422
Polihale State Park (K), 422, 430
Polihua Beach (L), 364
Polipoli Spring State Recreation Area (M), 320, 324
Polo Beach (M), 293
Pololu Valley Lookout (H), 188
Polynesian Cultural Center (Oa), 124
Pookela Church (M), 320
Poolenalena Beach Park (Paipu Beach Park) (M), 293
Pounders Beach (Oa), 130
Price ranges used in book: dining, 13; lodging, 11–12
Princeville (K): condos, 446; dining, 446–47; groceries, 449; lodging, 445–46; nightlife, 450; shopping, 449; sights, 442
Princeville beaches (K), 452
Puaakaa State Wayside (M), 305
Puako (H): groceries, 192
Puamana County Wayside Park (M), 265
Public transit: (H) 245–46; (K) 467; (M) 345; (Oa) 161–62
Pueone o Honokahua (cultural preserve) (M), 276
Pukalani (M): dining, 322; groceries, 323
Pukoo Beach (Mo), 379
Puna District (H), 230–33; beaches & parks, 233; camping, 233; dining, 232; groceries, 232–33; lodging, 231–32; map, 231; shopping, 233; sights, 230–31
Punalau Beach (Windmill Beach) (M), 280–81
Punaluu (H): dining, 220; lodging, 218
Punaluu (Oa): lodging, 126; shopping, 128
Punaluu Beach Park (H), 215, 223
Punaluu Beach Park (Oa), 129
Punchbowl (Oa), 104
Puohokamoa Falls (M), 304
Purdy's Natural Macadamia Nut Farm (Mo), 383
Puu o Hoku Ranch (Mo), 375
Puu o Makuka Heiau (Oa), 132

Puu Olai Beach (Little Beach) (M), 294
Puu Pehe (sea stack) (L), 359–60
Puu Poa Beach (K), 452
Puu Ualakaa Park (Oa), 106
Puu Ulaula Overlook (M), 326
Puuhonua o Honaunau National
  Historical Park (H), 211, 212, 214
Puuhonua o Honaunau Park (H), 211
Puukohola National Historic Site (H),
  187
Puunene (M): sights, 306

Queen Emma Summer Palace (Oa),
  98–99, 107
Queen Kapiolani Garden (Oa), 68
Queen Victoria's profile (K), 410
Queen's Surf (Oa), 66

Rabbit Island, 116, 119
Rafting: (M) 336–37
Rainbow Falls (H), 170
Red Sand Beach (Kaihalulu Beach) (M),
  316, 318
Reed's Bay Beach Park (H), 177
Restaurants, 13. *See also* Dining *in area
  and town entries; see also* Dining Index
Richardson's Ocean Park (H), 177–78
Riding stables: (H) 240; (K) 461; (L) 366;
  (M) 337–38; (Mo) 393–94; (Oa) 154
Rock Point (Pohakuloa Point) (Mo), 379
Royal Hawaiian Hotel (Oa), 65; lodging,
  75–76
Royal Mausoleum (Oa), 98, 104
Royal-Moana Beach (Oa), 65
Running Waters Beach (K), 409
Russian Fort Elizabeth State Historical
  Park (K), 421

Saddle Road area (H), 226–27
Sailing: (H) 236; (M) 333–35; (Mo) 393;
  (Oa) 153
St. Benedict's Painted Church (H), 214
St. Gabriel's Church (Wailua) (M), 305
St. Joseph Catholic Church (Kaunakakai)
  (Mo), 374
St. Peter's Catholic Church (Kailua-Kona
  area) (H), 199
St. Philomema Church (Kalaupapa) (Mo),
  389
Salt Pond Beach Park (K), 427–28
Sand Island State Recreation Area (Oa),
  103
Sandalwood Measuring Pit (Mo), 384–85
Sandy Beach (Oa), 116, 119
Sans Souci Beach (Oa), 68
Schofield Barracks (Oa), 145
Scuba diving. *See* Diving; Snuba
Sea kayaking. *See* Kayaking

Sea Life Park (Oa), 116
Sealodge Beach (K), 452
Seamen's Cemetery (M), 255
Seashell hunting (M), 317
Seaweed gathering, 32
Secret Beach (Kauapea Beach) (K), 451
Senator Fong's Plantation and Gardens
  (Oa), 122
Senior travelers, 17
Shark Island, 363
Sharks, 33
Shave ice, 135
Shell hunting: (M) 317
Shellfish gathering, 30, 32
Sheraton Moana Surfrider Resort (Oa),
  65–66; lodging, 75
Sheraton Waikiki (Oa), 65; nightlife,
  84–85
Shipwreck Beach (K), 419
Shipwreck Beach (L), 356, 357–58
Shrimp Shack (Oa), 125
Signature Theater (Oa), 93
Silversword plant, 24–25, 326
"69" Beach (H), 194–95
Skiing: (H) 239
Slaughterhouse Beach (Mokuleia Beach)
  (M), 280
Sliding Sands Trail (M), 328
Smith and Bronte Landing (Mo), 374
Smith's Tropical Paradise (K), 432
Snakes, 29
Snorkeling. *See* Diving; Snuba
Snuba: (Oa) 151
Soto Mission of Hawaii (Oa), 104
South Coast beaches (Mo), 390–91
South Point (H), 215
Southeast Lanai (L), 358–62; beaches &
  parks, 361–62; camping, 362; dining,
  361; lodging, 360–61; map, 359;
  nightlife, 361; sights, 358–60
Southeast Oahu (Oa), 114–20; beaches
  & parks, 118–20; camping, 119, 120;
  dining, 117–18; groceries, 118; map,
  115; shopping, 118; sights, 114–17
Southwest Lanai (L), 362–63; map, 363;
  sights, 362–63
Spearfishing, 30
Spelunking: (M) 334. *See also specific
  caves*
Spencer Beach Park (H), 195
Sporting clays: (L) 366
Sports, 29–34. *See also* Outdoor adven-
  tures *in island chapters*
Spouting Horn (lava tube) (K), 410–11,
  419
Squidding, 30
Star of the Sea Painted Church (H), 230
State Capitol Building (Oa), 88, 90

Stewart's Hoomau Ranch (H), 215
Sugar Cane Train (M), 255
Suisan Fish Market (H), 168
Sunrise Protea Farm (M), 320
Sunset Beach (Oa), 132, 140
Surfing: (H) 235; (K) 457–58; (M) 332; (Oa) 151–52. *See also* Beaches & parks *in area and town entries*
Swanzy Beach Park (Oa), 129
Swimming. *See* Beaches & parks *in area and town entries; see also* Ocean safety

Tantalus (Oa), 106
Tedeschi Vineyards (M), 319
Tennis: (H) 238; (M) 339–40; (Oa) 155–56
Tenrikyo Mission (Oa), 104
Thurston Lava Tube (H), 226
Time zone, 2
Toilet Bowl (tidepool) (Oa), 114–15
Torchfishing, 30
Tourist seasons, 4
Tours: (Mo) 396. *See also* Aerial tours; Boat tours; Jeep tours; Package tours; Walking tours
Trails. *See* Hiking
Transportation, 19–21. *See also* Transportation *in island chapters*
Tree Growth Research Area (M), 320
Tree Molds (fossils) (H), 224
Tree Tunnel (K), 410
Trees, 25
Tropical Gardens of Maui (M), 295
Tunnels Beach (K), 454
Twin Falls (M), 304

Ualapue Fishpond (Mo), 374
UCC Hawaii Coffee Factory Outlet (H), 212
Ulua Beach (M), 293
Ulupalakua Ranch (M), 309
Ulupo Heiau (Oa), 99, 120
University of Hawaii (Oa), 109
University of Hawaii Agricultural Station (M), 320
Upcountry (M), 319–24; beaches & parks, 324; camping, 324; dining, 322–23; groceries, 323; lodging, 320, 322; map, 321; nightlife, 324; shopping, 323–24; sights, 319–20
Upolu Airport (H), 244–45
U.S. Army Museum of Hawaii (Oa), 65
USS *Arizona* Memorial (Oa), 108
USS *Bowfin* Submarine Museum (Oa), 108
USS *Missouri* Memorial (Oa), 108

Vegetables and fruits, 25–27
Visitor information, 10
Volcano House and Art Center (H), 224
Volcano Village (H): dining, 229; groceries, 229; lodging, 228

Wahiawa (Oa): sights, 144–45
Wahiawa Botanical Gardens (Oa), 144–45
Wahikuli Wayside Park (M), 266
Waiahole Valley (Oa), 122
Waiakea Fishpond (H), 168
Waialae Beach Park (Oa), 114
Waialea Bay Beach (H), 194–95
Waialua (Oa): dining, 139; nightlife, 140
Waianae (Oa): dining, 146–47; groceries, 147; sights, 143
Waianapanapa Cave (M), 305
Waianapanapa State Park (M), 305, 316
Waihee (M): sights, 280
Waihee Beach Park (M), 302
Waikamoi Ridge (M), 304
Waikanaloa Wet Cave (K), 444
Waikane Valley (Oa), 122
Waikapalae Wet Cave (K), 444
Waikiki (Oa), 64–87; condos, 76–77; dining, 77–81; groceries, 82; lodging, 69–77; map, 67; nightlife, 84–87; shopping, 82–84; sights, 65–69
Waikiki Aquarium (Oa), 66, 68
Waikiki Shell (Oa), 68
Waikoko Beach (K), 453
Waikoloa (H): dining, 192; groceries, 193; lodging, 189–90; nightlife, 194; shopping, 193; sights, 187
Waikoloa Petroglyph Field (H), 187
Waikolu Valley Lookout and Picnic Grove (Mo), 385
Wailea area (M). *See* Kihei–Wailea–Makena area
Wailea Beach (M), 293
Wailoa River State Park (H), 168
Wailua (M): sights, 304–305
Wailua Falls (K), 402
Wailua Falls (M), 308
Wailua Homesteads (K), 433–34
Wailua–Kapaa area (K), 432–41; beaches & parks, 439–41; camping, 441; condos, 435–36; dining, 436–38; groceries, 438; lodging, 434–36; map, 433; nightlife, 439; shopping, 438–39; sights, 432–34
Wailuku area (M). *See* Kahului–Wailuku area
Waimanalo (Oa): dining, 117–18; groceries, 118; shopping, 118; sights, 117
Waimanalo Bay Beach Park (Oa), 119–20
Waimanalo Beach Park (Oa), 119–20

Waimea (Kamuela) (H), 183–86; dining, 185–86; groceries, 186; lodging, 184–85; map, 183; nightlife, 186; shopping, 186; sights, 183–84
Waimea area (K), 420–31; beaches & parks, 427–31; camping, 428, 429, 430, 431; dining, 424, 426; groceries, 426; lodging, 423–24; maps, 423, 431; shopping, 426–27; sights, 420–23
Waimea Bay (Oa), 132, 134
Waimea Bay Beach Park (Oa), 141
Waimea Canyon (K), 422
Waimea Falls (Oa), 132
Waimea-Kohala Airport (H), 245
Waimea Valley Adventure Park (Oa), 132
Waiohai Beach (K), 418
Waiohinu (H): lodging, 217–18
Waiola Cemetery (M), 254
Waiola Church (M), 254
Waioli Beach Park (K), 453
Waioli Mission House (K), 444
Waioli Tea Room (Oa), 109
Waiomao cave (M), 305
Waipahu (Oa): sights, 145
Waipio Valley (H): shopping, 182; sights, 179–80
Waipio Valley Lookout (H), 180
Waipouli (K): dining, 436; groceries, 438
Wakeboarding: (Oa) 151
Walking tours: (Oa) 92, 162

Wananalua Church (M), 308
Wastewater Reclamation Facility (Mo), 372
Waterskiing: (K) 460–61; (Oa) 151
Weather, 4–5
West End area (Mo). See Kaunakakai to West End area
Whalers Village Museum (M), 267
Whales and whale watching, 27; (H) 236; (M) 307, 333–35
White Hill (M), 326
Whittington Beach Park (H), 223
Windmill Beach (Punalau Beach) (M), 280–81
Windsurfing: (H) 235; (K) 457–58; (M) 332; (Oa) 151–52
Windward Coast (K). See Wailua–Kapaa area
Windward Coast (Oa), 120–31; beaches & parks, 128–31; camping, 129, 130, 131; dining, 126–27; groceries, 127–28; lodging, 125–26; map, 123; nightlife, 128; shopping, 128; sights, 120–25
Wo Hing Museum (M), 254
Women travelers, 15
Wood Valley (H), 216
Wood Valley Temple (H), 215–16; lodging, 218
World Botanical Gardens (H), 179

Yokohama Bay (Oa), 145, 148–49

Lodging Index

Ali'i Bluffs Bed & Breakfast, 125–26
Aloha Cottages, 310
Arnott's Lodge, 172–73
Aston Honolulu Prince Hotel, 73
Aston Kaanapali Shores, 269
Aston Keauhou Beach Resort, 202
Aston Kona By The Sea, 204
Aston Maui Islander Hotel, 258
Aston Maui Lu Resort, 284–85
Aston Pacific Monarch, 77
Aston Waikiki Banyan, 77
Aston Waikiki Beach Tower, 76–77
Aston Waikiki Circle Hotel, 74
Aston Waikiki Shore, 77
Atherton YMCA, 110

Backpacker's Vacation Inn, 136
Banana Bungalow, 298
Banyan Harbor Resort, 404
Best Inn Hukilau, 126
Best Western Pioneer Inn, 256
The Breakers, 71–72
Butterfly Inn, 232

Cabana at Waikiki, 74–75
Camp Keanae, 310
Camp Naue, 445
Camps at Molokai Ranch, 385–86
Castle Maui Park, 270
The Cliffs at Princeville, 446
Coconut Plaza, 74
Colony Surf Condominiums, 75
Countryside Cabins, 126

Diamond Head Beach Hotel, 75
Dolphin Bay Hotel, 172
Dragonfly Ranch, 217
Dreams Come True on Lanai, 352

Estates at Turtle Bay, 136
Ewa Hotel, 72

Fernhurst YWCA, 110
Four Seasons Resort Maui at Wailea, 285

Garden Island Inn, 404
Garden Isle Cottages Oceanfront, 412

Gloria's Spouting Horn Bed & Breakfast,
    412
Golden Bamboo Ranch, 311

H. Manago Hotel, 217
Hale Lihue, 404
Hale Maui, 270
Hale Ono Loa, 270
Hale Pua Nui, 71
Halfway to Hana House, 312
Hana Accommodations and Plantation
    Houses, 310–11
Hana Alii Holidays, 311
Hana Kai Maui Resort, 310
Hanalei Bay Resort, 445
Hanalei Colony Resort, 446
Hanalei Inn, 445
Hawaii Naniloa Hotel, 172
Hawaiiana Hotel, 74
Heavenly Hana Inn, 310
Hilo Bay Hotel, 170, 172
Hilo Seaside Hotel, 170
Hilton Hawaiian Village, 76
Hilton Turtle Bay Golf and Tennis
    Resort, 136
Holiday Inn Waikiki, 73–74
Honokowai Palms, 270
Hostelling International Honolulu, 110
Hostelling International—Waikiki, 70
Hotel Coral Reef, 434
Hotel Hana-Maui, 311
Hotel Honokaa Club, 180–81
Hotel Lanai, 350–51
Hotel Molokai, 376
Huelo Point Lookout, 312
Hyatt Regency Kauai Resort & Spa,
    412–13
Hyatt Regency Maui, 268

Interclub Waikiki, 70–71
Island Hostel/Hotel, 69

Jack & Tom's Condos or Cottage, 286
JW Marriott Ihilani Resort & Spa, 146

Kaanapali Alii, 268–69
Kaanapali Beach Hotel, 267
Kahana Reef All Oceanfront, 270–71

Kahili Mountain Park, 411
Kai Aloha Apartment Hotel, 71
Kailani Eco-Resort and Adventures, 231–32
Kailua Beachside Cottages, 125
Kailua Maui Gardens, 312
Kailua Plantation House, 202
Kaleialoha, 270
Kaluakoi Resort, 384
Kamalo Plantation Bed & Breakfast, 376
Kamaole Beach Royale, 286
Kamuela Inn, 184–85
Kapaa Sands Resort, 436
Kapalua Bay Hotel, 268
Kapulanikai, 286
Kauai Coast Resort at the Beachboy, 434–35
Kauai International Hostel, 435
Kauai Kailani, 436
Kauai Sands Hotel, 434
Kaulana Kai Resort at Waikiki, 76
Kaupoa Camp, 386
Ke Iki Hale, 137
Ke Nani Kai Resort, 384–85
Kealakekua Bay Bed and Breakfast, 217
Keapana Center Bed and Breakfast, 435
Kiahuna Plantation, 413
Kihei Kai, 285–86
Kilauea Lodge, 228
King Kamehameha Kona Beach Hotel, 201–202
Kohala Village Inn, 188
Kokee Lodge Cabins, 424
Kolo Cliffs, 386
Koloa Landing Cottages, 412
Kona Alii, 203
Kona Bali Hai, 203
Kona Bay Hotel, 200
Kona Hotel, 216
Kona Islander Inn, 200
Kona Magic Sands, 203
Kona Riviera Villa, 203
Kona Seaside Hotel, 200
Kona Tiki Hotel, 200
Kona Village Resort, 202–203
Kona White Sands Apartment Hotel, 200–201
Kuhio Shores, 414
Kula Lodge, 320

Lahaina Inn, 258
Lahaina Shores Hotel, 258–59
Lawai Beach Resort, 414
Leilani Kai, 285
Lihi Kai, 286
Lodge at Koele, 352
Lodge at Molokai Ranch, 385

Mahina Kai Ocean Villa, 435
Mahina Surf, 270
Makaha Shores, 146
Makaha Valley Towers, 146
Malihini Hotel, 71
Mana Kai Maui Resort, 286
Manele Bay Hotel, 360–61
Manoa Valley Inn, 110
Marc Molokai Shores Suites, 376–77
Marc Waikiki Grand Hotel, 74
Margo's Corner, 216
Maui Beach Hotel, 296, 298
Maui Coast Hotel, 285
Maui Oceanfront Inn, 285
Maui Sands, 269
Maui Seaside Hotel, 296
Mauna Lani Bay Hotel and Bungalows, 190
Mauna Lani Point, 190
Mohala Ke Ola, 435
Mokihana of Kauai, 436
Motel Lani, 404

Nalu Kai Lodge, 309–10
Napili Bay, 271
Napili Kai Beach Resort, 271
Napili Point Resort, 271
Napulani O'Hana, 312
New Otani Kaimana Beach Hotel, 75
Nona Lani Cottages, 284
Northshore Inn, 298
Nuuanu YMCA, 109–10

Ohana Coral Seas Hotel, 72
Ohana Edgewater Hotel, 72
Ohana Village, 73
Ohana Waikiki Surf, 72
Outrigger Waikoloan Beach, 189–90
Outrigger's Napili Shores Resort, 271

Paauhau Plantation House, 181
Pagoda Hotel, 93–94
Pahio at Kaeo Kai, 446
Paki Maui, 270
Pali Ke Kua, 446
Paniolo Camp, 386
Paniolo Hale, 385
Papakea Resort, 269
Patey's Place in Paradise, 199–200
Plantation Inn, 256, 258
Poipu Bed & Breakfast Inn, 412
Poipu Crater Resort, 413
Poipu Kai Resort, 413
Poipu Kapili, 413
Poipu Shores, 413
PollyMakena, 284
Polynesian Hostel Beach Club, 70
Polynesian Shores, 270

Princeville Hotel and Resort, 445–46
Puamana, 258

Queen Kapiolani Hotel, 74

Ramada Vacation Suites, 74
Royal Grove Hotel, 71
Royal Hawaiian Hotel, 75–76
Royal Kuhio, 76
Royal Lahaina Resort, 268

Schrader's Windward Marine Resort, 125
Sea Mountain at Punaluu, 218
Sea Village, 203
Sheraton Moana Surfrider Resort 75
Silver Cloud Ranch, 320, 322
Skirakawa Motel, 217–18
Sunseeker Resort, 286
Sunset Kahili Condominiums, 413–14

Teshima's Inn, 216
Tip Top Motel, 404
Town Inn, 94
Turtle Bay Condos, 136

Volcano House, 228

Waianapanapa State Park cabins, 311
Waikiki Hana Hotel, 72
Waikiki Prince Hotel, 71

Waikoloa Villa, 188
Wailua Bay View, 435–36
Waimea Country Lodge, 184
Waimea Plantation Cottages, 423–24
Waipio Treehouse, 180
Westin Hapuna Beach Prince Hotel, 190
Westin Maui Prince Hotel, 285
Wild Ginger Inn, 172
Winston's Waikiki Condos, 77
Wood Valley Temple, 218

YMCA Central Branch (Waikiki), 70

LODGING REFERRAL SERVICES
Affordable Accommodations, 12
All Islands Bed & Breakfast, 12
Bed and Breakfast Hawaii, 12, 76
Bed and Breakfast Honolulu (Statewide), 12
Bed and Breakfast Honolulu, 76
Condo Rentals of Waikiki, 77
Grantham Resorts, 414
Hanalei Vacations, 446
Hawaii's Best Bed & Breakfasts, 12, 76, 184
Hawaiian Islands Bed & Breakfast, 12
Marc Resorts, 77
Poipu Beach Resort Association, 414
R & R Realty & Rentals, Inc., 414
Volcano Accommodations, 228

Dining Index

Acqua, 79
Aioli's, 185
Aki's Cafe, 205
Alan Wong's Restaurant, 111
Aloha Café, 218
Aloha Diner, 437
Aloha Kauai Pizza, 436
Anna Bannana's, 111
Arancino's, 81
Auntie Pasto's, 96
Azeka's Market Snack Shop, 287
Azteca Mexican Restaurant, 112
Azul, 146

Baci Bistro, 126–27
Bali-by-the-Sea, 81
Bali Hai Restaurant, 447
Bamboo Restaurant, 191
Bangkok Cuisine, 313
Basil's Restaurant, 204
The Batik, 191
Bautista's Filipino Kitchen, 78
Bay Club, 274
Bay Terrace, 191–92
Beach House Restaurant, 416
Beach Hut, 406
Beachside Café, 78–79
Beachside Grill, 272
Betty's Chinese Kitchen, 204
Big Island Bistro, 174
Big Save Market, 407
Black Rock Cafe, 232
Blue Dolphin Restaurant, 191
Blue Ginger Café, 352–53
Brennecke's Beach Broiler, 415–16
Bubba Gump Shrimp Co., 260
Bubba's, 448
Buena Nalo, 126
Bull Shed, 436–37
Buzz's Steak & Lobster, 436

Cafe Ohia, 219
Café Haleiwa, 138
Café Pesto (Hilo), 175
Café Pesto (Kawaihae), 190
Café Portofino, 406
Cali Café, 300
Camp House Grill, 424

Canaan Deli, 219
Canoe House, 192
Canoes Café, 174
Canton Chef, 287
Carelli's On The Beach, 288
Casanova Italian Restaurant & Deli, 322
Cassandra's Greek Tavern, 205–206
Cathay Inn Chop Suey, 146
Cha Cha Cha Restaurant, 80
Chai's Island Bistro, 96
Cheeseburger in Paradise (Lahaina), 259
Cheeseburger in Paradise (Waikiki), 79
Chef Marro's, 97
Chez Paul, 261
China Boat, 272–73
Choi's Kitchen, 78
Cinnamon's Restaurant, 126
Coconut Willy's Bar & Grill, 78
Coffee Gallery, 138
Compadres (Honolulu), 95
Compadres (Lahaina), 260
Country Kitchen, 137
Crouching Lion Inn, 127

Da Imu Hut Café, 426
Davey Jones Ribs, 80
David Paul's Lahaina Grill, 261
Diamond Head Grill, 79–80
Dollie's Pub and Café, 272
Don's Grill, 175
Dondero's, 416–17
Double Eight Restaurant, 97
Duane's Ono CharBurger, 438
Durty Jake's Café and Bar, 207

Edelweiss, 185
Elsie's Fountain, 174
Erik's Seafood Grotto, 272
Ezogiku, 78

Fatty's Chinese Kitchen, 80
Fish Hut, 436
Fisherman's Wharf, 95–96
Flashbacks Bar and Grill, 205
Formal Dining Room, 353–54
Fujiya, 299

Gaylord's, 406–407
Gerard's Restaurant, 261
Giovanni's Aloha Shrimp Truck, 137
Great Wall Chopsui, 185
Greek Bistro, 288
Green Garden Restaurant, 424

Hakone, 289
Hale O'Java, 446
Hale Vietnam, 112
Haleiwa Beach Grill, 138
Haleiwa Joe's Seafood Grill, 127
Haliimaile General Store, 323
Hamura Saimin, 405
Hana Gion, 289
Hana Ranch Restaurant, 313
Hanalei Dolphin Restaurant and Fish
    Market, 448–49
Hanalei Gourmet, 447–48
Hanalei Mixed Plate, 448
Hanalei Wake-Up Cafe, 447
Hanamaulu Café, 406
Hanapepe Cafe and Espresso, 424, 426
Hannara Restaurant, 147
Hapa's Restaurant, 288
Happy Cat's Cafe, 174
Hard Rock Café (Lahaina), 260
Harley's Ribs-'n-Chicken, 436
Harrington's, 175
Hau Tree Lanai, 79
Hawaiian Style Cafe, 185
Henry Clay's Rotisserie, 352
Hilton Turtle Bay Golf and Tennis
    Resort, 137
Hong Kong Chop Suey, 219
Hotel Hana-Maui, 314
House of Seafood, 416
Hula Grill, 273
Hula Moons, 288–89
Hulopoe Court Restaurant, 361

Ihilani Dining Room, 361
Ilima Terrace, 417
Indigo, 98–99
Irifune, 110

J. J.'s Broiler, 406
Jacques Bistro, 312
Jameson's By the Sea (Haleiwa), 138
Jameson's By the Sea (Kailua-Kona), 207
John Dominus, 96
John's Place, 426
Jolene's Kau Kau Korner, 181
JW Marriott Ihilani Resort & Spa, 146

Kaanapali Mixed Plate Restaurant, 271
Kal Bi House, 287
Kalaheo Steak House, 424

Kamuela Deli, 204
Kapaa Fish & Chowder House, 437
Kau Kau Corner Food Lanai, 96
Kauai Chop Suey, 406
Kauai Kitchens, 414
Kawara Sobe Takase Restaurant, 272
Ken's House of Pancakes, 173–74
Keneke's, 117
Keo's in Waikiki, 80
Keoki's Paradise, 415
Kihei Prime Rib and Seafood House,
    288
Kilauea Lodge, 229
Kimo's, 260
Koa House Grill, 185
Koa Omelette House, 127
Kohala Coffee Mill, 191
Kokee Lodge, 426
Kona Inn, 206
Kona Ranch House, 206
Koo's Kitchen, 117–18
Kua Aina Sandwich, 137
Kula Lodge Restaurant, 323

La Bourgogne French Restaurant, 207
La Cascata, 446–47
La Mer, 81
Lava Rock Café, 229
Leilani's On The Beach, 272
Lighthouse Bistro, 448
Lihue Barbeque Inn, 405
A Little Bit of Saigon, 97
Longhi's, 260–61
Luigi's Pasta & Pizzeria, 271
Lulu's, 206–207
Luquin's Mexican Restaurant, 232

Mabuhay Cafe, 98
Magoo's, 111
Makai Market, 94
Makawao Steak House, 322
Mama's Fish House, 313
Manago Hotel, 218–19
Marco's Grill & Deli, 298
Margarita's Beach Cantina, 287
Ma's Family Restaurant, 404–405
Maui Tacos, 273
Maunakea Marketplace, 98
Maunaloa Village Grill, 386
McCully Chop Suey, 96–97
Meg's Drive-In, 138
Mermaid's Cafe, 437
Merriman's, 185
Mi Casita Mexican Restaurant, 414
Mister Bill's, 219
Molokai Pizza Cafe, 377
Mun Cheong Lau Chop Suey Restaurant,
    175

Naupaka, 146
Nick's Fishmarket, 77–78
Nick's Place, 322
19th Hole, 147
Norberto's El Café, 437

Ocean Seafood Chinese Restaurant, 204
Ocean Terrace, 78
Oceanview Inn, 204
Ohia Lodge, 386
Oki Diner, 405
Old Lahaina Luau, 260
Ono Hawaiian Foods, 111
Oodles of Noodles, 206
Orchid Snackshop, 137
Orchids, 81
Orient Express, 273
Outpost Natural Foods, 377
Oviedo's Lunch Counter, 378

A Pacific Café (Kauai), 437
A Pacific Café Maui, 287
A Pacific Café (Oahu), 95
Pae Thai, 96
Pagoda Floating Restaurant, 96
Paia Fish Market, 312
Palm Terrace, 137
Pancho & Lefty's Cantina &
    Restaurante, 206
Paniolo Plantation Inn, 181
Paniolo Country Inn, 185
Papaya's Natural Foods, 437
Paradise Bar & Grill, 446
Paradise Found Café, 138
Pattaya Asian Cafe, 415
Patti's Chinese Kitchen, 94
Pau Hana Pizza, 446
Pavilion, 191
Peking Garden, 78
People's Café, 97
Perry's Smorgy, 81
Pescatore, 174
Picnics, 313
Pioneer Grill and Bar, 259
Pioneer Inn Restaurant, 259
Pizza Paradiso, 271–72
Plantation House (Koloa), 415
Plantation House Restaurant (Kapalua),
    273
Poi Bowl, 94
Polli's Restaurant, 322–23
Polo Beach Grille and Bar, 289
Pool Grille, 361
Portofino, 139
Prince Court, 94

Rainbow Dining Room, 299
Rainbow Drive-In, 111

Ramon's, 299
Restaurant Kiibo, 405
Restaurant Kiku, 173
Restaurant Kintaro, 436
Restaurant Matsu, 298
Reuben's Mexican Food, 174
Rosie's Cantina, 138–39
Roussels, 192
Royal Siam, 175
Royal Thai Cuisine, 288
Roy's Kahana Bar and Grill, 272
Roy's Poipu Bar & Grill, 416
Roy's Restaurant, 117
Ryan's Grill, 95

S. T. Property, 352
Saeng's Thai Cuisine (Kailua), 126
Saeng's Thai Cuisine (Wailuku), 299
A Saigon Café, 299
Sam Choy (Honolulu), 110–11
Sam Choy's Restaurant (Kailua-Kona),
    207
Sam Choy's Breakfast, Lunch & Crab, 99
Sam Sato's, 299
Sandcastle Restaurant and Lounge, 289
Sawasdee Thai Cuisine, 232
Schlotzsky's Deli, 94
Scoozee's, 94
Seamountain Golf Course & Lounge,
    220
Seaside Bar & Grill, 80
Seasons, 289
Shaka Restaurant, 219
Shirokiya, 94
Shore Bird Beach Broiler, 81
Siam Thai Cuisine, 299
Sibu Café, 204
Siu's Chinese Kitchen, 298
Smokin' Bob Barr-B-Q, 127
Soda Fountain, 191
Spats Trattoria, 272
Stan's Restaurant, 204
Stella Blues Café & Delicatessen, 288
Suda's Store and Snack Shop, 286–87
Sugar Bar & Pizza Garden, 139
Sunrise Café, 259
Sunset Diner, 137–38
Sunset Grill, 95
Surfside Spirits and Deli, 287
Surt's, 229
Sushi Blues Grill, 449
Sushi Shop, 204
Swiss Inn, 117

Tahiti Nui Restaurant, 448
Tai Pan on the Boulevard, 95
Tasaka Guri Guri Shop, 298
TC's Island Grill, 436

The Terrace, 353
Teshima's, 218
Tidepools, 417
Times Coffee Shop, 126
Tip Top Café and Bakery, 405–406
Toi's Thai Kitchen, 426
Tokyo Tei, 300
Tom Kats Grill, 414
Tres Hombres Beach Grill (Kailua), 206
Tres Hombres Beach Grill (Kawaihae),
   190–91
Tropix Island Style Café and Bar, 438
Tsunami Grill and Tempura, 175
Tutu's At Hana Bay, 313

Uncle Billy's Fish and Steakhouse,
   174
Up Country Café, 322

Vegan Restaurant, 313
Vi's Restaurant, 298
Village Korean Barbeque, 271
Village Snack and Bakery, 447
Volcano House Restaurant, 228–29

Waikiki Broiler, 80
Waikiki Shopping Plaza, 78
Waipouli Delicatessen and Restaurant,
   436
Wakefield Gardens & Restaurant, 219
Woody's Oceanfront Grill, 259–60
Wranglers Steakhouse, 426

Yong Sing Restaurant, 97
Yong's Kalbi, 185

Zelo's Beach House, 448

Travel With Someone You Trust®

Wherever you go, it's good to have a guide. Someone who knows the territory. Someone who can help you find those hidden spots and great deals. For generations of travelers, AAA has been that guide.

When you join AAA, you gain access to a world of information: AAA TourBooks, TripTiks, and maps help you find exciting things to do and wonderful places to stay. As a member of one of the world's largest consumer organizations, you receive the best deals from the world's best travel providers as well as valuable discounts from a wide range of Show Your Card & Save® partners. In addition, AAA financial and insurance services provide the freedom to help you pay for your travels and enjoy peace of mind on the ride.

As a AAA member, you join a community that numbers over 42 million members and that provides partnerships with the biggest names in travel. We invite you to explore the world. Let AAA be your guide. With over 4000 offices nationwide, you can find us in many local communities or on the Web at www.aaa.com.

HIDDEN GUIDES

Adventure travel or a relaxing vacation?—"Hidden" guidebooks are the only travel books in the business to provide detailed information on both. Aimed at environmentally aware travelers, our motto is "Adventure Travel Plus." These books combine details on unique hotels, restaurants and sightseeing with information on camping, sports and hiking for the outdoor enthusiast.

THE NEW KEY GUIDES

Based on the concept of ecotourism, The New Key Guides are dedicated to the preservation of Central America's rare and endangered species, architecture and archaeology. Filled with helpful tips, they give travelers everything they need to know about these exotic destinations.

Ulysses Press books are available at bookstores everywhere. If any of the following titles are unavailable at your local bookstore, ask the bookseller to order them.

You can also order books directly from Ulysses Press
P.O. Box 3440, Berkeley, CA 94703
800-377-2542 or 510-601-8301
fax: 510-601-8307
www.ulyssespress.com
e-mail: ulysses@ulyssespress.com

Order Form

HIDDEN GUIDEBOOKS

____ Hidden Arizona, $15.95
____ Hidden Bahamas, $14.95
____ Hidden Baja, $14.95
____ Hidden Belize, $15.95
____ Hidden Boston and Cape Cod, $14.95
____ Hidden British Columbia, $17.95
____ Hidden Cancún & the Yucatán, $16.95
____ Hidden Carolinas, $17.95
____ Hidden Coast of California, $18.95
____ Hidden Colorado, $14.95
____ Hidden Disneyland, $13.95
____ Hidden Florida, $17.95
____ Hidden Florida Keys & Everglades, $12.95
____ Hidden Georgia, $16.95
____ Hidden Guatemala, $16.95
____ Hidden Hawaii, $18.95
____ Hidden Idaho, $14.95

____ Hidden Maui, $13.95
____ Hidden Montana, $15.95
____ Hidden New England, $18.95
____ Hidden New Mexico, $15.95
____ Hidden Oahu, $13.95
____ Hidden Oregon, $15.95
____ Hidden Pacific Northwest, $18.95
____ Hidden San Francisco & Northern California, $18.95
____ Hidden Southern California, $17.95
____ Hidden Southwest, $18.95
____ Hidden Tahiti, $17.95
____ Hidden Tennessee, $16.95
____ Hidden Utah, $16.95
____ Hidden Walt Disney World, $13.95
____ Hidden Washington, $14.95
____ Hidden Wine Country, $13.95
____ Hidden Wyoming, $15.95

THE NEW KEY GUIDEBOOKS

____ The New Key to Costa Rica, $17.95

____ The New Key to Ecuador and the Galápagos, $17.95

Mark the book(s) you're ordering and enter the total cost here ⇨ [ ]

California residents add 8% sales tax here ⇨ [ ]

Shipping, check box for your preferred method and enter cost here ⇨ [ ]

❑ BOOK RATE   **FREE! FREE! FREE!**

❑ PRIORITY MAIL $3.20 First book, $1.00/each additional book

❑ UPS 2-DAY AIR $7.00 First book, $1.00/each additional book   [ ]

Billing, enter total amount due here and check method of payment ⇨ [ ]

❑ CHECK   ❑ MONEY ORDER

❑ VISA/MASTERCARD _____ EXP. DATE _____

NAME _____ PHONE _____

ADDRESS _____

_____

CITY _____ STATE _____ ZIP _____

MONEY-BACK GUARANTEE ON DIRECT ORDERS PLACED THROUGH ULYSSES PRESS.

ABOUT THE AUTHOR

RAY RIEGERT is the author of eight travel books, including *Hidden San Francisco & Northern California*. His most popular work, *Hidden Hawaii*, won the coveted Lowell Thomas Travel Journalism Award for Best Guidebook as well a similar award from the Hawaii Visitors Bureau. In addition to his role as publisher of Ulysses Press, he has written for the *Chicago Tribune*, *Saturday Evening Post*, *San Francisco Chronicle* and *Travel & Leisure*. A member of the Society of American Travel Writers, he lives in the San Francisco Bay area with his wife, co-publisher Leslie Henriques, and their son Keith and daughter Alice.

ABOUT THE PHOTOGRAPHER

ROBERT HOLMES, born in England, launched his U.S. photography career in 1976 when Ansel Adams asked him to come work in the United States. His photographs have appeared in most of the major travel magazines including *National Geographic*, *Geo*, *Islands* and *Travel & Leisure*. In addition to his magazine credits, he has 15 books in print including The Thomas Cook Guides to California, Boston & New England, and Hawaii, as well as Fodor's *Essential California*. He lives in Mill Valley, California, with his wife and two daughters.